Basic4Android

Rapid App Development for Android

By Wyken Seagrave

Basic4Android

Rapid App Development for Android
by Wyken Seagrave
Published by Penny Press Ltd
176 Greendale Road, Coventry CV5 8AY, United Kingdom
sales@pennypress.co.uk

Please report errors to errors@Basic4Android.info

Copyrights

Trademarks

Notice of Rights

Notice of Liability

ISBN

9781871281200 (ebook)
9781491226735 (paperback)

Cover by Edgar 'Feo' Ibarra
Corrections:
Replaced missing # before #Region and #End Region in sample code

Table of Contents

Table of Contents 3
Foreword by Erel Uziel 4
Introduction 5
Part 1: Basics 12
1.1 Getting Started 13
1.2 The Integrated Development Environment 37
1.3 Upgrade to Full Version 59
Part 2: Creating Your App 67
2.1 The Project 68
2.2. Designing Your App 74
2.3 Communicating with your User 85
2.4 The Designer 92
2.5 Designer Scripts Reference 109
2.6 Compiling, Debugging & Testing 119
2.7 Graphics and Drawing 144
2.8 Databases 156
2.9 Process and Activity Life Cycle 173
2.10 Modules 180
2.11 Publishing and Monetizing Your App 193
2.12 Getting More Help 203
Part 3: Language and Core Objects 206
3.1 Basic4Android's Language 207
3.2 VB6 versus B4A 262
3.3 Core Objects 270
Part 4: Libraries 402
4.1 Libraries 403
4.2 Standard Libraries included with Full Version 408
4.3 Additional Libraries and Modules 524
Index 555

Foreword by Erel Uziel

I started developing Basic4ppc, a development tool for Pocket PC devices (later renamed to Windows Mobile) in 2005. It was a real challenge for me to build a new programming language and development environment. Five years later, when Microsoft decided to stop developing Windows Mobile in favor of a different platform, and with the first signs of the new Android operating system, I decided that it was time to change direction and Basic4Android was born. I had a rare opportunity to go back to the drawing board and then, with the many lessons learnt from the previous project, build a powerful and simple development tool for native Android applications.

In the last three years, since the first release, Basic4Android has improved dramatically. Today, Basic4Android supports 99% of the advanced features of Android. Features such as NFC, Wifi-Direct, serial ports, graphics and many more are supported, and all of the features are designed to be simple to use yet powerful enough to meet your real-world requirements.

Basic4Android is used by companies, organizations, educational institutes and individuals from all over the world. I honestly believe that Basic4Android is the best development tool for native Android applications available today

Over the years, a very active online community has evolved around Basic4Android. This community is the heart of Basic4Android. In our forums, there are almost 200 thousand messages with questions, answers, examples, bugs, tutorials, classes and libraries. The ecosystem around Basic4Android is huge.

Many customers have asked for a full, comprehensive book to help them with their own development. I was thrilled to hear that Wyken has taken on himself the challenging task of mapping this ecosystem. I'm happy to say that Wyken, an experienced software developer and author, has done a great job.

I'm sure that this book will help you to quickly get started with development of your own Android apps.

I'm looking forward to see you becoming part of our community!

Erel Uziel
CEO, Anywhere Software

Introduction

Basic4Android is widely recognized as the simplest and most powerful Rapid App Development tool available for Android. It is used by tens of thousands of enthusiastic developers. A complete list of its features and benefits can be found here (http://www.basic4ppc.com/android/why.html).

Who this Book is For

This book serves two audiences:

For the Beginner

For those new to Basic4Android, new to BASIC, or even new to programming, this book contains step-by-step tutorials for the complete beginner. It explains everything you need to know to use this exciting and easy application development environment design to create and sell your app on Android devices in the shortest possible time without having to climb the steep learning curve of learning Java.

For the Professional

For experienced Basic4Android developers, this book brings together a huge range of reference material never previously assembled in one place and organizes it into an easily accessible form.
It contains all the key terms used by the core language and its official libraries. It includes examples to show how the code is used and links to further on-line information.

What You Need to Run Basic4Android

You will need a PC running Windows with at least 512 Mb of RAM.
You can test your app on either an emulator (page 128) (a virtual device running on your PC) or a real device. We recommend you have a real device available as it usually takes less time to install your app there than on an emulator and apps running there usually excute faster.
If you use a real device it should be running Android 1.6 or above (that is Android 2.x, 3.x etc.).

Version of Basic4Android

This book covers the functionality of Version 3.00 of Basic4Android, which includes the amazing Rapid Debugger (page 124), a feature which is not available in any other native Android development tool.

How to Obtain this Book

You can buy copies of this in book in various formats.
As a Kindle book from the Amazon USA site go here (http://amzn.to/11FFWjP).
As a PDF or EPUB document from the Penny Press store go here (http://bit.ly/16ycjX1).
The EPUB version will also be available from the Barnes & Noble web store.

How this Book is Organized

Part 1 (page 12) – **Basics**
We begin with a tutorial which walks you gently through the process of installing the free Trial Version of Basic4Android, connecting it to your device, then writing, running, designing and debugging your very first Android app.
We explain every feature of the Integrated Development Environment and show you how to upgrade to the Full Version of Basic4Android. This will give you access to the Libraries discussed in Part 4.

Part 2 (page 67) – **Creating Your App**
Here we go in detail through the process of creating a real app, including the principles of design, how your app can communicate with the user, how you can use Designer Scripts to automatically modify your app to suit different devices, and how to compile, debug and test your app using either real or virtual devices.
We discuss creating graphics and databases. We examine how processes, services and activities live and die in Android. We look at the various types of modules you can create, examine ways you can make money from your app and finally explore ways you can get more help in using Basic4Android.

Part 3 (page 206) – **Language and Core Objects**
Parts 3 and 4 form the reference sections of this book.

Part 3 includes two chapters of reference material which cover every part of Basic4Android's language and core objects (that is, objects accessible from every app).

We also compare Basic4Android's language with Microsoft's Visual Basic.

Part 4 (page 402) – **Libraries**
In this reference section we discuss libraries (only available if you have upgraded to the Full Version of Basic4Android), and explain how to create your own libraries and share them with others (should you wish to).
We give full details of the Standard Libraries included in the Full Version installation. We also discuss some of the many Additional Libraries and Modules, including all the "Official" ones created by Anywhere Software, which you can download from the Basic4Android website.

Conventions Used in this Book

Code

Examples of Basic4Android code are shown indented, like this:

```
Sub Globals
  'These global variables will be redeclared each time the
activity is created.
  'These variables can only be accessed from this module.
End Sub

Sub Activity_Create(FirstTime As Boolean)
  'Do not forget to load the layout file created with the visual
designer. For example:
 Msgbox("Welcome to Basic4Android!", "")
End Sub
```

Code which is shown within the text is often shown like this: **`Sub Process_Globals`**. However, this is not always possible, since the electronic versions of this book include many links (to make it easy to find related parts of the book), which overlap code and have a different font.

We also use the same font to highlight options in on-screen dialog boxes.

Specifying Menus

We specify menus within Basic4Android by surrounded by [square brackets] and separating the parts by a greater than symbol ">" and. So the following would be shown as [Edit > Copy]:

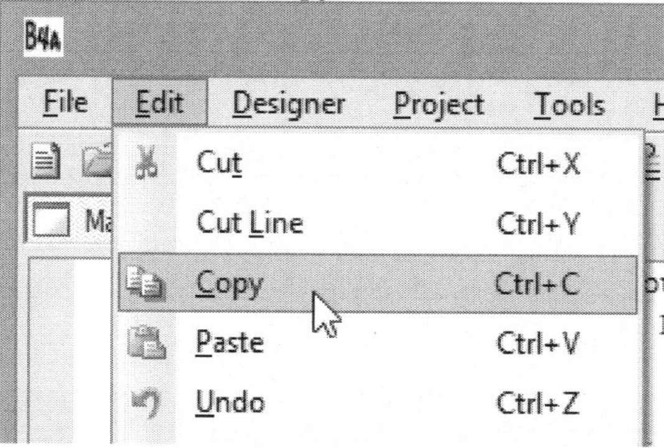

Specifying Functional Arguments

When we specify the types of the arguments which are used to call functions, we adopt a different convention than that used in the Basic4Android on-line documentation. On-line they include the full path to the argument types, for example:

DrawBitmap (Bitmap1 As android.graphics.Bitmap, SrcRect As android.graphics.Rect, DestRect As android.graphics.Rect)

We find this difficult to read, so in this book we simply write:

DrawBitmap (Bitmap1 As Bitmap, SrcRect As Rect, DestRect As Rect)

The reason that the full paths are specified on-line is that Basic4Android types, such as Bitmap, are actually "wrappers" for the full Java class. This allows for greater flexibility in extending the Basic4Android language in the future. But in most cases you do not need to worry about this when developing your apps.

Icons

The following icons are used in this book and within the IDE:

Keywords and methods have a pink flying box

Key constants have a blue box

Functions defined in your code have a pink box with a lock

Global variables (defined in Process_Globals) have a blue box with a key

Local variables (defined in current Sub) have a blue box with a lock

Properties have a hand pointing to a list

Acronyms

We use the following acroynms in this book:

ADB	Android Debug Bridge
AES-256	Advanced Encryption Standard
ANSI	American National Standards Institute
API	Application Program Interface
APK	Filename extension for Android Package
.APK	Android Package (filename extension)
ARGB	Alpha,Red,Green,Blue (Color Specification)
ASCII	American Standard Code for Information Interchange
AVD	Android Virtual Device
B4A	Basic4Android
BA	A Basic4Android object which library developers can use to raise events and to get access to the user activity, application context and other resources.
.BAS	Filename extension for BASic files
BASIC	Beginner's All-Purpose Symbolic Instruction Code
BOM	Byte Order Mark
C2DM	Cloud To Device Messaging
CPU	Central Processing Unit
CSV	Comma-Separated Values
DBMS	DataBase Management System
dip	density independent pixel
DOS	Disk Operating System
dpi	dots per inch
DSA	Digital Signature Algorithm
DTMF	Dual-tone multi-frequency
EAS	Embedded Audio Synthesizer
.EXE	Filename extension for an EXEcutable file

FTP	File Transfer Protocol
GMT	Greenwich Mean Time
GPS	Global Positioning System
GPU	Graphics Processing Unit
HD	High Definition
HDPI	High-density Dots Per Inch
HSV	Hue, Saturation and Value (Color Specification)
HTML	HyperText Markup Language
HTTP	HyperText Transfer Protocol
IDE	Integrated Development Environment
IME	Input Method Editor
IP	Internet Protocol (as in "IP address")
.JAR	File extension for Java ARchive
JDK	Java Development Kit
JET	The SONiVOX interactive music engine.
JSON	JavaScript Object Notation
LDPI	Low-density Dots Per Inch
MAC	Media Access Control address of a device
MDPI	Medium-density Dots Per Inch
MIDI	Musical Instrument Digital Interface
MIME	Multi-Purpose Internet Mail Extensions
NDEF	NFC Data Exchange Format
NFC	Near-Field Communication
NMEA	National Marine Electronics Association
OEM	Original Equipment Manufacturer
OS	Operating System
PC	Personal Computer
.PNG	Filename extension for a Portable Network Graphic
POP3	Post Office Protocol 3
PPC	Pocket Personal Computer
PRN	Pseudo-Random Number
px	pixels (page 109)
RAM	Random Access Memory
RFCOMM	Radio Frequency COMMunication
RGB	Red,Green,Blue (Color Specification)
SAX	Simple API for XML
SD	Secure Digital
SDK	Software Development Kit
SFTP	SSH File Transfer Protocol or Secured File Transfer Protocol
SIM	Subscriber Identity Module
SIP	Session Initiation Protocol
SKU	Stock Keeping Unit
SMS	Short Message Service
SQL	Structured Query Language
SSH	Secure Shell Protocol
SSL	Secure Sockets Layer

TCP/IP	Transmission Control Protocol/Internet Protocol
TTS	Text to Speech
TTS	Text-To-Speech
UDP	User Datagram Protocol
UI	User Interface: the images, sounds, keyboards and other objects which allow the user to communicate with the device.
URI	Uniform Resource Identifier
URL	Uniform Resource Locator
USB	Universal Serial Bus
UTC	Coordinated Universal Time (equivalent to Greenwich Mean Time).
UTF-16	16-bit Universal Character Set Transformation Format
UTF-8	8-bit Universal Character Set Transformation Format
UUID	Universal Unique Identifier
VB6	Visual Basic 6.0
VM	Virtual Memory
VOIP	Voice Over Internet Protocol
WYSIWYG	What You See Is What You Get
XHDPI	Extra-High-density Dots Per Inch
XLS	Microsoft Excel Spreadsheet (File Extension)
XML	eXtensible Markup Language

Support

Resources to support this book can be found at resources.Basic4Android.info (http://resources.basic4android.info/)
The main source of support is the active community of enthusiastic developers around the world who already use Basic4Android and are very happy to support others who have problems.
See the Getting More Help Chapter (page 203) for details.

Acknowledgements

We would like to thank the creator of Basic4Android, Erel Uziel, for his help in creating this book, and Klaus Christl who wrote the original Beginner's Guide and User Guide which have been the inspiration for this book. We also thank those who have reviewed drafts of the book and made constructive comments, especially Bob Paehr.

We'd Like to Hear from You

We hope you will enjoy this book and find it useful. If you have any comments, we would be very happy to hear them. Please write to info@Basic4Android.info
We would also be very grateful if you would take the time to rate it on the main Amazon website: USA Amazon site (http://amzn.to/11FFWjP)

About the Author

Wyken Seagrave is a professional developer of applications and websites using Visual Basic, Visual Basic for Applications, PHP and MySQL, among other languages. He has taught computer programming at college and university, and written many user manuals for the applications he has developed.

His great passion in life is to bring knowledge of the history of the universe to a wider public. To this end he has written books and websites dealing with the subject both as fact and fiction, including the History of the Universe (http://historyoftheuniverse.com/) website (also available as an eBook on Amazon (http://amzn.to/1446HTw)) and the Time Crystal (http://timecrystal.co.uk/) series.

Part 1: Basics

We begin with a tutorial which walks you gently through the process of installing the free Trial Version of Basic4Android, connecting it to your device, then writing, running, designing and debugging your very first Android app.

We explain every feature of the Integrated Development Environment.

Then we show you how to upgrade to the Full Version of Basic4Android. This will give you access to the Libraries discussed in Part 4.

1.1 Getting Started

Note: Basic4Android runs on PCs with Windows 2000 and above, including Windows 8. Both 32-bit and 64-bit systems are supported.

Two Versions

There are two versions of Basic4Android: the trial and the full version. The main differences are in brief:

Price: the trial version is FREE! The price of the full version depends upon which flavor you purchase.

Remote Compilation Mode (page 23) which makes compiling your apps simple and painless only runs under the free trial. This means you do not need to install the Java JDK and Android SDK packages if you are running the free version, although you may if you wish. They are both required for the full version.

Note that Basic4Android includes a Rapid Debugger (page 124) which can greatly shorten development times. You can use this feature with both the trial and full versions, but in both cases it requires that you install the Java JDK, even when you use Remote Compilation with the trial version.

Advanced features: the full version supports libraries (page 403) and other advanced features missing from the trial.

Installing the Trial Version

In the tutorials, we assume you will be using the free trial version of Basic4Android. We also assume you will not want to install the Java JDK to begin with, so we will postpone explanation of the Rapid Debugger (page 124) until Chapter 2.

Download Basic4Android Trial

Download the latest version of the Basic4Android Trial version from here: http://www.basic4ppc.com/android/downloads.html

Install and Run the Trial

Installing .NET Framework

Basic4Android requires .NET Framework 3.5. If it is not present on your machine, you will be prompted to download and install it.

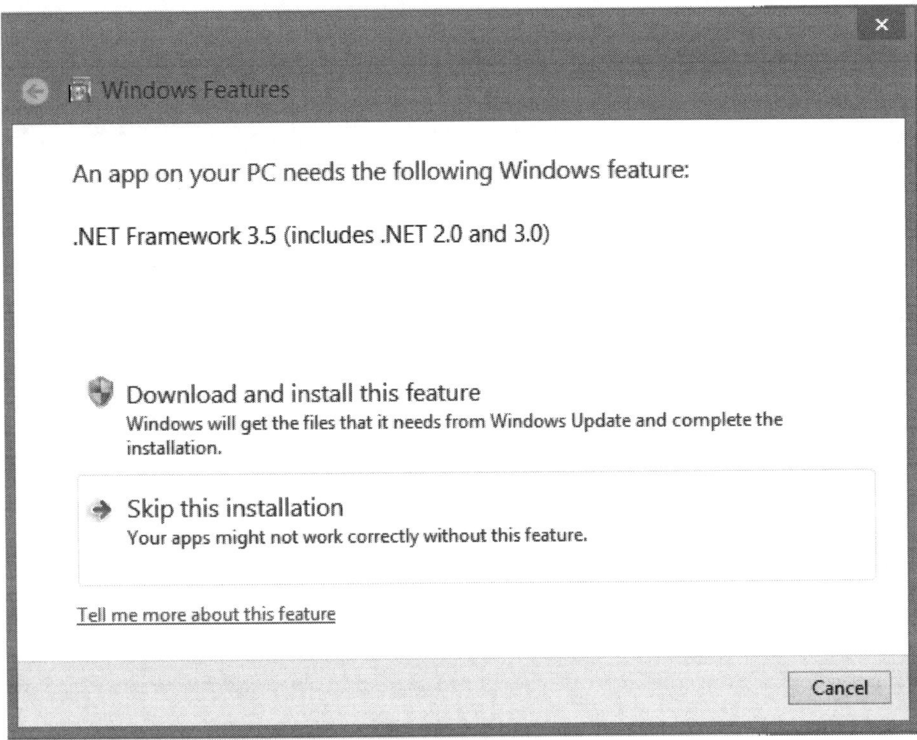

After you run the Trial, you will see this screen:

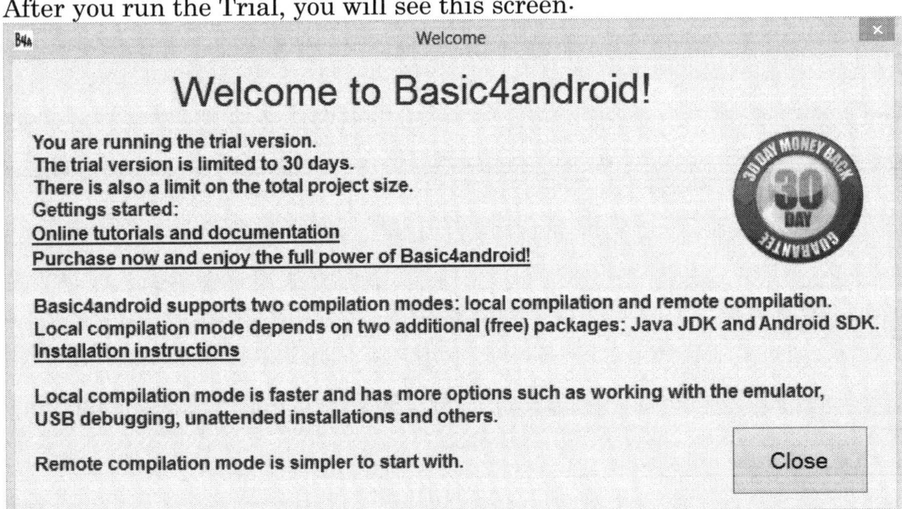

We will say more about local and remote compilation soon.
Click **Close**
You then see the IDE (Integrated Development Environment).

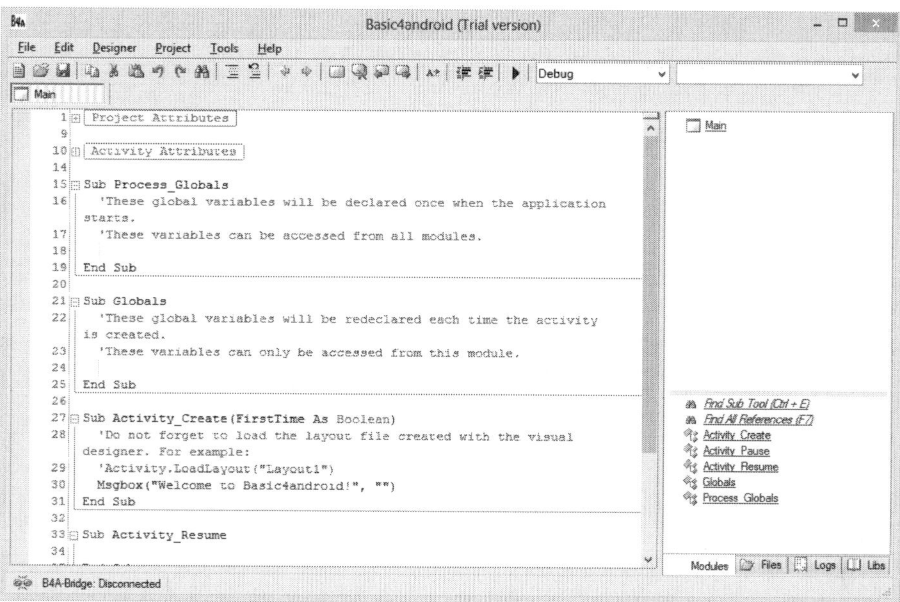

This is where you create, test and compile your apps. Apps are developed within projects (page 68) and projects are stored in folders.

Your First App

When you create a new Basic4Android app, a sample project is already loaded, allowing you to run this simple app without any additional code. The code should be as follows. If your code is different, you can either copy this or edit your code to be the same, or download “Your First App” from this book’s resource page (http://resources.basic4android.info/) and unzip it to a new folder within your projects folder.

```
#Region  Project Attributes
 #ApplicationLabel: B4A Example
 #VersionCode: 1
 #VersionName:
 'SupportedOrientations possible values: unspecified, landscape
or portrait.
 #SupportedOrientations: unspecified
 #CanInstallToExternalStorage: False
#End Region

#Region  Activity Attributes
 #FullScreen: False
 #IncludeTitle: True
#End Region

Sub Process_Globals
 'These global variables will be declared once when the
application starts.
 'These variables can be accessed from all modules.
End Sub

Sub Globals
 'These global variables will be redeclared each time the
activity is created.
 'These variables can only be accessed from this module.
End Sub

Sub Activity_Create(FirstTime As Boolean)
 'Do not forget to load the layout file created with the visual
designer. For example:
 Msgbox("Welcome to Basic4Android!", "")
End Sub

Sub Activity_Resume
End Sub

Sub Activity_Pause (UserClosed As Boolean)
End Sub
```

This is just about the minimum code required to create an app.
Before you can run the app, first you must save the code into a project folder.

Save the program

Use the [File > Save] menu

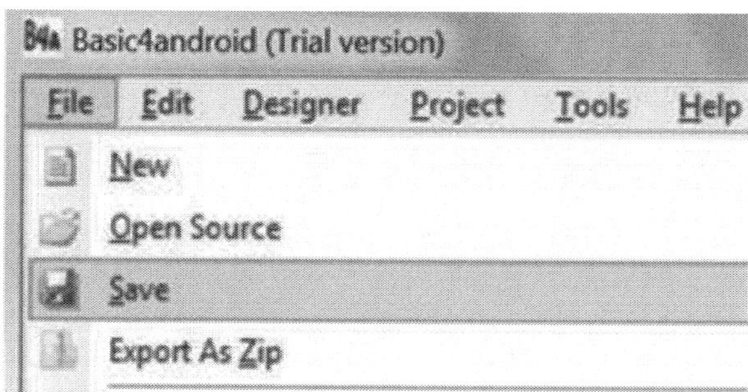

We recommend you create a folder to hold all your Basic4Android projects, and within this folder, create separate folders, one for each project. When you create a new program, Basic4Android will create sub-folders called **Files** and **Objects** in the selected folder. For this reason you must put every program in a separate sub-folder of your projects folder.
The project folder for this program, we will call "B4A Example".

B4A-Bridge

Before you can run the program, you need to connect Basic4Android to a device or an emulator (page 128). There are several options (see Testing Options (page 127)), but as a first step we recommend using B4A-Bridge to connect to your device. B4A-Bridge is a free app which runs on an Android mobile phone or tablet. It was built using Basic4Android! The source code is available here (http://bit.ly/141A2MC).
B4A-Bridge is made of two components. One component runs on the device and allows the second component (which is part of the IDE) to connect and communicate with the device. The connection is done over the local network or with a Bluetooth connection. Once connected, B4A-Bridge supports all of the IDE features which include: installing applications, viewing the logs, debugging and the visual designer (taking screenshots is not supported).
Android doesn't allow applications to quietly install other applications. Therefore, when you run your application using B4A-Bridge, you will see a dialog asking you to approve the installation.

Notes on Bluetooth Connection

Many devices, especially older devices running Android 2.1 or 2.2, can have problems with Bluetooth connections and especially with multiple connections. All kinds of workarounds were implemented because of these issues. However, there are devices (HTC desire for example) that do not work reliably enough.
If there are connection problems, the **Reset Bluetooth** button within B4A-Bridge might help. It disables and then re-enables the Bluetooth adapters. If your connection is still not stable, you should avoid using the debugger and designer on your device; both require an additional connection.

Install the B4A-Bridge app on your device

B4A-Bridge is available free in Google Play and Amazon Market. Search for: B4A Bridge. Install the app on your device (Android mobile phone or tablet).

Run B4A-Bridge on your device

It will display a screen similar to:

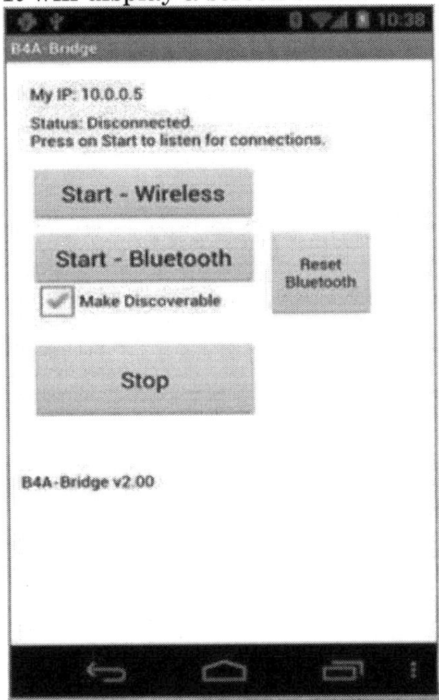

You should choose either **Start - Wireless** or **Start - Bluetooth** depending on the working mode. The **Make Discoverable** checkbox will make your device Bluetooth discoverable for 5 minutes. This is only needed if the device and computer weren't paired before.

Note: the **My IP**: address at the top of the app. This is what you will need in the next step.

Connect the IDE to the device

Go back to the Basic4Android IDE running on your PC.

Go to [Tools > B4A-Bridge] and choose either **Connect Wireless** or **Connect Bluetooth**.

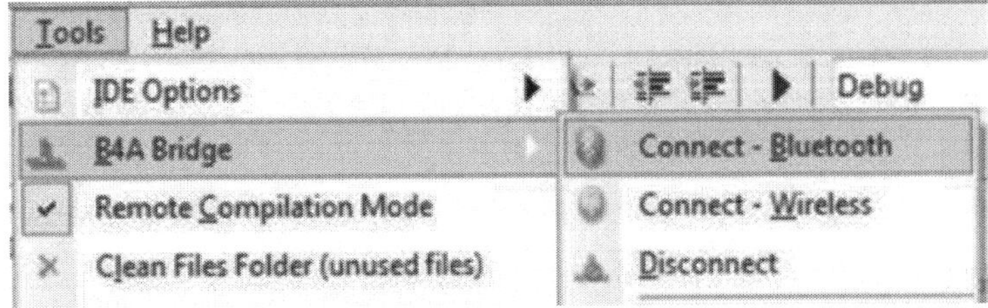

When using the trial version, checking the **Remote Compilation Mode** option will allow rapid compilation without installing any further software.

Wireless connections

If you selet [Tools > B4A Bridge > Connect – Wireless] you will see a list of up to five IP addresses previously selected, and and option to enter another address:

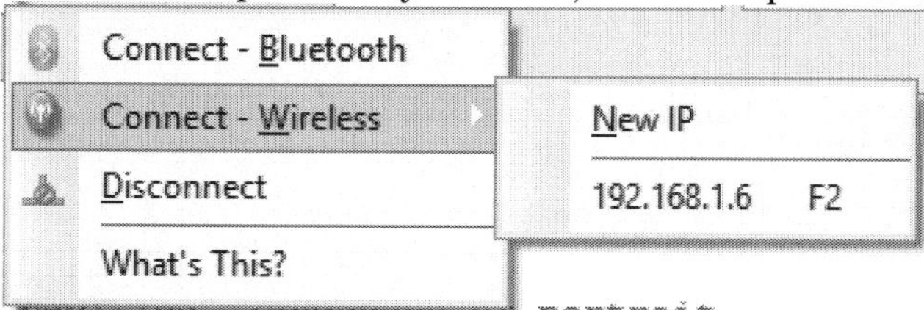

You can quickly connect to the last IP address using F2.
The IP address which you need to enter for a new connection is displayed in the B4A Bridge app on the device. In some cases, the address displayed may be the mobile network address. In that case you can find the local wireless address in the wireless advanced settings page.

Bluetooth connections

Most devices include Bluetooth, although many PCs do not. Verify that your PC has Bluetooth. If not, and if you wish to use Bluetooth, dongles are available to provide this facility. To connect to your PC to your device using Bluetooth, you must turn Bluetooth on, using Wireless and Networks Settings, and also make your device discoverable using the Bluetooth Settings. Discoverability might only last for a minute or two.
When you select [Tools > B4A-Bridge > Connect Bluetooth] within Basic4Android, you will see a dialog box. Click **Find Devices**.

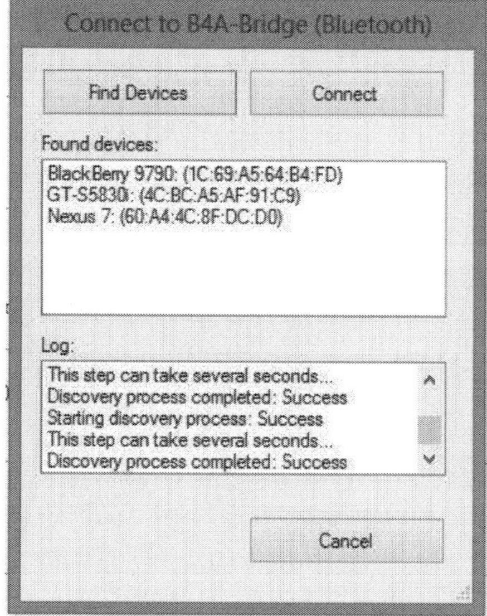

All paired devices, and new devices in discoverable mode, will be listed. You should choose the correct one and click **Connect**. If the connection succeeds, the dialog will close. The status bar at the bottom of the IDE screen shows the current status:

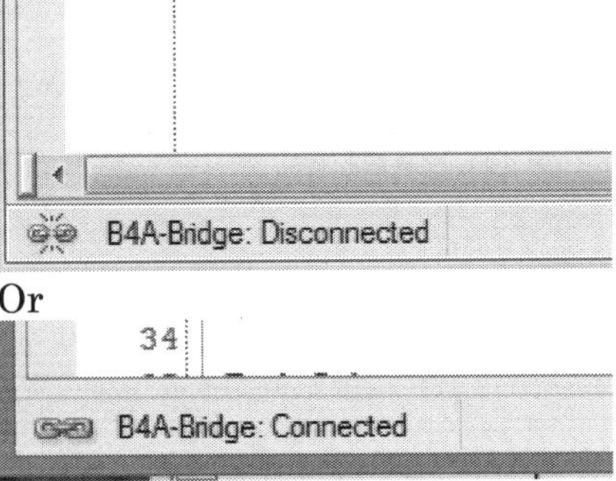

Or

B4A Designer

When B4A-Bridge gets connected, it first checks if another App, B4A Designer, needs to be updated. B4A Designer allows you to design your app directly on your device. If B4A Designer has not been installed, B4A-Bridge will ask whether to install it. You might see a screen something like this:

Select **Verify and install**, so Google can check the app for viruses. You will then see the following:

Click on **Install**. The app will be installed and you will see the confirmation page.

At this point, you do not need to open the designer, but you can do so as it will be useful soon. B4A-Bridge should then continue to install your app. However, it may have "timed out" (got tired and stopped trying), in which case you need to start the install again from the IDE.

As the install proceeds, you might see the Complete Action Using dialog again, because now B4A-Bridge is trying to install your test app. You can click on either option in that dialog.

Stopping B4A-Bridge

B4A-Bridge keeps running as a service until you press on the Stop button. You can always reach it by pulling down the notifications screen from the notification bar at the top of the device's screen.

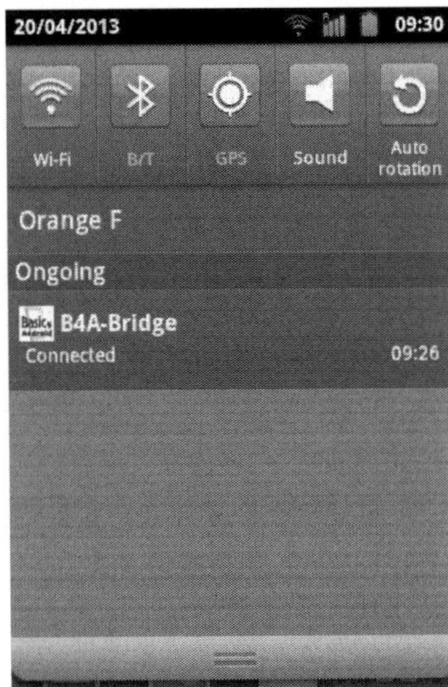

Pressing on the B4A-Bridge notification will open the main screen.

Running your new app

Now you can compile your app (that is, convert it into Java) and run it on your device. There are a number of ways to do this. Let's start with the simplest:

Compile and Run

In the toolbar of the IDE on your PC, first ensure that **Debug (legacy)** is selected in the compile options dropdown list (as shown below), then either select [Project > Compile & Run] or type Alt+1 or click on the blue triangle in the toolbar:

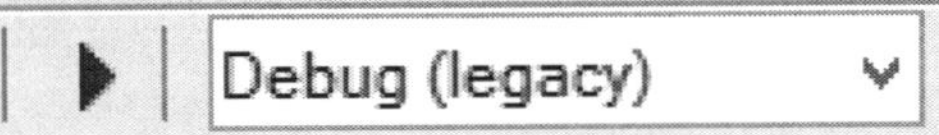

Note: Basic4Android includes a Rapid Debugger (page 124) feature, but to use it you need to install the Java JDK. To keep things simple for this introduction, we explain the older form of the debugger.

During compilation you'll see a dialog box:

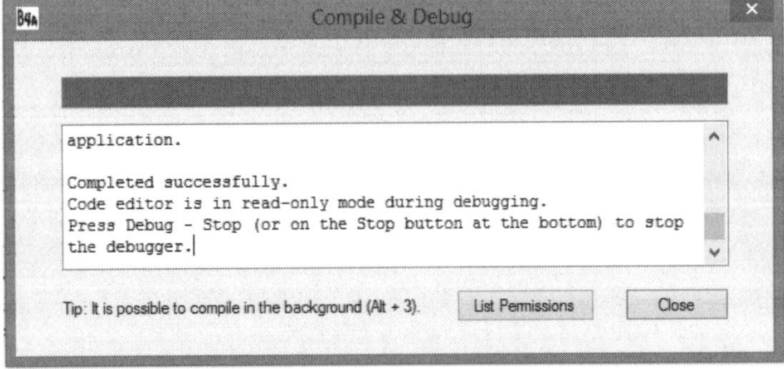

This is for information only. Either click **Close** or click on another window and the dialog will close automatically.

Remote Compilation

The Trial Version of Basic4Android includes a facility called Remote Compilation. This works by compiling your code over the web using Basic4Android servers. This means that you can compile your app without installing the Java JDK or Android SDK.

However, Remote Compilation has limits to the size of code it will compile. If you get an error message saying the limit has been reached, you can install the Java JDK and the Android SDK (as described in Upgrade to Full Version (page 59)) and compile locally. You do **NOT** need to buy the full version to do this.

Also note that, with Remote Compilation, you cannot use the Rapid Debugger unless you install the Java JDK on your PC. For the purpose of this tutorial, therefore, we will use the legacy debugger and introduce the Rapid Debugger later (page 124).

Approve the app on your device

As mentioned above, when you run an application, you are required to approve it. You might see the Complete Action Using (page 20) dialog.

Note: If you have already run this app before on your device, you would see the following:

If you saw this, you would click on **OK**. If this is your first run, that screen will not be shown. In any case, you will then see the following screen:

Note: the Bluetooth permission and Internet permission are automatically added in debug mode. Click on **Install**.

Having installed the app, you will see the following:

Click on **Open**

You should then see the app running on the device. There might be a delay while the IDE debugger connects to the app. This is to allow you to debug your app, as we discuss later.

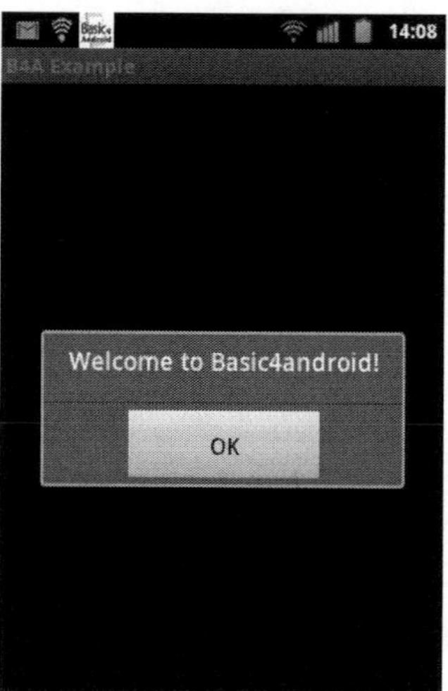

Rotate your device

When you rotate your device you should see the app rotate. How does this happen? Let's try debugging the app and find out!

Debugging

To learn more about the above events and discover how to debug an app, we are going to look at setting breakpoints and logging events. Note that Basic4Android has an amazing feature called the Rapid Debugger (page 124), but to use it with Remote Compilation, you would need to install the Java JDK. For the purposes of keeping things simple during this introduction, we will use the legacy debugger, and introduce the Rapid Debugger later (page 124).

Setting a breakpoint

We now explain how to debug your app using the legacy debugger.
Return to the IDE on your PC. If you can still see the Compile & Debug window:

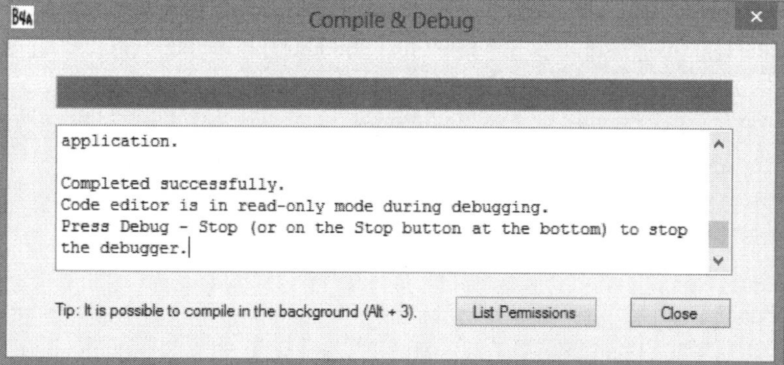

Click **Close**. You can then see the IDE in debug mode.

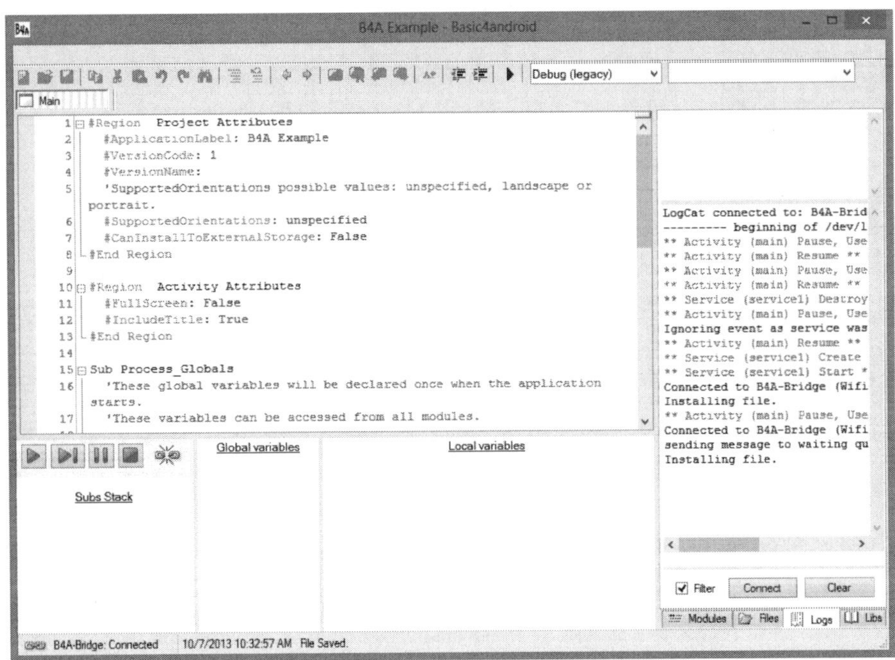

Notice the debug area near the bottom-left corner. The code is now “read only”.
We are trying to discover why the message box is shown when the device is rotated.
Clearly the following line of code must be executed:

```
Msgbox("Welcome to Basic4Android!", "")
```

You will find it in the

```
Sub Activity_Create(FirstTime As Boolean)
```

As we discuss below (page 175), this subroutine runs whenever the orientation of the screen changes. To verify this, and gain some experience in debugging, let’s add a breakpoint at this statement. Click in the grey column on the left side of the screen at the **Msgbox** line. A red dot appears and the line is highlighted in red:

```
Sub Activity_Create(FirstTime As Boolean)
    'Do not forget to load the layout file created with the
visual designer. For example:
    'Activity.LoadLayout("Layout1")
    Msgbox("Welcome to Basic4Android!", "")
End Sub
```

In addition, a red bar appears in the scroll-bar on the right of the code area to indicate the position of the breakpoint. Now try rotating your device again. A message will be shown on the device:

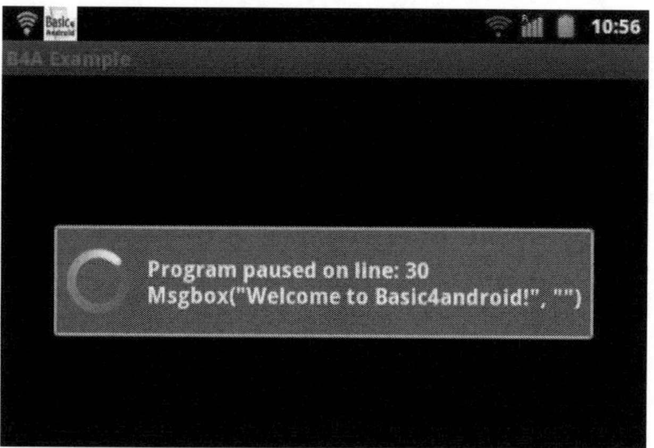
10:56
B4A Example
Program paused on line: 30
Msgbox("Welcome to Basic4android!", "")

Execution of the program in the IDE will stop at the breakpoint:

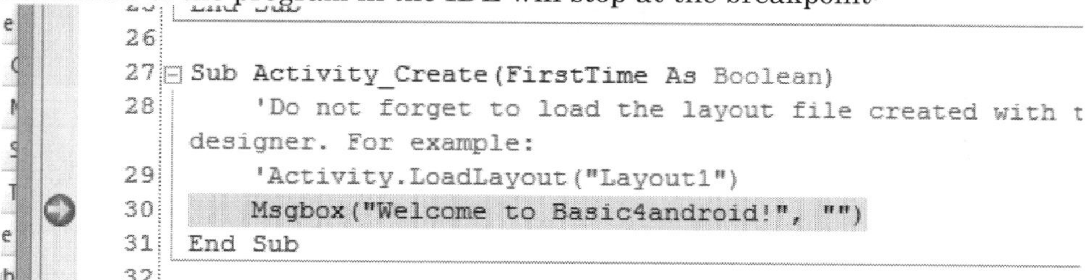
Sub Activity_Create(FirstTime As Boolean)
'Do not forget to load the layout file created with t
designer. For example:
'Activity.LoadLayout("Layout1")
Msgbox("Welcome to Basic4android!", "")
End Sub

Click on the **Run** icon or press **F5** to continue execution of the program:

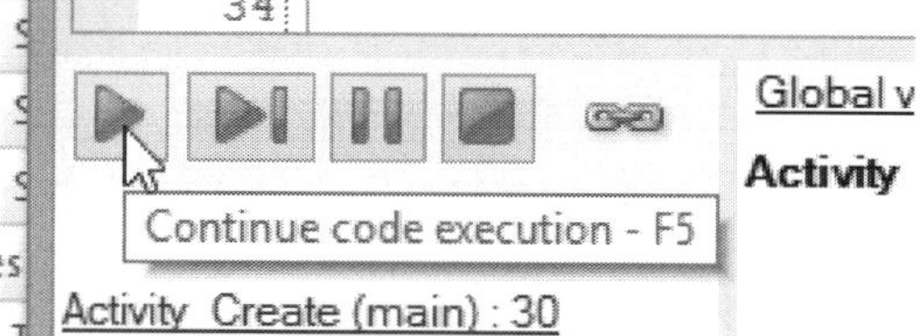
Global v
Activity
Continue code execution - F5
Activity_Create (main) : 30

The program will continue on the device and the Msgbox will be shown.

When the User Rotates a Device

Note: that when the user rotates the device, Android calls Activity_Pause, Activity_Create and Activity_Resume, in that order.

More about Debugging

For more information, see the Debugging (page 123) section.

Logging Events

You can also write into the IDE Log in order to keep track of events while the app is running. Let's try it. To do that we need to add some code. Stop the debugger by clicking on the **Debug Stop** button or by pressing **F11**:

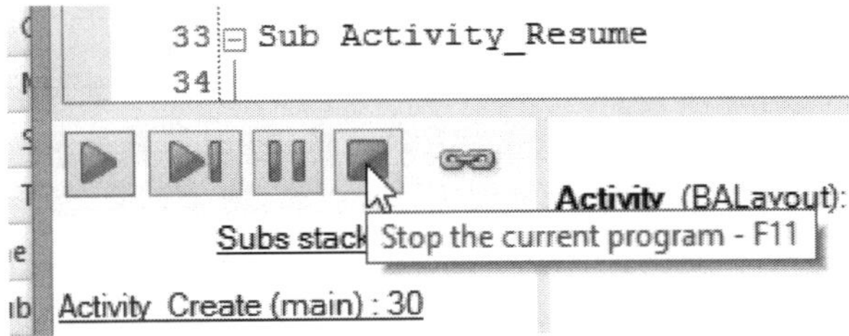

Scroll down to the line

```
Msgbox("Welcome to Basic4Android!", "")
```

And add the line

```
Log ( "Height = " & Activity.Height)
```

Now run the app and, once it is running, rotate the device. Click on the **Logs** tab in the IDE:

In the Detail Area above the Tabs you will then see something like the following:

```
Installing file.
PackageAdded: package:b4a.example
** Activity (main) Create, isFirst = true **
Height = 430
** Activity (main) Resume **
** Activity (main) Pause, UserClosed = false **
** Activity (main) Create, isFirst = false **
Height = 270
** Activity (main) Resume **
** Activity (main) Pause, UserClosed = false **
** Activity (main) Create, isFirst = false **
Height = 430
** Activity (main) Resume **
```

The IDE is logging information. You can use this method to record information while the app is running and so help debug your app. **Note**: you might need to click on the **Connect** button in the logging area. It will be easier to see just activity from your app if you select the **Filter** checkbox:

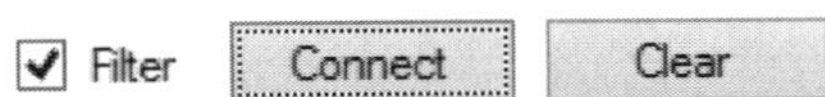

We will now try changing the appearance of the app. This will be the first step towards designing an effective user interface.

Your Second App: Using the Designer

We are going to make this app more interesting by adding a button.

The View and Layout Concepts

First a few key concepts. In Basic4Android, a page displayed to a user is called an **`Activity`** and a control which can be added to the Activity is called a **`View`**. The details of Views are collected in a file called a **`Layout`**.

The code which controls the Layout is called an **Activity Module**. To be visible to the user, the Layout must be loaded into the Activity. This normally happens within the **`Activity_Create`** sub.
The tool we normally use to create a Layout is the **Designer**. So next, we learn to use the Designer.

Running the Designer

Run the Designer by clicking Designer in the main menu. The Designer and Abstract Designer Windows appear:

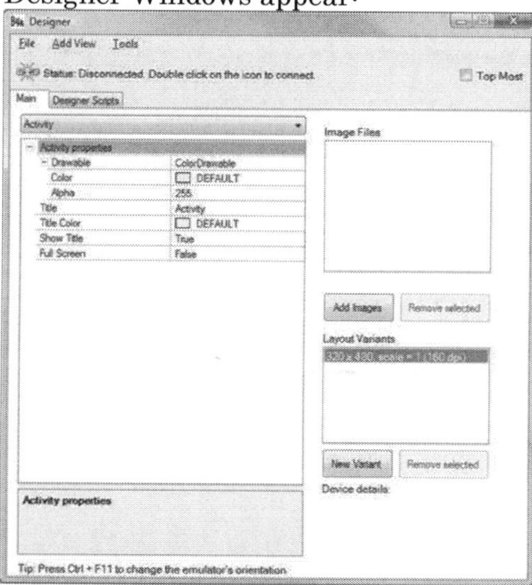

This is where you add views (controls) and configure their properties.

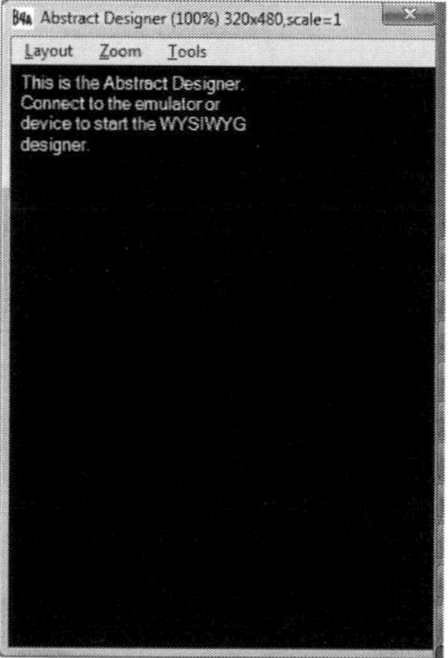

Here you will see the Views of the Layout, but note the Abstract Designer (page 103) is NOT "What you see is what you get" (WYSIWYG). So how do you see your Layout as the user will see it?

Connect the Designer to your device.

To see the Layout in WYSIWYG, you need to connect Basic4Android to either a device or an emulator (page 128). In this tutorial, we will use your device and B4A-Bridge. (We describe how to use the emulator in Testing Your App (page 127).)
First start B4A-Bridge on your device if it is not already running. Then connect Basic4Android to your device, if it is not already connected. You can do this from the IDE as described above (page 18).
Now connect the Designer to your device within the Designer menu [Tools > Connect to Device / Emulator] or by double-clicking the broken chain:

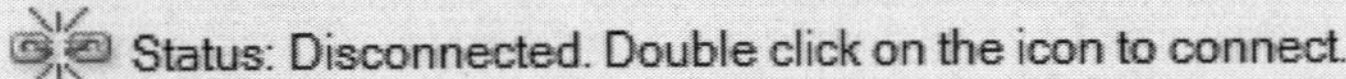

The B4A Designer app will start on your device and a blank screen appears on your device since the layout has no views.

Add a button

In the Designer Window click [Add View > Button]

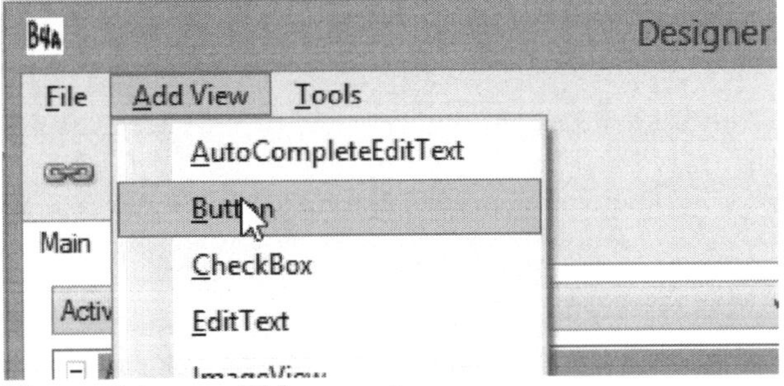

Three things will happen:

You will see the parameters of your button in the Designer:

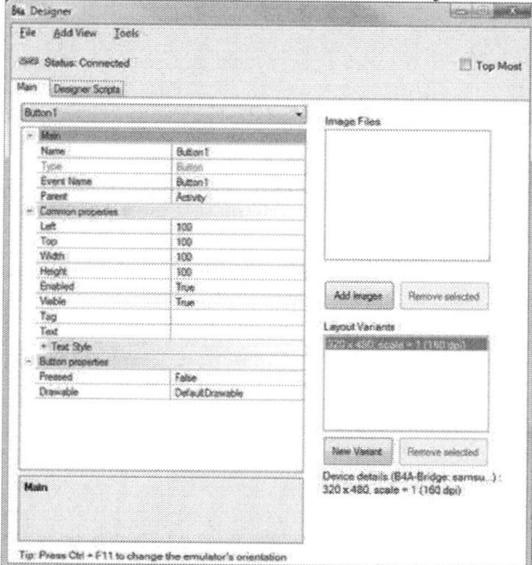

You will see the button in the Abstract Designer

And you will see it on your device as WYSIWYG (What You See Is What You Get).

Configure your button

You can resize and reposition the button either in the Abstract designer or on your device. You can also set its position in the Designer (using **Common Properties: Left, Top**, **Width** and **Height**) but normally you use the Designer to change the name, colors and other features. **Note**: Basic4Android offers a more powerful way of controlling the position of Views using Designer Scripts. We describe this in a separate chapter (page 109).

We recommend you change the name of the button to something like **`btnTest`**. (This type of name uses the so-called Hungarian naming convention (page 215).)

Use the Designer to change the **Text** field to "Click Me!". This is what will be displayed to the user.

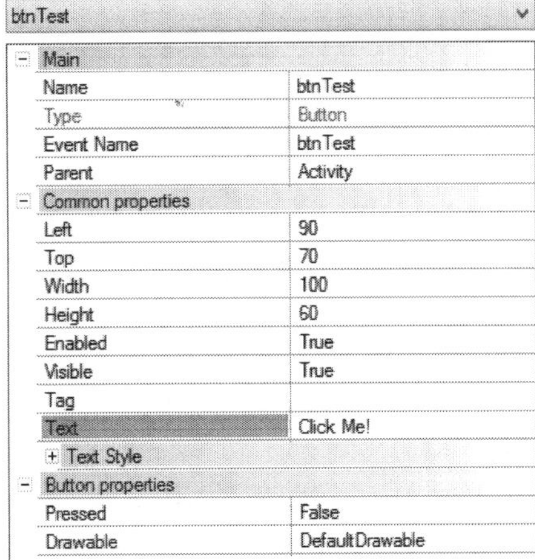

Save your layout by clicking [File > Save] in the Designer. You can choose any name, but it makes sense to use the same name as the **Activity Module**, in this case "Main". (This will create a file called "main.bal" within the Files folder of your project.)

Generate Members

In order to control the button in code, we need to declare it in the relevant **Activity Module**. The best way to make sure you do this correctly is to ask the either Designer or the Abstract Designer to generate this code for you.
First make sure the correct **Activity** tab is selected in the IDE, since any code you generate will be added to the current activity.

If your app only has one activity, then you should select the Main tab.

Using the Designer Tools

Select your new button and use the Designer's [Tools > Generate Members] option. This will display the following (you might need to expand the **`btnTest`** list by clicking the + sign:

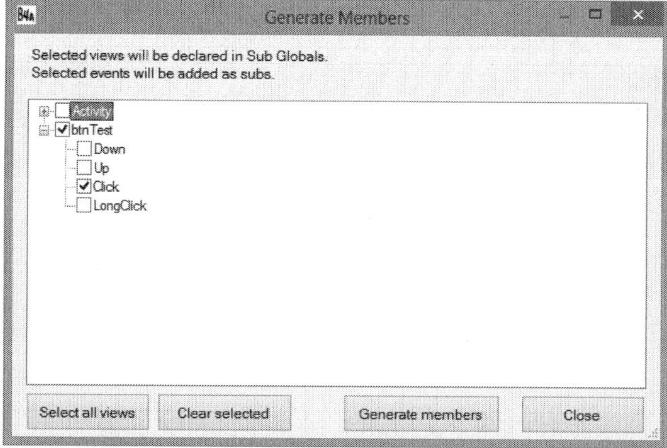

Check **btnTest** and **Click**, as shown.
Click **Generate members** and **Close**.
Two entries will be generated within your code. The first is a new line within **`Sub Globals`**:

```
Sub Globals
  'These global variables will be re-declared each time the
activity is created.
  'These variables can only be accessed from this module.
  Dim btnTest As Button
End Sub
```

This tells your code what type of object btnTest is. The reason why view variables **must** be declared in **`Sub Globals`** and not in **`Sub Process_Globals`** is explained here (page 222).
The **Generate Members** dialog will also generate a new empty Sub:

```
Sub btnTest_click
End Sub
```

Explanation of Sub's name

You might wonder why this sub has to be called **`btnTest_Click`**. This code is an example of an **event handler**. We explain how events work here (page 233). Essentially, some objects can generate events, for example when a user does something, and your code has to handle that event. The first part of the event handler name "**`btnTest`**" tells Basic4Android which object generated the event. The "**`Click`**" part of the name specifies which event we are responding to. These two parts have to be joined by an underscore to create the name of the event handler sub.

Using the Abstract Designer

An alternative way to generate these two pieces of code is to use the Abstract Designer's context (or popup) menu. If you right-click on **`btnTest`** in the Abstract Designer, the following menu appears:

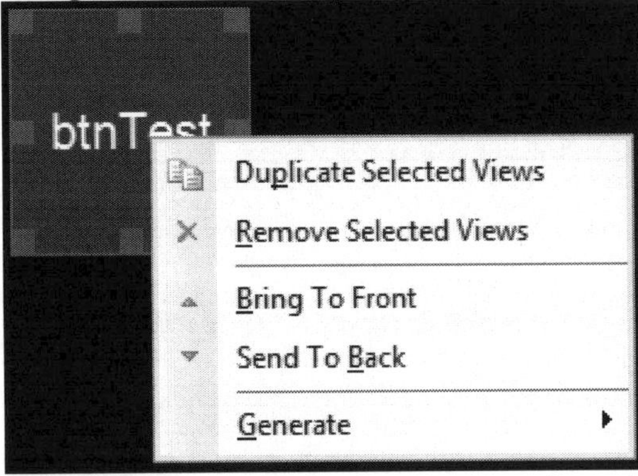

By hovering over **Generate**, you see the sub-menu:

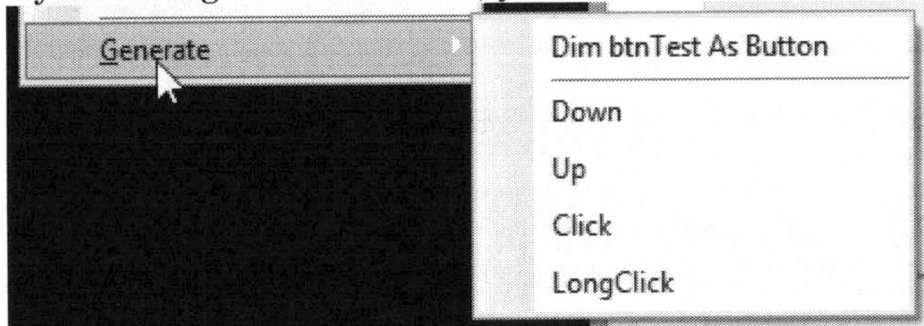

First, select [Dim btnTest as Button], then repeat the process and select [Click]. This will achieve the same result as before. **Note**: there is no danger about asking the Designer or Abstract Designer to generate the code twice. If the code already exists in your Activity, the request will be ignored.

Add code to button

Now we are going to write the code to handle this event. Move the existing **`Msgbox`** code from the **`Sub Activity_Create`** into the new sub. It should now read

```
Sub btnTest_Click
 Msgbox("Welcome to Basic4Android!", "")
End Sub
```

Load the Layout

To make this work we need to load this new layout when the app starts.
Edit **Activity_Create** to read:

```
Sub Activity_Create(FirstTime As Boolean)
 Activity.LoadLayout("Main")
End Sub
```

Note: you need to use the same name which was used to save the Layout in the Designer.

Run your app

This time B4A Bridge will ask:

Click **OK**. You should now see your button and the message when you click it.

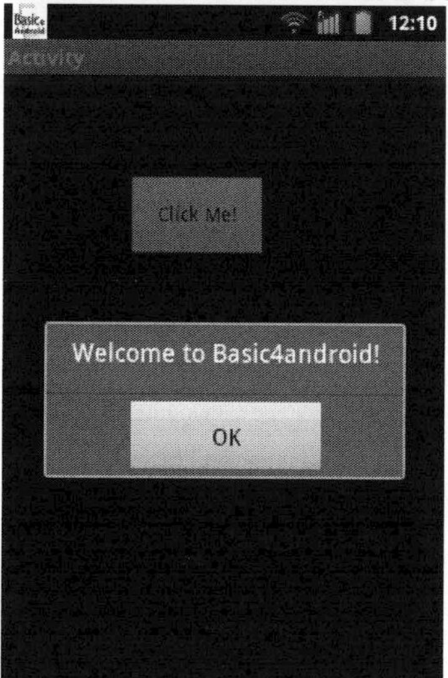

Your Third App

Now let's see if you can create an app on your own! You are going to create an app which will show the time when the user clicks a button. To do this, you need to add a label to your view. A label is an object (a "view" in Android jargon) which can display text. Call it **Label1**.

Use the designer to declare the label (that is, add a **Dim** statement to your code). Now change your app so that your **btnText** will run the following code when the user clicks it:

```
Label1.Text = "The time now is " & DateTime.Time(DateTime.Now)
```

This defines the message which **Label1** will show. **DateTime** is a Basic4Android object which provides a wide range of time-related and date-related functions. For example: **DateTime.Now** returns the number of milliseconds since 1-1-70, and **DateTime.Time** converts this number into the current time.

It may sound a bit complex but you do not need to understand the details at this stage. It's just to give an example program, so see if you can make it work. If you get stuck, you can download the solution (Your Third App) from this book's resource page (http://resources.basic4android.info/).

Stopping B4A-Bridge

After you have finished developing, you should navigate to B4A-Bridge on your device and press on the **Stop** button, in order to save its battery.

More about Designer

For more details about the Designer see the Designer Chapter (page 92).

1.2 The Integrated Development Environment

Now we will look more closely at the parts of the **I**ntegrated **D**evelopment **E**nvironment (IDE). This is what you use to develop your app. The IDE consists of the following areas:

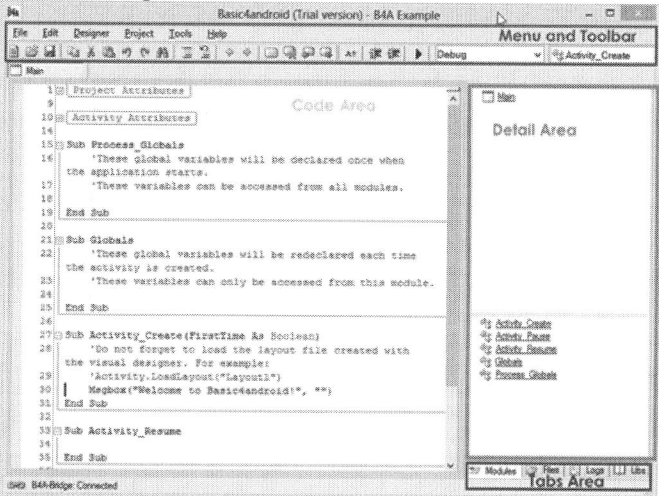

Menu and Toolbar
Code Area (page 44)
Detail Area (page 53)
Tabs Area (page 53)

Menu and Toolbar

File menu

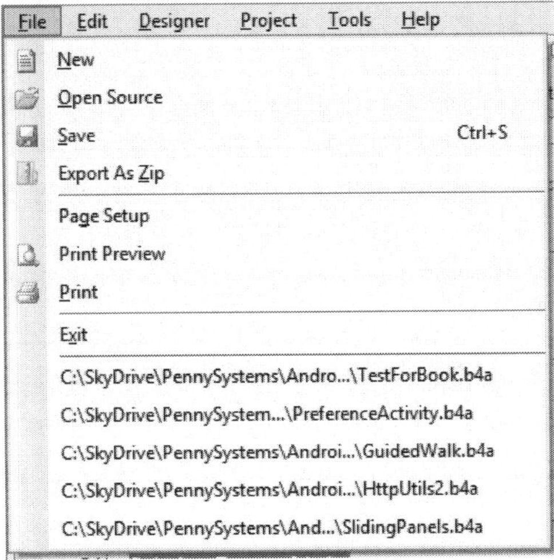

New
Generate a new empty project (page 68).

Open Source
Load a project.

Save
Save the current project.

Export As Zip
Export the whole project in a zip file.

Page Setup
Page setup for printing

Print Preview
Show a print preview.

Print
Print the code.

Exit
Leave the IDE.

Below this is a list of the last loaded programs.

Edit menu

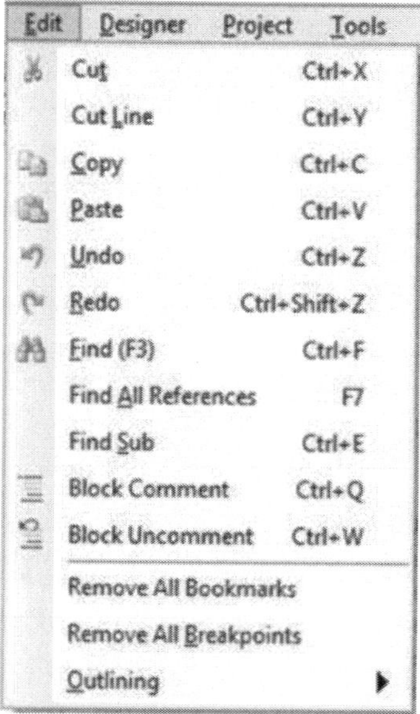

Cut (Ctrl+X)
  Cut the selected text and copy it to the clipboard.

Cut Line (Ctrl+Y)
  Cut the line at the cursor position. **Note**: in other programs, Ctrl+Y often redoes the previous action, which is Ctrl+Shift+Z in Basic4Android.

Copy (Ctrl+C)
  Copy the selected text to the clipboard.

Paste (Ctrl+V)
  Paste the text in the clipboard at the cursor position.

Undo (Ctrl+Z)
  Undo the last operation.

Redo (Ctrl+Shift+Z)
  Redo the previous operation.

Find (F3 or Ctrl+F)
  Activate the **Find and Replace** function.

Find All References (F7)
  Show a list of all references to the selected string. You can click a reference to quickly go to that line of code.

Block Comment
  Set the selected lines as comments (page 47).

Block Uncomment
  Uncomment the selected lines. (page 47)

Remove All Bookmarks
  Bookmarks (page 47).

Remove All Breakpoints
  Breakpoints (page 121).

Outlining

Open a sub-menu containing three functions to expand or collapse code:
- **Toggle All** (Ctrl-Shift-o) - Expand collapsed code and collapse extended code.
- **Expand All** - Expand all code.
- **Collapse All** - Collapse all code.

Designer

This menu option opens the Designer (page 92).

Project menu

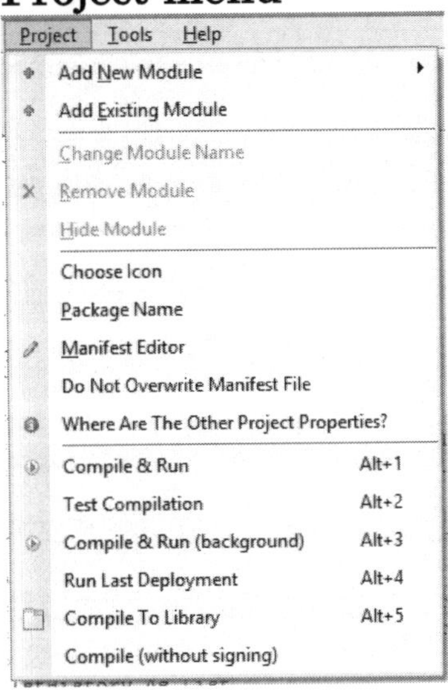

Modules

The first five options deal with Modules (page 180):

Add New Module

lets you choose which type of module to create:

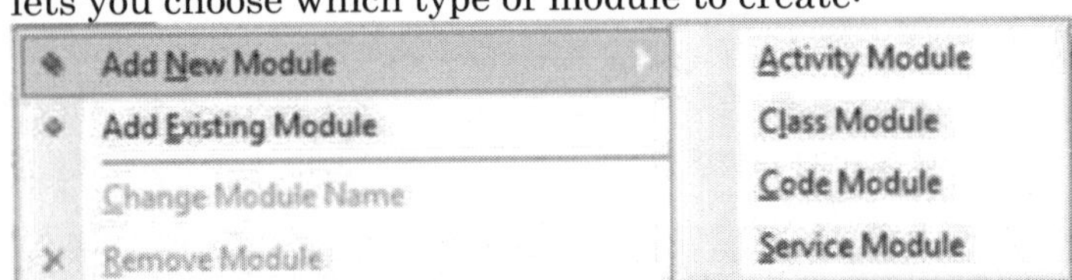

Add Existing Module

lets you select a module (probably from another project) which will then be copied into this project. It will be added to the list of modules in the Modules Tab and shown as the active module.

The following 3 options are available only if a module other than Main is active:

Change Module Name

Change the name used in the IDE

Remove Module

This will not delete the module, merely remove it from the list of active modules in the Modules Tab (page 54).

Hide Module

When a Module is hidden it will still be visible in the Modules Tab (page 54). Clicking there will make it visible in the editor.

Package Options

The next 5 options in the Project menu deal with the overall program:

Choose Icon

Choose an icon (page 193) for the program,

Package Name

Change the package name (page 69)

Manifest Editor

Run the Manifest Editor (page 70).

Do Not Overwrite Manifest (page 70) **File**

This option is available only for backwards compatibility. It is recommended to use the Manifest Editor (page 70) instead.

Where Are the Other Object Properties?

This is for backward compatibility and takes you to a web page which explains about Project Attributes (page 68) and Activity Attributes (page 180).

Compile Options

The bottom options in the Project Menu deal with the different compiling options.

Compile & Run (Alt+1)

has the same effect as pressing the run icon ▶. The result will depend upon which compile mode (page 119) is selected in the IDE.

For example, it will produce these files in the Objects folder if the Debug mode is selected:

bin
gen
res
src
AndroidManifest
classes.dex
TestForBook_DEBUG.apk

Test Compilation (Alt+2)

Run the Warning Engine (page 56) which helps find errors in your code.

Compile & Run (background) (Alt+3)

The same as Compile & Run except no progress dialog box is shown.

Run Last Deployment (Alt+4)

Re-run the code installed already on the device, without recompiling or re-installing.

Compile to Library (Alt+5)

Compile your project into a library which you can use in other projects and share with other users. More details can be found at How to Compile a Library (page 406).

Compile (without signing)

Compile the code but do not produce an apk file in the **Objects** folder. You might want to do this, for example, if you want to sign an app with a non-Basic4Android keystore. See here (http://bit.ly/17rLYeo) for a tutorial on how to do this, and here (page 197) for more about keystores.

Tools menu

IDE Options

These are explained below.

B4A Bridge

See the B4A-Bridge section (page 17) for details of this method of designing and debugging your app on a real Android device. B4A-Bridge must be running on the device before you can connect. The options are to connect via Bluetooth or Wireless, or to disconnect the device.

Clean Files Folder (unused files)

Delete files that are located under the **Files** folder but are not used by the project. It will not delete any file referenced by any of the project layouts. A list of unused files will be displayed before deletion, and you will be allowed to cancel the operation.

Be careful: copies of deleted files are NOT kept in the Recycle Bin!

Clean Project

Delete all files that are generated during compilation.

Run AVD Manager

See Using the AVD Manager (page 128) for details.

Configure Paths

Tell Basic4Android the location of your javac.exe, android.jar and (optionally) your additional libraries.

See the Configure Paths (page 64) section for details

Restart ADB Server

In some cases the connected emulator (page 128) or device fails to respond and you might need to end the link and restart it. The link is managed by the ADB (Android Debug Bridge) server process, hence the name of this menu option. See here for details about the ADB server from the Android Developer site (http://developer.android.com/tools/help/adb.html).

Private Sign Key

Allows you to create and sign your app to make it ready for publication. See the Publishing Your App chapter (page 193) for details.

Take Screenshot

You can capture screens from the emulator and perhaps from devices connected via USB, but not from devices connected via B4A-Bridge. For USB connections to devices, see here (http://bit.ly/141xVIP).

The Take Screenshot function can also be called from:

- Tools menu when the IDE is in edit mode

- Debug menu when the IDE is in debug mode

These options start the following dialog:

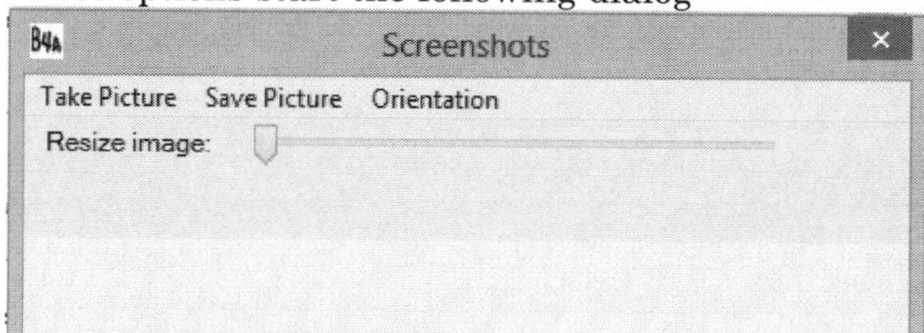

Click on **Take Picture** to take the screenshot from the device or the emulator. If several devices are connected, you will be asked to select which one to use for the screenshot.

You can resize the image, change the orientation of the picture, save it as a PNG file or copy it to the clipboard by right-clicking on the image. A **Copy to clipboard** button will pop up:

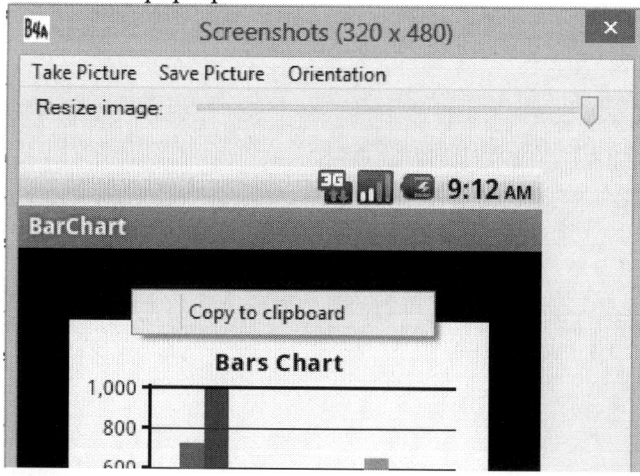

IDE Options Sub-Menu

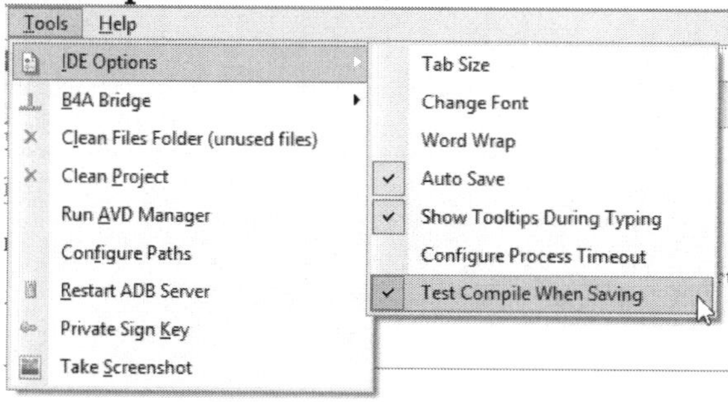

Tab Size

Set the size of the indent when you press the tab key in the editor. The default is 4 (although 2 is probably a better value).

Change Font

Shows the following dialog box:

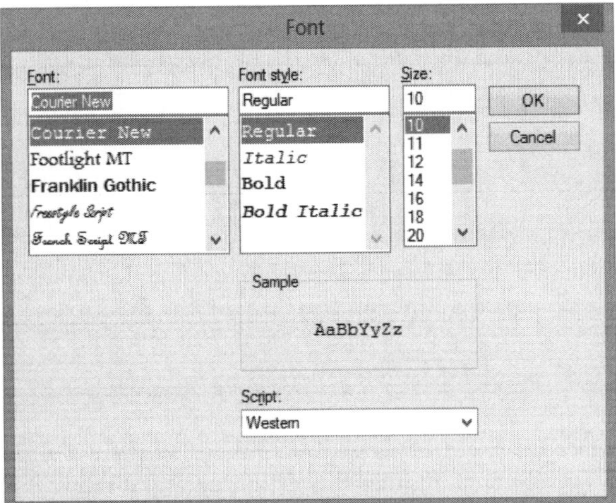

Word wrap

Without word wrap, long lines may extend beyond the visible window. With word wrap, such lines are wrapped to the next line.

Auto Save

Saves the program and the layout in the Designer whenever you run the app on a connected device or emulator.

Show Tooltips During Typing

Tooltips are hints and prompts for data you can enter:

```
    btnAction.Text(
                   Text As String
```

You can create your own tooltips. See Comments As Documentation (page 51)

Configure Process Timeout

Specify how many seconds the IDE should wait as it tries to connect to the emulator. After this number of seconds, the IDE will show an error message in the **Compile & Debug** dialog box. This is called a Process Timeout. The default is 30 seconds.

Test Compile When Saving

With this option selected, the IDE runs a test compilation every time the project is saved.

Help Menu

This contains a link to the on-line help and tutorials (http://www.basic4ppc.com/android/documentation.html), and an **About** option which shows the version number, copyright and other information about Anywhere Software.

Toolbar

Generates a new empty project (page 68).

Loads a project.

Saves the current project.

Copies the selected text to the clipboard.
Cuts the selected text and copies it to the clipboard.
Pastes the text in the clipboard at the cursor position.
Undoes the last edit.
Redoes the previous "Undo".
Activates the Find and Replace function.
Sets the selected lines as comments.
Uncomments the selected lines.
Navigate backwards
Navigate forwards
Adds a bookmark.
Removes a bookmark.
Go back to the previous bookmark.
Go forward to the next bookmark.
Autocomplete function (page 49) (Ctrl+space).
Decrease the indentation of the selected lines (page 48).
Increase the indentation of the selected lines (page 48).
Runs the compiler using the mode selected in the compiler options list
Debug (rapid) Compiler options list. See Compilation Modes (page 119).
Process_Globals Select routine to edit.

Code area

Below the Toolbar is a row of tabs, one for each module (page 180) in the project.

Main | Person | utils | testService | testActivity | DBUtils

Clicking a tab brings the corresponding module to the front. This is where you edit your code. Code consists of some header information, such as **`Project Attributes`** and **`Activity Attributes`**. It then contains a series of Subroutines. This is typical of Basic programs.

Regions

For your convenience while editing, your code is divided into blocks called Regions. A Region is an area of your code which you can rapidly expand or collapse. You can do the same with Subroutines. You can expand or collapse regions and subs by clicking on the "+" and "–" signs on the left of the Code area:

```
Sub Process_Globals

Sub Globals

  Dim tgtspin As Spinn
  Dim myarray(4) As St

    Dim btnTest As Butt
  End Sub
```

You can define your own regions using **`#Region`** and **`#End Region`** and embed several subroutines within them. The benefit is that by collapsing the code, you make it easier to navigate to the required section.

Collapse the whole code

The [Edit > Outlining] menu contains three functions to expand or collapse code:

Toggle All (Ctrl-Shift-o)- Expands collapsed code and simultaneously collapses extended code.

Expand All - Expands the whole code

Collapse All - Collapses the whole code.

Hovering over Collapsed Code

Hovering with the mouse over a collapsed Region or subroutine shows the beginning of its content.

Code header

There are two pre-defined Regions in the Main Module: **`Project Attributes`** and **`Activity Attributes`**, which we describe next.

Project Attributes Region

This Region contains attributes valid for the whole project. It is displayed only in the Main module.

```
#Region  Project Attributes
  #ApplicationLabel: B4A Example
  #VersionCode: 1
  #VersionName:
 'SupportedOrientations possible values: unspecified, landscape or portrait.
  #SupportedOrientations: unspecified
  #CanInstallToExternalStorage: False
#End Region
```

For details see the Project Attributes section (page 68).

Activity Attributes Region

This Region determines attributes of the current activity.

```
#Region  Activity Attributes
  #FullScreen: False
  #IncludeTitle: True
#End Region
```

See Activity Attributes (page 180) for details.

Service Attributes

When you add a new Service, you'll find the **Service Attributes** header:

```
#Region  Service Attributes
  #StartAtBoot: False
#End Region
```

See Service Attributes (page 190) for details.

Commenting and uncommenting code

A selected part of the code can be set to comment lines or set to normal.
Original code:

```
    Dim btnAction, btn0 As Button
    Dim lblResult As Label
    Dim lblComments As Label
    Dim lblMathSign As Label
    Dim lblNumber1 As Label
    Dim lblNumber2 As Label
```

Select the code and click on .

```
    Dim btnAction, btn0 As Button
    Dim lblResult As Label
    Dim lblComments As Label
    Dim lblMathSign As Label
    Dim lblNumber1 As Label
    Dim lblNumber2 As Label
```

The lines are now set as comments.

```
  ' Dim btnAction, btn0 As Button
  ' Dim lblResult As Label
  ' Dim lblComments As Label
  ' Dim lblMathSign As Label
  ' Dim lblNumber1 As Label
  ' Dim lblNumber2 As Label
```

To reset the lines to normal, select the lines and click on .

Bookmarks

You can set 'bookmarks' anywhere in the code and jump between these bookmarks.
To set a bookmark, position the cursor on the desired line:

```
Dim btnAction, btnO As Button
Dim lblResult As Label
Dim lblComments As Label
Dim lblMathSign As Label
```

Click on or type Ctrl-M. The bookmark sign is displayed in the left margin:

```
Dim btnAction, btnO As Button
Dim lblResult As Label
Dim lblComments As Label
Dim lblMathSign As Label
```

To remove a bookmark, position the cursor on the line and click on .

Click on to jump forward to the next bookmark.

Click on to jump backward to the previous bookmark.

You can remove all bookmarks with [Edit > Remove All Bookmarks]

Indentation

A good practice is to use the Tab key to indent code and so make its structure (of subroutines, loops etc.) more obvious and easier to verify. The indentation size created by the Tab key can be set in the Tools menu (page 43). For example consider the following:

```
Sub btnAction_Click
If btnAction.Text = "O K" Then
If lblResult.Text="" Then
Msgbox("No result entered","E R R O R")
Else
CheckResult
End If
Else
New
btnAction.Text = "O K"
lblResult.Text = ""
End If
End Sub
```

This is clearer if the text is indented to reveal its logical structure:

```
Sub btnAction_Click
  If btnAction.Text = "O K" Then
    If lblResult.Text="" Then
      Msgbox("No result entered","E R R O R")
    Else
      CheckResult
    End If
  Else
    New
    btnAction.Text = "O K"
    lblResult.Text = ""
  End If
End Sub
```

Whole blocks of code can be indented forth and back at once by selecting the code block and clicking or , or by selecting the block and pressing the tab key to indent or shift-tab to un-indent.

Autocomplete

The autocomplete function helps you write your code. Enter the first few letters of a keyword or variable name and press Ctrl+Space, or click on . For example, if you type “ty” and Ctrl+Space you will see:

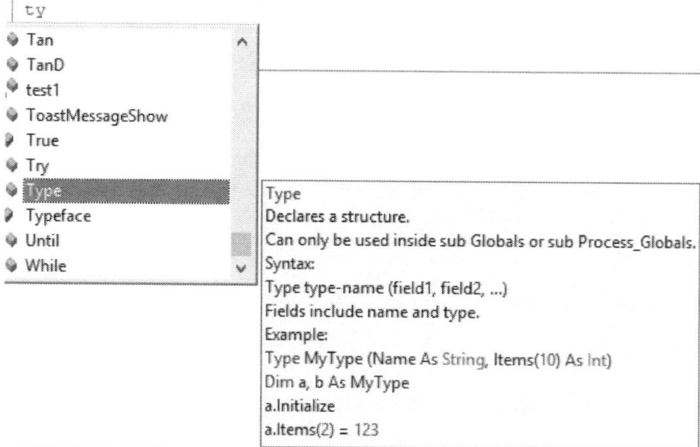

The popup menu shows all variables, views and property names beginning with “ty”, plus online help for the highlighted variable, view or property name.

Note: if there are no property names, views, or variables that match what you have started to type before pressing CTRL+Space, a popup list will not appear. Also, if there is only one entry in the popup list that matches what you have typed, the IDE assumes that this is what you want autocompleted, and that entry will be typed out completely for you, without showing the popup list.

Icons

The following icons are used here (or in other parts of the IDE):

Keywords and methods have a pink flying box
Key constants have a blue box
Functions defined in your code have a pink box with a lock

- Global variables (defined in **`Sub Process_Globals`**) have a blue box with a key
- Local variables (defined in current Sub) have a blue box with a lock
- Properties have a hand pointing to a list

Select the required word by using the mouse or the arrow keys, then press Enter or Return.

Autocomplete Properties and Methods

Once a variable or object name has been selected, type a dot. All properties and methods are displayed in a popup menu:

```
lblNumber1.
```

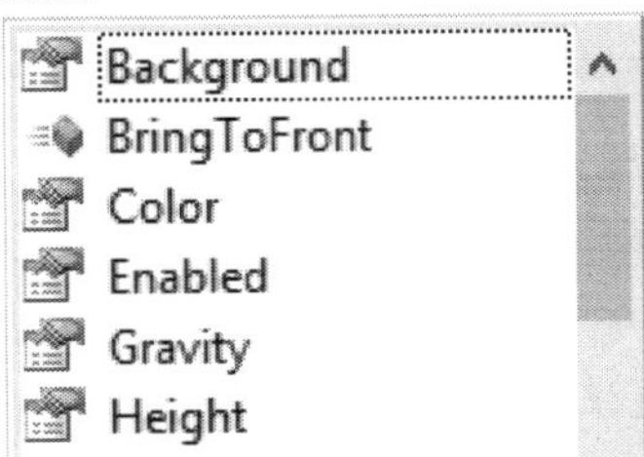

Properties have a hand icon and methods have a pink box.

Autocomplete event subroutines

A second Autocomplete function allows you to create Event (page 233) subroutines **with the correct arguments**. Enter the Sub word plus a blank character and press the Tab key. A list of available types is displayed:

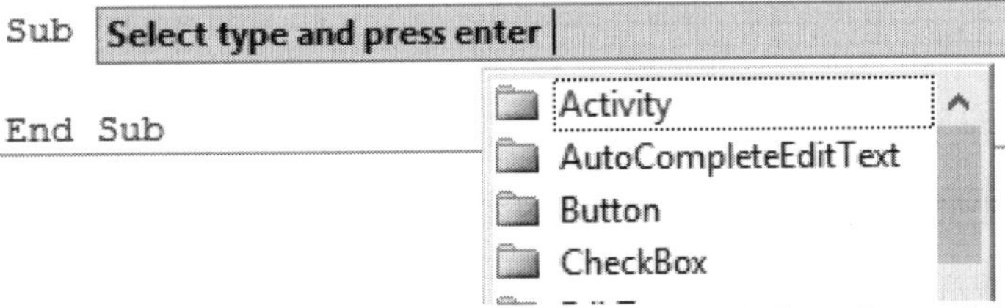

Select the required type and press Enter. A list of possible events is then displayed:

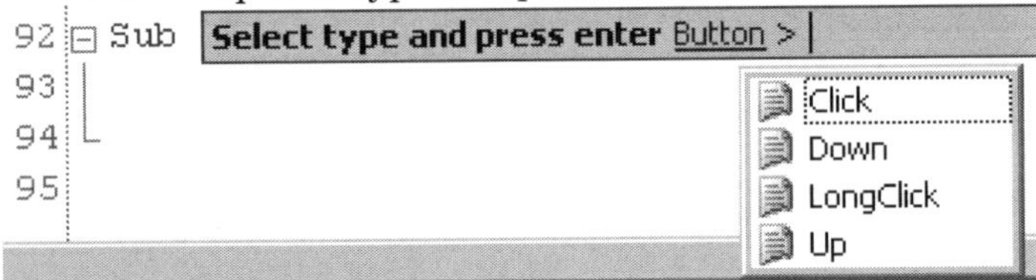

Select the type and press Enter. The Sub name is automatically created together with its arguments:

```
Sub EventName_Click

End Sub
```

Now you must enter the EventName. This will have been specified when the source object was Initialized.

Comments as Documentation

The documentation feature built into Basic4Android is very useful. Comments (page 207) above subs, such as:

```
' Split strCurrent into substrings using strDelimiter
'  and return a list
' strCurrent - the string to split
' strDelimiter - the character(s) to use to split strCurrent
' Example: <code>
' lst = splitString("Abcdefcghi", "c")
' </code>
Sub splitString(strCurrent As String, strDelimiter As String) As List
    Dim splitResult As List
```

will automatically appear in the popup window:

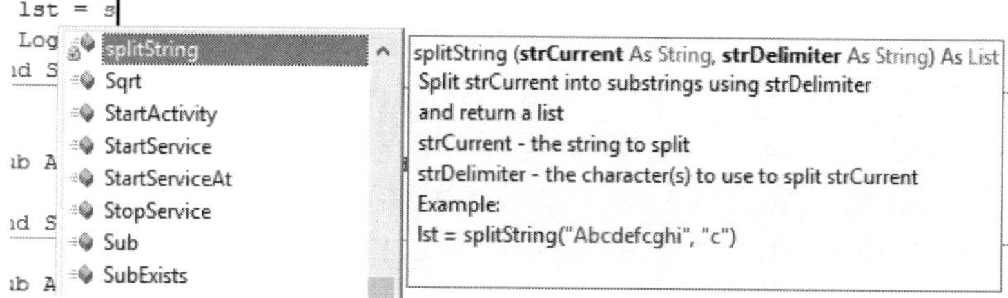

Any comment immediately before **`Sub Process_Globals`** is treated as the main module comment.

Context Menu

Right-clicking in the Code Area produces the Context Menu:

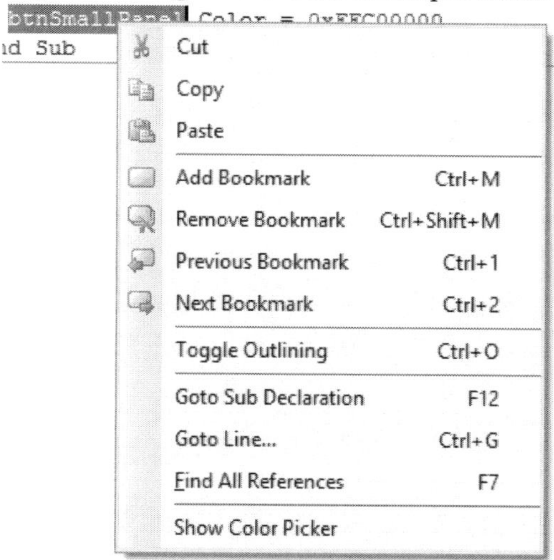

Many of these occur in the Edit menu (page 39).

Note: Cut and Copy apply to any text which is selected and beneath the cursor when you right-click, such as btnSmallPanel in the example above. If no text was selected, the line at the cursor will be cut or copied.

Other items in the Context Menu are:

Goto Sub Declaration

Sometimes it is useful to jump from a subroutine call to the subroutine definition. This can easily be done from [Goto Sub Declaration] in the context menu.

Find All References

This shows a modal dialog box with a list of all lines in the code which contain the selected word.

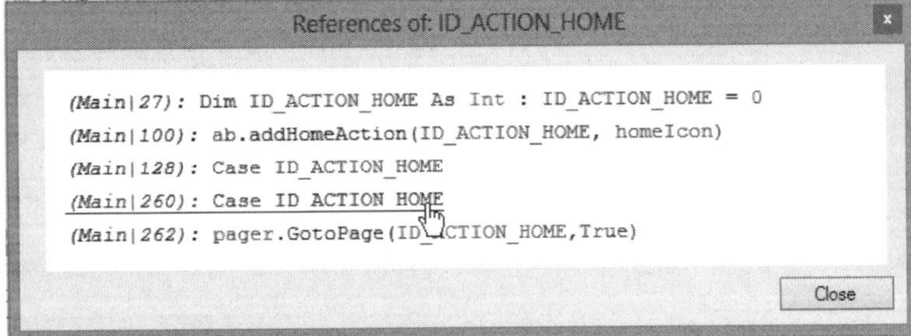

You can quickly go to any of these by clicking the line.

Color Picker

Selecting this option from the Context Menu shows:

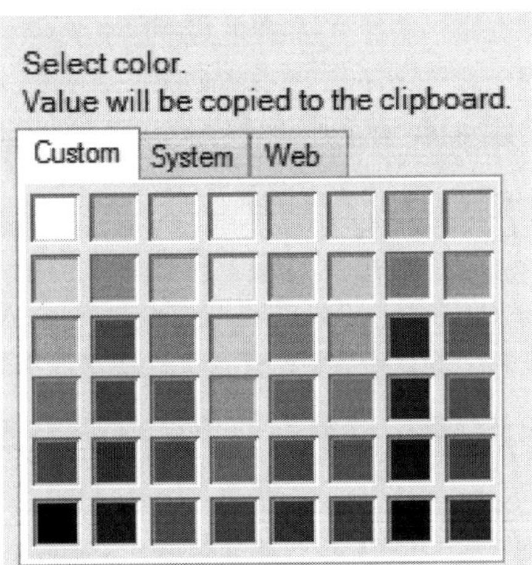

Clicking on a color will copy the color to the clipboard as a hexadecimal quadruplet, that is, a hex literal (page 210) with four bytes or eight digits. The format is the same as given by the Colors.ARGB (page 281) function, that is, Alpha channel, Red, Green and Blue values. For example:

0xFFFFFFFF = fully opaque white

0xFF000000 = fully opaque black
0xFFFF0000 = fully opaque red

Highlighting occurrences of words

When selecting a word, the word is highlighted in dark blue (A in the following diagram) and all other occurrences in the code are highlighted in light blue (B) while the scrollview on the right side indicates the position of this word (A) in the document (C) in light blue.

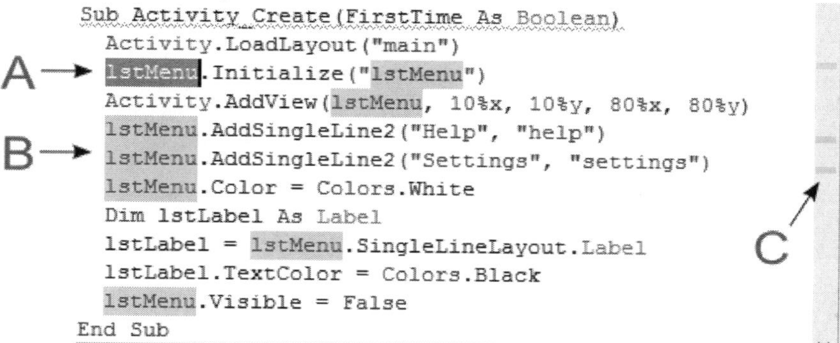

With the slider, you can move up or down the code to go to the other occurrences. Breakpoints (page 121) are also marked on the scrollview, this time in red (D).

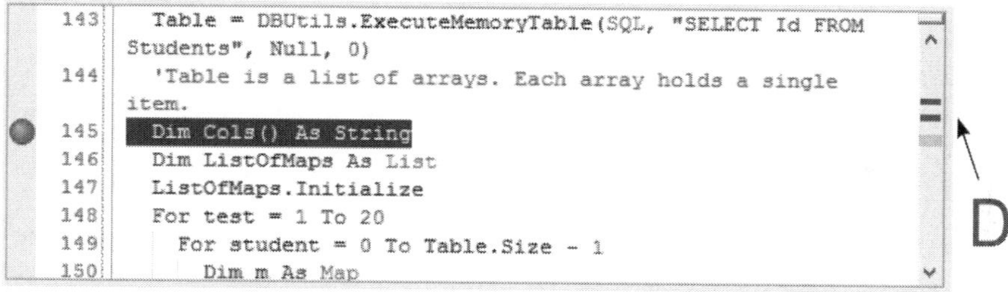

Detail Area

The content of this area depends upon which of the tabs has been selected. We therefore show the detail area in the following Tabs section.

Tabs

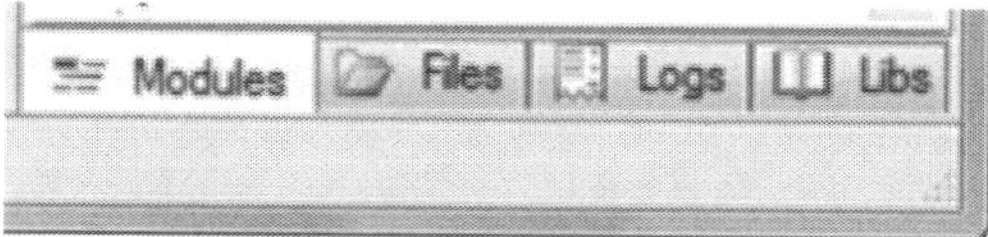

There are 4 tabs at the bottom right corner of the IDE that display the following information.

Modules Tab

An app can contain several modules (pieces of code). Clicking on the Modules Tab shows a list of the modules in the top of the Detail Area, and a list of Subroutines below it.

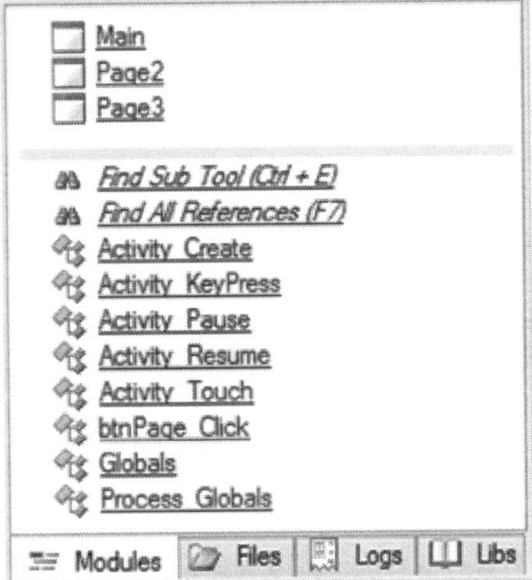

List of Modules

List of Subroutines within current module

Clicking on one of the module names brings that module to the top. Clicking on one of the subroutine names moves the cursor directly to the selected routine.

Files Tab

Clicking on the Files Tab brings into the Detail Area a list of all the files that have been added to the project.

horse.png
Main.bal
menuIcon.png
myFile.txt
question.png
smith.jpg
temp.bal
test.txt
testActivity.bal

Add Files | Remove Selected

Click on **Add Files** to add files to the list. These can be any kind of files: layouts, images, texts, etc. On your PC, the selected files will be copied to the **Files** folder of your project. On the device, these files will be saved in the Files.DirAssets (page 307) folder.
Checking one or more files in the list enables the **Remove Selected** button.

horse.png
Main.bal
menuIcon.png
myFile.txt
question.png
smith.jpg
temp.bal
test.txt
testActivity.bal

Add Files   Remove Selected

Clicking on the **Remove Selected** button shows the following dialog:

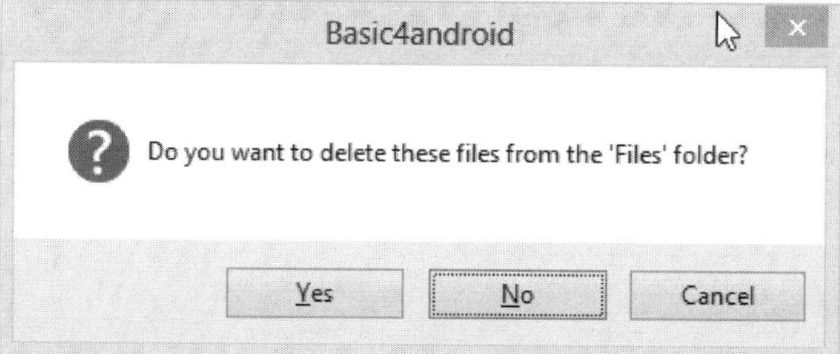

Yes: removes the selected files from the list and from the **Files** folder of the project. **Make sure to have a copy of the files you remove, because they are removed from the Files folder, but not transferred to the recycle bin. This means they are definitively lost if you don't have a copy.**
No: removes the selected files from the list but does not delete them from the project's **Files** folder.
See Files (page 303) chapter for file handling.

Logs Tab

Clicking on the Logs tab displays in the Detail Area a list of comments generated by the program when it is running. We explain its use in the Logging (page 126) section.

Warning Area

An area at the top of the Logs Tab. See the Warning Engine below for details.

Libs Tab

This option is only available in the Full version of Basic4Android.
Clicking on the Libs tab brings into the Detail Area a list of the available libraries (page 403) that can be used in the project.

Referenced libraries

Download More Libraries

- [ ] DateUtils
- [ ] Daydream
- [x] Dialogs (version: 2.92)
- [ ] GameView
- [ ] Geocoder
- [ ] GoogleMaps
- [ ] GPS

This includes a link here (http://bit.ly/16H9C7s) that allows you to download more libraries including user-generated ones. More information about libraries can be found in this book here (page 403).

Check the libraries you need to reference in your project. All projects reference the Core Library (page 270). Some other libraries (the Standard Libraries (page 408)) are included with the installation. Others are Additional Libraries (page 524), generated both by Anywhere Software (the makers of Basic4Android) and by users.

The Warning Engine

Basic4Android version 2.7 introduces the Warning Engine which helps find errors in and warnings about your code. It gives a warning after you choose one of the compile options in the Project menu or type Alt+1, Alt+2, Alt+3 or Alt+5, or when you save the project (if the [Tools > IDE Options > Test Compile When Saving] option is selected).

The offending lines of code are underlined in green (A in the following diagram), their position is marked in green in the scrollbar (B) and they are listed in the Warning Area of the Logs Tab (C).

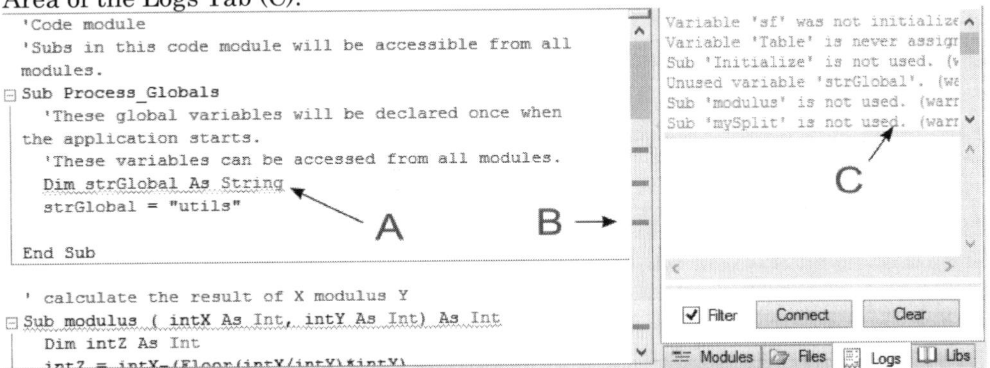

Warnings are too long to fit in the space, but hovering over a warning reveals the full text and clicking on a warning will take you to the relevant line in the source code. These lines are also highlighted in the editor, as described next.

Editor Highlighting

The Warning Engine highlights errors and warnings. Errors are underlined in red in the Editor. If you hover your mouse near an error, you see its error message:

```
yourAge = myAg * 2
                         Undeclared variable 'myag' is used before it was assigned any value.
nd Sub
```

Warnings are underlined in green, and the warning revealed when you hover:

```
strest = "test"
Dim myAge, you Undeclared variable 'strest'. (warning #8)
myAge = 16
```

Ignoring Warnings

You can disable warnings, either for specific lines or for a specific type of warning in a module. To ignore warnings for a line, add a comment with the word "ignore":

```
Sub Activity_KeyPress(KeyCode As Int) As Boolean 'ignore
```

To disable specific types of warnings in a module, add the **`#IgnoreWarning`** attribute.

For example, to disable warnings #10 and #12 in an **Activity module**:

```
#Region Activity Attributes
 #FullScreen: False
 #IncludeTitle: True
 ' add the following line
 #IgnoreWarnings: 10, 12
#End Region
```

For modules which have no Attributes Region, add the line near the top of the code, for example:

```
'Class Person module
 IgnoreWarnings: 12
```

The warnings

1: Unreachable code detected.
2: Not all code paths return a value.
3: Return type (in Sub signature) should be set explicitly.
4: Return value is missing. Default value will be used instead.
5: Variable declaration type is missing. String type will be used.
6: The following value misses screen units ('dip' or %x / %y): {1}.
7: Object converted to String. This is probably a programming mistake.
8: Undeclared variable '{1}'.
9: Unused variable '{1}'.
10: Variable '{1}' is never assigned any value.
11: Variable '{1}' was not initialized.
12: Sub '{1}' is not used.
13: Variable '{1}' should be declared in **`Sub Process_Globals`**.
14: File '{1}' in Files folder was not added to the **Files** tab. You should either delete it or add it to the project. You can choose Tools - Clean unused files.
15: File '{1}' is not used.

16: Layout file '{1}' is not used. Are you missing a call to **`Activity.LoadLayout`**?
17: File '{1}' is missing from the **Files** tab.
18: TextSize value should not be scaled as it is scaled internally.
19: Empty Catch block. You should at least add Log(LastException.Message).
20: View '{1}' was added with the designer. You should not initialize it.
21: Cannot access view's dimension before it is added to its parent.
22: Types do not match.
23: Modal dialogs are not allowed in **`Sub Activity_Pause`**. It will be ignored.
24: Accessing fields from other modules in **`Sub Process_Globals`** can be dangerous as the initialization order is not deterministic.

In addition, Basic4Android gives the following **runtime warnings:**
1001: **`Panel.LoadLayout`** should only be called after the panel was added to its parent.
1002: The same object was added to the list. You should call **`Dim`** again to create a new object.
1003: Object was already initialized.
1004: **`FullScreen`** or **`IncludeTitle`** properties in layout file do not match the activity attributes settings.

1.3 Upgrade to Full Version

Once you have tried Basic4Android free for 30 days, you might want to upgrade to a Full Version. There are several of these:

About Full Versions

They support libraries (an important part of Basic4Android) and give you full access to the Basic4Android forum. Applications developed with Basic4Android are royalty free. You can sell any number of developed applications. The full version only supports local compilation, not remote compilation mode. Licenses are per developer. Each developer requires a single license.

Basic4Android Standard Version

A single developer license with 2 months of free upgrades and full access to Basic4Android forum. Buy Now (http://bit.ly/14uTuGS)

Basic4Android Enterprise Version

2 years of free upgrades with a single developer license. Buy Now (http://bit.ly/1e4kAZD)

Basic4Android Site License

2 years of free upgrades for up to 30 developers on a single site, each with full access to the Basic4Android forum. Buy Now (http://bit.ly/1e4kHV5)

Academic Licenses

Academic licenses (for students, teachers and researchers) are available for half the price. Please contact support@basic4ppc.com and include your academic details.

Purchase

You can use Paypal to purchase any of the above versions from:
http://www.basic4ppc.com/android/purchase.html

Java JDK and Android SDK Installation

The full version does not support remote compilation, only local compilation, so you must install Java JDK and Android SDK. (These are optional with the trial version.) So we must now visit the murky world of Java. Luckily you have chosen Basic4Android so our visit will be brief!

Check if the Java JDK is already installed

You might want to verify whether the Java JDK is already installed on your PC.

Open [Control Panel > Programs and Features] and search for the JDK. Confusingly, this will be called "Java SE Development Kit N Update X" where N and X are numbers.

If you already have JDK 64 Bit

In some cases, the Android SDK installer fails to find JDK 64bit. Therefore, it is recommended to install the 32bit version of the JDK. However, if the SDK is already installed, then it should work. Skip the next step and proceed to install the Android SDK. If it finds the JDK then it's fine. If it fails, then come back to the step below and install the 32bit version.

Install the 32 bit Java JDK

For all machines, even 64 bit, it is recommended to select 32bit **"Windows x86"** in the platforms list. This is because in some cases the Android SDK installer fails to find JDK 64bit. See the note above if you already have the 64bit JDK.

Installation

The first step should be to install the Java JDK, also known as the Java SE Development Kit. **Note**: there is no problem with having several versions of Java installed on the same computer. The steps are:
- Goto the Java SE Development Kit download web page at http://bit.ly/1cUdx1r
- Check the **Accept License Agreement** radio button.
- Find the Java SE Development Kit NuNN section (N will vary depending on the latest version available).

Note: Demos and Samples are not needed.
- Download the relevant exe (X86 recommended, see above) and run it.
- **Note the folder in which you install the JDK**. You will need this information later.

Install the Android SDK and a platform

The Android software development kit (SDK) is a comprehensive set of development tools including a debugger, libraries, a device emulator (page 128), documentation, sample code, and tutorials. It provides the API libraries and developer tools to build, test, and debug apps for Android, and is required in order to use the full version of Basic4Android. With the trial version it is optional.
You need to install the SDK but do not need the ADT Bundle (which includes a version of the Eclipse IDE, since you will be using the (far superior) Basic4Android!).

Install the SDK

Goto the SDK page http://developer.android.com/sdk/index.html
Do not click "Download the SDK ADT Bundle for Windows" since you do not need the ADT! Instead, scroll down, click "DOWNLOAD FOR OTHER PLATFORMS" and select the "SDK Tools Only" option. We recommend you select the installer_rNNNN.exe
Agree to the terms and conditions. If necessary, select the appropriate version then download and run the installer.
If asked whether to "install for anyone using this computer" or "just for me", select whichever seems more appropriate.

The SDK doesn't always behave properly when it is installed in a path with spaces (like "Program Files"). It is recommended to install it to a custom folder similar to C:\android-sdks.

Note the folder where you install it. You will need this information later.

You now need to download the required packages. You should automatically see the Android SDK Manager, as shown below. (You can also run this from the SDK folder).

Android SDK Manager

Packages Tools

SDK Path: C:\android-sdks

Packages

Name	API	Rev.	Status
☐ Tools			
☐ Android SDK Tools		22.0.1	Installed
☑ *Android SDK Platform-tools*		17	*Not installed*
☑ *Android SDK Build-tools*		17	*Not installed*
☑ Android 4.2.2 (API 17)			
☑ *Documentation for Android SDK*	17	2	*Not installed*
☑ *SDK Platform*	17	2	*Not installed*
☑ *Samples for SDK*	17	1	*Not installed*
☑ *ARM EABI v7a System Image*	17	2	*Not installed*
☑ *Intel x86 Atom System Image*	17	1	*Not installed*
☑ *MIPS System Image*	17	1	*Not installed*
☑ *Google APIs*	17	3	*Not installed*
☑ *Sources for Android SDK*	17	1	*Not installed*
☐ Android 4.1.2 (API 16)			
☐ Android 4.0.3 (API 15)			
☐ Android 4.0 (API 14)			
☐ Android 3.2 (API 13)			
☐ Android 3.1 (API 12)			
☐ Android 3.0 (API 11)			
☐ Android 2.3.3 (API 10)			
☑ Android 2.2 (API 8)			
☐ Android 2.1 (API 7)			
☐ Android 1.6 (API 4)			
☐ Android 1.5 (API 3)			

Show: ☑ Updates/New ☑ Installed ☐ Obsolete Select New or Updates [Install 15 packages...]

Sort by: ◉ API level ○ Repository Deselect All [Delete packages...]

Done loading packages.

You need the Android SDK Tools and SDK Platform-tools. In the above example, the Android SDK Tools have already been installed. The platform tools and the latest platform image (API) are selected for installation by default. Platform images are named "Android VVV (API NN)" where VVV is the version and NN is the API

number. Select any older ones you need, depending on the hardware you wish to emulate. In the example, API 8 has been chosen.
For each API, the SDK Platform is needed. The ARM, Intel and MIPS System Images will be used by the emulator (page 128).
Note: installation might take a very long time if you have select many APIs, especially if you have a slow Internet connection, since each one has to be downloaded to your PC.
The Google APIs are also needed. Documentation, Samples and Sources are not required.
Under "Extras", you can also install the Google USB Driver, if you need to connect a physical device with USB.

☐ Extras		
☐ *Android Support Repository*	1	*Not installed*
☑ *Android Support Library*	13	*Not installed*
☐ *Google AdMob Ads SDK*	11	*Not installed*
☐ *Google Analytics App Tracking SDK*	3	*Not installed*
☐ *Google Cloud Messaging for Android Library*	3	*Not installed*
☐ *Google Play services*	7	*Not installed*
☐ *Google Repository*	1	*Not installed*
☐ *Google Play APK Expansion Library*	3	*Not installed*
☐ *Google Play Billing Library*	4	*Not installed*
☐ *Google Play Licensing Library*	2	*Not installed*
☑ *Google USB Driver*	7	*Not installed*
☐ *Google Web Driver*	2	*Not installed*
☐ *Intel x86 Emulator Accelerator (HAXM)*	3	*Not installed*

Information about OEM drivers is available here (http://developer.android.com/intl/fr/sdk/oem-usb.html).
Note: Basic4Android allows you to connect to any device over the local network by using the B4A-Bridge tool (http://bit.ly/14C3DMz).
You can install more packages later.
Click **Install NN Selected** to install your selected packages.
A dialog box is shown. Click on **Accept License** and **Install**.

Install and configure Basic4Android

When you install a full version, you do **NOT** need to uninstall the trial version. The full version overwrites it.

Download and install Basic4Android

When you purchase the full version, you will receive an email containing a link to the download, with a username and password, plus a text file containing your license.

Open Basic4Android

The first time you run Basic4Android, it will check to see if .Net Framework is installed and if not, it will show a dialog box shown previously (page 13). You must download and install .Net Framework or Basic4Android will not run.

Common Windows XP Error

Windows XP users might see an error on start-up of Basic4Android:
"Basic4Android.exe Application could not be initialised correctly error 0xc0000135"
This is because Basic4Android requires .Net Framework 2.0 or above.
Windows XP users who didn't install it before should first install the framework (http://bit.ly/15IDe60).

License

The email you receive contains a license file (b4a-license.txt) which you should store on your computer. On the first run, Basic4Android will ask you to first locate the license file and afterwards it will ask you for the email address you have used when you purchased Basic4Android.

Notes

The license is not a text file, so you should not open it with a text editor.
It is a good idea to save a copy in a different folder, since the license will be deleted after it is authenticated. This will allow you to re-install if you move to a different version of Windows, for example.

Configure Paths

Once B4A has installed and is running, you need to configure several path options for the system to work correctly.
Select menu [Tools > Configure Paths]. The following dialog appears:

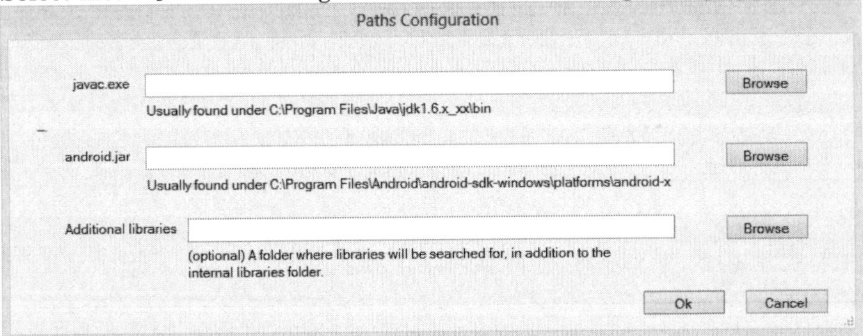

To complete this, you will need the paths which you noted during the installation process.

Javac.exe

This is typically C:\Program Files\Java\jdk1.7.0_09\bin\javac.exe
- Use the browse buttons to locate "javac.exe" and "android.jar"
javac is located under <java folder>\bin.

Android.jar

This file is located under <android-sdk-windows>\platforms\android-**17**
The folder depends where you installed the Android SDK.
You might have recorded this location when you installed the SDK. If not, you will need to find it. It could be:
C:\Android\platforms\android-17\android.jar or C:\Android\platforms\android-8\android.jar.
The number depends on the Android version you loaded.
On older versions it could be under:
C:\Android\android-sdk-windows\platforms\android-8\android.jar.
On Windows 64 bit, Java will probably be installed under C:\Program Files (x86).
You might have have several android.jar files, for example:
D:\android-sdks\platforms\android-10
D:\android-sdks\platforms\android-17
In that case, you need to select one of these, for example:
D:\android-sdks\platforms\android-10\android.jar

Additional Libraries

The Full Version of Basic4Android allows you to download Additional Libraries which provide extra functionality. For example, there are libraries for OpenGL, Camera access, Barcode Readers, FTP and HTTP functions, to name but a few. More details in Additional libraries Chapter (page 524).
You use the "Additional Libraries" option to tell B4A where those downloaded library files are stored on your computer.
If you have the trial version or do not have any additional libraries, you can leave the "Additional Libraries" option blank for initial testing.
It is recommended to use a specific folder for Additional libraries.
Now your Paths Configuration dialog box will look something like this:

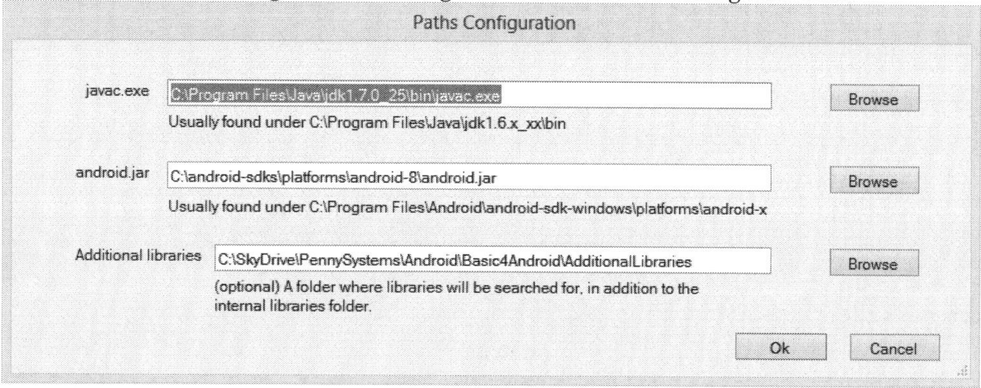

Click **OK**.
That completes the installation of the files required for B4A to run. Much of what follows will work with the trial version. The main difference is that Libraries are only available in the full version.

Updating to a new version

When a new version is released, you will receive an email with the subject "Basic4Android vNNN is released" containing a link to the download.

Part 2: Creating Your App

Here we go through the process of creating a real app, including the principles of design, how your app can communicate with the user, how you can use Designer Scripts to automatically modify your app to suit different devices, and how to compile, debug and test your app using either real or virtual devices.

We discuss creating graphics and databases. We examine how processes, services and activities live and die in Android. We look at the various types of modules you can create, examine ways you can make money from your app and finally explore ways you can get more help in using Basic4Android.

2.1 The Project

Every Project has an **Activity Module** called "Main" and a number of project attributes, some of which are specified within the Main module.

Project Attributes

Project Attributes are valid for the whole project but are displayed only in the **Main Activity Module**:

```
#Region  Project Attributes
   #ApplicationLabel: B4A Example
   #VersionCode: 1
   #VersionName:
  'SupportedOrientations possible values: unspecified, landscape
or portrait.
   #SupportedOrientations: unspecified
   #CanInstallToExternalStorage: False
#End Region
```

These attributes will be added automatically to existing projects when they are first loaded with the latest version of Basic4Android. Available project attributes are:

ApplicationLabel:

The application label, a string which will appear in lists of applications on the device, for example in [Settings > Apps].

CanInstallToExternalStorage:

Whether the application can be installed to external storage. Values: `True` or `False`

CustomBuildAction:

The build process is made of a number of steps. You can add additional steps that will run as part of the build process. For example, you can run a batch file that will copy the latest resource files from some folder before the files are packed.
Note: you can add any number of build actions.
CustomBuildAction should be added to the main activity.
The running folder is set to the program objects folder.

Syntax

The syntax is:
<step id>, <program to run>, <program arguments>

step id can be one of the following:
1 - Before the compiler cleans the objects folder (it happens after the code is parsed).
2 – Before the R.java file is generated.
3 - Before the package is signed (the APK file at this point is: bin\temp.ap_).
4 - Before the APK is installed.

5 - After the APK is installed.

Example

To mark all files under the **res** folder as read-only (and so prevent the compiler from deleting them):

```
CustomBuildAction: 1, c:\windows\system32\attrib.exe, +r res\*.*
/s
```

SupportedOrientations:

Sets the orientations supported by this app. Values (case is important): unspecified, portrait or landscape

VersionCode:

Must be an integer

VersionName:

Is a string

Library compilation attributes

In addition to the project attributes mentioned above, there exist Library compilation attributes which are covered in the library compilation (page 405) section.

Project Icon

This icon (called the Launcher Icon in Android documentation) can be set with the menu [Project > Choose Icon]. More details in the Launcher Icon (page 194) section.

Package name

Every app needs a unique Package Name. The package name is a unique identifier for the application and the default name for the application process. In Basic4Android, it can be set with the menu
[Project > Package Name].

Unique name

The name must be unique. To avoid conflicts with other developers, you should use an Internet domain which you own as the basis for your package names, written in reverse, for example:
uk.co.pennypress.Basic4Android_book
You can register a domain name with a Domain Name Registrar.

Allowed Characters

The name may contain dots, lower case letters ('a' through 'z' but see Note below), numbers, and underscores ('_'). Individual package name parts (between dots) may

only start with letters. Package names should contain at least two components separated with "." (a dot).
Note: the use of lower case is a convention. Upper case letters A through Z are also accepted but can occasionally lead to problems, so it is safer to use only lower case. The name you enter will be validated before it is accepted.

Google Play URL

The Package Name will be used by Google Play to determine the URL of your app. So if the package name is uk.co.pennypress.abc, it will appear on Google Play as:
https://play.google.com/store/apps/details?id=uk.co.pennypress.abc

Caution: Name cannot be changed

Once you publish your application, you cannot change the package name. The package name defines your application's identity, so if you change it, then it is considered to be a different application and users of the previous version cannot update to the new version.

The Manifest

Every app running on an Android device requires a file named AndroidManifest.xml. Basic4Android compiler stores this code in the project's b4a file and generates the XML file automatically. In most cases, there is no need to change anything. However, in some cases, especially when using third-party libraries (ads for example), the developer is required to add some elements to the manifest file. This can be achieved with the Manifest Editor.

Manifest Editor

Basic4Android includes a Manifest Editor (available from the menu [Project > Manifest Editor]) which allows you to add or modify elements in the manifest while also allowing the compiler to add the standard elements.
If you open the Manifest Editor (which is a modal dialog, so you will not be able to use the IDE or Designer while it is open), you will see something like:

```
'This code will be applied to the manifest file during
compilation.
'You do not need to modify it in most cases.
'See this link for for more information:
http://www.basic4ppc.com/forum/showthread.php?p=78136
AddManifestText(
<uses-sdk android:minSdkVersion="4"
android:targetSdkVersion="14"/>
<supports-screens android:largeScreens="true"
  android:normalScreens="true"
  android:smallScreens="true"
  android:anyDensity="true"/>)
SetApplicationAttribute(android:icon, "@drawable/icon")
SetApplicationAttribute(android:label, "$LABEL$")
'End of default text.
```

You can modify these elements or add other elements as needed. To make it easier to add multiline strings and strings that contain quote characters, the manifest editor treats all characters between the open parenthesis and the closing parenthesis or comma (for commands with multiple parameters) as a single string.

Escaping end of string characters

If you need to write a string with a comma, you should write two commas: ,, The same thing is true for strings with closing parenthesis:))

Editor commands

You can add commands at the bottom of the manifest. There are several types of commands: commands that add an additional text inside an element, commands that set the value of an attribute (replacing the old value if it already exists) and two other commands which will be discussed later.
Note: you can call 'add text' commands multiple times.

AddApplicationText

Can be used to add permissions, although this is normally achieved with **AddPermission**.

AddManifestText

These commands add text. Both expect a single parameter which is the text to add.

AddActivityText

AddServiceText

AddReceiverText

These commands expect two parameters: component name and the text to add. For example, to use C2DM push framework you should add some text to the receiver.
Note: a Service module in Basic4Android is actually made of a native service and a native receiver. The name of the receiver is the same as the service module.
Example:

```
AddReceiverText(PushService,
<intent-filter>
<action android:name="com.google.android.c2dm.intent.RECEIVE" />
<category android:name="anywheresoftware.b4a.samples.push" />
</intent-filter>
<intent-filter>
<action
android:name="com.google.android.c2dm.intent.REGISTRATION" />
<category android:name="anywheresoftware.b4a.samples.push" />
</intent-filter>)
```

SetActivityAttribute

SetReceiverAttribute

SetServiceAttribute

These commands set attributes. **Note**: the attributes keys are case sensitive. They expect three parameters: component name, attribute key and attribute value. For example, the following command can be used to set the orientation of a specific activity:

```
SetActivityAttribute(Main, android:screenOrientation,
"portrait")
```

SetManifestAttribute

SetApplicationAttribute

These commands expect two parameters: attribute key and attribute value. For example if you wish to use accelerated hardware, you would add the line:

```
SetApplicationAttribute(android:hardwareAccelerated, "true")
```

AddReplacement

This method allows you to declare a string that will be replaced with a second string. The compiler automatically adds the following declarations: $PACKAGE$ (replaced with the package name), $LABEL$ (replaced with the application label) and $ORIENTATION$ (replaced with the orientation value).
The string replacement happens as the last step. You can use it to delete other strings by replacing them with an empty string.
Syntax: AddReplacement (OldString, NewString)

AddPermission

Adds a permission if it doesn't already exist. You can also add permissions using AddApplicationText. The advantage of AddPermission is that it makes sure to only add each permission once.
Syntax: AddPermission (Permission)
Example: AddPermission (android.permission.INTERNET)

Tips

- Deleting the whole text will restore the default text (after you reopen the manifest editor).
- As stated above, in most cases you do not need to add anything to the manifest editor.

- Open AndroidManifest.xml to better understand how it is built.

More information

For more about the Android Manifest see
http://developer.android.com/guide/topics/manifest/manifest-intro.html

Do Not Overwrite Manifest File Option

This option (available from the Project Menu) is available only for backwards compatibility. It is recommended to use the Manifest Editor instead.

Project Menu

The IDE has a Project Menu (page 40) for setting properties of and compiling Projects.

2.2. Designing Your App

Fulfilling Wants and Needs

Any successful product has to fulfill the wants and needs of a specific audience. Before you begin to design your app, therefore, it is wise to think about these questions and talk to potential customers to understand what they really need and want.
You should also look at other similar apps on the market and identify where there is a gap, evaluate their strengths and weaknesses and decide how your app will be better.

Evolving Environment

One of the main problems about creating Android apps is that the environment is rapidly changing. New versions of the Android API appear on a regular basis, introducing new features, while there are still many devices which have old versions. You must decide whether you want to use the new features or design your app for one of the old versions. Android 2.x is a fairly safe basis on which to start if you want your app to be compatible with a wide range of devices.

Backward Compatible

Note: Android is backward compatible. You can use the latest API and it will still work on devices with an earlier version. **But your app will have problems if your users try to use new features not available in the old API**.

Play Store Compatibility Check

To ensure compatibility, Play Store checks the version of the user's device and will not allow downloads of apps built with incompatible APIs.
Note: Play Store uses the "minSDKversion" value in your project's manifest to determine its SDK version. An example from a manifest showing default values:

```
<uses-sdk android:minSdkVersion="4"
android:targetSdkVersion="14"/>
```

You can change these values. See Manifest Editor (page 70) for details.

Discovering the API of the current device

How to cope with this situation? You could use the most up-to-date SDK and then use the Phone library SdkVersion (page 466) to discover the API level of the user's device. You could then use features appropriate to that type of device. But be aware of the comment above regarding Play Store's compatibility check. See here (http://developer.android.com/guide/topics/manifest/uses-sdk-element.html) for a list of API levels.

Playing Safe

If you want to be safe, you might decide to use an old API. This prevents compilation if you try to add new features. You tell Basic4Android which version of the API you wish to use by specifying it in the "android.jar" entry of the Paths Configuration (page 64) dialog.

The Android Screen

The appearance of the screen within which your app runs will vary depending not just on the size of the device but the version of Android.
We discuss how to cope with different screen sizes in the Designer Scripts Reference (page 109).
The parts of the screen surrounding your app will normally consist of the Status Bar at the top of the screen and, for Android 4.x, a Navigation Bar at the bottom.

Status Bar

The Status Bar at the top of the screen shows pending Notifications (page 329) on the left and status information (such as time, battery level, and signal strength) on the right.

You should not hide the Status Bar (by using Activity Attribute (page 180) **#FullScreen:True**) unless absolutely necessary.

Navigation Bar

For devices running Android 4.x, a Navigation Bar is shown at the bottom of the screen (if the device does not have the traditional hardware keys). It houses the device navigation controls Back, Home, and Recents, and also displays a menu for apps written for Android 2.3 or earlier.

Notifications

The user can swipe down from the status bar to show notification details.
Consider whether your app needs to give Notifications (page 329) to the user.

App Design Step by Step

You want your app to be appealing and useful, so you need to think about the user interface early in the design process.

Basic Design Principles

Make your app **visually appealing**. Where possible, use graphics instead of words, and if you must use words, keep them brief.
Always offer your user a **consistent experience**, for example, when moving between screens. Be faithful to the Android experience, for example, by swiping to navigate.
Break your app into **logical chunks** and offer each on a separate screen. Organize your screens logically and let your users know where they are and how to get somewhere else.

Title Bar

If the #IncludeTitle Activity Attribute (page 180) is set to **`True`**, an activity will display a Title Bar below the Status Bar at the top of the screen. On later versions of Android, it also includes the Launcher Icon (page 194):

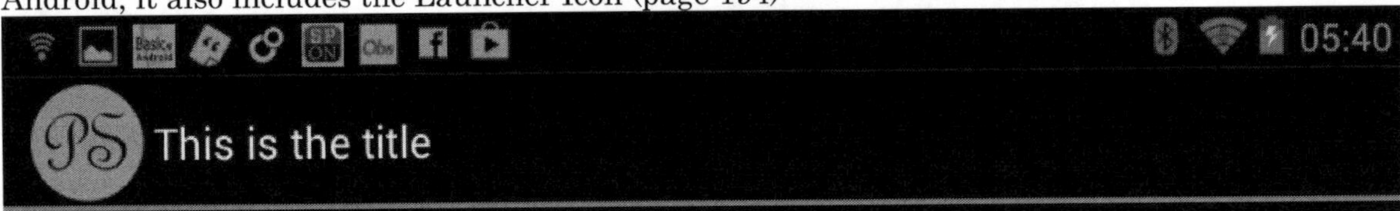

Action Bar

You might want an **Action Bar** at the top of your app to let your user select the action to take.

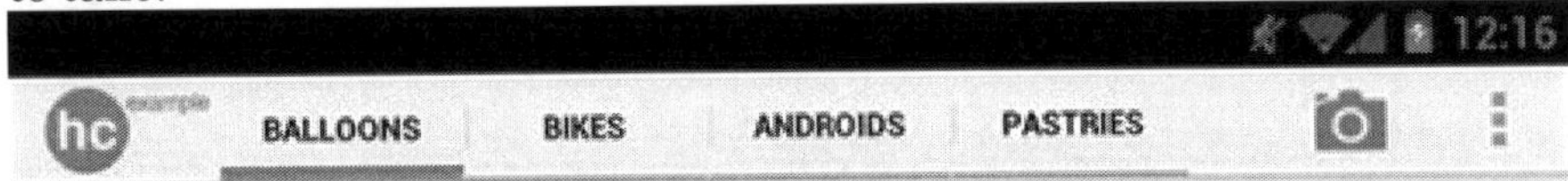

The Android Action Bar was introduced with Android 3.0 (API level 11). Read more about this here (http://developer.android.com/guide/topics/ui/actionbar.html).

AHActionBar

The AHActionBar Library available here (http://bit.ly/176cKvc) lets you create an Action Bar on older devices. (**Note**: the Full Version of Basic4Android is required to use libraries.)

Menu

An easy way of allowing your user to make selections is by adding a menu. The menu is shown if the user presses the Menu button (on older devices) or selects the overflow symbol (3 vertical dots) on the Action Bar, as in the previous image.
The Activity.AddMenuItem (page 274) commands (with 3 variants) allow you to do this easily.
If you use AddMenuItem3 (page 275) (which tries to install an entry directly in the Action Bar), it will still work when run on Android 2.x, but will appear in the Menu instead, revealed by the device's Menu button.

Tabbed Views

TabHost (page 388) is a View which allows you to create a row of tabs which call different pages.
TabHostExtras Library (page 552) is a user-generated extension of this view which gives you more power over its appearance.

Sliding Pages

There is another library, AHViewPager, which allows the user to slide pages sideways. It works with Android 2.x and allows you to use tabs to activate the pages. The library and sample project are available here (http://bit.ly/1bAV9Iu).

You can also combine the above Action Bar and View Pager into a single app which uses the action bar to select a page:

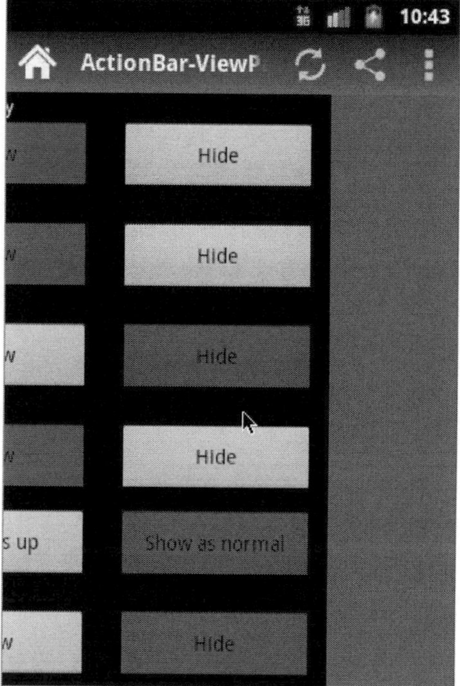

It can be downloaded from this book's resource page (http://resources.basic4android.info/).

Navigation Drawer

A navigation drawer is a panel that slides in from the left edge of the screen and displays the app's main navigation options. The user can bring the navigation drawer onto the screen by swiping from the left edge of the screen or by touching the application icon on the action bar.

At present, there is no navigation drawer which is backward compatible with early versions of Android, but you might consider using Sliding Pages, Tabbed Views or simply use a ListView as a popup menu (page 365).

Advertising

If you are going to include advertising in your app, you need to plan the screen layout to allow space for them. See here (page 198) for more about advertising plans.

Android Themes

Themes are Android's mechanism for applying a consistent style to an app or activity. The style specifies the visual properties of the elements that make up your user interface, such as color, height, padding and font size. For more about Themes, see here (http://bit.ly/1gvrvtm).

For a Basic4Android tutorial which shows you how to select an android theme based on what version of Android the device is using, see here (http://bit.ly/17j7KOL).

More Advice

The Android Developer website has a lot of advice on how to design an effective app. Start from http://developer.android.com/design/index.html

Managing Settings

Editing Settings

Your app will almost certainly need to have settings, that is, user preferences and details. You will need to allow the user to change them. There is an easy way to do this in Basic4Android: the Preference Activity Library (page 484). There is a tutorial here (http://bit.ly/11jIyFd) about how to use it.

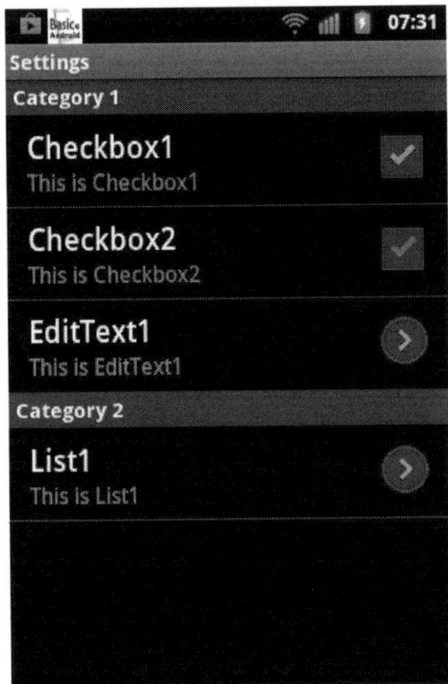

Saving and Retrieving Settings

StateManager (page 528) is a code module you can add to your projects to handle saving user settings to persistent storage and retrieving them when needed.

Screens and Layouts

With the large and increasing number of devices available on the market, all with different screen sizes and resolutions (page 109), it becomes increasingly difficult to design an app that looks good on all of them.

There is no universal rule to manage this problem. It depends on:

- What kind of project you are designing
- What devices and screen sizes you are targeting
- What you want to show on the different screens

For example, it might be enough to show the same layout simply stretched according to the different screen sizes. Or you might need different layout variants for the different sizes. A layout which looks good on a small screen seldom appeals on a big one, where increased space means that more views (such as both the View Control and the Content Area) can be displayed at the same time.
The same layout might not look good in both portrait and landscape orientations, although your work will be simpler if you can design one which does.

Multiple activities

If you have complex coding for each page then it would be better to have separate activity modules. You would normally create a separate layout for each activity.
In order to call the second activity from the first, use **`StartActivity(Activity2)`**.
The second activity automatically runs **`Sub Activity_Create`** which will load the relevant Layout by calling **`Activity.LoadLayout("Layout2")`**

Returning from an Activity

To return to the first activity, the second would typically:

- Save any data to return in a **`Process_Globals`** variable
- Close the current activity with **`Activity.Finish`**

In Activity1 you could use **`Sub Activity_Resume`** to check the value of the saved data.

Overlays

Menu Overlay

You might want to have a menu popup over an Activity. The simplest way to do this is to use a **`ListView`**, as we describe here (page 365).

Layout as Overlay

You can also call a second layout from within the first Activity, using **`Activity.LoadLayout("Layout2")`**. In this case the second layout will be seen floating above the first. To hide parts of the first, the second must have opaque panels (Alpha set to 255). It is probably rare to use such a strategy.

The Designer

The most common way to create a layout is to use the Designer. We describe this in detail in the next chapter (page 92).

How to Detect the Display Type

LayoutValues

Use **LayoutValues** to get information about the screen. This object holds values related to the display. For more details, see the LayoutValues main entry (page 317).
You can get the values of the current display by calling `GetDeviceLayoutValues`
For example:

```
Dim lv As LayoutValues
lv = GetDeviceLayoutValues
Log(lv)
```

This will print the following line to the log:
320 x 480, scale = 1.0 (160 dpi)
Note: **Activity.LoadLayout** and **Panel.LoadLayout** return a **LayoutValues** object with the values of the chosen layout variant.

You can use **LayoutValues.scale** to check the device type. This returns the scale (page 110), where 1 is a screen with 160 dpi.
For example, you could then use **TextSizeRatio** to scale text on the screen:

```
Dim TextSizeRatio As Float
Dim LayoutVals As LayoutValues

LayoutVals = GetDeviceLayoutValues
TextSizeRatio = GetDeviceLayoutValues.Scale
lblSample.TextSize = lblSample.TextSize * TextSizeRatio
```

Detecting Device Orientation

You may need to know whether the screen is portrait or landscape.
You could use either:

```
If Activity.Width > Activity.Height Then
```

Or the equivalent but longer:

```
Dim lv As LayoutValues
lv = GetDeviceLayoutValues
If lv.Width > lv.Height Then
```

Allowed Screen Orientation

The screen orientation values which an app can support can be set to portrait only, landscape only or both. These orientations can be defined either 1) in the Project Attributes (page 68) or 2) using the Phone Library.

1) Using Project Attribute

```
#Region  Project Attributes
  #ApplicationLabel: MyFirstProgram
  #VersionCode: 1
  #VersionName:
  #SupportedOrientations: unspecified
  #CanInstallToExternalStorage: False
#End Region
```

where #SupportedOrientations can have the values **portrait**, **landscape** or **unspecified** (meaning both portrait and landscape).

2) With the Phone library

Or your project can use the Phone Library (page 453) to set the allowed screen orientation:

```
Dim Phone1 As Phone
Phone1.SetScreenOrientation (-1)
```

Possible values are **0** (Landscape only), **1** (Portrait only) or **-1** (Both)

Adding views by code

Layouts are most commonly defined using the Designer (page 92), but it is also possible to create and modify views directly in your Activity code.

Advantage: you have full control of the view.

Disadvantage: you have to define almost everything. For example, you must initialize any view added in code, as shown in the following:

Example

The source code for an example project, AddViewsByCode, is in this book's Resource web page (http://pennypress.co.uk/?p=86). This is part of it:

```
Sub Globals
 Dim lblTitle As Label
End Sub

Sub Activity_Create(FirstTime As Boolean)
 lblTitle.Initialize("")
 lblTitle.Color = Colors.Red
 lblTitle.TextSize = 20
 lblTitle.TextColor = Colors.Blue
 lblTitle.Gravity = Gravity.CENTER_HORIZONTAL +
Gravity.CENTER_VERTICAL
 lblTitle.Text = "Title"
 Activity.AddView(lblTitle, 20%x, 10dip, 60%x, 30dip)
End Sub
```

dips

To write code, you need to be aware of **D**ensity **I**ndependent **P**ixels (dips (page 110)).

Dips are a way of solving the uncertainty caused by the variety of screen resolutions available on different devices. Dips are defined so that, on all devices
160dip = 1 inch
Thus, if you want a button to be 2 inches wide on any device, you would write:
```
btnStop.Width = 320dip
```
Any number followed by the string dip will be converted. **Note**: no spaces are allowed between the number and the word **dip**. Read more about dips here (page 110).

DipToCurrent(Length as Int)

You can also set the size of a view using **DipToCurrent**. This function converts Length, given in dips, into a value for the current screen. For example, the following code will set the width value of this button to be 1 inch wide on all devices.
```
EditText1.Width = DipToCurrent(160)
```
You might consider that simply saying 160dip is easier!

Percentage of Activity

As well as specifying the absolute size of an object, you can set the size as a percentage of the screen (actually of the current **Activity**).

PerXToCurrent (Percentage As Float) As Int

Returns the given percentage of the activity width, converted to dip (page 110).
Example: set the width of Button1 to 50% of the width of the current activity:
```
EditText1.Width = PerXToCurrent(50)
```
A shorthand syntax for this method is available. See below.
PerYToCurrent performs a similar function for the height.

%x and %y

These are shorthand ways of achieving the same result. 50%x means 50% of the width of the current activity, converted to dip (page 110). So the previous code is equivalent to:
```
EditText1.Width = 50%x
```
Note: there is no space between the number and the `%`.
To specify 5% of the height of the screen: `EditText1.Height = 5%y`

Does the device have a keyboard?

You can find out with the following code. This requires the Reflection Library (page 543).
```
Dim r As Reflector
r.Target = r.GetContext
r.Target = r.RunMethod("getResources")
r.Target = r.RunMethod("getConfiguration")
Dim keyboard As Int = r.GetField("keyboard")
Log ("keyboard=" & keyboard)
```
The possible values of keyboard are:
1 = KEYBOARD_NOKEYS
2 = KEYBOARD_QWERTY

3 = KEYBOARD_12KEY

App or Widget ?

Basic4Android supports the creation of miniature application views called App Widgets that can be embedded in other applications (such as the Home screen) and receive periodic updates. These views are referred to as Widgets in the user interface. An application component that is able to hold other App Widgets is called an App Widget host, which is typically the home screen.
Because another application is hosting your widget, it is not possible to directly access the widget's views. Instead, you must use a special object called RemoteViews (page 332) which gives you indirect access to the widget's views.
You create a RemoteViews object based on the layout file using ConfigureHomeWidget (page 246).

```
Sub Process_Globals
  Dim rv As RemoteViews
End Sub

Sub Service_Create
   rv = ConfigureHomeWidget("LayoutFile", "rv", 0, "Widget Name")
End Sub
```

Each widget is tied to a Service module. The widget is created and updated through this module.
Widgets do not support all view types. The following views are supported:

- Button (default drawable)
- Label (**ColorDrawable** or **GradientDrawable**)
- Panel (**ColorDrawable** or **GradientDrawable**)
- ImageView
- ProgressBar (both modes)

All views support the **Click** event and **no other event**.
The widget layout and configuration must be defined with XML files. During compilation, Basic4Android reads the layout file created with the designer and generates the required XML files. For a tutorial on creating widgets with Basic4Android, see here (http://bit.ly/14Lm40H) for part 1 and an example program. For part 2 of the tutorial, building a more extensive example, see here (http://bit.ly/16TSq09).

Managing Permissions

When an Android app is installed, it must tell the user what resources and data it needs to access on the device, and the user has the opportunity to cancel the installation. This is achieved by your app including a list of the required permissions in the Manifest (page 70) file.
Normally, Basic4Android will create this Manifest for you, automatically detecting the required permissions. We list these required permissions in this book, within the documentation for objects which need them.

However, it might be that you need to manually add permissions to the Manifest. You achieve this by using the AddPermission (page 72) command in the Manifest editor.

2.3 Communicating with your User

As your program runs, you will need to send messages to your user from time to time. We deal here with the methods of doing this. Of course, there are many Views (such as buttons) which allow the user to take actions during an **Activity**, but here we are thinking about how you can take specific actions to gain your user's attention.

Modal Dialogs

There are several ways to show your user a message in a dialog box which remains visible until the user clicks (sometimes called "modal" or "blocking" dialogs). The program will not continue and timers will be suspended until the user responds. See the section below about how to handle modal dialogs if Android interrupts your app, for example when the user rotates the device.

Msgbox

Use the Msgbox (page 254) keyword to show a simple message without any options. You can specify the message and the box title:

```
Msgbox ("Please select a route first", "Error")
```

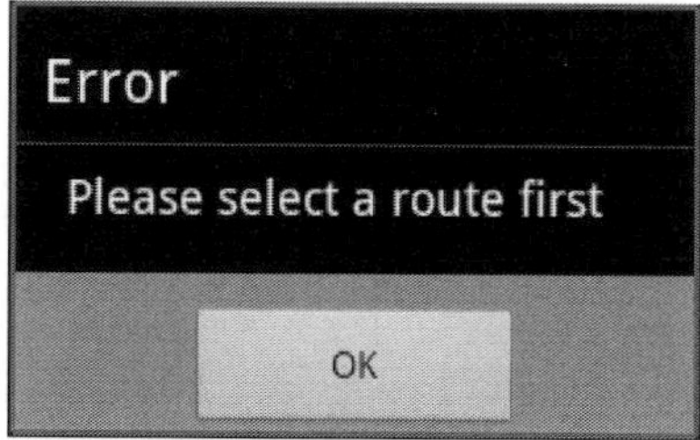

Msgbox2

If you want to show more options, Msgbox2 (page 254) allows you to include any combination of the following: a positive button, a negative button, a cancel button and/or an icon. It will return one of the DialogResponse (page 281) constants, and you can detect the user's response and act accordingly:

```
Dim bmp As Bitmap
Dim choice As Int
bmp.Initialize(File.DirAssets, "question.png")
choice = Msgbox2("Would you like to select a route?", "Please
specify your choice", "Yes please", "", "No thank you", bmp)
If choice = DialogResponse.POSITIVE Then ...
```

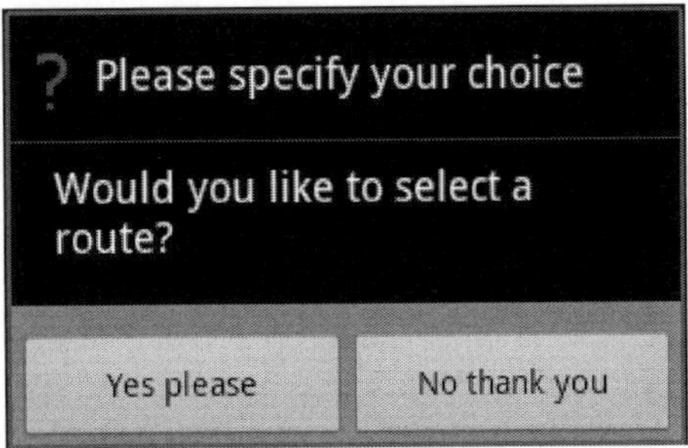

InputList

InputList (page 250) shows the user a modal dialog with a list of options. It ends when the user clicks on an option and returns either the index of the selected item, or **DialogResponse.Cancel** if the user presses the back key.

```
Dim choice As Int
Dim lst As List
lst.Initialize2(Array As String("1", "More than 10", "I don't
care"))
choice = InputList(lst, "How many friends do you want?", 1)
```

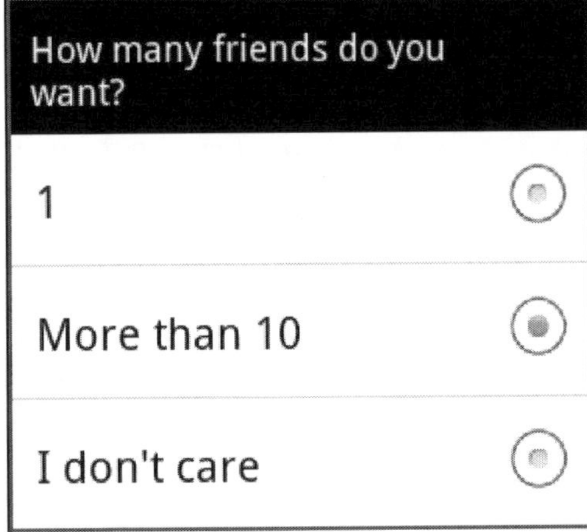

InputMultiList

InputMultiList (page 251) lets you show a list from which the user can select multiple items before returning.

```
Dim choice As Int
Dim lstInput, lstOutput As List
lstInput.Initialize2(Array As String("Apples", "Bananas",
"Mangos", "Oranges"))
lstOutput = InputMultiList (lstInput, "Select all the fruits you
want")
For Each index As Int In lstOutput
 Log (index)
Next
```

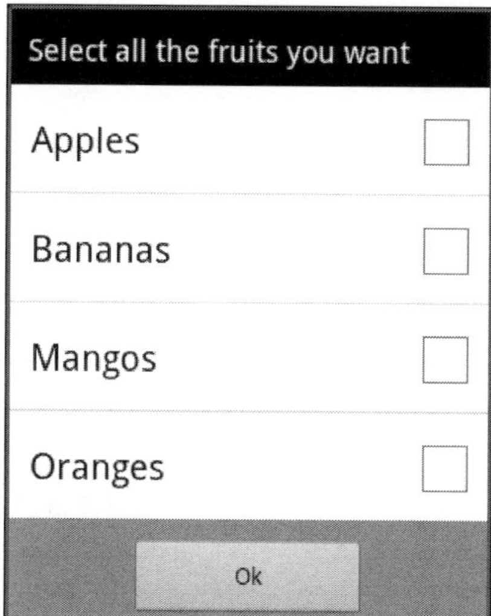

If Bananas and Oranges are selected, the numbers 1 and 3 will be logged.

InputMap

This looks and acts much like an **InputMultiList**, but items in the list can be pre-selected and the result is returned in a different way.

```
Dim m As Map
m.Initialize
m.Put("Apples", True)
m.Put("Bananas", False)
m.Put("Mangos", False)
m.Put("Oranges", True)
InputMap(m, "Select all the fruits you want")
```

This will show an input list with the **True** items pre-selected:

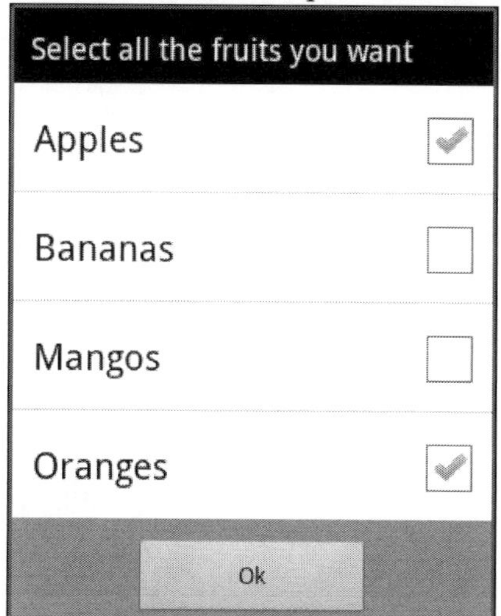

To process the result, check the map:

```
For Each fruit As String In m.Keys
 If m.Get( fruit ) Then
 Log( fruit )
 End If
Next
```

Handling Long Lists

`InputList`, **`InputMultiList`** and **`InputMap`** can all display long lists, but if the list is too long to fit on the screen, parts of it will be hidden so that not all the items will be visible. Although the user can drag the list to reveal hidden items, there is no visual indication of this to the user. This is normal with Android. It might be wise to add a message indicating this to the user:

```
Dim choice As Int
Dim lst As List
lst.Initialize
For i = 0 To 9
 lst.Add ( "Item " & i)
Next
choice = InputList (lst, "Select all the items you want (drag
up/down for more)", 1)
```

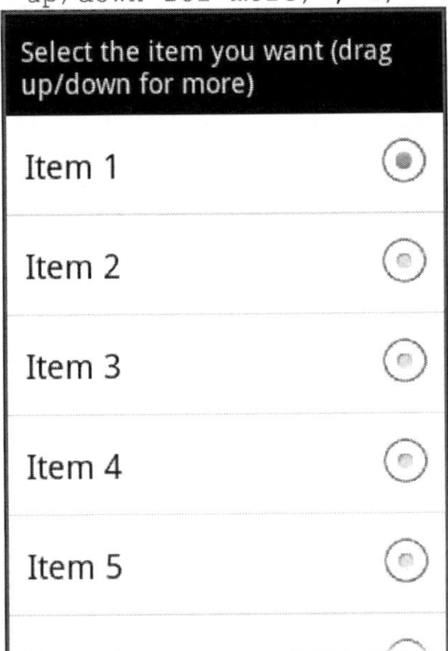

Notice also thqthe list has already scrolled down to show the selected item.

Dialogs Library

This library, written by Andrew Graham, contains several modal dialogs (meaning they remain visible until the user takes some action). They are useful if you need your user to enter data. At present, they are an InputDialog for text, a TimeDialog for times, a DateDialog for dates, both a ColorDialog and a ColorPickerDialog for colors, a NumberDialog for numbers, a FileDialog for folders and file names, and a CustomDialog. We describe them in the Dialogs Library (page 530) section.

Handling Modal Dialogs when your App Pauses

Android does not provide modal dialogs, but a special mechanism in Basic4Android permits them. The Android Activity lifetime system makes this support complicated because Activities can be created and destroyed at will by Android. To avoid stack runaway on the GUI thread when an Activity is destroyed, the stack must be unwound to the lowest level. The Basic4Android modal mechanism does this by closing any modal dialog being shown and exiting the Sub that called the dialog, and any Sub that called that Sub and so on, in order to return the main thread to the message loop.

This means that the application does not necessarily receive a return value from the dialog and has its expected flow of execution interrupted. This will probably most often happen if the device is rotated while a modal dialog is displayed, so the Activity is destroyed and rebuilt with a new layout.

Because this may happen unexpectedly, applications (depending upon their logical structure) may need code in the **`Pause`** and **`Resume`** Subs to deal with the fact that modal dialog closure may not always be detected. Setting a variable defined in **`Sub Process_Globals`** when a modal dialog is shown, and clearing it when it returns with some checking code in the Resume Sub, is one way of dealing with this possibility.

The above discussion applies to Dialogs Library objects as well as the Basic4Android modal dialogs **`InputList`**, **`InputMultiList`**, **`Msgbox`** and **`Msgbox2`**.

ToastMessageShow

ToastMessageShow (page 260) shows a message to the user which lasts for only a few seconds.

```
ToastMessageShow ("No messages received", False)
```

You can make it last a bit longer by setting the last parameter to **`True`**.

Alarms

You can create a Service module (page 188) which will sound an alarm and perhaps show a notification at a certain time. You can use the StartServiceAt (page 259) method to schedule when your service will start. See Simple Alarm (http://bit.ly/14yNI4n) for an example of how to implement this type of alarm. You could also use a Timer (page 338) to do something similar, but a service will continue to run even when your app is not running.

Notifications

Both activities and services can display status bar notifications. For services; it is their main way of interacting with the user.
The notification displays an icon in the status bar.

When the user swipes the bar down, she or he sees the notification. The user can press on the message, which will open an activity as configured by the Notification object (page 329).

ProgressDialog

You can use ProgressDialogShow (page 256) to show a dialog with a circular spinning disc and the specified text, telling the user that a long-running task it in progress.

```
ProgressDialogShow("Please wait while we fetch your
information")
```

Unlike Msgbox (page 254) and InputList (page 250) methods, the code will not be blocked; so the activity can continue to run until the task is completed.

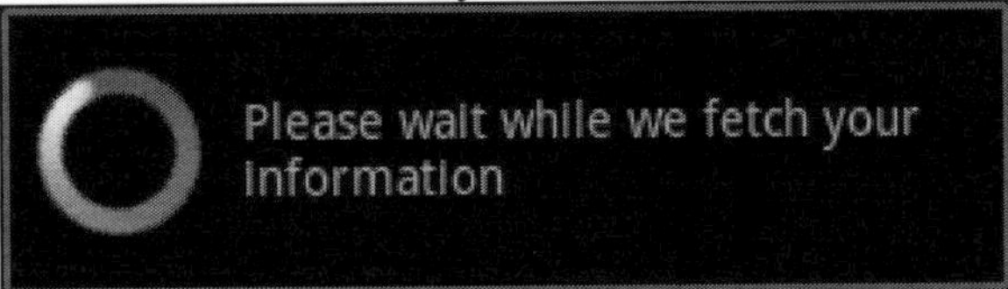

You should call ProgressDialogHide to remove the dialog. The dialog will also be removed if the user presses on the Back key. However by using **`ProgressDialogShow2`** you can prevent this.

```
ProgressDialogShow2("Please wait while we fetch your
information", False)
```

The second argument specifies whether the user can dismiss the dialog by pressing on the Back key.

ProgressBar

Unlike a **`ProgressDialog`**, which floats above an activity, a **`ProgressBar`** belongs to the **`Activity`**. It gives your user information about how far a long-running process has progressed. The exact nature of the visible bar depends upon the device. Here is one example

Example code:

```
Sub Activity_Create(FirstTime As Boolean)
 Activity.LoadLayout("Main")
 ProgressBar1.Progress = 0
 Timer1.Initialize("Timer1", 1000)
 Timer1.Enabled = True
End Sub

Sub timer1_Tick
 'Handle tick events
 ProgressBar1.Progress = ProgressBar1.Progress + 10
 If ProgressBar1.Progress = 100 Then
 Timer1.Enabled = False
 End If
End Sub
```

See ProgressBar (page 374) for more details.

2.4 The Designer

We introduced the Designer in an earlier tutorial (page 28). It allows you to generate layouts and see how they look on either an emulator (page 128) or a real device. We describe how to connect to one of these in Testing Your App (page 127). We recommend that for designing, the emulator is the preferred option since the screen on a real device will normally blank out after a minute or two to save battery.
In the following sections remember that; in Basic4Android; a **View** is a component on a page. Start the Designer using the Basic4Android Designer menu. The Designer looks like this:

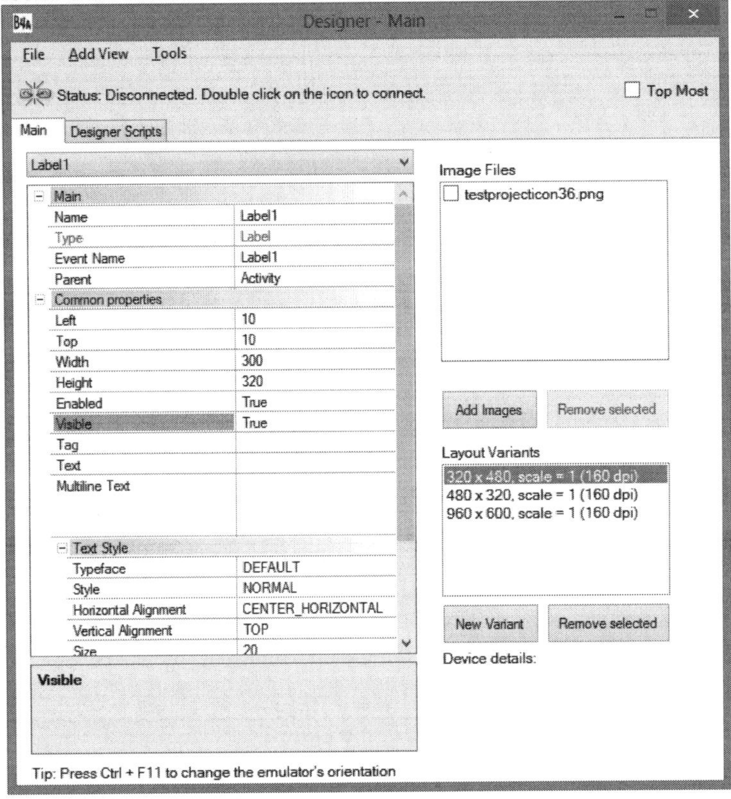

File menu

This menu allows you to open and save layouts. It also lists the layouts in the current project (page 68).

AddView menu

This menu allows you to select the view (object) you want to add on the current layout on the device or the Emulator. The views you can add are: AutoCompleteEditText (page 341), Button (page 346), CheckBox (page 349), CustomView (page 351), EditText (page 352), ImageView (page 359), HorizontalScrollView (page 357), Label (page 362), ListView (page 364), Panel (page 370) , ProgressBar (page 374), RadioButton (page 376), ScrollView (page 379), SeekBar (page 382), Spinner (page 384), TabHost (page 388), ToggleButton (page 392), WebView (page 398)

Tools Menu

The Designer Tools Menu contains the following items:

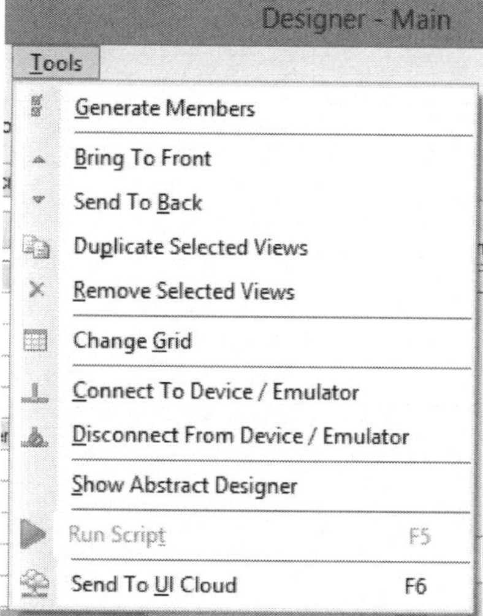

We explain these next. **Note**: some of these options can also be achieved by right-clicking the view in the Abstract Designer (page 103) and using the popup context menu.

Generate Members

Generates **`Dim`** statements and skeleton Subroutines within the code editor. Select the Views for which you wish the Dim statements to be created (in **`Sub Globals`**), and the Events for which you want to generate a skeleton Sub.

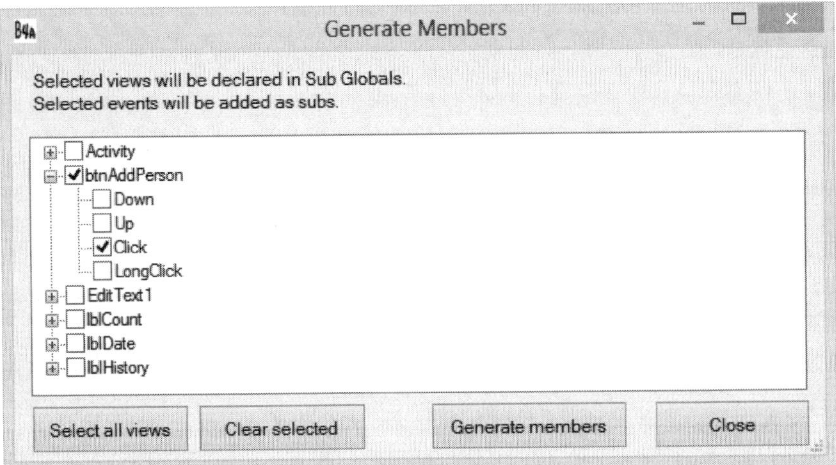

Click **Generate members** then **Close**.
This will add the following to the **Activity module**:

```
Sub Globals
 Dim btnAddPerson As Button
End Sub
```

And

```
Sub btnAddPerson_Click

End Sub
```

Bring To Front and Send To Back

Change the layering position of overlapping Views. This is especially useful for large Panels.

Selecting Views

Select a view by either chosing from the Designer drop-down menu:

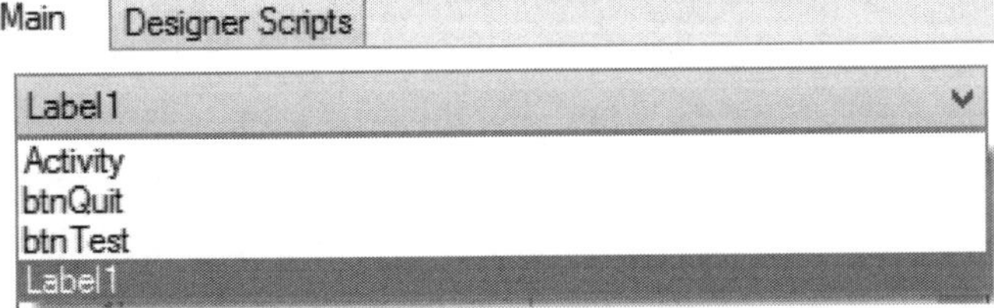

or by clicking on the view in the Abstract Designer or in the emulator or a connected device (see "Connect to Device or Emulator" below).
You can select multiple views by dragging the cursor around them in the Abstract Designer, or by control-clicking them. They become highlighted in yellow.

Duplicate Selected View

First, select the view or views you want to duplicate, then use this option to duplicate it/them.

Remove Selected View

First, select the view or views to remove.
Note: Be careful: you will not be asked to confirm you want to remove the view(s) and the action cannot be undone!

Change grid

The (invisible) grid determines the minimum distance (in pixels) which a View moves when you drag it in the Abstract Designer or in a connected device or emulator. This option lets you change the grid size. The default is 10 pixels.

Connect to Device or Emulator

Note: if the Designer is already connected to a device or emulator (page 128), then this option has no effect. You first need to use the "Disconnect from Device".
The way a layout looks in the Abstract Designer is not exactly the same as on a real device, as shown below:

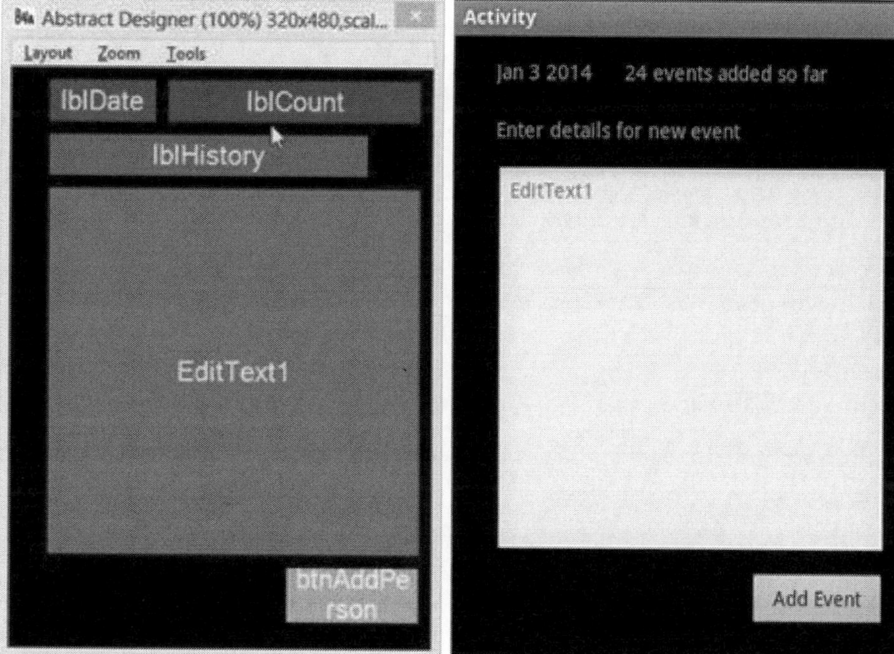

It is therefore very useful to connect the Designer to a device or an emulator to see how your layout will look when in use.
To connect the Designer, you first need to start the emulator(s) (using the [Tools > Run AVD Manager] in the IDE) or connect the device to Basic4Android using [Tools > B4A Bridge]. **Note**: many emulators can be running simultaneously but only one device can be connected at any one time. If different devices or Emulators are connected when you select [Tools > Connect to Device] (or Connect to Emulator) in the Designer, you will be asked which you want to connect to.

Note also: once a device or emulator is connected, you can select, move and resize the views there as well as in the Abstract Designer.

Disconnect From Device

This option disconnects the Designer from the Device or Emulator.

Show Abstract Designer

See the Abstract Designer (page 103) section below.

Run Script

Runs the script code in the Designer Scripts (page 109) tab. This is only available when this tab is active.

Send To UI Cloud

The Designer [Tools > Send To UI Cloud] menu allows you to see how layouts look on different devices. The layout file will be sent to the Basic4Android site and, after a short delay, a page will be opened in your web-browser showing your layout on different devices with different screen resolutions and densities. It's a very convenient tool to check the layout look without needing to have physical devices.

Example of a UI Cloud screen

The top of a typical web page looks like this:

Basic4android UI Cloud

Useful links:

- Supporting Multiple Screens - tips and best practices
- Designer Scripts Tutorial
- Designer Scripts & AutoScale Tutorial

Build a robust layout in 3 steps:

- **Scale** - Call `AutoScaleAll` keyword to scale the views based on the device physical size
- **Adjust** - Adjust the views position (for example views that need to be docked to the bottom, right or center)
- **Fill** - Use `SetLeftAndRight` and `SetTopAndBottom` methods to resize the views that should fill the available space

This is a temporary link. It will expire in several minutes.

Number of connected devices: 9
Total process time: 5.62 seconds

Galaxy Note (5.3" phone)

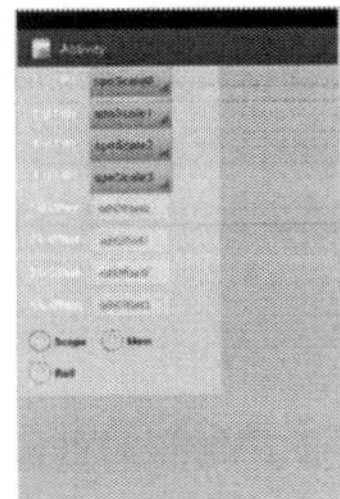

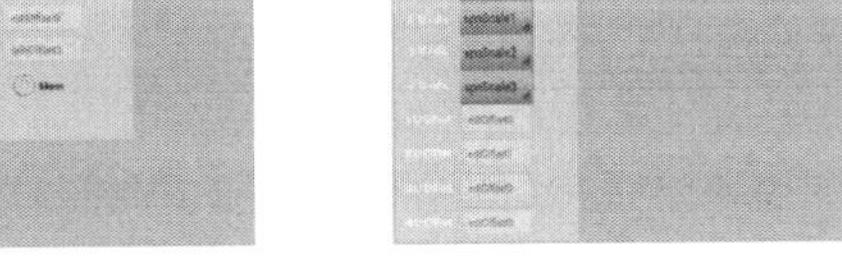

Process time: 2.75 seconds

Note: in the web-browser, you can click on an image to show it full-size, and you can scroll down to see the layout on many other devices.

Designer Status Line

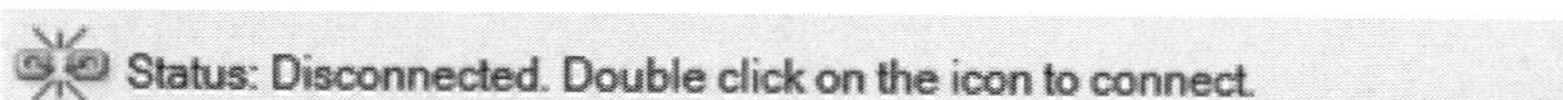

Connection Status

Below the Designer Menu there is a status line to show whether the Designer is connected to a device or emulator. To connect, first start the emulator (in the Basic4Android IDE [Tools > Run AVD Manager] menu) or B4A Bridge on your device and run IDE [Tools > B4A Bridge]. Then connect by either double-clicking on the Designer's Disconnected icon or select the Designer menu [Tools > Connect to Device / Emulator].

Top Most

The Designer window can be set to stay always on top of all other windows by selecting the "Top Most" checkbox in the Status line, shown above.

Designer Main Tab

Below the Status Line there are two tabs: **Main** and **Designer Scripts**.
The **Main** tab consists of the following parts:

Properties Editor

This consists of the following parts:

View Selector

EditText1

This drop-down list contains all the views in the activity, and the Activity itself, allowing you to select which you wish to edit. If you select a view in the Abstract Designer or a connected device or emulator (page 128), the same view is automatically selected here.

Properties list

This lists all the properties of the selected view (or the Activity, if selected) organized in groups, and allows you to modify them.

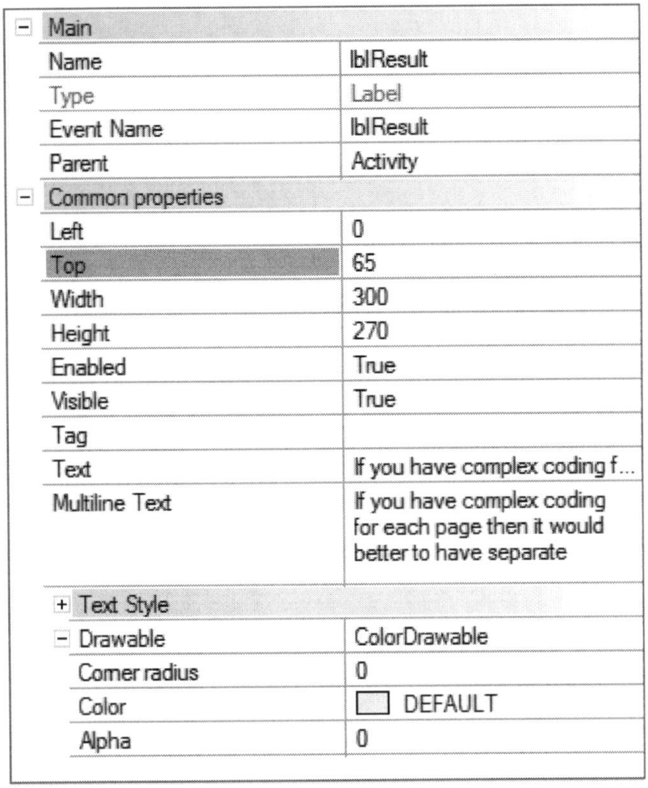

Main	
Name	lblResult
Type	Label
Event Name	lblResult
Parent	Activity
Common properties	
Left	0
Top	65
Width	300
Height	270
Enabled	True
Visible	True
Tag	
Text	If you have complex coding f...
Multiline Text	If you have complex coding for each page then it would better to have separate
Text Style	
Drawable	ColorDrawable
Corner radius	0
Color	DEFAULT
Alpha	0

Main Properties

These properties can be changed by entering data or selecting items from drop-down lists in the column on the right.

Name: Name of the view. It is good practice to give meaningful names. Common usage is to give a 3 character prefix and add the purpose of the view. In the example, the view is of type Label and its purpose is to enter a result. So we give it the name "lblResult", "lbl" for Label and "Result" for the purpose. This does not take much time during the design of the layout but saves a lot time during coding and maintenance of the program.

Type: Type of the view, not editable. It is not possible to change the type of a view. If you need to, you must remove the view and add a new one.

Event Name: Prefix for the subroutines which manage this view's events. By default the Event Name is the same as the view's name. Thus, for a label called lblResult, the Designer menu [Tools > Generate Members] would generate a sub such as

```
Sub lblResult_Click
```

The Events of several Views can be redirected to a single subroutine. In that case, you must enter the name of that routine in the Event Name field.

Parent: Name of the parent view (Activity in the example). The parent view can be changed by selecting a new one from the pull-down list:

Main	
Name	lblResult
Type	Label
Event Name	lblResult
Parent	Activity
Common properties	Activity
Left	pnlTest

Left: X coordinate of the left edge of the View from the left edge of its parent View, in dips (page 110).
Top: Y coordinate of the upper edge of the View from the upper edge of its parent View, in dips (page 110).
Width: Width of the View in dips (page 110).
Height: Height of the View in dips (page 110).
Enabled: Enables or disables the use of the View
Visible: Determines if the View is visible to the user or not.
Tag: This is a place holder which can be used to store additional data. Tag can simply be text but can also be any other kind of object when accessed in code.
Warning: If you want to set both the Width and the Right side, set the Width first. Similarly you should set the Height before setting the Bottom. This can be summarized as: set the internal dimensions before the external position.

Help area

When a property is selected, a gray box at the foot of the Main tab shows help information about what the property does. For example, if the "Tag" property is selected, the following appears in the help area:

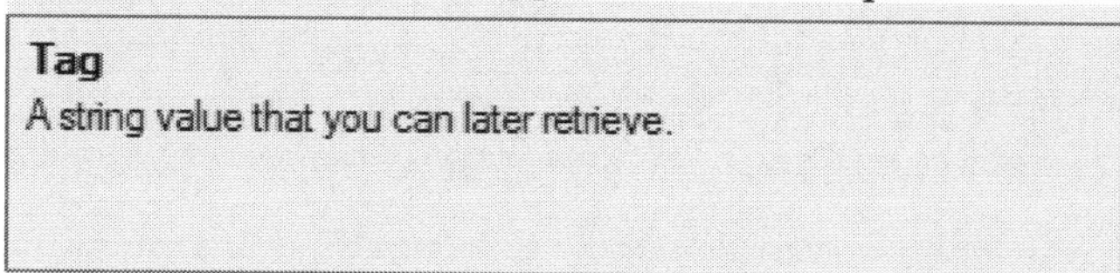
Tag
A string value that you can later retrieve.

Note that the Help Area can be expanded or contracted by clicking and dragging on the space between the Help Area and the overall properties box area. If you only see the word "Tag", you can click and drag the top of the Help Area upward to see the rest of the Help information.

Image files

This area of the Main tab allows you to add (or remove) images on the layout:

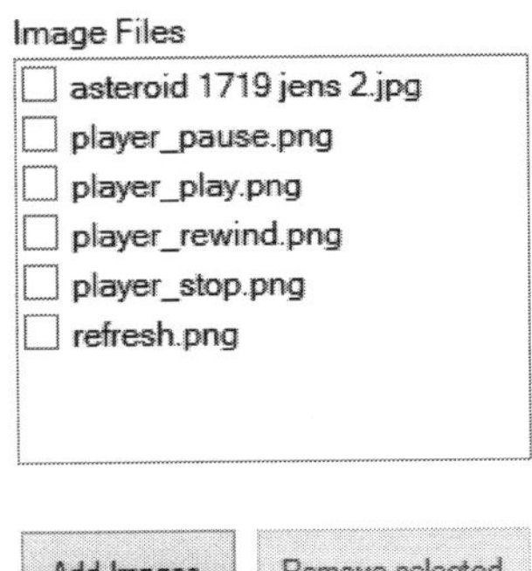

Add Images: Allows you to select an image, which will be copied to the Files folder of the project. Once added, you can add an **`ImageView`** to your layout and select the required image in the Image file property.
Remove Selected: shows the following dialog:

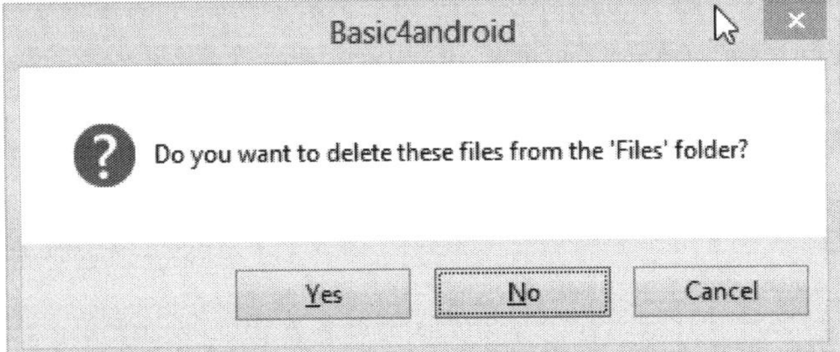

Yes: removes the selected files from the list and from the **Files** folder of the project.
Make sure to have a copy of the files you remove, because they are removed from the Files folder, but not transferred to the recycle bin. This means they are definitively lost if you don't have a copy.
No: removes the selected files from the list but does not delete them from the project's **Files** folder.

Layout variants

One of the most common issues that Android developers face is the need to adapt the user interface to devices with different screen sizes and orientations.
One solution is to create multiple layout variants, one to match every different device, and to adapt to changes in device orientation.
Note that it is neither feasible nor recommended to create many layout variants. A better solution is to use the minimum number of variants, perhaps one for portrait and one for landscape, and adapt them using the AutoScale function (page 114) **in Designer Scripts.**
Nevertheless, it is often necessary to create different variants to suit different sized devices. It's probably not the best solution to have the same layout stretched for all screen sizes. It could be more interesting to show more views on bigger screens.

Multiple variants can all be managed in a single layout file.

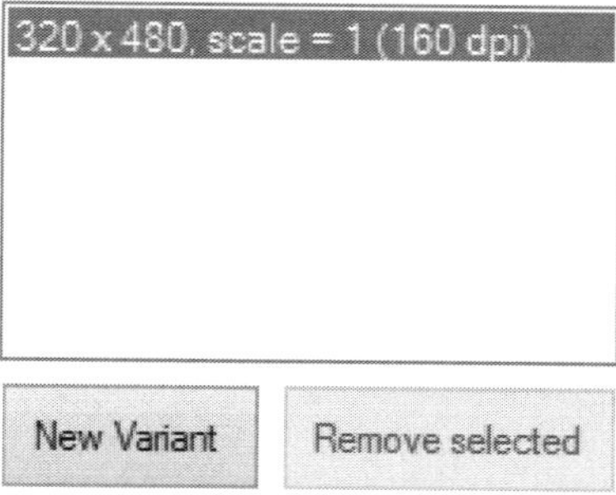

Device details:

New Variant: shows the following dialog:

Create new layout variant

Standard Values:

Phone (portrait): 320x480, scale=1

Phone (landscape): 480x320, scale=1

7" Tablet (portrait): 600x960, scale=1

7" Tablet (landscape): 960x600, scale=1

10" Tablet (portrait): 800x1280, scale=1

10" Tablet (landscape): 1280x800, scale=1

Other: Width Height Scale

Ok Cancel

You can select a pre-defined standard value or define a new one.

Standard Variant

The default or standard variant or standard screen (page 110) used by Basic4Android is 320 x 480 pixels with a scale of 1.

Adding a Standard Variant

You can pick one of the other standard values and click **OK**. This is then added to your variant list.

Adding Other Variants

It is possible to select Other and add the Width and Height (in pixels) and the Scale (page 110). The new variant will be added to the Layout Variants list.

Do not add too many variants

Note that in most cases it is not recommended to add variants other than these recommended ones. It is all too easy to create many variants, but they are very difficult to maintain. Instead, you should use the designer script feature to adjust (or fine tune) your layout.

Normalized Variants

Normalized variants are variants with a scale of 1.0. The layout you create with the designer is scaled (not stretched or resized) automatically. This means that the layout will look exactly the same on two phones with the same physical size. The scale doesn't matter.
It is highly recommended to design your layout with normalized variants only. For example, a variant of 480x800, scale=1.5, matches the normalized variant: 320x533, scale=1.0 (divide each value by the scale value). Now it is easy to see that this device is slightly longer than the "standard" variant: 320x480, scale=1.0.

Add Only Normalized Variants

It is recommended only to create variants with scales (page 110) of 1.0. When you add such a variant, you will be given an option to add a normalized variant instead with a scale of 1.0.

Why this recommendation?

Consider a device (such as the Samsung Galaxy Nexus phone) whose screen data is 720x1184 at 320 dpi (scale 2). It may seem completely different from the default phone which is 320x480 at 160 dpi (scale 1), but if you calculate the normalized values of the Galaxy Nexus to scale 1, its layout actually matches: 360x592 at 160 dpi. This means that it is slightly wider and longer than the default phone size. It should be easier to handle these differences in the designer script.

Rotating the Emulator

If the layout selected is in landscape, you will need to change your Emulator to the same mode. Select the Emulator and press Ctrl + F11 to change its orientation.

Warning: Bug in Emulator

There is a bug in the Emulator using Android 2.3.x (API 9 or 10) for the AVD. It can get stuck in a certain orientation so that pressing Ctrl + F11 repeatedly can cause the Emulator to become confused, rotating the text on its screen but not resizing correctly:

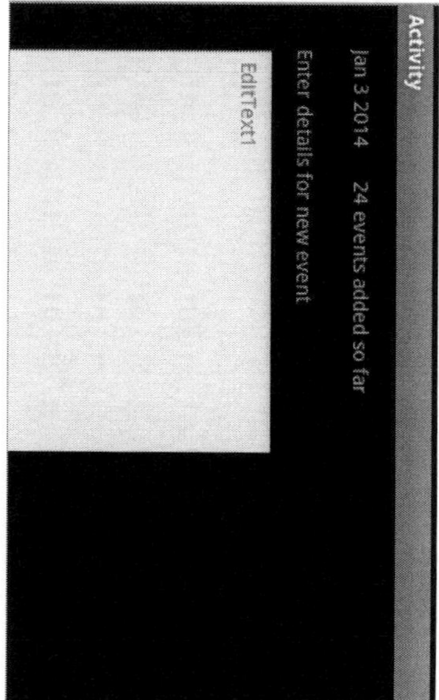

One solution is to create a new AVD with the same specifications but using a different API level (such as 7 or 8). Or use B4A-Bridge to connect to a real device.

Designer Scripts Tab

Every layout file can include script code. The script is written in the Designer Scripts tab:

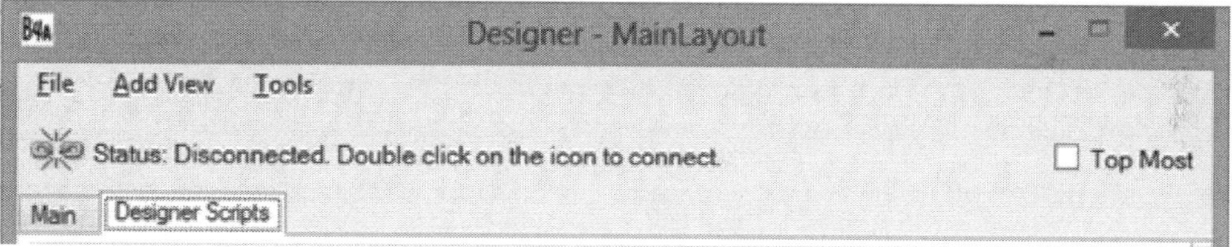

We describe Designer Scripting in the Designer Scripting Reference (page 109) Chapter.

The Abstract Designer

The Abstract Designer shows the layout you are creating in the Designer. Its main purpose is to help you create your layout and its variants. The different views are not shown with their exact shape but only as colored rectangles. Clicking on a view shows its properties in the Designer.

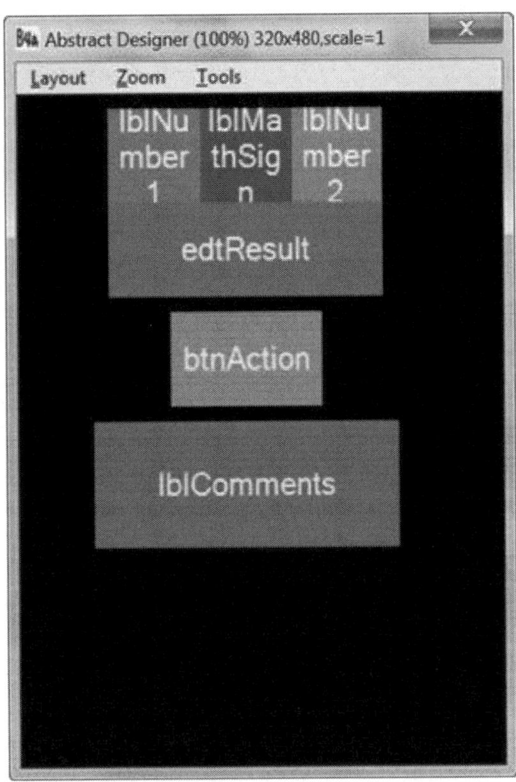

Layout Menu

It allows you to quickly match the size of the Abstract Designer with the variant selected in the Designer Main tab, or match the size of the Connected Device.
It also lists the most popular current screen sizes and resolutions.

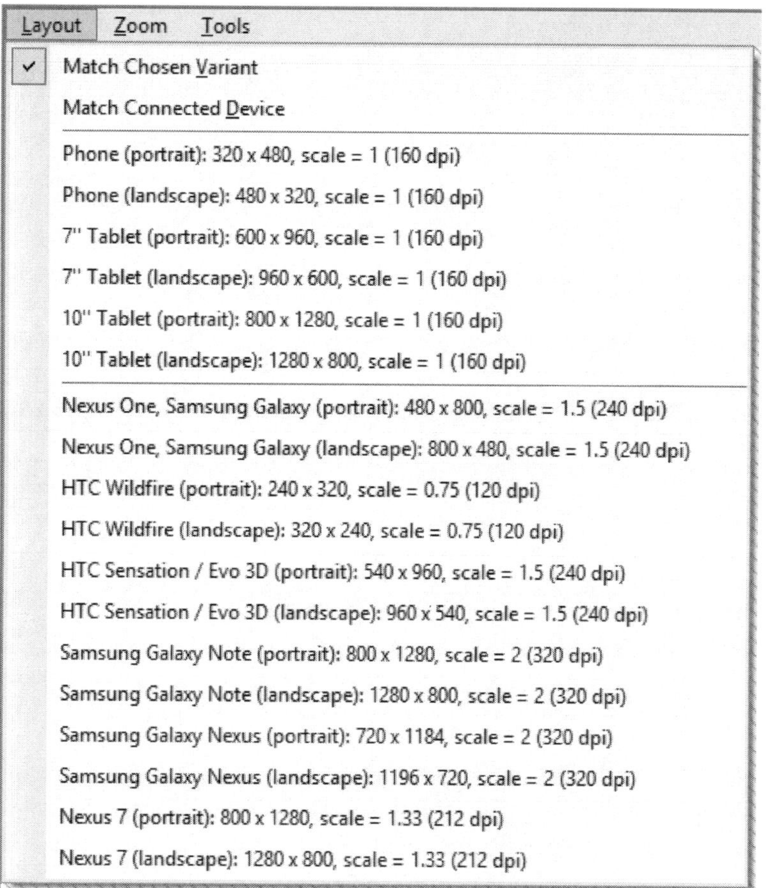

After you select your target variant, you can position the views according to the new dimensions and scale.

Zoom Menu

You can use the Abstract Designer full-size or reduced by 50%.

Tools Menu

You can resize the form (window) to fit the layout, and add the current layout (selected in the Layout Menu) as a new layout variant in the Designer.

Context menus

Clicking with the right button on a view in the Abstract Designer shows a context menu which has the options:

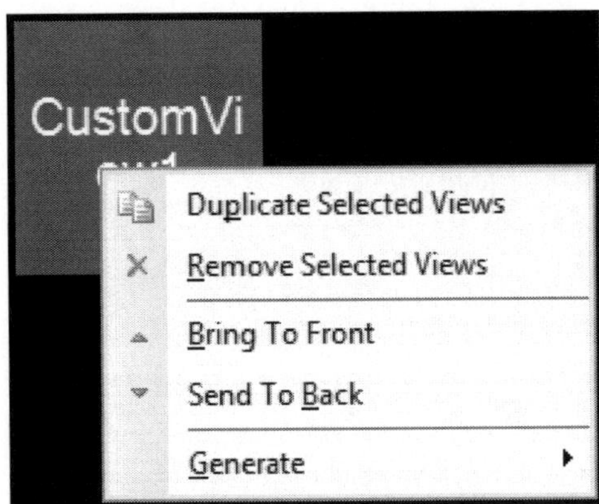

Generate: Generates the `Dim` statement or an event routine for the selected View. It is very similar to the Designer [Tools > Generate Members (page 93)] menu.

Selecting views

The selected views have a yellow border. You can select a single view by clicking on the view. Select several views by clicking on the first view, holding the Ctrl key and selecting more views or by dragging the cursor around them in the Abstract Designer.

After making a selection you can:

- Move the selected views with the arrow keys of the keyboard in the four directions.
- Use the Context menu (as described above).

With several views selected in the Abstract Designer, you can change various properties for them all in the Designer:

Multiple Views Selected	
Event Name	
Parent	
Left	0
Top	0
Width	0
Height	0

Example

Suppose we have a layout in portrait mode:

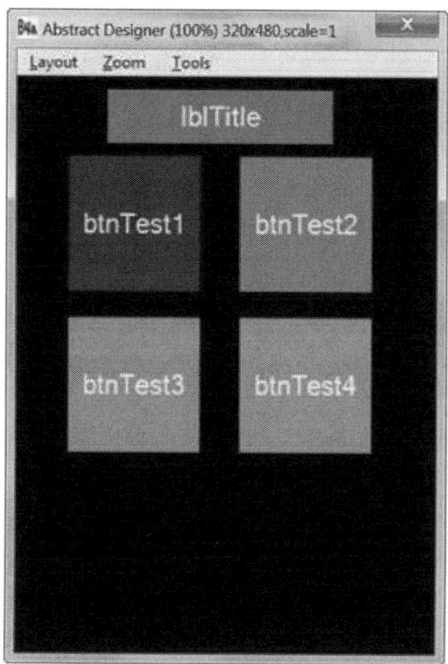

To make a landscape variant, click on [Layout > Phone (landscape)…]

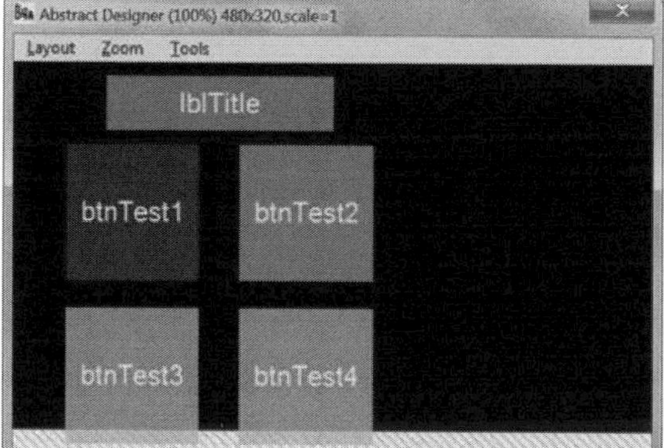

Now rearrange the views to fit the new orientation. Select Abstract Designer [Tools menu > Resize Form To Fit Layout] to see exactly what the user will see.

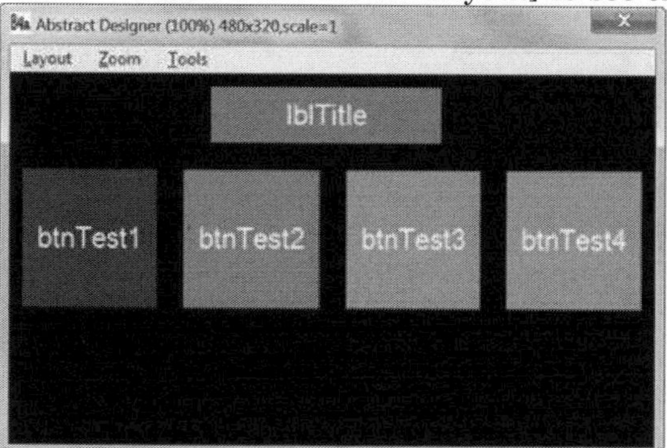

When the user rotates their phone, you want them to automatically see this layout, so you must add this as a new variant using the Abstract Designer menu [Tools > Add Current Layout As New Variant]. The new variant appears in the Designer Main tab:

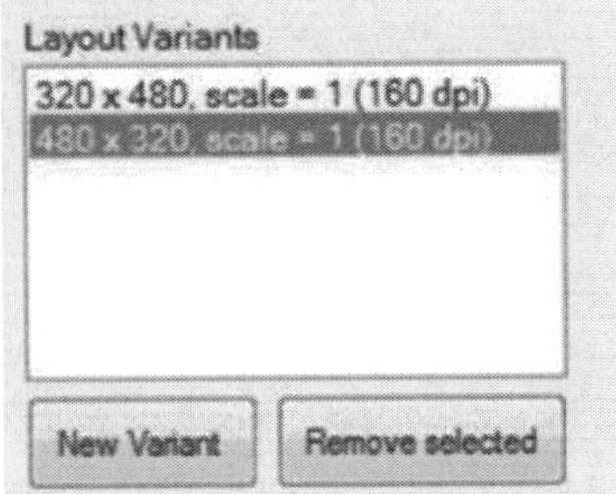

When you select a different variant in this list you will see it reflected in the Abstract Designer.

Designer Scripts

As well as the Main tab (page 97), the Designer includes a Designer Scripts tab. This is explained in the Designer Scripts chapter.

Adding views by code

Instead of using the Designer, it is also possible to create and modify views directly in your Activity code. See the section below (page 81) for details.

2.5 Designer Scripts Reference

Background

One of the most common issues that Android developers face is the need to adapt the user interface to devices with different screen sizes. As described in the Designer Chapter (page 92), you can create multiple layout variants (page 100) to match different devices. However, it is neither feasible nor recommended to create and maintain a lot of layout variants.
To solve this problem, Basic4Android supports designer scripts which help you fine-tune your layout and easily adjust it to different screens and resolutions. The idea is to combine the usefulness of the visual designer with the flexibility and power of programming code.
You can write a simple script to adjust the layout based on the dimensions of the current device and immediately see the results on a connected device or emulator (page 128). There is no need to compile and install the full program each time. You can also immediately see the results in the Abstract Designer (page 103). This allows you to quickly test your layout on many different screen sizes.

Designer Scripts and Activity Code

Note: a designer script runs before the code in your activity. If, for example, you have designer scripts for different orientation variants, when the user rotates the screen, the designer script will run first, then your activity code will be run as explained in Process and Activity Life Cycle (page 173).

Key Concepts

First, we define some key concepts for working with layouts and devices.

Pixel

A pixel (or picture element) is the smallest addressable physical element on a screen. It corresponds to a glowing dot of light.

Resolution

The number of pixels on the device, for example, 320 x 480

dpi : dots per inch

Dots per inch (also called dpi or pixels per inch or ppi or density) is a measure of the physical number of pixels in one inch of a device. A pixel is the smallest addressable element of the display. dpi will vary from one device to another, and vertical and horizontal dpi may differ on a single device. Things can get pretty complicated! Basic4Android developers do not need to worry about this, however! See **dip** below.

Screen Size

Typically the diagonal dimension of a screen is quoted in inches.

dip

We now come to a key concept. Suppose you want a button in your app to always be ½ inch wide. If you know the device will 160 dpi then you know the button should be 80 pixels wide. Your code might be:

```
Button1.Width = 80 'This can cause a problem
```

But what if your app runs on a device with a screen resolution of 240 dpi? Your button will only be 1/3 inch wide! This is the problem for which dips were created to solve.

dips are **D**ensity **I**ndependent **P**ixels (sometimes called **D**evice **I**ndependent **P**ixels). They are abstract units that are independent of the dpi of the device. One dip is defined as equal to 1/160 inch. It is equal in size to one pixel on a 160 dpi screen. 160 dips will always measure exactly one inch, no matter what the density of the device. 80 dips are always half an inch. Magic! So your code should say:

```
Button1.Width = 80dip   'Always 1/2 inch wide!
```

Use dip units for all specified sizes (except TextSize - see below).

By using dip units, the values will be sized correctly on devices with higher or lower resolution. You should always use dips when specifying the size or position of a view (control). This way the view's *physical* position and size will be the same on any device. This is true for both regular code and designer script.

Text Size

Note: text size is measured in physical units: you should **not** use dips with text size values.

Standard Screen

The Standard Screen is assumed to have a density of 160 dpi and a resolution of 320 x 480 pixels. This is the same as the Designer's Standard Variant (page 101).

Scale

The standard screen resolution is 160 dpi. This is said to have a scale of 1. To calculate the scale of a specific device, divide the dpi by 160. So, a phone with 320 dpi has a scale of 320/160 = 2 and a screen with 240 dpi has a scale of 240/160 = 1.5. Typical scale values are: 0.75, 1.0, 1.5 and 2. Most phones today have 240 dpi, so their scale is 1.5. Most tablets have a scale of 1.0.

Should you want to, you can convert dips to physical pixels by multiplying by the scale. So, 80dip on a device with scale 2 would be 160 pixels.

You can find the scale value for the current device by using the Scale property (page 318) of a LayoutValues object.

Dock and Fill Strategy

A common way of designing a layout is to dock some views to the edges of the screen, then use the other views to fill in the space between them. You can dock a button, for example, with the Designer Script:

```
button1.Right = 100%x
```

It is often useful to dock a panel and then fill it with views, such as buttons in a ToolBox Panel.

Designer Scripting Basics

The top of the Designer Scripts tab includes the following items:

Run Script Button

Run Script (F5) Current Variant 320 x 480, scale = 1 (160 dpi) What's This?

If you click this button (or press F5), the current script will be run and the results will be shown on the connected device / emulator (page 128) and in the Abstract Designer (page 103). The same thing happens when you run your compiled program. The (now compiled) script is executed after the layout is loaded. The general script is first executed followed by the variant script specific to the device and orientation. The system will automatically decide which variant to apply.

Current Variant Option

If you have added more than one variant in the Layout Variants (page 100) section of the Designer's Main Tab (page 97), then here you can select which variant you wish to use for the script. Changing this will update the Abstract Designer to show the selected variant and also update the Variant Specific Script area of the Designer Script Tab.

Scripting Areas

There are two scripting areas: All Variants (at top) and Variant Specific

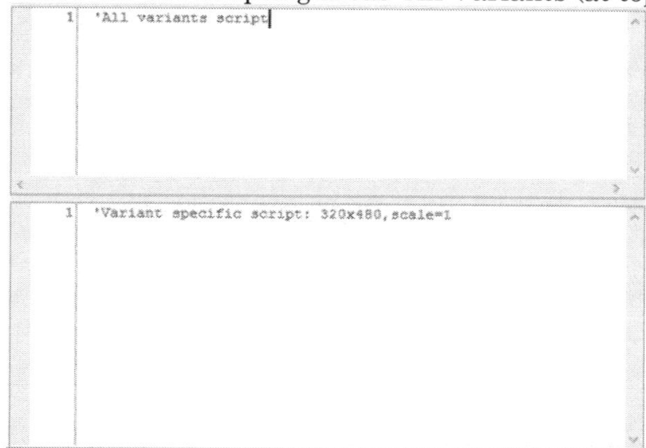

All Variants Script Area

The script written here will be applied to all variants.

Variant Specific Script Area

The lower half of the Designer Scripts screen provides a script which is specific for the Current Variant.

Activating Designer Scripts

There are two tabs in the Designer window, **Main** and **Designer Scripts**:

Main | Designer Scripts

What you see in the Abstract Designer (and in a device or emulator connected to the Designer) depends on which of these tabs is selected.
If **Main** is selected, the Views are in their original position.
If **Designer Scripts** is selected, the Views move to the positions specified by the relevant scripts.

Script Language

The script language is simple and is optimized for managing layouts.

Variables

You can use variables in Designer Scripts. You do not need to declare the variables before using them. There is no **`Dim`** keyword in the script.

```
gap = 3dip
cmd0.Left = gap
```

%x and %y

50%x means 50% of the maximum width available.
100%y means 100% of the height available.
These values are relative to the view that loads the layout. Usually it will be the activity (page). However, if you use **`Panel.LoadLayout`**, then it will be relative to this panel.
Note: **`ScrollView`** inner panel width is set to **`-1`**. This is a special value that causes the panel to fill its parent's available size.
If you want to load a layout file (with a script) to the inner panel then you will need to first set the panel width:

```
ScrollView1.Panel.Width = ScrollView1.Width
```

Screen Size

The screen width is 100%x and its height is 100%y. So to set view EditText1 at the bottom of the screen, you would use:

```
EditText1.bottom = 100%y
```

Properties Within Scripts

You can get or set a view's position using the properties **Width, Height, Left, Right, Top, Bottom, HorizontalCenter, VerticalCenter.**
For example:

```
EditText1.Left = 0
EditText1.Top = 0
lblTitle.Right = 100%x
lblTitle.Bottom = 100%y
```

Warning: Set Internal Properties before External

It is important that you set internal properties (Width or Height) BEFORE you set the external properties (**Left, Right, Top, Bottom, HorizontalCenter, VerticalCenter**). If you set the external properties first, then the view will be positioned wrongly. For example, suppose you want a button positioned at the bottom of the screen.
You might use the script:

```
btnTest.Bottom = 100%y
btnTest.Height = 10%x
```

But this will produce the following in the Abstract Designer:

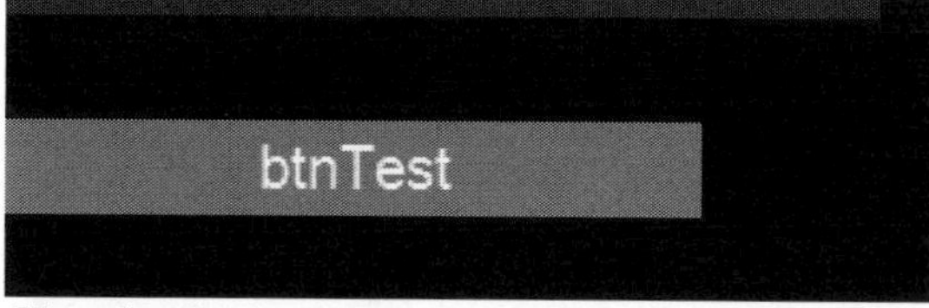

Clearly the button is not at the bottom of the screen! The reason is that you have specified the external property (**Bottom**) before the internal (**Height**). If you swap them round:

```
btnTest.Height = 10%x
btnTest.Bottom = 100%y
```

the button will be positioned correctly:

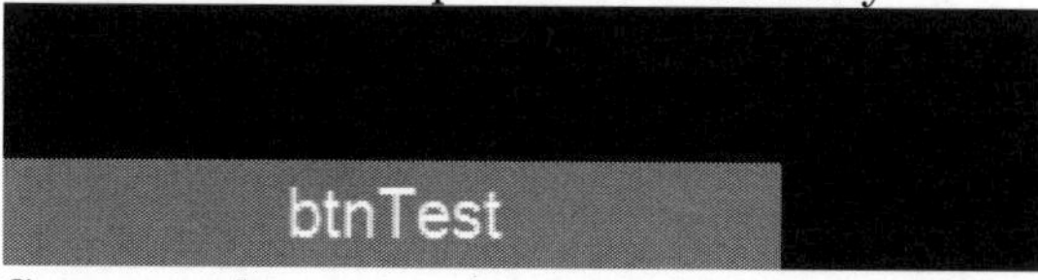

So remember to set internal before external properties. The letters "IE" might help to remind you of this. Alternatively, you could use **SetLeftAndRight** or **SetTopAndBottom**. See below for details.

Text Properties

You can get or set the text size and textual content of views such as labels and buttons which show text:
- **TextSize** - Gets or sets the text size.

You should not use 'dip' units with this value as it is already measured in physical units.
- **Text** - Gets or sets the view's text.

Other Properties

- **Image** - Sets the image file (write-only). Only supported by ImageView.
- **Visible** - Gets or sets the view's visible property.

Methods

- **SetLeftAndRight** (Left, Right) - Sets the view's left and right properties. This method changes the width of the view based on the two values.
- **SetTopAndBottom** (Top, Bottom) - Sets the view's top and bottom properties. This method changes the height of the view based on the two values.

Other Keywords

- **Min / Max** - Same as the standard Min / Max keywords.
- **ActivitySize** - Returns the approximate activity size measured in inches.
- **If ... Then** condition blocks

Both single line and multiline statements are supported. The syntax is the same as for regular If blocks.

Activity Methods

Activity.RerunDesignerScript (LayoutFile As String, Width As Int, Height As Int)

A Designer Script will be called automatically when your app starts and if the device orientation changes (see Note below), but in some cases it may be desirable to run the script again while your app is executing. For example, you may want to update the layout when the soft keyboard becomes visible. The `Activity.RerunDesignerScript` method allows you to run the script again and specify the width and height that will represent 100%x and 100%y. In order for this method to work, all the views referenced in the script must be declared in `Sub Globals`.

Note: this method should **not** be used to handle screen orientation changes. When the device's orientation changes, the activity will automatically be recreated and the script will run during the `Activity.LoadLayout` call.

AutoScale: Layouts for Different Sized Devices

Larger devices offer a lot more available space. The result is that, if the physical size of a view is the same, it looks smaller. Some developers use %x and %y to specify the view's size. However, the result is far from perfect. The layout will just be stretched.

The solution is to combine the dock and fill strategy (page 111) with a smart algorithm that increases the view's size and text size based on the running device's physical size.
Note: **`AutoScale`** is the only way to automatically change the **`TextSize`**.

How AutoScale works

Basic4Android internally calculates the values given below. You do not need to understand these calculations, but we include them here for reference:
Delta: a measure of the ratio of the current screen compared to the standard variant, calculated by the formula

```
delta = ((100%x + 100%y) / (320dip + 480dip) - 1)
```

Rate: How much we want to stretch the views. Normally a value between 0.3 and 1 is used. The default is 0.3, but this can be changed with the **`AutoScaleRate()`** function.
Scale: The multiplication factor applied to individual views, calculated by

```
scale = 1 + rate * delta
```

These values have no effect until either **`AutoScale`** or **`AutoScaleAll`** are called by the Designer Script.

How to See the Effect of AutoScale

AutoScale bases its calculations upon the standard variant: resolution 320 x 480, 160 dpi, scale = 1. Therefore, when used with this variant, **`AutoScale`** will have no effect.
To see the effect of **`AutoScale`**, you need to add a different sized variant. Go to the **Main** tab in the Designer and do the following:
1) add a New Variant, such as 960 x 600, then
2) select the variant in the Layout Variants list:

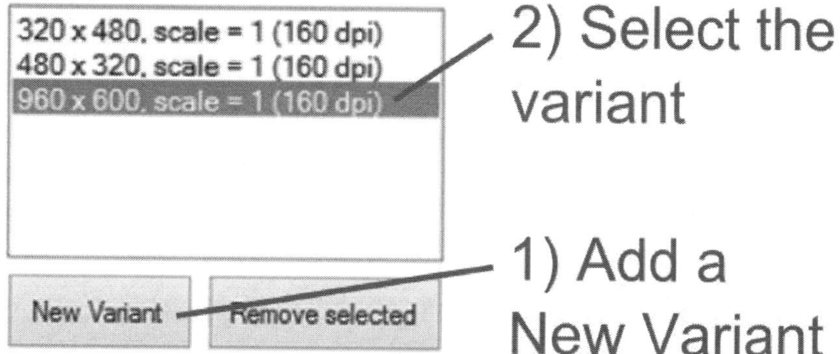

You can also select the **Current Variant** (step 2) in the **Designer Scripts** tab of the Designer:

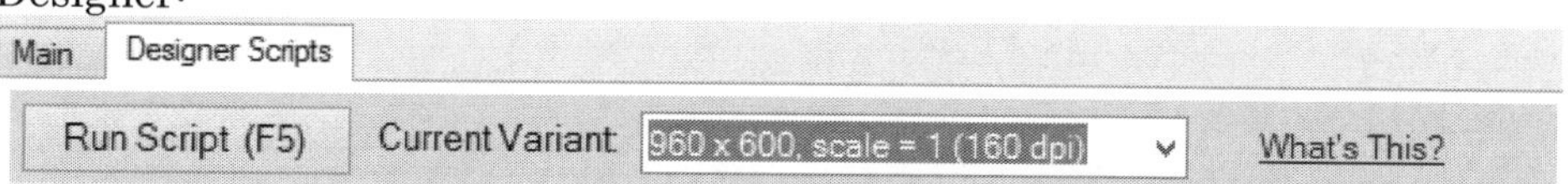

Now you can use the **`AutoScale`** commands, as described next, and see their effect.

How to See the Effect of AutoScale on Text Size

Note: because the Abstract Designer is not WYSIWYG, you will not see the effect of **`AutoScale`** on text size. You must attach the Designer to an emulator or a real device to see the actual results. **Note also**: the device will ignore the **Current Variant** you have selected and automatically select the variant suitable to the device.

How to Use AutoScale

Often your script will select the **`AutoScaleRate`** and then you will **`AutoScaleAll`** so that all views are scaled. So your script might be something like this:

```
AutoScaleRate(0.5)
AutoScaleAll
```

By changing the value for **`AutoScaleRate`**, you can find the best value for different variants. Occasionally you might need to scale individual views, in which case you would use the **`AutoScale`** function. We describe these functions next:

AutoScaleRate(rate)

Sets the rate value for above scale calculation. The rate determines the change amount in relation to the device physical size. Example:

```
AutoScaleRate(0.5)
```

Value of 0 means no change at all. Value of 1 is almost similar to using %x and %y: If the physical size is twice the size of the standard phone, then the size will be twice the original size. Values between 0.2 to 0.5 seem to give good results. If this is not called, **rate** defaults to 0.3.

If a view has a **`Text`** property, its **`TextSize`** is also multiplied by the scale value.

Note: **`AutoScaleRate`** cannot be called by Basic4Android code, only by a Designer Script.

AutoScaleAll

Scales all the views in the selected layout using the algorithm shown above. Normally you call it after **AutoScaleRate**.

AutoScale(View)

Scales the specified view using the scale value calculated as explained above.

Example: `AutoScale(btnTest1)`

This is equivalent to:

```
btnTest1.Left = btnTest1.Left * scale
btnTest1.Top = btnTest1.Top * scale
btnTest1.Width = btnTest1.Width * scale
btnTest1.Height = btnTest1.Height * scale
btnTest1.TextSize = btnTest1.TextSize * scale
```

AutoScale multiplies the **`Left/Top/Width`** and **`Height`** properties by the scale value.

Note: "scale" is not a keyword so it cannot be used in your scripts.

Different Layouts for Portrait and Landscape

A layout rarely looks good in both portrait and landscape mode. For example, a row of buttons might look better along the bottom in portrait but down the side in landscape. Therefore, it can be a good idea to create different layouts, one for each orientation. Suppose we have already created a Designer Script for portrait mode. To make it work for both portrait and landscape, the Designer Script code must be changed.

For the portrait variant, we keep only the most general code in the `All variants script` area of the Main layout file. For example:

```
'All variants script
AutoScaleRate(0.5)
AutoScaleAll
```

All the other code is moved to the `Variant specific script` areas.

Scaling strategy

You should decide what will happen with your layout when it runs on a larger device. Usually some views will be docked to the edges. This can be done easily with a designer script. For example, to dock a button to the right side:

```
Button1.Right = 100%x
```

Some views should fill the available area.

This is done with the **SetTopAndButtom** and **SetLeftAndRight** methods:

```
'Make an EditText fill the available height between two buttons:
EditText1.SetTopAndBottom(Button1.Bottom, Button2.Top)

'Make a Button fill the entire PARENT panel:
Button1.SetLeftAndRight(0, Parent1.Width)
Button1.SetTopAndBottom(0, Parent1.Height)
```

Editing Views in a program

As well as using the Designer to create a Layout, you can create or modify Views in code.

Example

Here is some code which will produce the following screen:

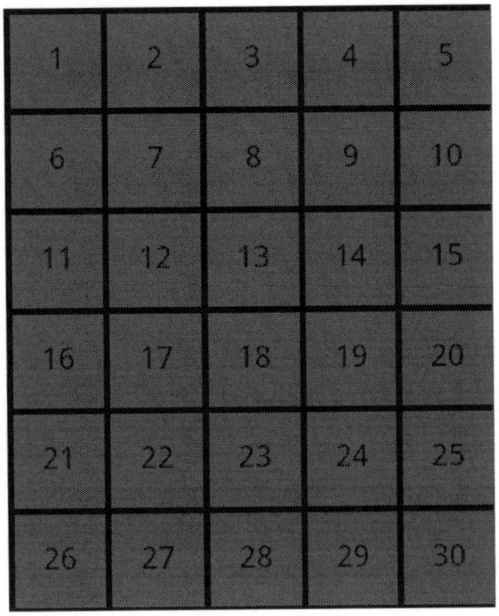

```
Sub Activity_Create(FirstTime As Boolean)
 Dim i, j, k, nx, ny, x0, x1, x2 As Int

 x0 = 4dip
 x1 = 60dip
 x2 = x0 + x1

 nx = Floor(Activity.Width / x2) - 1
 ny = Floor(Activity.Height / x2) - 1
 k = 0
 For j = 0 To ny
  For i = 0 To nx
   k = k + 1
   Dim btn As Button
   btn.Initialize("btn")
   btn.Color = Colors.Red
   Activity.AddView(btn, x0 + i * x2, x0 + j * x2, x1, x1)
   btn.Text = k
   btn.TextSize = 20
  Next
 Next
End Sub
```

2.6 Compiling, Debugging & Testing

Compiling

To test and later distribute your project, you must compile it either using the Project menu, the ▶ Run icon or Alt-3 (Compile and Run).

Compilation Modes

There are four compilation modes which are selected by a drop-down list box at the top of the IDE:

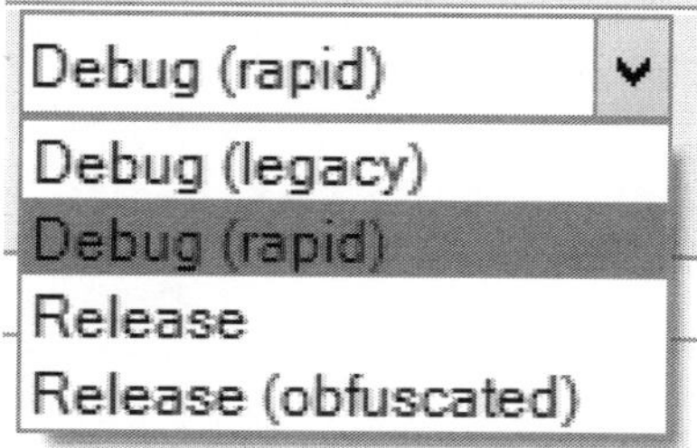

Debug Legacy Mode

This mode requires a device or emulator (page 128) to be attached to the IDE. This option will sign the package file with a debug key, ready for debugging, and produce a file **projectname_DEBUG.apk** in the **project\Objects** folder. If no device is attached, it will still compile the code, but produce an error message. See Legacy Debugging (page 123) for details.

Debug Rapid Mode

This mode requires a device or emulator (page 128) to be attached to the IDE. This option will sign the package file with a debug key, ready for debugging, and produce a file **projectname_RAPID_DEBUG.apk** in the **project\Objects** folder. If no device is attached, it will still compile the code, but produce an error message. See Rapid Debugging (page 124) for details.

Release Mode

In this mode, the debugger code will not be added to the apk file.

Release (obfuscated)

Basic4Android includes a code obfuscation feature. During compilation, Basic4Android generates Java code which is then compiled with the Java compiler and converted to Dalvik (Android byte code format). There are tools that people can use to decompile the Dalvik byte code which Basic4Android creates back into Java code. The purpose of obfuscation is to make the decompiled code less readable, harder

to understand and make it more difficult to extract strings like developer account keys.
It is important to understand how the obfuscator works.
When compiled in this mode, the debugger code will not be added to the apk file, but the program file will be modified, as follows:

Strings obfuscation

Any string written in **`Sub Process_Globals`** (and only in this sub) will be obfuscated, making it much harder to extract important keys. The strings are deobfuscated at runtime. **Note**: several keys are used during obfuscation including the package name, version name and version code. Modifying these values with the manifest editor will break the deobfuscation process, so your code will not run.

Renaming of Variables

The names of global variables and subs are converted to meaningless strings. Local variables are not affected as their names are lost anyway during the compilation.
The following identifiers are **not** renamed:
- Identifiers that contain an underscore (which is required for handlers of events).
- Subs that appear in **`CallSub`** statements. If the sub name appears as a static string, the identifier will not be renamed.
- Names of Designer views.

Tip: If, for some reason, you need to prevent the obfuscator from renaming an identifier, you should add an underscore in the identifier name.
A file named **`ObfuscatorMap.txt`** will be created under the Objects folder. This file maps the original names of identifiers to their obfuscated names. This mapping can be helpful to analyze crash reports.

Debugging

Debugging is the process of finding "bugs" or faults in your code.
The two major methods for debugging are setting Breakpoints and Logging (page 126). There are two debugging modes in Basic4Android: Legacy Debugging and Rapid Debugging. We describe these next.
Select the required mode from the toolbar:

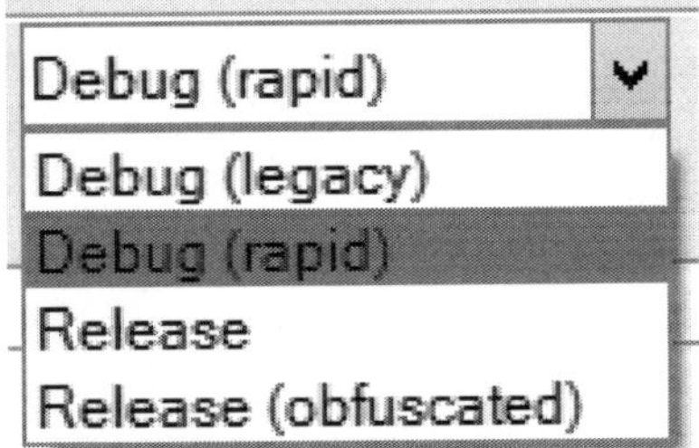

Then either select [Project > Compile & Run] or type Alt+1 or click on the blue triangle in the toolbar, to compile and run the app.

Breakpoints

You can create "breakpoints" in your code. When the program runs, it stops when it meets a breakpoint.
You can mark lines of code as breakpoints. This is done by clicking on the grey margin at the left of the IDE. The breakpoint is shown as a red dot in the left margin, as a line of code highlighted in red, and as a red bar in the scroll-bar at the right:

```
        Activity.LoadLayout("Main")
        timer1.Initialize("timer1", 1000)
        timer1.Enabled = True
    End If
    Dim lv As LayoutValues
    Log(lv.Scale)
End Sub

Sub timer1 Tick
```

When the program has stopped at a breakpoint, the breakpoint line is highlighted in yellow in the IDE:

```
        timer1.Enabled = True
    End If
    Dim lv As LayoutValues
    Log(lv.Scale)
End Sub
```

In the app, a blocking dialog with a circular spinning disc and the line number and code at the breakpoint is shown:

Program paused on line: 48
tm = DateTime.Now + 3600 * 1000

Breakpoint Limitations

- Breakpoints in the following subs will be ignored: **`Globals`**, **`Process_Globals`** and **`Activity_Pause`**.
- Services - Breakpoints that appear after a call to StartService will be ignored.
- Breakpoints set in **`Service_Create`** and **`Service_Start`** will pause the program for up to a specific time (about 12 seconds). This is to avoid Android from killing the Service.
- Events that fire when the program is paused will be executed. Breakpoints in the event code will be ignored (only when the program is already paused).

Debugger Control

When in either of the debug modes, buttons are available to control the execution of your program while debugging:

 Continue code execution (equivalent to F5)

Step to the next line (equivalent to F8). This steps through the program line by line, very useful to see the real program flow and the evolution of variable values.

Pause the code as soon as possible.

Stop the current program (equivalent to F11). Also stops the program in the Emulator. **Note**: stopping the program in the Emulator or on a device does not stop it in the IDE.

If you are using the Legacy Debugger, you will see the Connected Icon which tells you that the debugger is connected to a device or emulator. Click the icon to detach.

If you are using the Rapid Debugger, you will see the Restart Program icon, which forces the code to reload and execute from the beginning.

Debugger Menus

Once the debugger is running, you will see the Debug Menu, the Help Menu and perhaps the Edit Menu at the top of the IDE.
The **Edit Menu (page 39)** is visible only if you are using the Rapid Debugger.
The **Debug Menu** is:

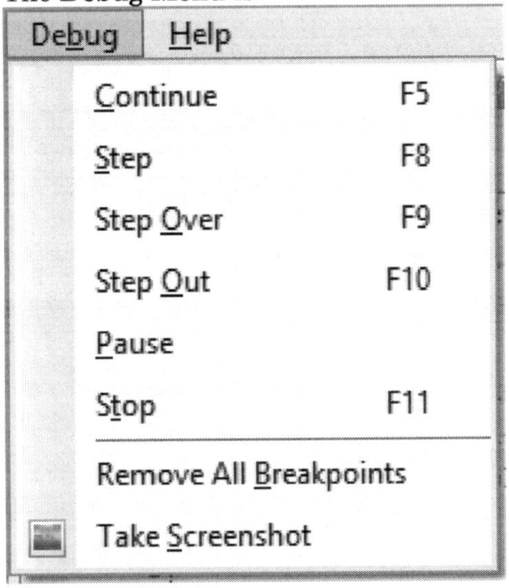

Debug Help
Continue F5
Step F8
Step Over F9
Step Out F10
Pause
Stop F11
Remove All Breakpoints
Take Screenshot

Continue (F5)
Makes the app continue to run until the next breakpoint.

Step (F8)
Steps to the next line of code. If the current line calls a sub, the first line of the sub will be executed.

Step Over (F9)
This will step over a sub. So, if the current line calls a sub, the whole sub will be executed without stepping through each line, and the code will stop at the line

after the sub call. If the current line does not call a sub, the result will be the same as Step (F8).

Step Out (F10)

This steps out of the current sub. The code will run until execution has left the current sub.

Pause

Pause the code as soon as possible.

Stop

Stop the current program (equivalent to F11). Also stops the program in the Emulator. **Note**: stopping the program in the Emulator or on a device does not stop it in the IDE.

Remove All Breakpoints

This will clear any breakpoints you have set in the code.

Take Screenshot

This calls the Screenshots (page 42) dialog box.

The **Help Menu** is the standard one (page 44) for Basic4Android.

Legacy Debugging

To use legacy debugging, you must activate the **Debug (legacy)** option at the top of the IDE, as shown above. If this option is selected, then the compiled code will contain debugging code.

The debugging code allows the IDE to connect to the program and inspect it while it runs. When the program starts, it will wait for up to 10 seconds for the IDE to connect. Usually the IDE will connect immediately. However, if you run your program manually from the phone, you will see it waiting.

The name of the compiled APK file will end with `_DEBUG.apk`. You should not distribute this apk file as it contains the debugging code which adds a significant overhead. To distribute files, you must select the **Release** option.

Legacy Debugger Information Area

When the program stops at a breakpoint in legacy mode, you find information about variables at the bottom of the IDE:

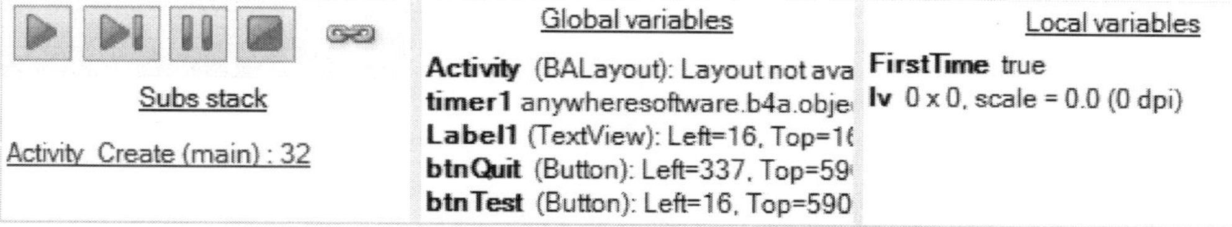

The meaning of the icons on the left are explained under Debugger Control below.

Global variables in Legacy Debugger

This list of the global objects and variables used by the program with their values and properties can be useful. Hover over the list to see more details.

Note: data sent from the device to the IDE is limited in size, so long strings may be truncated.

When the legacy debugger is running, the code in the IDE is read-only. You cannot change any of the program text. However, using the Rapid Debugger you can do exactly that.

Local variables in Legacy Debugger

Local variables (variables defined within the current sub) are also listed at the bottom of the IDE while in debug mode. In addition, you can see the value of variables by hovering the mouse over a variable within the code:

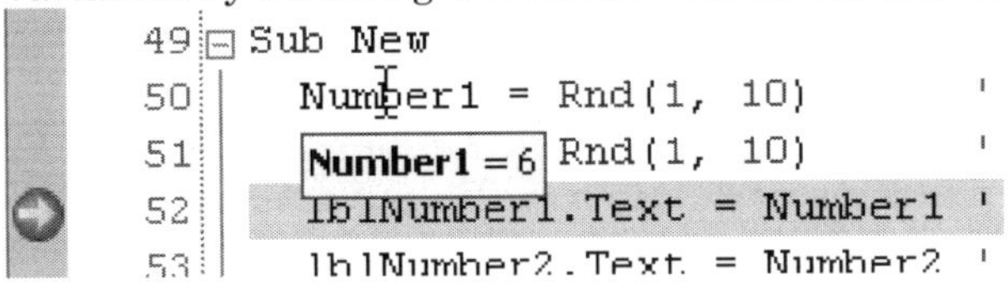

```
Sub New
  Number1 = Rnd(1, 10)        '
  Number1 = 6 Rnd(1, 10)      '
  lblNumber1.Text = Number1   '
  lblNumber2.Text = Number2   '
```

Hovering the mouse over an object shows its properties:

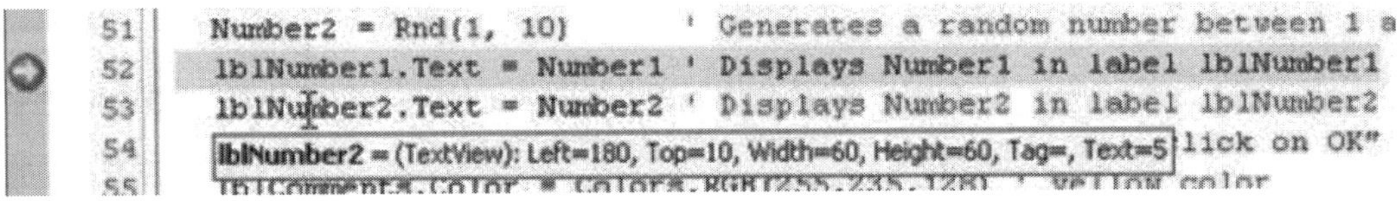

```
Number2 = Rnd(1, 10)        ' Generates a random number between 1 a
lblNumber1.Text = Number1 ' Displays Number1 in label lblNumber1
lblNumber2.Text = Number2 ' Displays Number2 in label lblNumber2
lblNumber2 = (TextView): Left=180, Top=10, Width=60, Height=60, Tag=, Text=5 lick on OK"
lblComments.Color = Colors.RGB(255,235,128) ' yellow color
```

Rapid Debugging

Version 3 of Basic4Android introduced a very powerful tool, the Rapid Debugger, which provides features not available in any other native Android development tool. Using this feature, you can compile and install your app on your device very quickly, usually within a few seconds. You can modify your code while your app is running and re-deploy it to your device immediately; you will not need to reinstall it. Similarly, the next time you start Basic4Android, you will not need to re-install the app to the device.

Limitations of the Rapid Debugger

- If you are using the free Trial Version of Basic4Android, then you will need to install Java JDK version 6 or 7 on your PC before the Rapid Debugger option will work. See here (page 60) for how to install the JDK.
- Execution of apps using the Rapid Debugger is slower than using any of the other compile options. It is not recommended to use the Rapid Debugger for any apps which require a lot of computation or graphics manipulation such as games.
- You cannot add or remove Globals variables when using the Rapid Debugger.
- You cannot run the app on a device if it is not connected to the IDE. The reason is that the app actually runs in a Debugger Engine within the IDE, as explained

below.

How the Rapid Debugger Works

The Rapid Debugger sends a simple "Shell App" to the device. This handles the user interface but provides no other functionality. Your app actually runs in a "Debugger Engine" which is a virtual device running on your PC, as shown in the following diagram:

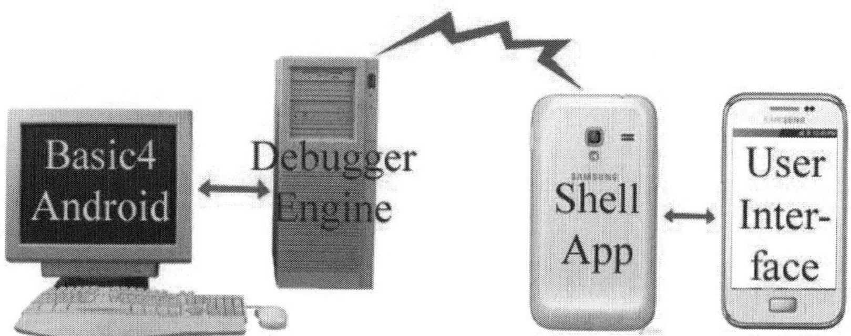

Thus, when you modify your app, only the code within the Debugger Engine needs to be changed. This is why deployment is so incredibly quick.
Note that if you add files to your app or modify the manifest, then a new Shell App will need to be uploaded to the device, but you will not need to re-approve the installation on the device, so this upload will be rapid.
Note also that, if you are using the Trial Version of Basic4Android and using remote compilation, the remote server will only need to be accessed in those rare circumstances when the Shell App needs to be changed. So modifying your app will usually be extremely rapid, as you normally only change the code in the Debugger Engine. See the limitations section above for more about using the Rapid Debugger with the Trial Version.

Rapid Debugger Information Area

When the Rapid Debugger meets a breakpoint, information similar to the following is displayed at the foot of the IDE:

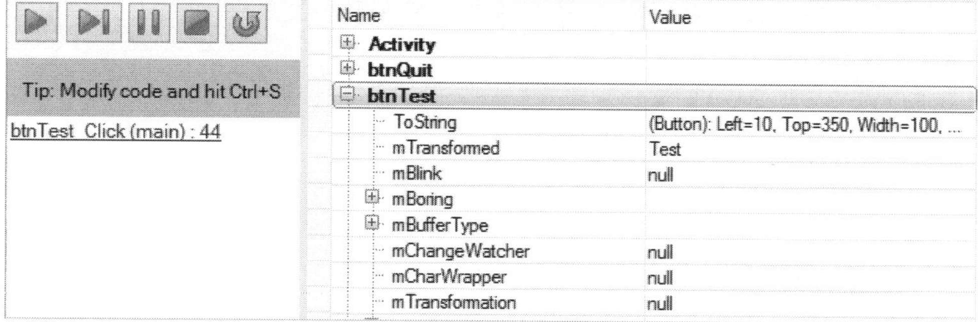

The control icons on the left are described under Debugger Control (page 121).
The area on the right contains a tree showing details about all current variables.

If you hover the mouse over a variable name in your code, the tree will automatically scroll to the corresponding variable.

Editing Code using the Rapid Debugger

The great benefit that the Rapid Debugger offers over the legacy debugger is that the code is not frozen. You can modify the code and very quickly recompile it simply by saving it (by using Control + S). This will send the new code to the Debugger Engine and show the message "Hot code swap completed successfully" at the foot of the IDE. You can do this whether the code is stopped at a breakpoint or not.

Logging

The other useful way of debugging your app is to use logging. This produces messages in the Logs tab at the right of the IDE:

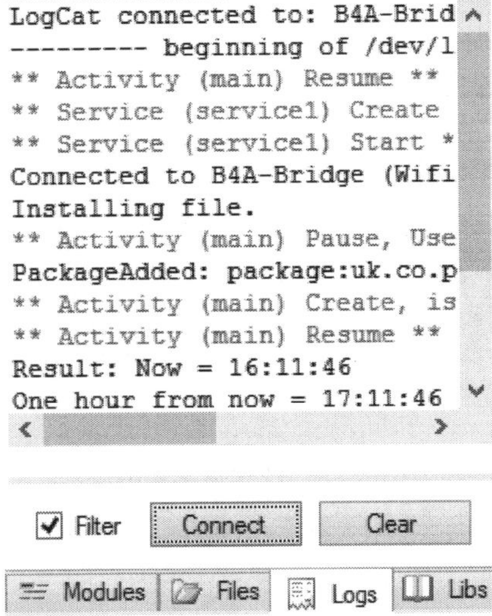

It shows messages related to the components life cycle (for example when a **Sub Activity_Create** runs) and it can also show messages that you specify with the Log keyword.

Consider the following Sub:

```
Sub btnTest_Click
    Log ("Button pressed at " & DateTime.Time(DateTime.Now))
    Msgbox ("Test for book", "It works")
End Sub
```

Run the program. If you are running several devices or emulators you will need to click on **Connect** in the Logs tab to connect the logger to the correct device. In the Logs Tab, you will see the flow of the program:

```
LogCat connected to: B4A-Bridge: asus Nexus 7-
--------- beginning of /dev/log/main
Installing file.
PackageAdded: package:pennypress.TestForBook
** Activity (main) Create, isFirst = true **
** Activity (main) Resume **
Button pressed at 13:29:00
```

When **Filter** is checked (see the image above), you will only see messages related to your program. When it is unchecked, you will see all the messages running in the system. If you are encountering an error and do not see any relevant message in the log, it is worth unchecking the filter option and looking for an error message.
Click **Clear** to delete the data in the Logs window. **Note**: the log is maintained by the device. When you connect to a device, you will also see previous messages.

Testing your App

There are several options for testing your app:

- Connect to a real device with B4A-Bridge.
- Connect to a real device in USB debugging mode
- Android emulator

B4A-Bridge

B4A-Bridge is a way to debug your app on a real device. You need to connect your PC to the device via wireless connections over the local network or Bluetooth connections. This is the recommended option. It is easier than USB connection and faster than an emulator. We explain the details in this tutorial (page 17).

USB Debugging

Unfortunately, not all devices support USB debugging. In that case, you should use one of the following options. To use USB debugging, you will need to first configure your device to support USB debugging. You might find this in one of the following, or perhaps something similar, depending how menus are configured on your device:

[Settings > Development > USB debugging]
[Settings > Developer Options > USB debugging]
[Settings > Applications > Development > USB debugging]

You will also need to install a Windows driver specific to your device. You should download the Google USB Driver in the Android SDK Manager (page 60). If this driver doesn't work, you must search for a specific driver for your device. There are more details about connecting your device via USB here (http://bit.ly/141xVIP) and here (http://bit.ly/141zLJG).

The Emulator or Android Virtual Device (AVD) Manager

Another way to run your app is by using an emulator. These are created and managed by the AVD Manager. **Note**: an emulator can be quite memory-hungry.

Introduction

The AVD (Android Virtual Device) Manager is a utility provided by Google as part of the Android SDK which allows you to create emulated Android devices. You can run the AVD from the IDE by clicking on [Tools > Run AVD Manager].
You can create as many devices as you require, with different hardware specifications and with different screen resolutions. You are not restricted to running just one emulated device at a time. You can start as many devices as you need (dependent upon the memory on your computer of course) and you can keep those devices running as you edit and compile your code within Basic4Android. But note that emulators can consume a lot of memory.

How Basic4Android interacts with Emulated Devices

On successful code compilation, Basic4Android will look for any active Device Emulators, or real devices which have been connected to your computer and will provide a list of those devices. You can then choose which device - real or emulated - to run the compiled code on from that list.
Since you can have multiple emulated devices running at one time, this means that you can test your code against several different devices in a reasonably fast manner - you just run your code against each device in the list.

Using the Android Virtual Device Manager

In the IDE, select [Tools > Run AVD Manager]. A window similar to the following appears:

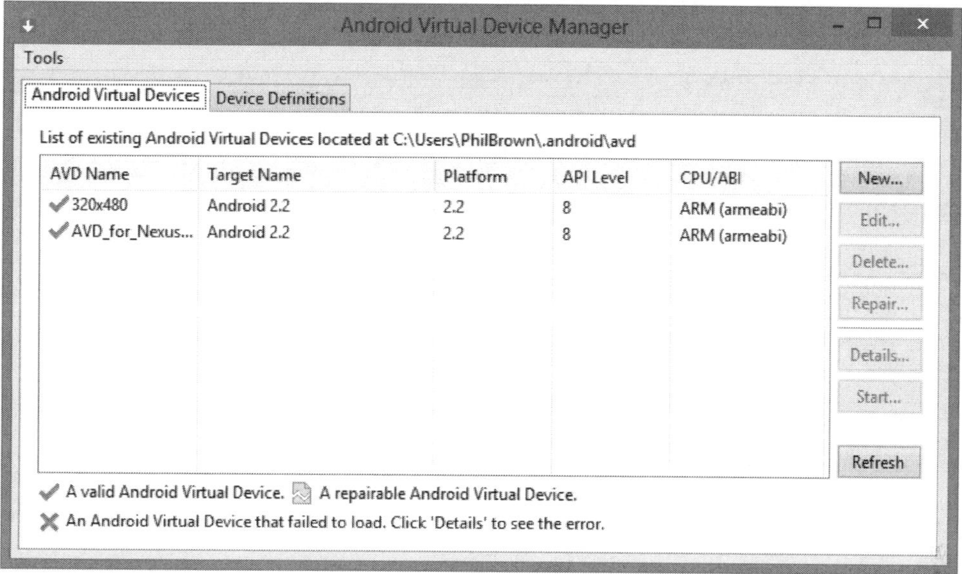

Missing Tabs

Exactly what you see will depend on which Revision of the Android SDK Tools you have installed on your PC. Those with newer versions will see the two tabs, **Android Virtual Devices** and **Device Definitions**, below the menu. Those with older versions will simply see a list of the existing Android Virtual Devices.

How to upgrade

If you need access to the Device Definitions tab, described below, then you should use the [Tools > Manage SDK...] menu and upgrade to a later version of the Android SDK Tools, for example 22.n.n:

Android Virtual Devices (AVDs)

The emulators you will run are Android Virtual Devices (AVD). Each one is based upon a Device Definition. Initially, the AVD list will be empty, but there is a pre-populated list of Device Definitions.

Creating an AVD

Every virtual device is based upon a Device Definition. The emulator comes with a list of device definitions pre-defined, and you can create new ones using the Device Definitions tab. Choose "New". A dialog box will open for creating a new emulator:

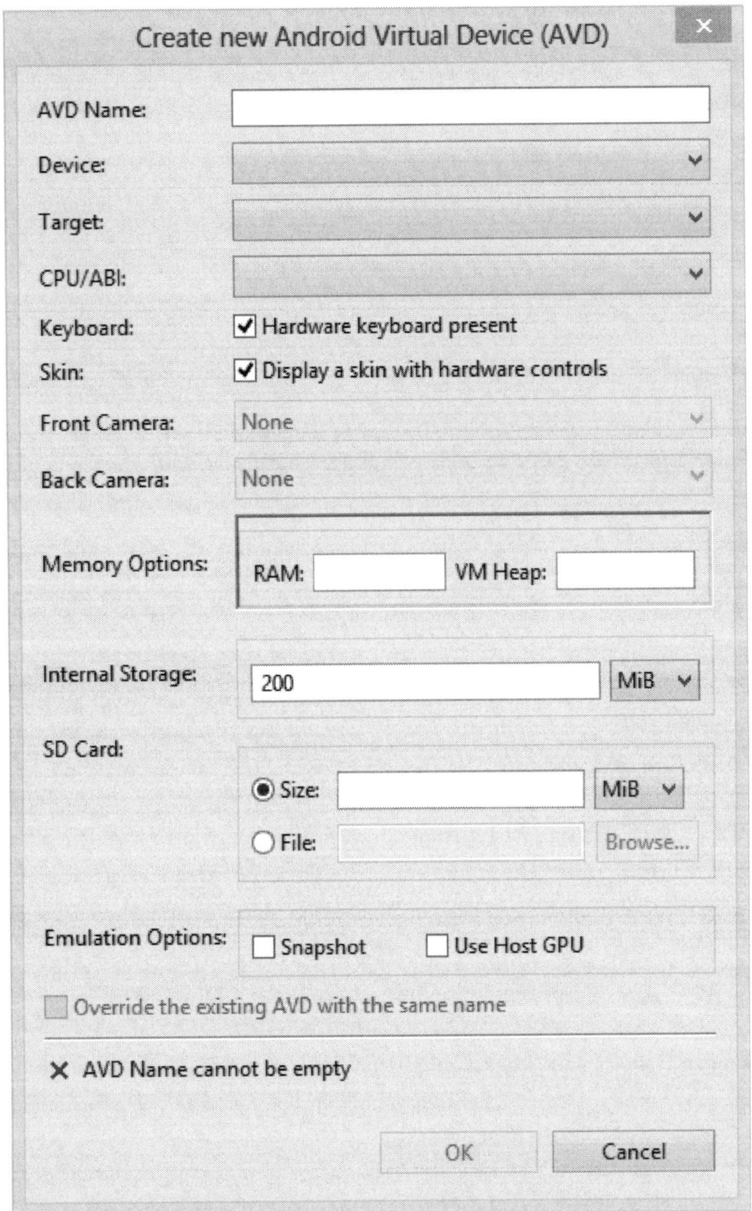

AVD Name

A name for your Virtual device. Spaces are not allowed in this field. You can give it a name like “HTCDesireHD” or “Xoom10.1”, but since you can use a particular size to emulate different devices which have the same specs, you may want to use names like “480x320x160” and “800x480x240”, where the last number is the pixel density of the layout.

Device

Choose the device upon which this AVD will be based. **Note**: you can also create new devices using the Device Definitions tab in the AVD Manager.

Target

The options available here depend upon which Android APIs you have installed using the Android SDK Manager. Basic4Android supports all versions of the API from 1.6.

CPU / ABI

Keyboard

This option is intended for devices which have an external hardware keyboard.
It is recommended to leave this option selected. This allows you to use the keyboard on your computer to enter data into fields in the emulator. Otherwise, you have to use the emulator's keyboard.

Skin

If you select this option, you will see a keyboard to the right of the emulator screen

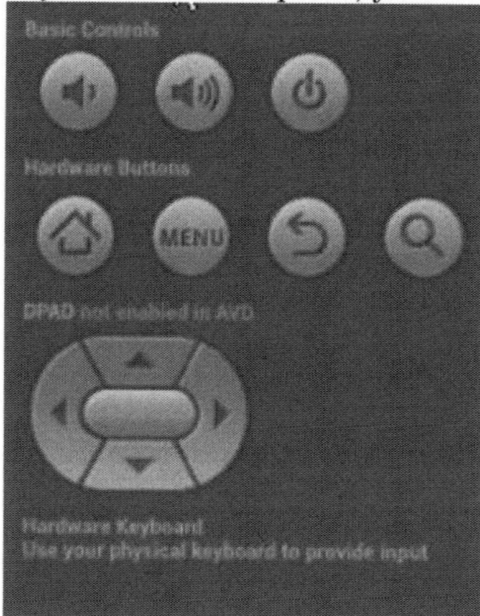

The **keyboard** option determines whether these keys are active.

Front / Back Camera

This allows you to specify whether a front and/or back camera (if present in this Device Definition) is inactive, emulated or uses a webcam attached to the computer on which the AVD is running.

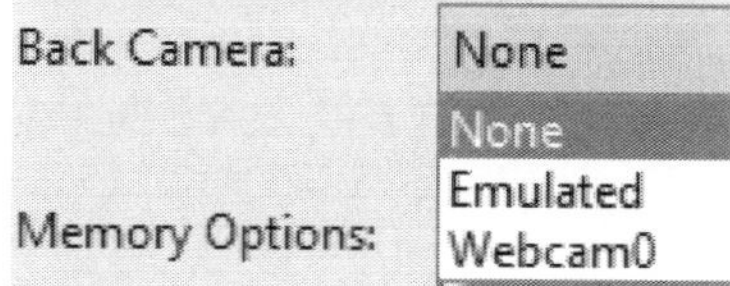

Memory Options

These will be set by the Device Definition you have selected but can be over-ridden.

RAM

Set the amount of RAM in Mb. Under Windows, emulating RAM greater than 768 Mb might fail if you do not have enough RAM available on your PC. If the emulator fails to run, reduce the amount of RAM allocated.

VM Heap

The VM Heap specifies the heap size of the virtual machine in MB. You should increase the heap size if you allocate more RAM. The heap is used to store instance variables of instantiated class objects. Garbage collection is used by the VM to free the heap space.

Internal Storage

This assumes a default value of 200 Mb but can be changed. Enter the number and select the units (Kb, Mb or Gb).

SD Card

Size

This allows you to specify the size of the SD card fitted to your device. **Note**: this will consume hard disk space, so don't be tempted to create a 32GB card by entering 32000 or else you will be waiting a long time as the SDK creates the SD card, and consumes 32GB of your drive!
The minimum size is 9Mb, and a useful size is probably 16 or 32 MB. Enter the number and select the units (Kb, Mb or Gb). It might be useful to have an emulator without an SD card so you can check that your app will still work.

File

This allows you to specify a File which represents an SD card. This allows you to share virtual SD cards between emulators.
In order to create a File, you need to use a tool which is provided by the Android SDK, "mksdcard", and a reference to this tool can be found in the Android Documentation here:
http://developer.android.com/guide/developing/tools/mksdcard.html

For example, if you wanted to create a file with a volume name of "mySDCard", and a size of 128M, you would follow these steps:

- Open a Command Prompt Window (on Windows 7, this is found under "All Programs-Accessories-Command Prompt")
- If your computer's Path does not contain the Android SDK (which it probably doesn't), you will need to navigate to the folder "C:\Program Files (x86)\Android\android-sdk-windows\tools" using DOS commands. On 32-bit systems, the path will be "C:\Program Files\Android\android-sdk-windows\tools".
- Enter "mksdcard -l mySDCard 128M mySDCardFile.img"

- This will create a file called **mySDCardFile.img**. You can then use this as your SD Card file in the AVD Manager.

For Mac users, If you are running Basic4Android inside a Virtual machine running a Windows O/S, you can go back to the Mac O/S and mount this SD image file. This allows you to copy files onto the SD Card. These files will be available on the SD Card when viewed on a Virtual Device using this SD Card file.

Emulation Options

Snapshot

Taking a snapshot means that the emulator will launch to that saved state, thus launching faster. For example, adding the Snapshot option can change the startup time from 24 seconds to 2 seconds! The first time it runs after you enble this option, the launch dialog box shows options to save snapshop and launch from the snapshop:

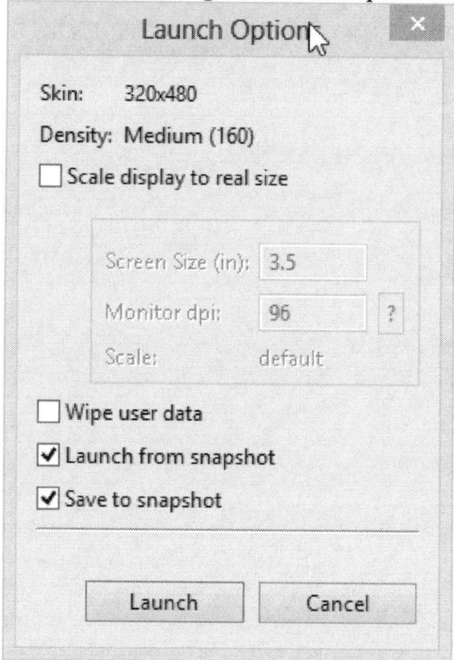

The first time it runs, the emulator starts normally. But when it closes, a snapshot will be saved so the next time it starts, this saved state will be used to launch the emulator much more quickly.

Use Host GPU

This option allows the emulator to use the graphics processing unit (GPU) of the host machine the emulator is running on. This results in a faster emulator. This option is not available in some older version of the SDK.

Creating a Device Definition

As well as using the pre-defined device definitions, you can create your own. Within the AVD Manager, click **Device Definitions** tab and click the **New Device...** button:

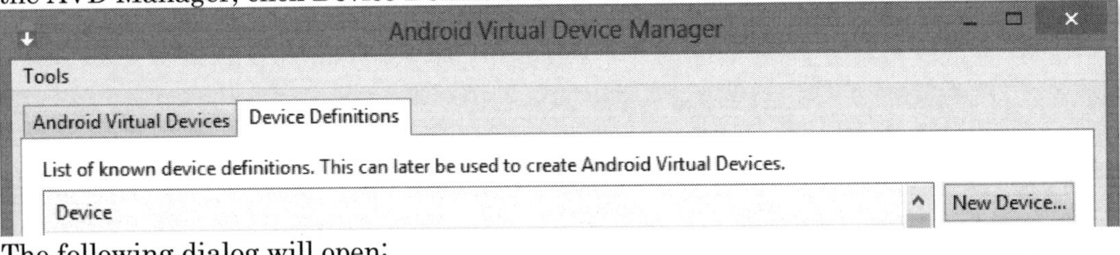

The following dialog will open:

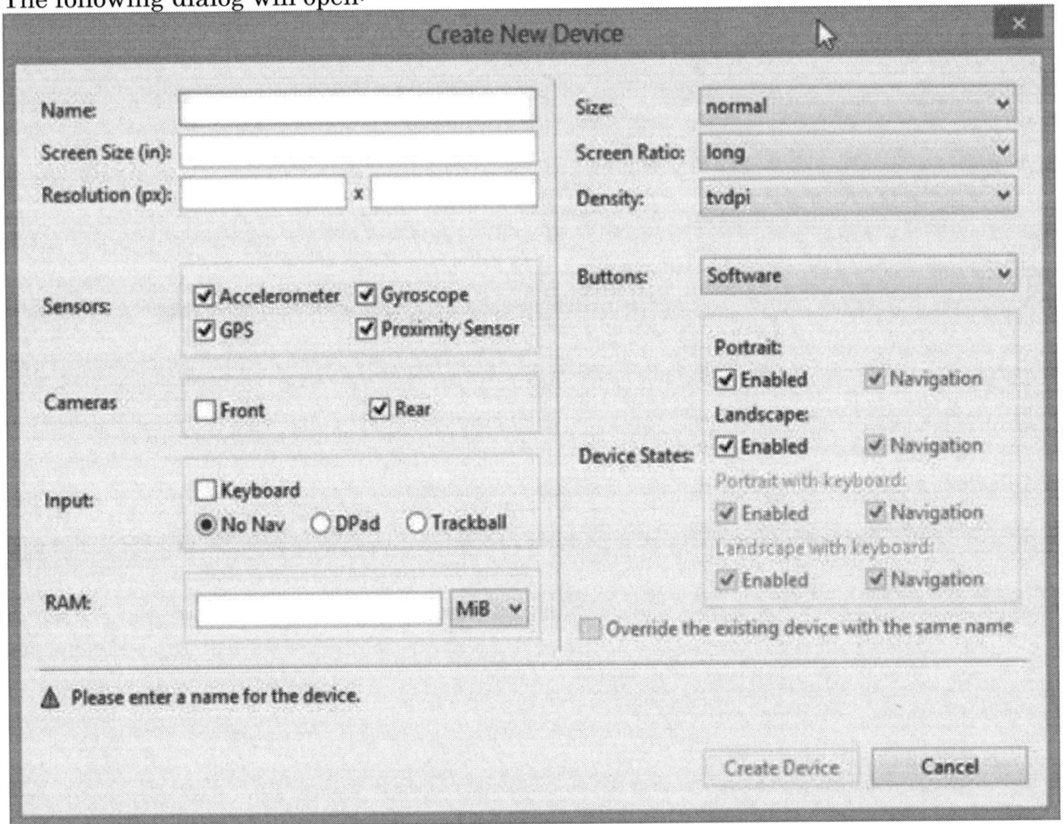

The main parameters you need to set are `Name`, `Screen Size` (in inches) and `Resolution` (width and height in pixels). The `Size`, `Screen Ratio` and `Density` parameters on the right are not critical. More information can be found at http://developer.android.com/guide/practices/screens_support.html

Running a Virtual Device and scaling for Real Size Emulation

From the "Virtual Devices" section of the Android SDK AVD Manager, select the Virtual Device that you want to run from the list of defined devices, and then click "Start". You will be presented with the Launch Options dialog box (shown above). This is where you can set the size of your Virtual device screen as it appears on your computer monitor.

The dialog box will tell you what the screen resolution has been set to - this refers to the Virtual Device resolution. It will also tell you what the pixel density is for that device. These parameters are the parameters that were entered when the device was set up.

You have two options as to how AVD Manager will present your Virtual Device on your computer monitor: **`No Scaling`** and **`Scale display to real size`**. These are described next.

No Scaling

If you leave the **`Scale display to real size`** option unchecked, then AVD Manager will directly map the Virtual Device screen's pixels to your monitor's pixels, one for one. A 1280 by 800 screen will therefore take up 1280x800 pixels on your monitor. A 480 by 800 screen will take up 480 by 800 pixels on your monitor. This could create problems for you - for example, if you're running on a 1024 by 768 monitor and you try and run a 1280 by 800 Virtual device, the Virtual Device screen will be bigger than your monitor, so you'll only see part of the Virtual Device screen.

Scale display to real size

If you select the **`Scale display to real size`** option, then AVD Manager will attempt to scale your device so that it shows with the correct physical dimensions on your computer monitor. To do this, AVD Manager needs some more information about your requirement, so you need to fill in the following fields:

Screen Size (inches)

This is the length of the diagonal measured from top left to bottom right across your desired device screen. (This is the standard used when quoting screen sizes). So if you want to emulate an HTC Desire HD, you would enter 4.3 here as that device has a 4.3in screen. For something like the Xoom, you would enter 10.1, as that device has a 10.1 inch screen. The emulator will try and make your emulated device screen match that size on your computer monitor.

Monitor dpi

Scaling involves interpolating between real pixel sizes (on your computer monitor) and emulated device pixel sizes (on your emulated device), so AVD Manager needs to know about your monitor. Click on the "?" next to this option, and you will see the **`Monitor Density`** dialog box. These values refer to your computer monitor, not the emulated device. This little dialog will try and work out a monitor density for you.

The resolution shown in the **`Resolution`** dropdown menu should match your computer monitor's resolution. The one bit that this dialog doesn't know is your computer monitor size - so you need to enter that into the **`Screen Size`** dropdown box. With that piece of information, AVD Manager can now scale the Virtual Device correctly so that it appears to be the correct size on your computer monitor.
Having set up all the required parameters, click on **`Launch`** to launch the desired Virtual Device. There will be a delay as the Virtual Device is created (if this is the first time it has been used) or launched. Be patient - this can take some time.
Eventually your device will appear in a window of its own. You may have to unlock the device by sliding the green Android button across the screen.

Interacting with your Virtual Device

When the emulator is running, you can interact with the emulated mobile device just as you would an actual mobile device, except that you use your mouse pointer to "touch" the touchscreen and your keyboard keys to "press" the simulated device keys. The table below summarizes the mappings between the emulator keys and and the keys of your keyboard.
One of the most useful functions is CTRL-F11 - this rotates the Virtual Display from landscape to portrait and back.

PC Keyboard Shortcuts

Emulator Function	PC Keyboard Key
Home	Home
(left softkey)	F2 or Page-up button
Star (right softkey)	Shift-F2 or Page Down
Back	ESC
Call/dial button	F3
Hangup/end call button	F4
Search	F5
Power button	F7
Audio volume up button	KEYPAD_PLUS, Ctrl-5
Audio volume down button	KEYPAD_MINUS, Ctrl-F6
Camera button	Ctrl-KEYPAD_5, Ctrl-F3
Switch to previous layout orientation (for example, portrait, landscape)	KEYPAD_7, Ctrl-F11
Switch to next layout orientation (for example, portrait, landscape)	KEYPAD_9, Ctrl-F12
Toggle cell networking on/off	F8
Toggle code profiling	F9 (only with -trace startup option)
Toggle fullscreen mode	Alt-Enter
Toggle trackball mode	F6
Enter trackball mode temporarily (while key is pressed)	Delete
DPad left/up/right/down	KEYPAD_4/8/6/2
DPad center click	KEYPAD_5
Onion alpha increase/decrease	KEYPAD_MULTIPLY(*) / KEYPAD_DIVIDE(/)

Mac Keyboard Shortcuts

The following assumes you are using Parallels (http://www.parallels.com/) to run Windows on a Mac.

Emulator Function	Mac Keyboard Key (in Parallels)
(left softkey)	fn-F2
Back	ESC
Call/dial button	fn-F3
Hangup/end call button	fn-F4
Search	fn-F5
Power button	fn-F7
Toggle cell networking on/off	fn-F8
Toggle code profiling	fn-F9

Enabling Hardware Buttons

By default, the buttons on the emulator are disabled in the AVD, as shown by the following:

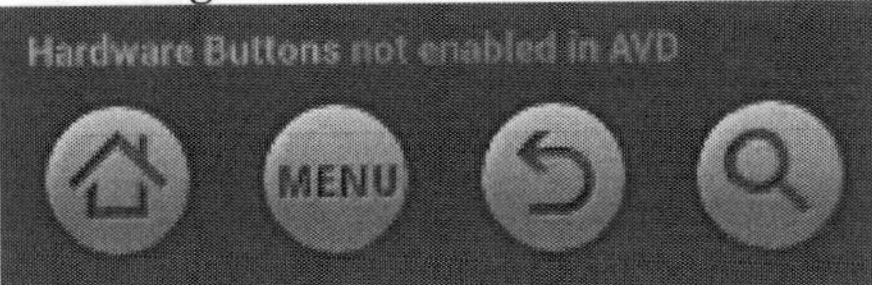

You cannot use the above keys. If you want to activate these Hardware Buttons, you need to modify the Device Definitions. To do this, find the **`Device Definitions`** tab in the Android Virtual Device Manager. Every AVD is based upon a Device Definition. Select the Device Definition for the AVD you want to modify.

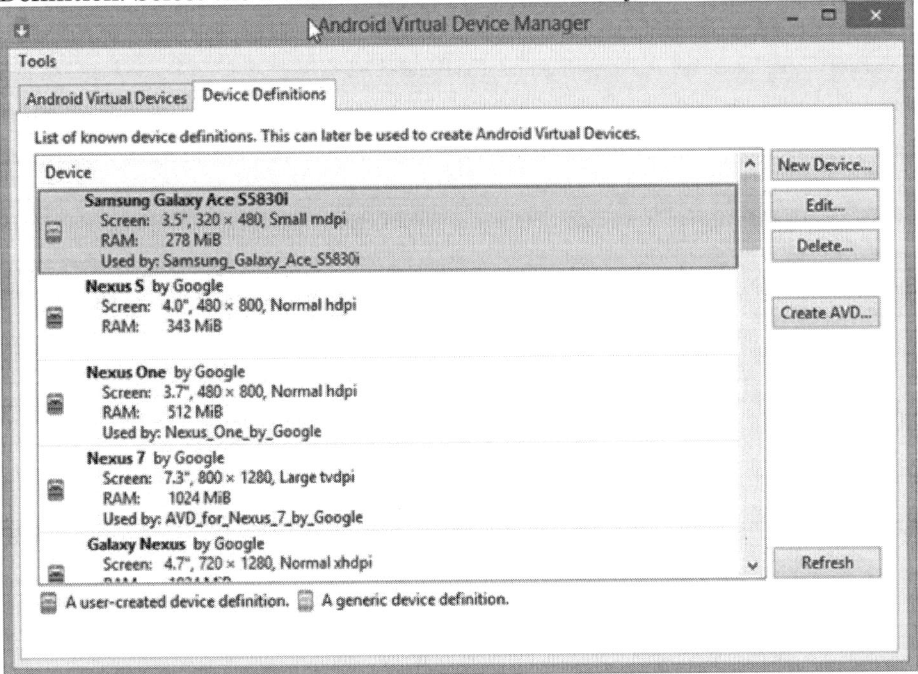

Select the device you're using and click **Edit...**. You will see the following

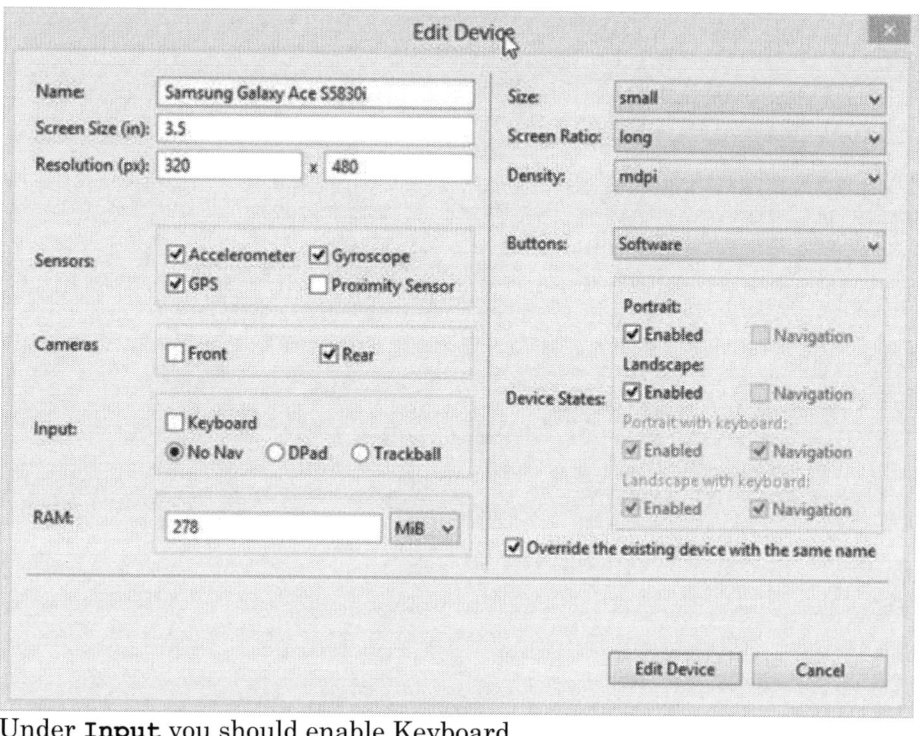

Under **`Input`** you should enable Keyboard.

Input: Keyboard
No Nav DPad Trackball

Now when you run an AVD based on this device, the keys will work.

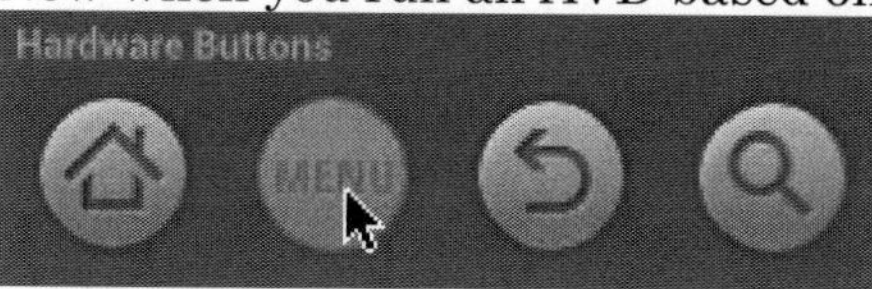

You enable them with the option "Display a skin with hardware controls":

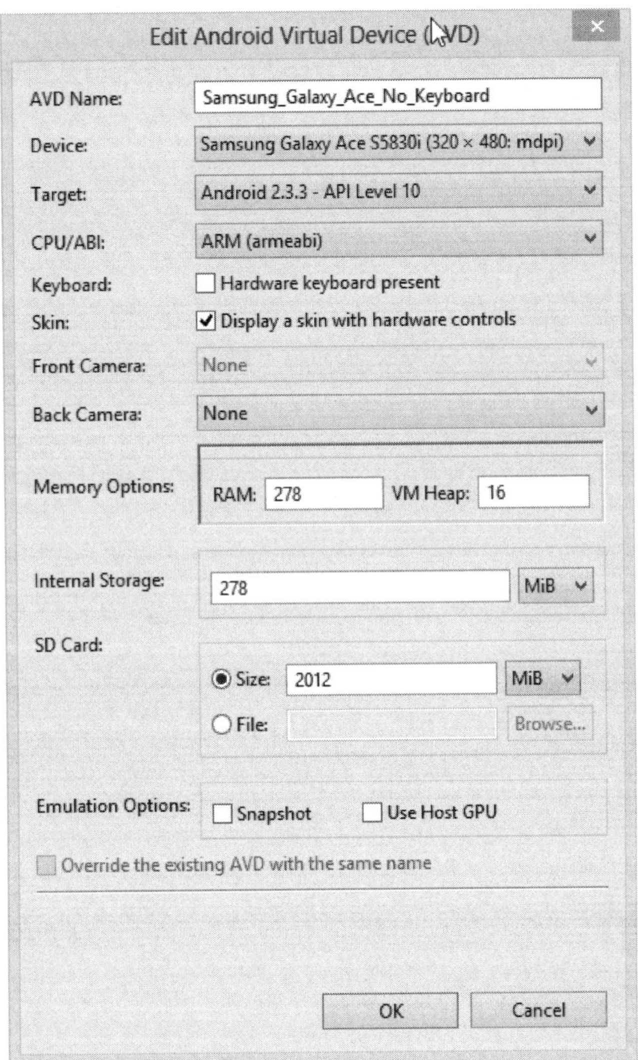

Exchanging files with the PC

To get access to files in the Emulator, you can use the **Dalvik Debug Monitor**. The name is **ddms.bat** and it is located in the folder where you copied the Android SDK, for example **C:\android-sdks\tools**

Make sure that an Emulator is running. Run the **ddms.bat** file. A window like this one will appear:

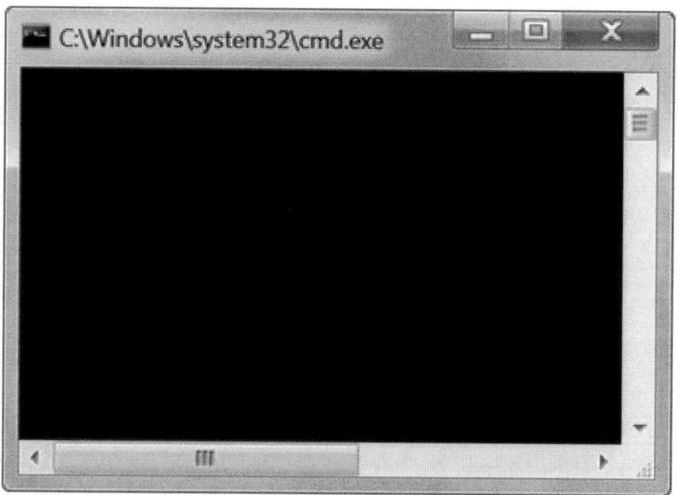

Wait a moment and the Dalvik Debug Monitor will be displayed. You might see a message from Google asking if you are willing to send them certain statistics. You can decide whether you agree or not. Then you should see something like this:

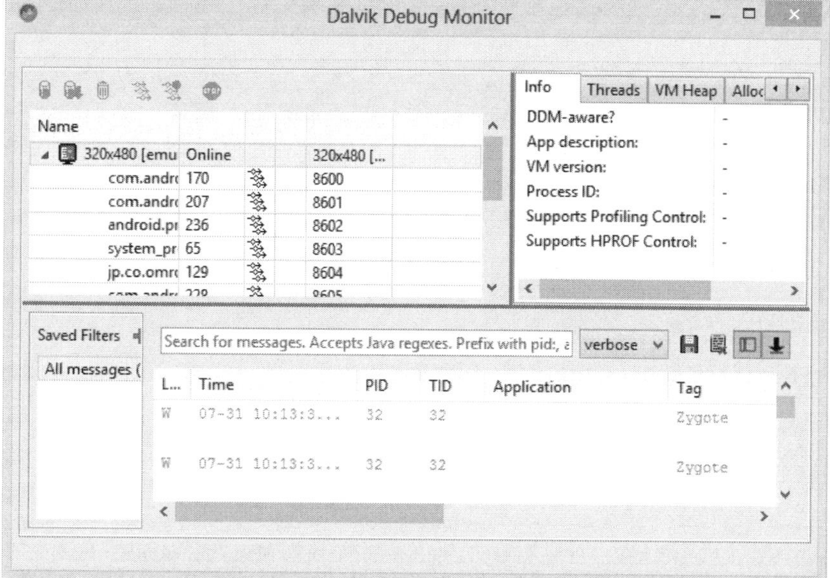

In the upper-left panel you should see a reference to the currently running Emulator. Select it. Then select the menu [Device > File Explorer...]
The Device File Explorer will be displayed, something like this:

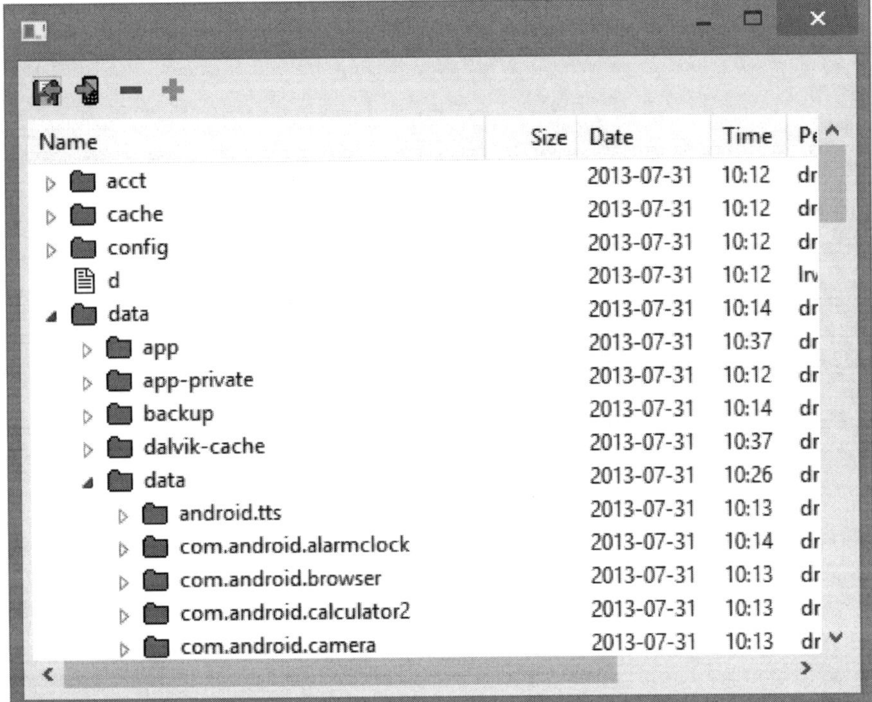

In **data\data** , you will find files your app has copied to **`File.DirAssets`**. You need to search for the Package Name you gave your app in the IDE [Project > Package Name] menu. In the **mnt\sdcard** folder, you will find files your app has created in **`File.DirRootExternal`**.

In the upper left corner you see three icons:

Pull file from device, copies the file to the PC

Push file onto device, copies a file to the device

Deletes the file

Clicking on either or shows the standard Windows file explorer to select the destination or source folder for the selected file.

If the Dalvik Debug Monitor doesn't run, you will need to add the path where the **ddms.bat** file is located to the environment variables.

- From the desktop, right-click **`My Computer`** and click **`Properties`**.
- In the System Properties window, click on the **`Advanced tab`**.
- In the Advanced section, click the **`Environment Variables`** button.
- Finally, in the Environment Variables window, highlight the **`Path`** variable in the Systems Variable section and click the **`Edit`** (Modifier) button. Add or modify the path lines with the paths you wish the computer to access. **Note**: directories are separated with a semicolon.

Troubleshoot Connection Problems

Sometimes when you run an app or try connect to the Emulator, you will see the following error:

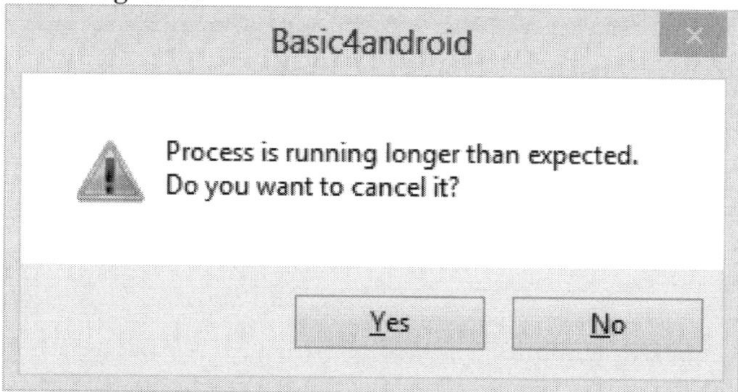

This indicates that Emulator is still running a program or that the Emulator is still connected to another project. In this case try one of the following:

- Use the [Tools > Restart ADB Server (page 42)] menu option
- Go to the Emulator and press the Back button until you reach the Emulator's home screen, then try to connect again.
- Close the Emulator and start another.
- If this problem happens repeatedly, try increasing the Process Timeout in the [Tools > Configure Process Timeout (page 44)] menu.

2.7 Graphics and Drawing

The details of the core Basic4Android drawing types (page 289) are explained in the Core Objects (page 270) chapter. Here we explain how to use them.

Canvas Object

To draw graphics, we normally use a **Canvas** object. A **Canvas** is an object that draws on other views or editable (also called "mutable") bitmaps.

Initializing a Canvas

When we initialize the **Canvas**, we must specify which view or bitmap it can draw onto. The simplest case is to draw onto the **Activity** background:

```
Dim Canvas1 As Canvas
Canvas1.Initialize(Activity)
```

Then we can draw onto the **Canvas**:

```
Canvas1.DrawLine(20dip, 20dip, 160dip, 20dip, Colors.Red, 3dip)
```

When our drawing is complete, we make the **Canvas** draw itself onto its target by making the target invalid:

```
Activity.Invalidate
```

More Details

When the **Canvas** is initialized and set to draw on a view, a new mutable bitmap is created for that view background, the current view's background is first copied to the new bitmap and the **Canvas** is set to draw on the new bitmap. In this way, we can prepare our drawing over the top of the old background.

Canvas drawings are not immediately updated on the screen. You should call the target view **Invalidate** method to make it refresh the view. This is useful as it allows you to make several drawings and only refresh the display when everything is ready.

The **Canvas** can be temporarily limited to a specific region (and thus only affect this region). This is done by calling **ClipPath**. Removing the clipping is done by calling RemoveClip.

You can get the bitmap that the **Canvas** draws on with the **Bitmap** property.

This is an **Activity** object; it cannot be declared under **Sub Process_Globals**.

A **Canvas** can draw onto the following views:

Activity (page 271), ImageView (page 359), Panel (page 370) and Bitmap (page 289)

A bitmap must be "mutable" in order for a **Canvas** to draw upon it.

Most common Canvas functions

See the Canvas (page 291) object for details.

DrawBitmap (Bitmap1 As Bitmap, SrcRect As Rect, DestRect As Rect)

Draws a source bitmap (or part of it) onto a destination. If the source and destination sizes are different, the destination drawing is stretched or shrunk.

DrawBitmapRotated (Bitmap1 As Bitmap, SrcRect As Rect, DestRect As Rect, Degrees As Float)

Same functionality as DrawBitmap, but with a rotation around the centre of the bitmap.

DrawCircle (x As Float, y As Float, Radius As Float, Color As Int, Filled As Boolean, StrokeWidth As Float)

Draws a circle with left edge of x and top of y. It can be filled with a given color (page 280) and, if filled, the perimeter can be outlined with a stroke of a given width.

DrawColor (Color As Int)

Fills the whole view with the given color. The color can be Colors.Transparent making the whole view transparent.

DrawLine (x1 As Float, y1 As Float, x2 As Float, y2 As Float, Color As Int, StrokeWidth As Float)

Draw a straight line from (x1,y1) to (x2,y2) with specified color (page 280) and stroke width (in dips (page 110)).

DrawRect (Rect1 As Rect, Color As Int, Filled As Boolean, StrokeWidth As Float)

Draw a rectangle with given size, color, whether filled, and line width.

DrawRectRotated (Rect1 As Rect, Color As Int, Filled As Boolean, StrokeWidth As Float, Degrees As Float)

Same as `DrawRect`, but rotated by the given angle

DrawText (Text As String, x As Float, y As Float, Typeface1 As Typeface, TextSize As Float, Color As Int, Align1 As Align)

Draws the given text in the given typeface, size and color.
Align1 is the alignment relative to the chosen position, and can have one of the following values: **`LEFT`**, **`CENTER`**, **`RIGHT`**.

DrawTextRotated (Text As String, x As Float, y As Float, Typeface1 As Typeface, TextSize As Float, Color As Int, Align1 As Align, Degree As Float)

Same as **DrawText**, but with the text rotated.

Full details of all **Canvas** methods can be found here (page 291).

Example Program

In this example, we draw some sample shapes on the Main Activity. We put the code in the **Sub Activity_Resume** because this is always run whenever the app starts or restarts. Thus, we do not need to call **Activity.Invalidate**. We also add a button and draw a circle when it is pressed. In this case, we need to call **Activity.Invalidate** so that the **Canvas** will be transferred to the **Activity**'s background.

```
Sub Globals
 Dim cvsActivity As Canvas
 Dim btnTest As Button
End Sub

Sub Activity_Create(FirstTime As Boolean)

End Sub

Sub Activity_Resume
 ' create a button
 btnTest.Initialize("btnTest")
 Activity.AddView(btnTest,10dip, 240dip, 200dip, 50dip)
 btnTest.Text = "Draw Another Circle"
 ' initialize the canvas
 cvsActivity.Initialize(Activity)
 ' draw a horizontal line
 cvsActivity.DrawLine(20dip, 20dip, 160dip, 20dip, Colors.Red,
3dip)
 ' draw an empty rectangle
 Dim rect1 As Rect
 rect1.Initialize(50dip, 40dip, 150dip, 100dip)
 cvsActivity.DrawRect(rect1, Colors.Blue, False, 3dip)
 ' draw an empty circle
 cvsActivity.DrawCircle(50dip, 200dip, 30dip, Colors.Green,
False, 3dip)
 ' draw a text
 cvsActivity.DrawText("Test text", 50dip, 150dip,
Typeface.DEFAULT, 20, Colors.Yellow, "LEFT")
 ' draw a filled circle with a boarder
```

```
 cvsActivity.DrawCircle(50dip, 340dip, 30dip, Colors.Green,
True, 3dip)
 ' the above will always be drawn because
 '  the Activity is automatically redrawn on activity_resume
End Sub

Sub btnTest_Click
 cvsActivity.DrawCircle(100dip, 40dip, 30dip, Colors.Green,
False, 3dip)
 ' make the drawing visible
 Activity.Invalidate
End Sub
```

The resulting screen is:

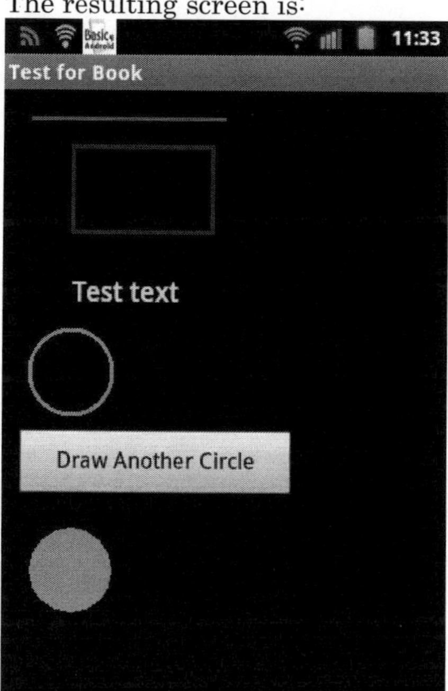

More Complex Examples

A good way to learn is to play with projects and figure out how they work. You can download several graphics example projects from this book's resource page (http://resources.basic4android.info/). The RotatingNeedle project will draw a compass which will rotate either the compass or the needle.

It uses a **Timer** to control the rotation.

The SimpleDrawFunctions project uses more common drawing functions and Panels which can be shown or hidden with buttons.

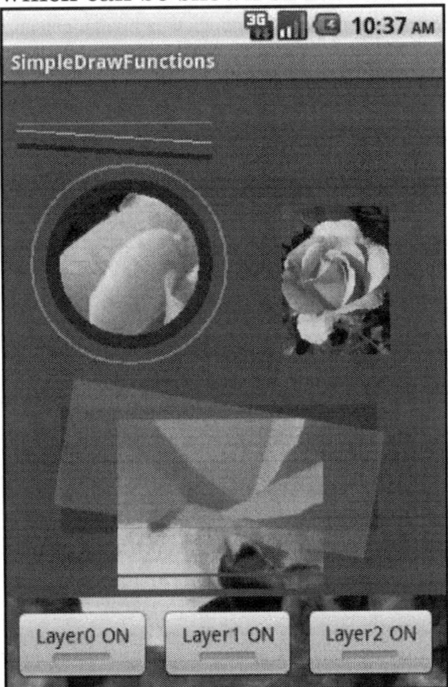

The blue circle with a transparent center can be dragged around the screen.

Drawing Methods

There are three main ways you can draw:

- By setting the properties of View Drawables
- By copying **BitMaps** to Panels or ImageViews (page 152)
- By drawing lines or other shapes (page 153)

View Drawables

Views (page 395) are the objects shown on an Activity (page 271). They each have default backgrounds when they are defined either in the Designer or by code.

Drawables

Objects such as **BitmapDrawable, ColorDrawable, GradientDrawable, StateListDrawable** and the background of a **View** are termed "drawables" in Android, which is a concept meaning "capable of being drawn".
These objects can be drawn onto a canvas in various ways, for example, using **Canvas.DrawDrawable**.

Background Property

There exist three drawables which can be assigned to the **Background** property of various objects, such as the **Activity** itself:

ColorDrawable

The **ColorDrawable** object has a solid single color. The corners can be rounded or not.

GradientDrawable

The **GradientDrawable** object has two colors with a gradient change from the first to the second color.

BitmapDrawable (page 291)

The **BitmapDrawable** object has two properties: **Bitmap** and **Gravity**. The **BitmapDrawable** object has no rounded corner property; if you want rounded corners; they must be part of the bitmap.

You can define all of these properties in the Designer, but in the following example; we define them in code as backgrounds of panels. (If you want to run this you will need to provide your own background.png file, which you would add to the Files folder of your project).

Example Code

```
Sub Globals
 Dim pnlColor As Panel
 Dim pnlGradient As Panel
 Dim pnlBitmap As Panel
```

```
End Sub

Sub Activity_Create(FirstTime As Boolean)
 pnlColor.Initialize("")
 Activity.AddView(pnlColor, 10%x, 40dip, 80%x, 80dip)
 Dim cdwColor As ColorDrawable
 cdwColor.Initialize(Colors.Red, 5dip)
 pnlColor.Background = cdwColor

 pnlGradient.Initialize("")
 Activity.AddView(pnlGradient, 10%x, 140dip, 80%x, 80dip)
 Dim gdwGradient As GradientDrawable
 Dim Cols(2) As Int
 Cols(0) = Colors.Blue
 Cols(1) = Colors.White
 gdwGradient.Initialize("TOP_BOTTOM", Cols)
 gdwGradient.CornerRadius = 10dip
 pnlGradient.Background = gdwGradient

 pnlBitmap.Initialize("")
 Activity.AddView(pnlBitmap, 10%x, 250dip, 80%x, 80dip)
 Dim bdwBitmap As BitmapDrawable
 bdwBitmap.Initialize(LoadBitmap(File.DirAssets,
"background.png"))
 bdwBitmap.Gravity = Gravity.FILL
 pnlBitmap.Background = bdwBitmap
End Sub
```

The result would be:

StateListDrawable

A **StateListDrawable** is a drawable object that holds other drawables and chooses the current one based on the view's state. It can be defined either in code:

```
Dim sld As StateListDrawable
```

or in the Designer as the **Background** property of **Buttons**.

There are two options for the **Drawable** property of a button:

- **DefaultDrawable**, which is set by default and uses default colors
- **StatelistDrawable**, which allows you to chose custom colors

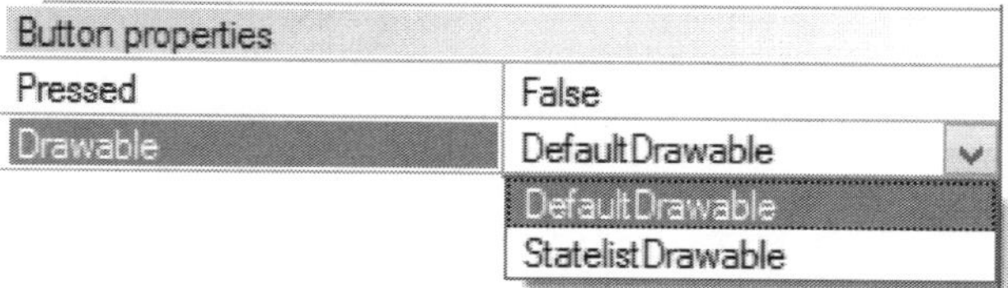

A button with the StatelistDrawable property has three states:

- Enabled Drawable – What you see when the button is enabled
- Disabled Drawable – What you see when it's disabled
- Pressed Drawable – What it looks like when pressed

Each state has its own Drawable, which could be either **ColorDrawable**, **GradientDrawable** or **BitmapDrawable**.

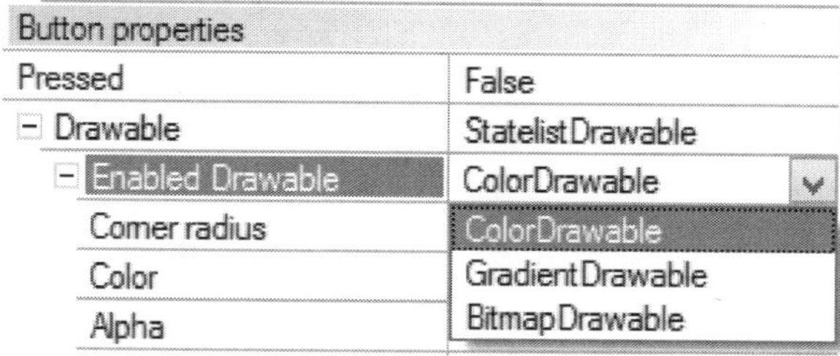

Example Project

For a sample project which uses both code and a Designer-created layout to create buttons with a **StateListDrawable** set to **ColorDrawable, GradientDrawable** and **BitmapDrawable**, download the ButtonStateDrawables project from this book's resources page (http://resources.basic4android.info/). It produces the following:

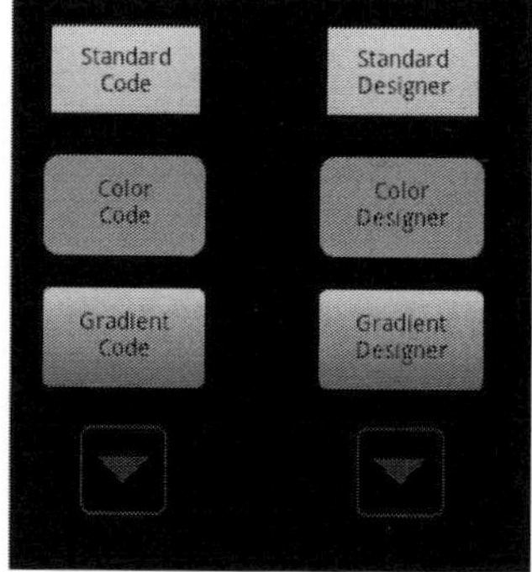

NinePatchDrawable

Android supports a special format of PNG images that can be resized by replicating specific parts of the image. These images also include padding information. Such images are named "nine-patch images". You can read more about this format here (http://developer.android.com/guide/topics/graphics/2d-graphics.html).
The Android SDK includes a tool named **draw9patch.bat** that can help you with building and modifying such images. This tool is available in the Tools folder of your Android SDK. You can read more about it here (http://developer.android.com/intl/fr/guide/developing/tools/draw9patch.html).

Example Project

NinePatchExample is a simple example of a project which uses SetNinePatchDrawable to demonstrate the power and usage of NinePatchDrawable.
Note: this project requires the use of the Reflection library (page 543), so it cannot be run with the Trial Version of Basic4Android. The project is available from this book's resources page (http://resources.basic4android.info/), and produces the result shown below:

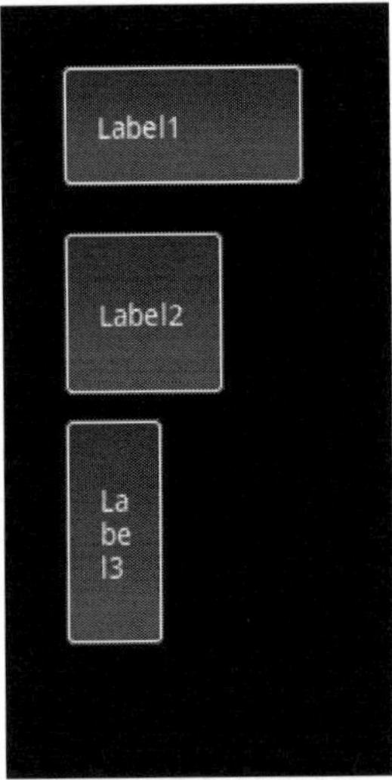

Drawing Bitmaps on Panels or ImageViews

The second main way to draw is by using a **`Canvas`** to draw a bitmap (page 289) onto a **`Panel`** or **`ImageView`**. Several layers may be needed to achieve the required effect. If the image needs to be changed often, then you would draw onto a canvas first. The code to draw is essentially:

```
Dim cvs As Canvas
Dim imv As ImageView
Dim img As Bitmap
Dim Rect1 As Rect
```

```
imv.Initialize("")
Activity.AddView(imv, 0, 0, 100%x, 100%y)
cvs.Initialize(imv)
img.Initialize(File.DirAssets, "horse.png")
Rect1.Initialize(0, 45%y, img.Width, 45%y + img.Height)

cvs.DrawBitmap(img, Null, Rect1)
imv.Invalidate2(Rect1)
```

"Layers" is an example project, whose source code is available from this book's resource webpage (http://pennypress.co.uk/?p=86). It uses **DrawBitmap** with two **ImageViews** to animate a horse galloping across a moving background.

The **ImageView**, which shows the horse, is transparent and is drawn by a **Canvas**. The background **ImageView** merely moves so it does not require a **Canvas**. There are two **Timers** to control the movements of horse and background.

Diagrams / Charts

The third main way to draw is by drawing lines, circles, etc., to create the required images. The **Canvas** object has the following methods which allow you to draw: DrawCircle (page 295), DrawLine (page 296), DrawOval (page 296), DrawOvalRotated (page 296), DrawPath (page 296), DrawPoint (page 297), DrawRect (page 297), DrawRectRotated (page 297), DrawText (page 297) and DrawTextRotated (page 298). You can specify their positions, colors, width of the line and (for closed shapes) whether they are filled.

Oscilloscope is a demonstration of this technique, written by Klaus Christl.

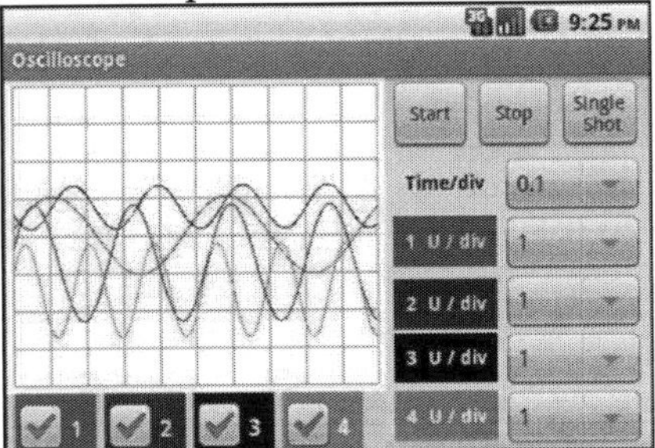

The project can be downloaded from the Basic4Android Book page (http://resources.basic4android.info/)

Charts Framework

The Charts Framework module allows to draw several types of diagrams:

- Pie charts
- Bar charts
- Stacked Bar charts
- Curves

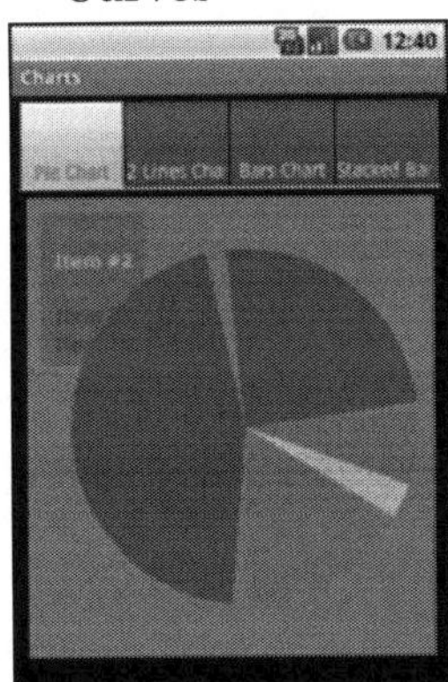

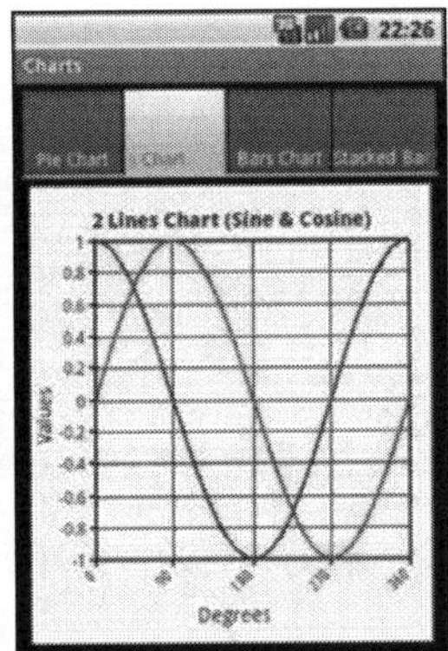

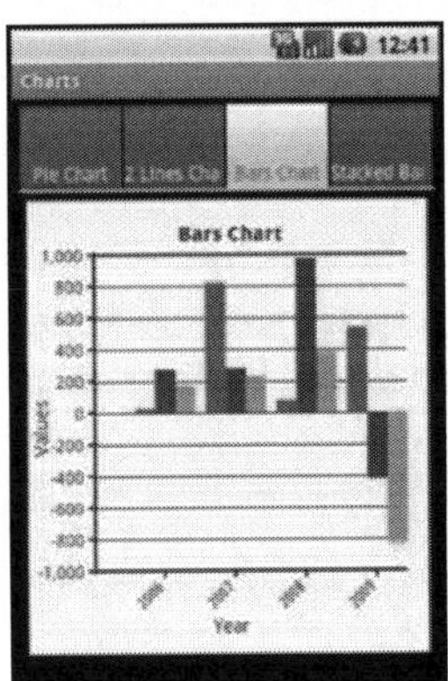

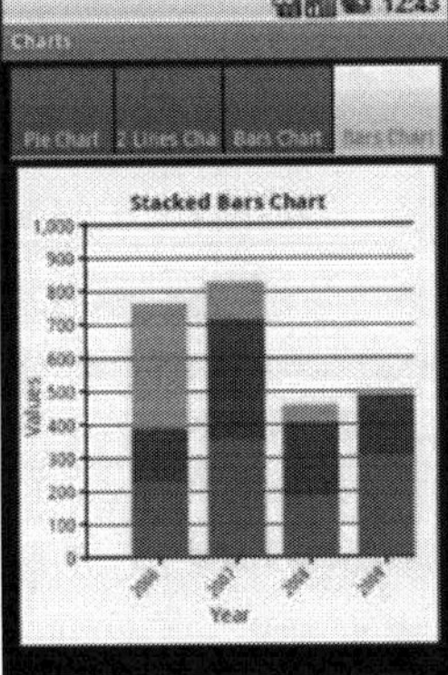

The Charts Framework is a code module (not a library) **charts.bas** which must be included in your project if you wish to use it. It can be downloaded here: Charts Framework (http://bit.ly/10enSTK)

2.8 Databases

Database fundamentals

Android supports the SQLite database engine which your app can use to store data on the device. Basic4Android provides DBUtils which allow you to easily manipulate tables and data without any special knowledge. If you need something more sophisticated, you can write commands in the SQL database manipulation language. First, let's look at some fundamental facts about databases.

Database

A database is a collection of data organised into tables, fields and records. A database management system (DBMS) such as SQLite allows the creation of these structures and lets you input and retrieve data.

Table

Data within a database is organised into tables. A table corresponds to an object about which data is to be stored. For example, a table could contain information about cities or countries.

Record

A record is the data about one object in a table. Thus, the city table might contain one record for Toyko and a different one for London.
A table is often pictured as an array, like a spreadsheet in which the rows contain the records.

Field

The fields within a table are the individual pieces of information which need to be stored for the objects in the table. For example, the city table might store City Name, Country and Population fields.
If a table is pictured like a spreadsheet, then the columns would contain the fields:

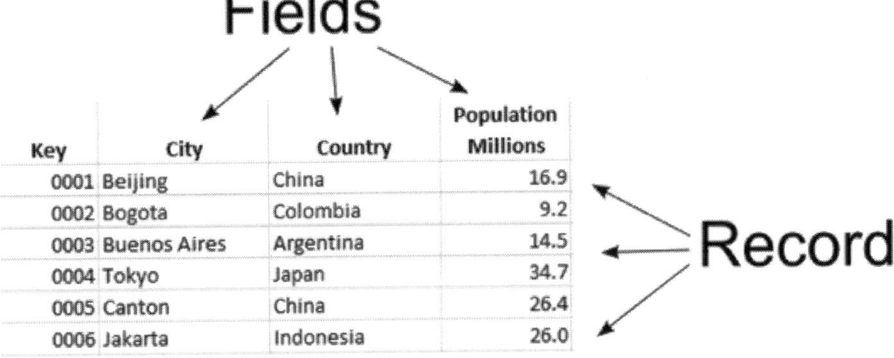

Key	City	Country	Population Millions
0001	Beijing	China	16.9
0002	Bogota	Colombia	9.2
0003	Buenos Aires	Argentina	14.5
0004	Tokyo	Japan	34.7
0005	Canton	China	26.4
0006	Jakarta	Indonesia	26.0

Primary Key

Every table should contain one special field, called the primary key, which is used to quickly identify and locate a single record. In the country table, we might want to use the city name as the key, but that would cause a problem if two cities in different countries share the same name. So it is safest to create a special key field, using an integer, which is usually incremented automatically when a new record is added.

Field Type

The DBMS needs to know what type of data will be added to each field. Typical types are:

NULL: The value is a `Null` value.

INTEGER: The value is a signed integer, stored in 1, 2, 3, 4, 6, or 8 bytes depending on the magnitude of the value.

REAL: The value is a floating point value, stored as an 8-byte IEEE floating point number.

TEXT: The value is a text string, stored using the database encoding (UTF-8 by default for Android).

BLOB: The value is a blob of data, stored exactly as it was input.

Relational Data

Let us look again at our Country table.

Key	City	Country	Population Millions
0001	Beijing	China	16.9
0002	Bogota	Colombia	9.2
0003	Buenos Aires	Argentina	14.5
0004	Tokyo	Japan	34.7
0005	Canton	China	26.4
0006	Jakarta	Indonesia	26.0

Because countries contain many cities, the name of each country occurs more than once. So if the name of the country changes, we would need to change many records. Also, it would be very slow to find every city belonging to a particular country. A better way to store this data would be to have two tables, one for cities and one for countries:

City Table			
Key	**Name**	**Country**	**Population Millions**
0001	Beijing	0001	16.9
0002	Bogota	0002	9.2
0003	Buenos Aires	0003	14.5
0004	Tokyo	0004	34.7
0005	Canton	0001	26.4
0006	Jakarta	0005	26.0

Country Table	
Key	**Name**
0001	China
0002	Colombia
0003	Argentina
0004	Japan
0005	Indonesia

One of the benefits of most DBMS is that you can establish links (or relationships) between tables. Thus, for example, you might have a city table and a country table. Instead of the name of the country, we store only its key in the city table. To find which country a city belongs to, we look up its country key in the country table.

Database Files

In SQLite, a database is contained within a single file. You can create this file before you publish your app, or your app can create the database from scratch. If you want to ship your database file with your app, you should copy the file into the Files folder of your project.

Your app will need to copy the database to a writable location because it is not possible to access a database located in File.DirAssets. You can use CopyDBFromAssets (page 161) **to copy it.**

KeyValueStore Class

Note: the additional KeyValueStore (page 527) class provides a useful way to easily store data to persistent storage using an SQLite database in a transparent fashion. It can be used, for example, to store user preferences before Android calls **`Activity_Pause`**, then restore them on **`Activity_Resume`**.

Encrypting Databases

The SQLCipher (http://bit.ly/165Z6Uq) additional library allows you to encrypt the SQLite database file.

Database Administration

DBMS Tools

While it is possible to create a database from within your app using SQL, it is sometimes necessary to create it during the development process and ship it with your app (see the previous section). The easiest way to create a database is to use one of the following tools.

SQLiteBrowser

SQLite Database Browser is a freeware, public domain, open source visual tool used to create, design and edit database files compatible with SQLite. It is meant to be used for users and developers that want to create databases, and edit and search data using a familiar spreadsheet-like interface, without the need to learn complicated SQL commands.
It has an excellent GUI which lets you create and manipulate SQLite databases without SQL, but also lets you run SQL against them.
This tool is not currently being maintained, but it is very valuable nevertheless.
http://sourceforge.net/projects/sqlitebrowser/

SQLiteSpy

For those who know SQL, if you want an SQL-based database management tool to create SQLite databases, try SQLiteSpy, a fast and compact GUI database manager for SQLite. It reads SQLite3 files and executes SQL against them. Its graphical user interface makes it very easy to explore, analyze, and manipulate SQLite3 databases. It is frequently updated. The problem with it is that it relies entirely upon SQL. Unlike SQLiteBrowser, it has no GUI tools for table manipulation.
http://bit.ly/1agKxQx

SQL Object

This is the main object which accesses a database. It is defined in the SQL Library (page 505). Before you can use SQL, you need to reference the library and declare the object, as follows.

Reference SQL Library

Your project needs to reference the SQL library, even if you do not want to write SQL yourself, since DBUtils needs it. Use the Libs Tab (page 55) within the IDE to create the reference.

Declare SQL Object

For the SQL Library to work, you need to declare an SQL object in `Process_Globals`:

```
Sub Process_Globals
 Dim SQL1 As SQL
End Sub
```

Initialize SQL Object

As well as declaring the SQL Object, you must initialize it. This ties the SQL to the named database file and opens the database file.
Note that a new database will be created if it does not exist and only if Initialize's third parameter `CreateIfNecessary` is true.
You can have several database files open by using multiple SQL Objects. See the File Location (page 303) section for information on where to store your files.

Example

```
Sub Activity_Create(FirstTime As Boolean)
 If FirstTime Then
  SQL1.Initialize(File.DirRootExternal, "1.db", True)
 End If
End Sub
```

DBUtils

DBUtils Fundamentals

DBUtils is a code module which lets you manipulate databases without writing much SQL. However, it is probable you will still need a little SQL, which we explain in the SQLite (page 167) Reference section.

Installing DBUtils

DBUtils is a code module and not a library, so you have to include it in your project:

- First, see here (http://bit.ly/1cUgfEi) to find the DBUtils web page, scroll down to the bottom of the tutorial and download the zip file.
- Unzip the file into a folder. You might want to study the project contained in that folder to learn about how to use DBUtils.
- When you want to use it in your own project, add **DBUtils.bas** to your project with the menu [Project > Add Existing Module]. Navigate to the DBUtils project and select DBUtils.bas.
- Click Open. A message will appear telling you the file has been copied to your project, and "DBUtils" will appear in the Modules tab (on the right of the IDE) and in the modules tabs (near the top of the IDE).

Preliminary SQL Steps

SQL Object

You need to reference the SQL Library and declare the object, as described above.

Versioning

Your database structure might change over time.

DBUtils introduces the concept of database version, so that your code can set and test the version number of the database and update it if necessary. Use the functions **GetDBVersion** and **SetDBVersion** to control the version of your database.

DBUtils Field Types

DBUtils includes the following which are used as constants for defining field types:

```
DB_BLOB
DB_INTEGER
DB_REAL
DB_TEXT
```

For an example, see CreateTable

DBUtils Functions

CopyDBFromAssets (FileName As String) As String

If you have shipped your database file with your app (by adding it in the Files tab), then the database must be copied to a writable location because it is not possible to access a database located in **File.DirAssets**. You can use **CopyDBFromAssets** to copy it. **Note**: If the database file already exists, then no copying is done.

Location of Database

If the storage card is available, this method copies the database to the storage card folder **File.DirDefaultExternal**. If the storage card is not available, the file is copied to the internal folder **File.DirInternal**. The target folder is returned.

Creating Tables

You can use a DBMS tool to create your database and its tables before shipping your app, then use CopyDBFromAssets to move it into storage, or you can create tables when the app is running using **CreateTable**.

CreateTable (SQL As SQL, TableName As String, FieldsAndTypes As Map, PrimaryKey As String)

This function creates a new table with the given name within the file previously opened when the **SQL** object was initialized.

FieldsAndTypes – A map with the field names as keys and the types as values. You can use the DBUtils Field Types for the types.

PrimaryKey – The column that will be the primary key (page 157). Pass an empty string if not needed.

Example:

```
Dim m As Map
m.Initialize
m.Put("Id", DBUtils.DB_INTEGER)
m.Put("First Name", DBUtils.DB_TEXT)
m.Put("Last Name", DBUtils.DB_TEXT)
m.Put("Birthday", DBUtils.DB_INTEGER)
DBUtils.CreateTable(SQL, "Students", m, "Id")
```

DeleteRecord (SQL As SQL, TableName As String, WhereFieldEquals As Map)

Deletes the specified record in **TableName**.
WhereFieldEquals is a map in which the field names are the keys and the values to search for are the map's values.

DropTable (SQL As SQL, TableName As String)

Deletes the given table.

ExecuteHtml(SQL As SQL, Query As String, StringArgs() As String, Limit As Int, Clickable As Boolean) As String

Creates HTML which, when viewed in a **WebView**, displays the data in a table. This method can be used rapidly to visualize data during development, or to show reports to users. You can change the table style by modifying the Cascading Style Sheet (CSS) variable **HtmlCSS** within **Process_Globals** of the DBUtils module.
StringArgs() – Values to replace question marks in the query. Pass **Null** if not needed.
Limit – Limits the number of records returned. Pass **0** to get all the records.
Clickable – Defines whether the values will be clickable or not. If the values are clickable, you should catch the WebView_OverrideUrl event to find the clicked cell.
Example:

```
Sub WebView1_OverrideUrl (Url As String) As Boolean
  'parse the row and column numbers from the URL
  Dim values() As String
  values = Regex.Split("[.]", Url.SubString(7))
  Dim col, row As Int
  col = values(0)
  row = values(1)
  ToastMessageShow("User pressed on column: " & col & " and row:
" & row, False)
  Return True 'Don't try to navigate to this URL
End Sub
```

You might want to change **HtmlCSS** to make it obvious that there is a hyperlink. By default, hyperlinks are not differentiated from other text. Thus, you might change the CSS code from the default:

```
a { text-decoration:none; color: #000;}
```

to make hyperlinks underlined and blue with the following:

```
a { text-decoration:underline; color: #0000FF;}
```

ExecuteJSON(SQL As SQL, Query As String, StringArgs() As String, Limit As Int, DBTypes As List) As Map

Executes the given query and creates a Map that you can pass to JSONGenerator and generate JSON text.
StringArgs() – Values to replace question marks in the query. Pass **Null** if not needed.
Limit – Limits the number of records returned. Pass 0 to get all the records.
DBTypes – Lists the type of each column in the result set.
Usage example (requires a reference to the JSON library):

```
Dim gen As JSONGenerator
gen.Initialize(DBUtils.ExecuteJSON(SQL, "SELECT Id, Birthday
FROM Students", Null, 0, Array As String(DBUtils.DB_TEXT,
DBUtils.DB_INTEGER)))
Dim JSONString As String
JSONString = gen.ToPrettyString(4)
Msgbox(JSONString, "")
```

ExecuteListView(SQL As SQL, Query As String, StringArgs() As String, Limit As Int, ListView1 As ListView, TwoLines As Boolean)

Executes the **Query** and fills the ListView (page 364) with the values, one row for each record.
StringArgs() – Values to replace question marks in the **Query**. Pass **Null** if not needed.
Limit – Limits the number of records returned. Pass **0** to get all the records.
TwoLines – if **True**, then the first column in the ListView is mapped to the first field and the second column is mapped to the second field.
Example:

```
'Find all tests of this student with grade lower than 55.
DBUtils.ExecuteListView(SQL, "SELECT test, grade FROM Grades
WHERE id = ? AND grade <= 55", Array As String(StudentId), 0,
lstFailedTest, True)
```

The result will be as follows, depending on whether TwoLines is **True** or **False**

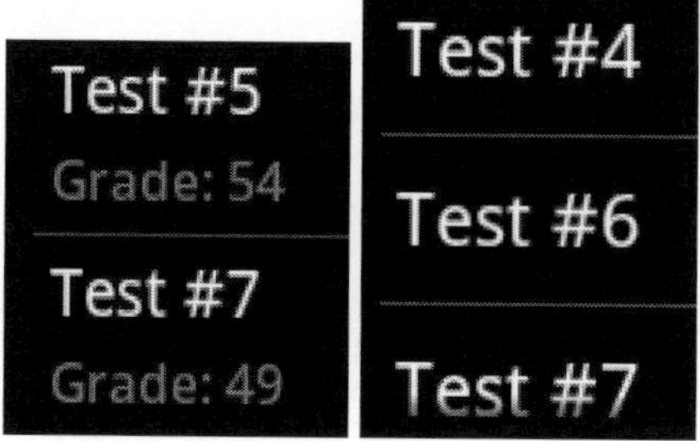

ExecuteMap(SQL As SQL, Query As String, StringArgs() As String) As Map

Executes **Query** and returns a **Map** with the column names as the keys and the first record values as the map's values.
StringArgs() – Values to replace question marks in the **Query**. Pass **Null** if not needed.
The keys are lower-cased. Returns **Null** if no results found.
Example:

```
mFirstRecord = DBUtils.ExecuteMap(SQL, "SELECT Id, [First Name],
[Last Name], Birthday FROM students WHERE id = ?", Array As
String(Value))
```

ExecuteMemoryTable(SQL As SQL, Query As String, StringArgs() As String, Limit As Int) As List

Executes the **Query** and returns the result as a **List** of arrays. Each item in the list is an array of strings.
StringArgs() – Values to replace question marks in the **Query**. Pass **Null** if not needed.
Limit – Limits the number of records returned. Pass **0** to get all the records.
Example:

```
Dim lstTable As List
Dim strFields() As String
Dim lstRecords As List
Dim iCountStudents As Int

'lstTable is a list of string arrays. Each array holds a single
record.
lstTable = DBUtils.ExecuteMemoryTable(SQL, "SELECT Id, [First
Name] FROM Students", Null, 0)
lstRecords.Initialize
For iCountStudents = 0 To lstTable.Size - 1
 strFields = lstTable.Get(iCountStudents)
 Log("Id: " & strFields(0))
 Log("Name: " & strFields(1))
Next
```

Example using **StringArgs**:

```
lstTable = DBUtils.ExecuteMemoryTable(SQL, "SELECT Id FROM
Students where Id > ?", Array As String(intMinID), 0)
```

ExecuteSpinner(SQL As SQL, Query As String, StringArgs() As String, Limit As Int, Spinner1 As Spinner)

Executes the **Query** and fills the **Spinner** with the values in the first column.
StringArgs() – Values to replace question marks in the query. Pass Null if not needed.
Limit – Limits the results. Pass 0 for all results.
Examples:

```
'If parameter is known to developer
DBUtils.ExecuteSpinner(SQL, "SELECT * FROM Students WHERE Id <
40000", Null, 0, spnrStudentId)
'If parameter is a variable Value
DBUtils.ExecuteSpinner(SQL, "SELECT * FROM Students WHERE Id =
?", Array As String(Value), 0, spnrStudentId)
```

GetDBVersion(SQL As SQL) As Int

Gets the current version (page 160) of the database.
If the DBVersion table does not exist within the initialized database, it is created and the current version is set to version 1.

Example:

```
Dim DBVersion, CurrentDBVersion As Int
DBVersion = DBUtils.GetDBVersion(SQL)
CurrentDBVersion = 2
Do While DBVersion < CurrentDBVersion
 Select DBVersion
 Case 1
 UpdateDB1_2(SQL)
 Case 2
 UpdateDB2_3
 End Select
 DBVersion = DBUtils.GetDBVersion(SQL)
Loop
```

InsertMaps (SQL As SQL, TableName As String, ListOfMaps As List)

This is the way to insert one or more records into a table. The data is passed as a **List** that contains maps as items. Each map holds the fields for one record and their values.

ListOfMaps – A list with maps as items. Each **Map** represents a record, where the map keys are the field names and the map values are the values.

Note: you should create a new map for each record (this can be done by calling **Dim** to redim the map). Example:

```
Dim allRecords As List
allRecords.Initialize
Dim id As Int
For id = 1 To 40
 Dim oneRecord As Map
 oneRecord.Initialize
 oneRecord.Put("Id", id)
 oneRecord.Put("First Name", "John")
 oneRecord.Put("Last Name", "Smith" & id)
 allRecords.Add(oneRecord)
Next
DBUtils.InsertMaps(SQL, "Students", allRecords)
```

SetDBVersion(SQL As SQL, Version As Int)

Sets the database version (page 160) to the given version number.

UpdateRecord(SQL As SQL, TableName As String, Field As String, NewValue As Object, WhereFieldEquals As Map)

Update (that is change) an existing record in the database.
TableName – The table where the record exists.
Field – The name of the field to update.
NewValue – The new value.
WhereFieldEquals – This identifies which record to update. It is a Map, where the keys are the column names and the map values are the values to look for.
Example:

```
Dim WhereFields As Map
WhereFields.Initialize
WhereFields.Put("id", spnrStudentId.SelectedItem)
WhereFields.Put("test", spnrTests.SelectedItem)
DBUtils.UpdateRecord(SQL, "Grades", "Grade", txtGrade.Text,
WhereFields)
```

UpdateRecord2(SQL As SQL, TableName As String, Fields As Map, WhereFieldEquals As Map)

Update (that is change) several fields in an existing record in the database.
TableName – The table where the record exists.
Fields – A map of the fields to update, where the field names to update are the keys and the values are the new values these fields should be given.
WhereFieldEquals – This identifies which record to update. It is a Map where the keys are the column names and the map values are the values to look for.
Example:

```
Dim mapNewFieldsValues As Map
mapNewFieldsValues.Initialize
mapNewFieldsValues.Put("tries", iTries + 1)
Dim mapWhere As Map
mapWhere.Initialize
mapWhere.Put("id", iRandRecord)
mapNewFieldsValues.Put("correct", iCorrect + 1)
DBUtils.UpdateRecord2(SQL1, "aorde", mapNewFieldsValues,
mapWhere)
```

Sample DBUtils Program

A sample project using DBUtils is **SQLiteViewer**, an Android-based database browser. It is available from this book's online resource page (http://resources.basic4android.info/). Screen shots:

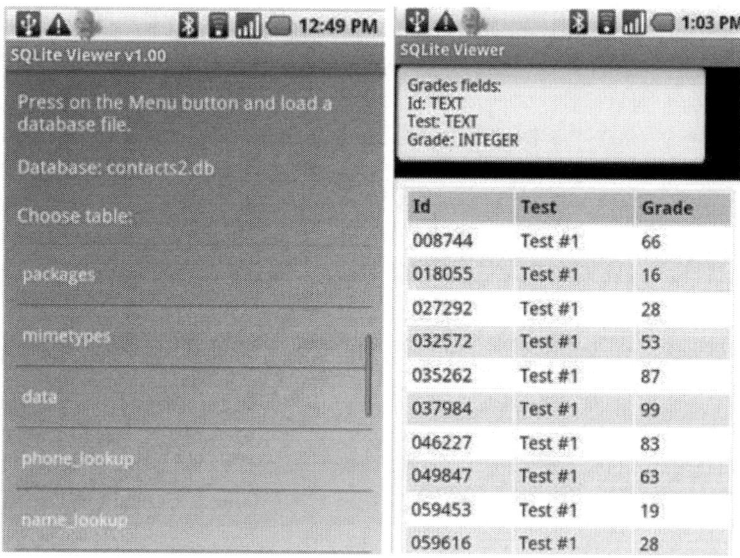

SQLite

SQL

If DBUtils is not adequate for your needs, you are going to have to write code in your app using Structured Query Language (SQL). This allows you to create tables, define their fields and other attributes, and add, retrieve and manipulate records.
There are many websites which help you to learn SQL, for example W3Schools SQL (http://www.w3schools.com/sql/).

SQLite

SQLite is the DBMS built into Android. It is the most widely deployed SQL DBMS in the world. Below, we give an outline of how to write SQLite without using DBUtils (page 160).

More Information on SQLite

You can find more about SQLite here: http://www.sqlite.org/. Here you will find the SQLite syntax: SQLite syntax (http://www.sqlite.org/lang.html). See here (http://www.sqlite.org/lang_keywords.html) for details of keywords and commands.

Sample SQLite Program

SQLExample is a demonstration program, available from this book's Resource page (http://resources.basic4android.info/), which uses SQLite to create and manipulate a database.

Manifest Typing

Most DBMS use "static typing", in which one datatype is associated with each field in a table, and only values of that particular datatype are allowed to be stored in that field. SQLite, on the other hand, uses "manifest typing".
In "manifest typing", the datatype is a property of the value itself, not of the field in which the value is stored. SQLite thus allows you to store any value of any datatype into any field regardless of the declared type of that field.
There are some exceptions to this rule: An INTEGER PRIMARY KEY field may only store integers. And SQLite attempts to coerce values into the declared datatype of the field when it can.

SQLiteExceptions

Because interacting with SQLite might raise runtime exceptions, it might be wise to wrap your code in **`TRY-CATCH`** blocks so you can handle any problems.

SQL Library

In order to use SQLite, you need to enable the SQL library in your project. See here (page 404) for the method of referencing a library. For details of all SQL types and functions, see the SQL Library reference section (page 505).

SQL Object

You need to declare an SQL object and initialize it, as described above (page 159).

ExecQueries and ExecNonQueries

Basic4Android SQL functions consist largely of queries which return results (**`ExecQueries`**), or commands which perform actions on the database but do not return results (**`ExecNonQueries`**). Several flavors are available in each category.

Cursor

A **`Cursor`** is the object returned from an **`ExecQuery`**. It consists of a set of records and a pointer to the current record. It is similar to a **recordset** in Visual Basic. More details in the SQL Library section (page 505).

Transactions

A transaction consists of a set of SQL statements. No changes will be made to the database unless all the statements are completed successfully. This ensures the integrity of the database. Statements inside a transaction will be executed significantly faster than separate statements.
It is very important to close transactions in order to commit the changes. This is a situation where the Try-Catch block (page 239) is useful.
Example:

```
SQL.BeginTransaction
Try
 'block of statements
 For i = 1 To 10
 SQL.ExecNonQuery2("INSERT INTO demo VALUES (?,?)", Array As
Object(i, "Tom Brown"))
 Next
 SQL.TransactionSuccessful
Catch
 Log(LastException.Message) 'no changes will be made
End Try
SQL.EndTransaction
```

Note: a transaction is implicitly created for every normal statement and automatically closed.

SQLite Commands

Note that what follows is only an introduction to SQL programming. Consult the SQLite website (http://www.sqlite.org/lang.html) for complete details of the language.

Database Creation

You can create a database (that is, a file containing all the tables of the database) using the **`SQL.Initialize`** statement, for example:

```
SQL.Initialize(File.DirRootExternal, "mydatabase.db", True)
```

Note: if the database file already exists, it will be opened rather than created.

Table creation

Having created your database, you need to add tables using the SQLite command **`CREATE TABLE`**. A simple example would be:

```
CREATE TABLE TableName(ID INTEGER PRIMARY KEY, Col1 TEXT, Col2
REAL)
```

Execute this command with the ExecNonQuery (page 509) function, or the ExecNonQuery2 (page 509) function which allows you to easily parameterize this type of command.

The parameters of **`CREATE TABLE`** are:

TableName: It is usually an error to attempt to create a new table in a database that already contains a table, index or view of the same name.

Field List: TableName is followed by parentheses, containing a list of fields separated by commas. Thus, the example above defines 3 fields.

Field Definition: Each field is defined by its name and, optionally, a type and a contraint.

Field Type: This is the word after the field name. It is optional except in the case of INTEGER PRIMARY KEYS. As mentioned above, SQLite uses Manifest Typing, so the type specification is not necessary. If you specify it, variables of other types can still be stored here but will be converted to the specified type.

The declaration merely determines the **Type Affinity** of the field, the preferred type of data. The type affinities available are: TEXT, NUMERIC, INTEGER, REAL and NONE.
A field with TEXT affinity stores all data using storage classes NULL, TEXT or BLOB. If numerical data is inserted into a field with TEXT affinity, it is converted into text form before being stored.
IF NOT EXISTS: It is usually an error to attempt to create a new table in a database that already contains a table, index or view of the same name. However, if the **`IF NOT EXISTS`** clause is specified as part of the **`CREATE TABLE`** statement and a table or view of the same name already exists, the **`CREATE TABLE`** command simply has no effect (and no error message is returned).

```
CREATE TABLE IF NOT EXISTS TableName(etc)
```

An error is still returned if the table cannot be created because of an existing index, even if the **`IF NOT EXISTS`** clause is specified.
PRIMARY KEY: A primary key is one or more fields which are indexed to ensure rapid access and are required to contain unique data. Usually it is an integer.
Example:

```
CREATE TABLE IF NOT EXISTS Students (Id INTEGER PRIMARY KEY,
Name TEXT, etc)
```

To specify a composite key, you need to add a primary key clause:

```
CREATE TABLE TableName (ID1 INTEGER, ID2 INTEGER, Col1 TEXT,
Col2 REAL, CONSTRAINT PrimaryKeyName PRIMARY KEY (ID1, ID2))
```

Adding records

Use the **`INSERT INTO`** command to add records to a table. There are two main ways to specify the data to add.
1) Either you specify the names of specific fields and the values to inserted, for example:

```
INSERT INTO TableName (col1) VALUES ( 'Fred' )
```

In this case, a new record will be inserted into table called "TableName", the "col1" field will be set to the value "Fred" and the primary key will be automatically incremented.
2) Or you specify the values of all fields in the correct sequence, in which case you do not need to include their names:

```
INSERT INTO TableName VALUES (NULL, 'Tom', 26)
```

Note: passing **`NULL`** will automatically increment the integer primary key for this record.
Execute this command with the ExecNonQuery (page 509) function, or the ExecNonQuery2 (page 509) function which allows you to easily parameterize this type of command.

Updating records

You can change one or more fields in an existing record:

```
UPDATE TableName Set Col1 = 'Fred', Col2 = 32 WHERE  ID = 2
```

Execute this command with the ExecNonQuery (page 509) function, or the ExecNonQuery2 (page 509) function which allows you to easily parameterize this type of command.

Retrieving data

The SQL command **SELECT** is used to retrieve data from a database. Specify the fields you want and which table to read:

```
SELECT col1, col2 FROM table1
```

To select all fields from a table, use an asterisk (*):

```
SELECT * FROM TableName
```

Processing the SQL

In Basic4Android, execute the **SELECT** command with the ExecQuery (page 509) function, which returns a Cursor (page 505) object:

```
Dim Cursor1 As Cursor
Cursor1 = SQL.ExecQuery("SELECT col1, col2 FROM table1")
For i = 0 To Cursor1.RowCount - 1
  Cursor1.Position = i
  Log(Cursor1.GetString("col1"))
  Log(Cursor1.GetInt("col2"))
Next
```

Parameterize the Command

Use ExecQuery2 (page 509) to parameterize the **SELECT** command with variables:

```
Dim Cursor1 As Cursor
Cursor1 = SQL.ExecQuery2("SELECT col1 FROM table1 WHERE id = ?",
Array As String(intId))
```

Filtering

Specify which records you want to read using **WHERE**:

```
SELECT id, col1 FROM Tablename WHERE id >= 2
```

The percent character (%) can be used as a wildcard, substituting zero or more characters:

```
SELECT * FROM TableName WHERE  Col1 LIKE  'T%'
SELECT * FROM Customers WHERE City LIKE '%es%'
```

Max and Min Values

Find the maxiumum/minimum value of a field:

```
SELECT MAX(Col1) FROM TableName
SELECT MIN(Col1) FROM TableName
```

Count Records

Find the total number of records in a table:

```
SELECT COUNT() FROM TableName
```

Ordering

Specify how you want the results sorted, either in ascending order:

```
SELECT * FROM TableName ORDER BY Col1
```

or in descending order:

```
SELECT * FROM TableName ORDER BY Col1 DESC
```

ExecQueryAsync

If a query will take a long time to run, you can issue an ExecQueryAsync (page 510) command which will raise an event when it finishes.

Deleting data

Delete selected records from a table:

```
DELETE FROM TableName WHERE ID = idVal
```

Delete ALL records from a table!

```
DELETE FROM TableName
```

Execute this command with the ExecNonQuery (page 509) function.

Rename a table

Rename a given table with:

```
ALTER TABLE TableName RENAME TO NewTableName
```

Execute this command with the ExecNonQuery (page 509) function.

Add a field

Add a new field to a table.

```
ALTER TABLE TableName ADD COLUMN Age REAL
```

Execute this command with the ExecNonQuery (page 509) function.

2.9 Process and Activity Life Cycle

Process

Each Basic4Android program runs in its own process. A process has one main thread (also named the **UI thread**) which lives as long as the process lives. A process can also have more threads which are useful for background tasks.
A process starts when the user launches your application (assuming it is not running already in the background). The end of the process is more variable. It will happen sometime after the user or system has closed all the activities.
If, for example, you have one activity and the user pressed on the back key, the activity gets closed. Later, when the phone gets low on memory (and eventually it will happen), the process will quit. If the user launches your program again and the process was not killed, then the same process will be reused.
A Basic4Android application is made of one or more activities. Android supports several other "main" components. These will be added to Basic4Android in the future.

Services

Within Android, code written in an activity module is paused once the activity is not visible. So, by only using activities, it is not possible to run any code while your application is not visible. A service, on the other hand, is (almost) unaffected by the currently visible activity. This allows you to run tasks in the background.
See the Service Module (page 188) section for details.

The Activity Concept

A fundamental concept within most apps is the `Activity`. This corresponds to a page which is displayed to the user. It might have a Layout (created with the Designer) which determines the views (elements of the page) and their position, or they might be created in code and added to the activity.

Activity_Pause and Activity_Resume

When an activity is not in the foreground, Android can kill it to preserve memory. Before it kills your app, Android will call your `Sub Activity_Pause`. You will usually want to use this to save the state of the activity either in persistent storage or in memory. Later, when Android calls your `Sub Activity_Resume`, you can restore this data.
The same thing happens when the user rotates the device. Thus, in `Sub Activity_Resume`, you might need to check the screen dimensions, or you might have a Designer Script (page 109) to handle this.

Activity Module

There is one Module for every Activity. If you want a new Activity in your app, you would use the menu [Project > Add New Module > Activity Module].
For details of an **Activity Module**'s events and members, see the Activity (page 271) reference section in the Core Views Chapter. For more about the **Activity Module** code, see Activity Module (page 180) in the Modules Chapter.

The Activity Template

When you create a new activity, you will start with the following code template:

```
Sub Process_Globals
 'These global variables will be declared once when the
application starts.
 'These variables can be accessed from all modules.
End Sub

Sub Globals
 'These global variables will be redeclared each time the
activity is created.
 'These variables can only be accessed from this module.
End Sub

Sub Activity_Create(FirstTime As Boolean)
 'Do not forget to load the layout file created with the visual
designer. For
   example:
 'Activity.LoadLayout("Layout1")
End Sub

Sub Activity_Resume
End Sub

Sub Activity_Pause (UserClosed As Boolean)
End Sub
```

Activity Attributes

Every activity has Attributes, which are described here (page 180).

Variables within an Activity

Variables can be either local or global.

Local Variables

Local variables are variables that are declared inside a **`Sub`** other than **`Process_Globals`** or **`Globals`**.

Local variables are local to the containing **Sub**. Once the **Sub** ends, these variables no longer exist.

Global Variables

Global variables can be accessed from all subs. There are two types of global variables: Process variables (page 221) and Activity variables (page 222). See the relevant sections for details.

Activity Globals

Every **Activity Module** has two subs dealing with global variables.

Sub Process_Globals

This code is executed once, when the application starts. It is dedicated to the declaration of **Sub Process_Globals** variables.

```
Sub Process_Globals
 Dim lstHistory As List
End Sub
```

This sub is a place where you declare **Sub Process_Globals** variables. These are variables that are valid during the whole lifetime of the process (normally the same as the app). These variables are accessible from every module in the program. You declare variables here and use them inside Subroutines. You can also initialize primitive type (page 209) **Process_Globals** (such as integers) here.

```
Dim bFreeVersion As Boolean = True
```

It is recommended to initialize more complex types within **Sub Activity_Create** when the Activity first runs (check this using the **FirstTime** parameter).

Sub Globals

This sub contains global variables which are valid only during the lifetime of this activity and accessible only inside it.

```
Sub Globals
 Dim EditText1 As EditText
 Dim strTest As String
End Sub
```

As soon as the activity is paused, these variables are no longer available. If the activity is resumed, these variables will be declared again. You can initialize primitive type globals here:

```
Dim intMaxRuns As Int = 20
```

Sub Activity_Create (FirstTime As Boolean)

This sub is automatically called when the activity is created.
The activity is created when:

- the user first launches the application
- the device configuration has changed (user rotated the device) and the activity

was destroyed
- the activity was in the background and the operating system decided to destroy it in order to free memory.

The primary purpose of this sub is to initialize activity variables and load or create the layout.

```
Sub Activity_Create(FirstTime As Boolean)
 Activity.LoadLayout("Main")
 If FirstTime Then
  LoadLstHistory
 End If
End Sub
```

FirstTime parameter

The **FirstTime** parameter tells the app if this is the first time that this activity has been created during the current process. If the user exits the app, or restarts the device, then the next time the app runs, **FirstTime** is reset to **True**. You can use **FirstTime** to initialize those variables or objects which must be initialized only once, such as process variables. For example, suppose you have a file with a list of values that you need to read. You can read the file if **FirstTime** is **True** and store the list as a process variable by declaring the list variable within **Process_Globals** so it will be available as long as the process lives. There will be no need to reload it when the activity is recreated.
To summarize, you can test whether **FirstTime** is **True** and then initialize the process variables that are declared in **Sub Process_Globals**.

Sub Activity_Pause (UserClosed As Boolean)

This Sub is called when the activity is going to be paused. Here you need to save activity parameters you want to get back when the activity is resumed.

When is Activity_Pause called?

Activity_Pause is called when one of the following happens:

- A different activity was started. Note that when you open a different activity (by calling StartActivity (page 258)), the current activity is first paused and then the other activity will be created if needed and will run its own version of **Activity_Resume**.
- The Home button was pressed
- A configuration changed event was raised (device rotated for example). This is one of the most frequent reasons that **Activity_Pause** is called. In this case, the current activity is 'paused' and re-activated with the new orientation. It then goes through the subs **Globals**, **Activity_Create** (with **FirstTime** set to **False**) and **Activity_Resume**.
- The Back button was pressed.
- **Activity_Create** finishes.
- Any time the Activity moves from the foreground to the background.

How to use Activity_Pause

`Activity_Pause` is the last place to save important information before the app pauses.

UserClosed parameter

The parameter **`UserClosed`** can be used to decide whether the Activity has been paused by the Operating System (for example by an orientation change) or by the user (for example by a back button click). The **`UserClosed`** parameter will be **`True`** either when the user clicks the Back button or when the program calls **`Activity.Finish`**. You can use the **`UserClosed`** parameter to decide which data to save and whether to reset any related process variables to their initial state, as we discuss next.

Saving Data

`Activity_Pause` is the last place to save important information. Generally there are two types of mechanisms that allow you to save the activity state:

- Information that is only relevant to the current run of the application can be stored in one or more **process variables**.
- Information which you want to keep between one run of your app and the next, for example the user's settings, should be saved to **persistent storage** (a file or database).

One way to store data to persistent storage is provided by the KeyValueStore (page 527) class. But you might prefer to use StateManager (page 528) to save the current state as well as settings. For example, if the user has entered some text in an **`EditText`** view, then you might want to keep this text and restore it when the activity resumes.

Sub Activity_Resume

This routine is called every time an activity is launched or re-activated. **`Activity_Resume`** is automatically called right after **`Activity_Create`** finishes and after resuming a paused activity, typically when an activity moved to the background and then it returns to the foreground. Here you can restore any activity parameters which you stored when **`Activity_Pause`** was called.

Note: when you open a different activity (by calling StartActivity (page 258)), the current activity is first paused and then the other activity will be created if needed and (always) resumed.

StartActivity (Activity As Object)

You can start an **`Activity`** or bring it to front if it already exists. The **`Activity`** can be a string with the target activity name, or it can be the actual activity. An **Activity Module** with this name must exist.

Examples:

```
StartActivity(Activity2)
StartActivity("Activity2")
```

The target activity will be started once the program is free to process its message queue. After this call, the current activity will be paused and the target activity will be resumed. This method can also be used to send Intents (page 314) objects to the system.
Note: contrary to some documentation on the Basic4Android website, it IS possible to call StartActivity from a Service.

Activity.Finish vs ExitApplication

There are two ways to end your app: **`Activity.Finish`** and **`ExitApplication`**. Most applications should **not** use **`ExitApplication`** but prefer **`Activity.Finish`**, which lets Android decide when the process is killed. You should only use **`ExitApplication`** if you really need to fully kill the process. An interesting article about the functioning of Android can be found here: Multitasking the Android way (http://android-developers.blogspot.com/2010/04/multitasking-android-way.html). Should we use **`Activity.Finish`** before starting another activity? Consider first the following example, which shows the flow of execution of code which does not use **`Activity.Finish`**:

Main activity
StartActivity(SecondActivity)
  SecondActivity activity
  StartActivity(ThirdActivity)
    ThirdActivity activity
    Click on Back button
    Android goes back to previous activity, SecondActivity
  SecondActivity activity
  Click on Back button
  Android goes back to previous activity, Main
Main activity
Click on Back button
Android leaves the program

Now consider following example, which calls **`Activity.Finish`** before each **`StartActivity`**:
Main activity
Activity.Finish
StartActivity(SecondActivity)
  SecondActivity activity
  Activity.Finish
  StartActivity(ThirdActivity)
    ThirdActivity activity
    Click on Back button

Android leaves the program

We should use **`Activity.Finish`** before starting another activity only if we don't want to go back to this activity with the Back button.

2.10 Modules

An app consists of chunks of code called modules. At least one module exists, the main one. Its name is always **Main** and cannot be changed. There are four different types of modules:

- Activity modules
- Class modules (page 183)
- Code modules (page 188)
- Service modules (page 188)

Creating or Adding Modules

You can add either an existing module or a new module.
To add a new module, select the IDE menu [Project > Add New Module]:

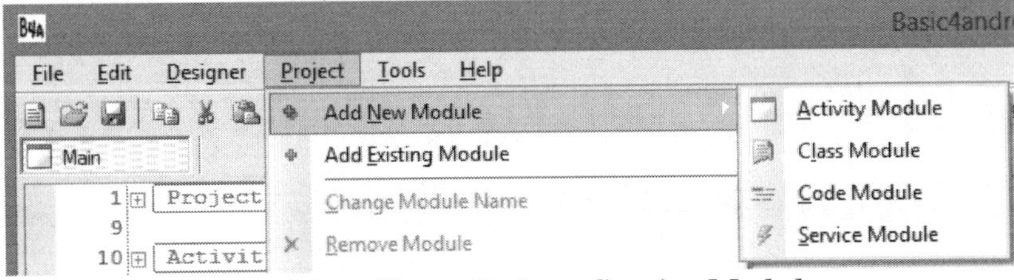

Click on either Activity, Class, Code or Service Module.
To bring in an existing module (and so reuse the code), click on [Project > Add Existing Module] in the IDE menu.
Each module (except **Main**) is saved in a **.bas** file within the project folder. Main is part of the **.b4a** file.

Activity Module

This is where you write the code for an Activity. Every Basic4Android app must have at least one `Activity` called Main. Activities have three special life-cycle related events: Activity_Create (page 175), Activity_Pause (page 176) and Activity_Resume (page 177). See Process and Activity Life Cycle (page 173) for more information about activities and the process's life cycle.

Activity Attributes

You can set attributes which are valid for the current activity within the Activity Attributes Region at the top of an **Activity Module**.

Defaults

By default, Attributes are set as follows:

```
#Region  Activity Attributes
 #FullScreen: False
 #IncludeTitle: True
#End Region
```

FullScreen

Whether to show the Status Bar (page 75) at the top of the screen. Values: **True** or **False**, default **False**. You should not hide the Status Bar unless absolutely necessary.

IncludeTitle

Whether to include a Title Bar (page 76) at the top of your app. Values: **True** or **False**. Default value **True**.

Creating the Page

An Activity can either have a Layout which determines the views (elements of the page) and their position, or the views can be created in the code itself. You load a layout file with **LoadLayout**. You can add views to this activity with AddView (page 275), and remove them with RemoveViewAt (page 277).

Activity Events

The Activity can respond to several user events, for example:

Touch (Action As Int, X As Float, Y As Float) Event

The Touch (page 272) event can be used to handle user touches.
Action: specifies the user's action. It's values can be:

- **Activity.ACTION_DOWN**: The user has touched the screen at **X,Y**.
- **Activity.ACTION_MOVE**: The user's touch has moved to **X,Y**.
- **Activity.ACTION_UP**: The user has stopped touching the screen at **X,Y**.

KeyPress and KeyUp

The KeyPress (page 272) and KeyUp (page 272) events occur when the user presses or releases a key on a physical keyboard attached to the device or on Android's-on-screen keyboard. **Note**: it is possible for a view (such as a **EditText**) to consume this event, in which case the Activity will not see it. When handling the **KeyPress** or **KeyUp** event, you should return a boolean value which tells whether the event has been consumed by our code. For example, if the user pressed on the Back key and you return **True** then Android will not see the back key and so will not close your activity.

```
Sub Activity_KeyPress (KeyCode As Int) As Boolean
 If Keycode = KeyCodes.KEYCODE_BACK Then
     Return True
  Else
     Return False
  End If
End Sub
```

For a complete list of Activity events, see here (page 272).

Creating a Menu

You can add menu items to the activity with Activity.AddMenuItem (page 274) method. The menu is shown if the user presses the Menu button (on older devices) or selects the overflow symbol (3 vertical dots) on the Action Bar. **Note**: **AddMenuItem** should only be called inside the **Activity_Create** event.

Activities vs Windows Forms

Activities are similar to what are called Forms in Microsoft Visual Basic. One major difference is that, while an activity is not in the foreground, it can be killed in order to preserve memory. Usually, you will want to save the state of the activity before the data is lost. It can be stored either in persistent storage or in memory that is associated with the process. Later, this activity will be recreated when needed. Another delicate point happens when there is a major configuration change in the device. The most common is an orientation change (the user rotates the device). When such a change occurs, the current activities are destroyed and then recreated by calling **Activity_Create()**. Then it is possible to create the activity according to the new configuration (for example, the new screen dimensions).

Variables in other Activity Modules

If there are several Activity Modules in an application, they can access the **Process_Globals** variables in other modules using references such as

```
Main.Value2
```

where Main is an activity name.

More Information

See Process and Activities Life Cycle (page 173) for more information about Activities and Processes Life Cycle.

Multiple Activity Modules

An app might need several different screens. Each one of these will (normally) require its own activity module. To access any object or variable in a module other than the module where they were declared, you must add the module name as a prefix to the object or variable name separated by a dot. For example, suppose variables Value1 and Value2 are declared in Main module in **Sub Process_Globals**:

```
Sub Process_Globals
 Dim Value1, Value2, Value3 As String
End Sub
```

To access these variables from another module, the variable name is Main.Value1 or Main.Value2.

```
Sub Activity_Pause (UserClosed As Boolean)
 Main.Value2 = edtValue2_P2.Text
End Sub
```

It is not possible to access any view from another activity module, because when a new activity is started, the current activity is paused and it is no longer accessible.

Class module

What is a Class?

A class represents an object such as a person, place or thing and encapsulates the data and functionality of that object. For example, a "Customer" class would represent your customers. A single, particular customer would be an **instance** of the "Customer" class, an object of the type "Customer".

A class contains **properties**, such as strForeName, which gives the state of a particular instance, and **methods**, such as AddOrder ( ), which allow the properties of an instance to be manipulated or queried.

Benefits of Classes

Writing code which focuses on the objects involved is called object-oriented programming. There are number of benefits to this style of coding:

- It provides a clear, modular structure, which makes it good for defining abstract datatypes where implementation details are hidden and the unit has a clearly defined interface.
- It simplifies code maintenance, as new objects can be created with small differences to existing ones.
- It delivers a framework for code libraries where supplied software components can be easily adapted and modified.

Example

We give here an example of a class module. (You can download the complete Classes example project here (http://resources.basic4android.info/)). Consider a "Person" class. We want to store a person's forename, last name and date of birth. We want to make it easy to change the two names, so we make these values public. The date of birth will be stored as a `Long` so we can do calculations. Therefore, this value must be hidden and accessed through functions within the class.

When we create a Person, we need to state their two names and their date of birth as a string:

```
'Class Person module
Sub Class_Globals
 Public FirstName, LastName As String
 Private BirthDate As Long
End Sub

Sub Initialize (strFirstName As String, strLastName As String,
strBirthDate As String)
 FirstName = strFirstName
 LastName = strLastName
 Try
  BirthDate = DateTime.DateParse(strBirthDate)
 Catch
  Msgbox (strBirthDate, "Invalid Date Format")
 End Try
End Sub

Public Sub GetName As String
 Return FirstName & " " & LastName
End Sub

Public Sub GetCurrentAge As Int
 Return GetAgeAt(DateTime.Now)
End Sub

Public Sub GetAgeAt(Date As Long) As Int
 Dim diff As Long
 diff = Date - BirthDate
 Return Floor(diff / DateTime.TicksPerDay / 365)
End Sub
```

Main module.

```
Sub Activity_Create(FirstTime As Boolean)
 Dim Fred As Person
 Fred.Initialize("Fred", "Smith", "1/2/1950")
 Log (Fred.GetName & " is aged " & Fred.GetCurrentAge)
 Fred.LastName = "Jones"
 Log (Fred.GetName & " is aged " & Fred.GetCurrentAge)
End Sub
```

The log shows

```
Fred Smith is aged 63
Fred Jones is aged 63
```

Public vs Private Variables

Public variables can be read and written to directly:

```
Fred.LastName = "Jones"
```

Private variables are hidden, and we must provide special functions to access them:

```
Fred.GetCurrentAge
```

We might do this because we want to store the data in a special format which the user would never want to access, for example storing the date of birth as a **`Long`**.

Classes vs Types

Basic4Android allows you to declare simple data structures using the **`Type`** keyword, as explained here (page 219).
What are the similaries and differences between a class module and a type (http://bit.ly/13uxb1r)?

- Both **classes** and **types** are templates. From these templates, you can instantiate any number of objects.
- **Type** fields are similar to the global variables of a **class**. However, unlike types which only define the data structure, classes also define the data's behavior. The behavior is defined in the class's subs.

Classes vs Code Modules

How does a class module compare with a code module (http://bit.ly/15IAy8o)?

- A **code module** is a collection of subs, unlike a **class**, which is a template for an object.
- A **code module** always runs in the context of the calling sub (the activity or service that called the sub) and the code module doesn't hold a reference to any context. For that reason, it is impossible to handle events or use **`CallSub`** within code modules.
  A **class**, on the other hand, stores a reference to the context of the activity or service module that called the Initialize sub. This means that class objects share the same life cycle as the service or activity that initialized them.

Adding a class module

Add a new or existing class module by choosing [Project > Add New Module > Class Module] or [Project > Add Existing Module]. Like other modules, classes are saved as files with a "bas" extension.

Classes structures

Classes must have the following two subs:
`Sub Class_Globals` - This sub is similar to the activity Globals sub. These variables will be the class global variables (sometimes referred to as instance variables or instance members).
`Sub Initialize` - A class object should be initialized before you can call any other sub. Initializing an object is done by calling the **`Initialize`** sub. When you call **`Initialize`**, you set the object's context (the parent activity or service).
Note that you can chose the arguments you need to instantiate an instance of your class. In the above code, we created a class named Person and later instantiated an object of this type:

```
Dim Fred As Person
Fred.Initialize("Fred", "Smith", "1/2/1950")
```

Note that **`Initialize`** is not required if you make a copy of an object which was already initialized:

```
Dim p2 As Person
p2 = Fred 'both variables now point to the same Person object.
Log(p2.GetCurrentAge)
```

Polymorphism

Polymorphism allows you to treat different classes of objects that adhere to the same interface in the same way. As an example, we will create two classes named: Square and Circle. Each class has a sub named Draw that draws the object on a canvas:

Class Square module

```
Sub Class_Globals
 Private mx, my, mLength As Int
End Sub

'Initializes the object. You can add parameters to this method
if needed.
Sub Initialize (x As Int, y As Int, length As Int)
 mx = x
 my = y
 mLength = length
End Sub

Sub Draw(c As Canvas)
 Dim r As Rect
 r.Initialize(mx, my, mx + mLength, my + mLength)
 c.DrawRect(r, Colors.White, False, 1dip)
End Sub
```

Class Circle module

```
Sub Class_Globals
 Private mx, my, mRadius As Int
End Sub

'Initializes the object. You can add parameters to this method
if needed.
Sub Initialize (x As Int, y As Int, radius As Int)
 mx = x
 my = y
 mRadius = radius
End Sub

Sub Draw(cvs As Canvas)
 cvs.DrawCircle(mx, my, mRadius, Colors.Yellow, False, 1dip)
End Sub
```

In the main module

Create a list with Squares and Circles. We then go over the list and draw all the objects:

```
Sub Process_Globals
End Sub

Sub Globals
 Dim shapes As List
 Dim cvs As Canvas
End Sub

Sub Activity_Create(FirstTime As Boolean)
 cvs.Initialize(Activity)
 Dim sq1, sq2 As Square
 Dim circle1 As Circle
 sq1.Initialize(100dip, 100dip, 50dip)
 sq2.Initialize(2dip, 2dip, 100dip)
 circle1.Initialize(50%x, 50%y, 100dip)
 ' add the items to the list
 shapes.Initialize
 shapes.Add(sq1)
 shapes.Add(sq2)
 shapes.Add(circle1)
 DrawAllShapes
End Sub

Sub DrawAllShapes
 For i = 0 To shapes.Size - 1
   Log(shapes.Get(i))
   CallSub2(shapes.Get(i), "Draw", cvs)
 Next
 Activity.Invalidate
End Sub
```

We do not need to know the specific class of each object in the list. We know that it has a Draw method that expects a single Canvas argument. Later we can easily add more classes of shapes. You can use the **SubExists** keyword to check whether an object includes a specific sub. You can also use the **Is** keyword to check if an object is of a specific type.

Self reference

The **Me** keyword returns a reference to the current object. **Me** can only be used inside a class module. Consider the above example. We could have passed the shapes list to the **Initialize** sub and then added each object to the list from the **Initialize** sub:

```
Sub Initialize (Shapes As List, x As Int, y As Int, radius As
Int)
 mx = x
 my = y
 mRadius = radius
 Shapes.Add(Me)
End Sub
```

In that case, the calls from Main to Initialize would have been:

```
sq1.Initialize(shapes, 100dip, 100dip, 50dip)
```

Classes and Activity Object

Android UI elements such as views hold a reference to the parent activity. But, since Android is allowed to kill background activities in order to free memory, UI elements cannot be declared as **`Sub Process_Globals`** variables because these variables live as long as the process lives. They should be declared in **`Sub Globals`** instead. This is discussed further in the Process and Activities Life Cycle (page 173) chapter.
The same is true for instances of a class. If one or more of the class global variables is of a UI type (or any activity object type), then the class will be treated as an "activity object", meaning that instances of this class cannot be declared as **`Sub Process_Globals`** variables.

Limitations of Classes

Basic4Android's implementation of classes is only partial. For example, it does not support inheritance, overriding or overloading.

Code module

Code modules contain only code. No Activity is allowed in Code modules. The purpose and advantage of code modules is that they allow the same code to be shared in different programs, mainly for calculations or other general management.
Examples of code modules are:
DBUtils (page 160), database management utilities.
StateManager (page 528), helps managing Android application settings and states.

Service Module

Why use a Service

If you want to run code when your app is not visible, you need to use a service. Activity modules are paused when they are not visible, so it is not possible to run any code while your application is not visible if you only use activities. A service is almost unaffected by the currently visible activity. This allows you to run tasks in the background.
Services usually use status bar notifications to interact with the user. They do not have any other visible elements. Services cannot show any dialog (except toast messages (page 260)).

Note: when an error occurs in a service code module, you will not see the "Do you want to continue?" dialog. Android's regular "Process has crashed" message will appear instead.

Alternative to an Activity

Because a service is never paused or resumed, and because services are not recreated when the user rotates the screen, services are often easier to code than activities.
There is nothing special about the code written in a service.
Code in a service module runs in the same process and the same thread as all other code.

When Does Android Kill a Process?

When Android is low on memory, it will select a process to kill. If the process is needed later, it will be re-created. It is important to understand how Android chooses which process to kill. A process can be in one of the three following states:
Paused - There are no visible activities and no started services.
Paused processes are the first to be killed when needed.
Background - None of the activities of the process are visible, however there is a started service.
If there is still not enough memory, background processes will be killed.
Foreground - The user currently sees one of the process activities.
Foreground processes will usually not be killed. A service can bring a process to the foreground.

Android's View of Services

For more about how Android sees services, consult
http://developer.android.com/reference/android/app/Service.html

How to Start a Service

Call StartService (page 259) during **`Activity_Create`**. This will run **`Sub Service_Create`** followed by **`Sub Service_Start`** (see below).
You can then use the service's code.

Service Code

Adding a service module is done using the menu [Project > Add New Module > Service Module].
This creates a new service with the skeleton code:

```
#Region  Service Attributes
 #StartAtBoot: False
#End Region
```

```
Sub Process_Globals
 'These global variables will be declared once when the
application starts.
 'These variables can be accessed from all modules.
End Sub

Sub Service_Create
End Sub

Sub Service_Start (StartingIntent As Intent)
End Sub

Sub Service_Destroy
End Sub
```

Service Attributes

These are defined in the #Region at the top of the code.
The possible options are:

- #StartAtBoot: Whether this service should start automatically after boot. Values: **`True`** or **`False`**. Defaults to **`False`**.
- #StartCommandReturnValue: (advanced) Sets the value that will be returned from onStartCommand. The default value is android.app.Service.START_NOT_STICKY. For possible values, see Android's view of services (http://developer.android.com/reference/android/app/Service.html).

SubRoutines

Every service module must include at least the following subs:

Sub Process_Globals

The place to declare the service global variables. Unlike an Activity, there is no Globals sub as Services do not support Activity objects. **`Sub Process_Globals`** should only be used to declare variables. It should not run any other code as it might fail. This is true for other modules as well. **Note**: Process_Globals variables are kept as long as the process runs and are accessible from other modules.

Sub Service_Create

This is called when the service is first started. This is the place to initialize and set the **`Sub Process_Globals`** variables. Once a service is started, it stays alive until you call **`StopService`**, or until the whole process is destroyed.

Sub Service_Start (StartingIntent As Intent)

This is called **each time** you call StartService (page 259) (or StartServiceAt (page 259)). It can also be called if this service is a broadcast receiver. For more on this, see this page (http://bit.ly/12QWZBw). When this sub runs, the process is moved to the foreground state, which means that Android will not kill your process until this sub finishes running. If you want to run some code periodically, you should schedule the next task with **`StartServiceAt`** inside this sub.

StartingIntent: The argument will be set by Android if this service is a broadcast receiver. For more information, see this page (http://bit.ly/12QWZBw) on the Basic4Android website. See here (page 314) for more on `Intent`s.

Sub Service_Destroy

This is called when you call StopService. The service will not be running until you call StartService again.

When to Use a Service

There are probably four main use-cases for services:

1) Separating the user interface (UI) code from logical code.

Writing the non-UI code in a service is easier than implementing it inside an Activity module as the service is not paused and resumed and it will usually not be recreated (whereas an Activity can be).

You can call StartService (page 259) during `Activity_Create` and from then-on work with the service module.

A good design is to make the activity fetch the required data from the service in Sub `Activity_Resume`. The activity can fetch data stored in a `Sub Process_Globals` variable or it can call a service Sub with the `CallSub` method.

2) Running a long operation.

For example, downloading a large file from the internet. In this case you can call `Service.StartForeground` (from the service module). This will move your service to the foreground state and will make sure that Android doesn't kill it. Make sure to eventually call `Service.StopForeground`.

3) Scheduling a repeating task.

By calling StartServiceAt (page 259), you can schedule your service to run at a specific time. You can call `StartServiceAt` in `Sub Service_Start` to schedule the next time and create a repeating task (for example, a task that checks for updates every couple of minutes).

4) Run a service after the device boots, that is, when it powers up.

Your service will run after boot is completed if you set:

```
#Region  Service Attributes
 #StartAtBoot: True
#End Region
```

Notifications

Both activities and services can display status bar notifications, but for services it is their main way of interacting with the user.

The notification displays an icon in the status bar.

The user can swipe down the notifications screen and press on the notification.

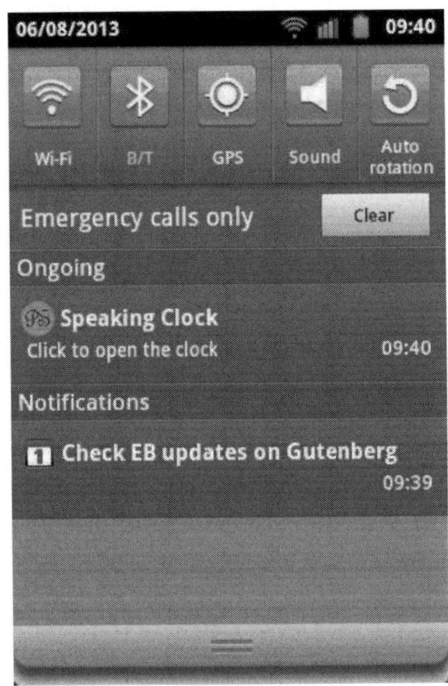

The user can press on the message, which will open an activity as configured by the Notification object (page 329).

Accessing other modules

`Sub Process_Globals` objects are public and can be accessed from other modules. Using the **`CallSub`** method you can also call a sub in a different module, provided the other module is not paused. You can use **`IsPaused`** to check if the target module is paused.

This means that one activity can never access a sub of a different activity as there could only be one running activity. However, an activity can access a running service and a service can access a running activity. **Note**: if the target component is paused, then an empty string is returned. No exception is thrown. For example, suppose a service has finished downloading some new information. It can call:

```
CallSub(Main, "RefreshData")
```

If the Main activity is running, it can fetch the data from the service **`Process_Globals`** variables and update the display. It is also possible to pass the new information to the activity sub, but it is better to keep the information as a **`Process_Globals`** variable. This allows the activity to call the required sub (in this case RefreshData) whenever it wants and fetch the information (as the activity might be paused when the new information arrived).

Note: it is NOT possible to use **`CallSub`** to access subs of a Code module.

Sample Projects Using Services

Examples of projects using services are available from the Basic4Android website:
Downloading a file using a service module (http://bit.ly/17yeXPZ)
Periodically checking Twitter feeds (http://bit.ly/17yfyRP)

2.11 Publishing and Monetizing Your App

Once you have developed your app, you will want to distribute it. This can be done either through the Google Play website or one of the other distribution channels such as Amazon, or by distributing the APK file from a website or via email.
This chapter will take you through the whole process of preparing your app for publication, including ways to make money from it, then sending it out into the world.

User Help

Users will probably need help about how to use your app most effectively. You can provide some information in a splash screen (http://bit.ly/13WB1xW), in an activity or on a web page which you display in a WebView (page 398).

Branding and Marketing

Before you begin to distribute your app, you will need to think about what to call it, whether it needs its own website, and if so, whether the domain name is available, the design of your logo, whether you need to register the trademark, and how you are going to advertise and market the product. To do all these things effectively requires a different set of skills from development, and you might want to find a partner who can spend time on these important aspects of app distribution.

Setting Your Project Parameters

Before generating the APK, you should check that the following parameters are set correctly:

Package Name

This is set in [Project > Package Name]. See Package Name (page 69) for what is required.

Project Attributes

A number of attributes should be set in the Project Attributes Region at the top of the Main Activity. See here (page 68) for details.

Setting Icons

Your app will need a number of icons before it can be distributed. There are several sorts of icons you might consider: launcher, menu, action bar, status bar, tab, dialog and list view icons are all possible. Your app may also need to display icons in the Notification Area (page 329). We discuss some of these below. For more details, see here (http://developer.android.com/guide/practices/ui_guidelines/icon_design.html).

See here for Launcher Icon tips
(http://developer.android.com/guide/practices/ui_guidelines/icon_design_launcher.html)
See here for a wider view of Android Icons
(http://developer.android.com/design/style/iconography.html)

Google Play Store Icon

For the Google Play Store you will need an icon 512x512 pixels, 32-bit PNG with an alpha channel and maximum size of 1024KB (more details here (http://support.google.com/googleplay/android-developer/answer/1078870?hl=en)).

Launcher Icon

Every app needs a Launcher Icon so the user can identify and run it.
The Launcher icon incorporated into the app is always 48x48 pixels.
This icon will be shown in several places on the user's device:

- on the installation panel
- in the Title Bar (for later versions of Android)
- on the Home page
- in the [Settings > Apps] list

A 512x512 pixel version is also required for Google Play.

[Project > Choose Icon]

You set the Launcher Icon with the menu [Project > Choose Icon]. You can navigate to any folder and choose any file with an extension of BMP, JPG, GIF or PNG. The file will be copied into the project's **Objects\res\drawable** folder and automatically renamed to icon.xxx, where xxx is the original filename extension. Android will search for a file with this name to use for the Launcher, therefore you should not rename it once it has been copied, although you can select a new Launcher Icon at any time.

Creating Icons

An icon is a file in BMP, JPG, GIF or PNG format.
You can create a PNG file using the free Inkscape program (http://inkscape.org/).
This allows you to control the opacity (alpha channel) of your image, which is important in achieving a good result, as explained here (http://developer.android.com/guide/practices/ui_guidelines/icon_design_launcher.html).
Tip: Use filenames which contain only lower case letters, numbers and underscores so when you export the image to PNG, it's name will be acceptable to Basic4Android.

Sources of Icons

You can find some ready-made icons at http://www.iconarchive.com/

Notification Icon Recommendations

Notification icons are shown in the notification area at the top of the screen. For notification icons, the recommended practice is to use half the size of the corresponding launcher icon. You can specify which icon to use using the notification Icon (page 331) property.

Icon Sizes

Provide icons for use within your app in all prescribed sizes to make sure it looks good at all resolutions. Otherwise, Android can downsize large images, but that may result in jagged edges. More information here (http://developer.android.com/guide/practices/screens_support.html). Also, if you use large icons, they might be trimmed instead of resized when shown in the notifications pull-down list, resulting in inappropriate images. However, if for some reason you can only provide a single icon, 48x48 is the best size to use. It looks passable on most devices.

Prescribed Resolutions

There are 4 prescribed resolutions, and each have their own recommended icon sizes, as shown below. **Note**: "**px**" means pixels.

LDPI

dpi 120
Screen Resolution (px) 240x320
Notification Icon Size (px) 18x18
Launcher Icon Size (px) 36x36
Folder .... drawable-ldpi

MDPI

dpi 160
Screen Resolution (px) 320x480
Notification Icon Size (px) 24x24
Launcher Icon Size (px) 48x48
Folder .... drawable-mdpi

HDPI

dpi 240
Screen Resolution (px) 480x800
Notification Icon Size (px) 36x36
Launcher Icon Size (px) 72x72
Folder .... drawable-hdpi

XHDPI

dpi 320
Screen Resolution (px) .... 720x1280 and above
Notification Icon Size (px) 48x48
Launcher Icon Size (px) 96x96
Folder .... drawable-xhdpi

Installing Icons

This is how to include your other icons into the project:

- In your project's **Objects\res** folder, create one sub-folder for each desired resolution. They must be named drawable-ldpi, drawable-mdpi, drawable-hdpi and drawable-xhdpi.

- For each of the desired icon sizes, create icons with the desired size. Their file names must contain only lower case letters a-z, numbers 0-9, underscore or period(.)
- Copy the icons into their appropriate folder.
- Make sure you mark all those files and folders as read only (otherwise they will get deleted during compilation).

Now when you install the app on a device, the Android system will use the icons in the folder corresponding to the device's screen resolution.

Generating Your APK

Now you are ready to create your APK.

APK File

The APK is a package which contains the compiled source code and the assets files.

Keys and Certificates

Electronic documents (such as APKs) can be "signed" using other electronic documents called Certificates. Certificates contain the identity of the owner and a key. Certificates occur in pairs, one containing a private key, the other a public key. Some certificates are issued by certificate authorities, who authenticate the owner's identity. Other certificates are simply generated by the owner, without any authentication.

Signing

Android requires that all installed apps are signed before they can be installed. Details from the Android Developer website (http://developer.android.com/tools/publishing/app-signing.html). Android devices will not install an unsigned APK. The Android system uses certificates as a means of identifying the author of an application and establishing trust relationships between applications. The certificate is not used to control which applications the user can install.

The developer signs his app using the private key and then distributes it along with the certificate containing the public key. After an app is signed, it is not possible to modify it without the private key that was used to sign it.

Debugging Certificates

To test and debug your app, Basic4Android signs it with a special debug key that is created by the Android SDK build tools. Basic4Android uses a default "debug key" to sign apps. This key is fine during debugging. However, Google Play doesn't accept APK files signed with this key.

For an app called "abc", the debug key would be stored in a file called **abc_DEBUG.apk** in the **Objects** folder of the **abc** project.

Signing for Distribution

An Android certificate does not need to be signed by a certificate authority; it is perfectly allowable, and typical, for Android applications to use self-signed certificates, but before you can distribute your app, you must sign it with a certificate whose private key you hold. Also, it is very important that you keep this certificate safe. See below.

Creating A Private Key

You therefore need to create your own private key. Basic4Android makes it easy to create such a key.
Select [Tools > Private Sign Key] to see the following dialog:

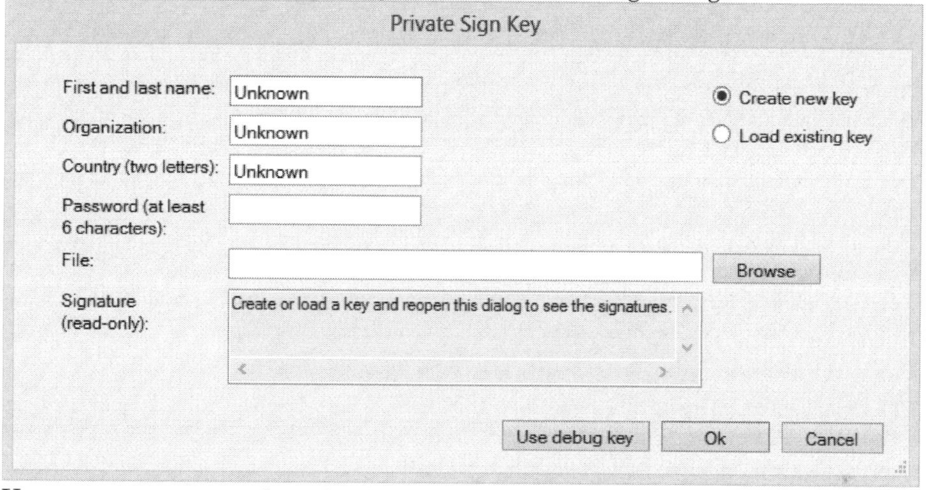

Private Sign Key

First and last name: Unknown
Organization: Unknown
Country (two letters): Unknown
Password (at least 6 characters):
File: Browse
Signature (read-only): Create or load a key and reopen this dialog to see the signatures.

◉ Create new key
○ Load existing key

Use debug key | Ok | Cancel

You can create a new key, load an existing one or use the debug key.

Creating a New Key

If you create a new key, you need to provide your two-letter Country Code. There is a list of codes here (http://www.digicert.com/ssl-certificate-country-codes.htm). See below for more about keystores.
The private key which Basic4Android generates will have an expiry date set to the maximum allowed by the certificate system, a date about 38 years in the future.
Basic4Android uses the DSA 1024 algorithm to generate keys.

The KeyStore

Keys are stored in a "keystore" file. You can store the key in any file with any name you wish. It might be a good idea to give it the extension "keystore" so you will know what it is. It is not possible to read such a file without its password, so make sure you can remember the password.
Once you have created a new keystore file, Basic4Android will use this key for all your projects. **You should be very careful with this file. If you lose this file, you will not be able to update your applications in the market. You will need to publish updates as new applications.** Therefore, it is recommended to backup this file.

Note: while it is possible to have several keystores, it then becomes difficult to keep track of which key is in which keystore. It is probably best to use a single key in a single keystore to sign all your apps. However, problems might arise if you wish to sell your app to another developer in the future, as you would then need to give them a copy of your keystore and its password.
After signing, you can continue to debug. Your private key will then be used to sign the APK. If you wish, you can revert to using a debug key, but there is no need.

Keystore Explorer

If you need to, Keystore Explorer 4.01 allows you to explore your keystore. Download it free (http://www.lazgosoftware.com/kse/).

Compiling the APK

Compile your app, either in Release Mode or Release Obfuscated Mode. See the Compilation Modes (page 119) section for details.
This will create an APK file in the Objects folder of your project.

Monetising Your App

Before you publish your app, you need to consider whether you are going to try to make money from it. If not then you can skip this section.

Ways of Monetizing Your App

There are a number of ways you can earn money from your app:

- Give your app away but include advertisements
- Sell it, perhaps as an add-free alternative
- Ask for donations if people find your app useful
- Use in-app billing
- Verify the user is licensed to use the app
- Find a sponsor and link your app to their site
- Write an app for a client and sell your time
- Use the PayPal library (page 528)

Libraries Supporting Advertising

There are several Basic4Android libraries which allow you to easily include advertisements in your app. They are all official libraries (that is, produced by Anywhere Software) but are not included in the core distribution, so they require the library (or wrapper) to be downloaded.
Note that advertisements take up space on the device's display, so you need to consider the implications when designing the user interface.

AdMob

Google is perhaps the best-known source of advertising. Use the AdMob library to display Google ads in your applications. This has the benefit that you can also use Google Analytics to analyse your results.

Library and Tutorial

Download the AdMob library here (http://bit.ly/19UeAy4). This library also requires configuration. Of course, in order to get your ads and get paid, you will need to register with Google's Admob site. See here (http://bit.ly/19UeDcY) for a tutorial with all the details.

AdiQuity

AdiQuity is another advertisement solution. See here (http://adiquity.com/app-developer/) for details of Adiquity and see here (http://bit.ly/19UgZbZ) for the library and a tutorial.

Matomy

This is another provider of mobile ads. For details of the service see here (http://publishers.matomymobile.com/join.mat?ref=3), and for the library go here (http://bit.ly/19UkLSx).

TapForTap

Tap for Tap offers a way to promote your app and a way of generating ad revenue, or perhaps to do both. When users "tap" on a link in your app and install an app advertised on the tap exchange, you can either earn credits (and hence have your app advertised) or you can make money; or you can choose a mix of these options.

For more information about the service, see here (https://tapfortap.com/). See here (http://bit.ly/14Lhsrc) for the Basic4Android wrapper around the SDK.

Selling Your App

Google Play (https://play.google.com/store) is the main place users go to find new apps, although you can distribute your app through other channels. If you charge for your app, then the distributor will charge you a transaction fee.

Note: once you publish an app as free on Google Play, you can't change it to a paid app later. However you can sell a license within your app via in-app billing.

In-App Billing

Google Play provides an in-app billing service which you can use to accept payments from within your app. You define your products (using Google Play Developer Console) including product type, SKU, price, description, and so on. This could include a key which removes advertisements.

In-app products, which are declared in the Google Play Developer Console, can include licenses, subscriptions and managed items which your app can consume. You would typically implement consumption for items that can be purchased multiple times (such as in-game currency, fuel, or magic spells). Once purchased, a managed item cannot be purchased again until you consume the item, by sending a consumption request to Google Play. Read the official documentation here (http://developer.android.com/google/play/billing/api.html). Get the library here (http://bit.ly/19UimHB) and read the tutorial here (http://bit.ly/19UidUJ).

Licensing

A good way to protect your app is to use Google Play App Licensing, a service that lets you enforce licensing policies for applications that you publish on Google Play. Your app can query Google Play at run time to obtain the licensing status for the current user, then allow or disallow further use as appropriate. This way you can be sure that the user has the right to use your app. For more information about licensing, see here (http://bit.ly/14Li2VV). To download the library see here (http://bit.ly/14LiaF2). For a tutorial on how to use it, follow this link (http://bit.ly/14LikMx).

Registering as a Google Play Developer

Whether you want to sell your app or give it away, the best outlet for Android Apps is the Google Play store, and before you can publish there, you must register as a Developer. This has a one-time registration fee of $25. Any number of apps can be distributed once you have registered.

Register as a Google Play Developer

Go to the Google Play Developer sign-up page: https://play.google.com/apps/publish/signup/.
Review and agree to the Google Play Developer distribution agreement: https://play.google.com/about/developer-distribution-agreement.html. This includes important information about user privacy and legal rights.
Review the distribution countries where you can distribute and sell applications to ensure you can sell into your target markets.
Check if you can have a merchant account in your country.
Pay your one-time registration fee of $25. You will need a credit card if you have not already registered one with Google Wallet (http://www.google.com/wallet/).

Merchant Account

If you are planning to sell apps or in-app products, you will need a Merchant Account. Before you register as a developer, you need to check if you can have a merchant account in your country. If you have a Google Wallet (http://www.google.com/wallet/), this will automatically be used as your merchant account.

Prepare Your App's Google Play Page

You must upload at least two screenshots of your app in approved formats, and a large 512 x 512-pixel icon for your app, as well as listing details.
It's worth spending some time on these details, since they'll represent the entirety of your "shopfront" in Google Play.

User Support

Before you begin selling your app (or even distributing it free), consider how you are going to support your users. On Google Play for example, you will be solely responsible for support and maintenance of your products and any complaints about them. Your contact information will be displayed in each application detail page and made available to users for customer support purposes. You need to respond to these complaints quickly, otherwise your ratings will go down.

Google Play Developer Console

For information on how to use the Google Play Developer Console to upload and manage your app, see the following page:
https://developer.android.com/distribute/googleplay/publish/console.html

Upload your App to Google Play

You will need to choose a title and decide whether to just upload the APK or prepare a store listing. An app you upload is a draft until you publish it, at which time Google Play makes your store listing page and app available to users. You can unpublish the app at any time.

Distributing Apps elsewhere

There are several other ways to distribute your app in addition to Google Play.

Preparing the User's Device

If they obtain the app from anywhere other than Google Play, users will need to allow their device to run it by selecting
either: [Settings > Applications > Unknown sources]
or: [Settings > Security > Unknown sources]
(This might frighten some users!)

Amazon Appstore

The Amazon Mobile App Distribution Program enables developers to make their apps available for sale on any Android device running Android 2.2 and higher. This costs $99 per year, although the first year may be free.
Details from https://developer.amazon.com/help/faq.html
Full terms and conditions from https://developer.amazon.com/help/da.html
To install your app, users need to install an app called "Appstore for Android". It is pre-installed on Kindle Fire devices or can be downloaded from the Amazon website to other Android devices. The sites are
http://www.amazon.co.uk/appstore-web or
http://www.amazon.com/appstore-web

By Email

If you attach your app to an email, when a user running Gmail on Android 4 tries to download the attachment, they will be asked whether they want to install it.

Downloading from a website

If you upload your app to a web-server, then you can publish a link to your app on any web page. If a user clicks the link, it will be saved by their browser, then their device will show a notification (in the status bar at the top of the screen) which they can tap to install the app.

Other App Publishers

Other places you might want to consider publishing your app include the following. You will have to pay to advertise on some of these. Their appearance in this list is NOT meant as an endorsement of these sites:

pandaapp.com (http://download.pandaapp.com/?controller=android)
android.brothersoft.com (http://android.brothersoft.com/)
appsapk.com (http://www.appsapk.com/)
freewarelovers.com (http://www.freewarelovers.com/)
appszoom.com/android (http://www.appszoom.com/android)
androidfreedownload.net (http://www.androidfreedownload.net/)

2.12 Getting More Help

Anywhere Software

The producers of Basic4Android provide an excellent level of service, usually answering queries very rapidly via the Forum (see below). In addition, there is a lively on-line community of enthusiastic Basic4Android developers who not only contribute their own Additional Libraries (page 524), but also support other users by answering questions.
The on-line documentation for Basic4Android is available here (http://www.basic4ppc.com/android/documentation.html).

Forum

The main place to find help and support is http://www.basic4ppc.com/forum/
Here you can find information on updates, get answers to questions and, if you have bought a copy of Basic4Android, download the Additional Libraries.

Chat Room

You can chat live with other Basic4Android enthusiasts and get help and support at http://jonsap.com/b4achat/. When you see the sign-on screen...

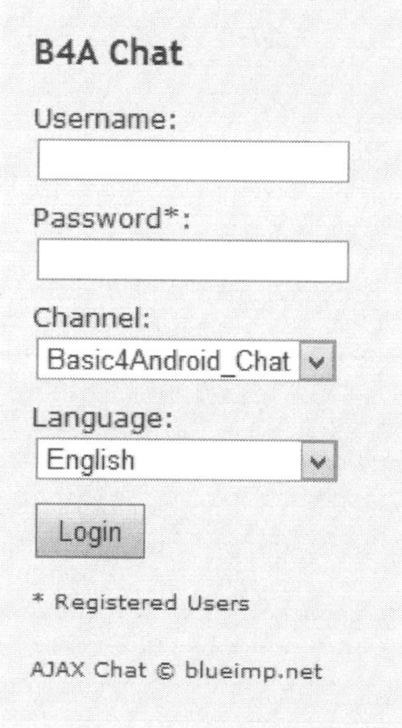

...simply enter a Username. You can enter without a password.

The busiest times are between 17:00 and 00:00 GMT. To convert 17:00 GMT to your local time, you could use http://www.timebie.com/std/gmt.php?q=17

Video Tutorials

Andy McAdam has published several tutorials on YouTube (http://www.youtube.com/amcadam26). Erel Uziel has also put some videos on YouTube (http://bit.ly/15IGy13).

On-Line Tutorials

The Basic4Android website includes many tutorials covering many aspects of developing apps and using the IDE. See here (http://www.basic4ppc.com/search?query=tutorial) for a list. Andy McAdam is a developer who is so keen to help others to use Basic4Android that he has created a website containing tutorials (http://easyandroidcoding.wordpress.com/).

Twitter

Basic4Android has a Twitter account (https://twitter.com/Basic4android) @Basic4Android.

Linked In

There is a small LinkedIn group called Basic4Android Developers.

On-line Documentation

The main on-line source for documentation is: http://www.basic4ppc.com/android/documentation.html

PDF Guides

Although most of the material is covered in this book, you might want to refer to the valuable assistance with using Basic4Android which can be found in the following two guides, written by Klaus Christl: Beginner's Guide (http://www.basic4ppc.com/android/files/guide.zip), a zip file which includes many example programs and a pdf with tutorials; and User's Guide (http://www.basic4ppc.com/android/files/UserGuide.zip) which explains advanced features and also includes example programs and accompanying files.

Library Browsers

The XML files that describe a library to Basic4Android contain descriptions of object members and sometimes an overall description of the library itself and of each object within the library. This information is shown in the online help but is not accessible in the IDE. There are two programs you can download to your PC which will browse through the library XML files:

B4a Object Browser

Vader (http://www.basic4ppc.com/forum/members/vader.html) has produced the B4A Object Browser (http://bit.ly/12RRrcI) (also called the DocLoader Help Documentation) which allows you to browse the help information contained in the XML files in your Basic4Android installation library, similar to the Visual Studio Object Browser. It requires .NET Framework 3.5 and Basic4Android to be installed on your PC.

B4AHelp

B4AHelp is another XML browser program written by Andrew Graham (agraham) which shows this help information. It can be downloaded here (http://bit.ly/13uEAxN).

Part 3: Language and Core Objects

Part 3 includes two chapters of reference material which cover every part of Basic4Android's language and core objects (that is, objects accessible from every app).

We compare Basic4Android's language with Microsoft's Visual Basic.

3.1 Basic4Android's Language

BASIC

Basic4Android is a dialect of BASIC (Beginner's All-purpose Symbolic Instruction Code), a family of high-level programming languages designed to be easy to use. Created in 1964 at a time when writing programs was still technically difficult, BASIC was designed to be easy to use and became widespread as microcomputers were introduced.
Many dialects appeared and the ones written by the young Microsoft were especially popular. The company's Visual Basic is widely used to develop programs for Windows.

Basic4Android

In 2005, Israeli company Anywhere Software created "Basic for PPC", a system for developing apps for Pocket PC computers. In 2010, a version appeared which could create apps for Android devices and this evolved into Basic4Android in 2011.

Lexical Rules

Lexical rules determine how code should be written. Ground rules are:

- Basic4Android is not case sensitive. The editor will automatically change the case of keywords.
- Unlike some languages, a semi-colon(;) is not required at the end of each line. They are simply terminated by a carriage return.

Statement Separator

Two statements can be written on one line by separating them with a colon:

```
Dim intX As Int: If intY > 3 Then intX = 2 Else intX = 9
```

(You might consider your code would be easier to read if such code were placed on separate lines.)

Comments

For many apps, more time is spent maintaining and enhancing the code than was originally spent writing them, so it is essential that they are easy to read and understand. For this purpose, comments are important. They explain the purpose of variables and subs. The single quote is used to add a comment on a line. For example:

```
'Send a POST request with the given file as the post data.
'This method doesn't work with assets files.
Public Sub PostFile(Link As String, Dir As String, FileName As
String)
 If Dir = File.DirAssets Then ' Dir is not valid
  Msgbox("Cannot send files from the assets folder.", "Error")
     Return
 Else
  '...
 End If
End Sub
```

This illustrates some important principles which will help improve the ease of maintenance of your code:

Meaningful names

Choose meaningful names for variables and subs, so their function is clear.

Comments as Documentation

Document your subs by adding comments before them. See here for more information (page 51).

Splitting Long Lines

Long lines of code are difficult to read:

```
Sub dblSecsToJ2000 (intYear As Int, intMonth As Int, intDay As
Int, intHour As Int, intMin As Int, intSec As Int, floLat As
Float, floLong As Float, bRound As Boolean) As Double
```

The underscore character can be used to split long lines. For example:

```
Sub dblSecsToJ2000 ( _
 intYear As Int, intMonth As Int, intDay As Int, _
 intHour As Int, intMin As Int, intSec As Int, _
 floLat As Float, floLong As Float, bRound As Boolean _
) As Double
```

Variables

A **variable** is a symbolic name given to some quantity or information to allow the data to be easily manipulated and changed.

Constants

Unlike Visual Basic, Basic4Android does not allow you to define constants, but you can use a variable as if it were a constant. You might want to use the prefix “const”, or use UPPERCASE names, to remind yourself that this is a constant.

Types

The **type** of a variable is the sort of data which it can contain. The Basic4Android type system is derived directly from the Java type system. There are two types of variables: primitive and non-primitive types.

Primitive Types

These are the fundamental types in Basic4Android.
In the following list of primitive types with their ranges, "~" means "approximately equal to"

Boolean

Type .... boolean
min value................................ FALSE
max value .... TRUE

Byte

Type .... 8 bits (1 byte signed)
min value................................ $-2^{7} = -128$
max value .... $2^{7} - 1 = 127$

Short

Type .... integer 16 bits (2 bytes signed)
min value................................ $-2^{15} = -32768$
max value .... $2^{15} - 1 = 32767$

Int

Type .... integer 32 bits (4 bytes signed)
min value................................ $-2^{31} = -2147483648$
max value .... $2^{31} - 1 = 2147483647$

Long

Type .... long integer 64 bits (8 bytes signed)
min value................................ $-2^{63} = -9,223,372,036,854,775,808$
max value .... $2^{63} - 1 = 9,223,372,036,854,775,807$

Float

Type .... floating point number 32 bits (4 bytes, ~7 digits)
max negative value.................. $-(2 - 2^{-23}) * 2^{127} \sim -3.4028235*10^{38}$
min negative value .... $-2^{-149} \sim -1.4*10^{-45}$
min positive value.................... $2^{-149} \sim 1.4*10^{-45}$
max positive value .... $(2 - 2^{-23}) * 2^{127} \sim 3.4028235*10^{38}$

Double

Type .... double precision number .... 64 bits (8 bytes, ~15 digits)
max negative value.................. $-(2 - 2^{-52}) * 2^{1023} \sim -1.7976931348623157*10^{308}$
min negative value .... $-2^{-1074} \sim -2.2250738585072014*10^{-308}$
min positive value.................... $2^{-1074} \sim 2.2250738585072014*10^{-308}$
max positive value .... $(2 - 2^{-52}) * 2^{1023} \sim 1.7976931348623157*10^{308}$

Char
Type .... character, 2 bytes unsigned

String
Type .... array of characters

Hex Literals
Basic4Android supports the writing of integers in hexadecimal notation, (often shortened to "hex"). For more details about hex, see here (http://en.wikipedia.org/wiki/Hexadecimal).
You must prefix the number with 0x (the 0 is the number zero). Thus you can write

```
Dim iSize As Int
iSize = 0x2C
Log (iSize) ' produces 44
```

Non-Primitive Types
All other types, including arrays (page 216) of primitive types, are categorized as non-primitive types.

Core Types
In the following sections, we give details of the non-primitive types built into Basic4Android; the so-called Core Types.

Reference to Non-Primitives
When you pass a non-primitive to a Sub, or when you assign a non-primitive to a different variable, a copy of the reference is passed. This means that the data itself isn't duplicated. For examples, see below Pass by Reference (page 214).

Type Conversion
In Basic4Android, variable types are automatically converted as needed. For example:

```
Dim str As String
Dim i As Int
i = 3
str = i ' automatic type conversion
Log (str) ' produces 3

' conversion string to int
str = "4"
i = str ' automatic type conversion
Log (i) ' produces 4
```

Note that type conversion does not always work

```
str = "hello"
i = str
```

The last line cannot be executed and produces a runtime error (page 238): NumberFormatException

This problem can be solved by using code like:

```
If IsNumber(str) Then
 i = str
End If
```

Rank

You might sometimes see a compile-time error such as:

```
Cannot cast type: {Type=Int,Rank=0} to: {Type=Int,Rank=1}
```

Rank=0 is a simple variable, Rank=1 means an array (page 216).

Creating Your Own Types

You can create a new type using the Type keyword. See here for details (page 219).

Objects

An Object is a useful concept in computer programming which allows us to represent real-world objects in our code. This helps us to design better and more robust apps. Objects can have attributes (also called properties) and behaviours (also called functions or methods). In Basic4Android, these are collectively called Members.
In addition, an object can respond to user actions by raising Events, which we describe elsewhere (page 233).
For example, a Button has attributes of **`Left`** and **`Top`** (which determine its position on the screen), and it has behaviours which determine how it responds to commands.

```
Dim btn As Button
btn.Initialize("Menu")
btn.Left = 20dip
btn.BringToFront
```

If we are not sure what type of variable we will be dealing with, we can declare a variable to be an Object. An Object can contain any type of variable.

```
Dim objThing As Object
```

Later we can test its type:

```
If objThing Is Bitmap Then
```

If one variable containing an Object is assigned to a second variable, they both refer to the same Object:

```
Dim btnTest As Button
Dim btnCopy As Button
btnCopy = btnTest
```

Now anything you do to btnCopy also affects btnTest. This is an example of passing by reference (page 214).
A collection, such as a **`List`** or a **`Map`**, works with objects and therefore can store any type of data. It is not necessary that all its elements contain the same type. On the other hand, an array (page 216) can store only a single type in all of its elements.

Initialization of Objects

Objects must be initialized (i.e. assigned a value) before use. Otherwise they cannot be used. Consider a button, for example. First we declare it:

```
Sub Globals
 Dim btnAddRoute As Button
End Sub
```

Then we initialize it and declare the event name which will be used to handle its events:

```
Sub Activity_Create(FirstTime As Boolean)
 btnAddRoute.Initialize("GetPath")
End Sub
```

Then we create subs to handle each required event:

```
Sub GetPath_click
 ' do something
End Sub
Sub GetPath_LongClick
 ' do something
End Sub
```

The IDE provides an easy way to create these subs (page 50) and ensures we have the correct arguments.

Declaring Variables

The "declare a variable" means "to tell Android the name, type and (perhaps) number of dimensions of a variable".

Dim Statement

The way you declare a variable is to use the **Dim** statement. The word "Dim" comes from "dimension" because, if you wish to use an array (page 216), it has to be declared and the number of dimensions specified.

In Basic4Android, it is not essential to declare a variable before you use it, but it is good practice to do so. This is a good way to reduce logical errors within your code, because it tells the compiler to only allow values of a specific type to be assigned to that variable. If you do not declare a variable before you use it, Basic4Android assumes it is a **String** type.

Variables are declared with the **Dim** keyword followed by the variable name, the **As** keyword and the variable's **type (page 209)**. If it is an array, the variable name is followed by parentheses enclosing the number of dimensions. Variables can also be initialized when they are declared. Examples:

```
Dim dblCapital As Double
Dim i = 0 As Int
Dim intData(3, 5, 10) As Int
```

Variables of the same type can be declared together with their names separated by commas and followed by the type declaration. They can be initialized at the same time:

```
Dim dblCapital, dblInterest, dblRate As Double
Dim i = 0, j = 2, k = 5 As Int
```

Variables of different types can be declared on the same line:

```
Dim txt As String, value As Double, flag As Boolean
```

However, this can be difficult to read:

```
Dim txt = "test" As String, value = 1.05 As Double, flag = False
As Boolean
```

These might be better spread over several Dim statements. It is usually best to make your code as easy as possible for humans to read and understand, in particular yourself, when you have to maintain your own app!

No Option Explicit

Programmers can sometimes waste time searching for errors caused by mis-spelt variable names. Unlike Microsoft Visual Basic, there is no Option Explicit in Basic4Android. Option Explicit required that all variables were declared using the Dim statement before they were used, but you do not have to declare variables in Basic4Android. Thus the following lines will compile without problem with Basic4Android:

```
Sub Activity_Create(bFirstTime As Boolean)
  intX = 16
  Log (intX)
End Sub
```

Note: the IDE editor highlights an undeclared variable in red (**`intX`** in this case) as a warning, and also puts a message in the Warning Area (page 55), but the code will nevertheless compile.

Note also: **`intX`** will be automatically declared as a **`String`**, which is clearly not the programmer's intention!

Allocating Values

To allocate a value to a variable, write its name followed by the equal sign and followed by the value, like:

```
Capital = 1200
LastName = "SMITH"
```

Note: the values of strings (page 334), such as `LastName`, must be written between double quotes.

Type Checking

The main benefit of declaring a variable is that, if you try to assign the wrong type (page 209) of data to a variable (which indicates a logical error on your part), there will be a run-time error and the program will stop, highlighting the error in the code:

```
Dim myAge, yourAge As Int
myAge = 16
yourAge = "Seventeen"
```

An exception will be raised and shown at the foot of the IDE:

Local variables

FirstTime true
myAge 16
yourAge 0
LastException java.lang.NumberFormatException: Seventeen

Such errors should be caught during testing, if your testing is effective.

Use of Unassigned Variables

Variables, whether declared or not, cannot be used before they are assigned a value. The following (which mis-types the variable name) will produce an error when you try to compile the code:

```
myAge = 16
yourAge = myAg * 2
```

The error produced will be:

```
Error parsing program.
Error description: Undeclared variable 'myag' is used before it
was assigned any value.
Occurred on line: 33
yourAge = myAg * 2
```

Pass by Value

Primitive types are always passed by value to other subs or when assigned to other variables. The alternative, passing a reference to a primitive variable, is not implemented. This means you cannot alter the original value from within a subroutine.

Example:

```
Sub S1
 Dim A As Int
 A = 12
 ' pass a copy of A's value to routine S2
 S2(A)
 Log(A)
 ' Prints 12. This value of A is unchanged
End Sub

Sub S2(A As Int)
 ' This A Is a local copy
 A = 45
 ' Only the value of the local copy is changed
End Sub
```

Pass by Reference

Non-primitive types, such as arrays, are always passed to other subs by reference[1]. For example:

---

1 Technically this is not passing by reference, since only a copy of the reference is passed. You cannot change the reference, only the original object.

```
Sub S1
 Dim A(3) As Int
 A(0) = 12
 ' pass a reference A to routine S2
 S2(A)
 Log(A(0))
 ' Prints 45
End Sub

Sub S2(B() As Int)
 ' This B Is a reference to the original
 B(0) = 45
 ' The original value A(0) is changed
End Sub
```

The same is true when a non-primitive such as an array is assigned to another variable. The second variable is a reference to the first. Example:

```
Dim A(3), B(3) As Int
A(0) = 12
B = A
' B is a reference to A
Log(B(0)) ' prints 12
' Change both A and B
A(0) = 45
Log(B(0)) ' prints 45
```

The same is true for any non-primitive, such as an object:

```
Dim lbl1, lbl2 As Label
lbl1.Initialize("")
lbl2.Initialize("")
lbl1.TextSize = 20
Log (lbl1.TextSize) ' prints 20
lbl2 = lbl1
' lbl2 is a reference to lbl1
' if change lbl2 we also change lbl1
lbl2.TextSize = 40
Log (lbl1.TextSize) ' prints 40
```

Naming of Variables

You must identify your variables by giving them names. A variable name must begin with a letter and must be composed of the following characters: A-Z, a-z, 0-9, and underscore "_". You cannot use spaces, brackets, etc.

Variable names are not case-sensitive. This means that "Index" and "index" refer to the same variable. You cannot use reserved words (keywords listed in this chapter) as variable names. You can use Object types such as Bitmap (but see the note below). Thus:

```
Dim Int As Int              ' this is an error
Dim Bitmap As Bitmap        ' this is OK, although not good
practice
Dim Bitmap1 As Bitmap       ' this is good
Dim bmpMyPhoto As Bitmap ' this is perfect
```

Note: using Object types as variable names (**Bitmap**, for example) is widely regarded as bad practice, since it can cause confusion; for example, the IDE will color-code the variable wrongly. The best practice is to use Hungarian notation (see below).

Hungarian Notation

It can help to remember which type of data a variable needs by using the so-called Hungarian notation. In Hungary (and other cultures), the family name is cited before the given name. So, in variables which use this convention, the first part of the variable's name tells you what type of object you are handling. For example, an integer could be named intMyAge, a string could be called strMyName and so on.
More examples:

```
Dim intAge As Int
Dim strName As String
Dim dblWeight As Double
Dim bMale As Boolean
Dim lblCapital As Label
Dim edtInterest As EditText
Dim btnNext As Button
```

For a suggested list of prefixes, see http://support.microsoft.com/kb/173738

Arrays

An array is a collection of values or objects of the same type. These elements are held within the array in a fixed order and individual elements can be selected by specifying their position using an index number.

Dimensions

Arrays can have multiple dimensions. Think of a one-dimensional array as a row of objects. You pick one of them by counting along the row until you find the one you want. A two-dimensional array is like a chequer-board with each square containing an object. To pick one of them, you must specify two numbers, one for the horizontal position and one for the vertical. This plan can be extended to any number of dimensions, although they get increasing difficult to imagine!

Declaring an Array

A one-dimensional array is declared as follows:

```
Dim strLastName(50) As String
```

The declaration contains the `Dim` keyword followed by the variable name `strLastName`, the dimensions between brackets `(50)`, the keyword `As` and the variable type `String`.
This array can hold a total of 50 Strings.

Other Examples

Two dimensional array of Doubles, total number of items 9:

```
Dim dblMatrix(3, 3) As Double
```

Three dimensional array of integers, total number of items 150:

```
Dim intData(3, 5, 10) As Int
```

Saving and Retrieving Data

To store data in an array, you have to specify at which position you want to store it. You do this by giving an index-number, starting with 0 as the first position.

```
Dim strLastName(2) As String
strLastName(0) = "Jones"
strLastName(1) = "Smith"
```

You can read data from an array if you know its position within the structure. For example, to pick the first item, you would say:

```
Dim strPatient As String
strPatient = strLastName(0)
```

Now strPatient will be `"Jones"`

The first index of each dimension in an array is 0:

```
strLastName(0), dblMatrix(0,0), intData(0,0,0)
```

The last index is equal to the number of items in each dimension minus 1.

```
Dim dblMatrix(3,3) As Double
dblMatrix(2,2) = 1.233
Dim intData(3,5,10) As Int
intData(2,4,9) = 36676
```

The following example shows how to access all items in a three dimensional array:

```
Dim intData(3,5,10) As Int
For i = 0 To 2
 For j = 0 To 4
  For k = 0 To 9
   intData(i,j,k) = i + j + k
  Next
 Next
Next
```

Variable Can Specify Dimensions

The above example demonstrates that you can use variables (i, j and k) to specify the index when you store or retrieve data. You can also use variables to specify the number of elements when you declare an array, as shown in the last line of this code:

```
Dim intFriends As Int
' read number of friends from user input
intFriends = txtNumFriends.Text
' declare array to hold friends names
Dim strLastName(intFriends) As String
```

Filling an array using the Array keyword

An array can be declared without specifying its length:

```
Dim strNames() As String
```

At this point, the **Length** of the array is zero.

```
Log(strNames.Length) ' shows 0
```

The array can then be filled using the Array keyword:

```
strNames = Array As String("Miller", "Smith", "Johnson",
"Jordan")
```

The array now has length of 4.

You can declare and fill an array at the same time:

```
Dim strName() As String = Array As String("a", "b", "c")
```

Arrays of Objects

Views or other objects can be stored in an Array. An example is given in the Shared Event Handler (page 234) section.

Array Dimensions are Fixed

One of the limitations of arrays is that their dimensions are fixed. Once you have created an array, the number of elements it can hold is fixed. You cannot later decide to make it bigger unless you replace it with a new array:

```
strNames = Array As String("Jones", "Windor")
' replace the original data with some new strings
strNames = Array As String("Miller", "Smith", "Johnson",
"Jordan")
```

The array has changed its dimensions but the original data is lost.

This limitation can be overcome by using **Lists** or **Maps**, which allow you to add data to existing structures:

Lists

Lists are similar to arrays but they are dynamic: you can add and remove items from a list and it will change its size accordingly:

```
List1.Add(Value)
```

Lists resemble arrays in that you access their elements by using an index number:

```
number = List1.Get(i)
List1.RemoveAt(12)
```

There are other benefits of using lists. For example, lists can hold any type of object.

A detailed description of all functions is in the List section (page 318).

Maps

A **Map** resembles a **List**, but you access its members not with an index number but with a key. A key can be a string or a number. Like a **List**, a **Map** can store any type of object.

```
Dim mapPerson As Map
Dim photo As Bitmap
...
mapPerson.Put("name", "smith")
mapPerson.Put("age", 23)
mapPerson.Put("photo", photo)
```

More details in the Map section (page 323).

Type variables

The **Type** keyword is used to create your own types or structures. You can use such types to create simple structures that group some values. However, you can also use it to create more complex collections. Define a type with the Type keyword:

```
Sub Process_Globals
 Type Person( _
 LastName As String, FirstName As String, _
 Address As String, City As String _
 )
End Sub
```

We can declare either single variables or arrays of this type:

```
Dim CurrentUser As Person
Dim User(intUsers) As Person
```

To access a particular item, we use the variable name and its data item, separated by a period:

```
CurrentUser.FirstName = "Wyken"
CurrentUser.LastName = "Seagrave"
```

If the variable is an array, then the name is followed by the desired index between parentheses:

```
User(1).LastName = "Seagrave"
```

It is possible to assign a typed variable to another variable of the same type:

```
CurrentUser = User(1)
```

Declaring Types

Types must be declared in Process_Globals.

A Type cannot be private. Once declared, it is available everywhere (similar to Class modules).

Recursive Types

It is possible to use the current type as a type for one of the variable's fields.

```
Sub Process_Globals
 Type Element (NextElement As Element, Val As Int)
 Dim Head As Element 'declare a variable of that type
 Dim Last As Element
End Sub
```

The ability to declare such recursive types is very powerful. The above example could be used for a linked list, as explained in this on-line tutorial (http://bit.ly/13uxb1r)

Initializing a Recursive Type

Before we can access any of the type fields in a recursive type, it should be initialized by calling its Initialize method:

```
Head.Initialize
```

Note: if your type only includes numeric fields and strings, then there is no need to call Initialize (although there is no harm in calling it).

Casting

Casting means changing an object's type (page 209). Basic4Android casts types automatically as needed. It also converts numbers to strings and vice versa automatically. In many cases, you need to explicitly cast an Object to a specific type. For example, you might have an event handler which needs to read data from the object which raised the event. You can get a reference to that object by using the "Sender" keyword, but to use the properties of that object, you must cast it to the correct type. This can be done by assigning the Object to a variable of the required type.

```
Sub Btn_Click
  ' Create an object of the correct type so we can access its
properties
  Dim btn As Button
  ' Copy the Object which raised this event.
  '  This will cast its type to Button
  btn = Sender
  ' Now we can access its properties
  btn.Color = Colors.RGB(Rnd(0, 255), Rnd(0, 255), Rnd(0, 255))
End Sub
```

Visibility and Lifetime of Variables and Subs

This section will cover the rules which determine from where a variable or a sub can be accessed. This is called "visibility" or "scope". We will also discuss how long they endure.
First we will deal with visibility between modules. Then we will explain visibility inside modules.

Visibility Between Modules

There are two access modifiers which determine the visibility of variables and subroutines between modules: `Public` and `Private`. `Public` means that the object can be accessed from other modules as well as the one in which it is declared. **Private** means it is hidden from other modules. You can declare them with:

```
Private intLocal As Int
Public intGlobal As Int
```

Default

The default accessibility is **Public**. Therefore this modifier is not needed:

```
' The following are identical
Dim intGlobal As Int
Public intGlobal As Int
```

You might choose to use **Public** instead of **Dim** if you have a mixture of public and private variables and want the difference to be clear to other programmers (or to yourself in later months).

Sub Process_Globals

Public by Default

Variables defined in **Sub Process_Globals** of activity, service and code modules are public by default, but you can hide them by using the **Private** modifier:

```
Sub Process_Globals
 ' define a variable visible from any module
 Dim strThisIsAPublicVariable As String
 ' define a variable only visible in this module
 Private strThisIsAPrivateVariable As String
End Sub
```

Process_Globals variables are the only public variables.

Lifetimes of Process_Globals Variables

Sub Process_Globals is called once when the process (page 173) starts. This is true for all activities, not just the first activity. Variables declared inside **Sub Process_Globals** live as long as the process lives.

Rotating Device

Note: if you need variables to retain their value after the user rotates the device, you should put the variables in **Process_Globals** and not in **Globals**.

How to Access Process_Globals Variables

To access **Process_Globals** variables in other modules than the module where they were declared, their names must be prefixed by the name of the module they were declared in. Example:

In MyModule

```
'declare the variable
Sub Process_Globals
 Dim MyVar As String
End Sub
...
'use the variable
MyVar = "Text"
```

In OtherModule

```
'use the variable
MyModule.MyVar = "Text"
```

Sub Globals

Always Private

Activity Global Variables

Variables defined in **Sub Globals** of a module are always private within this module and can only be accessed from within the current activity module. All object types can be declared as activity variables. Every time the activity is created, **Sub Globals** is called (before **Activity_Create**). These variables exist as long as the activity exists.

View Variables Must be Here

Views must be declared inside the **Sub Globals**, not **Sub Process_Globals** nor within any other Sub. The reason is as follows. We do not want to hold a reference to objects that should be destroyed together with the activity. When the activity is destroyed, all of the views which are contained in the activity are destroyed as well. If we hold a reference to a **Process_Globals** view, the garbage collector would not be able to free the resource and we will have a memory leak. Therefore, the Basic4Android compiler enforces this requirement! Likewise, views cannot be local variables as such variables only endure while the sub is running, whereas views endure while the activity exists.
Summary: views must be declared inside the **Sub Globals**.

Class_Globals

Variables declared in **Sub Class_Globals** of a class module are public by default, but can be hidden by using the **Private** modifier, as above.

Subroutines

Subs declared in Activity and Service modules are private.
Subs declared in Code modules and Class modules are public by default, but they can be hidden by using the **Private** modifier, so they are visible only in this module:

```
Private Sub ThisIsAPrivateSub(x As Int)
' code here can only be run within this module
End Sub
```

The **Public** modifier can also be used, although it doesn't have any effect.

Running Subs in other modules

CallSub (page 244) and CallSubDelayed (page 244) can be used to call subs in other services, activities and classes. These methods can be used to access both private and public subs.

Variables in Subs

Local variables

Variables that are declared inside a Sub (other than **Process_Globals** or **Globals**) are local to this subroutine. They are "private" and can only be accessed from within the subroutine where they were declared. Once the sub ends, these variables no longer exist. All object types can be declared as local variables. At each call of the subroutine, the local variables are initialized to their default value or to any other value you have defined in the code and are 'destroyed' when the subroutine ends.

Expressions and Operators

An expression is a combination of values, constants, variables, operators, and functions which are combined using operators to produce a value, for example:

```
2 + intAge
strName.Length - 1
```

Mathematical expressions

The mathematical operators ("+", "-" etc) have to be executed in a particular order. This is called their precedence. **Precedence 1 is highest.** Precedence Level is abbreviated PL in the following table:

Operator	Example	PL	Operation
`Power`	`Power(x,y)`	1	Power of, x^y
`Mod`	`x Mod y`	2	Modulo
`*`	`x * y`	2	Multiplication
`/`	`x / y`	2	Division
`+`	`x + y`	3	Addition
`-`	`x - y`	3	Subtraction

Thus, for example, in the expression 4 + 5 * 3 + 2, the multiplication is evaluated first, to produce 4 + 15 + 2, so the returned value is 21.

Power means multiplying a number by itself several times, so Power(2,3) means 2 * 2 * 2.

Mod (short for modulo or modulus) returns the remainder after a division. Thus, 11 Mod 4 is the remainder of 11 / 4, so it returns 3.

Relational Operators

Relational operators compare two values and decide if they are equal, if one is larger than the other, etc. These operators return **True** or **False**.

Operator	Example	Returns **True** if
=	x = y	the two values are equal
<>	x <> y	the two values are not equal
>	x > y	the value of the left expression is greater than that of the right
<	x < y	the value of the left expression is less than that of the right
>=	x >= y	the value of the left expression is greater than or equal to that of the right
<=	x <= y	the value of the left expression is less than or equal to that of the right

Logical Operators

Logical or "Boolean" operators are used to determine whether an expression is **True** or **False**. They are typically used in conditional statements such as **If-Then**. They return values of **True** or **False**

Operator	Example	Returns **True** if
Or	X Or Y	if either X or Y is **True**, or if both are **True**
And	X And Y	**True** only if both X and Y are **True**
Not ( )	Not(X)	**True** only if X is **False**

Regular Expressions

Regular Expressions occur several times in Basic4Android, and provide a very powerful (although not very programmer-friendly) method of specifying a pattern (sometimes very complex) to search for within a string. For example:

- to search for a tab character you would use the expression "\t"
- to match any single character you use a dot "."
- to match one or more characters you would use ".*"

Thus, for example:

- "c.t" would match "cat" and "cot" but not "cart"
- "c.*t" would match "cat", "cot" and "cart" but not "ct"

There are many of these rules. Regular expressions are used in the delimiters of the String Functions Library (http://bit.ly/15HuBDW).

Getting Help with Regular Expressions

For an on-line primer see here (http://docs.activestate.com/komodo/4.4/regex-intro.html).

You can test your expressions on-line using http://gskinner.com/RegExr/

If you need to use regular expressions regularly, I recommend you invest in RegexBuddy (http://www.regexbuddy.com/). It not only provides a tool for creating and testing regular expressions, but it has useful (although not easily digested) tutorials to explain the more abstruse parts of the arcane syntax.

Conditional statements

Different conditional statements are available in Basic4Android.

If – Then – Else – End If

The **`If-Then-Else-End If`** structure allows you to operate conditional tests and execute different code sections according to the test result.
General case:

```
If test1 Then
  ' code1
Else If test2 Then
  ' code2
' more tests are possible
Else
  ' codeN
End If
```

The **`If-Then-Else`** structure works as follows:

- When reaching the line with the **`If`** keyword, "test1" is evaluated. The test can be any kind of conditional test with two possibilities: **`True`** or **`False`**.
- If the test result is **`True`**, then "code1" is executed until the line with the **`Else If`** keyword, then execution jumps to the line following the **`End If`** keyword and continues.
- If the result of test1 is **`False`**, then "test2" is evaluated.
- The same thing is repeated.
- If all tests fail, then the code after the **`Else`** keyword is executed.

Example of If-Then

```
If intA = 20 Then
  intA = intA - 3
End If
```

If only simple code is to be executed when the condition is **`True`**, then it can be placed on the same line as the If statement:

```
If intA = 20 Then intA = intA - 3
```

Note that in this case, the **`End If`** is not needed.

Example of If-Then-Else

```
If intA = 20 Then
  intA = intA - 3
Else
  intA = intA + 1
End If
```

This could be written as

```
If intA = 20 Then intA = intA - 3 Else intA = intA + 1
```

But you might decide that having the structure spread over several lines makes the code more readable.

Differences between Basic4Android and Visual Basic

1. B4A uses **`Else If`** whereas VB uses: **`ElseIf`**
2. The following line is interpreted differently in B4A and VB:

```
If b = 0 Then a = 0: c = 1
```

In B4A this is equivalent to:

```
If b = 0 Then
  a = 0
End If
c = 1
```

But in VB it is:

```
If b = 0 Then
  a = 0
  c = 1
End If
```

Select – Case

The **`Select - Case`** structure allows you to compare a test expression with other expressions and to execute different code sections according to the matches with the test expression:

```
Select TestExpression
  Case ExpressionList1
     ' code1
  Case ExpressionList2
     ' code2
  Case Else
     ' code3
End Select
```

"TestExpression" is any expression or value.
"ExpressionList1" is a list of any expressions or values, separated by commas.
The **`Select - Case`** structure works as follows:

- "TestExpression" is evaluated.
- If one element in the "ExpressionList1" matches "TestExpression", then "code1" is executed and control passes to the line following the **`End Select`** keyword.
- If one element in the "ExpressionList2" matches "TestExpression", then "code2" is executed and control passes to the line following the **`End Select`** keyword.
- If no expression matches "TestExpression", then "code3" is executed and control continues at the line following the **`End Select`** keyword.

Note: the type of each value in each ExpressionList has to be the same as the type of the TestExpression. If not, either a compiletime error or a runtime error will result.
Some examples:

```
Dim intA As Int
intA  = Rnd(1,100)
Select intA
 Case 1, 2, 99
 ' code
 Case 5
 ' code
 Case Else
 ' code
End Select
```

Note: if you accidentally use the same expression in two lists, a compile error is reported. Some more examples:

```
Dim intA  As Int
intA  = Rnd(1,100)
Select intA  < 10
Case True
 Log("small")
Case False
 Log("big")
End Select
'----------
Dim intA, intB  As Int
intA = Rnd(1,100)
intB = Rnd(1,100)
Select intA + intB
Case 1,2,3,4,5
 Log("small")
Case Else
 Log("big")
End Select
'----------
Dim strCode As String
Select strCode
 Case "walk"
 ' code
 Case "run"
 ' code
 Case Else
 ' code
End Select
'----------
Sub Activity_Touch (Action As Int, X As Float, Y As Float)
 Select Action
  Case Activity.ACTION_DOWN
   ' code
  Case Activity.ACTION_MOVE
   ' code
  Case Activity.ACTION_UP
   ' code
```

```
  End Select
End Sub
```

Differences between Basic4Android and Visual Basic:

- B4A uses **Select**, where VB uses **Select Case**.
- B4A allows only a list for example: **Case 1,2,3**, where VB also allows a range for example: **Case 1 To 3**

Loop structures

Various loop structures are available in Basic:

For – Next

In a **For-Next** loop, the same code will be executed a number of times controlled by a variable called an "iterator". For example:

```
For i = 1 To 10 Step 2
  ' your code
Next
```

In this case **i** is the iterator. This is how the code is executed:

- Iterator **i** set to the first value **1** and **your code** will be executed.
- When execution reaches **Next**, execution will return to the **For** statement and **i** will be incremented by the **Step** value **2** to 1+2 or 3.
- If **i** is less than or equal to the upper value **10**, then your code will be executed again.
- This will be repeated until **i** is greater than the upper value
- Control then passes the line after **Next**.

So **your code** in the above example will execute exactly five times, when **i** = 1,3,5,7 and 9.

If the iterator variable **i** was not previously declared, it will be of type **Int**.

Note: the loop limits (in the above case, 1 and 10) might be expressions which depend on variables. In that case, they will only be calculated once, before the first iteration.

Step Value

Note: if the **Step** value is omitted, then it is assumed to be 1, no matter what the starting value of the iterator. So:

```
For i = 1 To 10
```

is the same as

```
For i = 1 To 10 Step 1
```

Step variable can be negative:

```
For i = 10 To 6 Step -1
```

Non-integer Iterators

Note that the iterator (**i** in the above examples) is assumed to be in integer, unless it is declared beforehand. But if declared correctly, then any numeric value can be used as the iterator:

```
Dim i As Float
For i = 1.1 To 1.4 Step 0.1
 ' your code
Next
```

Exit

It is possible to exit a **For-Next** loop with the **Exit** keyword. When code execution meets the **Exit** keyword, it continues on the line after **Next**. The following will log 1-4:

```
For i = 1 To 10
 If i = 5 Then Exit
 Log (i)
Next
```

Continue

If you want to stop executing the current iteration but continue with the next one, use **Continue**. The following will log 1-4 and 6-10, but not 5:

```
For i = 1 To 10
 If i = 5 Then Continue
 Log (i)
Next
```

Differences between Basic4Android and Visual Basic

- B4A uses **Next**, whereas VB uses **Next i**
- B4A uses **Exit**, VB uses **Exit For**

For-Each

For-Each is a variant of the **For-Next** loop, but while **For-Next** is limited to using an integer to control the loop, **For-Each** can use arrays, lists, maps or any other "IterableList" you may create. Example:

```
Dim strName() As String = Array As String("a", "b", "c")
For Each name As String In strName
 Log (name)
Next
```

Each value of strName is assigned, in turn, to the variable name, so the result is:

```
a
b
c
```

An example iterating over a **Map**:

```
Dim balances As Map
balances.Initialize
balances.Put("Fred", 123.45)
balances.Put("Tom", 543.21)
Dim value As Float
For Each Person As String In balances.Keys
 value = balances.Get(Person)
 Log (Person & " has balance " & value)
Next
```

The views in an activity are an IterableList:

```
For Each vw As View In Activity
 ' check its type
 If vw Is Button Then
 ' need object with correct type so
 '  can gain access to properties
 Dim btn As Button
 ' make copy of original view
 btn = vw
 Log (btn.Text)
 End If
Next
```

Do-While

You can loop while a certain condition is **`True`**. For example, this will randomly decrease a number starting with 10000 and log the result while it is greater than 0:

```
Dim i As Int = 10000
Do While i > 0
 ' randomly decrease i
 i = i - Rnd(20, 200)
 Log (i)
Loop
```

`Do-While` is useful if you know the starting condition when the loop starts. For example, when you read a text file. The following reads a text file and uses it as the text for a **`Label`**:

```
Dim lbl As Label
Dim strLines As String
Dim tr As TextReader
tr.Initialize(File.OpenInput(File.DirAssets, "test.txt"))
lbl.Initialize("")

strLines = tr.ReadLine
Do While strLines <> Null
 lbl.Text = lbl.Text & CRLF & strLines
 strLines = tr.ReadLine
Loop
tr.Close
Activity.AddView(lbl, 10dip, 10dip, 100dip, 100dip)
```

Do-While may not be executed

Note: in some languages, such as C, the syntax causes a do-while loop to always be executed at least once, because the condition which controls the loop is not tested until **after** the code is run. For example:

```
// Example of C code
do {
 /* "Hello, world!" is printed at least one time
 even though the condition is false */
 printf( "Hello, world!\n" );
} while ( x != 0 );
```

In Basic4Android, on the other hand, the condition is tested **before** the loop is executed. For example, the following B4A code will produce NO log entries:

```
Dim i As Int = 0
Do While i > 3
 Log (i)
 i = i - 1
Loop
```

Do-Until

Sometimes, we do not know the initial value which we want to use. We only know when we want to stop the loop. In this case, we use the **`Do Until`** loop:

```
i = Rnd(20, 200)
Do Until i <= 0
 ' randomly decrease i
 i = i - Rnd(20, 200)
 Log (i)
Loop
```

Exit a Loop

It is possible to exit either of these Do-Loop structures by using the **`Exit`** keyword.

```
Dim i As Int = 10000
Dim magicNumber As Int = 1234
Do While i > 0
 ' randomly decrease i
 i = i - Rnd(20, 200)
 Log (i)
 If i = magicNumber Then
  Log ("Hit magic number so ending loop")
  Exit
 Else
  Log (i)
 End If
Loop
```

Differences between Basic4Android and Visual Basic

In Visual Basic, the loop type is specified after **`Exit`**, for example, **`Exit Loop`**
In Basic4Android, only **`Exit`** is used.
Visual Basic also accepts the following loops:

```
Do ... Loop While test
Do ... Loop Until test
```

These are NOT supported in Basic4Android.

Subs

A Subroutine ("**Sub**") is a piece of code. It has a distinctive name and a defined visibility (as discussed earlier (page 222)). In Basic4Android, a subroutine is called **Sub**, and is equivalent to procedures, functions, methods and subs in other programming languages. Example:

```
Sub CalcInterest(Capital As Double, Rate As Double) As Double
 Return Capital * Rate / 100
End Sub
```

Using Subs to encapsulate logical units of your code can help it to be more readable and more robust, since you can test each **Sub** separately from all the other code. It is not recommended to have Subs that are too long; they get less readable.

Declaring a Sub

A Sub is declared in the following way:

```
Sub CalcInterest(Capital As Double, Rate As Double) As Double
 ' code goes here
End Sub
```

It starts with the keyword **Sub**, followed by the Sub's name **CalcInterest**, followed by a parameter list enclosed in parentheses **(Capital As Double, Rate As Double)**, followed by the return type **Double**. This is followed by the code which the sub executes. The sub ends with the keywords **End Sub**.

There is no limit on the number of subs you can add to your program, but you are not allowed to have two subs with the same name in the same module.

Subs are always declared at the top level of the module. That is so say, you CANNOT nest two Subs one inside the other.

Naming

For a **Sub**, you can use any name that's legal for a variable (page 215). It is highly recommended to name the **Sub** with a meaningful name so that your code is self-documenting.

Calling a Sub

When you want to execute a Sub in the same module, you simply use the Sub's name.

```
Sub Activity_Resume
 doSomething
End Sub

Sub doSomething
 ' code goes here
End Sub
```

Calling a Sub from another module

A subroutine declared in a code module can be accessed from any other module by prefixing the name of the module where the **Sub** was declared to the name of the sub, joined by a dot:

```
MyModule.mySub
```

Parameters

Input parameters can be transmitted to the Sub. This allows you to make the sub do different things depending on its inputs. The parameter list is enclosed in parentheses, and their types are required:

```
Sub CalcInterest(Capital As Double, Rate As Double) As Double
 Return Capital * Rate / 100
End Sub
```

To invoke a sub which needs parameters, add the parameters to the call:

```
Interest = CalcInterest(1234.56, 3.2)
```

If a sub needs no parameters, then the parentheses are not required when the sub is defined or called:

```
i = getRate
...
Sub getRate
 Return 3
End Sub
```

Returned value

A sub can return a value. This can be any object. Returning a value is done with the **Return** keyword. The type of the return value is defined after the parameter list. So the following will return a **Double**

```
Sub CalcInterest(Capital As Int, Rate As Int) As Double
```

Creating Tooltips for Subs

You can create a tooltip to remind yourself what a Sub does. See Comments As Documentation (page 51) for more information.

Events

In Object-oriented programming, objects can react to things called Events. These could be actions by the user or system-generated events. The number and the type of events an object can raise depends on the type of the object.

Core Object Events

Many Core Objects generate events. Examples are **Animation**, **AudioRecordApp**, **Camera**, **DayDream**, **GameView**, **GPS**, **HTTPClient**, **IME**, **MediaPlayerStream**, **Timer**, etc. Consult the documentation for each of these objects to discover what events they can raise.

Reacting to an Event

To react to an event, you must write a subroutine with the correct name. You must write a **Sub** with the name of the object which is raising the event, followed by an underscore followed by the event name. For example:

```
Sub Timer1_Tick
```

Timer1 is the name of the object which is raising the event. You decide this name when you initialize the object, for example

```
Timer1.Initialize("Timer1", 1000)
```

The **Tick** part of the subroutine name is the name of the event. This is determined by the object itself. You need to consult the object's documentation to discover what events it can raise. Some objects can raise several events.
You must join these two parts of the name together with an underscore _, for example **Timer1_Tick**.
Note: the IDE provides a way of easily autocompleting Event Subroutines (page 50).

Example

To give a concrete example, a **Timer** will run in the background until it has finished its task, then it will raise an event (in this case **Tick**) which your code needs to respond to. For example, **Timer1_Tick** as in the following sample:

```
Sub Process_Globals
 ' declare here so dont get multiple timers when activity
recreated
 Dim Timer1 As Timer
End Sub

Sub Globals
End Sub

Sub Activity_Create(FirstTime As Boolean)
 ' make the timer last 1000 milliseconds
 Timer1.Initialize("Timer1", 1000)
 ' start the timer
 Timer1.Enabled = True
End Sub

Sub Timer1_Tick
 ' timer has ended
 Log ("Timer finished")
End Sub
```

Shared Event Handler

You can use a single Sub to handle the events of many objects. For example, you might have several buttons, all of which perform a similar function, so you only need a single event handler. You can determine which object raised the event by using the **Sender** keyword. The following produces a column of buttons labeled Test 1 to Test 7, all of which share the same handler **Buttons_Click**:

```
Sub Globals
 Dim b1, b2, b3, b4, b5, b6, b7 As Button
 Dim Buttons() As Button
End Sub

Sub Activity_Create(FirstTime As Boolean)
 ' index to handle buttons
 Dim i As Int
 Buttons = Array As Button(b1, b2, b3, b4, b5, b6, b7)

 For i = 0 To 6
 ' all buttons share same event handler
 Buttons(i).Initialize("Buttons")
 ' use index to position buttons correctly
 Activity.AddView(Buttons(i), 10dip, 10dip + i * 60dip, 150dip,
50dip)
 ' add tag so can identify which button this is
 Buttons(i).Tag = i + 1
 Buttons(i).Text = "Test " & (i + 1)
 Next
End Sub

Sub Buttons_Click
 ' event handler for all buttons
 Dim btn As Button
 btn = Sender
 Activity.Title = "Button " & btn.Tag & " clicked"
End Sub
```

View Events

Many events are raised by Views (page 395) which are handled by your code in the same way as Core Object Events. The Designer is able to generate the skeleton subs (page 93) for you, such as:

```
Sub btnTest_Click
  ' add your code here
End Sub
```

Here is a summary of the events for different views:

Views	Events														
	Click	LongClick	Touch	Down	Up	KeyPress	ItemClick	ItemLongClick	CheckedChange	EnterPressed	FocusChanged	TextChanged	ValueChanged	TabChanged	PageFinished
Activity	■	■	■			■									
Button	■	■		■	■										
CheckBox									■						
EditText										■	■	■			
ImageView	■	■													
Label	■	■													
ListView							■	■							
Panel	■	■	■												
RadioButton									■						
SeekBar													■		
Spinner							■								
TabHost	■	■												■	
ToggleButton									■						
WebView															■

Commonest View Events

The most common events are as follows. Note that the events supported vary with the type of view:

Click

Event raised when the user clicks on the view. Example:

```
Sub Button1_Click
  ' Your code
End Sub
```

LongClick

Event raised when the user clicks on the view and holds it pressed for about one second. Example:

```
Sub Button1_LongClick
  ' Your code
End Sub
```

Touch(Action As Int, X As Float, Y As Float)

Event raised when the user touches the screen.
Three different actions are handled:

- Activity.Action_DOWN: the user touches the screen.
- Activity.Action_MOVE: the user moves the finger without leaving the screen.
- Activity.Action_UP: the user stops touching the screen.

The X and Y coordinates of the finger position are given. Example:

```
Sub Activity_Touch (Action As Int, X As Float, Y As Float)
 Select Action
 Case Activity.ACTION_DOWN
  ' Your code for DOWN action
 Case Activity.ACTION_MOVE
  ' Your code for MOVE action
 Case Activity.ACTION_UP
  ' Your code for UP action
 End Select
End Sub
```

CheckChanged (Checked As Boolean)

Event raised when the user clicks on a **CheckBox** or a **RadioButton**.
Checked is equal to **True** if the view is checked or **False** if not checked.
Example:

```
Sub CheckBox1_CheckedChange(Checked As Boolean)
 If Checked = True Then
  ' Your code if CheckBox1 is checked
 Else
  ' Your code if CheckBox1 is not checked
 End If
End Sub
```

KeyPress (KeyCode As Int) As Boolean

This event (which only belongs to the **Activity** object) is raised when the user presses a physical or virtual key (except the Home key, which calls **Activity_Pause**).
KeyCode is the code of the pressed key, you can get a list of them in the IDE by typing **KeyCodes** and a dot:

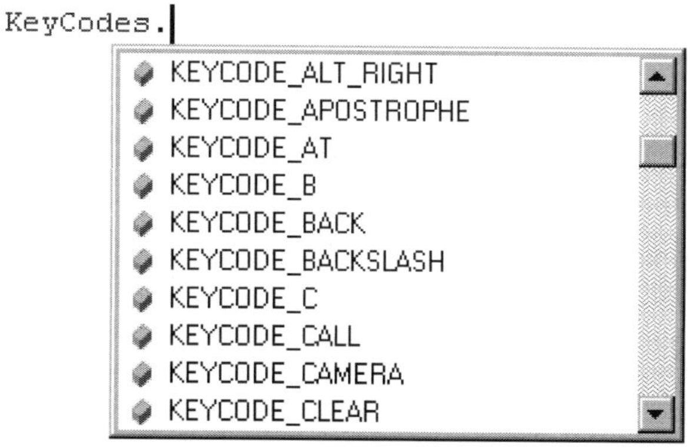

```
KeyCodes.
  KEYCODE_ALT_RIGHT
  KEYCODE_APOSTROPHE
  KEYCODE_AT
  KEYCODE_B
  KEYCODE_BACK
  KEYCODE_BACKSLASH
  KEYCODE_C
  KEYCODE_CALL
  KEYCODE_CAMERA
  KEYCODE_CLEAR
```

The **KeyPress** event returns either **True**, in which case the event is consumed and never seen by the operating system, or **False**, in which case the event is transmitted to the system for further action.
Example:

```
Sub Activity_KeyPress(KeyCode As Int) As Boolean
 ' Confirm user wants to quit if press back key
 Dim Answ As Int
 Dim Txt As String

 ' Check if KeyCode is BackKey
 If KeyCode = KeyCodes.KEYCODE_BACK Then
  ' Confirm user wants to quit
  Txt = "Do you really want to quit the program ?"
  Answ = Msgbox2(Txt, "A T T E N T I O N", "Yes", "", "No",
Null)
  If Answ = DialogResponse.POSITIVE Then
   ' User wants to quit
   Return False
  Else
   ' Do not quit
   Return True
  End If
 End If
End Sub
```

Error Handling

Runtime Errors

Some errors are caught by the compiler, but some more subtle errors are only revealed when the code runs. Such a "runtime error" is produced by the following example:

```
Dim str As String
Dim i As Int
str = "hello"
i = str
```

The last line produces a runtime error because Java (which is what Android uses) cannot convert a non-numeric string to a number.

Exceptions

When a runtime error occurs, a Java language Exception (page 303) is raised. You can add Try-Catch code to your app to handle Exceptions. If you have not added this code when an Exception occurs, the program stops and an error is shown on the device or emulator, as described next.

Uncaught Runtime Exceptions

If a runtime error occurs outside a Try-Catch block, what the user sees will depend on how you have distributed the app. If you distribute your application directly with an apk file and it crashes without any error handling, the user will see an error crash report and asked if they wish to continue.

On the other hand, if you distribute via Google Play, when your application crashes outside a **Try-Catch** block, the user will be asked to send a crash report. This happens automatically. You can see the reports in Google Play Developer Console.

Try-Catch

Basic4Android provides a mechanism to handle runtime errors, called a **Try-Catch** block. Example:

```
Try
  'block of statements
Catch
  Log(LastException.Message)
  'handle the problem if necessary
End Try
```

Now when the Exception occurs in the **Try** block, control moves to the **Catch** block. Your program can take steps to handle the problem.

When to use a Try-Catch

Try-Catch should not be used to protect from programming mistakes. You should make sure your code is logically and syntactically correct by testing before distribution.

Try-Catch should only be used when there might be a problem which you cannot control. For example, when you parse a downloaded feed, the feed itself might have problems. Or when you try to update a database using a Transaction (page 168) and there is a problem. For example:

```
SQL.BeginTransaction
Try
 'block of statements
 For i = 1 To 10
 SQL.ExecNonQuery2("INSERT INTO demo VALUES (?,?)", Array As
Object(i, "Tom Brown"))
 Next
 SQL.TransactionSuccessful
Catch
 Log(LastException.Message) 'no changes will be made
End Try
SQL.EndTransaction
```

Try-Catch is of use mainly during development.

Note: if an error is caught in the middle of a large subroutine, you cannot make a correction and resume within the code you were executing. Only the code in the **Catch** block gets executed.

String manipulation

Basic4Android allows string manipulations like other Basic languages, but with some differences. These manipulations can be done directly on a string.

Example:

```
strTxt = "123,234,45,23"
strTxt = strTxt.Replace(",", ";")
```

Result: `123;234;45;23`

Mutable Strings

Repetitive manipulation of strings can be very slow. Since they are immutable (page 334), a new string has to be created every time you want to change a string. If you are doing extensive string manipulation, you should consider using StringBuilder (page 337).

The String functions

Here we list the string functions. For more details, see below (page 334).

CharAt(Index)

Returns the character at the position given by **Index**, where the first character is at 0.

CompareTo(Other)

Lexicographically compares the string with the **Other** string.

Contains(SearchFor)

Returns **True** if the string contains the given **SearchFor** string.

EndsWith(Suffix)

Returns **True** if the string ends with the given **Suffix** substring.

EqualsIgnoreCase(Other)

Returns **True** if both strings are equal ignoring their case. Example:

```
If firstString.EqualsIgnoreCase("Abc") Then
```

GetBytes(Charset)

Encodes the `Charset` string into a new array of bytes.

IndexOf(SearchFor)

Returns the index of the first occurrence of `SearchFor` in the string, or `-1` if not found.

IndexOf2(SearchFor, Index)

Returns the index of the first occurrence of `SearchFor` in the string, or `-1` if not found. Starts searching from the given `Index`.

LastIndexOf(SearchFor)

Returns the index of the first occurrence of SearchFor in the string, or `-1` if not found. Starts searching from the end of the string.

Length

Returns the number of characters in the string.

Replace(Target, Replacement)

Returns a new string resulting from the replacement of all the occurrences of Target with Replacement.

StartsWith(Prefix)

Returns `True` if this string starts with the given `Prefix`.

Substring(BeginIndex)

Returns a new string which is a substring of the original string. The new string will include the character at `BeginIndex` and will extend to the end of the string.

Substring2(BeginIndex,EndIndex)

Returns a new string which is a substring of the original string. The new string will include the character at `BeginIndex` and will extend to the character before `EndIndex`.

ToLowerCase

Returns a new string which is the result of lower casing this string.

ToUpperCase

Returns a new string which is the result of upper casing this string.

Trim

Returns a copy of the original string without any leading or trailing white spaces.

Number formatting

Numbers can be displayed as strings with different formats. There are two keywords: `NumberFormat` and `NumberFormat2`.

NumberFormat (page 255) (Number As Double, MinimumIntegers As Int, MaximumFractions As Int)

Follow the link for the meaning of the arguments. Examples:

```
NumberFormat(12345.6789, 0, 2)
' produces 12,345.68
NumberFormat(1, 3 ,0)
' produces 001
NumberFormat(Value, 3 ,0)
' variables can be used.
NumberFormat(Value + 10, 3 ,0)
' arithmetic operations can be used.
NumberFormat((lblscore.Text + 10), 0, 0)
' parentheses needed If one variable Is a String.
```

NumberFormat2 (page 255)(Number As Double, MinimumIntegers As Int, MaximumFractions As Int, MinimumFractions As Int, GroupingUsed As Boolean)

Follow the link for the meaning of the arguments. Example:

```
NumberFormat2(12345.67, 0, 3, 3, True)
' This will produce "12,345.670".
```

Keywords

In this section we list alphabetically the keywords used by Basic4Android and define their functions. We list separately the objects (page 270) which are included in the core of the language.

Abs (Number As Double) As Double

Returns the absolute value of a number, that is, the value of the number but with negative numbers changed to positive. Thus both of the following produce 123.45:

```
Log (Abs(123.45))
Log (Abs(-123.45))
```

ACos (Value As Double) As Double

Given a cosine, this function returns the angle, measured as radians. Thus

```
Log (ACos(0.5))
```

will produce 1.0471975511965979 since 60° is just over 1 radian.

ACosD (Value As Double) As Double

Given a cosine, this returns the angle measured in degrees. Thus

```
Log (ACosD(0.5))
```

will produce 60 (or something very close).

Array

Creates a one-dimensional array of the specified type.
The syntax is: Array As type (list of values).
Example

```
Dim Days() As String
Days = Array As String("Sunday", "Monday", ...)
```

See Arrays (page 216) for more details.

Asc (Char As Char) As Int

Returns the unicode code point (http://bit.ly/10alZFl) of the given character or first character in the given string. Thus, `Log (Asc("A"))` and `Log (Asc("ABC"))` will both produce 65. See http://unicode-table.com/en/ for a list of characters and their codes.

ASin (Value As Double) As Double

Given the sine of an angle, this function returns the angle measured in radians.

ASinD (Value As Double) As Double

Given the sine of an angle, this function returns the angle measured in degrees.

ATan (Value As Double) As Double

Given the tangent of an angle, this function returns the angle measured in radians. Thus, the following returns 0.7853981633974483

```
Log (ATan(1))
```

ATan2 (Y As Double, X As Double) As Double

Given the opposite Y and adjacent X sides of a right-triangle, this function returns the tangent of the angle measured in radians. Thus, `Log (ATan2(1,1))` returns 0.7853981633974483

ATan2D (Y As Double, X As Double) As Double

Given the opposite Y and adjacent X sides of a right-triangle, this function returns the angle measured in degrees. Thus, `Log (ATan2D(1,1))` returns 45

ATanD (Value As Double) As Double

Given the tangent of an angle, this function returns the angle measured in degrees. Thus, `Log (ATanD(1))` returns 45

BytesToString (Data() As Byte, StartOffset As Int, Length As Int, CharSet As String) As String

Decodes the given byte array as a string.
Data - The byte array.
StartOffset - The first byte to read.
Length - Number of bytes to read.
CharSet - The name of the character set. See Text Encoding (page 304) for details.
The following example will produce ABCDE:

```
Dim Buffer() As Byte = Array As Byte(65,66,67,68,69)
Dim str As String
str = BytesToString(Buffer, 0, Buffer.Length, "UTF-8")
Log (str)
```

CallSub (Component As Object, Sub As String) As String

CallSub allows an activity to call a Sub in a service module or a service to call a Sub in an activity. CallSub can also be used to call subs in the current module. Pass an empty string as the component in that case.
Component - name of a module. Should not be a string.
Sub – name of Sub to call. Must be a string.

Example

```
CallSub(Main, "RefreshData")
```

Restrictions

A sub will only be called if the called module is not paused. But if it is paused, an empty string will be returned. This is why one activity cannot call a sub of a different activity since the other activity will certainly be paused. You can use **IsPaused** to test whether a module is paused.
Nor is it possible to use this function to call Subs of code modules. To call a Sub in a code module, use a call like **moduleName.subName**.

CallSub2 (Component As Object, Sub As String, Argument As Object) As String

Similar to **CallSub**. Calls a sub with a single argument.

CallSub3 (Component As Object, Sub As String, Argument1 As Object, Argument2 As Object) As String

Similar to **CallSub**. Calls a sub with two arguments.

CallSubDelayed (Component As Object, Sub As String)

CallSubDelayed is a combination of **StartActivity**, **StartService** and **CallSub**.
Unlike CallSub (which only works with currently running components), CallSubDelayed will first start the target component if needed.
CallSubDelayed can also be used to call subs in the current module. Instead of calling these subs directly, a message will be sent to the message queue.
The sub will be called when the message is processed. This is useful in cases where you want to do something "right after" the current sub (usually related to UI events).
Note: if you call an Activity while the whole application is in the background (no visible activities), the sub will be executed once the target activity is resumed.

CallSubDelayed2 (Component As Object, Sub As String, Argument As Object)

Similar to CallSubDelayed. Calls a sub with a single argument.

CallSubDelayed3 (Component As Object, Sub As String, Argument1 As Object, Argument2 As Object)

Similar to **CallSubDelayed**. Calls a sub with two arguments.

CancelScheduledService (Service As Object)

Cancels previously scheduled tasks for this service.

Catch

Any exception thrown inside a **Try** block will be caught in the **Catch** block.
Call LastException to get the caught exception. See Try-Catch (page 239) for details.
Syntax

```
Try
...
Catch
...
End Try
```

cE As Double

e (natural logarithm base) constant, approximately 2.718281828459045

Ceil (Number As Double) As Double

Returns the smallest whole number that is greater than or equal to the specified number. Thus, **Ceil(4.321)** will return 5. The word is an abbreviation of "ceiling". For the opposite function, see Floor (page 248).

CharsToString (Chars() As Char, StartOffset As Int, Length As Int) As String

Creates a new String by copying the characters from the array **Chars()**.
Copying starts from **StartOffset** and the number of characters copied is specified by **Length**. The following will produce "cd":

```
Dim chars() As Char
chars = Array As Char("a", "b", "c", "d", "e")
Log (CharsToString(chars, 2,2))
```

Chr (UnicodeValue As Int) As Char

Returns the character that is represented by the given unicode value. Thus, **Log (Chr(65))** will produce "A". See http://unicode-table.com/en/ for a list of characters and their codes.

ConfigureHomeWidget (LayoutFile As String, EventName As String, UpdateIntervalMinutes As Int, WidgetName As String) As RemoteViews

At compile time, the compiler generates the required XML files based on the arguments of this keyword. At runtime, this command creates a **RemoteViews** object based on the **LayoutFile**. Note that all parameters must be strings or numbers (not variables) so they can be read by the compiler.

LayoutFile - The widget layout file.

EventName - Sets the **Sub** that will handle events from **RemoteViews**, such as **RequestUpdate** event in the example below.

UpdateIntervalMinutes - Sets the update interval in minutes. Pass **0** to disable automatic updates. Otherwise, the minimum value is 30.

WidgetName - The name of the widget as it appears in the widgets list.

Example

```
Sub Process_Globals
 Dim rv As RemoteViews
End Sub

Sub Service_Create
 rv = ConfigureHomeWidget("LayoutFile", "rv", 0, "Widget Name")
End Sub

Sub rv_RequestUpdate
 rv.UpdateWidget
End Sub
```

Reference

See here for more information (page 83) about Widgets.

Continue

Stops executing the current iteration and continues with the next one. The following will log 1-4 and 6-10 but not 5:

```
For i = 1 To 10
 If i = 5 Then Continue
 Log (i)
Next
```

Compare to Exit.

Cos (Radians As Double) As Double

Calculate the cosine of the angle given in radians.

CosD (Degrees As Double) As Double

Calculate the cosine of the angle given in degrees.

cPI As Double

The constant PI, approximately 3.141592653589793

CRLF As String

The line feed character whose value is Chr(10).
Note: The name CRLF sometimes causes confusion. Despite its name, this is NOT the combination of
CR = Carriage Return = Chr(13) and LF = Line Feed =Chr(10)
which Windows uses in its documents! Android is a Linux-based system in which lines are terminated just by a LF.

Density As Float

Returns the screen's density, which is number of dots per inch / 160.
More information about the screen can be found using GetDeviceLayoutValues

Dim

Declares a variable.
To declare a single variable:
Dim variable name [As type]

```
Dim intSize As Int
```

The default type is String.

To declare and initialize a single variable, two alternatives are possible:
Dim variable name [As type] [= expression]
Dim variable name [= expression] [As type]

```
Dim intA As Int = 1
Dim intB = 2 As Int
```

To declare multiple variables, all of the same type:
Dim variable1 [= expression], variable2 [= expression], ..., [As type]

```
Dim intA, intB, intC As Int
Dim intA = 1, intB = 2, intC = 3 As Int
```

Declare an array and specify the size of each dimension:
Dim variable(size1, size2, ...) [As type]

```
Dim strDayNames(7) As String
```

The size can be omitted for zero length arrays:

```
Dim payments() As Long
Log(payments.Length) ' this will produce 0
```

DipToCurrent (Length As Int) As Int

DipToCurrent(Length as Int) scales Length given in dips (page 110). For example, the following code will set the width value of an EditText to be 1 inch wide on all devices.

```
EditText1.Width = DipToCurrent(160)
```

Note: a shorthand syntax for this method is available. Any number followed by the string dip (page 110) will be converted in the same manner (no spaces are allowed between the number and "dip").
So the previous code is equivalent to

```
EditText1.Width = 160dip
```

DoEvents

Processes waiting messages in the message queue. DoEvents can be called inside lengthy loops to allow your app to update the screen. Other waiting events will not be handled by DoEvents.

Exit

Exits the inner -most loop. The following will log 1-4:

```
For i = 1 To 10
 If i = 5 Then Exit
 Log (i)
Next
```

Compare to Continue.

ExitApplication

Immediately ends the application and stops the process. Most applications should not use this method, with the use of **`Activity.Finish`** being the preferred method to allow Android to decide when the process will be killed. See Activity.Finish vs ExitApplication (page 178) for a discussion.

False As Boolean

A constant which can be used to compare or set logical values, for example:

```
#Region  Activity Attributes
 #FullScreen: False
 #IncludeTitle: True
#End Region
```

File As File

File-related methods. See the File Object (page 306) for details of its members and here (page 303) for a discussion of its usage.

Floor (Number As Double) As Double

Returns the largest whole number that is smaller than or equal to the specified number. Thus, `Floor(123.456)` is 123.
For the opposite function, see Ceil (page 245).

For

Begins a loop controlled by a variable called an "iterator". Syntax:

```
For variable = value1 To value2 [Step interval]
  ...
Next
```

Step is optional. If not specified it defaults to 1. Example:

```
For i = 1 To 10
  Log(i) 'Will print 1 to 10 (inclusive).
Next
```

If the iterator variable **i** was not previously declared, it will be of type **Int**.

Note: the loop limits will only be calculated once, before the first iteration.

For Each

Iterates a loop over an IterableList. Syntax:

```
For Each variable As Type In collection
  ...
Next
```

Examples

```
Dim strName() As String = Array As String("a", "b", "c")
For Each name As String In strName
  Log (name)
Next

For Each vw As View In Activity
  If vw Is Button Then
  ...
  End If
Next
```

GetDeviceLayoutValues As LayoutValues

Returns the device LayoutValues (page 317). For example:

```
Dim lv As LayoutValues
lv = GetDeviceLayoutValues
Log(lv)
Dim scale As Float
scale = lv.Scale
```

This will print the following line to the log:

320 x 480, scale = 1.0 (160 dpi)

GetType (object As Object) As String

Returns a string representing the object's java type.

If

Single line

```
If condition Then true-statement [Else false-statement]
```

Multiline

```
If condition Then
 statements
 ...
Else If condition Then
 statements
 ...
Else
 statements
 ...
End If
```

InputList (Items As List, Title As String, CheckedItem As Int) As Int

Shows a modal dialog with a list of items and radio buttons. Pressing on an item will close the dialog and return the index of the selected item or **`DialogResponse.Cancel`** if the user pressed on the **Back** key.

List - Items to display.

Title - Dialog title.

CheckedItem - The index of the item that will be preselected. If you want the top item to be selected, set this to **`0`**. Pass **`-1`** if no item should be preselected.

Example which makes a label act like a spinner (page 384):

```
Sub tgtLabel_Click
 Dim myarray(4) As String
 myarray(0)="January"
 myarray(1)="February"
 myarray(2)="March"
 myarray(3)="May"
 choice = InputList(myarray, "Select Month", 1)
 tgtlabel.Text = myarray(choice)
End Sub
```

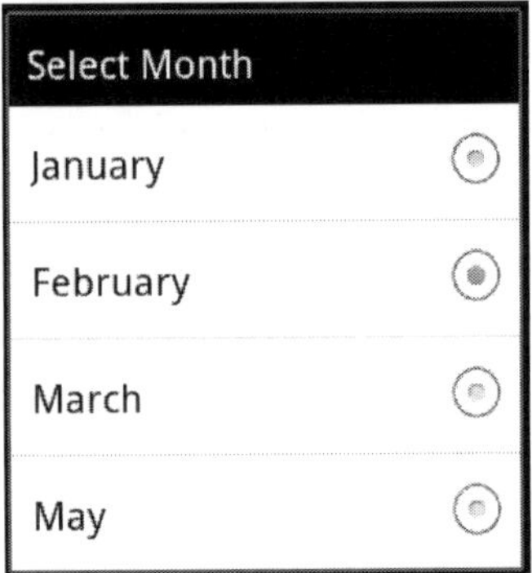

InputMap (Items As Map, Title As String)

Shows a modal dialog with a title, a list of items and checkboxes, and an **Ok** button . The user can select multiple items. The dialog closes when the user presses **Ok** or the **Back** button.

The text displayed are the keys of the **Items** map. The values of this map determine whether they are checked. Items with a value of **`True`** will be checked.

When the user checks or unchecks an item, the related item value gets updated.

The updated values are returned whether the user presses **Ok** or **Back**.

Items - A map object with the items as keys and their checked state as values.

Example:

```
Dim m As Map
m.Initialize
m.Put("Apples", True)
m.Put("Bananas", False)
m.Put("Mangos", False)
m.Put("Oranges", True)
InputMap(m, "Select all the fruits you want")
```

The InputMap looks something like this:

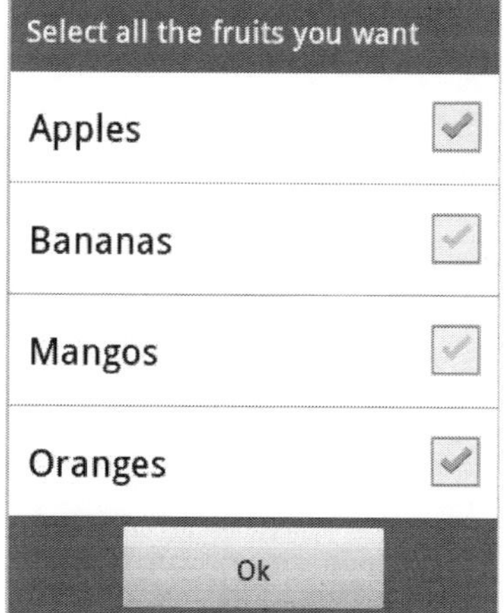

Its exact appearance will vary, depending on the device and the version of Android running.

InputMultiList (Items As List, Title As String) As List

Shows a modal dialog with a title, a list of items and checkboxes, and an **Ok** button. The user can select multiple items. The dialog is closed when the user presses **Ok** or **Back**.

If the user presses **Ok**, it returns a list with the indices of the selected items, sorted in ascending order.

It returns an empty list if the user has pressed on the **Back** key.

```
Dim choice As Int
Dim lstInput, lstOutput As List
lstInput.Initialize2(Array As String("Apples", "Bananas",
"Mangos", "Oranges"))
lstOutput = InputMultiList (lstInput, "Select all the fruits you
want")
For Each index As Int In lstOutput
 Log (index)
Next
```

The **InputMultiList** will appear to the user as:

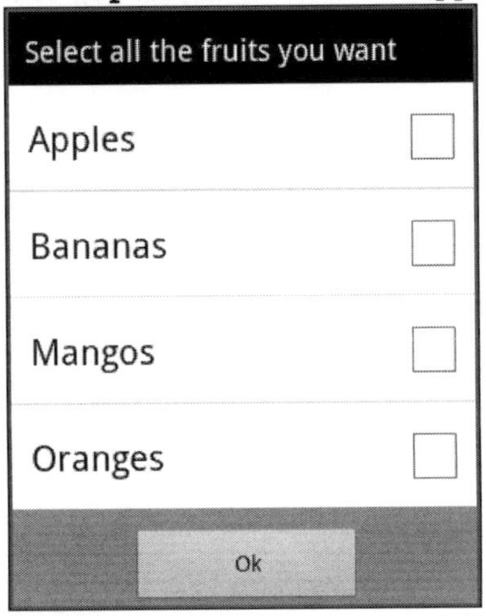

Select all the fruits you want

Apples

Bananas

Mangos

Oranges

Ok

If Bananas and Oranges are selected, the numbers 1 and 3 will be logged.

Is

Returns **TRUE** if the object is of the given type. Example:

```
For i = 0 To Activity.NumberOfViews - 1
If Activity.GetView(i) Is Button Then
 Dim b As Button
 b = Activity.GetView(i)
 b.Color = Colors.Blue
End If
Next
```

IsBackgroundTaskRunning (ContainerObject As Object, TaskId As Int) As Boolean

Returns **TRUE** if a background task is running which was submitted by the container object and with the specified id. Example:

```
Dim hc As HttpClient
Dim req As HttpRequest
Dim TaskID As Int = 1

req.InitializePost2("http://abc.com/query.php",
Query.GetBytes("UTF8"))
hc.Execute(req, TaskId)

If IsBackgroundTaskRunning(hc, TaskId) Then
 ToastMessageShow("Wait for previous call to finish.", False)
End If
```

IsNumber (Text As String) As Boolean

Returns **TRUE** if the specified string can be converted to a number.

IsPaused (Component As Object) As Boolean

Returns **TRUE** if the given component is paused. Will also return **True** for components that were not started yet. Example:

```
If IsPaused(Main) = False Then CallSub(Main, "RefreshData")
```

LastException As Exception

Returns the last exception (page 303) that was caught (if such exists). If there has not been an exception, **LastException** will be uninitialized. Thus you should only check for **LastException** inside the **Catch** block of a Try-Catch (page 239). Example:

```
Try
 'block of statements
Catch
 Log(LastException.Message)
 'handle the problem if necessary
End Try
```

LoadBitmap (Dir As String, FileName As String) As Bitmap

Loads the bitmap (page 289). **Note**: the Android file system is case sensitive. You should consider using LoadBitmapSample if the image size is large. The actual file size is not relevant as images are usually stored compressed. Example:

```
Activity.SetBackgroundImage(LoadBitmap(File.DirAssets,
"SomeFile.jpg"))
```

LoadBitmapSample (Dir As String, FileName As String, MaxWidth As Int, MaxHeight As Int) As Bitmap

Loads the bitmap (page 289). The decoder will sub-sample the bitmap if either MaxWidth or MaxHeight is smaller than the bitmap dimensions. This can save a lot of memory when loading large images. The width / height ratio is preserved. Example:

```
Activity.SetBackgroundImage(LoadBitmapSample(File.DirAssets,
"SomeFile.jpg", Activity.Width, Activity.Height))
```

Log (Message As String)

Logs a message. When debugging, the log can be viewed in the Logs tab. When the app is released, this command has no effect.

Logarithm (Number As Double, Base As Double) As Double

The power you need to raise Base to in order to create Number. Examples:
`Logarithm(10,10) is 1, Logarithm(8,2) is 3 and Logarithm(100,10) is 2.`

Max (Number1 As Double, Number2 As Double) As Double

Returns the larger number of two numbers.

Me As Object

For classes: returns a reference to the current instance.
For activities and services: returns a reference to an object that can be used with CallSub, CallSubDelayed and SubExists keywords. Example:

```
CallSub(Me, "test")
```

Cannot be used in code modules.

Min (Number1 As Double, Number2 As Double) As Double

Returns the smaller of two numbers.

Msgbox (Message As String, Title As String)

Shows a modal message box with the specified message and title.
The dialog will show one OK button.
Example:

```
Msgbox("Hello world", "This is the title")
```

See Modal Dialogs (page 85) for more.

Msgbox2 (Message As String, Title As String, Positive As String, Cancel As String, Negative As String, Icon As Bitmap) As Int

Shows a modal message box with the specified message and title.
Message - The dialog message.
Title - The dialog title.
Positive - The text to show for the "positive" button. Pass "" if you don't want to show the button.
Cancel - The text to show for the "cancel" button. Pass "" if you don't want to show the button.
Negative - The text to show for the "negative" button. Pass "" if you don't want to show the button.

Icon - A bitmap that will be drawn near the title. Pass Null if you don't want to show an icon.
Returns one of the DialogResponse values. Example:

```
Dim bmp As Bitmap
Dim choice As Int
bmp.Initialize(File.DirAssets, "question.png")
choice = Msgbox2("Would you like to select a route?", "Please
specify your choice", "Yes please", "", "No thank you", bmp)
If choice = DialogResponse.POSITIVE Then ...
```

See Modal Dialogs (page 85) for more.

Not (Value As Boolean) As Boolean

Inverts the value of the given boolean. Example:

```
If Not (startMarker.IsInitialized) Then
```

Null As Object

The value of an object which does not exist. It will be returned, for example, if you try to access a non-existent key in a map. In the following, **obj** has the value null:

```
Dim m As Map
m.Initialize
Dim obj As Object
obj = m.Get("test")
If obj = Null Then …
```

NumberFormat (Number As Double, MinimumIntegers As Int, MaximumFractions As Int) As String

Converts **Number** to a string with at least **MinimumIntegers** integer digits and at most **MaximumFractions** decimal digits. Examples:

```
NumberFormat(12345.6789, 0, 2) '12,345.68
NumberFormat(1, 3 ,0)          '001
```

NumberFormat2 (Number As Double, MinimumIntegers As Int, MaximumFractions As Int, MinimumFractions As Int, GroupingUsed As Boolean) As String

Converts **Number** to a string with at least **MinimumIntegers**, at most **MaximumFractions** decimal digits and at least **MinimumFractions** decimal digits.
GroupingUsed - Determines whether to group every three integers. Example:

```
NumberFormat2(12345.67, 0, 3, 3, false) ' 12345.670
NumberFormat2(12345, 0, 2, 2, True)     ' 12,345.00
```

PerXToCurrent (Percentage As Float) As Int

Returns the actual size of the given percentage of the activity width.
Example: set the width of Button1 to 50% of the width of the current activity:

```
EditText1.Width = PerXToCurrent(50)
```

A shorthand syntax for this method is available. Any number followed by %x will be converted in the same manner.
So the previous code is equivalent to

```
EditText1.Width = 50%x
```

Note: there is no space between the 0 and the %.

PerYToCurrent (Percentage As Float) As Int

Returns the actual size of the given percentage of the activity height.
Example: set the height of Button1 to 50% of the current activity:

```
EditText1.Height = PerYToCurrent(50)
```

A shorthand syntax for this method is available. Any number followed by %y will be converted in the same manner.
So the previous code is equivalent to

```
EditText1.Height = 50%y
```

Note: there is no space between the 0 and the %.

Power (Base As Double, Exponent As Double) As Double

Returns the Base value raised to the Exponent power.

ProgressDialogHide

Hides a visible progress dialog. Does not do anything if no progress dialog is visible.

ProgressDialogShow (Text As String)

Shows a dialog with a circular spinning bar and the specified **Text**.
Unlike `Msgbox` and `InputList` methods, the code will not block, or in other words, the program will continue to run and not wait for the user to take some action.
You should call ProgressDialogHide to remove the dialog.
The dialog will also be removed if the user presses on the **Back** key.

ProgressDialogShow2 (Text As String, Cancelable As Boolean)

Shows a dialog with a circular spinning bar and the specified **Text**.

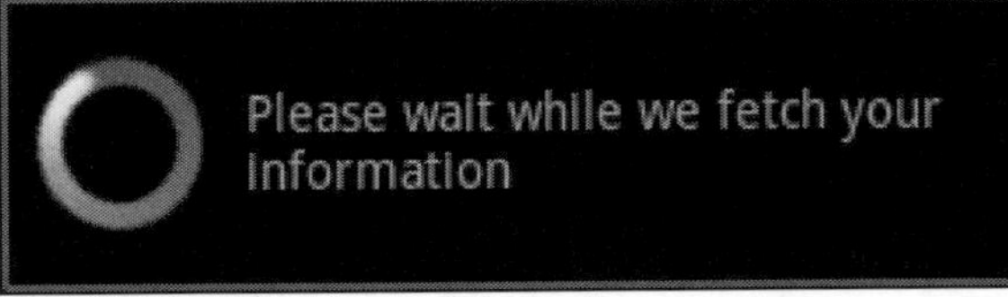

Unlike `Msgbox` and `InputList` methods, the code will not block, or in other words, the program will continue to run and not wait for the user to take some action.
You should call `ProgressDialogHide` to remove the dialog.
Cancelable - Whether the user can dismiss the dialog by pressing on the **Back** key.

QUOTE As String

Quote character. The value of Chr(34).

Regex As Regex

Regular expression (page 224) related methods. Follow the link for more on this subject.
The following example requires the Reflection library (page 543).
Suppose we want to replace the "a" with "x" in the string "abcde":

```
Sub Activity_Resume
 Log (RegexReplace("a", "abcde", "x"))
 Activity.Finish
End Sub

Sub RegexReplace(Pattern As String, Text As String, Replacement
As String) As String
 Dim m As Matcher
 m = Regex.Matcher(Pattern, Text)
 Dim r As Reflector
 r.Target = m
 Return r.RunMethod2("replaceAll", Replacement,
"java.lang.String")
End Sub
```

The result is "xbcde".
This will also work for more complex regular expressions, such as

```
RegexReplace("abc(d)(e)", "abcde", "$2 $1")
```

This will produce "e d"

Return

Returns from the current sub and optionally returns the given value.
Syntax: Return [value]

Rnd (Min As Int, Max As Int) As Int

Returns a random integer between Min (inclusive) and Max (exclusive).

RndSeed (Seed As Long)

Sets the random seed value.
This method can be used for debugging as it allows you to get the same results each time.

Round (Number As Double) As Long

Returns the closest long number to the given number.

Round2 (Number As Double, DecimalPlaces As Int) As Double

Rounds **Number**, retaining **at most** the specified number of decimal digits.

```
Log(Round2(1234.5678, 2)) ' result is 1234.57
Log(Round2(1234, 2)) ' result is 1234
```

Select

Compares a single value to multiple values.
Example

```
Dim value As Int
value = Rnd(-10, 10)
Log("Value = " & value)
Select value
 Case 1
   Log("One")
 Case 2, 4, 6, 8
   Log("Positive even")
 Case 3, 5, 7, 9
   Log("Positive odd")
 Case Else
  If value < 1 Then
   Log("Less than 1")
  Else
   Log("Larger than 9")
  End If
End Select
```

Sender As Object

Returns the object that raised the event. Only valid while inside the event sub.
Example:

```
Sub Button_Click
 Dim b As Button
 b = Sender
 b.Text = "I've been clicked"
End Sub
```

Sin (Radians As Double) As Double

Calculates the trigonometric sine function. Angle measured in radians.

SinD (Degrees As Double) As Double

Calculates the trigonometric sine function. Angle measured in degrees.

Sqrt (Value As Double) As Double

Returns the positive square root.

StartActivity (Activity As Object)

Starts an activity or brings it to the front if it already exists.
The target activity will be started once the program is free to process its message queue.
Activity can be a string with the target activity name or it can be the actual activity.

After this call, the current activity will be paused and the target activity will be resumed.
This method can also be used to send Intents (page 314) objects to the system.
Note: you should usually **not** call **`StartActivity`** from a Service.
Example: `StartActivity (Activity2)`

StartService (Service As Object)

Starts the given **Service**. The **Service** will be first created if it was not previously started.
The target **Service** will be started once the program is free to process its message queue.
Service - The service module or the service name.
Note: you cannot show a Msgbox after this call and before the service starts.
Example: `StartService(SQLService)`

StartServiceAt (Service As Object, Time As Long, DuringSleep As Boolean)

Schedules the given **Service** to start at the given **Time**. This is an alternative to using a timer (page 338).
Service - The service module or service name. Pass an empty string when calling from a service module that schedules itself.
Time - The time to start the service, specified as a **`Long`**. You can use the DateTime (page 285) object to calculate this, for example, to specify 1 hour from now:

```
DateTime.Now + 3600 * 1000
```

If the selected time has already passed, the **Service** will be started immediately.
DuringSleep - Whether to start the **Service** when the device is sleeping. If set to **`False`** and the device is sleeping at the specified time, the **Service** will be started when the device wakes up.
`StartServiceAt` can be used to schedule a repeating task. You should call it under **`Sub Service_Start`** to schedule the next task. This call cancels previous scheduled tasks (for the same service).
Example:

```
StartServiceAt(SQLService, DateTime.Now + 30 * 1000, false)
'will start after 30 seconds.
```

StopService (Service As Object)

Stops the given service. **`Sub Service_Destroy`** will be called. Calling **`StartService`** afterwards will first create the **Service**.
Service - The service module or service name. Pass an empty string to stop the current service (from the service module).
Example:

```
StopService(SQLService)
```

Sub

Declares a sub with the parameters and return type. Syntax:

```
Sub name [(list of parameters)] [As return-type]
```

Any parameters which are given must include a name and type. You can pass an array as a parameter but it must be one-dimensional. The size of the dimension should not be included. Multi-dimensional arrays are not allowed. For example, a sub which requires a parameter **iScores** which is a one-dimensional array would be declared as:

```
Sub dWeightedMean (strName As String, iScores() As Int) As
Double
```

A sub can return an object of any type. It can also return a one-dimensional array. For example, a sub which returns an array of Double would be declared as:

```
Sub getArray (iCount As Int) As Double()
```

SubExists (Object As Object, Sub As String) As Boolean

Returns **TRUE** if the **Object** includes the specified method.

Returns **False** if the **Object** was not initialized, or is not an instance of a user class.

TAB As String

Tab character equivalent to Chr(9).

Tan (Radians As Double) As Double

Calculates the trigonometric tangent function. Angle measured in radians.

TanD (Degrees As Double) As Double

Calculates the trigonometric tangent function. Angle measured in degrees.

ToastMessageShow (Message As String, LongDuration As Boolean)

Shows a small message that fades automatically.

Message - The text message to show.

LongDuration - If **True**, shows the message for a long period. If **False**, shows the message for a short period.

True As Boolean

A constant which can be used to compare or set logical values, for example:

```
ToastMessageShow("Email sent", True)
```

Try

Any exception thrown inside a **Try** block will be caught in the **Catch** block.

Call **LastException** to get the caught exception. Syntax:

```
Try
...
Catch
...
End Try
```

See Try-Catch (page 239) for more details.

Type

Declares a structure. Can only be used inside sub Globals or **Sub Process_Globals**. Syntax:

```
Type type-name (field1, field2, ...)
```

Fields must include their name and type. Example:

```
Type MyType (Name As String, Items(10) As Int)
Dim a, b As MyType
a.Initialize
a.Items(2) = 123
```

See here for details (page 219).

Until

Loops until the condition is **True**. Syntax:

```
Do Until condition
...
Loop
```

See Do-Until (page 231) for more details.

While

Loops while the condition is **True**. Syntax:

```
Do While condition
...
Loop
```

See Do-While (page 230) for more details.

3.2 VB6 versus B4A

There are some differences between Basic4Android and Visual Basic from Microsoft. The following analysis of the differences between Basic4Android and Visual Basic 6 is extracted from work by nfordbscndrd (http://www.basic4ppc.com/forum/members/nfordbscndrd.html), a member of the Basic4Android forum. It highlights some of the differences between the two IDEs and their languages. It might be useful for experienced VB6 programmers.

Controls vs. Views

The objects which Basic4Android calls Views (page 395) (buttons, edittext, labels, etc.) are called Controls in Visual Basic.
In the VB6 code window, the top left drop-down list contains all the controls you have placed in the current form and the right list contains all the events for each control.
The equivalent in Basic4Android can be found by clicking on the Designer menu [Tools > Generate Members]. Once you have created Subs in the program coding window, the tab “Modules” on the right side will list each of the Subs.
In Basic4Android, you start by typing “Sub” followed by a space. The IDE will then prompt you for details. We describe this in the Autocomplete Event Subroutines (page 50) section.
In VB6, you can leave ".Text" off the names of controls when assigning text to them, but this is not allowed in B4A.

Dim

VB6: Dim name(n) will give you n+1 elements with index 0 to n. For example, `Dim strName(12)` will give you 13 strings.
B4A: Dim name(n) will give you n elements with index 0 to n-1. This can be confusing since, for `Dim strName(12)`, the last element is actually `strName(11)`.

ReDim

VB6: ReDim name(n) does not exist in B4A, where you would simply use another `Dim name(n)`. Likewise, VB6 “ReDim Preserve” does not exist. If you need this, you would be better to use a list or map.

Boolean Operations

Suppose the following have been declared in either language:

```
Dim i Int
Dim b as Boolean
```

Not

VB6 does not require parentheses: "If Not b Then"
In B4A, parentheses are reqired: **`If Not(b) Then`**

Using Integers as Boolean

In VB6, an integer that equals zero is considered as the same as a Boolean FALSE; anything non-zero is TRUE. For example: "If i Then"
In Basic4Android, a Boolean value CANNOT be used in a math function. Instead, you must test the value of a variable, for example:

```
If i > 0 Then
```

Global Const

Basic4Android does not have a Global Const function.
In VB6 you can say

```
Global Const x=1
```

In Basic4Android you say
Sub Globals

```
Dim x as Int = 1
```

However, x is not a constant. Its value can be changed.

Repeating Structures

For...Next

VB6: For i...Next i
B4A: For i...Next

Loops, If-Then, Select Case

VB6: Loop...Until, Loop...While
This structure is not allowed in Basic4Android. You can, however, use the alternative form:
B4A: Do While...Loop, Do Until... Loop
See Do-While (page 230) and Do-Until (page 231) for more details.

Exit

VB6: Exit Do/For
B4A: Exit

ElseIf/EndIf

VB6: ElseIf/EndIf
B4A: Else If/End If

Colors

In VB6, colors have names such as “vbRed”. In B4A, you use the Colors object, for example: **`Colors.Red`**

Subroutines

Declaring a Sub

VB6: Sub SubName()
B4A: Sub SubName() As Int/String/etc.

Calling a sub

VB6: SubName x, y
B4A: SubName(x, y)

Functions

Functions do not exist in Basic4Android. Instead, any **`Sub`** can be used as a Function by adding a variable type.
VB6: Function FName() As Int
B4A: **`Sub FName() As Int`**
If no **`Return`** is given, then zero or **`False`** or "" is returned.

Exit Sub

Exit Sub does not exist in Basic4Android. Use Return instead.
VB6: Exit Sub / Exit Function
B4A: Return / Return [value]

DoEvents

While **`DoEvents`** exists in Basic4Android, calling DoEvents in a loop consumes a lot of resources and uses excessive battery power because Android will never get back to the main “idle loop” where the hardware power saving measures are invoked. Also, **`DoEvents`** doesn’t allow the system to process all waiting messages properly. In short, **looping for long periods should be avoided where possible on mobile devices**.

Format

VB6: Format()
B4A: NumberFormat (page 255) & NumberFormat2 (page 255)

InputBox

In VB6, InputBox() shows a dialog box and waits for the user to input text or click a button, and then returns a string containing the contents of the text box.
B4A has no dialog box which allows the user to enter text. Instead, you create something similar using an EditText on a layout. Alternatively, you could use one of the following:

- The user-created Dialogs Library (page 530), which offers InputDialog for text, a TimeDialog for times, a DateDialog for dates, both a ColorDialog and a ColorPickerDialog for colors, a NumberDialog for numbers, a FileDialog for folders and file names, and a CustomDialog.
- InputList (page 250) to show a modal dialog with a list of choices and radio buttons and return an index indicating which one the user has selected.
- InputMultiList (page 251) to show a list from which the user can select multiple items before returning.
- InputMap (page 251) to show a modal dialog with a list of items and checkboxes. The user can select multiple items.

MsgBox

VB6: MsgBox "text" / i=MsgBox()
B4A: has several alternatives:
MsgBox (page 254)("text", "title")
MsgBox2 (page 254)(Message, Title, Positive, Cancel, Negative, Icon) as Int
ToastMessageShow (page 260)(text, b)

Random Numbers

Random numbers generated by computers are not really random. They are “pseudo-random” and are created using an algorithm which starts from one number, the “seed”, to generate the next.

Rnd

In VB6, **Rnd()** returns a float < 1.
In B4A, **Rnd(min, max)** returns an integer >= min and < max.

RndSeed

If # is a number, then in VB6, Rnd(-#) sets the “seed” of the random number generator to #. After this call, Rnd will return the same series of numbers every time.
In B4A, **RndSeed(#)** sets the random number generator seed in the same way. # must be a **Long** type number.

Randomize

If # is a number, then in VB6, Randomize(#) uses # to initialize the Rnd function's random number generator, using # as the new seed value. Randomize() without the

number uses the value returned by the system timer as the new seed value. If Randomize is not used, the Rnd function (with no arguments) always uses the same number as a seed the first time it is called, and thereafter uses the last-generated number as a seed value.
In Basic4Android, there is no equivalent of Randomize, because the seed of Rnd is always randomized automatically.

Round

VB6: Round(n) where n is a floating point number.
B4A: **`Round(n)`** or **`Round2(n, x)`** where n is a **`Double`** and x=number of decimal places

---

Val()

VB6: i = Val(string)
B4A: If IsNumber(string) Then i = string Else i = 0
An attempt to use i=string throws a NumberFormatException if the string is not a valid number.

SetFocus

VB6: control.SetFocus
B4A: **`view.RequestFocus`**

Divide by Zero

VB6 throws an exception for division by 0. Basic4Android returns either 2147483647 or Infinity, depending whether the result is set to an integer or a string:

```
Dim i As Int
i = 12/0
Log (i) ' 2147483647

Dim str As String
str = 12/0
Log (str) ' Infinity
```

Shell

VB6: x = Shell("...")
B4A: See "Intent (page 314)".
This is not a complete replacement, but allows code such as the following:

```
Dim Intent1 As Intent
Intent1.Initialize(Intent1.ACTION_MAIN, "")
Intent1.SetComponent("com.google.android.youtube/.HomeActivity")
StartActivity(Intent1)
```

Timer

VB6: t = Timer
B4A: **`t = DateTime.Now`**, which returns the number of milliseconds since 1-1-70

TabIndex

In VB6, TabIndex can be set to control the order in which controls get focus in a form when Tab is pressed.
On an Android device, Android handles the sequence according to their position. However, in the Designer or in code, you can set **`EditText.ForceDone`** to **`True`** in all your EditTexts: **`EditText1.ForceDoneButton = True`**. This forces the virtual keyboard to show the Done button. You can then catch the **`EditText_EnterPressed`** event and explicitly set the focus to the next view (with **`EditText.RequestFocus`**).

Setting Label Transparency

You can control the transparency of a label as follows:
VB6: [Properties > Back Style]
B4A Designer: [Drawable > Alpha]

Constants

There are a number of useful predefined constants in VB6, for example,
VB6: vbCr, vbCrLf
B4A: CRLF (page 247) (Android's equivalent of Windows CRLF, although in fact it is the Line Feed character Chr(10)).

String "Members"

VB6 uses a character position pointer starting with 1.
Basic4Android function CharAt() uses a character Index pointer starting with 0.
All the following produce "a":
VB6: Mid$("abcde", 1)
VB6: Mid$("abcde", 1, 1)
B4A: "abcde".CharAt(0)
B4A: "abcde".SubString2(0,1)
The following produce "abc":
VB6: Mid$("abcde", 1, 3)

B4A: "abcde". SubString2(0, 3)

Left$ and Right$

These do not exist in Basic4Android. You can recreate them as follows:

VB6: Left$("abcde", 3)
B4A: "abcde".SubString2(0, 3)

VB6: Right$("abcde", 2)
B4A: "abcde".SubString("abcde".Length - 2)

VB6: If Right$(text, n) = text2
B4A: If text.EndsWith(text2)...

VB6: If Left$(text, n) = text2
B4A: If text.StartsWith(text2)...

VB6: If Lcase$(text) = Lcase$(text2)
B4A: If text.EqualsIgnoreCase(text2)

Len

VB6: x = Len(text)
B4A: x = text.Length

Replace

VB6: text = Replace(text, str, str2)
B4A: text.Replace(str, str2)

Case

VB6: Lcase(text)
B4A: text.ToLowerCase
VB6: Ucase(text)
B4A: text.ToUpperCase

Trim

VB6: Trim(text)
B4A: text.Trim
There is no LTrim or RTrim in Basic4Android

Instr

VB6: Instr(text, string)
B4A: text.IndexOf (page 336)(string)

VB6: Instr(int, text, string)
B4A: text.IndexOf2 (page 336)(string, int)

VB6: If Lcase$(x) = Lcase$(y)
B4A: If x.EqualsIgnoreCase(y)

VB6: text = Left$(text, n) & s & Right$(Text, y)
B4A: text.Insert(n, s)

Error Trapping

VB6

```
Sub SomeSub
  On [Local] Error GoTo ErrorTrap
   ...some code...
  On Error GoTo 0 [optional end to error trapping]
  ...optional additional code...
  Exit Sub [to avoid executing ErrorTrap code]
ErrorTrap:
  ...optional code for error correction...
  Resume [optional: "Resume Next" or "Resume [line label]".
End Sub
```

Basic4Android

```
Sub SomeSub
  Try
   ...some code...
  Catch [only executes if error above]
   Log(LastException) [optional]
   ...optional code for error correction...
  End Try
  ...optional additional code...
End Sub
```

With Basic4Android, if you get an error caught in the middle of a large subroutine, you CANNOT make a correction and resume within the code you were executing. Only the code in "Catch" gets executed. That would seem to make **`Try-Catch-End Try`** of use mainly during development.

"Immediate Window" vs. "Logs" Tab

Comments, variable values, etc., can be displayed in VB6's Immediate Window by entering into the code "Debug.Print ...".
In Basic4Android, show values of variables, etc. in the Logs tab (page 27).
Both VB6 and Basic4Android allow single-stepping through the code while it is running and viewing the values of variables. VB6 also allows changing the value of variables, changing the code, jumping to other lines from the current line, etc. Because Basic4Android runs on a PC while the app runs on a separate device, Basic4Android is currently unable to duplicate all of these VB6 debug features.

3.3 Core Objects

These objects are in the core library of the IDE and can be used without referring to any other libraries. These are included in both the Trial and the Full versions of Basic4Android.
For example your code can simply say:

```
Sub Globals
 Dim map1 As Map
 Dim match1 As Matcher
 Dim mediaPlayer1 As MediaPlayer
End Sub
```

List of Core Objects

In the following lists, we group the core objects (and constants) according to their function where possible. The remainder we group under "General".

General

Activity
Bit (page 278)
DateTime (page 285)
Exception (page 303)
Intent (page 314)
LayoutValues (page 317)
List (page 318)
Map (page 323)
MediaPlayer (page 327)
Notification (page 329)
RemoteViews (page 332)
Service (page 333)
String (page 334)
StringBuilder (page 337)
Timer (page 338)

Constants

Colors (page 280)
DialogResponse (page 281)
Gravity (page 282)
KeyCodes (page 282)
Typeface (page 284)

Drawing Objects

Bitmap (page 289)
BitmapDrawable (page 291)

Canvas (page 291)
ColorDrawable (page 299)
GradientDrawable (page 299)
Path (page 300)
Rect (page 300)
StateListDrawable (page 151)

File Objects

File (page 306)
InputStream (page 310)
OutputStream (page 311)
TextReader (page 312)
TextWriter (page 313)

Views

Activity
AutoCompleteEditText (page 341)
Button (page 346)
CheckBox (page 349)
EditText (page 352)
HorizontalScrollView (page 357)
ImageView (page 359)
Label (page 362)
ListView (page 364)
Panel (page 370)
ProgressBar (page 374)
RadioButton (page 376)
ScrollView (page 379)
SeekBar (page 382)
Spinner (page 384)
TabHost (page 388)
ToggleButton (page 392)
View (page 395)
WebView (page 398)

Activity

Activity is the main component of your application. We describe its usage in the Activity Concept (page 173) Chapter. In the following section, we detail its events and members.
If you iterate over an Activity, you will find each of the views it consists of:

```
For Each vw As View In Activity
 ' check its type
 If vw Is Button Then
  ' need object with correct type so
  '  can gain access to properties
  Dim btn As Button
  ' make copy of original view
  btn = vw
  Log (btn.Text)
 End If
Next
```

Activity Events

Click

This event is generated when the user touches the screen, provided that no other view has consumed the event (such as an **EditText**), and provided that no handler exists for the **Touch** event. **Touch** takes priority over **Click**.

KeyPress and KeyUp Events

The **KeyPress** and **KeyUp** events occur when the user presses or releases a key on the Android keyboard, assuming that no other view has consumed this event (like EditText). When handling the KeyPress or KeyUp event, you should return a boolean value which tells whether the event was consumed. Return **True** to consume the event. For example, if the user pressed on the Back key and you return **True**, then Android will not close your activity.

```
Sub Activity_KeyPress (KeyCode As Int) As Boolean
 If Keycode = KeyCodes.KEYCODE_BACK Then
   Return True
 Else
   Return False
 End If
End Sub
```

LongClick

This event is generated when the user touches the screen for a long time (about one second) provided that no other view has consumed the event (such as an **EditText**), and provided that no handler exists for the **Touch** event. **Touch** takes priority over **LongClick**.

Touch (Action As Int, X As Float, Y As Float)

The Touch event can be used to handle user touches. If a handler exists for the Touch event, then handlers for the **Click** and **LongClick** events will not work.

The **Action** parameter values can be:

- Activity.ACTION_DOWN: The user has touched the screen at X,Y.
- Activity.ACTION_MOVE: The user's touch has moved to X,Y.

- Activity.ACTION_UP: The user has stopped touching the screen at X,Y.

Use this value to find the user current action.

Activity Members

- ACTION_DOWN As Int
- ACTION_MOVE As Int
- ACTION_UP As Int
- AddMenuItem (Title As String, EventName As String)
- AddMenuItem2 (Title As String, EventName As String, Bitmap1 As Bitmap)
- AddMenuItem3 (Title As String, EventName As String, Bitmap1 As Bitmap, AddToActionBar As Boolean)
- AddView (View1 As View, Left As Int, Top As Int, Width As Int, Height As Int)
- Background As Drawable
- CloseMenu
- Color As Int [write only]
- Finish (page 276)
- GetAllViewsRecursive (page 276) As IterableList
- GetStartingIntent (page 276) As Intent
- GetView (page 276) (Index As Int) As View
- Height (page 276) As Int
- Initialize (page 276) (EventName As String)
- Invalidate (page 276)
- Invalidate2 (page 276) (Rect As Rect)
- Invalidate3 (page 276) (Left As Int, Top As Int, Right As Int, Bottom As Int)
- IsInitialized (page 277) As Boolean
- Left (page 277) As Int
- LoadLayout (page 277) (Layout As String) As LayoutValues
- NumberOfViews (page 277) As Int [read only]
- OpenMenu (page 277)
- RemoveAllViews (page 277)
- RemoveViewAt (page 277) (Index As Int)
- RequestFocus (page 277) As Boolean
- RerunDesignerScript (page 277) (Layout As String, Width As Int, Height As Int)
- SendToBack (page 277)
- SetActivityResult (page 278) (Result As Int, Data As Intent)
- SetBackgroundImage (page 278) (Bitmap1 As Bitmap)
- SetLayout (page 278) (Left As Int, Top As Int, Width As Int, Height As Int)
- Tag (page 278) As Object
- Title (page 278) As CharSequence
- TitleColor (page 278) As Int

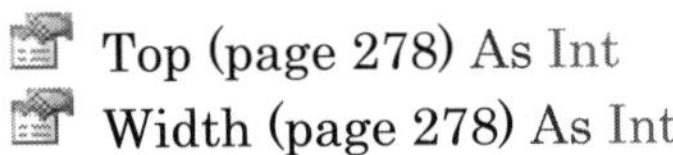
Top (page 278) As Int
Width (page 278) As Int

ACTION_DOWN As Int

ACTION_MOVE As Int

ACTION_UP As Int

AddMenuItem (Title As String, EventName As String)

Adds a menu item to the activity. On devices running Android less than 3.0, the menu is evoked by pressing the menu key. On 3.0 and above it is shown as an overflow symbol (3 vertical dots) on the Action Bar.

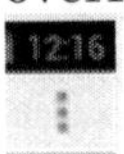

See here (http://developer.android.com/guide/topics/ui/menus.html) for more about the options menu and here (http://developer.android.com/guide/topics/ui/actionbar.html) for more about the Action Bar in Android 3.0+.
Title – Text shown in menu.
EventName - The prefix name of the sub that will handle the click event.
This method should only be called inside **`Sub Activity_Create`**.
Note: the `Sender (page 258)` keyword inside the click event equals to the clicked menu item text.
Example:

```
Activity.AddMenuItem("Test Menu", "TestMenu")
' ...
Sub TestMenu_Click
 Log (Sender) ' will log "Test Menu"
End Sub
```

AddMenuItem2 (Title As String, EventName As String, Bitmap1 As Bitmap)

Adds a menu item with a **`Bitmap`** to the activity. See previous topic for more details.
Title – Text shown in menu.
EventName – The prefix name of the sub that will handle the click event.
Bitmap – Bitmap to draw as the item background.
Only the first five (or six if there are six total) menu items display icons.
This method should only be called inside **`Sub Activity_Create`**.
Note: the **`Sender`** keyword inside the click event equals to the clicked menu item text.
Example:

```
Activity.AddMenuItem2("Open File", "OpenFile",
LoadBitmap(File.DirAssets, "SomeImage.png"))
...
Sub OpenFile_Click
...
End Sub
```

AddMenuItem3 (Title As String, EventName As String, Bitmap1 As Bitmap, AddToActionBar As Boolean)

Adds a menu item with a **Bitmap** to the activity, with the option to add the action bar on Android 3.00+ devices. See below for more details.
Title – Text shown in menu.
EventName – The prefix name of the sub that will handle the click event.
Bitmap – Bitmap to draw as the item background.
AddToActionBar – if **True**, then the item will be displayed in the action bar (on Android 3.0+ devices) if there is enough room. If there is not enough room, then the item will be displayed together with the other menu items in the overflow options.
See here (http://bit.ly/19E7ppF) for more about the options menu in Android 3.0+
Note: the **Sender** keyword inside the click event equals to the clicked menu item text.
Example

```
Dim bm As Bitmap
bm.Initialize (File.DirAssets, "menuIcon.png")
Activity.AddMenuItem3 ( "Open File", "OpenFile", bm, True)
...
Sub OpenFile_click()
...
End Sub
```

AddView (View1 As View, Left As Int, Top As Int, Width As Int, Height As Int)

Adds a view to this activity.

Background As Drawable

Gets or sets the background drawable.

CloseMenu

Programmatically closes the menu.

Color As Int [write only]

Sets the background of the view to be a **ColorDrawable** with the given color. If the current background is of type **GradientDrawable** or **ColorDrawable**, the round corners will be kept.

Finish

Closes this activity. See Activity.Finish vs ExitApplication (page 178) for details of when you should use Finish.

GetAllViewsRecursive As IterableList

Returns an iterator that iterates over all the views belonging to the Activity, including views which are children of other views. Example:

```
For Each vw As View In Activity.GetAllViewsRecursive
  vw.Color = Colors.RGB(Rnd(0,255), Rnd(0,255), Rnd(0,255))
Next
```

GetStartingIntent As Intent

(Advanced) Gets the intent object that started this Activity.
This can be used together with **`SetActivityResult`** to return results to 3rd party applications.

GetView (Index As Int) As View

Gets the view that is stored at the specified index.

Height As Int

Gets or sets the Activity's height.

Initialize (EventName As String)

Initializes the Activity and sets the subs that will handle the events.
Note: this function is never needed since the Activity will be automatically initialized. It only exists because, technically, Activity is a sub-type of View.

Invalidate

Invalidates the whole Activity, forcing the view to redraw itself. Redrawing will only happen when the program can process messages, usually when it finishes running the current code.
If you only need to redraw part of the view, it is usually quicker to use **`Invalidate2`** or **`Invalidate3`**.

Invalidate2 (Rect1 As Rect)

Invalidates anything inside the given rectangle that is part of this Activity. Redrawing will only happen when the program can process messages, usually when it finishes running the current code.

Invalidate3 (Left As Int, Top As Int, Right As Int, Bottom As Int)

Invalidates anything inside the given rectangle that is part of this Activity. Redrawing will only happen when the program can process messages, usually when it finishes running the current code.

IsInitialized As Boolean

This always returns **True**. It only exists because, technically, Activity is a sub-type of View.

Left As Int

This is always 0 for an Activity.

LoadLayout (Layout As String) As LayoutValues

Loads a layout file (.bal). Returns the LayoutValues of the actual layout variant that was loaded.

NumberOfViews As Int [read only]

Returns the number of child views.

OpenMenu

Programmatically opens the menu.

RemoveAllViews

Removes all child views.

RemoveViewAt (Index As Int)

Removes the view that is stored at the specified index. Example:

```
Dim vw As View
For i = 0 To Activity.NumberOfViews - 1
 vw = Activity.GetView(i)
 If vw.Tag = "btnNew" Then
  Activity.RemoveViewAt(i)
 End If
Next
```

RequestFocus As Boolean

This function is never needed. It will always return **False**. It only exists because, technically, Activity is a sub-type of View.

RerunDesignerScript (Layout As String, Width As Int, Height As Int)

Runs the designer script again with the specified width and height. See the designer scripts (page 109) chapter for more information.

SendToBack

This function is never needed. It only exists because, technically, Activity is a sub-type of View.

SetActivityResult (Result As Int, Data As Intent)

This advanced feature allows an Activity to return a result to an external app that calls **startActivityForResult** to start the app and get a result. For example, you can use it to build a file chooser app with a defined external API.
SetActivityResult sets the result that the calling Activity will get after calling **StartActivityForResult**.
Note: **IOnActivityResult**, **OnActivityResult**, **SetActivityResult** and **StartActivityForResult** are all advanced features which are beyond the scope of this book. For more information, see here (http://bit.ly/1gvOvso).

SetBackgroundImage (Bitmap1 As Bitmap)

SetLayout (Left As Int, Top As Int, Width As Int, Height As Int)

Changes the view position and size.

Tag As Object

Gets or sets the Activity's Tag value. This can be used to store additional data.

Title As CharSequence

Gets or sets the Activity's title.

TitleColor As Int

Gets or sets the title color.
Note: the title color doesn't have any effect on devices using the holo style, which was introduced in Android 4. For more about Themes, see here (page 77).

Top As Int

This is always 0 for an Activity.

Width As Int

Gets or sets the view's width.

Bit

Bit is a predefined object containing bitwise related methods.
Example:

```
Dim flags As Int
flags = Bit.Or(100, 200)
```

Bitwise Operations

In bitwise operations, the numbers are first converted to their binary form (which consists of 1 and 0 digits). Then the operation is performed on each pair of binary digits, and the result assembled into a new binary number which is then converted back into a decimal form. For example, **3 AND 6** would be processed as follows to produce the decimal number 2:

- 3 is converted to binary 011
- 2 is converted to binary 110
- The left-hand digits are ANDED together: 0 AND 1 evaluate to 0
- The middle two digits are ANDED; 1 AND 1 = 1
- The right-hand digits are ANDED; 1 AND 0 evaluate to 0
- The three results are assembled to make the binary number 010
- The binary number 010 is converted to decimal 2

Members:

- And (N1 As Int, N2 As Int) As Int
- Not (N As Int) As Int
- Or (N1 As Int, N2 As Int) As Int
- ParseInt (Value As String, Radix As Int) As Int
- ShiftLeft (N As Int, Shift As Int) As Int
- ShiftRight (N As Int, Shift As Int) As Int
- ToBinaryString (N As Int) As String
- ToHexString (N As Int) As String
- ToOctalString (N As Int) As String
- UnsignedShiftRight (N As Int, Shift As Int) As Int
- Xor (N1 As Int, N2 As Int) As Int

And (N1 As Int, N2 As Int) As Int

Returns the bitwise **AND** of the two values. For each pair of corresponding bits in N1 and N2, the result is 1 if both both bits are 1, otherwise it is 0.

Not (N As Int) As Int

Returns the bitwise complement of the given value. For each bit in N, the corresponding bit in the result has the opposite value (1s are replace by 0s and 0s by 1s).

Or (N1 As Int, N2 As Int) As Int

Returns the bitwise **OR** of the two values. For each pair of corresponding bits in N1 and N2, the result is 0 if both both bits are 0, otherwise it is 1.

ParseInt (Value As String, Radix As Int) As Int

Converts **Value** from base **Radix** to base 10. So the following example will convert 100 in base 2 to base 10, and produce the result 4:

```
Log ( Bit.ParseInt("100",2))
```

Radix should be from 2 to 36. Other examples:

```
Log ( Bit.ParseInt("100",8)) ' 64
Log ( Bit.ParseInt("100",10)) ' 100
Log ( Bit.ParseInt("100",13)) ' 169
```

ShiftLeft (N As Int, Shift As Int) As Int

Shifts the bits in N to the left. The new right-most bits are set to 0.
Shift - Number of positions to shift.

ShiftRight (N As Int, Shift As Int) As Int

Shifts the bits in N to the right. Keeps the original value sign, meaning that the new left-most bits have the same value as the original left-most bit.
Shift - Number of positions to shift.

ToBinaryString (N As Int) As String

Returns a string representation of N in base 2.

ToHexString (N As Int) As String

Returns a string representation of N in base 16.

ToOctalString (N As Int) As String

Returns a string representation of N in base 8.

UnsignedShiftRight (N As Int, Shift As Int) As Int

Shifts **N** right and inserts a zero in the left-most position for each shift performed.
Shift - Number of positions to shift.

Xor (N1 As Int, N2 As Int) As Int

Returns the bitwise "exclusive or" of the two values. For each pair of bits, the result is 1 if only one of the two is 1, otherwise the result is 0.

Constants

Colors

A predefined object containing color constants.
For example: `Activity.Color = Colors.Green`

Members:

- ARGB (Alpha As Int, R As Int, G As Int, B As Int) As Int
- Black As Int
- Blue As Int
- Cyan As Int
- DarkGray As Int
- Gray As Int

- Green As Int
- LightGray As Int
- Magenta As Int
- Red As Int
- RGB (R As Int, G As Int, B As Int) As Int
- Transparent As Int
- White As Int
- Yellow As Int

ARGB (Alpha As Int, Red As Int, Green As Int, Blue As Int) As Int
Returns an integer value representing the color built from the three components **Red**, **Green** and **Blue**, and with the specified **Alpha** value, which determines the transparency of the color. Each component should be a value from 0 to 255 (inclusive).
Alpha - A value from 0 to 255, where 0 is fully transparent and 255 is fully opaque.
Note: you can get the same result by using a hex literal (page 210). Thus Colors.ARGB(255,0,0,0) is the same as 0xFF000000.

Black As Int

Blue As Int

Cyan As Int

DarkGray As Int

Gray As Int

Green As Int

LightGray As Int

Magenta As Int

Red As Int

RGB (Red As Int, Green As Int, Blue As Int) As Int
Returns an integer value representing the color built from the three components **Red**, **Green** and **Blue**. Each component should be a value from 0 to 255 (inclusive). This is the same as ARGB with Alpha set to 255 (opaque).
Note: you can get the same result by using a hex literal (page 210). Thus Colors.RGB(255,0,0) is the same as 0xFF0000.

Transparent As Int

White As Int

Yellow As Int

DialogResponse

A predefined object containing the possible values that dialogs return. For example:

```
Dim result As Int
result = Msgbox2("Save changes?", "", "Yes", "", "No", Null)
If result = DialogResponse.POSITIVE Then
  'save changes
End If
```

- **CANCEL** As Int
- **NEGATIVE** As Int
- **POSITIVE** As Int

Gravity

Predefined object containing "gravity" values. These values affect the alignment of text or images. Example:

```
Dim EditText1 As EditText
EditText1.Initialize("")
EditText1.Gravity = Gravity.CENTER
```

- **BOTTOM** As Int
- **CENTER** As Int
- **CENTER_HORIZONTAL** As Int
- **CENTER_VERTICAL** As Int
- **FILL** As Int
- **LEFT** As Int
- **NO_GRAVITY** As Int
- **RIGHT** As Int
- **TOP** As Int

KeyCodes

A predefined object with the **KeyCode** constants. These constants are passed to the **Activity KeyPressed** event, for example:

```
Sub Activity_KeyPress(KeyCode As Int) As Boolean
 If KeyCode = KeyCodes.KEYCODE_BACK Then
  Log ("KEYCODE_BACK")
  Return False
 End If
End Sub
```

Events

None

Members

All the following are integer constants:

KEYCODE_0 **KEYCODE_1**

KEYCODE_2
KEYCODE_3
KEYCODE_4
KEYCODE_5
KEYCODE_6
KEYCODE_7
KEYCODE_8
KEYCODE_9
KEYCODE_A
KEYCODE_ALT_LEFT
KEYCODE_ALT_RIGHT
KEYCODE_APOSTROPHE
KEYCODE_AT
KEYCODE_B
KEYCODE_BACK
KEYCODE_BACKSLASH
KEYCODE_C
KEYCODE_CALL
KEYCODE_CAMERA
KEYCODE_CLEAR
KEYCODE_COMMA
KEYCODE_D
KEYCODE_DEL
KEYCODE_DPAD_CENTER
KEYCODE_DPAD_DOWN
KEYCODE_DPAD_LEFT
KEYCODE_DPAD_RIGHT
KEYCODE_DPAD_UP
KEYCODE_E
KEYCODE_ENDCALL
KEYCODE_ENTER
KEYCODE_ENVELOPE
KEYCODE_EQUALS
KEYCODE_EXPLORER
KEYCODE_F
KEYCODE_FOCUS
KEYCODE_G
KEYCODE_GRAVE
KEYCODE_H
KEYCODE_HEADSETHOOK
KEYCODE_HOME
KEYCODE_I
KEYCODE_J
KEYCODE_K
KEYCODE_L
KEYCODE_LEFT_BRACKET
KEYCODE_M
KEYCODE_MEDIA_FAST_FORWARD
KEYCODE_MEDIA_NEXT
KEYCODE_MEDIA_PLAY_PAUSE
KEYCODE_MEDIA_PREVIOUS
KEYCODE_MEDIA_REWIND
KEYCODE_MEDIA_STOP
KEYCODE_MENU
KEYCODE_MINUS
KEYCODE_MUTE
KEYCODE_N
KEYCODE_NOTIFICATION
KEYCODE_NUM
KEYCODE_O
KEYCODE_P

KEYCODE_PERIOD
KEYCODE_PLUS
KEYCODE_POUND
KEYCODE_POWER
KEYCODE_Q
KEYCODE_R
KEYCODE_RIGHT_BRACKET
KEYCODE_S
KEYCODE_SEARCH
KEYCODE_SEMICOLON
KEYCODE_SHIFT_LEFT
KEYCODE_SHIFT_RIGHT
KEYCODE_SLASH
KEYCODE_SOFT_LEFT
KEYCODE_SOFT_RIGHT
KEYCODE_SPACE
KEYCODE_STAR
KEYCODE_SYM
KEYCODE_T
KEYCODE_TAB
KEYCODE_U
KEYCODE_UNKNOWN
KEYCODE_V
KEYCODE_VOLUME_DOWN
KEYCODE_VOLUME_UP
KEYCODE_W
KEYCODE_X
KEYCODE_Y
KEYCODE_Z

Typeface

`Typeface` is a predefined object that holds the typeface styles and the default installed fonts.
Note: unlike most other predefined objects, you can declare new objects of this type.
Example:

```
EditText1.Typeface = Typeface.DEFAULT_BOLD
```

Events

None

Members

- CreateNew (Typeface1 As Typeface, Style As Int) As Typeface
- DEFAULT As Typeface
- DEFAULT_BOLD As Typeface
- IsInitialized As Boolean
- LoadFromAssets (FileName As String) As Typeface
- MONOSPACE As Typeface
- SANS_SERIF As Typeface
- SERIF As Typeface
- STYLE_BOLD As Int
- STYLE_BOLD_ITALIC As Int

- STYLE_ITALIC As Int
- STYLE_NORMAL As Int

CreateNew (Typeface1 As Typeface, Style As Int) As Typeface
Returns a typeface with the specified **Style**. Example:
```
Typeface.CreateNew(Typeface.MONOSPACE, Typeface.STYLE_ITALIC)
```
DEFAULT As Typeface

DEFAULT_BOLD As Typeface

IsInitialized As Boolean
Whether this object has been initialized by calling **LoadFromAssets**.

LoadFromAssets (FileName As String) As Typeface
Loads a font file that was added with the file manager. Example:
```
Dim MyFont As Typeface
MyFont = Typeface.LoadFromAssets("MyFont.ttf")
EditText1.Typeface = MyFont
```
MONOSPACE As Typeface

SANS_SERIF As Typeface

SERIF As Typeface

STYLE_BOLD As Int

STYLE_BOLD_ITALIC As Int

STYLE_ITALIC As Int

STYLE_NORMAL As Int

DateTime

Date and time related methods. DateTime is a predefined object. You should not declare it yourself. Date and time values are stored as ticks.

Ticks

Ticks are the number of milliseconds since January 1, 1970 00:00:00 UTC (Coordinated Universal Time). **This value is too large to be stored in an Int variable. It should only be stored in a Long variable.** The methods **DateTime.Date** and **DateTime.Time** convert the ticks value to a string. You can get the current time with **DateTime.Now**.
Example:

```
Dim now As Long
now = DateTime.Now
Msgbox("The date is: " & DateTime.Date(now) & CRLF & _
  "The time is: " & DateTime.Time(now), "")
```

Members:

- Add (Ticks As Long, Years As Int, Months As Int, Days As Int) As Long
- Date (Ticks As Long) As String
- DateFormat As String
- DateParse (Date As String) As Long
- DateTimeParse (Date As String, Time As String) As Long
- DeviceDefaultDateFormat As String [read only]
- DeviceDefaultTimeFormat As String [read only]
- GetDayOfMonth (Ticks As Long) As Int
- GetDayOfWeek (Ticks As Long) As Int
- GetDayOfYear (Ticks As Long) As Int
- GetHour (Ticks As Long) As Int
- GetMinute (Ticks As Long) As Int
- GetMonth (Ticks As Long) As Int
- GetSecond (Ticks As Long) As Int
- GetTimeZoneOffsetAt (Date As Long) As Double
- GetYear (Ticks As Long) As Int
- Now As Long [read only]
- SetTimeZone (OffsetHours As Int)
- TicksPerDay As Long
- TicksPerHour As Long
- TicksPerMinute As Long
- TicksPerSecond (page 289) As Long
- Time (page 289) (Ticks As Long) As String
- TimeFormat (page 289) As String
- TimeParse (page 289) (Time As String) As Long
- TimeZoneOffset (page 289) As Double [read only]

Add (Ticks As Long, Years As Int, Months As Int, Days As Int) As Long

Returns a ticks value which is the result of adding the specified time spans to the given **Ticks** value. Pass negative values if you want to subtract the values. Example:

```
Dim Tomorrow As Long
Tomorrow = DateTime.Add(DateTime.Now, 0, 0, 1)
Log("Tomorrow's date is: " & DateTime.Date(Tomorrow))
```

Date (Ticks As Long) As String

Returns a string representation of the date (which is stored as ticks). The date format can be set with the DateFormat keyword. Example:

```
Log("Today is: " & DateTime.Date(DateTime.Now))
```

DateFormat As String

Gets or sets the format used to parse date strings. See this page for the supported patterns: formats (http://bit.ly/15IH0fK). The default pattern is MM/dd/yyyy (04/23/2002 for example).

DateParse (Date As String) As Long

Parses the given **Date** string and returns its ticks representation. An exception will be thrown if parsing fails. Example:

```
Dim SomeTime As Long
SomeTime = DateTime.DateParse("02/23/2007")
```

DateTimeParse (Date As String, Time As String) As Long

Parses the given date and time strings and returns the ticks representation.

DeviceDefaultDateFormat As String [read only]

Returns the default date format based on the language used by the Android device.

DeviceDefaultTimeFormat As String [read only]

Returns the default time format based on the language used by the Android device.

GetDayOfMonth (Ticks As Long) As Int

Returns the day of month component from the ticks value.
Values are from 1 to 31.

GetDayOfWeek (Ticks As Long) As Int

Returns the day of week component from the ticks value.
Values are from 1 to 7, where 1 means Sunday.
You can use the AHLocale library if you need to change the first day.

GetDayOfYear (Ticks As Long) As Int

Returns the day of year component from the ticks value.
Values are from 1 to 366.

GetHour (Ticks As Long) As Int

Returns the hour of day component from the ticks value.
Values are from 0 to 23.

GetMinute (Ticks As Long) As Int
Returns the minutes within an hour component from the ticks value.
Values are from 0 to 59.

GetMonth (Ticks As Long) As Int
Returns the month of year component from the ticks value.
Values are from 1 to 12.

GetSecond (Ticks As Long) As Int
Returns the seconds within a minute component from the ticks value.
Values are from 0 to 59.

GetTimeZoneOffsetAt (Date As Long) As Double
Returns the difference, measured in hours, between the time used by the Android device and UTC (Coordinated Universal Time, equivalent to Greenwich Mean Time). You can specify which **Date** you want to use for the calculation. The offset can change due to daylight-saving settings. For example, if you were in Paris in the summer, then the following would give the result of 2, because France is 1 hour ahead of UTC in winter and another hour ahead in the summer:

```
Log(DateTime.GetTimeZoneOffsetAt(DateTime.Now))
```

GetYear (Ticks As Long) As Int
Returns the year component from the ticks value.

ListenToExternalTimeChanges
Creates a dynamic broadcast receiver that listens to the "time-zone changed" event and "time set" event. By calling this method, the time-zone will update automatically when the device time-zone changes. The **DateTime_TimeChanged** event will be raised when the time-zone changes or when the time is set.

Now As Long [read only]
Gets the current time as ticks (number of milliseconds since January 1, 1970).

SetTimeZone (OffsetHours As Int)
Sets the time zone which your application uses to convert dates to ticks and vice versa. **Note**: the time zone used by the Android device is not changed.

TicksPerDay As Long
Contains the number of milliseconds in a day: 86400000

TicksPerHour As Long
Contains the number of milliseconds in an hour: 3600000

TicksPerMinute As Long
Contains the number of milliseconds in a minute: 60000

TicksPerSecond As Long
Contains the number of milliseconds in a second: 1000

Time (Ticks As Long) As String
Returns a string representation of the time (which is stored as ticks).
The time format can be set with the TimeFormat keyword.
Example:
```
Log("The time now is: " & DateTime.Time(DateTime.Now))
```

TimeFormat As String
Gets or sets the format used to parse time strings. The default pattern is HH:mm:ss (23:45:12 for example). See this page for the supported patterns: formats (http://docs.oracle.com/javase/1.4.2/docs/api/java/text/SimpleDateFormat.html).

TimeParse (Time As String) As Long
Parses the given **Time** string and returns its ticks representation, based on today's date. Example:
```
Log(DateTime.TimeParse("13:45:57"))
```
Note: if the format of Time does not match the format specified by **`DateTime.TimeFormat`**, then a ParseException will be raised and the app will crash.

TimeZoneOffset As Double [read only]
Returns the current offset measured in hours from UTC (Coordinated Universal Time).

Drawing Objects

Bitmap
An object that holds a bitmap image. The bitmap can be loaded from a file or other input stream, or can be set from a different bitmap. Loading large bitmaps can easily lead to out-of-memory exceptions. This is true even if the file is compressed and not large, as the bitmap is stored uncompressed in memory. For large images, you can call **`InitializeSample`** and load a subsample of the image. The whole image will be loaded with a lower resolution.

Members:

- GetPixel (x As Int, y As Int) As Int
- Height As Int [read only]
- Initialize (Dir As String, FileName As String)
- Initialize2 (InputStream As java.io.InputStream)
- Initialize3 (Bitmap As Bitmap)
- InitializeMutable (Width As Int, Height As Int)

InitializeSample (Dir As String, FileName As String, MaxWidth As Int, MaxHeight As Int)
IsInitialized As Boolean
Width As Int [read only]
WriteToStream (OutputStream As java.io.OutputStream, Quality As Int, Format As Bitmap.CompressFormat)

GetPixel (x As Int, y As Int) As Int

Returns the color of the pixel at the specified position.

Height As Int [read only]

Returns the bitmap height.

Initialize (Dir As String, FileName As String)

Reads the image from the given file and uses it to create the **Bitmap**. Note that the image will be downsampled if there is not enough memory available. Example:

```
Dim Bitmap1 As Bitmap
Bitmap1.Initialize(File.DirAssets, "X.jpg")
```

Initialize2 (InputStream As java.io.InputStream)

Initializes the bitmap from the given stream.

Initialize3 (Bitmap1 As Bitmap)

Initializes the bitmap with a copy of the original image (copying is done if necessary).

InitializeMutable (Width As Int, Height As Int)

Creates a new mutable bitmap with the specified dimensions. You can use a Canvas object to draw on this bitmap.

InitializeSample (Dir As String, FileName As String, MaxWidth As Int, MaxHeight As Int)

Initializes the bitmap from the given file. The decoder will subsample the bitmap if **MaxWidth** or **MaxHeight** are smaller than the bitmap dimensions. This can save a lot of memory when loading large images. Note that the actual dimensions may be larger than the specified values.

IsInitialized As Boolean

Whether the **Bitmap** has been initialized using one of the **Initialize** methods.

Width As Int [read only]

Returns the bitmap width.

WriteToStream (OutputStream As java.io.OutputStream, Quality As Int, Format As CompressFormat)

Writes the bitmap to the output stream.
Quality - Value from 0 (smaller size, lower quality) to 100 (larger size, higher quality), which is a hint for the compressor for the required quality.
Format – can be "JPEG" or "PNG". Any other format will produce a runtime exception.

Notes: "JPG" is not an allowed format, but you can use ".jpg" as the filename extension if you wish. Also you can read an image in format and write it in the other.
Example:

```
Dim bm As Bitmap
bm.Initialize(File.DirAssets, "horse.png")
Dim Out As OutputStream
Out = File.OpenOutput(File.DirRootExternal, "horse.jpg", False)
bm.WriteToStream(Out, 100, "JPEG")
Out.Close
```

BitmapDrawable

A drawable that draws a bitmap. The bitmap is set during initialization. You can change the way the bitmap appears by changing the Gravity (page 282) property.
Example:

```
Dim bd As BitmapDrawable
bd.Initialize(LoadBitmap(File.DirAssets, "SomeImage.png"))
bd.Gravity = Gravity.FILL
Activity.Background = bd
```

This is an **`Activity`** object; it cannot be declared under **`Sub Process_Globals`**.

Members:

- Bitmap As Bitmap [read only]
- Gravity As Int
- Initialize (Bitmap1 As Bitmap)
- IsInitialized As Boolean

Bitmap As Bitmap [read only]

Returns the internal Bitmap.

Gravity As Int

Gets or sets the gravity value. This value affects the way the image will be drawn.
Example:

```
BitmapDrawable1.Gravity = Gravity.FILL
```

Initialize (Bitmap1 As Bitmap)

IsInitialized As Boolean

Whether the **`BitmapDrawable`** has been initialized using one of the **`Initialize`** methods.

Canvas

A **`Canvas`** is an object that draws on other views or bitmaps which are editable (also called "mutable"). When the canvas is initialized and set to draw on a view, a new mutable bitmap is created for that view's background, the current view's background is copied to the new bitmap and the canvas is set to draw on the new bitmap.
The canvas drawings are not immediately updated on the screen. You should call the target view's **`Invalidate`** method to make it refresh the view. This is useful as it allows you to make several drawings and only then refresh the display.

The canvas can be temporarily limited to a specific region (and thus only affect this region). This is done by calling **ClipPath**. Removing the clipping is done by calling **RemoveClip**. You can get the bitmap that the canvas draws on with the **Bitmap** property.
This is an **Activity** object; it cannot be declared under **Sub Process_Globals**.

Members:

Bitmap As Bitmap [read only]

ClipPath (Path1 As Path)

DrawBitmap (Bitmap1 As Bitmap, SrcRect As Rect, DestRect As Rect)

DrawBitmapFlipped (Bitmap1 As Bitmap, SrcRect As Rect, DestRect As Rect, Vertically As Boolean, Horizontally As Boolean)

DrawBitmapRotated (Bitmap1 As Bitmap, SrcRect As Rect, DestRect As Rect, Degrees As Float)

DrawCircle (page 295) (x As Float, y As Float, Radius As Float, Color As Int, Filled As Boolean, StrokeWidth As Float)

DrawColor (page 295) (Color As Int)

DrawDrawable (page 295) (Drawable1 As Drawable, DestRect As Rect)

DrawDrawableRotate (page 295) (Drawable1 As Drawable, DestRect As Rect, Degrees As Float)

DrawLine (page 296) (x1 As Float, y1 As Float, x2 As Float, y2 As Float, Color As Int, StrokeWidth As Float)

DrawOval (page 296) (Rect1 As Rect, Color As Int, Filled As Boolean, StrokeWidth As Float)

DrawOvalRotated (page 296) (Rect1 As Rect, Color As Int, Filled As Boolean, StrokeWidth As Float, Degrees As Float)

DrawPath (page 296) (Path1 As Path, Color As Int, Filled As Boolean, StrokeWidth As Float)

DrawPoint (page 297) (x As Float, y As Float, Color As Int)

DrawRect (page 297) (Rect1 As Rect, Color As Int, Filled As Boolean, StrokeWidth As Float)

DrawRectRotated (page 297) (Rect1 As Rect, Color As Int, Filled As Boolean, StrokeWidth As Float, Degrees As Float)

DrawText (page 297) (Text As String, x As Float, y As Float, Typeface1 As Typeface, TextSize As Float, Color As Int, Align1 As Align)

DrawTextRotated (page 298) (Text As String, x As Float, y As Float, Typeface1 As Typeface, TextSize As Float, Color As Int, Align1 As Align, Degree As Float)

Initialize (page 298) (Target As View)

Initialize2 (page 298) (Bitmap1 As Bitmap)

MeasureStringHeight (page 298) (Text As String, Typeface1 As Typeface, TextSize As Float) As Float

MeasureStringWidth (page 298) (Text As String, Typeface1 As Typeface, TextSize As Float) As Float

RemoveClip (page 299)

Bitmap As Bitmap [read only]

Returns the bitmap that the canvas draws to. The following example saves the drawing to a file:

```
Dim Out As OutputStream
Out = File.OpenOutput(File.DirRootExternal, "Test.png", False)
Canvas1.Bitmap.WriteToStream(out, 100, "PNG")
Out.Close
```

ClipPath (Path1 As Path)

Clips the drawing area to the given path.

Example: Fills a diamond shape with gradient color.

```
Dim Canvas1 As Canvas
Dim DestRect As Rect
Dim Gradient1 As GradientDrawable
Dim Clrs(2) As Int
Clrs(0) = Colors.Black
Clrs(1) = Colors.White
Gradient1.Initialize("TOP_BOTTOM", Clrs)
Dim Path1 As Path
Path1.Initialize(50%x, 100%y)
Path1.LineTo(100%x, 50%y)
Path1.LineTo(50%x, 0%y)
Path1.LineTo(0%x, 50%y)
Path1.LineTo(50%x, 100%y)
Canvas1.Initialize(Activity)
Canvas1.ClipPath(Path1) 'clip the drawing area to the path
DestRect.Initialize(0%y,0%y,100%x,100%y)
Canvas1.DrawDrawable(Gradient1, DestRect) 'fill the drawing area
with the gradient.
Activity.Invalidate
```

DrawBitmap (Bitmap1 As Bitmap, SrcRect As Rect, DestRect As Rect)

Draws a bitmap.
SrcRect - The subset of the bitmap that will be drawn. If **`Null`**, then the complete bitmap will be drawn.
DestRect - The rectangle that the bitmap will be drawn to.
The following example first draws the whole bitmap, then draws just the left half . The image must be included in the Files folder of the project:

```
Dim Canvas1 As Canvas
Canvas1.Initialize(Activity)

'draw the whole bitmap to the top half of the Activity
Dim Bitmap1 As Bitmap
Bitmap1.Initialize(File.DirAssets, "horse.png")
Dim DestRect As Rect
DestRect.Initialize(0, 0, 100%x, 50%y)
Canvas1.DrawBitmap(Bitmap1, Null, DestRect)

' draw the left half of the bitmap to bottom half of Activity
Dim SrcRect As Rect
SrcRect.Initialize(0, 0, Bitmap1.Width / 2, Bitmap1.Height)
DestRect.Top = 50%y
DestRect.Bottom = 100%y
Canvas1.DrawBitmap(Bitmap1, SrcRect, DestRect)
Activity.Invalidate
```

DrawBitmapFlipped (Bitmap1 As Bitmap, SrcRect As Rect, DestRect As Rect, Vertically As Boolean, Horizontally As Boolean)

Flips the bitmap and draws it.
SrcRect - The subset of the bitmap that will be drawn. If **Null**, then the complete bitmap will be drawn.
DestRect - The rectangle that the bitmap will be drawn to.
Vertically - Whether to flip the bitmap vertically.
Horizontally - Whether to flip the bitmap horizontally.
Example:

```
Canvas1.DrawBitmapFlipped(Bitmap1, Null, DestRect, False, True)
```

DrawBitmapRotated (Bitmap1 As Bitmap, SrcRect As Rect, DestRect As Rect, Degrees As Float)

Rotates the bitmap and draws it.
SrcRect - The subset of the bitmap that will be drawn. If **Null**, then the complete bitmap will be drawn.
DestRect - The rectangle that the bitmap will be drawn to.
Degrees - Number of degrees to rotate the bitmap clockwise. Negative numbers will rotate anti-clockwise.
Example:

```
Dim Canvas1 As Canvas
Canvas1.Initialize(Activity)
Dim Bitmap1 As Bitmap
Bitmap1.Initialize(File.DirAssets, "horse.png")
Dim DestRect As Rect
DestRect.Initialize(0, 0, 100%x, 50%y)
' draw the bitmap rotated by 70 degrees
Canvas1.DrawBitmapRotated(Bitmap1, Null, DestRect, 70)
```

DrawCircle (x As Float, y As Float, Radius As Float, Color As Int, Filled As Boolean, StrokeWidth As Float)
Draws a circle.
x - the left edge of the circle
y - the top of the circle
Filled - Whether the circle will be filled.
StrokeWidth - The stroke width (only relevant when Filled = `False`)
Example:

```
Dim Canvas1 As Canvas
Canvas1.Initialize(Activity)
Canvas1.DrawCircle(150dip, 150dip, 20dip, Colors.Red, False,
10dip)
```

DrawColor (Color As Int)
Fills the entire canvas with the given color.
Example:

```
'fill with semi-transparent red color
Canvas1.DrawColor(Colors.ARGB(100, 255, 0, 0))
Activity.Invalidate
```

DrawDrawable (Drawable1 As Drawable, DestRect As Rect)
Draws a Drawable into the specified rectangle.
Example:

```
' Fill a rectangle with a Gradient
Dim Canvas1 As Canvas
Dim DestRect As Rect
Dim Gradient1 As GradientDrawable
Dim Clrs(2) As Int

Canvas1.Initialize(Activity)
DestRect.Initialize(0, 0, 100%x, 100%y)
Clrs(0) = Colors.Green
Clrs(1) = Colors.Blue
Gradient1.Initialize("TOP_BOTTOM", Clrs)
Canvas1.DrawDrawable(Gradient1, DestRect)
Activity.Invalidate
```

DrawDrawableRotate (Drawable1 As Drawable, DestRect As Rect, Degrees As Float)
Rotates and draws a Drawable into the specified rectangle.
Degrees - Number of degrees to rotate clockwise. Negative numbers will rotate anti-clockwise.

DrawLine (x1 As Float, y1 As Float, x2 As Float, y2 As Float, Color As Int, StrokeWidth As Float)
Draws a line from (x1, y1) to (x2, y2). StrokeWidth determines the width of the line.
Example:

```
Canvas1.DrawLine(100dip, 100dip, 200dip, 200dip, Colors.Red,
10dip)
Activity.Invalidate
```

DrawOval (Rect1 As Rect, Color As Int, Filled As Boolean, StrokeWidth As Float)

Draws an oval shape.
Filled - Whether the rectangle will be filled.
StrokeWidth - The stroke width. Relevant only when Filled = **False**.
Example:

```
Dim Rect1 As Rect
Rect1.Initialize(100dip, 100dip, 200dip, 150dip)
Canvas1.DrawOval(Rect1, Colors.Gray, False, 5dip)
Activity.Invalidate
```

DrawOvalRotated (Rect1 As Rect, Color As Int, Filled As Boolean, StrokeWidth As Float, Degrees As Float)

Rotates the oval and draws it.
Filled - Whether the rectangle will be filled.
StrokeWidth - The stroke width. Relevant when Filled = **False**.
Degrees - Number of degrees to rotate the oval clockwise. Negative numbers will rotate anti-clockwise.

DrawPath (Path1 As Path, Color As Int, Filled As Boolean, StrokeWidth As Float)

Draws the path.
Filled - Whether the path will be filled.
StrokeWidth - The stroke width. Relevant when Filled = **False**.
Example:

```
' Draw a magenta diamond
Dim Canvas1 As Canvas
Dim DestRect As Rect
Dim Path1 As Path

Canvas1.Initialize(Activity)
DestRect.Initialize(0, 0, 100%x, 50%y)
Path1.Initialize(50%x, 100%y)
Path1.LineTo(100%x, 50%y)
Path1.LineTo(50%x, 0%y)
Path1.LineTo(0%x, 50%y)
Path1.LineTo(50%x, 100%y)
Canvas1.DrawPath(Path1, Colors.Magenta, False, 10dip)
```

DrawPoint (x As Float, y As Float, Color As Int)

Draws a point at the specified position and color. Example to draw a point in the middle of the screen:

```
Dim Canvas1 As Canvas
Canvas1.Initialize(Activity)
Canvas1.DrawPoint(50%x, 50%y, Colors.Yellow)
```

DrawRect (Rect1 As Rect, Color As Int, Filled As Boolean, StrokeWidth As Float)

Draws a rectangle.
Filled - Whether the rectangle will be filled.
StrokeWidth - The stroke width. Relevant when Filled = **False**
Example to draw an outlined rectangle:

```
Dim Canvas1 As Canvas
Dim Rect1 As Rect
Canvas1.Initialize(Activity)
Rect1.Initialize(100dip, 100dip, 200dip, 150dip)
Canvas1.DrawRect(Rect1, Colors.Gray, False, 5dip)
Activity.Invalidate
```

DrawRectRotated (Rect1 As Rect, Color As Int, Filled As Boolean, StrokeWidth As Float, Degrees As Float)

Rotates the rectangle and draws it.
Filled - Whether the rectangle will be filled.
StrokeWidth - The stroke width. Relevant when Filled = **False**.
Degrees - Number of degrees to rotate the rectangle clockwise. Negative numbers will rotate anti-clockwise.

DrawText (Text As String, x As Float, y As Float, Typeface1 As Typeface, TextSize As Float, Color As Int, Align1 As Align)

Draws the text.
Text - The text to be drawn.
x, y - The origin point.
Typeface1 - Typeface (font) to use.
TextSize - This value will be automatically scaled, so do not scale it yourself.
Color - Text color.
Align - The alignment related to the origin. One of the following values: "LEFT", "CENTER", "RIGHT". Example to draw text in middle of screen:

```
Dim Canvas1 As Canvas
Canvas1.Initialize(Activity)
Canvas1.DrawText("Basic4Android is fantastic!", _
 50%x, 50%y, Typeface.DEFAULT_BOLD, 20, Colors.Blue, "CENTER")
Activity.Invalidate
```

DrawTextRotated (Text As String, x As Float, y As Float, Typeface1 As Typeface, TextSize As Float, Color As Int, Align1 As Align, Degree As Float)

Rotates the text and draws it.
Text - The text to be drawn.
x, y - The origin point.
Typeface1 - Typeface (font) to use.

TextSize - This value will be automatically scaled, so do not scale it yourself.
Color - Text color.
Align - The alignment related to the origin. One of the following values: "LEFT", "CENTER", "RIGHT".
Degrees - Number of degrees to rotate clockwise. Negative numbers will rotate anti-clockwise.
Example to draw rotated text in middle of screen:

```
Dim Canvas1 As Canvas
Canvas1.Initialize(Activity)
Canvas1.DrawTextRotated("Basic4Android is fantastic!", _
 50%x, 50%y, Typeface.DEFAULT_BOLD, 20, Colors.Blue, "CENTER",
90)
Activity.Invalidate
```

Initialize (Target As View)

Initializes the canvas for drawing on a view.
The view background will be drawn on the canvas during initialization.
Note that you should not change the view's background after calling this method.
Example:

```
Dim Canvas1 As Canvas
Canvas1.Initialize(Activity) 'this canvas will draw on the
activity background
```

Initialize2 (Bitmap1 As Bitmap)

Initializes the canvas for drawing on this bitmap. The bitmap must be mutable.
Bitmaps created from files or input streams are NOT mutable.

MeasureStringHeight (Text As String, Typeface As Typeface, TextSize As Float) As Float

Returns the height of the given text. Example of drawing a blue text with white rectangle as the background:

```
Dim Canvas1 As Canvas
Dim Rect1 As Rect
Dim width, height As Float
Dim t As String
Canvas1.Initialize(Activity)
t = "Text to write"
width = Canvas1.MeasureStringWidth(t, Typeface.DEFAULT, 14)
height = Canvas1.MeasureStringHeight(t, Typeface.DEFAULT, 14)
Rect1.Initialize(100dip, 100dip, 100dip + width, 100dip +
height)
Canvas1.DrawRect(Rect1, Colors.White, True, 0)
Canvas1.DrawText(t, Rect1.Left, Rect1.Bottom, Typeface.DEFAULT,
14, Colors.Blue, "LEFT")
Activity.Invalidate
```

MeasureStringWidth (Text As String, Typeface1 As Typeface, TextSize As Float) As Float

Returns the width of the given text. See MeasureStringHeight above for an example.

RemoveClip
Removes previous clipped region.

ColorDrawable
A drawable that has a solid color and can have round corners. Example to color a button green:

```
Dim Button1 As Button
Dim cd As ColorDrawable
Button1.Initialize("test")
Activity.AddView(Button1, 10dip, 10dip, 80dip, 50dip)
cd.Initialize(Colors.Green, 5dip)
Button1.Background = cd
Button1.Text = "Test"
Activity.Invalidate
```

This is an **Activity** object; it cannot be declared under **Sub Process_Globals**.

Initialize (Color As Int, CornerRadius As Int)
Initializes the drawable with the given color and corner radius.

IsInitialized As Boolean
Whether the **ColorDrawable** has been initialized using the **Initialize** method.

GradientDrawable
A drawable that has a gradient color and can have round corners.
This is an **Activity** object; it cannot be declared under **Sub Process_Globals**.
Example to draw a gradient, with rounded corners, within a panel:

```
' create the panel to receive the gradient
Dim pnlTest As Panel
pnlTest.Initialize("")
Activity.AddView(pnlTest,20dip,20dip,100dip,100dip)
' create gradient colors
Dim cols(2) As Int
cols(0) = Colors.Red
cols(1) = Colors.Blue
' create the gradient
Dim gd1 As GradientDrawable
gd1.Initialize("TL_BR",cols)
gd1.CornerRadius = 20dip
' add gradient to panel
pnlTest.Background=gd1
```

Members:
- CornerRadius As Float [write only]
- Initialize (Orientation1 As Orientation, Colors() As Int)
- IsInitialized As Boolean

CornerRadius As Float [write only]
Sets the radius of the "rectangle" corners. Set to 0 for square corners. Example:

```
Gradient1.CornerRadius = 20dip
```

Initialize (Orientation1 As Orientation, Colors() As Int)

Initializes this object.
Orientation - The gradient orientation. Can be one of the following value:
"TOP_BOTTOM"
"TR_BL" (Top-Right to Bottom-Left)
"RIGHT_LEFT"
"BR_TL" (Bottom-Right to Top-Left)
"BOTTOM_TOP"
"BL_TR" (Bottom-Left to Top-Right)
"LEFT_RIGHT"
"TL_BR" (Top-Left to Bottom-Right)
Colors - An array with the gradient colors.
Example:

```
Dim Gradient1 As GradientDrawable
Dim Clrs(2) As Int
Clrs(0) = Colors.Black
Clrs(1) = Colors.White
Gradient1.Initialize("TOP_BOTTOM", Clrs)
```

IsInitialized As Boolean

Whether the **GradientDrawable** has been initialized using the **Initialize** method.

Path

A **Path** is a collection of points that represent a connected path. The first point is set when the path is initialized, and then other points are added with **LineTo**.

Members:

Initialize (x As Float, y As Float)

Initializes the path and sets the value of the first point.

IsInitialized As Boolean

Whether the **Path** has been initialized using the **Initialize** method.

LineTo (x As Float, y As Float)

Adds a line from the last point to the specified point.

Rect

Holds four coordinates which represent a rectangle.

Members:

- Bottom As Int
- CenterX As Int [read only]
- CenterY As Int [read only]
- Initialize (Left As Int, Top As Int, Right As Int, Bottom As Int)
- IsInitialized As Boolean

Left As Int
Right As Int
Top As Int

Bottom As Int

CenterX As Int [read only]
Returns the horizontal center.

CenterY As Int [read only]
Returns the vertical center.

Initialize (Left As Int, Top As Int, Right As Int, Bottom As Int)

IsInitialized As Boolean
Whether the **Rect** has been initialized using the **Initialize** method.

Left As Int

Right As Int

Top As Int

StateListDrawable

A drawable that holds other drawables and chooses the current one based on the view's state, such as **State_Checked**. This is an **Activity** object; it cannot be declared under **Sub Process_Globals**. Example:

```
' create button to use StateListDrawable as background
Dim tb As ToggleButton
tb.Initialize("")
tb.Checked = False
tb.TextColor = Colors.Blue
tb.TextSize = 20
tb.Typeface = Typeface.DEFAULT_BOLD
' create colorDrawables
Dim checked, unchecked As ColorDrawable
checked.Initialize(Colors.Green, 10dip)
unchecked.Initialize(Colors.Red, 10dip)
' create StateListDrawable
Dim sld As StateListDrawable
sld.Initialize
' add colorDrawables to StateListDrawable
sld.AddState(sld.State_Checked, checked)
sld.AddState(sld.State_Unchecked, unchecked)
' add StateListDrawable to button
tb.Background = sld
' show button
Activity.AddView(tb, 100dip, 100dip, 100dip, 100dip)
```

Members:

AddCatchAllState (Drawable1 As Drawable)

- AddState (State As Int, Drawable1 As Drawable)
- AddState2 (State() As Int, Drawable1 As Drawable)
- Initialize
- IsInitialized As Boolean
- State_Checked As Int
- State_Disabled As Int
- State_Enabled As Int
- State_Focused As Int
- State_Pressed As Int
- State_Selected As Int
- State_Unchecked As Int

AddCatchAllState (Drawable1 As Drawable)

Adds the **Drawable** that will be used if no other state matched the current state.
Note: this should always be the last state. States added after this one will never be used.

AddState (State As Int, Drawable1 As Drawable)

Adds a **State** and **Drawable** pair. Example (see above for complete code):

```
sld.AddState(sld.State_Checked, checked)
```

Note: if you add the same state twice, the first one added will be used.

AddState2 (State() As Int, Drawable1 As Drawable)

Adds a **State** and **Drawable** pair. The state is made from a combination of states.
Note: You should not reuse the array specified as it is used internally by `StateListDrawable`.
Note also: the order of states is very important. The first state that matches will be used.

Initialize

Initializes the object.

IsInitialized As Boolean

Whether the `StateListDrawable` has been initialized using the `Initialize` method.

State_Checked As Int

State_Disabled As Int

State_Enabled As Int

State_Focused As Int

State_Pressed As Int

State_Selected As Int

State_Unchecked As Int

Exception

Holds a thrown exception. You can access the last thrown exception by calling **LastException**.

Example:

```
Try
  Dim in As InputStream
  in = File.OpenInput(File.DirInternal, "SomeMissingFile.txt")
  ' etc
Catch
  ' come here if there is an exception
  Log(LastException.Message)
End Try
If in.IsInitialized Then in.Close
```

Members:

IsInitialized As Boolean

Message As String [read only]

IsInitialized As Boolean

Whether the **Exception** has been initialized. Example:

```
If LastException.IsInitialized Then
```

Message As String [read only]

File Object

Many applications require access to persistent storage. The two most common storage types are files and databases. We deal with files here. Databases have a chapter of their own (page 156).

Filenames

Android file names allow the following characters:

a to z, A to Z, 0 to 9 . _ + - % &

Spaces, "*" and "?" are not allowed.

Note that Android file names are case sensitive , so "MyFile.txt" is different from "myfile.txt".

Adding Files to your Project

You must add files to your app by using the Files tab in the IDE and clicking "Add Files". This will place a copy of the selected file in the Files folder of your project.

File locations

There are several important locations where you can retrieve and perhaps store files: the folder where your app is installed; the main memory; or an external storage card.

File.DirAssets

The assets folder includes the files that were added with the file manager in the IDE. It's created from the Files folder in your project.
These files are read-only.
Your app cannot create new files in this folder (which is actually located inside the apk file).
If you have a database file in the DirAssets folder, you need to copy it to another folder before you can use it. You can use the DBUtils.CopyDBFromAssets (page 161) function to achieve this.

File.DirInternal / File.DirInternalCache

These two folders are stored in the main memory of the device and are private to your application. Other applications cannot access these files. The cache folder may get deleted by Android if it needs more space.

Storage Card Folders

The next two locations are on the storage card. You can check if there is a storage card and whether it is available with **File.ExternalReadable** and **File.ExternalWritable**.
Using either of the following will add the EXTERNAL_STORAGE permission to your application.

File.DirRootExternal

The storage card root folder: mnt\sdcard.

File.DirDefaultExternal

The default folder for your application in the SD card.
The folder is: <storage card>/Android/data/<package>/files/
It will be created if required.

Text encoding

Sometimes it is useful to read or write text files using Basic4Android. There are two objects to help you to do this: TextReader (page 312) and TextWriter (page 313). Here we describe how text is encoded and stored within a file. Since your app might deal with different languages and might import files with various formats, basic understanding can help overcome some possible problems.
Encoding is a way of converting a set of characters into binary data in a standard format so the data can be exchanged between systems.
Originally, (back in 1963), English characters were encoded in ASCII. As computing spread to other languages, the Unicode system was invented (in 1988), allowing all the world's languages to be encoded.
See http://unicode-table.com/en/ for a list of characters and their Unicode codes.
Unicode can be implemented by different encoding systems (also called Code Pages or Character Sets). The most commonly used encodings are UTF-8 and UTF-16.

Android Character Sets

Android can use following character sets:

- UTF-8 default character-set

- UTF-16
- UTF-16 BE
- UTF-LE
- US-ASCII ASCII character set
- ISO-8859-1 almost equivalent to the ANSI character-set
- Windows-1252

The default character set in Android is Unicode UTF-8.

Windows Character Sets

In Windows, the most common character sets are ASCII and **Windows-1252** (often called ANSI).

ASCII is a 7 bit encoding, allowing definitions for 128 characters. 33 are non-printing control characters (now mostly obsolete) that affect how text and space is processed.

Windows-1252

Windows-1252 or CP-1252, (often called **ANSI**), is a character encoding of the Latin alphabet, used by default in the legacy components of Microsoft Windows in English and some other Western languages with 256 definitions (one byte). The first 128 characters are the same as in the ASCII encoding.

Many files generated by Windows programs are encoded with the Windows-1252 character-set in western countries, for example, Excel CSV files and Notepad files by default. (Note that Notepad can also save files with UTF-8 encoding.)

To read Windows files encoded with Windows-1252, you should use the Windows-1252 character-set. If you need to write files for use with Windows, you should also use the Windows-1252 character-set.

To read or write files with a different encoding, you must use the TextReader (page 312) or TextWriter (page 313) objects with the **`Initialize2`** methods.

End-of-Line Character(s)

Another difference between Windows and Android is the end-of-line character. In Android (following the Linux model), only the LF (Line Feed) character, Chr(10), is added at the end of a line. In Windows, two characters, CR (Carriage Return Chr(13)) and LF Chr(10), are added at the end of a line. If you need to write files for Windows, you must add CR yourself.

The symbol for the end-of-line is **`CRLF`** = Chr(10). Its name can be slightly confusing, since it is actually only the LF character. The name was chosen because it has the same effect as CR+LF in Windows.

Reading and Writing Excel Files

Excel can save spreadsheets in CSV ("Comma Separated Values") format. There are two functions, **`LoadCSV`** and **`LoadCSV2`** in the StringUtils library, which can read CSV files and one which can save a CSV file. See the StringUtils (page 511) library documentation for examples. You do NOT need to change the format of the files when you move these CSV files between a Windows PC and an Android device.

Notepad and Notepad++

When you save a file with NotePad, three additional bytes are added. These bytes are called BOM characters (Byte Order Mark). In *UTF-8* they are represented by this

byte sequence: `0xEF,0xBB,0xBF`. A text editor or web browser interpreting the text as *Windows-1252* will display the characters `ï»¿`.
To avoid this, you can use Notepad++ (http://notepad-plus-plus.org/) instead of *NotePad* and use the menu [Encoding > Encode in *UTF-8* without BOM].
Another possibility to change text from *Windows-1252* to *UTF-8* is to use this code:

```
Dim var, result As String
var = "Gestió"
Dim arrByte() As Byte
arrByte = var.GetBytes("Windows-1252")
result = BytesToString(arrByte, 0, arrByte.Length, "UTF8")
```

File

File is a predefined object that holds methods for working with files. The File object includes several methods for writing to files and reading from files. To be able to write to a file or to read from a file, it must be opened.
"Predefined" means that you do not need to declare it yourself. Thus, for each of the following, you would prefix the method with File. For example, **`File.Exists`**.
Note: the Android file system is case sensitive.

Members:

- Combine (Dir As String, FileName As String) As String
- Copy (DirSource As String, FileSource As String, DirTarget As String, FileTarget As String)
- Copy2 (In As java.io.InputStream, Out As java.io.OutputStream)
- Delete (Dir As String, FileName As String) As Boolean
- DirAssets As String [read only]
- DirDefaultExternal As String [read only]
- DirInternal As String [read only]
- DirInternalCache As String [read only]
- DirRootExternal As String [read only]
- Exists (Dir As String, FileName As String) As Boolean
- ExternalReadable As Boolean [read only]
- ExternalWritable As Boolean [read only]
- GetText (Dir As String, FileName As String) As String
- IsDirectory (Dir As String, FileName As String) As Boolean
- LastModified (Dir As String, FileName As String) As Long
- ListFiles (Dir As String) As List
- MakeDir (Parent As String, Dir As String)
- OpenInput (page 309) (Dir As String, FileName As String) As InputStream
- OpenOutput (page 309) (Dir As String, FileName As String, Append As Boolean) As OutputStream
- ReadList (page 309) (Dir As String, FileName As String) As List
- ReadMap (page 309) (Dir As String, FileName As String) As Map

- ReadMap2 (Dir As String, FileName As String, Map As Map) As Map
- ReadString (Dir As String, FileName As String) As String
- Size (Dir As String, FileName As String) As Long
- WriteList (page 310) (Dir As String, FileName As String, List As List)
- WriteMap (page 310) (Dir As String, FileName As String, Map As Map)
- WriteString (page 310) (Dir As String, FileName As String, Text As String)

Combine (Dir As String, FileName As String) As String

Returns the full path to the given file.
This method does not support files in the assets folder.

Copy (DirSource As String, FileSource As String, DirTarget As String, FileTarget As String)

Copies the specified source file to the target file name.
Note: it is not possible to copy files to the Assets folder.

Copy2 (In As java.io.InputStream, Out As java.io.OutputStream)

Copies all the available data from the input stream into the output stream.
The input stream is automatically closed at the end.

Delete (Dir As String, FileName As String) As Boolean

Deletes the specified file **FileName** in the specified directory **Dir**. If FileName is the name of a directory, then it must be empty in order to be deleted. Returns **True** if the file was successfully deleted. Example:

```
File.MakeDir(File.DirRootExternal, "A123Test")
If File.Delete(File.DirRootExternal, "A123Test") Then
 ToastMessageShow("Success", False)
Else
 ToastMessageShow("Success", False)
End If
```

Note: files in the assets folder cannot be deleted.

DirAssets As String [read only]

Returns a reference to the files added to the Files tab. These files are read-only.

DirDefaultExternal As String [read only]

Returns the application default external folder which is based on the package name.
The folder is created if needed.

DirInternal As String [read only]

Returns the folder in the device internal storage that is used to save application private data.

DirInternalCache As String [read only]

Returns the folder in the device internal storage that is used to save application cache data.
This data will be deleted automatically when the device runs low on storage.

DirRootExternal As String [read only]

Returns the root folder of the external storage media.

Exists (Dir As String, FileName As String) As Boolean

Returns **True** if the specified FileName exists in the specified Dir.

Note that the Android file system is case sensitive.

Example:

```
If File.Exists(File.DirDefaultExternal, "MyFile.txt") Then ...
```

ExternalReadable As Boolean [read only]

Returns **TRUE** if the external storage media can be read from.

ExternalWritable As Boolean [read only]

Returns **TRUE** if the external storage media can be written to (and also read from)

```
Dim directory As String
If File.ExternalWritable Then
 directory = File.DirDefaultExternal
Else
 directory = File.DirInternal
End If
```

GetText (Dir As String, FileName As String) As String

Reads the entire file and returns its text. The file is assumed to be encoded with UTF8.

IsDirectory (Dir As String, FileName As String) As Boolean

Returns **TRUE** if the specified file is a directory.

LastModified (Dir As String, FileName As String) As Long

Returns the last modified date of the specified file. This method does not support files in the assets folder. Example:

```
Dim d As Long
d = File.LastModified(File.DirRootExternal, "1.txt")
Msgbox(DateTime.Date(d), "Last modified")
```

ListFiles (Dir As String) As List

Returns a read only list with all the files and directories which are stored in the specified path. Example:

```
Dim List1 As List
List1 = File.ListFiles(File.DirRootExternal)
```

List1 can be declared in **Sub Globals**.

An uninitialized list will be returned if the folder is not accessible.

MakeDir (Parent As String, Dir As String)

Creates the given folder. Example:

```
File.MakeDir(File.DirInternal, "Pictures")
```

Can also create a subfolder. All folders will be created as needed. Example:

```
File.MakeDir(File.DirInternal, "music/90/pop/favorites")
```

To access a file in the folder use either

```
ImageView1.Bitmap = LoadBitmap(File.DirInternal &
"/music/90/pop/favorites", "test1.png")
```

Or

```
ImageView1.Bitmap = LoadBitmap(File.DirInternal, "
music/90/pop/favorites/test1.png")
```

OpenInput (Dir As String, FileName As String) As InputStream

Opens the file for reading. The file, specified by **FileName, is** located in the folder specified by **Dir**.
Note: the Android file system is case sensitive.

OpenOutput (Dir As String, FileName As String, Append As Boolean) As OutputStream

Opens (or creates) the file specified by **FileName** which is located in the **Dir** folder for writing. If **Append** is **True**, then the new data will be written at the end of the existing file. If the file doesn't exist, it will be created.
Example:

```
Dim outFile As TextWriter
outFile.Initialize(File.OpenOutput(strMyFolder,"temp.txt",False)
)
outFile.Write("hello")
outFile.Close
```

ReadList (Dir As String, FileName As String) As List

Reads the entire file and returns all lines as a List of strings.
Example:

```
Dim List1 As List
List1 = File.ReadList(File.DirDefaultExternal, "1.txt")
For i = 0 to List1.Size - 1
  Log(List1.Get(i))
Next
```

ReadMap (Dir As String, FileName As String) As Map

Reads a file which has been previously written by **File.WriteMap**. **ReadMap** parses each line as a key-value pair (of strings) and adds them to a Map object, which it then returns.

```
mapCopy = File.ReadMap(File.DirDefaultExternal, "savedMap")
```

The original mapCopy is over-written by the saved data. Note that the order of entries returned might be different than the original order.

ReadMap2 (Dir As String, FileName As String, Map As Map) As Map

Same as **ReadMap** except the items retrieved from the file are appended to the existing Map.

ReadString (Dir As String, FileName As String) As String

Reads the file and returns its content as a string. Example:

```
Dim text As String
text = File.ReadString(File.DirRootExternal, "1.txt")
```

Size (Dir As String, FileName As String) As Long

Returns the size in bytes of the specified file. This method does not support files in the assets folder.

WriteList (Dir As String, FileName As String, List As List)
Writes each item in the **List** as a single line in the output file. All values are converted to string type if required. Each value will be stored in a separate line.
Note: a value in **List** containing CRLF, or a new-line character, will be saved as two lines. When subsequently reading the file with **`ReadList`**, they will be read as two items.
Example:
```
File.WriteList (File.DirInternal, "mylist.txt", List1)
```

WriteMap (Dir As String, FileName As String, Map1 As Map)
Takes a **Map** object (holding pairs of key and value elements), converts all values to strings, creates a new text file and stores the key-value pairs, each pair as a single line. This file format makes it easy to edit the file manually.
One common usage of **`File.WriteMap`** is to save a map of "settings" to a file.
You can use **`File.ReadMap`** to read this file.

WriteString (Dir As String, FileName As String, Text As String)
Writes the given text to a new file.
Example:
```
File.WriteString(File.DirRootExternal, "1.txt", "Some text")
```

InputStream
A stream that you can read from. Usually you will pass the stream to a "higher level" object like **`TextReader`** that will handle the reading. You can use **`File.OpenInput`** to get a file input stream. Example:
```
Dim streamInput As InputStream
streamInput = File.OpenInput(File.DirAssets, "test.txt")
Dim tr As TextReader
tr.Initialize(streamInput)
```

Members:

BytesAvailable As Int
Returns an estimation of the number of bytes available.
Note: if you call **`InputStream.ReadBytes`** on a network stream, then the thread will wait for at least a single byte to be available. In most cases this will cause your app to crash! So you should always use **`InputStream.BytesAvailable`** before calling **`ReadBytes`**, to avoid blocking the main thread.

Close
Closes the stream.

InitializeFromBytesArray (Buffer() As Byte, StartOffset As Int, MaxCount As Int)
Use **`File.OpenInput`** to get a file input stream. This method should be used to initialize the input stream and set it to read from the the **Buffer()** byte-array.
StartOffset - The first byte that will be read.
MaxCount - Maximum number of bytes to read.

IsInitialized As Boolean
Whether the InpuStream has been initialized using **`InitializeFromBytesArray`**.

ReadBytes (Buffer() As Byte, StartOffset As Int, MaxCount As Int) As Int
Reads up to **MaxCount** bytes from the stream and writes it to the given **Buffer**. The first byte will be written at **StartOffset**. Returns the number of bytes actually read. Returns **`-1`** if there are no more bytes to read. Otherwise, returns at least one byte.
Note: if you call **`InputStream.ReadBytes`** on a network stream, then the thread will wait for at least a single byte to be available. In most cases this will cause your app to crash! So you should always use **`InputStream.BytesAvailable`** before calling **`ReadBytes`**, to avoid blocking the main thread. Example:

```
Dim buffer(1024) As byte
count = InputStream1.ReadBytes(buffer, 0, buffer.length)
```

OutputStream

A stream that you can write to. Usually, you will pass the stream to a "higher level" object like **`TextWriter`** which will handle the writing.
Use **`File.OpenOutput`** to get a file output stream.

Members:

- Close
- Flush
- InitializeToBytesArray (StartSize As Int)
- IsInitialized As Boolean
- ToBytesArray As Byte()
- WriteBytes (Buffer() As Byte, StartOffset As Int, Length As Int)

Close
Closes the stream.

Flush
Flushes any buffered data.

InitializeToBytesArray (StartSize As Int)
Use **`File.OpenOutput`** to get a file output stream. This method should be used to write data to a byte-array.
StartSize - The starting size of the internal byte-array. The size will increase if needed.

IsInitialized As Boolean
Whether the **`OutputStream`** has been initialized using **`InitializeFromBytesArray`**.

ToBytesArray As Byte()
Returns a copy of the internal byte-array. Can only be used when the output stream was initialized with **`InitializeToBytesArray`**.

WriteBytes (Buffer() As Byte, StartOffset As Int, Length As Int)
Writes the buffer to the stream. The first byte to be written is Buffer(StartOffset), and the last is Buffer(StartOffset + Length - 1).

TextReader
Reads text from the underlying stream. Example:
```
Dim streamInput As InputStream
streamInput = File.OpenInput(File.DirAssets, "test.txt")
Dim tr As TextReader
tr.Initialize(streamInput)
Dim strLine As String
strLine = tr.ReadLine
Do While strLine <> Null
 Log (strLine)
 strLine = tr.ReadLine
Loop
streamInput.Close
```
Members:

Close
Closes the stream.

Initialize (InputStream As java.io.InputStream)
Initializes a TextReader by wrapping the given InputStream using the UTF8 encoding (page 304).
Example:
```
In = File.OpenInput(File.DirAssets, "myFile.txt")
txtReader.Initialize(In)
strRead = txtReader.ReadAll
```
Initialize2 (InputStream As java.io.InputStream, Encoding As String)
Initializes this object by wrapping the given InputStream using the specified encoding (page 304). Example:
```
Dim txt As String
Dim tr As TextReader
tr.Initialize2(File.OpenInput(File.DirAssets, "TestCSV1_W.csv"),
"Windows-1252")
txt = tr.ReadAll
tr.Close
```
IsInitialized As Boolean
Whether the `TextReader` has been initialized using one of the Initialize methods.

Read (Buffer() As Char, StartOffset As Int, Length As Int) As Int
Reads characters from the stream and into the **Buffer**. Reads up to **Length** characters and puts them in the Buffer starting at **StartOffset**. Returns the actual number of characters read from the stream. Returns `-1` if there are no more characters available.

ReadAll As String
Reads all of the remaining text and closes the stream.

ReadLine As String
Reads the next line from the stream. Any new-line characters at the end of the line are not returned. Returns Null if there are no more characters to read. Example:

```
Dim Reader As TextReader
Reader.Initialize(File.OpenInput(File.InternalDir, "1.txt"))
Dim line As String
line = Reader.ReadLine
Do While line <> Null
 Log(line)
 line = Reader.ReadLine
Loop
Reader.Close
```

ReadList As List
Reads the remaining text and returns a List object filled with the lines. Closes the stream when done.

Ready As Boolean
Returns **TRUE** if there is at least one character ready for reading without stopping execution of the program (sometimes called blocking).

Skip (NumberOfCharacters As Int) As Int
Skips the specified number of characters. Returns the actual number of characters that were skipped (which may be less than the specified value).

TextWriter
Writes text to the underlying stream.
Example:

```
Dim Writer As TextWriter
Writer.Initialize(File.OpenOutput(File.DirDefaultExternal,
"1.txt", False))
Writer.WriteLine("This is the first line.")
Writer.WriteLine("This is the second line.")
Writer.Close
```

Members:
- Close
- Flush
- Initialize (OutputStream As java.io.OutputStream)
- Initialize2 (OutputStream As java.io.OutputStream, Encoding As String)
- IsInitialized As Boolean
- Write (Text As String)
- WriteLine (Text As String)
- WriteList (List As List)

Close
Closes the stream.

Flush
Flushes any buffered data.

Initialize (OutputStream As java.io.OutputStream)
Initializes this object by wrapping the given **OutputStream** using the UTF8 encoding (page 304). Example:

```
Writer.Initialize(File.OpenOutput(File.DirRootExternal,
"Test.txt" , False))
```

Initialize2 (OutputStream As java.io.OutputStream, Encoding As String)
Initializes this object by wrapping the given **OutputStream** using the specified encoding (page 304).

```
Dim strText As String
strText = "Hello World"
Dim tw As TextWriter
tw.Initialize2(File.OpenOutput(File.DirInternal, "Test.txt",
False), "ISO-8859-1")
tw.Write(strText)
tw.Close
```

IsInitialized As Boolean
Whether the **`TextWriter`** has been initialized using one of the Initialize methods.

Write (Text As String)
Writes the given Text to the stream.

WriteLine (Text As String)
Writes the given Text to the stream followed by a new-line character Chr(10). Example:

```
Dim Writer As TextWriter
Writer.Initialize(File.OpenOutput(File.DirDefaultExternal,
"1.txt", False))
Writer.WriteLine("This is the first line.")
Writer.WriteLine("This is the second line.")
Writer.Close
```

WriteList (List As List)
Writes each item in the **List** as a single line. All values will be converted to strings. **Note**: a value containing CRLF will be saved as two lines (which will return two items when read with **`ReadList`**).

Intent

Intent objects are messages which you can send to Android in order to do some external action. A service can also receive an Intent from Android if it is a Broadcast Receiver. For more about this, see this page (http://bit.ly/12QWZBw) on the

Basic4Android website. The Intent object should be sent with the **StartActivity** keyword. See this page (http://developer.android.com/reference/android/content/Intent.html) for a list of Android's standard constants. Example to launch a YouTube application:

```
Dim Intent1 As Intent
Intent1.Initialize(Intent1.ACTION_MAIN, "")
Intent1.SetComponent("com.google.android.youtube/.HomeActivity")
StartActivity(Intent1)
```

Members:

- Action As String
- ACTION_APPWIDGET_UPDATE As String
- ACTION_CALL As String
- ACTION_EDIT As String
- ACTION_MAIN As String
- ACTION_PICK As String
- ACTION_SEND As String
- ACTION_VIEW As String
- AddCategory (Category As String)
- ExtrasToString As String
- Flags As Int
- GetData As String
- GetExtra (Name As String) As Object
- HasExtra (Name As String) As Boolean
- Initialize (Action As String, URI As String)
- Initialize2 (URI As String, Flags As Int)
- IsInitialized As Boolean
- PutExtra (Name As String, Value As Object)
- SetComponent (Component As String)
- SetType (Type As String)
- WrapAsIntentChooser (Title As String)

Action As String

Gets or sets the Intent action.

ACTION_APPWIDGET_UPDATE As String

See here for more information (page 83) about Widgets and here for more (http://developer.android.com/reference/android/appwidget/AppWidgetManager.html) about the Android AppWidgetmanager.

ACTION_CALL As String

ACTION_EDIT As String

ACTION_MAIN As String

ACTION_PICK As String

ACTION_SEND As String

ACTION_VIEW As String

AddCategory (Category As String)

Adds a category describing the intent required operation.

ExtrasToString As String

Returns a string containing the extra items. This is useful for debugging.

Flags As Int

Gets or sets the **Flags** component.

GetData As String

Retrieves the data component as a string.

GetExtra (Key As String) As Object

Returns the item value with the given **Key**.

HasExtra (Key As String) As Boolean

Returns **TRUE** if an item with the given **Key** exists.

Initialize (Action As String, URI As String)

Initializes the object using the given **Action** and data **URI**.
Action - can be one of the action constants or any other string.
URI – a "Uniform Resource Identifier" identifying the resource to initialize. Pass an empty string if a URI is not required.

Initialize2 (URI As String, Flags As Int)

Initializes the object by parsing the URI.
URI – the "Uniform Resource Identifier" identifying the resource to initialize.
Flags - Additional integer value. Pass 0 if it is not required.
Example:

```
Dim Intent1 As Intent
Intent1.Initialize2("http://www.basic4ppc.com", 0)
StartActivity(Intent1)
```

IsInitialized As Boolean

Whether the **Intent** has been initialized using one of the Initialize methods.

PutExtra (Name As String, Value As Object)

Adds extra data to the intent.

SetComponent (Component As String)

Explicitly sets the component that will handle this intent.

SetType (Type As String)

Sets the MIME type (the Internet media type). See here (http://bit.ly/1f1wI8U) for details of MIME types.
Example:

```
Intent1.SetType("text/plain")
```

WrapAsIntentChooser (Title As String)

Wraps the intent in another "chooser" intent. A dialog will be displayed to the user with the available services that can act on the intent.
WrapAsIntentChooser should be the last method called before sending the intent.

LayoutValues

This object holds values related to the display. You can get the values of the current display by calling **GetDeviceLayoutValues**. For example:

```
Dim lv As LayoutValues
lv = GetDeviceLayoutValues
Log(lv) 'will print the values to the log
Dim scale As Float
scale = lv.Scale
```

This will print the following line to the log:

```
320 x 480, scale = 1.0 (160 dpi)
```

Activity.LoadLayout and **Panel.LoadLayout** return a **LayoutValues** object with the values of the chosen layout variant.

Members:

- ApproximateScreenSize As Double [read only]
- Height As Int
- Scale As Float
- toString As String
- Width As Int

ApproximateScreenSize As Double [read only]
Returns the approximate diagonal screen size in inches.

Height As Int
The display height (in pixels).

Scale As Float
The device scale value which is equal to 'dots per inch' / 160.

toString As String

Width As Int
The display width (in pixels).

List
Lists are similar to dynamic arrays. You can add and remove items from a list and it will change its size accordingly. A list can hold any type of object. However, if a list is declared as a **Process_Globals** object, it cannot hold activity objects (such as views). Basic4Android automatically converts regular arrays to lists. So, when a List parameter is expected, you can pass an array instead. For example:

```
Dim List1 As List
List1.Initialize
List1.AddAll(Array As Int(1, 2, 3, 4, 5))
```

Use the **Get** method to get an item from the list.

```
number = List1.Get(i)
```

Lists can be saved and loaded from files using **File.WriteList** and **File.ReadList**.
You can use a **For** loop to iterate over all the values:

```
For i = 0 To List1.Size - 1
 Dim number As Int
 number = List1.Get(i)
 ...
Next
```

How to use a List
We summarise the main points here. Details are given in the reference section below.

Initialize
Before it can be used, a list must be initialized with the **Initialize** method. This initializes an empty list:

```
Dim List1 As List
List1.Initialize
List1.AddAll(Array As Int(1, 2, 3, 4, 5))
```

Add Elements

You can add and remove items from a list and it will change its size accordingly.
To add a value at the end of the list:

```
List1.Add(Value)
```

To add all elements of an array at the end of the list:

```
List1.AddAll(Array As Int(1, 2, 3, 4, 5))
```

To insert the specified element at the specified index, and shift down all items with larger index to make room:

```
List1.InsertAt(5, Value)
```

To insert all elements of an array in the list starting at the given position:

```
List1.AddAllAt(3, Array As Int(1, 2, 3, 4, 5))
```

Remove Elements

Remove a specified element at the given position from the list.

```
List1.RemoveAt(12)
```

Retrieve Elements

Use the **Get** method to get an item from the list with:

```
number = List1.Get(i)
```

Change an Element

A single item can be changed with:

```
List1.Set(12, Value)
```

Get the size of a List

```
List1.Size
```

Iterate a List

Either you can use a **For** loop to iterate over all the values:

```
Dim List1 As List
List1.Initialize2(Array As Int(1, 2, 3, 4, 5))
For i = 0 To List1.Size - 1
 Log( List1.Get(i) )
Next
```

Or you can use a **For Each** loop:

```
Dim List1 As List
List1.Initialize2(Array As Int(1, 2, 3, 4, 5))
For Each i As Int In List1
 Log (i)
Next
```

Save to and Load from Files

Lists can be saved to and loaded from files:

```
File.WriteList(File.DirRootExternal, "Test.txt", List1)
List1 = File.ReadList(File.DirRootExternal, "Test.txt")
```

Sort a List

A List whose items are numbers or strings can be sorted with:

```
List1.Sort(True)          'sort ascending
List1.Sort(False)         'sort descending
List1.SortCaseInsensitive(True)
```

Clear a List

```
List1.Clear
```

Convert Array to List

You can convert an array to a list using

```
Initialize2 (SomeArray)
```

Note that if you pass a list to this method, then both objects will share the same list, and if you pass an array, the list will be of a fixed size, meaning you cannot later add or remove items.

Members:

- Add (Item As Object)
- AddAll (List As List)
- AddAllAt (Index As Int, List As List)
- Clear
- Get (Index As Int) As Object
- IndexOf (Item As Object) As Int
- Initialize
- Initialize2 (Array As List)
- InsertAt (Index As Int, Item As Object)
- IsInitialized As Boolean
- RemoveAt (Index As Int)
- Set (Index As Int, Item As Object)
- Size As Int [read only]
- Sort (Ascending As Boolean)
- SortCaseInsensitive (Ascending As Boolean)
- SortType (FieldName As String, Ascending As Boolean)
- SortTypeCaseInsensitive (FieldName As String, Ascending As Boolean)

Add (Item As Object)

Adds an **Item** at the end of the list.

AddAll (List As List)

Adds all elements in the specified **List** to the end of the list.
Note that you can add an array directly.
Example:

```
List.AddAll(Array As String("value1", "value2"))
```

AddAllAt (Index As Int, List As List)

Adds all elements in the specified collection starting at the specified index.

Clear

Removes all the items from the list.

Get (Index As Int) As Object

Gets the item at the specified index. The item is not removed from the list.

IndexOf (Item As Object) As Int

Returns the index of the specified item, or `-1` if it was not found.

Initialize

Initializes an empty list.

Initialize2 (Array As List)

Initializes a list with the given values. This method should be used to convert arrays to lists. Note that if you pass a list to this method, then both objects will share the same list, and if you pass an array, the list will be of a fixed size, meaning that you cannot later add or remove items. Example:

```
Dim List1 As List
List1.Initialize2(Array As Int(1,2,3,4,5))
Example:
Dim List1 As List
Dim SomeArray(10) As String
'Fill array...
List1.Initialize2(SomeArray)
```

InsertAt (Index As Int, Item As Object)

Inserts the specified **Item** at the specified index. As a result, all items with an index larger than the specified **Index** are shifted down to make room.

IsInitialized As Boolean

Whether the **`List`** has been initialized using one of the Initialize methods.

RemoveAt (Index As Int)

Removes the item at the specified index.

Set (Index As Int, Item As Object)

Replaces the current item at the specified index with the new item.

Size As Int [read only]

Returns the number of items in the list.

Sort (Ascending As Boolean)

Sorts the list. The items must all be numbers or strings.
Ascending - **`True`** to sort ascending, **`False`** to sort descending.

SortCaseInsensitive (Ascending As Boolean)

Lexicographically sorts the list, ignoring the characters' case. The items must all be numbers or strings.

Ascending - **True** to sort ascending, **False** to sort descending.

SortType (FieldName As String, Ascending As Boolean)

Sorts a list with items of user defined type. The list is sorted based on the specified field.
FieldName - The case-sensitive field name that will be used for sorting. Field must contain numbers or strings.
Ascending - **True** to sort ascending, **False** to sort descending.
Example:

```
Sub Process_Globals
 Type Person(Name As String, Age As Int)
End Sub

Sub Activity_Create(FirstTime As Boolean)
 Dim Persons As List
 Persons.Initialize
 For i = 1 To 50
  Dim p As Person
  p.Name = "Person" & i
  p.Age = Rnd(0, 121)
  Persons.Add(p)
 Next
 Persons.SortType("Age", True) 'Sort the list based on the Age
field
 For i = 0 To Persons.Size - 1
  Dim p As Person
  p = Persons.Get(i)
  Log(p)
 Next
End Sub
```

SortTypeCaseInsensitive (FieldName As String, Ascending As Boolean)

Sorts a list with items of user defined type. The list is sorted based on the specified field.
FieldName - The field name that will be used for sorting. The case of strings in this field will be ignored. Field must contain numbers or strings.
Ascending - Whether to sort ascending or descending.
Example:

```
Sub Process_Globals
  Type Person(Name As String, Age As Int)
End Sub

Sub Activity_Create(FirstTime As Boolean)
 Dim Persons As List
 Persons.Initialize
 Persons.Add(makePerson("dick"))
 Persons.Add(makePerson("Harry"))
 Persons.Add(makePerson("alex"))
 Persons.Add(makePerson("Brigit"))
 Persons.Add(makePerson("tom"))
 ' sort the people by name case insensitive
 Persons.SortTypeCaseInsensitive("Name", True)
 For i = 0 To Persons.Size - 1
  Dim p As Person
  p = Persons.Get(i)
  Log(p.Name & "," & p.age)
 Next
End Sub

Sub makePerson(strName As String) As Person
 ' create person with given name and random age
 Dim p As Person
 p.Initialize
 p.Name = strName
 p.Age = Rnd(0, 121)
 Return p
End Sub
```

Map

A collection that holds pairs of keys and values. Keys can be strings or numbers. The strings are case-sensitive. Keys are unique, which means that if you add a key/value pair and the collection already holds an entry with the same key, the previous entry will be removed from the map. Similar to a list, the values of a map can be any type of object.

```
Dim mapPerson As Map
mapPerson.Initialize
Dim photo As Bitmap
photo.Initialize(File.DirAssets, "smith.bmp")
mapPerson.Put("name", "smith")
mapPerson.Put("age", 23)
mapPerson.Put("photo", photo)
```

Fetching an item is done by looking for its key.

```
photo = mapPerson.Get("photo")
```

This is usually a very fast operation compared to using an array because a Map uses a system called "hashing". A Map is sometimes referred to as a Dictionary, Hashtable or HashMap. Usually you will use **`Put`** to add items and **`Get`** or **`GetDefault`** to get the values based on the key. If you need to iterate over all the items, you can use a **`For Each`** loop:

```
For Each key As String In mapPerson.Keys
 Log (key)
Next
```

Note that this iteration does not necessarily return items in the same order as they were added. Similar to a list, a map that is a **`Process_Globals`** variable cannot hold activity objects (such as views). Maps are very useful for storing applications settings.

You can save and load maps with **`File.WriteMap`** and **`File.ReadMap`**.

How to use a Map

We summarise the main points here. Details are given in the reference section below.

Initialize

A map must be initialized before it can be used.

```
Dim Map1 As Map
Map1.Initialize
```

Adding Entry

Add a new entry with Put(Key As Object, Value As Object)

```
Map1.Put("Language", "English")
```

Retrieve Entry

Get(Key As Object)

```
Language = Map1.Get("Language")
```

Iteration

You can retrieve each of the items in a map in two different ways:

Method 1

`GetKeyAt` and **`GetValueAt`** retrieve items with a given index and can be used to iterate over all the items:

```
For i = 0 To mapPerson.Size - 1
 Log("Key: " & mapPerson.GetKeyAt(i))
 Log("Value: " & mapPerson.GetValueAt(i))
Next
```

Method 2

```
For Each key As String In mapPerson.Keys
 Log ("Key: " & key)
 Log ("Value: " & mapPerson.Get(key))
Next
```

The order in which the items are retrieved may be different for these two methods.

Check if a Map contains an entry

```
If Map1.ContainsKey("Language") Then ...
```

Remove an entry

```
Map1.Remove("Language")
```

Clear all items from the map

```
Map1.Clear
```

Save to and Load from a File

The File (page 306) object contains some useful functions for reading and writing maps.
Save a map to a file:

```
File.WriteMap(File.DirInternal, "settings.txt", mapSettings)
```

Read it back from the file:

```
mapSettings = File.ReadMap(File.DirInternal, "settings.txt")
```

The order in which the elements in a map read from the file will not necessarily be the same as the order in the original map. Normally this is not a problem. If you want to fix the order, see below.

Appending to a Map

You can use **`File.ReadMap2`** to add items to a Map.

```
mapCopy.Put("newItem", "someValue")
mapCopy = File.ReadMap2(File.DirDefaultExternal, "savedMap",
mapCopy)
```

The elements read from the file are appended to the existing elements. If an existing element has the same name as an element in the file, its value is overwritten.

Fixing Order in a Map

Normally we do not care about the order in which elements are stored in a Map. However, if this is important to you, you can use **`File.ReadMap2`** to force the elements to be added in a particular order. The trick is to first create a Map with the keys in the order you want but with no values. Then read the data from a file. The values from the file will be added to the keys you have specified, (assuming the keys are the same).

```
Dim mapCopy As Map
mapCopy.Initialize
' add empty elements to fix their order in the map
mapCopy.Put("Item #1", "")
mapCopy.Put("Item #2", "")
' now read elements from file
mapCopy = File.ReadMap2(File.DirInternal, "settings.txt",
mapCopy)
```

Members:

- Clear
- ContainsKey (Key As Object) As Boolean
- Get (Key As Object) As Object

- GetDefault (Key As Object, Default As Object) As Object
- GetKeyAt (Index As Int) As Object
- GetValueAt (Index As Int) As Object
- Initialize
- IsInitialized As Boolean
- Keys As IterableList
- Put (Key As Object, Value As Object) As Object
- Remove (Key As Object) As Object
- Size As Int [read only]
- Values As IterableList

Clear

Clears all items from the map.

ContainsKey (Key As Object) As Boolean

Returns **TRUE** if there is an item with the given key.
Example:

```
If Map.ContainsKey("some key") Then ...
```

Get (Key As Object) As Object

Returns the value of the item with the given key. If the key does not exist, it returns **Null**.

GetDefault (Key As Object, Default As Object) As Object

Returns the value of the item with the given key. If no such item exists, the specified default value is returned.

GetKeyAt (Index As Int) As Object

Returns the key of the item at the given index. **GetKeyAt** and **GetValueAt** should be used to iterate over all the items. These methods are optimized for iterating over the items in ascending order. Example:

```
For i = 0 to Map.Size - 1
  Log("Key: " & Map.GetKeyAt(i))
  Log("Value: " & Map.GetValueAt(i))
Next
```

GetValueAt (Index As Int) As Object

Returns the value of the item at the given index. **GetKeyAt** and **GetValueAt** should be used to iterate over all the items. These methods are optimized for iterating over the items in ascending order. Example:

```
For i = 0 to Map.Size - 1
  Log("Key: " & Map.GetKeyAt(i))
  Log("Value: " & Map.GetValueAt(i))
Next
```

Initialize

Initializes the object.
Example:

```
Dim Map1 As Map
Map1.Initialize
```

IsInitialized As Boolean
Whether the **Map** has been initialized using the **Initialize** method.

Keys As IterableList
Returns an object which can be used to iterate over all the keys with a **For Each** loop. Example:

```
For Each k As String In map1.Keys
  Log(k)
Next
```

Put (Key As Object, Value As Object) As Object
Puts a key/value pair in the map, overwriting the previous item with this key (if such exists). Returns the previous item with this key or null if there was no such item. Note that if you are using strings as the keys, then the keys are case sensitive.
Example:

```
Map1.Put("Key", "Value")
```

Remove (Key As Object) As Object
Removes the item with the given key, if such exists. Returns the item removed or null if no matching item was found.

Size As Int [read only]
Returns the number of items stored in the map.

Values As IterableList
Returns an object which can be used to iterate over all the values with a **For Each** loop. Example:

```
For Each v As Int In map1.Values
  Log(v)
Next
```

MediaPlayer

The MediaPlayer can be used to play audio files. See the media player tutorial (http://www.basic4ppc.com/forum/basic4android-getting-started-tutorials/6591-mediaplayer-tutorial.html) for more information.
Note: The media player should be declared as a **Process_Globals** object.

Event: Complete
The **Complete** event is raised when playback completes. It will only be raised if you initialize the object with **Initialize2**.

Members:
- Duration As Int [read only]
- Initialize

- Initialize2 (EventName As String)
- IsPlaying As Boolean
- Load (Dir As String, FileName As String)
- Looping As Boolean
- Pause
- Play
- Position As Int
- Release
- SetVolume (Right As Float, Left As Float)
- Stop

Duration As Int [read only]

Returns the total duration of the loaded file (in milliseconds).

Initialize

Initializes the object. You should use **`Initialize2`** if you want to handle the Complete event. Example:

```
Dim MP As MediaPlayer 'should be done in Sub Process_Globals
MP.Initialize2("MP")
MP.Load(File.DirAssets, "SomeFile.mp3")
MP.Play
```

Initialize2 (EventName As String)

Similar to Initialize, but raises the **`Complete`** event when play-back completes.
EventName - The Sub that will handle the **`Complete`** event.

IsPlaying As Boolean

Returns **`True`** if the media player is currently playing.

Load (Dir As String, FileName As String)

Loads an audio file and prepares it for playing.

Looping As Boolean

Gets or sets whether the media player will restart playing automatically.

Pause

Pauses playback. You can resume playback from the current position by calling **`Play`**.

Play

Starts (or resumes) playing the loaded audio file.

Position As Int

Gets or sets the current position (in milliseconds).

Release

Releases all resources allocated by the media player.

SetVolume (Right As Float, Left As Float)

Sets the playing volume for each channel. The values should be from 0 to 1.

Stop

Stops playing. You must call **Load** before trying to play again.

Notification

A notification object allows an activity or a service to display an icon on the left of the Status Bar at the top of the device's screen:

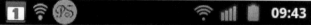

The user can swipe down the notifications screen and press on the notification.

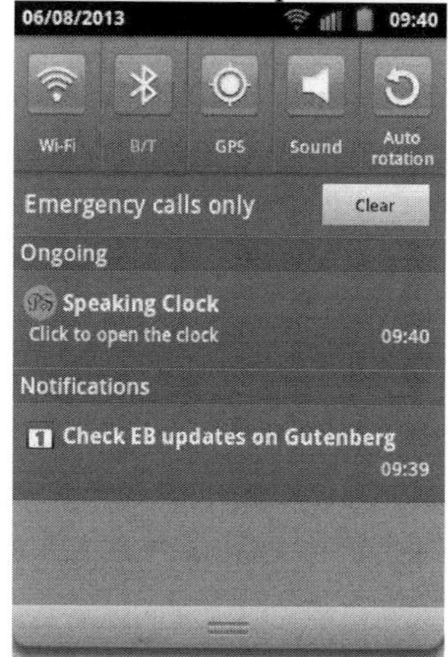

Ongoing notifications are not removed if the user presses “Clear”, whereas normal notifications are. Pressing the notification will start an activity as set by the notification object **SetInfo** command. Notifications are usually used by services because services are not expected to directly start activities. The notification **must** have an icon and its "info" **must** be set.

Example:

```
Dim n As Notification
n.Initialize
n.Icon = "icon"
n.SetInfo("This is the title", "and this is the body.", Main)
'Change Main to "" if this code is in the main module.
n.Notify(1)
```

Permissions:

android.permission.VIBRATE

Members:

AutoCancel As Boolean [write only]
Cancel (Id As Int)
Icon As String [write only]
Initialize
Insistent As Boolean [write only]
IsInitialized As Boolean
Light As Boolean [write only]
Notify (Id As Int)
Number As Int
OnGoingEvent As Boolean [write only]
SetInfo (Title As String, Body As String, Activity As Object)
SetInfo2 (Title As String, Body As String, Tag As String, Activity As Object)
Sound As Boolean [write only]
Vibrate As Boolean [write only]

AutoCancel As Boolean [write only]

Sets whether the notification will be canceled automatically when the user clicks on it.

Cancel (Id As Int)

Cancels the notification with the given Id.

Icon As String [write only]

Sets the icon displayed. The icon value is the name of the image file without the extension. **The name is case sensitive.**
Note: the image file must be manually copied to the following folder within your project:

```
\Objects\res\drawable
```

You can use "icon" to specify the application icon (which is also located in this folder):

```
n.Icon = "icon"
```

Initialize

Initializes the notification. By default, the notification plays a sound, shows a light and vibrates the phone.

Insistent As Boolean [write only]

Sets whether the sound will play repeatedly until the user opens the notifications screen.

IsInitialized As Boolean

Whether the **Notification** has been initialized using the **Initialize** method.

Light As Boolean [write only]

Sets whether the notification will show a light. Example:

```
n.Light = False
```

Notify (Id As Int)

Displays the notification.
Id - The notification id. This can be used to later update this **Notification** (by calling Notify again with the same Id), or to cancel the **Notification**.

Number As Int

Gets or sets a number that will be displayed on the icon. This is useful to represent multiple events in a single notification.

OnGoingEvent As Boolean [write only]

Sets whether this notification is an "ongoing event". The notification will be displayed in the ongoing section and it will not be cleared.

SetInfo (Title As String, Body As String, Activity As Object)

Sets the message text and action.
Title - The message title.
Body - The message body.
Activity - The activity to start when the user presses on the notification.
Pass an empty string to start the current activity (when calling from an activity module). Example:

```
n.SetInfo("Some title", "Some text", Main)
```

SetInfo2 (Title As String, Body As String, Tag As String, Activity As Object)

Similar to SetInfo. Also sets a string that can be later extracted in **Activity_Resume**.

Title - The message title.
Body - The message body.
Tag - An arbitrary string that can be later extracted when the user clicks on the notification.
Activity - The activity to start when the user presses on the notification.
Pass an empty string to start the current activity (when calling from an activity module). Example of extracting the tag:

```
Sub Activity_Resume
 Dim in As Intent
 in = Activity.GetStartingIntent
 If in.HasExtra("Notification_Tag") Then
  Log(in.GetExtra("Notification_Tag")) 'Will log the tag
 End If
End Sub
```

Sound As Boolean [write only]

Sets whether the notification will play a sound.
Example:

```
n.Sound = False
```

Vibrate As Boolean [write only]

Sets whether the notification will vibrate.
Example:

```
n.Vibrate = False
```

RemoteViews

RemoteViews allows indirect access to a home screen widget.
See here for more information (page 83) about Widgets.

Events:

RequestUpdate
Disabled

Members:

- HandleWidgetEvents (StartingIntent As Intent) As Boolean
- SetImage (ImageViewName As String, Image As Bitmap)
- SetProgress (ProgressBarName As String, Progress As Int)
- SetText (ViewName As String, Text As String)
- SetTextColor (ViewName As String, Color As Int)
- SetTextSize (ViewName As String, Size As Float)
- SetVisible (ViewName As String, Visible As Boolean)
- UpdateWidget

HandleWidgetEvents (StartingIntent As Intent) As Boolean

Checks if the intent starting this service was sent from the widget and raises events based on the intent. Returns **True** if an event was raised.
See here for more information (page 83) about Widgets.

SetImage (ImageViewName As String, Image As Bitmap)

Sets the image of the given ImageView. Example:

```
rv.SetImage("ImageView1", LoadBitmap(File.DirAssets, "1.jpg"))
```

SetProgress (ProgressBarName As String, Progress As Int)

Sets the progress value of the given ProgressBar. Value should be from 0 to 100.
Example:

```
rv.SetProgress("ProgressBar1", 50)
```

SetText (ViewName As String, Text As String)

Sets the text of the given view. Example:

```
rv.SetText("Label1", "New text")
```

SetTextColor (ViewName As String, Color As Int)

Sets the text color of the given button or label. Example:

```
rv.SetTextColor("Label1", Colors.Red)
```

SetTextSize (ViewName As String, Size As Float)

Sets the text size of the given button or label. Example:

```
rv.SetTextSize("Label1", 20)
```

SetVisible (ViewName As String, Visible As Boolean)

Sets the visibility of the given view. Example:

```
rv.SetVisibile("Button1", False)
```

UpdateWidget

Updates the widget with the changes done. This method is also responsible for configuring the events.
See here for more information (page 83) about Widgets.

Service

Each Service module (page 188) includes a Service object which is used to bring the service in and out of the foreground state. See the Services module section for more information.

Members:

StartForeground (Id As Int, Notification1 As Notification)

Brings the current service to the foreground state and displays the given notification.
Id - The notification Id (see the notification object documentation).
Notification - The notification that will be displayed.

StopForeground (Id As Int)

Takes the current service out of the foreground state and cancels the notification with the given **Id**.

String

Immutable Strings

Strings are immutable in Basic4Android, which means that you can change the value of a string variable, but you cannot change the text stored in a string object. So methods like **SubString**, **Trim** and **ToLowerCase** return a new string; **they do not change the value of the current string**. Typical usage:

```
Dim s As String
s = "some text"
s = s.Replace("a", "b")
```

You can use **StringBuilder** if you need a mutable string. **Note** that string literals are also string objects:

```
Log(" some text ".Trim)
```

Mutable Strings

Repetitive manipulation of strings can be very slow. Since they are immutable, a new string has to be created every time you want to change a string. If you are doing extensive string manipulation, you should consider using StringBuilder (page 337).

Number formatting

Numbers can be displayed as strings with different formats. There are two keywords:

- NumberFormat (page 255) (Number As Double, MinimumIntegers As Int, MaximumFractions As Int) As String
- NumberFormat2 (page 255) (Number As Double, MinimumIntegers As Int, MaximumFractions As Int, MinimumFractions As Int, GroupingUsed As Boolean) As String

String Functions Library

As well as the built-in members, the user-generated String Functions Library (http://bit.ly/15HuBDW) is useful.

Members:

CharAt (Index As Int) As Char

- CompareTo (Other As String) As Int
- Contains (SearchFor As String) As Boolean
- EndsWith (Suffix As String) As Boolean
- EqualsIgnoreCase (other As String) As Boolean
- GetBytes (Charset As String) As Byte()
- IndexOf (SearchFor As String) As Int
- IndexOf2 (SearchFor As String, Index As Int) As Int
- LastIndexOf (SearchFor As String) As Int
- LastIndexOf2 (SearchFor As String, Index As Int) As Int
- Length As Int
- Replace (Target As String, Replacement As String) As String
- StartsWith (Prefix As String) As Boolean
- SubString (BeginIndex As Int) As String
- SubString2 (BeginIndex As Int, EndIndex As Int) As String
- ToLowerCase As String
- ToUpperCase As String
- Trim As String

CharAt (Index As Int) As Char

Returns the character at the given index.

CompareTo (Other As String) As Int

Lexicographically compares the two strings, that is, as they would appear in a dictionary. Returns a value less than 0 if the current string comes before **Other**. Returns 0 if both strings are equal. Returns a value larger than 0 if the current string comes after **Other**. **Note:** upper case characters precede lower case characters. The exact value returned depends in part upon the unicode values of the strings involved. Examples:

```
"abc".CompareTo("da") ' < 0
"abc".CompareTo("Abc") ' > 0
"abc".CompareTo("abca")' < 0
```

Contains (SearchFor As String) As Boolean

Returns **`TRUE`** if the string contains the given string parameter.

EndsWith (Suffix As String) As Boolean

Returns **`True`** if this string ends with the given Suffix.

EqualsIgnoreCase (other As String) As Boolean

Returns **`True`** if both strings are equal (ignoring their case).

GetBytes (Charset As String) As Byte()

Encodes the string into a new array of bytes. Example:

```
Dim Data() As Byte
Data = "Some string".GetBytes("UTF8")
```

IndexOf (SearchFor As String) As Int

Returns the index of the first occurrence of **SearchFor** in the string. Returns `-1` if **SearchFor** was not found.

IndexOf2 (SearchFor As String, Index As Int) As Int

Returns the index of the first occurrence of **SearchFor** in the string. Starts searching from **Index**. Returns `-1` if **SearchFor** was not found.

LastIndexOf (SearchFor As String) As Int

Returns the index of the first occurrence of **SearchFor** in the string. The search starts at the end of the string and advances to the beginning.

LastIndexOf2 (SearchFor As String, Index As Int) As Int

Returns the index of the first occurrence of **SearchFor** in the string. The search starts at **Index** and advances to the beginning.

Length As Int

Returns the length of this string.

Replace (Target As String, Replacement As String) As String

Returns a new string resulting from the replacement of all the occurrences of **Target** with **Replacement**.

StartsWith (Prefix As String) As Boolean

Returns `True` if this string starts with the given Prefix.

SubString (BeginIndex As Int) As String

Returns a new string which is a substring of the original string. The new string will include the character at **BeginIndex** and will extend to the end of the string.
Example:

```
"012345".SubString(2) 'returns "2345"
```

SubString2 (BeginIndex As Int, EndIndex As Int) As String

Returns a new string which is a substring of the original. The new string will include the character at **BeginIndex**, where first character counts as index 0. The last character returned will be the one before **EndIndex**. Examples:

```
Log("ABCDEF".SubString2(0, 3)) 'result is "ABC"
Log("ABCDEF".SubString2(2, 4)) 'result is "CD"
```

ToLowerCase As String

Returns a new string which is the result of lower casing this string.

ToUpperCase As String

Returns a new string which is the result of upper casing this string.

Trim As String

Returns a copy of the original string without any leading or trailing white spaces.

StringBuilder

StringBuilder is a mutable string, unlike regular strings which are immutable. StringBuilder is especially useful when you need to concatenate many strings. The following code demonstrates the performance boosting of StringBuilder:

```
Dim start As Long
start = DateTime.Now
'Regular string
Dim s As String
For i = 1 To 5000
 s = s & i
Next
Log(DateTime.Now - start)
'StringBuilder
start = DateTime.Now
Dim sb As StringBuilder
sb.Initialize
For i = 1 To 5000
 sb.Append(i)
Next
Log(DateTime.Now - start)
```

Tested on a real device, the first 'for loop' took about 20 seconds and the second took less than one tenth of a second. The reason is that the code: **`s = s & i`** creates a new string each iteration because strings are immutable.
The method **`StringBuilder.ToString`** converts the object to a string.

Members:

- Append (Text As String) As StringBuilder
- Initialize
- Insert (Offset As Int, Text As String) As StringBuilder
- IsInitialized As Boolean
- Length As Int [read only]
- Remove (StartOffset As Int, EndOffset As Int) As StringBuilder

ToString As String

Append (Text As String) As StringBuilder

Appends the specified text at the end. Returns the same object, so you can chain methods. Example:

```
sb.Append("First line").Append(CRLF).Append("Second line")
```

Initialize

Initializes the object. Example:

```
Dim sb As StringBuilder
sb.Initialize
sb.Append("The value is:
").Append(SomeOtherVariable).Append(CRLF)
```

Insert (Offset As Int, Text As String) As StringBuilder

Inserts the specified text at the specified offset.

IsInitialized As Boolean

Whether the **StringBuilder** has been initialized using the Initialize method.

Length As Int [read only]

Returns the number of characters.

Remove (StartOffset As Int, EndOffset As Int) As StringBuilder

Removes the specified characters.
StartOffset - The first character to remove.
EndOffset - The ending index. This character will not be removed. Examples:

```
Dim sb As StringBuilder
sb.Initialize
sb.Append("ABCDEF")
Log(sb.Remove(0, 3)) 'result is "DEF"
sb.Initialize
sb.Append("ABCDEF")
Log(sb.Remove(2, 4)) 'result is "ABEF"
```

ToString As String

Converts the object to a string.

Timer

A **Timer** object generates **Tick** events at specified intervals. Using a timer is a good alternative to a long loop, as it allows the UI (page 10) thread to handle other events and messages. The timer **Enabled** property is set to **False** by default. To start the timer, you should change **Enabled** to **True**.

Note: timer events will not fire while the UI thread is busy running other code unless you call the **DoEvents** keyword within a loop. In addition, Timer events will not fire when the activity is paused, or if a blocking dialog (like Msgbox) is visible. An alternative approach, which overcomes this limitation, is to start a service (page 333) at a given time using StartServiceAt (page 259).

Timers should be declared in Sub Process_Globals. Otherwise you may get multiple timers running when the activity is recreated. It is **also important** to disable the timer when the activity is pausing and then enable it when it resumes. This will save CPU and battery.

The Timer must be declared in a Sub Process_Globals routine.

```
Sub Process_Globals
' declare here so dont get multiple timers when activity
recreated
 Dim Timer1 As Timer
End Sub
```

A Timer must be initialized in the Activity_Create routine in the module where the timer tick event routine is used.

```
Sub Activity_Create(FirstTime As Boolean)
 If FirstTime = True Then
  ' Call every 1000 milliseconds
  Timer1.Initialize("Timer1", 1000)
  Timer1.Enabled = True
 End If
End Sub
```

Event: Tick

When a timer is **Enabled**, the **Tick** event is called after the time interval set by the **Initialize** method. **Tick** will continue to be called until **Enabled** is set to **False**.

Example:

```
Timer1.Initialize("Timer1", 1000)
Timer1.Enabled = True
' ...
Sub Timer1_Tick
 'Handle tick events
 ProgressBar1.Progress = ProgressBar1.Progress + 10
 If ProgressBar1.Progress = 100 Then
  Timer1.Enabled = False
 End If
End Sub
```

Example:

You find an example of using a Timer in the RotatingNeedle example program available from this book's resources website (http://resources.basic4android.info/).

Members:

Enabled As Boolean

- Initialize (EventName As String, Interval As Long)
- Interval As Long
- IsInitialized As Boolean

Enabled As Boolean

Gets or sets whether the timer is enabled (ticking). **It is False by default**, which means to start a timer you must call:

```
Timer1.Enabled = True
```

Initialize (EventName As String, Interval As Long)

Initializes the timer with the event sub prefix and the specified interval (measured in milliseconds). **Important**: this object should be declared in **`Sub Process_Globals`**.
EventName - The name used for the Tick event, for example, **`Sub Timer1_Tick`**.
Interval - Sets the timer interval in milliseconds. Interval can be changed by calling **`TimerName.Interval = Interval`**, for example:

```
Sub Process_Globals
Dim timer1 As Timer
End Sub

Sub Activity_Create(FirstTime As Boolean)
 timer1.Initialize("Timer1", 1000)
 timer1.Enabled = True
End Sub

Sub Timer1_Tick
 'Handle tick events
 'Shorten the timer interval
 timer1.Interval = timer1.Interval - 10
 If Timer1.Interval <= 0 Then
  Timer1.Enabled = False
 End If
End Sub
```

Interval As Long

Gets or sets the interval between tick events, measured in milliseconds.

IsInitialized As Boolean

Whether the timer has been initialized.

Views

Most views are objects which can be added to a layout either using the Designer (page 92) or in code. Here we list all views and give their methods. The view types are:

AutoCompleteEditText, Button (page 346), CheckBox (page 349), CustomView (page 351), EditText (page 352), ImageView (page 359), HorizontalScrollView (page 357), Label (page 362), ListView (page 364), Panel (page 370) , ProgressBar (page 374), RadioButton (page 376), ScrollView (page 379), SeekBar (page 382), Spinner (page 384), TabHost (page 388), ToggleButton (page 392), WebView (page 398)

AutoCompleteEditText

An enhanced version of EditText which shows the user a drop down list with all items matching the currently entered characters. Items matching are items starting with the current input or items that include a word that starts with the current input (words must be separated by spaces).

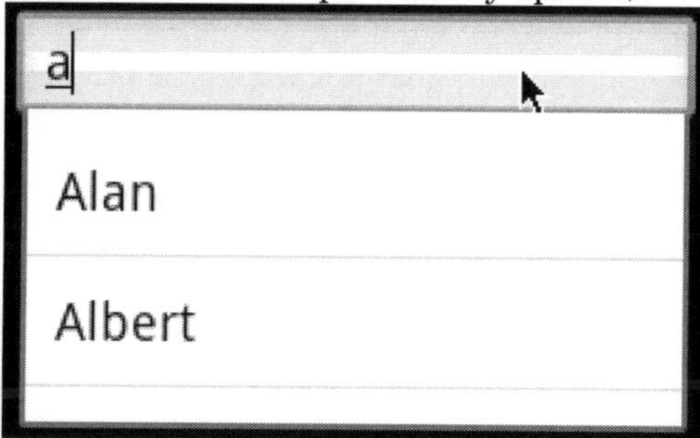

Call **SetItems** with the list of possible items.
Note: the SearchView (page 528) class offers similar functionality but with faster search and other benefits.
Example:

```
Sub Process_Globals
End Sub
Sub Globals
  Dim ACT As AutoCompleteEditText
End Sub
Sub Activity_Create(FirstTime As Boolean)
  ACT.Initialize("ACT")
  Activity.AddView(ACT, 10dip, 10dip, 500dip, 80dip)
  Dim people() As String
  people = Array As String( _
     "Alan", "Albert", "Algernon", "Alice", "Andorra")
  ACT.SetItems(people)
End Sub
Sub Activity_Pause (UserClosed As Boolean)
End Sub
```

Events:

ItemClick (Value As String)

The **ItemClick** event is raised when the user clicks on an item from the list.

TextChanged (Old As String, New As String)

This is raised every time the user edits the text in the AutoCompleteEditText. **Old** and **New** contain the text before and after the edit.

EnterPressed

This event is raised when the user presses the "Done" or "Enter" keys on the keyboard.

FocusChanged (HasFocus As Boolean)

This event is raised when the user touches the AutoCompleteEditText, in which case **HasFocus** will be `True`, or when the user moves from here to another view (when **HasFocus** will be `False`).

Members:

- Background As Drawable
- BringToFront
- Color As Int [write only]
- DismissDropDown
- Enabled As Boolean
- ForceDoneButton As Boolean [write only]
- Gravity As Int
- Height As Int
- Hint As String
- HintColor As Int
- Initialize (EventName As String)
- INPUT_TYPE_DECIMAL_NUMBERS As Int
- INPUT_TYPE_NONE As Int
- INPUT_TYPE_NUMBERS As Int
- INPUT_TYPE_PHONE As Int
- INPUT_TYPE_TEXT As Int
- InputType As Int
- Invalidate
- Invalidate2 (Rect1 As Rect)
- Invalidate3 (Left As Int, Top As Int, Right As Int, Bottom As Int)
- IsInitialized (page 345) As Boolean
- Left (page 345) As Int
- PasswordMode (page 345) As Boolean [write only]
- RemoveView (page 345)
- RequestFocus (page 345) As Boolean
- SelectAll (page 345)
- SelectionStart (page 345) As Int
- SendToBack (page 345)
- SetBackgroundImage (page 345) (Bitmap1 As Bitmap)
- SetItems (page 345) (Items As List)

SetItems2 (Items As List, Typeface1 As Typeface, Gravity As Int, TextSize As Float, TextColor As Int)
SetLayout (Left As Int, Top As Int, Width As Int, Height As Int)
ShowDropDown
SingleLine As Boolean [write only]
Tag As Object
Text (page 346) As String
TextColor (page 346) As Int
TextSize (page 346) As Float
Top (page 346) As Int
Typeface (page 346) As Typeface
Visible (page 346) As Boolean
Width (page 346) As Int
Wrap (page 346) As Boolean [write only]

Background As Drawable

Gets or sets the background drawable.

BringToFront

Changes the Z order of this view and brings it to the front.

Color As Int [write only]

Sets the background of the view to be a **ColorDrawable** with the given color. If the current background is of type **GradientDrawable** or **ColorDrawable**, the round corners will be kept.

DismissDropDown

Forces the drop down list to disappear.

Enabled As Boolean

If set to **True** then the **AutoCompleteEditText** will respond to events. If set to **False**, events are ignored.

ForceDoneButton As Boolean [write only]

By default, Android sets the virtual keyboard action key to display **Done** or **Next** according to the specific layout. You can force it to display **Done** by setting this value to **True**. Example:

```
EditText1.ForceDoneButton = True
```

Gravity As Int

Gets or sets the gravity (page 282) value. This value affects the way the text will be drawn.

Height As Int

Gets or sets the view's height.

Hint As String

Gets or sets the text that will appear when the EditText is empty. Example:

```
EditText1.Hint = "Enter username"
```

HintColor As Int

Gets or sets the hint text color.
Example:

```
EditText1.HintColor = Colors.Gray
```

Initialize (EventName As String)

Initializes the view and sets the subs that will handle the events.
Views added with the designer should NOT be initialized. These views are initialized when the layout is loaded.

INPUT_TYPE_DECIMAL_NUMBERS As Int

Numeric keyboard will be displayed. Numbers, decimal point and minus sign are accepted.

INPUT_TYPE_NONE As Int

No keyboard will be displayed. This could be useful, for example, if you use a read-only **AutoCompleteEditText** for which you do not want a keyboard to be displayed.

INPUT_TYPE_NUMBERS As Int

Numeric keyboard will be displayed. Only numbers are accepted.

INPUT_TYPE_PHONE As Int

Keyboard will be displayed in phone mode.

INPUT_TYPE_TEXT As Int

Default text mode.

InputType As Int

Gets or sets the input type flag. This flag is used to determine the settings of the virtual keyboard. **Note** that changing the input type will set the EditText to be in single line mode. Example:

```
EditText1.InputType = EditText1.INPUT_TYPE_NUMBERS
```

Invalidate

Invalidates the whole view forcing the view to redraw itself. Redrawing will only happen when the program can process messages, usually when it finishes running the current code.
If you only need to redraw part of the view, it is usually quicker to use **Invalidate2** or **Invalidate3**.

Invalidate2 (Rect1 As Rect)

Invalidates anything inside the given rectangle that is part of this view. Redrawing will only happen when the program can process messages, usually when it finishes running the current code.

Invalidate3 (Left As Int, Top As Int, Right As Int, Bottom As Int)

Invalidates anything inside the given rectangle that is part of this view. Redrawing will only happen when the program can process messages, usually when it finishes running the current code.

IsInitialized As Boolean
Whether this object has been initialized by calling `Initialize`.

Left As Int
Gets or sets the view's left position.

PasswordMode As Boolean [write only]
Sets whether the EditText should be in password mode and hide the actual characters.

RemoveView
Removes this view from its parent.

RequestFocus As Boolean
Tries to set the focus to this view.
Returns `True` if the focus was set.

SelectAll
Selects the entire text.

SelectionStart As Int
Gets or sets the selection start position (or the cursor position). Returns `-1` if there is no selection or cursor.

SendToBack
Changes the Z order of this view and sends it to the back.

SetBackgroundImage (Bitmap1 As Bitmap)

SetItems (Items As List)
Sets the list of possible items. The items' visual style will be the same as the style of the main text.

SetItems2 (Items As List, Typeface1 As Typeface, Gravity As Int, TextSize As Float, TextColor As Int)
Sets the list of possible items and specifies their style.
Gravity: sets the gravity (page 282) value. This value affects the way the text will be drawn.
Example:

```
Dim act As AutoCompleteEditText
act.Initialize("act")
Activity.AddView(act, 10dip, 10dip, 200dip, 80dip)
act.SetItems2(Array As String("aab", "abc"), act.Typeface,
Gravity.LEFT, 12, Colors.Green)
```

SetLayout (Left As Int, Top As Int, Width As Int, Height As Int)
Changes the view position and size.

ShowDropDown
Forces the drop down list to appear.

SingleLine As Boolean [write only]
Sets whether the EditText should be in single-line mode or multiline mode.

Tag As Object
Gets or sets the Tag value. This is a place holder which can be used to store additional data.

Text As String

TextColor As Int

TextSize As Float

Top As Int
Gets or sets the view's top position.

Typeface As Typeface

Visible As Boolean
Whether the user can see the object.

Width As Int
Gets or sets the view's width.

Wrap As Boolean [write only]
Sets whether the text content will wrap within the EditText bounds. Relevant when the EditText is in multiline mode. Example:

```
EditText1.Wrap = False
```

Button

A Button view. If you change the button's background, you will usually want to use **StateListDrawable** which allows you to set the "default" Drawable and the "pressed" drawable.
This is an **Activity** object; it cannot be declared under **Sub Process_Globals**.

Events:

Down
Occurs when the user first presses on the button.

Up
Occurs when the user releases the button.

Click
Occurs when the user presses and releases the button. The Down and Up events also fire. They are called in this sequence: Down, Up, Click.

LongClick
Occurs when the user presses on the button for roughly one second. The Down and Up events also fire. They are called in this sequence: Down, LongClick, Up.

Members:

- Background As Drawable
- BringToFront
- Color As Int [write only]

- Enabled As Boolean
- Gravity As Int
- Height As Int
- Initialize (EventName As String)
- Invalidate
- Invalidate2 (Rect1 As Rect)
- Invalidate3 (Left As Int, Top As Int, Right As Int, Bottom As Int)
- IsInitialized As Boolean
- Left As Int
- RemoveView
- RequestFocus As Boolean
- SendToBack
- SetBackgroundImage (Bitmap1 As Bitmap)
- SetLayout (Left As Int, Top As Int, Width As Int, Height As Int)
- Tag As Object
- Text As String
- TextColor As Int
- TextSize As Float
- Top As Int
- Typeface As Typeface
- Visible As Boolean
- Width As Int

Background As Drawable

Gets or sets the background drawable.

BringToFront

Changes the Z order of this view and brings it to the front.

Color As Int [write only]

Sets the background of the view to be a **`ColorDrawable`** with the given color. If the current background is of type **`GradientDrawable`** or **`ColorDrawable`**, the round corners will be kept.

Enabled As Boolean

If set to **`True`** then the **`Button`** will respond to events. If set to **`False`**, events are ignored.

Gravity As Int

Gets or sets the gravity (page 282) value. This value affects the way the text will be drawn.

Height As Int

Gets or sets the view's height.

Initialize (EventName As String)

Initializes the view and sets the subs that will handle the events.
Views added with the designer should NOT be initialized. These views are initialized when the layout is loaded.

Invalidate

Invalidates the whole view forcing the view to redraw itself. Redrawing will only happen when the program can process messages, usually when it finishes running the current code.
If you only need to redraw part of the view, it is usually quicker to use `Invalidate2` or `Invalidate3`.

Invalidate2 (Rect1 As Rect)

Invalidates anything inside the given rectangle that is part of this view. Redrawing will only happen when the program can process messages, usually when it finishes running the current code.

Invalidate3 (Left As Int, Top As Int, Right As Int, Bottom As Int)

Invalidates anything inside the given rectangle that is part of this view. Redrawing will only happen when the program can process messages, usually when it finishes running the current code.

IsInitialized As Boolean

Whether this object has been initialized by calling `Initialize`.

Left As Int

Gets or sets the view's left position.

RemoveView

Removes this view from its parent.

RequestFocus As Boolean

Tries to set the focus to this view. Returns `True` if the focus was set.

SendToBack

Changes the Z order of this view and sends it to the back.

SetBackgroundImage (Bitmap1 As Bitmap)

SetLayout (Left As Int, Top As Int, Width As Int, Height As Int)

Changes the view position and size.

Tag As Object

Gets or sets the Tag value. This is a place holder which can be used to store additional data.

Text As String

TextColor As Int

TextSize As Float

Top As Int

Gets or sets the view's top position.

Typeface As Typeface

Visible As Boolean

Whether the user can see the object.

Width As Int

Gets or sets the view's width.

CheckBox

A **CheckBox** view. Unlike **RadioButtons**, each CheckBox can be checked independently.

This is an **Activity** object; it cannot be declared under **Sub Process_Globals**.

Events:

CheckedChange(Checked As Boolean)

Members:

Background As Drawable

BringToFront

Checked As Boolean

Color As Int [write only]

Enabled As Boolean

Gravity As Int

Height As Int

Initialize (EventName As String)

Invalidate

Invalidate2 (Rect1 As Rect)

Invalidate3 (Left As Int, Top As Int, Right As Int, Bottom As Int)

IsInitialized As Boolean

Left As Int

RemoveView

RequestFocus As Boolean

SendToBack

SetBackgroundImage (Bitmap1 As Bitmap)

SetLayout (Left As Int, Top As Int, Width As Int, Height As Int)

Tag As Object

Text As String

TextColor As Int
TextSize As Float
Top As Int
Typeface As Typeface
Visible As Boolean
Width As Int

Background As Drawable
Gets or sets the background drawable.

BringToFront
Changes the Z order of this view and brings it to the front.

Checked As Boolean

Color As Int [write only]
Sets the background of the view to be a **ColorDrawable** with the given color. If the current background is of type **GradientDrawable** or **ColorDrawable**, the round corners will be kept.

Enabled As Boolean
If set to **True** then the **CheckBox** will respond to events. If set to **False**, events are ignored.

Gravity As Int
Gets or sets the gravity (page 282) value. This value affects the way the text will be drawn.

Height As Int
Gets or sets the view's height.

Initialize (EventName As String)
Initializes the view and sets the subs that will handle the events.
Views added with the designer should NOT be initialized. These views are initialized when the layout is loaded.

Invalidate
Invalidates the whole view forcing the view to redraw itself. Redrawing will only happen when the program can process messages, usually when it finishes running the current code.
If you only need to redraw part of the view, it is usually quicker to use **Invalidate2** or **Invalidate3**.

Invalidate2 (Rect1 As Rect)
Invalidates anything inside the given rectangle that is part of this view. Redrawing will only happen when the program can process messages, usually when it finishes running the current code.

Invalidate3 (Left As Int, Top As Int, Right As Int, Bottom As Int)
Invalidates anything inside the given rectangle that is part of this view. Redrawing will only happen when the program can process messages, usually when it finishes running the current code.

IsInitialized As Boolean
Whether this object has been initialized by calling `Initialize`.

Left As Int
Gets or sets the view's left position.

RemoveView
Removes this view from its parent.

RequestFocus As Boolean
Tries to set the focus to this view. Returns `True` if the focus was set.

SendToBack
Changes the Z order of this view and sends it to the back.

SetBackgroundImage (Bitmap1 As Bitmap)

SetLayout (Left As Int, Top As Int, Width As Int, Height As Int)
Changes the view position and size.

Tag As Object
Gets or sets the Tag value. This is a place holder which can be used to store additional data.

Text As String

TextColor As Int

TextSize As Float

Top As Int
Gets or sets the view's top position.

Typeface As Typeface

Visible As Boolean
Whether the user can see the object.

Width As Int
Gets or sets the view's width.

CustomView

A Custom View allows you to create your own types of views which you implement either as a class or in a library. Your class could also be compiled into a library.
First create the class (or library) and add it to your project. Now use the Designer menu [Add View > CustomView]
The custom type will be automatically added to the Custom Type list.
Ensure that the correct type is selected in the Custom Type list:

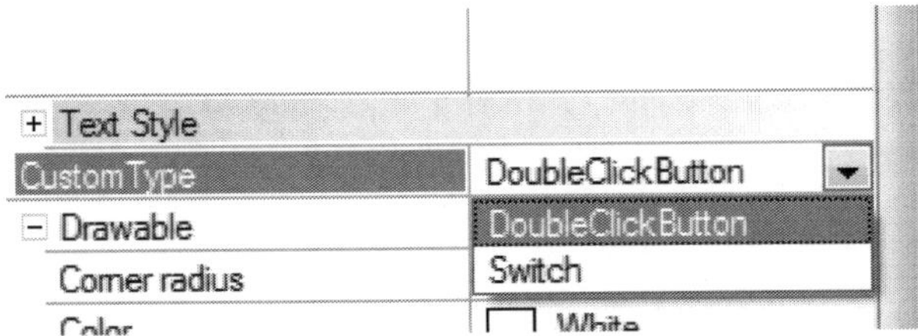

You can now set the view properties and also treat it like any other view in the designer script.
You must include a **Dim** statement in your **Activity Module** declaring every CustomView. The simplest way is to use either the Designer menu [Tools > Generate Members] or the context menu in the Abstract Designer (page 105)
In order for your object to be supported by the designer, your code must include the following two subs. When a layout file is loaded, the **Initialize** method will be called followed by a call to **DesignerCreateView**.

Sub Initialize (TargetModule As Object, EventName As String)

TargetModule - references the module that loads the layout file.
EventName - the event's name property.
These two parameters allow you to later raise events like all standard views.

Sub DesignerCreateView(Base As Panel, Lbl As Label, Props As Map)

Base - a panel that will be the parent for your custom view. The panel background and layout will be based on the values from the designer. Note that you are free to do whatever you need to do with this panel.
Lbl - the purpose of the label is to hold all the text-related properties. The label will not appear (unless you explicitly add it).
Props - a Map with additional entries. Currently, the only entry is an "activity" key that holds a reference to the parent Activity object.
Some sample code for using a Custom View with Designer support can be found here (http://bit.ly/17gbqCR).

EditText

EditText is a view that allows the user to write free text (similar to TextBox in VB forms). The EditText has two modes; **SingleLine** and **MultiLine**. You can set it to be multiline by calling **EditText1.SingleLine = False**
On most devices, the soft keyboard will show automatically when the user presses on the EditText. You can change the InputType property and change the type of keyboard that appears. For example:

```
EditText1.InputType = EditText1.INPUT_TYPE_NUMBERS
```

will cause the numeric keyboard to appear when the user presses on the EditText.
Note that it will also cause the EditText to only accept numbers. Note also that most views are not focusable. For example, pressing on a Button will not change the focus state of an EditText.
This is an **Activity** object; it cannot be declared under **Sub Process_Globals**.

TextChanged (Old As String, New As String)

The **TextChanged** event fires whenever the text changes and it includes the old and new strings.

EnterPressed

The **EnterPressed** event fires when the user presses on the enter key or action key (Done or Next).

FocusChanged (HasFocus As Boolean)

The FocusChanged event fires when the view is focused or loses focus. The **HasFocus** parameter value will be set accordingly.

Members:

Background As Drawable
BringToFront
Color As Int [write only]
Enabled As Boolean
ForceDoneButton As Boolean [write only]
Gravity As Int
Height As Int
Hint As String
HintColor As Int
Initialize (EventName As String)
INPUT_TYPE_DECIMAL_NUMBERS As Int
INPUT_TYPE_NONE As Int
INPUT_TYPE_NUMBERS As Int
INPUT_TYPE_PHONE As Int
INPUT_TYPE_TEXT As Int
InputType As Int
Invalidate
Invalidate2 (Rect1 As Rect)
Invalidate3 (Left As Int, Top As Int, Right As Int, Bottom As Int)
IsInitialized As Boolean
Left As Int
PasswordMode As Boolean [write only]
RemoveView (page 356)
RequestFocus (page 356) As Boolean
SelectAll (page 356)
SelectionStart (page 356) As Int
SendToBack (page 356)
SetBackgroundImage (page 356) (Bitmap1 As Bitmap)
SetLayout (page 356) (Left As Int, Top As Int, Width As Int, Height As Int)

SingleLine As Boolean [write only]
Tag As Object
Text As String
TextColor As Int
TextSize As Float
Top As Int
Typeface As Typeface
Visible As Boolean
Width As Int
Wrap As Boolean [write only]

Background As Drawable

Gets or sets the background drawable.

BringToFront

Changes the Z order of this view and brings it to the front.

Color As Int [write only]

Sets the background of the view to be a **ColorDrawable** with the given color. If the current background is of type **GradientDrawable** or **ColorDrawable**, the round corners will be kept.

Enabled As Boolean

If set to **True** then the **EditText** will respond to events. If set to **False**, events are ignored.

ForceDoneButton As Boolean [write only]

By default, Android sets the virtual keyboard action key to display Done or Next according to the specific layout. You can force it to display Done by setting this value to **True**.

Example:

```
EditText1.ForceDoneButton = True
```

Gravity As Int

Gets or sets the gravity (page 282) value. This value affects the way the text will be drawn.

Height As Int

Gets or sets the view's height.

Hint As String

Gets or sets the text that will appear when the EditText is empty.

Example:

```
EditText1.Hint = "Enter username"
```

HintColor As Int

Gets or sets the hint text color.

Example:

```
EditText1.HintColor = Colors.Gray
```

Initialize (EventName As String)

Initializes the view and sets the subs that will handle the events.
Views added with the designer should NOT be initialized. These views are initialized when the layout is loaded.

INPUT_TYPE_DECIMAL_NUMBERS As Int

Numeric keyboard will be displayed. Numbers, decimal point and minus sign are accepted.

INPUT_TYPE_NONE As Int

No keyboard will be displayed and clicking on the EditText will do nothing.

INPUT_TYPE_NUMBERS As Int

Numeric keyboard will be displayed. Only numbers are accepted.

INPUT_TYPE_PHONE As Int

Keyboard will be displayed in phone mode.

INPUT_TYPE_TEXT As Int

Default text mode.

InputType As Int

Gets or sets the input type flag. This flag is used to determine the settings of the virtual keyboard. **Note** that changing the input type will set the EditText to be in single line mode.
Example:

```
EditText1.InputType = EditText1.INPUT_TYPE_NUMBERS
```

Invalidate

Invalidates the whole view forcing the view to redraw itself. Redrawing will only happen when the program can process messages, usually when it finishes running the current code.
If you only need to redraw part of the view, it is usually quicker to use **`Invalidate2`** or **`Invalidate3`**.

Invalidate2 (Rect1 As Rect)

Invalidates anything inside the given rectangle that is part of this view. Redrawing will only happen when the program can process messages, usually when it finishes running the current code.

Invalidate3 (Left As Int, Top As Int, Right As Int, Bottom As Int)

Invalidates anything inside the given rectangle that is part of this view. Redrawing will only happen when the program can process messages, usually when it finishes running the current code.

IsInitialized As Boolean

Whether this object has been initialized by calling **`Initialize`**.

Left As Int

Gets or sets the view's left position.

PasswordMode As Boolean **[write only]**
Sets whether the EditText should be in password mode and hide the actual characters.

RemoveView
Removes this view from its parent.

RequestFocus As Boolean
Tries to set the focus to this view. Returns `True` if the focus was set.

SelectAll
Selects the entire text.

SelectionStart As Int
Gets or sets the selection start position (or the cursor position). Returns `-1` if there is no selection or cursor.

SendToBack
Changes the Z order of this view and sends it to the back.

SetBackgroundImage (Bitmap1 As Bitmap**)**

SetLayout (Left As Int**, Top As** Int**, Width As** Int**, Height As** Int**)**
Changes the view position and size.

SingleLine As Boolean **[write only]**
Sets whether the EditText should be in single-line mode or multiline mode.

Tag As Object
Gets or sets the Tag value. This is a place holder which can be used to store additional data.

Text As String

TextColor As Int

TextSize As Float

Top As Int
Gets or sets the view's top position.

Typeface As Typeface

Visible As Boolean
Whether the user can see the object.

Width As Int
Gets or sets the view's width.

Wrap As Boolean **[write only]**
Sets whether the text content will wrap within the EditText bounds. Relevant when the EditText is in multiline mode. Example:

```
EditText1.Wrap = False
```

HorizontalScrollView

HorizontalScrollView is a view that contains other views and allows the user to horizontally scroll those views. The HorizontalScrollView is similar to ScrollView which scrolls vertically. See the ScrollView tutorial (http://www.basic4ppc.com/forum/basic4android-getting-started-tutorials/6612-scrollview-example.html) for more information.
The HorizontalScrollView has an inner panel which actually contains the child views.
You can add views by calling: **`HorizontalScrollView1.Panel.AddView(...)`**
Note that it is not possible to nest scrolling views.
This is an **`Activity`** object; it cannot be declared under **`Sub Process_Globals`**.

Events:

ScrollChanged(Position As Int)

Members:

Background As Drawable
BringToFront
Color As Int [write only]
Enabled As Boolean
FullScroll (Right As Boolean)
Height As Int
Initialize (Width As Int, EventName As String)
Invalidate
Invalidate2 (Rect1 As Rect)
Invalidate3 (Left As Int, Top As Int, Right As Int, Bottom As Int)
IsInitialized As Boolean
Left As Int
Panel As Panel [read only]
RemoveView
RequestFocus As Boolean
ScrollPosition As Int
SendToBack
SetBackgroundImage (Bitmap1 As Bitmap)
SetLayout (Left As Int, Top As Int, Width As Int, Height As Int)
Tag As Object
Top As Int
Visible As Boolean
Width As Int

Background As Drawable

Gets or sets the background drawable.

BringToFront
Changes the Z order of this view and brings it to the front.

Color As Int [write only]
Sets the background of the view to be a **ColorDrawable** with the given color. If the current background is of type **GradientDrawable** or **ColorDrawable**, the round corners will be kept.

Enabled As Boolean
If set to **True** then the **HorizontalScrollView** will respond to events. If set to **False**, events are ignored.

FullScroll (Right As Boolean)
Set to **True** to scroll the view to the right. Set to **False** to scroll to the left.

Height As Int
Gets or sets the view's height.

Initialize (Width As Int, EventName As String)
Initializes the object.
Width - The width of the inner panel.
EventName - Sets the sub that will handle the event.

Invalidate
Invalidates the whole view forcing the view to redraw itself. Redrawing will only happen when the program can process messages, usually when it finishes running the current code.
If you only need to redraw part of the view, it is usually quicker to use **Invalidate2** or **Invalidate3**.

Invalidate2 (Rect1 As Rect)
Invalidates anything inside the given rectangle that is part of this view. Redrawing will only happen when the program can process messages, usually when it finishes running the current code.

Invalidate3 (Left As Int, Top As Int, Right As Int, Bottom As Int)
Invalidates anything inside the given rectangle that is part of this view. Redrawing will only happen when the program can process messages, usually when it finishes running the current code.

IsInitialized As Boolean
Whether this object has been initialized by calling **Initialize**.

Left As Int
Gets or sets the view's left position.

Panel As Panel [read only]
Returns the panel which you can use to add views to. Example:

```
HorizontalScrollView1.Panel.AddView(...)
```

RemoveView
Removes this view from its parent.

RequestFocus As Boolean
Tries to set the focus to this view. Returns **`True`** if the focus was set.

ScrollPosition As Int
Gets or sets the scroll position.

SendToBack
Changes the Z order of this view and sends it to the back.

SetBackgroundImage (Bitmap1 As Bitmap)

SetLayout (Left As Int, Top As Int, Width As Int, Height As Int)
Changes the view position and size.

Tag As Object
Gets or sets the Tag value. This is a place holder which can be used to store additional data.

Top As Int
Gets or sets the view's top position.

Visible As Boolean
Whether the user can see the object.

Width As Int
Gets or sets the view's width.

ImageView

A view that shows an image. You can assign a bitmap using the **`Bitmap`** property.
The **`Gravity`** property changes the way the image appears. The two most relevant values are:
`Gravity.FILL` (which will cause the image to fill the entire view)
and **`Gravity.CENTER`** (which will draw the image in the view's center).
This is an **`Activity`** object; it cannot be declared under **`Sub Process_Globals`**.

Events:

Click
Occurs when the user presses and releases the ImageView.

LongClick
Occurs when the user presses on the ImageView for roughly one second.

Members:

- Background As Drawable
- Bitmap As Bitmap
- BringToFront
- Color As Int [write only]
- Enabled As Boolean
- Gravity As Int

- Height As Int
- Initialize (EventName As String)
- Invalidate
- Invalidate2 (Rect1 As Rect)
- Invalidate3 (Left As Int, Top As Int, Right As Int, Bottom As Int)
- IsInitialized As Boolean
- Left As Int
- RemoveView
- RequestFocus As Boolean
- SendToBack
- SetBackgroundImage (Bitmap1 As Bitmap)
- SetLayout (Left As Int, Top As Int, Width As Int, Height As Int)
- Tag As Object
- Top As Int
- Visible As Boolean
- Width As Int

Background As Drawable

Gets or sets the background drawable.

Bitmap As Bitmap

Gets or sets the bitmap assigned to the ImageView.
Example:

```
ImageView1.Bitmap = LoadBitmap(File.DirAssets, "someimage.jpg")
```

BringToFront

Changes the Z order of this view and brings it to the front.

Color As Int [write only]

Sets the background of the view to be a **ColorDrawable** with the given color. If the current background is of type **GradientDrawable** or **ColorDrawable**, the round corners will be kept.

Enabled As Boolean

If set to **True** then the **ImageView** will respond to events. If set to **False**, events are ignored.

Gravity As Int

Gets or sets the gravity (page 282) assigned to the bitmap.
Example:

```
ImageView1.Gravity = Gravity.Fill
```

Height As Int

Gets or sets the view's height.

Initialize (EventName As String)

Initializes the view and sets the subs that will handle the events.

Views added with the designer should NOT be initialized. These views are initialized when the layout is loaded.

Invalidate

Invalidates the whole view forcing the view to redraw itself. Redrawing will only happen when the program can process messages, usually when it finishes running the current code.
If you only need to redraw part of the view, it is usually quicker to use **`Invalidate2`** or **`Invalidate3`**.

Invalidate2 (Rect1 As Rect)

Invalidates anything inside the given rectangle that is part of this view. Redrawing will only happen when the program can process messages, usually when it finishes running the current code.

Invalidate3 (Left As Int, Top As Int, Right As Int, Bottom As Int)

Invalidates anything inside the given rectangle that is part of this view. Redrawing will only happen when the program can process messages, usually when it finishes running the current code.

IsInitialized As Boolean

Whether this object has been initialized by calling **`Initialize`**.

Left As Int

Gets or sets the view's left position.

RemoveView

Removes this view from its parent.

RequestFocus As Boolean

Tries to set the focus to this view. Returns **`True`** if the focus was set.

SendToBack

Changes the Z order of this view and sends it to the back.

SetBackgroundImage (Bitmap1 As Bitmap)

SetLayout (Left As Int, Top As Int, Width As Int, Height As Int)

Changes the view position and size.

Tag As Object

Gets or sets the Tag value. This is a place holder which can be used to store additional data.

Top As Int

Gets or sets the view's top position.

Visible As Boolean

Whether the user can see the object.

Width As Int

Gets or sets the view's width.

Label

A Label view that shows read-only text.
This is an **Activity** object; it cannot be declared under **Sub Process_Globals**.

Events:

Click

Occurs when the user presses and releases the label.

LongClick

Occurs when the user presses on the label for roughly one second.

Members:

- Background As Drawable
- BringToFront
- Color As Int [write only]
- Enabled As Boolean
- Gravity As Int
- Height As Int
- Initialize (EventName As String)
- Invalidate
- Invalidate2 (Rect1 As Rect)
- Invalidate3 (Left As Int, Top As Int, Right As Int, Bottom As Int)
- IsInitialized As Boolean
- Left As Int
- RemoveView
- RequestFocus As Boolean
- SendToBack
- SetBackgroundImage (Bitmap1 As Bitmap)
- SetLayout (Left As Int, Top As Int, Width As Int, Height As Int)
- Tag As Object
- Text As String
- TextColor As Int
- TextSize As Float
- Top As Int
- Typeface As Typeface
- Visible As Boolean
- Width As Int

Background As Drawable

Gets or sets the background drawable.

BringToFront

Changes the Z order of this view and brings it to the front.

Color As Int [write only]
Sets the background of the view to be a **`ColorDrawable`** with the given color.
If the current background is of type **`GradientDrawable`** or **`ColorDrawable`**, the round corners will be kept.

Enabled As Boolean
If set to **`True`** then the label will respond to the **`Click`** and **`LongClick`** events. If set to **`False`**, these events are ignored.

Gravity As Int
Gets or sets the gravity (page 282) value. This value affects the way the text will be drawn.

Height As Int
Gets or sets the view's height.

Initialize (EventName As String)
Initializes the view and sets the subs that will handle the events.
Views added with the designer should NOT be initialized. These views are initialized when the layout is loaded.

Invalidate
Invalidates the whole view forcing the view to redraw itself. Redrawing will only happen when the program can process messages, usually when it finishes running the current code.
If you only need to redraw part of the view, it is usually quicker to use **`Invalidate2`** or **`Invalidate3`**.

Invalidate2 (Rect1 As Rect)
Invalidates anything inside the given rectangle that is part of this view. Redrawing will only happen when the program can process messages, usually when it finishes running the current code.

Invalidate3 (Left As Int, Top As Int, Right As Int, Bottom As Int)
Invalidates anything inside the given rectangle that is part of this view. Redrawing will only happen when the program can process messages, usually when it finishes running the current code.

IsInitialized As Boolean
Whether this object has been initialized by calling **`Initialize`**.

Left As Int
Gets or sets the view's left position.

RemoveView
Removes this view from its parent.

RequestFocus As Boolean
Tries to set the focus to this view.
Returns **`True`** if the focus was set.

SendToBack
Changes the Z order of this view and sends it to the back.

SetBackgroundImage (Bitmap1 As Bitmap)

SetLayout (Left As Int, Top As Int, Width As Int, Height As Int)
Changes the view position and size.

Tag As Object
Gets or sets the Tag value. This is a place holder which can be used to store additional data.

Text As String
Get or set the text which this label shows.

TextColor As Int
The color (page 280) of the text used by this label.

TextSize As Float
The size of the text this label uses.

Top As Int
Gets or sets the view's top position.

Typeface As Typeface
The typeface (page 284) this label uses.

Visible As Boolean
Whether the user can see this label.

Width As Int
Gets or sets the label's width.

ListView

ListView is a view that displays lists. The ListView can have one or two lines. A two-line item can also have an icon. You can mix all three types of lines in a single ListView:

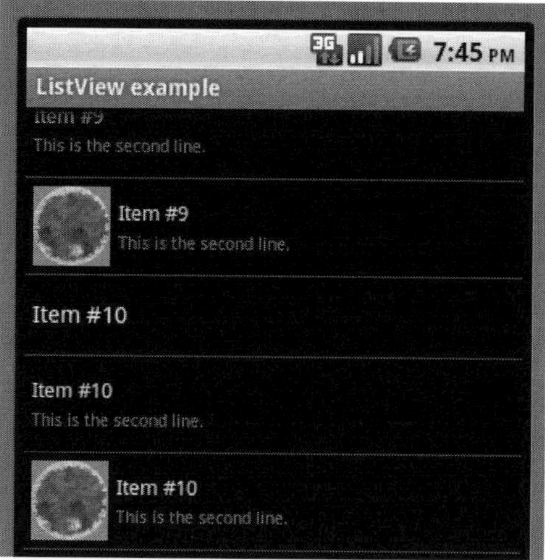

ListView has two events which allow you to determine which item the user clicked. Unfortunately, you cannot respond by changing the appearance of the selected item, so you might want to consider using a Custom List View (page 525) instead.
This is an **Activity** object; it cannot be declared under **Sub Process_Globals**.

Changing Text Appearance

You can change the appearance of each of these three types of line by editing the layout, for example:

```
Dim label1 As Label
label1 = ListView1.SingleLineLayout.Label
label1.TextSize = 20
label1.TextColor = Colors.Blue
```

This will change the appearance of all items in the list with SingleLineLayout.
Note that a TwoLine item has two labels, one for each line:

```
Dim Label1 As Label
Label1 = ListView1.TwoLinesLayout.SecondLabel
Label1.TextSize = 20
Label1.TextColor = Colors.Green
```

ListView as a Menu

You can use a ListView as a popup menu on any Activity. For example:

```
Sub Globals
  ' Could create either in Layout or here
  Dim lstMenu As ListView
End Sub

Sub Activity_Create(FirstTime As Boolean)
 Activity.LoadLayout("main")

 lstMenu.Initialize("lstMenu")
 Activity.AddView(lstMenu, 10%x, 10%y, 80%x, 80%y)
 lstMenu.AddSingleLine2("Help", "help")
 lstMenu.AddSingleLine2("Settings", "settings")
```

```
 ' Set colors since default background is transparent
 lstMenu.Color = Colors.White
 Dim lstLabel As Label
 lstLabel = lstMenu.SingleLineLayout.Label
 ' default text color is white
 lstLabel.TextColor = Colors.Black
 lstMenu.Visible = False
End Sub

Sub btnTest_Click
 ' StartActivity(test) will hide this activity
 ' Activity.LoadLayout("testActivity")
 lstMenu.Visible = True
End Sub

Sub lstMenu_ItemClick (Position As Int, Value As Object)
 Select Value
 Case "help"
  lstMenu.Visible = False
  StartActivity("help")
 Case "settings"
  lstMenu.Visible = False
  StartActivity("settings")
 End Select
End Sub
```

Tutorial

See the ListView tutorial (http://bit.ly/181bNV6) for more information.

Events:

ItemClick (Position As Int, Value As Object)

ItemClick is raised when an item is touched and released.

ItemLongClick (Position As Int, Value As Object)

ItemLongClick is raised when an item is touched and held.

Members:

- AddSingleLine (Text As String)
- AddSingleLine2 (Text As String, ReturnValue As Object)
- AddTwoLines (Text1 As String, Text2 As String)
- AddTwoLines2 (Text1 As String, Text2 As String, ReturnValue As Object)
- AddTwoLinesAndBitmap (Text1 As String, Text2 As String, Bitmap1 As Bitmap)
- AddTwoLinesAndBitmap2 (Text1 As String, Text2 As String, Bitmap1 As Bitmap, ReturnValue As Object)
- Background As Drawable
- BringToFront
- Clear

- Color As Int [write only]
- Enabled As Boolean
- FastScrollEnabled As Boolean
- GetItem (Index As Int) As Object
- Height As Int
- Initialize (EventName As String)
- Invalidate
- Invalidate2 (Rect1 As Rect)
- Invalidate3 (Left As Int, Top As Int, Right As Int, Bottom As Int)
- IsInitialized As Boolean
- Left As Int
- RemoveAt (Index As Int)
- RemoveView
- RequestFocus As Boolean
- ScrollingBackgroundColor As Int [write only]
- SendToBack
- SetBackgroundImage (Bitmap1 As Bitmap)
- SetLayout (Left As Int, Top As Int, Width As Int, Height As Int)
- SetSelection (Position As Int)
- SingleLineLayout (page 370) As SingleLineLayout [read only]
- Size (page 370) As Int [read only]
- Tag (page 370) As Object
- Top (page 370) As Int
- TwoLinesAndBitmap (page 370) As TwoLinesAndBitmapLayout [read only]
- TwoLinesLayout (page 370) As TwoLinesLayout [read only]
- Visible (page 370) As Boolean
- Width (page 370) As Int

AddSingleLine (Text As String)

Adds a single line item.
Example:

```
ListView1.AddSingleLine("Sunday")
```

AddSingleLine2 (Text As String, ReturnValue As Object)

Adds a single line item.
The specified return value will be returned when calling **GetItem** or in the **ItemClick** event.
Example:

```
ListView1.AddSingleLine2("Sunday", 1)
```

AddTwoLines (Text1 As String, Text2 As String)

Adds a two-lines item.
Example:

```
ListView1.AddTwoLines("This is the first line.", "And this is
the second")
```

AddTwoLines2 (Text1 As String, Text2 As String, ReturnValue As Object)

Adds a two-lines item. **ReturnValue** will be returned when calling **GetItem** or in the **ItemClick** event.

AddTwoLinesAndBitmap (Text1 As String, Text2 As String, Bitmap1 As Bitmap)

Adds two lines and a bitmap item.
Example:

```
ListView1.AddTwoLinesAndBitmap("First line", "Second line",
LoadBitmap( File.DirAssets, "SomeImage.png"))
```

AddTwoLinesAndBitmap2 (Text1 As String, Text2 As String, Bitmap1 As Bitmap, ReturnValue As Object)

Adds two lines and a bitmap item. **ReturnValue** will be returned when calling **GetItem** or in the **ItemClick** event.

Background As Drawable

Gets or sets the background drawable.

BringToFront

Changes the Z order of this view and brings it to the front.

Clear

Clears all items from the list.

Color As Int [write only]

Sets the background of the view to be a **ColorDrawable** with the given color.
If the current background is of type **GradientDrawable** or **ColorDrawable**, the round corners will be kept.

Enabled As Boolean

If set to **True** then the **ListView** will respond to the **ItemClick** and **ItemLongClick** events. If set to **False**, these events are ignored.

FastScrollEnabled As Boolean

Gets or sets whether the fast scroll icon will appear when the user scrolls the list.
The default is **False**.

GetItem (Index As Int) As Object

Returns the value of the item at the specified position. Returns the "return value" if it was set, and if not, returns the text of the first line.

Height As Int

Gets or sets the view's height.

Initialize (EventName As String)

Initializes the view and sets the subs that will handle the events.

Views added with the designer should NOT be initialized. These views are initialized when the layout is loaded.

Invalidate
Invalidates the whole view forcing the view to redraw itself. Redrawing will only happen when the program can process messages, usually when it finishes running the current code.
If you only need to redraw part of the view, it is usually quicker to use `Invalidate2` or `Invalidate3`.

Invalidate2 (Rect1 As Rect)
Invalidates anything inside the given rectangle that is part of this view. Redrawing will only happen when the program can process messages, usually when it finishes running the current code.

Invalidate3 (Left As Int, Top As Int, Right As Int, Bottom As Int)
Invalidates anything inside the given rectangle that is part of this view. Redrawing will only happen when the program can process messages, usually when it finishes running the current code.

IsInitialized As Boolean
Whether this object has been initialized by calling `Initialize`.

Left As Int
Gets or sets the view's left position.

RemoveAt (Index As Int)
Removes the item at the specified position.

RemoveView
Removes this view from its parent.

RequestFocus As Boolean
Tries to set the focus to this view. Returns `True` if the focus was set.

ScrollingBackgroundColor As Int [write only]
Sets the background color that will be used while scrolling the list. This is an optimization done to make the scrolling smoother. Set to `Colors.Transparent` if the background behind the list is not a solid color. The default is black.

SendToBack
Changes the Z order of this view and sends it to the back.

SetBackgroundImage (Bitmap1 As Bitmap)

SetLayout (Left As Int, Top As Int, Width As Int, Height As Int)
Changes the view position and size.

SetSelection (Position As Int)
Sets the currently selected item. Calling this method will make this item visible. If the user is interacting with the list with the keyboard or the wheel button, the item will also be visibly selected. Example:

```
ListView1.SetSelection(10)
```

SingleLineLayout As SingleLineLayout [read only]

Returns the layout that is used to show single line items. You can change the layout values to change the appearance of such items. Example:

```
Dim Label1 As Label
Label1 = ListView1.SingleLineLayout.Label
Label1.TextSize = 20
Label1.TextColor = Colors.Green
```

Size As Int [read only]

Returns the number of items stored in the list.

Tag As Object

Gets or sets the Tag value. This is a place holder which can be used to store additional data.

Top As Int

Gets or sets the view's top position.

TwoLinesAndBitmap As TwoLinesAndBitmapLayout [read only]

Returns the layout that is used to show items containing two lines and bitmap. You can change the layout values to change the appearance of such items. For example, if you want to remove the second label (in all items with this layout):

```
ListView1.TwoLinesAndBitmap.SecondLabel.Visible = False
```

TwoLinesLayout As TwoLinesLayout [read only]

Returns the layout that is used to show two-lines items.

You can change the layout values to change the appearance of such items. Example:

```
Dim Label1 As Label
Label1 = ListView1.TwoLinesLayout.SecondLabel
Label1.TextSize = 20
Label1.TextColor = Colors.Green
```

Visible As Boolean

Whether the user can see the object.

Width As Int

Gets or sets the view's width.

Panel

A Panel is a view that holds other child views. You can add child views programmatically or by loading a layout file. This is an **Activity** object; it cannot be declared under **Sub Process_Globals**.

Events:

Touch (Action As Int, X As Float, Y As Float)

When the user touches a Panel, it raises the Touch event. The first parameter of this event is the Action which is one of the Activity action constants. X and Y indicate where the panel was touched.
If the user keeps touching the panel, it will continue to raise the Touch event. Return `True` from the Touch event sub to consume the event (otherwise other views behind the Panel will receive the event).

Click

If there is no Touch event handler in your app, then Android will raise the Click event if the user touches the panel briefly.

LongClick

If there is no Touch event handler in your app, then Android will raise the LongClick event if the user touches the panel for an extended period.

Members:

- AddView (View1 As View, Left As Int, Top As Int, Width As Int, Height As Int)
- Background As Drawable
- BringToFront
- Color As Int [write only]
- Enabled As Boolean
- GetAllViewsRecursive As IterableList
- GetView (Index As Int) As View
- Height As Int
- Initialize (EventName As String)
- Invalidate
- Invalidate2 (Rect1 As Rect)
- Invalidate3 (Left As Int, Top As Int, Right As Int, Bottom As Int)
- IsInitialized As Boolean
- Left As Int
- LoadLayout (Layout As String) As LayoutValues
- NumberOfViews As Int [read only]
- RemoveAllViews
- RemoveView
- RemoveViewAt (Index As Int)
- RequestFocus As Boolean
- SendToBack
- SetBackgroundImage (Bitmap1 As Bitmap)
- SetLayout (Left As Int, Top As Int, Width As Int, Height As Int)
- Tag As Object

Top As Int
Visible As Boolean
Width As Int

AddView (View1 As View, Left As Int, Top As Int, Width As Int, Height As Int)
Adds a view to this panel.

Background As Drawable
Gets or sets the background drawable.

BringToFront
Changes the Z order of this view and brings it to the front.

Color As Int [write only]
Sets the background of the view to be a **ColorDrawable** with the given color. If the current background is of type **GradientDrawable** or **ColorDrawable**, the round corners will be kept.

Enabled As Boolean
If set to **True** then the Panel will respond to events. If set to **False**, events are ignored.

GetAllViewsRecursive As IterableList
Returns an iterator that iterates over all the views belonging to the panel, including views which are children of other views. Example:

```
For Each vw As View In pnlMain.GetAllViewsRecursive
  vw.Color = Colors.RGB(Rnd(0,255), Rnd(0,255), Rnd(0,255))
Next
```

GetView (Index As Int) As View
Gets the view that is stored at the specified index.

Height As Int
Gets or sets the view's height.

Initialize (EventName As String)
Initializes the view and sets the subs that will handle the events.
Views added with the designer should NOT be initialized. These views are initialized when the layout is loaded.

Invalidate
Invalidates the whole view forcing the view to redraw itself. Redrawing will only happen when the program can process messages, usually when it finishes running the current code.
If you only need to redraw part of the view, it is usually quicker to use **Invalidate2** or **Invalidate3**.

Invalidate2 (Rect1 As Rect)
Invalidates anything inside the given rectangle that is part of this view. Redrawing will only happen when the program can process messages, usually when it finishes running the current code.

Invalidate3 (Left As Int, Top As Int, Right As Int, Bottom As Int)
Invalidates anything inside the given rectangle that is part of this view. Redrawing will only happen when the program can process messages, usually when it finishes running the current code.

IsInitialized As Boolean
Whether this object has been initialized by calling `Initialize`.

Left As Int
Gets or sets the view's left position.

LoadLayout (Layout As String) As LayoutValues
Loads a layout file to this panel. Returns the value of the chosen layout variant.

NumberOfViews As Int [read only]
Returns the number of child views.

RemoveAllViews
Removes all child views.

RemoveView
Removes this view from its parent.

RemoveViewAt (Index As Int)
Removes the view that is stored at the specified index.

RequestFocus As Boolean
Tries to set the focus to this view. Returns `True` if the focus was set.

SendToBack
Changes the Z order of this view and sends it to the back.

SetBackgroundImage (Bitmap1 As Bitmap)

SetLayout (Left As Int, Top As Int, Width As Int, Height As Int)
Changes the view position and size.

Tag As Object
Gets or sets the Tag value. This is a place holder which can be used to store additional data.

Top As Int
Gets or sets the view's top position.

Visible As Boolean
Whether the user can see the object.

Width As Int
Gets or sets the view's width.

ProgressBar

A progress bar view which lets you show the progress of a long-running process.
Example:

```
Sub Activity_Create(FirstTime As Boolean)
 Activity.LoadLayout("Main")
 ProgressBar1.Progress = 0
 Timer1.Initialize("Timer1", 1000)
 Timer1.Enabled = True
End Sub

Sub timer1_Tick
 'Handle tick events
 ProgressBar1.Progress = ProgressBar1.Progress + 10
 If ProgressBar1.Progress = 100 Then
 Timer1.Enabled = False
 End If
End Sub
```

The exact nature of the visible bar depends upon the device and the size you have chosen. Here is one example:

The Progress property sets the progress value which is from 0 to 100.
This is an **Activity** object; it cannot be declared under **Sub Process_Globals**.

Members:

- Background As Drawable
- BringToFront
- Color As Int [write only]
- Enabled As Boolean
- Height As Int
- Indeterminate As Boolean
- Initialize (EventName As String)
- Invalidate
- Invalidate2 (Rect1 As Rect)
- Invalidate3 (Left As Int, Top As Int, Right As Int, Bottom As Int)
- IsInitialized As Boolean
- Left As Int
- Progress As Int
- RemoveView
- RequestFocus As Boolean
- SendToBack
- SetBackgroundImage (Bitmap1 As Bitmap)
- SetLayout (Left As Int, Top As Int, Width As Int, Height As Int)

Tag As Object
Top As Int
Visible As Boolean
Width As Int

Background As Drawable
Gets or sets the background drawable.

BringToFront
Changes the Z order of this view and brings it to the front.

Color As Int [write only]
Sets the background of the view to be a **ColorDrawable** with the given color. If the current background is of type **GradientDrawable** or **ColorDrawable**, the round corners will be kept.

Enabled As Boolean
This property has no effect since a **ProgressBar** has no events.

Height As Int
Gets or sets the view's height.

Indeterminate As Boolean
Gets or sets whether the progress bar is in indeterminate mode (cyclic animation).

Initialize (EventName As String)
Initializes the view and sets the subs that will handle the events.
Views added with the designer should NOT be initialized. These views are initialized when the layout is loaded.

Invalidate
Invalidates the whole view forcing the view to redraw itself. Redrawing will only happen when the program can process messages, usually when it finishes running the current code.
If you only need to redraw part of the view, it is usually quicker to use **Invalidate2** or **Invalidate3**.

Invalidate2 (Rect1 As Rect)
Invalidates anything inside the given rectangle that is part of this view. Redrawing will only happen when the program can process messages, usually when it finishes running the current code.

Invalidate3 (Left As Int, Top As Int, Right As Int, Bottom As Int)
Invalidates anything inside the given rectangle that is part of this view. Redrawing will only happen when the program can process messages, usually when it finishes running the current code.

IsInitialized As Boolean
Whether this object has been initialized by calling **Initialize**.

Left As Int
Gets or sets the view's left position.

Progress As Int
Gets or sets the progress value.

RemoveView
Removes this view from its parent.

RequestFocus As Boolean
Tries to set the focus to this view.
Returns `True` if the focus was set.

SendToBack
Changes the Z order of this view and sends it to the back.

SetBackgroundImage (Bitmap1 As Bitmap)

SetLayout (Left As Int, Top As Int, Width As Int, Height As Int)
Changes the view position and size.

Tag As Object
Gets or sets the Tag value. This is a place holder which can be used to store additional data.

Top As Int
Gets or sets the view's top position.

Visible As Boolean
Whether the user can see the object.

Width As Int
Gets or sets the view's width.

RadioButton

A RadioButton view. Only one RadioButton in a group can be checked. When a different RadioButton is checked, all others will automatically be unchecked.
Note that the `CheckedChange` event only runs for the button which has been checked.
Grouping is done by adding RadioButtons to the same activity or panel.
This is an `Activity` object; it cannot be declared under `Sub Process_Globals`.

Event:

CheckedChange(Checked As Boolean)

Note that the `CheckedChange` event only runs for the button which has been checked. Thus, **Checked** is never `False`, and your code should test whether each RadioButton has been checked.

Members:

Background As Drawable
BringToFront

Checked As Boolean
Color As Int [write only]
Enabled As Boolean
Gravity As Int
Height As Int
Initialize (EventName As String)
Invalidate
Invalidate2 (Rect1 As Rect)
Invalidate3 (Left As Int, Top As Int, Right As Int, Bottom As Int)
IsInitialized As Boolean
Left As Int
RemoveView
RequestFocus As Boolean
SendToBack
SetBackgroundImage (Bitmap1 As Bitmap)
SetLayout (Left As Int, Top As Int, Width As Int, Height As Int)
Tag As Object
Text As String
TextColor As Int
TextSize As Float
Top As Int
Typeface As Typeface
Visible As Boolean
Width As Int

Background As Drawable

Gets or sets the background drawable.

BringToFront

Changes the Z order of this view and brings it to the front.

Checked As Boolean

Color As Int [write only]

Sets the background of the view to be a **ColorDrawable** with the given color. If the current background is of type **GradientDrawable** or **ColorDrawable**, the round corners will be kept.

Enabled As Boolean

If set to **True** then the **RadioButton** will respond to events. If set to **False**, events are ignored.

Gravity As Int

Gets or sets the gravity (page 282) value. This value affects the way the text will be drawn.

Height As Int
Gets or sets the view's height.

Initialize (EventName As String)
Initializes the view and sets the subs that will handle the events.
Views added with the designer should NOT be initialized. These views are initialized when the layout is loaded.

Invalidate
Invalidates the whole view forcing the view to redraw itself. Redrawing will only happen when the program can process messages, usually when it finishes running the current code.
If you only need to redraw part of the view, it is usually quicker to use `Invalidate2` or `Invalidate3`.

Invalidate2 (Rect1 As Rect)
Invalidates anything inside the given rectangle that is part of this view. Redrawing will only happen when the program can process messages, usually when it finishes running the current code.

Invalidate3 (Left As Int, Top As Int, Right As Int, Bottom As Int)
Invalidates anything inside the given rectangle that is part of this view. Redrawing will only happen when the program can process messages, usually when it finishes running the current code.

IsInitialized As Boolean
Whether this object has been initialized by calling `Initialize`.

Left As Int
Gets or sets the view's left position.

RemoveView
Removes this view from its parent.

RequestFocus As Boolean
Tries to set the focus to this view. Returns `True` if the focus was set.

SendToBack
Changes the Z order of this view and sends it to the back.

SetBackgroundImage (Bitmap1 As Bitmap)

SetLayout (Left As Int, Top As Int, Width As Int, Height As Int)
Changes the view position and size.

Tag As Object
Gets or sets the Tag value. This is a place holder which can be used to store additional data.

Text As String

TextColor As Int

TextSize As Float

Top As Int

Gets or sets the view's top position.

Typeface As Typeface

Visible As Boolean

Whether the user can see the object.

Width As Int

Gets or sets the view's width.

ScrollView

ScrollView is a view that contains other views and allows the user to vertically scroll those views. See the ScrollView example (http://bit.ly/ZQMe5Q) for more information. The ScrollView has an inner panel which actually contains the child views. You can add views by calling: `ScrollView1.Panel.AddView(...)`

Note that it is not possible to nest scrolling views. For example, a multiline EditText cannot be located inside a ScrollView.

This is an **`Activity`** object; it cannot be declared under **`Sub Process_Globals`**.

Showing Tables

There is a tutorial here (http://bit.ly/16611bH) for a way of creating a table using a ScrollView.

Note: for showing large tables, the additional TableView (http://bit.ly/165ZUIM) class is a better alternative.

Events:

ScrollChanged(Position As Int)

Members:

Background As Drawable

BringToFront

Color As Int [write only]

Enabled As Boolean

FullScroll (Bottom As Boolean)

Height As Int

Initialize (Height As Int)

Initialize2 (Height As Int, EventName As String)

Invalidate

Invalidate2 (Rect1 As Rect)

Invalidate3 (Left As Int, Top As Int, Right As Int, Bottom As Int)

IsInitialized As Boolean

Left As Int
Panel As Panel [read only]
RemoveView
RequestFocus As Boolean
ScrollPosition As Int
SendToBack
SetBackgroundImage (Bitmap1 As Bitmap)
SetLayout (Left As Int, Top As Int, Width As Int, Height As Int)
Tag As Object
Top As Int
Visible As Boolean
Width As Int

Background As Drawable
Gets or sets the background drawable.

BringToFront
Changes the Z order of this view and brings it to the front.

Color As Int [write only]
Sets the background of the view to be a **`ColorDrawable`** with the given color. If the current background is of type **`GradientDrawable`** or **`ColorDrawable`**, the round corners will be kept.

Enabled As Boolean
If set to **`True`** then the **`ScrollView`** will respond to events. If set to **`False`**, events are ignored.

FullScroll (Bottom As Boolean)
Scrolls the scroll view to the top or bottom.

Height As Int
Gets or sets the view's height.

Initialize (Height As Int)
Initializes the ScrollView and sets its inner panel height to the given height. You can later change this height by calling ScrollView.Panel.Height.

```
Dim ScrollView1 As ScrollView
ScrollView1.Initialize(1000dip)
```

Initialize2 (Height As Int, EventName As String)
Similar to Initialize. Sets the Sub that will handle the ScrollChanged event.

Invalidate
Invalidates the whole view forcing the view to redraw itself. Redrawing will only happen when the program can process messages, usually when it finishes running the current code.

If you only need to redraw part of the view, it is usually quicker to use **`Invalidate2`** or **`Invalidate3`**.

Invalidate2 (Rect1 As Rect)
Invalidates anything inside the given rectangle that is part of this view. Redrawing will only happen when the program can process messages, usually when it finishes running the current code.

Invalidate3 (Left As Int, Top As Int, Right As Int, Bottom As Int)
Invalidates anything inside the given rectangle that is part of this view. Redrawing will only happen when the program can process messages, usually when it finishes running the current code.

IsInitialized As Boolean
Whether this object has been initialized by calling **`Initialize`**.

Left As Int
Gets or sets the view's left position.

Panel As Panel [read only]
Returns the panel which you can use to add views to. Example:

```
ScrollView1.Panel.AddView(...)
```

RemoveView
Removes this view from its parent.

RequestFocus As Boolean
Tries to set the focus to this view.
Returns **`True`** if the focus was set.

ScrollPosition As Int
Gets or sets the scroll position.

SendToBack
Changes the Z order of this view and sends it to the back.

SetBackgroundImage (Bitmap1 As Bitmap)

SetLayout (Left As Int, Top As Int, Width As Int, Height As Int)
Changes the view position and size.

Tag As Object
Gets or sets the Tag value. This is a place holder which can be used to store additional data.

Top As Int
Gets or sets the view's top position.

Visible As Boolean
Whether the user can see the object.

Width As Int
Gets or sets the view's width.

SeekBar

A view that allows the user to set a value by dragging a slider. Similar to WinForms TrackBar. The ValueChanged event is raised whenever the value is changed. The UserChanged parameter can be used to distinguish between changes done by the user and changes done programmatically.
This is an **`Activity`** object; it cannot be declared under **`Sub Process_Globals`**.

Events:

ValueChanged (Value As Int, UserChanged As Boolean)

Members:

- Background As Drawable
- BringToFront
- Color As Int [write only]
- Enabled As Boolean
- Height As Int
- Initialize (EventName As String)
- Invalidate
- Invalidate2 (Rect1 As Rect)
- Invalidate3 (Left As Int, Top As Int, Right As Int, Bottom As Int)
- IsInitialized As Boolean
- Left As Int
- Max As Int
- RemoveView
- RequestFocus As Boolean
- SendToBack
- SetBackgroundImage (Bitmap1 As Bitmap)
- SetLayout (Left As Int, Top As Int, Width As Int, Height As Int)
- Tag As Object
- Top As Int
- Value As Int
- Visible As Boolean
- Width As Int

Background As Drawable

Gets or sets the background drawable.

BringToFront

Changes the Z order of this view and brings it to the front.

Color As Int [write only]

Sets the background of the view to be a **`ColorDrawable`** with the given color. If the current background is of type **`GradientDrawable`** or **`ColorDrawable`**, the round corners will be kept.

Enabled As Boolean

If set to **`True`** then the **`SeekBar`** will respond to events. If set to **`False`**, events are ignored.

Height As Int

Gets or sets the view's height.

Initialize (EventName As String)

Initializes the view and sets the subs that will handle the events.
Views added with the designer should NOT be initialized. These views are initialized when the layout is loaded.

Invalidate

Invalidates the whole view forcing the view to redraw itself. Redrawing will only happen when the program can process messages, usually when it finishes running the current code.
If you only need to redraw part of the view, it is usually quicker to use **`Invalidate2`** or **`Invalidate3`**.

Invalidate2 (Rect1 As Rect)

Invalidates anything inside the given rectangle that is part of this view. Redrawing will only happen when the program can process messages, usually when it finishes running the current code.

Invalidate3 (Left As Int, Top As Int, Right As Int, Bottom As Int)

Invalidates anything inside the given rectangle that is part of this view. Redrawing will only happen when the program can process messages, usually when it finishes running the current code.

IsInitialized As Boolean

Whether this object has been initialized by calling **`Initialize`**.

Left As Int

Gets or sets the view's left position.

Max As Int

Gets or sets the maximum allowed value.

RemoveView

Removes this view from its parent.

RequestFocus As Boolean

Tries to set the focus to this view. Returns **`True`** if the focus was set.

SendToBack

Changes the Z order of this view and sends it to the back.

SetBackgroundImage (Bitmap1 As Bitmap)

SetLayout (Left As Int, Top As Int, Width As Int, Height As Int)

Changes the view position and size.

Tag As Object
Gets or sets the Tag value. This is a place holder which can be used to store additional data.

Top As Int
Gets or sets the view's top position.

Value As Int
Gets or sets the current value.

Visible As Boolean
Whether the user can see the object.

Width As Int
Gets or sets the view's width.

Spinner
A folded list that opens when the user clicks on it and allows the user to choose an item. Similar to WinForms ComboBox.
This is an **`Activity`** object; it cannot be declared under **`Sub Process_Globals`**.
A spinner behaves and looks like an InputList (page 250).

Example
```
Sub Globals
 Dim i As Int
 Dim tgtlabel As Label
 Dim tgtspin As Spinner
 Dim myarray(4) As String
End Sub

Sub Activity_Create(FirstTime As Boolean)
 Activity.LoadLayout("main")
 myarray(0)="January"
 myarray(1)="February"
 myarray(2)="March"
 myarray(3)="May"
 tgtspin.Initialize("spin")
 tgtspin.Prompt="Select Month"
 tgtspin.AddAll(myarray)
 Activity.AddView(tgtspin,10dip,10dip,200dip,40dip)
End Sub

Sub spin_ItemClick (Position As Int, Value As Object)
 ' what to do when the user selects an option
End Sub
```

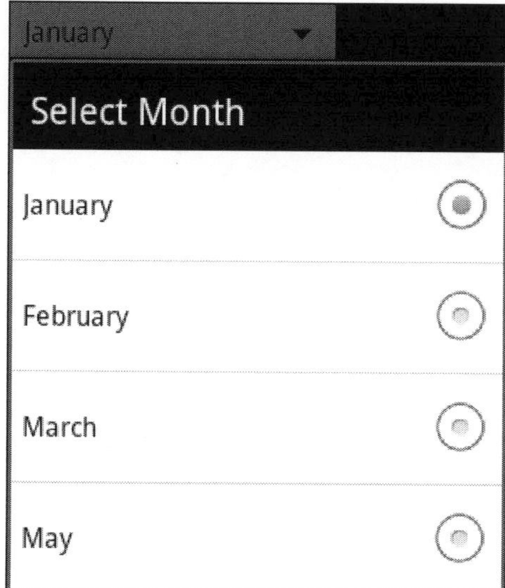

Event:

ItemClick (Position As Int, Value As Object)

The `ItemClick` event is raised each time a user presses on an item (even if the item is already selected). The arguments indicate which item has been clicked, both its position within the list of items and its value.

Members:

- Add (Item As String)
- AddAll (List As List)
- Background As Drawable
- BringToFront
- Clear
- Color As Int [write only]
- DropdownTextColor As Int
- Enabled As Boolean
- GetItem (Index As Int) As String
- Height As Int
- IndexOf (value As String) As Int
- Initialize (EventName As String)
- Invalidate
- Invalidate2 (Rect1 As Rect)
- Invalidate3 (Left As Int, Top As Int, Right As Int, Bottom As Int)
- IsInitialized As Boolean
- Left As Int
- Prompt As String

- RemoveAt (Index As Int)
- RemoveView
- RequestFocus As Boolean
- SelectedIndex As Int
- SelectedItem As String [read only]
- SendToBack
- SetBackgroundImage (Bitmap1 As Bitmap)
- SetLayout (Left As Int, Top As Int, Width As Int, Height As Int)
- Size As Int [read only]
- Tag As Object
- TextColor As Int
- TextSize As Float
- Top As Int
- Visible As Boolean
- Width As Int

Add (Item As String)

Adds an item.
Example:

```
Spinner1.Add("Sunday")
```

AddAll (List As List)

Adds multiple items.
Example:

```
Spinner1.AddAll(Array As String("Sunday", "Monday", ...))
```

Background As Drawable

Gets or sets the background drawable.

BringToFront

Changes the Z order of this view and brings it to the front.

Clear

Clears all items.

Color As Int [write only]

Sets the background of the view to be a **ColorDrawable** with the given color. If the current background is of type **GradientDrawable** or **ColorDrawable**, the round corners will be kept.

DropdownTextColor As Int

Gets or sets the color of the text of the spinner's dropdown items.

Enabled As Boolean

If set to **True** then the **Spinner** will respond to events. If set to **False**, events are ignored.

GetItem (Index As Int) As String
Returns the item at the specified index.

Height As Int
Gets or sets the view's height.

IndexOf (value As String) As Int

Initialize (EventName As String)
Initializes the view and sets the subs that will handle the events.
Views added with the designer should NOT be initialized. These views are initialized when the layout is loaded.

Invalidate
Invalidates the whole view forcing the view to redraw itself. Redrawing will only happen when the program can process messages, usually when it finishes running the current code.
If you only need to redraw part of the view, it is usually quicker to use `Invalidate2` or `Invalidate3`.

Invalidate2 (Rect1 As Rect)
Invalidates anything inside the given rectangle that is part of this view. Redrawing will only happen when the program can process messages, usually when it finishes running the current code.

Invalidate3 (Left As Int, Top As Int, Right As Int, Bottom As Int)
Invalidates anything inside the given rectangle that is part of this view. Redrawing will only happen when the program can process messages, usually when it finishes running the current code.

IsInitialized As Boolean
Whether this object has been initialized by calling `Initialize`.

Left As Int
Gets or sets the view's left position.

Prompt As String
Gets or sets the title that will be displayed when the spinner is opened.

RemoveAt (Index As Int)
Removes the item at the specified index.

RemoveView
Removes this view from its parent.

RequestFocus As Boolean
Tries to set the focus to this view. Returns `True` if the focus was set.

SelectedIndex As Int
Gets or sets the index of the selected item. Returns `-1` if no item is selected.

SelectedItem As String [read only]
Returns the value of the selected item.

SendToBack
Changes the Z order of this view and sends it to the back.

SetBackgroundImage (Bitmap1 As Bitmap)

SetLayout (Left As Int, Top As Int, Width As Int, Height As Int)
Changes the view position and size.

Size As Int [read only]
Returns the number of items.

Tag As Object
Gets or sets the Tag value. This is a place holder which can be used to store additional data.

TextColor As Int
Gets or sets the text color. The color should be set before adding items. Setting the color to transparent will make the spinner use the default text color.

TextSize As Float
Gets or sets the text size. The size should be set before adding items.

Top As Int
Gets or sets the view's top position.

Visible As Boolean
Whether the user can see the object.

Width As Int
Gets or sets the view's width.

TabHost

TabHost is a view that contains multiple tab pages. Each tab page contains other child views.

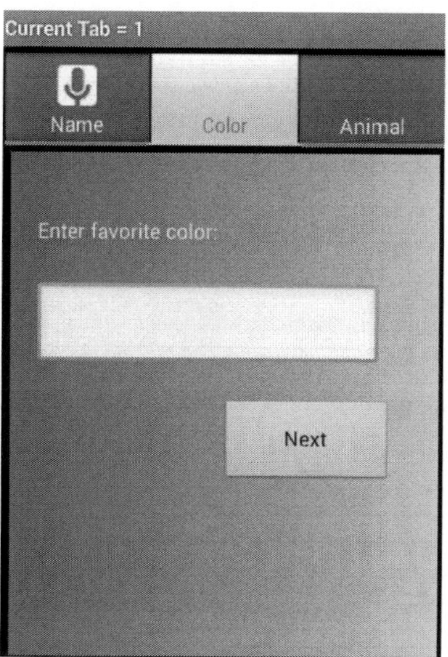

At present you can use the Designer to add a TabHost to a Layout, but you must use code to add pages to it. The simplest way to do this is to create separate layouts for each page. For example, if layout "main" contains TabHost1 and "page1", "page2" and "page3" contain the pages to be added to it, then your code might say:

```
Activity.LoadLayout("main")
TabHost1.AddTab("Name", "page1")
TabHost1.AddTab("Color", "page2")
TabHost1.AddTab("Animal", "page3")
```

A TabHost is an **`Activity`** object; it cannot be declared under **`Sub Process_Globals`**.

See the TabHost tutorial (http://www.basic4ppc.com/forum/basic4android-getting-started-tutorials/6721-tabhost-tutorial.html) for more information. **Note** that TabHostExtras Library (page 552) is a user-generated extension of this view which gives you more power over its appearance.

Events:

TabChanged

This event is raised when the user presses on the TabHost menu to select a different page.

Click

This event is never actually fired. It exists because it is inherited from the view object.

LongClick

This event is raised when the user presses and holds one of the pages of the TabHost.

Members:

- AddTab (Title As String, LayoutFile As String)
- AddTab2 (Title As String, View1 As View)

AddTabWithIcon (Title As String, DefaultBitmap As Bitmap, SelectedBitmap As Bitmap, LayoutFile As String)
AddTabWithIcon2 (Title As String, DefaultBitmap As Bitmap, SelectedBitmap As Bitmap, View1 As View)
Background As Drawable
BringToFront
Color As Int [write only]
CurrentTab As Int
Enabled As Boolean
Height As Int
Initialize (EventName As String)
Invalidate
Invalidate2 (Rect1 As Rect)
Invalidate3 (Left As Int, Top As Int, Right As Int, Bottom As Int)
IsInitialized As Boolean
Left As Int
RemoveView
RequestFocus As Boolean
SendToBack
SetBackgroundImage (Bitmap1 As Bitmap)
SetLayout (Left As Int, Top As Int, Width As Int, Height As Int)
TabCount As Int [read only]
Tag As Object
Top As Int
Visible As Boolean
Width As Int

AddTab (Title As String, LayoutFile As String)

Adds a tab page.
Title - The page title.
LayoutFile - A layout file describing the page layout.
Example:

```
TabHost1.AddTab("Page 1", "page1.bal")
```

AddTab2 (Title As String, View1 As View)

Adds a tab page.
Title - The page title.
View - The page content. Usually the view should be a panel containing other views.

AddTabWithIcon (Title As String, DefaultBitmap As Bitmap, SelectedBitmap As Bitmap, LayoutFile As String)

Adds a tab page. The tab title includes an icon.
Title - The page title.

DefaultBitmap - The icon that will be drawn when the page is not selected.
SelectedBitmap - The icon that will be drawn when the page is selected.
LayoutFile - A layout file describing the page layout.
Example:

```
Dim bmp1, bmp2 As Bitmap
bmp1 = LoadBitmap(File.DirAssets, "ic.png")
bmp2 = LoadBitmap(File.DirAssets, "ic_selected.png")
TabHost1.AddTabWithIcon("Page 1", bmp1, bmp2,"tabpage1.bal")
```

AddTabWithIcon2 (Title As String, DefaultBitmap As Bitmap, SelectedBitmap As Bitmap, View1 As View)

Adds a tab page. The tab title includes an icon.
Title - The page title.
DefaultBitmap - The icon that will be drawn when the page is not selected.
SelectedBitmap - The icon that will be drawn when the page is selected.
View - The page content. Usually the view should be a panel containing other views.

Background As Drawable

Gets or sets the background drawable.

BringToFront

Changes the Z order of this view and brings it to the front.

Color As Int [write only]

Sets the background of the view to be a **`ColorDrawable`** with the given color. If the current background is of type **`GradientDrawable`** or **`ColorDrawable`**, the round corners will be kept.

CurrentTab As Int

Gets or sets the current tab.
Example:

```
TabHost1.CurrentTab = (TabHost1.CurrentTab + 1) Mod
TabHost1.TabCount 'switch to the next tab.
```

Enabled As Boolean

If set to **`True`** then the **`TabHost`** will respond to events. If set to **`False`**, events are ignored.

Height As Int

Gets or sets the view's height.

Initialize (EventName As String)

Initializes the view and sets the subs that will handle the events.
Views added with the designer should NOT be initialized. These views are initialized when the layout is loaded.

Invalidate

Invalidates the whole view forcing the view to redraw itself. Redrawing will only happen when the program can process messages, usually when it finishes running the current code.

If you only need to redraw part of the view, it is usually quicker to use **Invalidate2** or **Invalidate3**.

Invalidate2 (Rect1 As Rect)
Invalidates anything inside the given rectangle that is part of this view. Redrawing will only happen when the program can process messages, usually when it finishes running the current code.

Invalidate3 (Left As Int, Top As Int, Right As Int, Bottom As Int)
Invalidates anything inside the given rectangle that is part of this view. Redrawing will only happen when the program can process messages, usually when it finishes running the current code.

IsInitialized As Boolean
Whether this object has been initialized by calling **Initialize**.

Left As Int
Gets or sets the view's left position.

RemoveView
Removes this view from its parent.

RequestFocus As Boolean
Tries to set the focus to this view. Returns **True** if the focus was set.

SendToBack
Changes the Z order of this view and sends it to the back.

SetBackgroundImage (Bitmap1 As Bitmap)

SetLayout (Left As Int, Top As Int, Width As Int, Height As Int)
Changes the view position and size.

TabCount As Int [read only]
Returns the number of tab pages.

Tag As Object
Gets or sets the Tag value. This is a place holder which can be used to store additional data.

Top As Int
Gets or sets the view's top position.

Visible As Boolean
Whether the user can see the object.

Width As Int
Gets or sets the view's width.

ToggleButton
A ToggleButton view. This view, which is similar to a button, has two modes: ON and OFF. When the user presses on it, it will change its mode. You can set the text with the **TextOn** and **TextOff** properties.

This is an **`Activity`** object; it cannot be declared under **`Sub Process_Globals`**.

Event:

CheckedChange(Checked As Boolean)

Members:

- Background As Drawable
- BringToFront
- Checked As Boolean
- Color As Int [write only]
- Enabled As Boolean
- Gravity As Int
- Height As Int
- Initialize (EventName As String)
- Invalidate
- Invalidate2 (Rect1 As Rect)
- Invalidate3 (Left As Int, Top As Int, Right As Int, Bottom As Int)
- IsInitialized As Boolean
- Left As Int
- RemoveView
- RequestFocus As Boolean
- SendToBack
- SetBackgroundImage (Bitmap1 As Bitmap)
- SetLayout (Left As Int, Top As Int, Width As Int, Height As Int)
- Tag As Object
- TextColor As Int
- TextOff As String
- TextOn As String
- TextSize As Float
- Top As Int
- Typeface As Typeface
- Visible As Boolean
- Width As Int

Background As Drawable

Gets or sets the background drawable.

BringToFront

Changes the Z order of this view and brings it to the front.

Checked As Boolean

Color As Int [write only]

Sets the background of the view to be a `ColorDrawable` with the given color. If the current background is of type `GradientDrawable` or `ColorDrawable`, the round corners will be kept.

Enabled As Boolean

If set to `True` then the `ToggleButton` will respond to events. If set to `False`, events are ignored.

Gravity As Int

Gets or sets the gravity (page 282) value. This value affects the way the text will be drawn.

Height As Int

Gets or sets the view's height.

Initialize (EventName As String)

Initializes the view and sets the subs that will handle the events.
Views added with the designer should NOT be initialized. These views are initialized when the layout is loaded.

Invalidate

Invalidates the whole view forcing the view to redraw itself. Redrawing will only happen when the program can process messages, usually when it finishes running the current code.
If you only need to redraw part of the view, it is usually quicker to use `Invalidate2` or `Invalidate3`.

Invalidate2 (Rect1 As Rect)

Invalidates anything inside the given rectangle that is part of this view. Redrawing will only happen when the program can process messages, usually when it finishes running the current code.

Invalidate3 (Left As Int, Top As Int, Right As Int, Bottom As Int)

Invalidates anything inside the given rectangle that is part of this view. Redrawing will only happen when the program can process messages, usually when it finishes running the current code.

IsInitialized As Boolean

Whether this object has been initialized by calling `Initialize`.

Left As Int

Gets or sets the view's left position.

RemoveView

Removes this view from its parent.

RequestFocus As Boolean

Tries to set the focus to this view. Returns `True` if the focus was set.

SendToBack
Changes the Z order of this view and sends it to the back.

SetBackgroundImage (Bitmap1 As Bitmap)

SetLayout (Left As Int, Top As Int, Width As Int, Height As Int)
Changes the view position and size.

Tag As Object
Gets or sets the Tag value. This is a place holder which can be used to store additional data.

TextColor As Int

TextOff As String
Gets or sets the text that will appear in the OFF mode.

TextOn As String
Gets or sets the text that will appear in the ON mode.

TextSize As Float

Top As Int
Gets or sets the view's top position.

Typeface As Typeface

Visible As Boolean
Whether the user can see the object.

Width As Int
Gets or sets the view's width.

View

View is a special type of object. You cannot create new View objects. However, all view types can be assigned to a view variable. This allows you to access the shared properties of all views. For example, this code hides all views of an activity:

```
For i = 0 To Activity.NumberOfViews - 1
  Dim v As View
  v = Activity.GetView(i)
  v.Visible = False
Next
```

This is an **Activity** object; it cannot be declared under **Sub Process_Globals**.

Events:

Click
This event is raised when the user presses on the View.

LongClick
This event is raised when the user presses on the View and holds for about one second.

Members:

- Background As Drawable
- BringToFront
- Color As Int [write only]
- Enabled As Boolean
- Height As Int
- Initialize (EventName As String)
- Invalidate
- Invalidate2 (Rect1 As Rect)
- Invalidate3 (Left As Int, Top As Int, Right As Int, Bottom As Int)
- IsInitialized As Boolean
- Left As Int
- RemoveView
- RequestFocus As Boolean
- SendToBack
- SetBackgroundImage (Bitmap1 As Bitmap)
- SetLayout (Left As Int, Top As Int, Width As Int, Height As Int)
- Tag As Object
- Top As Int
- Visible As Boolean
- Width As Int

Background As Drawable

Gets or sets the background drawable.

BringToFront

Changes the Z order of this view and brings it to the front.

Color As Int [write only]

Sets the background of the view to be a `ColorDrawable` with the given color. If the current background is of type `GradientDrawable` or `ColorDrawable`, the round corners will be kept.

Enabled As Boolean

If set to `True` then the `View` will respond to events. If set to `False`, events are ignored.

Height As Int

Gets or sets the view's height.

Initialize (EventName As String)

Initializes the view and sets the subs that will handle the events.
Views added with the designer should NOT be initialized. These views are initialized when the layout is loaded.

Invalidate
Invalidates the whole view forcing the view to redraw itself. Redrawing will only happen when the program can process messages, usually when it finishes running the current code.
If you only need to redraw part of the view, it is usually quicker to use **`Invalidate2`** or **`Invalidate3`**.

Invalidate2 (Rect1 As Rect)
Invalidates anything inside the given rectangle that is part of this view. Redrawing will only happen when the program can process messages, usually when it finishes running the current code.

Invalidate3 (Left As Int, Top As Int, Right As Int, Bottom As Int)
Invalidates anything inside the given rectangle that is part of this view. Redrawing will only happen when the program can process messages, usually when it finishes running the current code.

IsInitialized As Boolean
Whether this object has been initialized by calling **`Initialize`**.

Left As Int
Gets or sets the view's left position.

RemoveView
Removes this view from its parent. If this view has child views, then they are also removed.

RequestFocus As Boolean
Tries to set the focus to this view. Returns **`True`** if the focus was set.

SendToBack
Changes the Z order of this view and sends it to the back.

SetBackgroundImage (Bitmap1 As Bitmap)

SetLayout (Left As Int, Top As Int, Width As Int, Height As Int)
Changes the view position and size.

Tag As Object
Gets or sets the Tag value. This is a place holder which can be used to store additional data.

Top As Int
Gets or sets the view's top position.

Visible As Boolean
Whether the user can see the object.

Width As Int
Gets or sets the view's width.

WebView

The WebView view uses the internal WebKit engine to display HTML pages. The page displayed can be an online page loaded with **`LoadUrl`** or an HTML string loaded with **`LoadHtml`**. This is an **`Activity`** object; it cannot be declared under **`Sub Process_Globals`**.

Permissions:

android.permission.INTERNET

Events:

PageFinished (Url As String)

The PageFinished event is raised after the page loads.

OverrideUrl (Url As String) As Boolean

OverrideUrl is called before loading any URL. If this method returns **`True`**, then the given **Url** will not be loaded. You can use this event as a way to handle click events in your code.

UserAndPasswordRequired (Host As String, Realm As String) As String()

This event is raised when accessing a site that requires basic authentication. You should return an array of strings with the username as the first element and password as the second element. For example:

```
Return Array As String("someuser", "password123")
```

Returning **`Null`** will cancel the request. Sending incorrect credentials will cause this event to be raised again.

Members:

- Back
- Background As Drawable
- BringToFront
- CaptureBitmap As Bitmap
- Color As Int [write only]
- Enabled As Boolean
- Forward
- Height As Int
- Initialize (EventName As String)
- Invalidate
- Invalidate2 (Rect1 As Rect)
- Invalidate3 (Left As Int, Top As Int, Right As Int, Bottom As Int)
- IsInitialized As Boolean
- JavaScriptEnabled As Boolean
- Left As Int
- LoadHtml (HTML As String)

- LoadUrl (Url As String)
- RemoveView
- RequestFocus As Boolean
- SendToBack
- SetBackgroundImage (Bitmap1 As Bitmap)
- SetLayout (Left As Int, Top As Int, Width As Int, Height As Int)
- StopLoading
- Tag As Object
- Top As Int
- Url As String [read only]
- Visible As Boolean
- Width As Int
- Zoom (In As Boolean) As Boolean
- ZoomEnabled As Boolean

Back

Goes back to the previous URL.

Background As Drawable

Gets or sets the background drawable.

BringToFront

Changes the Z order of this view and brings it to the front.

CaptureBitmap As Bitmap

Returns the complete HTML page as a bitmap.

Color As Int [write only]

Sets the background of the view to be a **`ColorDrawable`** with the given color. If the current background is of type **`GradientDrawable`** or **`ColorDrawable`**, the round corners will be kept.

Enabled As Boolean

If set to **`True`** then the **`WebView`** will respond to events. If set to **`False`**, events are ignored.

Forward

Goes forward to the next URL.

Height As Int

Gets or sets the view's height.

Initialize (EventName As String)

Initializes the view and sets the subs that will handle the events.
Views added with the designer should NOT be initialized. These views are initialized when the layout is loaded.

Invalidate
Invalidates the whole view forcing the view to redraw itself. Redrawing will only happen when the program can process messages, usually when it finishes running the current code.
If you only need to redraw part of the view, it is usually quicker to use **Invalidate2** or **Invalidate3**.

Invalidate2 (Rect1 As Rect)
Invalidates anything inside the given rectangle that is part of this view. Redrawing will only happen when the program can process messages, usually when it finishes running the current code.

Invalidate3 (Left As Int, Top As Int, Right As Int, Bottom As Int)
Invalidates anything inside the given rectangle that is part of this view. Redrawing will only happen when the program can process messages, usually when it finishes running the current code.

IsInitialized As Boolean
Whether this object has been initialized by calling **Initialize**.

JavaScriptEnabled As Boolean
Gets or sets whether JavaScript is enabled.
JavaScript is enabled by default.

Left As Int
Gets or sets the view's left position.

LoadHtml (HTML As String)
Loads the given HTML. Example:
```
WebView1.LoadHtml("<html><body>Hello world!</body></html>")
```
You can use "file:///android_asset" to access files added with the file manager:
```
WebView1.LoadHtml("<html><body><img
src='file:///android_asset/someimage.jpg'/></body></html>")
```
Note that files added with the file manager should be accessed with a lower cased name.

LoadUrl (Url As String)
Loads the given **Url**. Example:
```
WebView1.LoadUrl("http://www.google.com")
```

RemoveView
Removes this view from its parent.

RequestFocus As Boolean
Tries to set the focus to this view.
Returns **True** if the focus was set.

SendToBack
Changes the Z order of this view and sends it to the back.

SetBackgroundImage (Bitmap1 As Bitmap)

SetLayout (Left As Int, Top As Int, Width As Int, Height As Int)
Changes the view position and size.

StopLoading
Stops the current load.

Tag As Object
Gets or sets the Tag value. This is a place holder which can be used to store additional data.

Top As Int
Gets or sets the view's top position.

Url As String [read only]
Returns the current URL.

Visible As Boolean
Whether the user can see the object.

Width As Int
Gets or sets the view's width.

Zoom (In As Boolean) As Boolean
Zooms in or out according to the value of **In**.
Returns `True` if zoom has changed.

ZoomEnabled As Boolean
Gets or sets whether the internal zoom feature is enabled.
The zoom feature is enabled by default.

Part 4: Libraries

In this reference section, we discuss libraries (only available if you have upgraded to the Full Version of Basic4Android), and explain how to create your own libraries and share them with others (should you wish to).

We give full details of the Standard Libraries included in the Full Version installation. We also discuss some of the many Additional Libraries and Modules, including all the "Official" ones created by Anywhere Software, which you can download from the Basic4Android website.

4.1 Libraries

Introduction

Libraries are key to gaining the full benefit of Basic4Android. Note that, apart from the Core Library, they are only available in the Full Version.

What is a library?

A Basic4Android library is an encapsulation of part or all of a project into a jar and an XML file which can easily be reused and shared with others. You can create your own, as described below.

Types of Libraries

There are several types of libraries in Basic4Android: The Core Library, Standard Libraries, Additional Official Libraries and Additional User Libraries.

Core Library

This is included in both the Trial and the Full versions of Basic4Android, and defines the Core Objects (page 270). Follow the link for more information.

Standard Libraries

When you upgrade from the Trial to the Full version, you get the Standard Libraries (page 408) which are saved in the Libraries folder in the B4A program folder. They are normally found in: C:\Program Files\Anywhere Software\Basic4Android\Libraries

Additional Official Libraries

Additional Official Libraries (page 524) are produced by Anywhere Software (the makers of Basic4Android) but are not included with the IDE. For a list of these, with links to the source for download, see the Additional Official Libraries (page 524) section.

Additional User Libraries

Additional User Libraries (page 529) have been produced by enthusiastic and generous users of Basic4Android who have published their own libraries for the benefit of others. These add significantly to the capabilities of the product.

Additional libraries folder

It is required that you set up a special folder to save additional libraries, for example: C:\Basic4Android\AddLibraries.

When you install a new version of B4A, all standard libraries are automatically updated, but the additional libraries are not included. The advantage of the special folder is that this folder is not affected when you install the new version of B4A.

Subscribing to Additional Library Updates

Because additional libraries are not systematically updated with new versions of B4A, you might want to subscribe here (http://bit.ly/18WJsgk) to be notified about updates.

Telling the IDE where to find Additional Libraries

When the IDE starts, it looks first for the available libraries in the Libraries folder of B4A and then in the folder for the additional libraries.
If you setup a special additional libraries folder, you must specify it in the IDE menu [Tools > Configure Paths]. The dialog allows you to specify the Additional Libraries folder.

Error message "Are you missing a library reference?"

If you get this message in the Compile & Debug dialog, it means that you either forgot to check the specified library in the Lib Tab list, or the library is missing from the folder.

Referencing Libraries

Before you can use the types and functions within a library, you need to add a reference to it in your project. Use the Libs Tab (page 55) within the IDE.

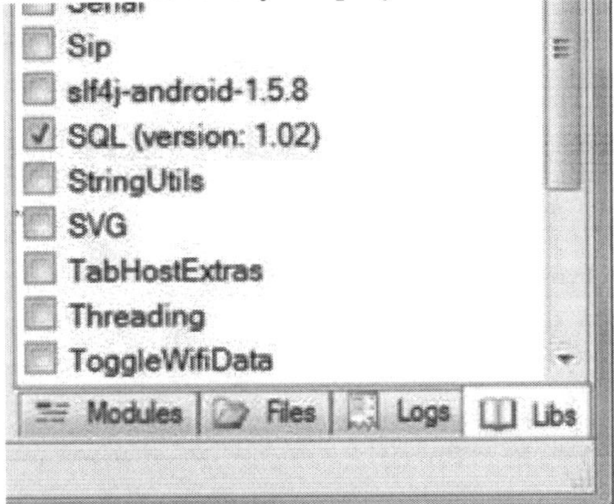

If it's an additional library, you might have to download and install it first. Note that it is worth checking periodically if you have the latest version, or subscribing to notifications about updates, as explained above.

Creating Libraries

You can create your own libraries and, if you wish, you can share them with other developers via the Basic4Android website.

There are two ways to build libraries: the easy way and the hard way.
The easy way is to compile modules from your project into a library. We describe this below.
The hard way is to write the code in Java and follow the instructions here (http://www.basic4ppc.com/forum/libraries-developers-questions/6810-creating-libraries-basic4android-2.html). Although more difficult, it allows you to add features not possible using the easy method.

More Information Creating Libraries

An on-line tutorial is available here (http://bit.ly/10GrdLE). A YouTube video on creating libraries can be found here (http://bit.ly/10GrYnU). Details of a Simple Library Compiler tool, which allows you to build simple libraries without Eclipse, is available here (http://bit.ly/10GrA91). You will still need to write the Java code, however.

Benefits of creating Libraries

There are several benefits from compiling your own library:
Modular code: If your project is large, it will be easier to create and maintain if you can break it into several smaller projects.
Reusable components: You can reuse modules in several projects.
Share components: You can share your work with other developers.
Protect your code: Once compiled, the library can be distributed to others without revealing the source code.
Create different versions: You can have various versions of an app, for example, “Free” and “Paid for”, by reusing the same core library.

Preparing Your Library

Main Activity Excluded

Except for the Project Attributes region, the Main Activity is not included in your library. This is necessary because the projects in which your library will be reused already contain a Main Activity.
The Main Activity in your development copy of the library can therefore be used to add code to test the library. You should add modules to contain the code of your library.
For details of what should be entered into the Project Attributes, see below.

Library specific attributes

The following attributes are specific for library compilation:

Project attributes

These are placed in the Project Attributes region of the main activity:
LibraryAuthor: The library author. This value is added to the library XML file.

LibraryName: The compiled library name. Sets the library name instead of showing the save dialog.
LibraryVersion: A number that represents the library version. This number will appear next to the library name in the libraries list.

Module Attributes

ExcludeFromLibrary: Whether to exclude this module during library compilation. Values: `True` or `False`.
Note that the Main activity is always excluded.

Classes Attributes

Event: Adds an event to the list of events. This attribute can be used multiple times. Note that the events list only affects the IDE events Autocomplete (page 49) feature.

How to Compile a Library

- First select the compilation mode (page 119) you wish to use: Release or Release Obfuscated (page 119). (Note that Strings will not be obfuscated.)
- Select menu [Project > Compile To Library] or type Alt+5. When you choose this option, all the modules except the main activity are compiled into a library. You can exclude other modules with the ExcludeFromLibrary attribute.
- The main activity (and the other excluded modules) can now be used to test the library.

You can reference the library from other projects and access the same functionality as in the original project. There is more information on creating your own libraries on the web here (http://www.basic4ppc.com/forum/libraries-developers-questions/6810-creating-libraries-basic4android.html).

Output

When you select menu [Project > Compile To Library], two files are created, both with the same name as the project:

- a jar (Java) file with the compiled code
- an XML file that includes the metadata that is required by the IDE.

These two files will be saved in the Additional Libraries folder specified in the [Tools > Configure Paths] menu dialog.

No Home Screen Widget Libraries

Services that host home screen widgets cannot be compiled into a library. See here for more information (page 83) about Widgets.

How to publish your library

Developers should edit the list of libraries at
http://www.basic4ppc.com/android/wiki/index.php/Libraries

and add their libraries. (Contact support@basic4ppc.com if you do not have write permission.) For information about the impact of using libraries, see this thread (http://www.basic4ppc.com/forum/basic4android-updates-questions/16171-what-performance-ramifications-adding-multiple-libraries-my-app.html).

4.2 Standard Libraries included with Full Version

Introduction

Libraries and official updates are only available for users who have purchased Basic4Android. If you have bought Basic4Android but cannot download files, then please contact support@basic4ppc.com and send the User name and Email address used when purchasing Basic4Android. See Libraries (page 403) for more information.

The following libraries are included in the Full version installation package. They are saved in the Libraries folder in the B4A program folder and are normally found in:
C:\Program Files\Anywhere Software\Basic4Android\Libraries
In order to use an object in one of these libraries, you need to reference its library in the library tab (page 55) of the IDE.
In fact, the Core library is also included in the installation, but since you do not need to reference it, we deal with its objects in the Core Objects Chapter (page 270).

List of Standard Libraries

Accessibility
Administrator
Animation (page 412)
Audio (page 415)
Camera (page 426)
Core (page 270)
Daydream (page 428)
GameView (page 429)
GPS (page 432)
HTTP (page 437)
IME (page 441)
JSON (page 443)
LiveWallpaper (page 445)
Network (page 447)
NFC (page 452)
Phone (page 453)
PreferenceActivity (page 484)
RandomAccessFile (page 489)
Serial (page 497)
Sip (page 502)
SQL (page 505)
StringUtils (page 511)
TTS (page 514)

USB (page 515)
XmlSax (page 522)

Accessibility Library

This library is included in the IDE installation package. It includes several accessibility related methods.

List of types:

Accessiblity (note the spelling).

Accessiblity

This library includes several accessibility related methods. The **SetNextFocus** methods allow you to explicitly set the focus order. This order is important when the user navigates your application with a directional controller (such as D-Pad). **SetContentDescription** sets the content that will be used by accessibility services such as TalkBack to describe the interface.

Members:

- GetUserFontScale As Float
- SetContentDescription (View1 As View, Content As CharSequence)
- SetNextFocusDown (ThisView As View, NextView As View)
- SetNextFocusLeft (ThisView As View, NextView As View)
- SetNextFocusRight (ThisView As View, NextView As View)
- SetNextFocusUp (ThisView As View, NextView As View)

GetUserFontScale As Float

Returns the user-set font scale. The user can adjust this scale in the device Settings. This scale is applied automatically to all text based views.

SetContentDescription (View1 As View, Content As CharSequence)

Sets the view's description. This text will be used by accessibility services to describe the view.

SetNextFocusDown (ThisView As View, NextView As View)

Sets the next view that will get the focus when the user presses on the down key (when this view is focused). Example:

```
Dim Access As Accessibility
Access.SetNextFocusDown(Button1, Button2) 'When the focus is on
Button1 and the user presses on the down key,
'the focus will move to Button2.
```

SetNextFocusLeft (ThisView As View, NextView As View)

Sets the next view that will get the focus when the user presses on the left key (when this view is focused).

SetNextFocusRight (ThisView As View, NextView As View)

Sets the next view that will get the focus when the user presses on the right key (when this view is focused).

SetNextFocusUp (ThisView As View, NextView As View)

Sets the next view that will get the focus when the user presses on the up key (when this view is focused).

Administrator Library

This library is included in the IDE installation package. Starting from Android 2.2 (api level 8), Android allows an application to be registered as an administrator. Administrator apps have the following special features

- Manually lock the screen
- Set the minimum password length and quality
- Wipe the entire device
- Set the maximum allowed time before the device locks
- Request the user to change password
- Manually set a new password
- Disable the camera
- Track password changes
- Some other security features as described here.

Note that the password is the screen lock password. Other passwords are not affected. The user needs to enable the admin app before it can have any special privileges. This is done either by calling Manager.Enable or from the Security settings page.

OnLine Link

For more details about using the Administrator Library, and an example program, see here (http://bit.ly/15k06pn).

List of types:

AdminManager

AdminManager

Members:

- Disable
- Enable (Explanation As String)
- Enabled As Boolean [read only]
- LockScreen
- MaximumTimeToLock As Long [write only]
- PASSWORD_QUALITY_ALPHABETIC As Int
- PASSWORD_QUALITY_ALPHANUMERIC As Int
- PASSWORD_QUALITY_NUMERIC As Int
- PASSWORD_QUALITY_UNSPECIFIED As Int
- PasswordSufficient As Boolean [read only]
- RequestNewPassword
- ResetPassword (NewPassword As String) As Boolean
- SetPasswordQuality (QualityFlag As Int, MinimumLength As Int)

Disable

Disables the admin policy.

Enable (Explanation As String)

Enables the admin policy. The user will be shown a dialog with the requested features. This method can only be called from an Activity context.
Explanation - A message shown at the top of the dialog.

Enabled As Boolean [read only]

Returns `True` if the admin policy is active.

LockScreen

Immediately locks the screen. Requires the force-lock tag in the policies file.

MaximumTimeToLock As Long [write only]

Sets the maximum time (measured in milliseconds) before the device locks. This limits the maximum length of time that the user can set in the Security menu: [Settings > Security > Automatically Lock]. This is not available on early versions of Android. Requires the force-lock tag in the policies file.

PASSWORD_QUALITY_ALPHABETIC As Int

PASSWORD_QUALITY_ALPHANUMERIC As Int

PASSWORD_QUALITY_NUMERIC As Int

PASSWORD_QUALITY_UNSPECIFIED As Int

PasswordSufficient As Boolean [read only]

Returns **TRUE** if the current password meets the requirements. Requires the limit-password tag in the policies file.

RequestNewPassword

Shows the new password activity. Note that the user might cancel the change.

ResetPassword (NewPassword As String) As Boolean

Sets the given password as the device password. Requires the reset-password tag in the policies file.

SetPasswordQuality (QualityFlag As Int, MinimumLength As Int)

Sets the minimum allowed length and quality for device passwords. These settings will affect new passwords. Requires the limit-password tag in the policies file.
QualityFlag - One of the password quality flags shown above.
MinimumLength - Password minimum length.
Example:

```
manager.SetPasswordQuality(manager.PASSWORD_QUALITY_ALPHANUMERIC
, 4)
```

Animation Library

This library is included in the IDE installation package.

Animation

The Animation object allows you to animate views (controls). These small animations can improve the user overall impression of your application. There are several types of animations. The **Initialize** methods determine the animation type.
This is an **Activity** object; it cannot be declared under **Sub Process_Globals**.
For a sample program demonstrating animations, see here (http://bit.ly/1dcOZ6u).

List of types:

Animation

Event: AnimationEnd

You can use this event to fire off another animation when the current one ends.
Example:

```
Dim a6, a7, a8 As Animation

a6.InitializeTranslate("Animation", 0, 0, 0dip, 200dip)

Sub Animation_AnimationEnd
 If Sender = a6 Then
  a7.Start(Button6)
 Else If Sender = a7 Then
  a8.Start(Button6)
 End If
End Sub
```

Members:

Duration As Long

InitializeAlpha (EventName As String, FromAlpha As Float, ToAlpha As Float)

InitializeRotate (EventName As String, FromDegrees As Float, ToDegrees As Float)

InitializeRotateCenter (EventName As String, FromDegrees As Float, ToDegrees As Float, View1 As View)

InitializeScale (EventName As String, FromX As Float, FromY As Float, ToX As Float, ToY As Float)

InitializeScaleCenter (EventName As String, FromX As Float, FromY As Float, ToX As Float, ToY As Float, View1 As View)

InitializeTranslate (EventName As String, FromDX As Float, FromDY As Float, ToDX As Float, ToDY As Float)

IsInitialized As Boolean

REPEAT_RESTART As Int

REPEAT_REVERSE As Int

RepeatCount As Int

RepeatMode As Int

Start (View1 As View)

Stop (View1 As View)

Duration As Long

Gets or sets the animation duration. Value is measured in milliseconds.
Example: `Animation1.Duration = 1000`

InitializeAlpha (EventName As String, FromAlpha As Float, ToAlpha As Float)

Initializes an alpha animation. This animation affects the view's transparency (fading effect). The **alpha** values are from 0 to 1, where 0 is fully transparent and 1 is fully opaque.
FromAlpha - The first frame value.
ToAlpha - The last frame value.

InitializeRotate (EventName As String, FromDegrees As Float, ToDegrees As Float)

Initializes a rotation animation. The view will rotate between the given values.
Rotation pivot is set to the top left corner.
FromDegrees - The first frame rotation value.
ToDegrees - The last frame rotation value.

InitializeRotateCenter (EventName As String, FromDegrees As Float, ToDegrees As Float, View1 As View)

Similar to `InitializeRotate`, with the pivot set to the given view's center.

InitializeScale (EventName As String, FromX As Float, FromY As Float, ToX As Float, ToY As Float)

Initializes a scale animation. The view will be scaled (resized) during the animation.
The scaling centre will be set to the view's top left corner.
FromX - The first frame horizontal scale.
FromY - The first frame vertical scale.
ToX - The last frame horizontal scale.
ToY - The last frame vertical scale.

InitializeScaleCenter (EventName As String, FromX As Float, FromY As Float, ToX As Float, ToY As Float, View1 As View)

Similar to `InitializeScale` with the scaling center set to the given view's center.

InitializeTranslate (EventName As String, FromDX As Float, FromDY As Float, ToDX As Float, ToDY As Float)

Initializes a translation animation. The view will move according to the given values.
FromDX - First frame horizontal position relative to the original position.
FromDY - First frame vertical position relative to the original position.
ToDX - Last frame horizontal position relative to the original position.
ToDY - Last frame vertical position relative to the original position.

IsInitialized As Boolean

Whether this object has been initialized by calling one of the `Initialize` methods.

REPEAT_RESTART As Int

A constant used by `RepeatMode`.

REPEAT_REVERSE As Int

A constant used by `RepeatMode`.

RepeatCount As Int

Gets or sets the number of times the animation will repeat after the first play. A value of 0 means that it will play once. A value of 1 means that it will play and then repeat once.
Set to `-1` for a non-stopping animation.
Example: `Animation1.RepeatCount = 1`

RepeatMode As Int

Gets or sets the repeat mode. Relevant only when RepeatCount is not 0. The default is REPEAT_RESTART, which means that the animation will restart each time. REPEAT_REVERSE causes the animation to repeat in reverse each time.
For example, if the animation moves the view to the right 100 pixels, in the next repeat it will move to the left. Example:

```
Animation1.RepeatMode = Animation1.REPEAT_REVERSE
```

Start (View1 As View)

Starts animating the given view. Note that a single animation should not be applied to more than one view at a time. Example:

```
Animation1.Start(Button1)
```

Stop (View1 As View)

Stops animating the given view.

Audio Library

This library is included in the IDE installation package.

List of types:

AudioRecordApp
Beeper
JetPlayer
MediaPlayerStream (page 419)
SoundPool (page 421)
VideoRecordApp (page 422)
VideoView (page 423)

AudioRecordApp

AudioRecordApp lets you use the default audio recorder application to record audio. After initializing the object, you should call **Record** to start recording. Example:

```
Sub Process_Globals
  Dim audioRecorder As AudioRecordApp
  Dim videoRecorder As VideoRecordApp
End Sub
Sub Globals
  Dim vv As VideoView
End Sub
Sub Activity_Create(FirstTime As Boolean)
  If FirstTime Then
   audioRecorder.Initialize("audioRecorder")
   videoRecorder.Initialize("videoRecorder")
  End If
  vv.Initialize("vv")
  Activity.AddView(vv, 0, 0, 100%x, 100%y)
  Activity.AddMenuItem("Record Video", "RecordVideo")
```

```
  Activity.AddMenuItem("Record Audio", "RecordAudio")
  ToastMessageShow("Press on Menu button...", True)
 End Sub
 Sub RecordVideo_Click
  videoRecorder.Record(File.DirRootExternal, "1.mp4")
 End Sub
 Sub RecordAudio_Click
  audioRecorder.Record(File.DirRootExternal, "1.3gpp")
 End Sub
 Sub videoRecorder_RecordComplete (Success As Boolean)
  Log(Success)
  If Success Then
   vv.LoadVideo(File.DirRootExternal, "1.mp4")
   vv.Play
  End If
 End Sub
 Sub audioRecorder_RecordComplete (Success As Boolean)
  Log(Success)
  If Success Then
   vv.LoadVideo(File.DirRootExternal, "1.3gpp")
   vv.Play
  End If
 End Sub
```

Event:

RecordComplete (Success As Boolean)
The RecordComplete event will be raised when recording completes.

Members:

- Initialize (EventName As String)
- Record (Dir As String, FileName As String)

Initialize (EventName As String)
Initializes the object and sets the sub that will handle the event.

Record (Dir As String, FileName As String)
Calls the recording application. **Dir** and **FileName** set the output file location.

Beeper

Plays a “beep” sound with the given duration and frequency. Example:

```
Dim b As Beeper
b.Initialize(300, 500)
b.Beep
```

Members:

- Beep
- Initialize (Duration As Int, Frequency As Int)
- Initialize2 (Duration As Int, Frequency As Int, VoiceChannel As Int)
- Release

- VOLUME_ALARM As Int
- VOLUME_MUSIC As Int
- VOLUME_NOTIFICATION As Int
- VOLUME_RING As Int
- VOLUME_SYSTEM As Int
- VOLUME_VOICE_CALL As Int

Beep

Plays the sound.

Initialize (Duration As Int, Frequency As Int)

Initializes the object with the given duration, measured in milliseconds, and the given frequency, measured in Hertz. The music volume channel will be used.

Initialize2 (Duration As Int, Frequency As Int, VoiceChannel As Int)

Similar to Initialize. Allows you to set the volume channel.

Release

Releases the resources used by this beeper.

VOLUME_ALARM As Int

Alarms channel.

VOLUME_MUSIC As Int

Music channel.

VOLUME_NOTIFICATION As Int

Notifications channel.

VOLUME_RING As Int

Phone ring channel.

VOLUME_SYSTEM As Int

System sounds channel.

VOLUME_VOICE_CALL As Int

Voice calls channel.

JetPlayer

JET is an interactive music player for small embedded devices. It works in conjunction with SONiVOX's Embedded Audio Synthesizer (EAS) which is the MIDI playback device for Android. Both the JET and EAS engines are integrated into the Android embedded platform through the JetPlayer class, as well as inherent in the JET Creator application. As such, the JET content author can be sure that the playback will sound exactly the same in both the JET Creator and the final Android application playing back on Android mobile devices. More details here (http://developer.android.com/guide/topics/media/jet/jetcreator_manual.html).

Events:

QueuedSegmentsCountChanged (Count As Int)

CurrentUserIdChanged (UserId As Int, RepeatCount As Int)

Members:

- ClearQueue
- CloseFile
- Initialize (EventName As String)
- IsInitialized As Boolean
- LoadFile (Dir As String, File As String)
- MaxTracks As Int [read only]
- Pause
- Play
- QueueSegment (SegmentNum As Int, LibNum As Int, RepeatCount As Int, Transpose As Int, MuteArray() As Boolean, UserId As Byte)
- Release
- SetMute (MuteArray() As Boolean, Sync As Boolean)
- SetTrackMute (Track As Int, Mute As Boolean, Sync As Boolean)

ClearQueue

Clears the segments queue.

CloseFile

Closes the resources related to the loaded file.

Initialize (EventName As String)

Initializes the object and sets the Subs that will handle the JetPlayer events.

IsInitialized As Boolean

Whether this object has been initialized by calling `Initialize`.

LoadFile (Dir As String, File As String)

Loads a JET file.

MaxTracks As Int [read only]

Returns the maximum number of simultaneous tracks.

Pause

Pauses playback.

Play

Starts playing the segments queue.

QueueSegment (SegmentNum As Int, LibNum As Int, RepeatCount As Int, Transpose As Int, MuteArray() As Boolean, UserId As Byte)

Adds a segment to the queue. No more than 3 segments are allowed.
SegmentNum - The segment identifier.

LibNum - The index of the sound bank associated with this segment. Pass `-1` if there is no sound bank.
RepeatCount - Number of times the segment will be repeated. 0 means that it will be played once. Pass `-1` to repeat indefinitely.
Transpose - The pitch transition. Should be from -12 to 12.
MuteArray - An array of booleans that sets the mute value of each track. The array length must be equal to MaxTracks value.
UserId - An id given to this segment. When the current segment changes, the **`CurrentUserIdChanged`** event is raised with this id (assuming that the id of the previous segment was different).

Release

Releases all resources allocated for the JetPlayer.

SetMute (MuteArray() As Boolean, Sync As Boolean)

Sets the tracks' mute state.
MuteArray - An array of booleans that sets the mute state of each track. The array length must be equal to MaxTracks value.
Sync - If **`False`**, the change will be applied as soon as possible, otherwise the change will be applied at the start of the next segment or next repeat.

SetTrackMute (Track As Int, Mute As Boolean, Sync As Boolean)

Similar to SetMute but only changes the state of a single track.

MediaPlayerStream

MediaPlayerStream is similar to MediaPlayer. Unlike MediaPlayer, which plays local files, MediaPlayerStream plays audio streams which are available online. Another difference between the objects is that, in this case, the **`Load`** method is asynchronous. Only when the file is ready, the **`StreamReady`** event will be fired and you can start playing. According to the Android documentation, the online resource must support progressive download.
Example:

```
Sub Process_Globals
  Dim mp As MediaPlayerStream
End Sub
Sub Globals
End Sub
Sub Activity_Create(FirstTime As Boolean)
  If FirstTime Then
     mp.Initialize("mp")
  End If
  mp.Load("http://www...")
End Sub
Sub mp_StreamReady
  Log("starts playing")
  mp.Play
End Sub
```

```
Sub mp_StreamError (ErrorCode As String, ExtraData As Int)
  Log("Error: " & ErrorCode & ", " & ExtraData)
  ToastMessageShow("Error: " & ErrorCode & ", " & ExtraData,
True)
End Sub
Sub mp_StreamBuffer(Percentage As Int)
  Log(Percentage)
End Sub
```

Permissions:

android.permission.INTERNET

Events:

StreamReady

Fired when the file is ready to play. Once this event has fired, call **Play** to start playing the stream.

StreamError (ErrorCode As String, ExtraData As Int)

This event is fired when there is an error with the stream. For example, if the target URL does not exist, you would get an error with ErrorCode= MEDIA_ERROR_UNKNOWN and ExtraData= -1004. For more about MediaPlayer errors, and lists of ErrorCodes and EstraData Constants, see here (http://bit.ly/GVziCW).

StreamBuffer(Percentage As Int)

Percentage of a stream which has been downloaded.

Complete

This event fires when the stream has finished playing.

Members:

- Duration As Int [read only]
- Initialize (EventName As String)
- IsPlaying As Boolean
- Load (URL As String)
- Looping As Boolean
- Pause
- Play
- Release
- SetVolume (Right As Float, Left As Float)
- Stop

Duration As Int [read only]

Initialize (EventName As String)

Initializes the object.
EventName - Name of Subs that will handle the events.

IsPlaying As Boolean

Load (Url As String)

Starts loading the resource from the given **Url**. **StreamReady** event will be raised when the stream is ready.

Looping As Boolean

Pause

Play

Release

SetVolume (Right As Float, Left As Float)

Sets the playing volume for each channel. The value should be from 0 to 1.

Stop

SoundPool

SoundPool holds a collection of short sounds which can be played with low latency. Each sound has two Id values which you should work with. The first is the **LoadId**, which is returned when loading the sound with **Load**. The second is the **PlayId**, which is returned when you call **Play**. When working with **SoundPool**, it is useful to watch the unfiltered (page 127) LogCat for messages (for example when the sound is too long).

Members:

- Initialize (MaxStreams As Int)
- IsInitialized As Boolean
- Load (Dir As String, File As String) As Int
- Pause (PlayId As Int)
- Play (LoadId As Int, LeftVolume As Float, RightVolume As Float, Priority As Int, Loop As Int, Rate As Float) As Int
- Release
- Resume (PlayId As Int)
- SetRate (PlayId As Int, Rate As Float)
- SetVolume (PlayId As Int, Left As Float, Right As Float)
- Stop (PlayId As Int)
- Unload (LoadId As Int)

Initialize (MaxStreams As Int)

Initializes the SoundPool and sets the maximum number of simultaneous streams.

IsInitialized As Boolean

Whether this object has been initialized by calling **Initialize**.

Load (Dir As String, File As String) As Int

Loads a sound file and returns the sound LoadId. Example:

```
Dim LoadId As Int
LoadId = SP.Load(File.DirAssets, "sound.wav")
```

Pause (PlayId As Int)
Pauses the stream with the given PlayId.

Play (LoadId As Int, LeftVolume As Float, RightVolume As Float, Priority As Int, Loop As Int, Rate As Float) As Int
Plays the sound with the matching LoadId and returns the PlayId. Returns 0 if there was an error.
LoadId - The value returned when loading the file.
LeftVolume / RightVolume - The volume value (0 - 1)
Priority - A priority value which you assign to this sound. The higher the value, the higher the priority. When the number of simultaneous streams is higher than the value set in **`Initialize`**, the lowest priority stream will be stopped.
Loop - Number of times to repeat. Pass **`-1`** to repeat indefinitely.
Rate - Playback rate (0 - 2).

Release
Releases all resources allocated to this object.

Resume (PlayId As Int)
Resumes the stream with the given PlayId.

SetRate (PlayId As Int, Rate As Float)
Sets the rate of the stream with the given PlayId. **`Rate`** is from 0 to 2.

SetVolume (PlayId As Int, Left As Float, Right As Float)
Sets the volume of the stream with the given PlayId. **`Left`** and **`Right`** are from 0 to 1.

Stop (PlayId As Int)
Stops the stream with the given PlayId.

Unload (LoadId As Int)
Unloads the stream with the given LoadId.

VideoRecordApp
VideoRecordApp lets you use the default video recorder application to record video. After initializing the object, you should call **`Record`** to start recording. Example:

```
Sub Process_Globals
  Dim audioRecorder As AudioRecordApp
  Dim videoRecorder As VideoRecordApp
End Sub
Sub Globals
  Dim vv As VideoView
End Sub
Sub Activity_Create(FirstTime As Boolean)
  If FirstTime Then
        audioRecorder.Initialize("audioRecorder")
```

```
      videoRecorder.Initialize("videoRecorder")
    End If
    vv.Initialize("vv")
    Activity.AddView(vv, 0, 0, 100%x, 100%y)
    Activity.AddMenuItem("Record Video", "RecordVideo")
    Activity.AddMenuItem("Record Audio", "RecordAudio")
    ToastMessageShow("Press on Menu button...", True)
  End Sub
  Sub RecordVideo_Click
    videoRecorder.Record(File.DirRootExternal, "1.mp4")
  End Sub
  Sub RecordAudio_Click
    audioRecorder.Record(File.DirRootExternal, "1.3gpp")
  End Sub
  Sub videoRecorder_RecordComplete (Success As Boolean)
    Log(Success)
    If Success Then
      vv.LoadVideo(File.DirRootExternal, "1.mp4")
      vv.Play
    End If
  End Sub
  Sub audioRecorder_RecordComplete (Success As Boolean)
    Log(Success)
    If Success Then
      vv.LoadVideo(File.DirRootExternal, "1.3gpp")
      vv.Play
    End If
  End Sub
  Sub Activity_Resume
  End Sub
  Sub Activity_Pause (UserClosed As Boolean)
  End Sub
```

Event RecordComplete (Success As Boolean)

The **RecordComplete** event will be raised when record completes.

Members:

- Initialize (EventName As String)
- Record (Dir As String, FileName As String)

Initialize (EventName As String)

Initializes the object and sets the sub that will handle the event.

Record (Dir As String, FileName As String)

Calls the recording application. **Dir** and **FileName** set the output file location.

VideoView

VideoView is a view that allows you to play video media inside your application. The VideoView optionally shows a media controller when the user touches the view. The

`Complete` event is raised when playback is completed. A simple example of using VideoView:

```
Sub Globals
  Dim vv As VideoView
End Sub
Sub Activity_Create(FirstTime As Boolean)
  vv.Initialize("vv")
  Activity.AddView(vv, 10dip, 10dip, 250dip, 250dip)
  vv.LoadVideo(File.DirRootExternal, "somefile.mp4")
  vv.Play
End Sub
Sub vv_Complete
  Log("Playing completed")
End Sub
```

This is an **`Activity`** object; it cannot be declared under **`Sub Process_Globals`**.

Event: Complete

The Complete event is raised when playback is completed.

Members:

- Background As Drawable
- BringToFront
- Color As Int [write only]
- Duration As Int [read only]
- Enabled As Boolean
- Height As Int
- Initialize (EventName As String)
- Invalidate
- Invalidate2 (arg0 As Rect)
- Invalidate3 (arg0 As Int, arg1 As Int, arg2 As Int, arg3 As Int)
- IsInitialized As Boolean
- IsPlaying As Boolean
- Left As Int
- LoadVideo (Dir As String, FileName As String)
- MediaControllerEnabled As Boolean [write only]
- Pause
- Play
- Position As Int
- RemoveView
- RequestFocus As Boolean
- SendToBack
- SetBackgroundImage (arg0 As Bitmap)
- SetLayout (arg0 As Int, arg1 As Int, arg2 As Int, arg3 As Int)

Stop
Tag As Object
Top As Int
toString As String
Visible As Boolean
Width As Int

Background As Drawable

BringToFront

Color As Int [write only]

Duration As Int [read only]

Gets the video duration (in milliseconds).

Enabled As Boolean

If set to **True** then the **VideoView** will respond to events. If set to **False**, events are ignored.

Height As Int

Initialize (EventName As String)

Initialize the object and sets the name of the subs that will handle the events.

Invalidate

Invalidates the whole view forcing the view to redraw itself. Redrawing will only happen when the program can process messages, usually when it finishes running the current code.
If you only need to redraw part of the view, it is usually quicker to use **Invalidate2** or **Invalidate3**.

Invalidate2 (Rect1 As Rect)

Invalidates anything inside the given rectangle that is part of this view. Redrawing will only happen when the program can process messages, usually when it finishes running the current code.

Invalidate3 (Left As Int, Top As Int, Right As Int, Bottom As Int)

Invalidates anything inside the given rectangle that is part of this view. Redrawing will only happen when the program can process messages, usually when it finishes running the current code.

IsInitialized As Boolean

Whether this object has been initialized by calling **Initialize**.

IsPlaying As Boolean

Returns **TRUE** if the video is currently playing.

Left As Int

LoadVideo (Dir As String**, FileName As** String**)**
Loads a video file and prepares it for playing. It is not possible to load files from the assets folder.
Advanced: you can pass "http" to the Dir parameter and then a full URL (including http) to the FileName. In this case, the online video will be streamed. Note that you need to add the INTERNET permission (page 83) for this to work.

MediaControllerEnabled As Boolean **[write only]**
Sets whether the media controller is enabled. It is enabled by default. **Note** that the media player gets attached to the VideoView parent.

Pause
Pauses the playback.

Play
Starts or resumes playing.

Position As Int
Gets or sets the playing position (in milliseconds).

RemoveView

RequestFocus As Boolean

SendToBack

SetBackgroundImage (arg0 As Bitmap**)**

SetLayout (arg0 As Int**, arg1 As** Int**, arg2 As** Int**, arg3 As** Int**)**

Stop
Stops the playback.

Tag As Object

Top As Int

toString As String

Visible As Boolean
Whether the user can see the object.

Width As Int

Camera Library

This library is included in the IDE installation package.

List of types:

Camera

Camera

The camera object allows you to access the device cameras. This library is supported by Android 1.6+. **Note**: if possible, it is recommended to work with the CameraEx (page 525) class that wraps this object and adds many features. The CameraEx class requires Android 2.3+.

Camera is an **`Activity`** object; it cannot be declared under **`Sub Process_Globals`**.

Permissions:

android.permission.CAMERA

Events:

Ready (Success As Boolean)

The Ready event will be raised when the Initialize action has finished opening the camera.

PictureTaken (Data() As Byte)

The PictureTaken event will be raised when the TakePicture action finishes and the picture is ready.

Preview (Data() As Byte)

Once the StartPreview action has been taken on a Camera, the Preview event is raised automatically whenever an image is ready.

FocusDone (Success As Boolean)

The FocusDone event will be raised when AutoFocus completes.

Members:

- AutoFocus
- CancelAutoFocus
- Initialize (Panel As ViewGroup, EventName As String)
- Initialize2 (Panel As ViewGroup, EventName As String, CameraId As Int)
- Release
- StartPreview
- StopPreview
- TakePicture

AutoFocus

Starts auto-focus function. The FocusDone event will be raised when the operation completes. You can check whether the "auto" focus mode is supported with CameraEx class.

CancelAutoFocus

Cancels the auto-focus operation. Does nothing if no such operation is in progress.

Initialize (Panel As ViewGroup, EventName As String)

Initializes the rear-facing camera. If the device only has one camera which is front-facing, use **`Initialize2`**.

Panel - The preview images will be displayed on the panel.

EventName - Events subs prefix.
The Ready event will be raised when the camera has finished opening.

Initialize2 (Panel As ViewGroup, EventName As String, CameraId As Int)

Same as **Initialize**, but you can specify which camera to use.
CameraId - the Id of the hardware camera. If there is only one camera on the device, its Id is 0. If there are two cameras, use 0 for the rear-facing camera, 1 for the front-facing one.
The Ready event will be raised when the camera has finished opening.
This method is only available from Android 2.3+.

Release

Releases the camera object and allows other processes to access the camera.

StartPreview

Starts displaying the preview images. Once the StartPreview action has been taken on a Camera, the Preview event is raised automatically whenever an image is ready.

StopPreview

Stops displaying the preview images.

TakePicture

Takes a picture. When the picture is ready, the **PictureTaken** event will be raised.
You should not call **TakePicture** while another picture is currently being taken.
The preview images are stopped after calling this method. You can call StartPreview to restart the preview images.
The image will be stored in the folder: /mnt/sdcard/DCIM/Camera.

Daydream Library

This library is included in the IDE installation package.

List of types:

Daydream

Daydream

Daydream is a new "screen saver" feature introduced in Android 4.2. See the Daydream tutorial (http://bit.ly/15mgqWA) for more information.

Events:

DreamStarted

SizeChanged

DreamStopped

Members:

Canvas As CanvasWrapper [read only]

- Finish
- FullScreen As Boolean
- Initialize (EventName As String)
- Interactive As Boolean
- Panel As PanelWrapper [read only]
- ScreenBright As Boolean

Canvas As CanvasWrapper [read only]
A placeholder for Canvas.

Finish
Manually finishes the dream.

FullScreen As Boolean
Gets or sets whether the system bar appears.

Initialize (EventName As String)
Initializes the object and sets the subs that will handle the events.

Interactive As Boolean
Gets or sets whether user interactions will be handled instead of finishing the dream.

Panel As PanelWrapper [read only]
Returns the main panel.

ScreenBright As Boolean
Gets or sets whether the screen should stay bright.

GameView Library
This library is included in the IDE installation package. GameView is a view that allows you to draw hardware accelerated graphics. Compared to software accelerated graphics, hardware accelerated graphics are many times faster. Using hardware accelerated graphics, it is possible to create smooth, real-time games.
Note: the acceleration method used by GameView is only available from Android 3.0 and above. This also means that, under [Tools > Configure paths], you need to reference android.jar on Android platform 11 or above.

Tutorial
For a tutorial on creating a 2D game using GameView see http://www.basic4ppc.com/forum/Basic4Android-getting-started-tutorials/20038-gameview-create-2d-android-games-part-i.html

List of types:
BitmapData
GameView

BitmapData

Members:

- Bitmap As BitmapWrapper
- Delete As Boolean
- DestRect As RectWrapper
- Flip As Int
- FLIP_BOTH As Int
- FLIP_HORIZONTALLY As Int
- FLIP_NONE As Int
- FLIP_VERTICALLY As Int
- Rotate As Int
- SrcRect As RectWrapper

Bitmap As BitmapWrapper

The bitmap that will be drawn.

Delete As Boolean

If Delete is **`True`**, then the BitmapData will be removed from the list when GameView is redrawn.

DestRect As RectWrapper

The target rectangle. Determines the location and size of the drawn bitmap.

Flip As Int

Flips the bitmap based on one of the FLIP constants.

FLIP_BOTH As Int

FLIP_HORIZONTALLY As Int

FLIP_NONE As Int

FLIP_VERTICALLY As Int

Rotate As Int

Number of degrees to rotate the bitmap.

SrcRect As RectWrapper

The source rectangle. Determines the bitmap's region that will be drawn. The complete bitmap will be drawn if the rectangle is uninitialized.

GameView

A view that draws itself with hardware accelerated graphics. Suitable for 2d games. See this tutorial (http://www.basic4ppc.com/forum/basic4android-getting-started-tutorials/20038-gameview-create-2d-android-games-part-i.html). The hardware acceleration method used is only available in Android 3.0 and above (API level 11 and above).
This is an **`Activity`** object; it cannot be declared under **`Sub Process_Globals`**.

Events:

Touch (Action As Int, X As Float, Y As Float)

Members:

- Background As Drawable
- BitmapsData As List [read only]
- BringToFront
- Color As Int [write only]
- Enabled As Boolean
- Height As Int
- Initialize (arg1 As String)
- Invalidate
- Invalidate2 (arg0 As Rect)
- Invalidate3 (arg0 As Int, arg1 As Int, arg2 As Int, arg3 As Int)
- IsHardwareAccelerated As Boolean [read only]
- IsInitialized As Boolean
- Left As Int
- RemoveView
- RequestFocus As Boolean
- SendToBack
- SetBackgroundImage (arg0 As Bitmap)
- SetLayout (arg0 As Int, arg1 As Int, arg2 As Int, arg3 As Int)
- Tag As Object
- Top As Int
- Visible As Boolean
- Width As Int

Background As Drawable

BitmapsData As List [read only]

Returns the list of BitmapData objects.

BringToFront

Color As Int [write only]

Enabled As Boolean

If set to **True** then the **GameView** will respond to events. If set to **False**, events are ignored.

Height As Int

Initialize (arg1 As String**)**

Invalidate

Invalidates the whole view forcing the view to redraw itself. Redrawing will only happen when the program can process messages, usually when it finishes running the current code.
If you only need to redraw part of the view, it is usually quicker to use **`Invalidate2`** or **`Invalidate3`**.

Invalidate2 (Rect1 As Rect**)**

Invalidates anything inside the given rectangle that is part of this view. Redrawing will only happen when the program can process messages, usually when it finishes running the current code.

Invalidate3 (Left As Int, **Top** As Int, **Right** As Int, **Bottom** As Int**)**

Invalidates anything inside the given rectangle that is part of this view. Redrawing will only happen when the program can process messages, usually when it finishes running the current code.

IsHardwareAccelerated As Boolean **[read only]**

Returns **`TRUE`** if hardware acceleration is supported.

IsInitialized As Boolean

Whether this object has been initialized by calling **`Initialize`**.

Left As Int

RemoveView

RequestFocus As Boolean

SendToBack

SetBackgroundImage (arg0 As Bitmap**)**

SetLayout (arg0 As Int, **arg1** As Int, **arg2** As Int, **arg3** As Int**)**

Tag As Object

Top As Int

Visible As Boolean

Whether the user can see the object.

Width As Int

GPS Library

This library is included in the IDE installation package. The GPS library allows you to get information from the phone's GPS device. There are three types of relevant objects:

- The main one is GPS. The GPS manages the connection and events.

- The second is Location. A Location is a structure that holds the data available regarding a specific "fix". The data includes the latitude and longitude coordinates, the time (expressed as ticks) of this fix and other information like bearing, altitude and so on. It may happen that not all information is available (due to poor reception for example). The Location also includes other functionalities like calculating the distance and bearing to another location and methods to convert the coordinates string formats. Usually you will work with Location objects passed to you in the LocationChanged events. However, you can also initialize such objects yourself (this is useful for calculating distance and bearing between locations).
- The third relevant object is GPSSatellite. This is a structure that holds various information regarding the currently known satellites. It is passed to you in the `GPSStatus` event.

See the GPS tutorial (http://bit.ly/18OcTkc) for more information about this library.

List of types:

GPS
GPSSatellite
Location

GPS

The main object that raises GPS events.
Note that this library requires Android 2.0 or above.

Permissions:

android.permission.ACCESS_FINE_LOCATION

Events:

GpsStatus (Satellites As List)

This event, which returns a list of GPSSatellite objects, is raised once per second, regardless of the **MinimumTime** parameter of the `Start` command.

LocationChanged (Location1 As Location)

This event is generated when the GPS detects that the device has moved. Its frequency depends upon the **MinimumDistance** of the `Start` command.
Location1 – The new location of the device.

NMEA (TimeStamp As Long, Sentence As String)

This event contains **Sentences** (lines of data) in NMEA format (as specified by the National Marine Electronics Association) containing details about the GPS sensor. These events are raised every few seconds.

UserEnabled (Enabled As Boolean)

This event is generated when the user changes the status of the GPS sensor.

Members:

GPSEnabled As Boolean [read only]
Initialize (EventName As String)

- IsInitialized As Boolean
- LocationSettingsIntent As Intent [read only]
- Start (MinimumTime As Long, MinimumDistance As Float)
- Stop

GPSEnabled As Boolean [read only]
Returns **TRUE** if the user has enabled the GPS.

Initialize (EventName As String)

IsInitialized As Boolean
Whether this object has been initialized by calling **Initialize**.

LocationSettingsIntent As Intent [read only]
Returns the intent that is used to show the global locations settings.
Example:

```
If GPS1.GPSEnabled = False Then
StartActivity(GPS1.LocationSettingsIntent)
```

Start (MinimumTime As Long, MinimumDistance As Float)
Starts listening for events.
MinimumTime - The shortest period (measured in milliseconds) between events (other than **GpsStatus**). Pass 0 for highest frequency.
MinimumDistance - The shortest change in distance (measured in meters) for which the **LocationChanged** event is raised. Pass 0 for highest frequency.

Stop
Stops listening to the GPS. You will usually want to call Stop inside **Sub Activity_Pause**.

GPSSatellite
The GPSSatellite object holds various information about a GPS satellite. A List with the available satellites is passed to the GpsStatus event.

Members:
- Azimuth As Float [read only]
- Elevation As Float [read only]
- IsInitialized As Boolean
- Prn As Int [read only]
- Snr As Float [read only]
- UsedInFix As Boolean [read only]

Azimuth As Float [read only]
Returns the satellite azimuth in degrees (0 - 360).

Elevation As Float [read only]
Returns the satellite elevation in degrees (0 - 90).

IsInitialized As Boolean
Whether this object has been initialized by calling **`Initialize`**.

Prn As Int [read only]
Returns the PRN (pseudo-random number) for the satellite.

Snr As Float [read only]
Returns the signal to noise ratio for the satellite.

UsedInFix As Boolean [read only]
Returns **`TRUE`** if this satellite was used to calculate the most recent fix.

Location
A Location object holds various information about a specific GPS fix. In most cases, you will work with locations that are passed to the GPS **`LocationChanged`** event. The Location object can also be used to calculate distance and bearing to other locations.

Members:
- Accuracy As Float
- AccuracyValid As Boolean [read only]
- Altitude As Double
- AltitudeValid As Boolean [read only]
- Bearing As Float
- BearingTo (TargetLocation As Location) As Float
- BearingValid As Boolean [read only]
- ConvertToMinutes (Coordinate As Double) As String
- ConvertToSeconds (Coordinate As Double) As String
- DistanceTo (TargetLocation As Location) As Float
- Initialize
- Initialize2 (Latitude As String, Longitude As String)
- IsInitialized As Boolean
- Latitude As Double
- Longitude As Double
- Speed As Float
- SpeedValid As Boolean [read only]
- Time As Long

Accuracy As Float
Gets or sets the fix accuracy (meters).

AccuracyValid As Boolean [read only]
Returns **`True`** if the fix includes accuracy value.

Altitude As Double
Gets or sets the fix altitude (meters).

AltitudeValid As Boolean [read only]
Returns **True** if the fix includes altitude value.

Bearing As Float
Gets or sets the bearing of the current location relative to the previous location. The value is given in degrees measured clockwise from true North. Check the value of **BearingValid** before using this value.

BearingTo (TargetLocation As Location) As Float
Calculates the bearing to **TargetLocation** from the current location, measured clockwise in degrees, starting from North.

BearingValid As Boolean [read only]
Returns **True** if the location includes bearing value.

ConvertToMinutes (Coordinate As Double) As String
Converts the given **Coordinate** to a string formatted with the following format:
[+-]DDD:MM.MMMMM (Minute = 1 / 60 of a degree)

ConvertToSeconds (Coordinate As Double) As String
Converts the given **Coordinate** to a string formatted with the following format:
[+-]DDD:MM:SS.SSSSS (Minute = 1 / 60 of a degree, Second = 1 / 3600 of a degree)

DistanceTo (TargetLocation As Location) As Float
Returns the distance from the current location to the given **TargetLocation**, measured in meters.

Initialize
Initializes an empty Location object.

Initialize2 (Latitude As String, Longitude As String)
Initializes the Location object with the given **Latitude** and **Longitude**.
Values can be formatted in any of the three formats:
Degrees: [+-]DDD.DDDDD
Minutes: [+-]DDD:MM.MMMMM (Minute = 1 / 60 of a degree)
Seconds: [+-]DDD:MM:SS.SSSSS (Second = 1 / 3600 of a degree)
Example:

```
Dim L1 As Location
L1.Initialize2("45:30:30", "45:20:15")
```

IsInitialized As Boolean
Whether this object has been initialized by calling one of the **Initialize** methods.

Latitude As Double
Gets or sets the fix latitude (degrees from -90 (South Pole) to 90 (North Pole)).

Longitude As Double
Gets or sets the fix longitude (degrees from -180 to 180, positive values represent the eastern hemisphere).

Speed As Float
Gets or sets the fix speed (meters / second).

SpeedValid As Boolean [read only]
Returns `True` if the fix includes speed value.

Time As Long
Gets or sets the time of the GPS fix, given in ticks (page 285).

HTTP Library

This library is included in the IDE installation package. It allows you to communicate with web services and to download resources from the web. Because network communication can be slow and fragile, this library handles the requests and responses in the background and raises events when a task is ready.
Note that two modules, available from HttpUtils2 (http://bit.ly/19SbQnA), extend the functionality of this library and make it easier to access web services.

List of types:

HttpClient
HttpRequest
HttpResponse (page 440)

HttpClient

HttpClient allows you to make HTTP requests. Instead of using HttpClient directly, it is recommended to use HttpUtil2 (http://bit.ly/19SbQnA) modules which are much simpler to use.

Permissions:

android.permission.INTERNET

Events:

ResponseSuccess (Response As HttpResponse, TaskId As Int)

ResponseError (Response As HttpResponse, Reason As String, StatusCode As Int, TaskId As Int)

Members:

Execute (HttpRequest As HttpRequest, TaskId As Int) As Boolean

ExecuteCredentials (HttpRequest As HttpRequest, TaskId As Int, UserName As String, Password As String) As Boolean

Initialize (EventName As String)

InitializeAcceptAll (EventName As String)

IsInitialized As Boolean

SetHttpParameter (Name As String, Value As Object)

SetProxy (Host As String, Port As Int, Scheme As String)

SetProxy2 (Host As String, Port As Int, Scheme As String, Username As String, Password As String)

Execute (HttpRequest As HttpRequest, TaskId As Int) As Boolean

Executes the HttpRequest asynchronously. `ResponseSuccess` or `ResponseError` events will be fired later. Note that in many cases the Response object passed in the `ResponseError` event will be `Null`. If there is a request with the same **TaskId** already running, then this method will return `False` and the new request will not be submitted.

ExecuteCredentials (HttpRequest As HttpRequest, TaskId As Int, UserName As String, Password As String) As Boolean

Same behavior as **Execute**. The **UserName** and **Password** will be used for Basic or Digest authentication. Digest authentication is only supported for GET requests.

Initialize (EventName As String)

Initializes this object. **IMPORTANT**: this object should be declared in `Sub Process_Globals`.
EventName - The prefix that will be used for ResponseSuccess and ResponseError events.

InitializeAcceptAll (EventName As String)

Similar to Initialize, with one important difference. All SSL certificates will be automatically accepted.
This method should only be used when trying to connect to a server located in a secured network.

IsInitialized As Boolean

Whether this object has been initialized by calling `Initialize`.

SetHttpParameter (Name As String, Value As Object)

Sets the value of the parameter with the given name.

SetProxy (Host As String, Port As Int, Scheme As String)

Sets the proxy to use for the connections.
Host - Proxy host name or IP.
Port - Proxy port.
Scheme - Scheme name. Usually "http".

SetProxy2 (Host As String, Port As Int, Scheme As String, Username As String, Password As String)

Sets the proxy to use for the connections, with the required credentials.

HttpRequest

Holds the target URL and other data sent to the web server.
The initial time-out is to 30000 milliseconds (30 seconds).

Members:

- InitializeDelete (Url As String)
- InitializeGet (Url As String)
- InitializeHead (Url As String)

InitializePost (Url As String, InputStream As java.io.InputStream, Length As Int)
InitializePost2 (Url As String, Data() As Byte)
InitializePut (Url As String, InputStream As java.io.InputStream, Length As Int)
InitializePut2 (Url As String, Data() As Byte)
RemoveHeaders (Name As String)
SetContentEncoding (Encoding As String)
SetContentType (ContentType As String)
SetHeader (Name As String, Value As String)
Timeout As Int [write only]

InitializeDelete (Url As String)

Initializes the request and sets it to be an HTTP Delete method.

InitializeGet (Url As String)

Initializes the request and sets it to be an HTTP Get method.

InitializeHead (Url As String)

Initializes the request and sets it to be an HTTP Head method.

InitializePost (Url As String, InputStream As java.io.InputStream, Length As Int)

Initializes the request and sets it to be an HTTP Post method. The specified **InputStream** will be read and added to the request.

InitializePost2 (Url As String, Data() As Byte)

Initializes the request and sets it to be an HTTP Post method. The specified **Data** array will be added to the request. Unlike `InitializePost`, this method will enable the request to retry and send the data several times in case of IO errors.

InitializePut (Url As String, InputStream As java.io.InputStream, Length As Int)

Initializes the request and sets it to be an HTTP Put method. The specified **InputStream** will be read and added to the request.

InitializePut2 (Url As String, Data() As Byte)

Initializes the request and sets it to be an HTTP Put method. The specified **Data** array will be added to the request.

RemoveHeaders (Name As String)

Removes all headers with the given name.

SetContentEncoding (Encoding As String)

Sets the encoding header of the request.
This method should only be used with Post or Put requests.

SetContentType (ContentType As String)

Sets the Mime header of the request. This method should only be used with Post or Put requests.

SetHeader (Name As String, Value As String)

Sets the value of the first header with the given name. If no such header exists, then a new header will be added.

Timeout As Int [write only]

Sets the request timeout (measured in milliseconds).

HttpResponse

An object that holds the response returned from the server. The object is passed in the ResponseSuccess event. You can choose to read the response synchronously or asynchronously. **It is important** to release this object when it is not used anymore by calling **`Release`**.

Events:

StreamFinish (Success As Boolean, TaskId As Int)

Members:

ContentEncoding As String [read only]

ContentLength As Long [read only]

ContentType As String [read only]

GetAsynchronously (EventName As String, Output As java.io.OutputStream, CloseOutput As Boolean, TaskId As Int) As Boolean

GetHeaders As Map

GetInputStream As InputStreamWrapper

GetString (DefaultCharset As String) As String

Release

StatusCode As Int [read only]

ContentEncoding As String [read only]

Returns the content encoding header.

ContentLength As Long [read only]

Returns the content length header.

ContentType As String [read only]

Returns the content type header.

GetAsynchronously (EventName As String, Output As java.io.OutputStream, CloseOutput As Boolean, TaskId As Int) As Boolean

Asynchronously reads the response and writes it to the given **OutputStream**. If there is a request with the same **TaskId** already running, then this method will return **`False`**, and the response object will be released. The **`StreamFinish`** event will be raised after the response has been fully read.

EventName - The sub that will handle the StreamFinish event.

Output - The stream from the server will be written to this stream.

CloseOutput - Whether to close the specified output stream when done.

TaskId - The task id given to this task.
Example:

```
Sub Http_ResponseSuccess (Response As HttpResponse, TaskId As
Int)
  Response.GetAsynchronously("ImageResponse", _
     File.OpenOutput(File.DirInternalCache, "image.jpg", False),
True, TaskId)
End Sub
Sub ImageResponse_StreamFinish (Success As Boolean, TaskId As
Int)
  If Success = False Then
     Msgbox(LastException.Message, "Error")
     Return
  End If
  ImageView1.Bitmap = LoadBitmap(File.DirInternalCache,
"image.jpg")
End Sub
```

GetHeaders As Map

Returns a Map object with the response headers. Each element is made of a key which is the header name and a value which is a list containing the values (one or more). Example:

```
Dim list1 As List
list1 = response.GetHeaders.Get("Set-Cookie")
For i = 0 To list1.Size - 1
  Log(list1.Get(i))
Next
```

GetInputStream As InputStreamWrapper

This method is deprecated and will not work properly on Android 4+ device.
Use GetAsynchronously instead.

GetString (DefaultCharset As String) As String

This method is deprecated and will not work properly on Android 4+ device.
Use GetAsynchronously instead.

Release

Frees resources allocated for this object.

StatusCode As Int [read only]

Returns the response HTTP code.

IME Library

Android has very good support for custom input method editors (IMEs). The downside for this powerful feature is that interacting with the soft keyboard can be sometimes quite complicated. This library, which is included in the IDE installation package, includes several utilities that will help you better handle the soft keyboard. A tutorial with a working example is available here (http://bit.ly/14hx2OB).

Example

```
Sub Globals
 Dim IME1 As IME
End Sub

Sub Activity_Create(FirstTime As Boolean)
 IME1.Initialize("IME")
End Sub
```

List of types:

IME

IME

This is an **Activity** object; it cannot be declared under **Sub Process_Globals**.

Events:

HeightChanged (NewHeight As Int, OldHeight As Int)

This event is raised when the height of the keyboard changes.

HandleAction As Boolean

This event is raised by the EditText which is specified by the member AddHandleActionEvent when the user clicks the action button (the button that shows Next or Done) on the keyboard. For an example, see below. The return value specifies whether to keep the keyboard visible. Returning **True** will keep it visible, returning **False** will close the keyboard.

Members:

- AddHandleActionEvent (EditText1 As EditText)
- AddHeightChangedEvent
- HideKeyboard
- Initialize (EventName As String)
- SetCustomFilter (EditText1 As EditText, DefaultInputType As Int, AcceptedCharacters As String)
- ShowKeyboard (View1 As View)

AddHandleActionEvent (EditText1 As EditText)

Adds the HandleAction event to the given EditText. Example:

```
Sub Activity_Create(FirstTime As Boolean)
 IME1.Initialize("IME1")
 IME1.AddHandleActionEvent(edtTextToSpeak)
End Sub
```

```
Sub IME1_HandleAction As Boolean
 Dim edtTxt As EditText
 edtTxt = Sender
 If edtTxt.Text.StartsWith("a") = False Then
  ToastMessageShow("Text must start with 'a'", True)
  'Consume the event.
  'The keyboard will not be closed
  Return True
 Else
  Return False 'will close the keyboard
 End If
End Sub
```

AddHeightChangedEvent

Enables the HeightChanged event. This event is raised when the soft keyboard state changes. You can use this event to resize other views to fit the new screen size.
Note that this event will not be raised in full screen activities (an Android limitation).

HideKeyboard

Hides the soft keyboard if it is visible.

Initialize (EventName As String)

Initializes the object and sets the subs that will handle the events.

SetCustomFilter (EditText1 As EditText, DefaultInputType As Int, AcceptedCharacters As String)

Sets a custom filter.
EditText - The target EditText.
DefaultInputType - Sets the keyboard mode.
AcceptedCharacters - The accepted characters.
Example: Create a filter that will accept IP addresses (numbers with multiple dots)

```
IME.SetCustomFilter(EditText1, EditText1.INPUT_TYPE_NUMBERS,
"0123456789.")
```

ShowKeyboard (View1 As View)

Sets the focus to the given view and opens the soft keyboard.
The keyboard will only show if the view has received the focus.

JSON Library

This library is included in the IDE installation package.

List of types:

JSONGenerator
JSONParser

JSONGenerator

This object generates JSON strings. It can be initialized with a Map or a List. Both can contain other Maps or Lists. See the JSON tutorial (http://bit.ly/18clue0).

Members:

- Initialize (Map As Map)
- Initialize2 (List As List)
- ToPrettyString (Indent As Int) As String
- ToString As String

Initialize (Map As Map)

Initializes the object with the given Map.

Initialize2 (List As List)

Initializes the object with the given List.

ToPrettyString (Indent As Int) As String

Creates a JSON string from the initialized object. The string will be indented and easier for reading. **Note** that the string created is a valid JSON string.
Indent - Number of spaces to add to each level.

ToString As String

Creates a JSON string from the initialized object. This string does not include any extra whitespace.

JSONParser

Parses JSON formatted strings. See here (http://www.json.org/) for a description of JSON. JSON objects are converted to Maps and JSON arrays are converted to Lists. After initializing the object, you will usually call NextObject to get a single Map object. If the JSON string top level value is an array, you should call NextArray. Afterward, you should work with the Map or List and fetch the required data. See the JSON tutorial (http://bit.ly/18clue0) for more information. Typical code:

```
Dim JSON As JSONParser
Dim Map1 As Map
JSON.Initialize(File.ReadString(File.DirAssets, "example.json"))
'Read the text from a file.
Map1 = JSON.NextObject
```

Members:

- Initialize (Text As String)
- IsInitialized As Boolean
- NextArray As List
- NextObject As Map
- NextValue As Object

Initialize (Text As String)

Initializes the object and sets the text that will be parsed.

IsInitialized As Boolean
Whether this object has been initialized by calling **`Initialize`**.

NextArray As List
Parses the text assuming that the top level value is an array.

NextObject As Map
Parses the text assuming that the top level value is an object.

NextValue As Object
Parses the text assuming that the top level value is a simple value.

LiveWallpaper Library

This library is included in the IDE installation package.

List of types:

LWEngine
LWManager

LWEngine

Represents a wallpaper instance.
A tutorial is available here (http://www.basic4ppc.com/forum/basic4android-getting-started-tutorials/12605-android-live-wallpaper-tutorial.html).

Members:

- Canvas As CanvasWrapper [read only]
- CurrentOffsetX As Int [read only]
- CurrentOffsetY As Int [read only]
- FullWallpaperHeight As Int [read only]
- FullWallpaperWidth As Int [read only]
- IsInitialized As Boolean
- IsPreview As Boolean [read only]
- IsVisible As Boolean [read only]
- Rect As RectWrapper
- Refresh (DirtyRect As Rect)
- RefreshAll
- ScreenHeight As Int [read only]
- ScreenWidth As Int [read only]
- Tag As Object

Canvas As CanvasWrapper [read only]
Returns the canvas which is used to draw on the wallpaper.
Changes will not be visible till you call Refresh or RefreshAll.

CurrentOffsetX As Int [read only]
Returns the current horizontal offset related to the full wallpaper width.

CurrentOffsetY As Int [read only]
Returns the current vertical offset related to the full wallpaper height.

FullWallpaperHeight As Int [read only]
Returns the full wallpaper height.

FullWallpaperWidth As Int [read only]
Returns the full wallpaper width. A wallpaper can be made of several screens.

IsInitialized As Boolean
Returns **TRUE** if this object is initialized.

IsPreview As Boolean [read only]
Returns **TRUE** if this wallpaper is running in "preview mode".

IsVisible As Boolean [read only]
Returns **TRUE** if this wallpaper is visible.

Rect As RectWrapper
A convenient Rect object which you can use. This object is not used internally.

Refresh (DirtyRect As Rect)
Refreshes the given region.

RefreshAll
Refreshes the complete screen.

ScreenHeight As Int [read only]
Returns the screen height.

ScreenWidth As Int [read only]
Returns the screen width.

Tag As Object
Gets or sets the Tag value. This is a place holder which can be used to store additional data.

LWManager

Manages the wallpaper events and the timer. A tutorial is available here (http://bit.ly/17dre8v).

Events:

SizeChanged (Engine As LWEngine)

Touch (Engine As LWEngine, Action As Int, X As Float, Y As Float)

VisibilityChanged (Engine As LWEngine, Visible As Boolean)

EngineDestroyed (Engine As LWEngine)

Tick (Engine As LWEngine)

OffsetChanged (Engine As LWEngine)

Members:

- Initialize (EventName As String, TouchEventsEnabled As Boolean)
- StartTicking (IntervalMs As Int)
- StopTicking

Initialize (EventName As String, TouchEventsEnabled As Boolean)

Initializes the object.
EventName - Sets the Subs that will handle the events.
TouchEventsEnabled - Whether the wallpaper should raise the Touch event when the user touches the screen.

StartTicking (IntervalMs As Int)

Starts the internal timer.
IntervalMs - Interval (in milliseconds).

StopTicking

Stops the internal timer.

Network Library

This library, which is included in the IDE installation package, includes two objects for working with TCP (`Socket` and `ServerSocket`) and two objects for working with UDP (`UDPSocket` and `UDPPacket`).
Using a `Socket`, you can communicate with other devices and computers over TCP/IP. `ServerSocket` allows you to listen for incoming connections. Once a connection is established, you will receive a `Socket` object that will be used for handling this specific connection. See the Network tutorial (http://bit.ly/17c4yY7) for more information.
A `UDPSocket` supports sending and receiving `UDPPackets`.

List of types:

ServerSocket
Socket
UDPPacket (page 450)
UDPSocket (page 451)

ServerSocket

The ServerSocket object allows other machines to connect to this machine.
The ServerSocket listens to a specific port. Once a connection arrives, the NewConnection event is raised with a Socket object. This Socket object should be used to communicate with this client. You may call Listen again and receive more connections. A single ServerSocket can handle many connections. For each connection, there should be one Socket object.

Permissions:

android.permission.INTERNET
android.permission.ACCESS_WIFI_STATE

Event: NewConnection (Successful As Boolean, NewSocket As Socket)

Members:

- Close
- GetMyIP As String
- GetMyWifiIP As String
- Initialize (Port As Int, EventName As String)
- IsInitialized As Boolean
- Listen

Close

Closes the ServerSocket. This will not close any other sockets.
You should call Initialize if you want to use this object again.

GetMyIP As String

Returns the server's IP. Will return "127.0.0.1" (localhost) if no other IP is found.
This method will return the wifi network IP if it is available.

GetMyWifiIP As String

Returns the IP address of the wifi network. Returns "127.0.0.1" (localhost) if not connected.

Initialize (Port As Int, EventName As String)

Initializes the ServerSocket.
Port - The port that the server will listen to. Note that you should call Listen to start listening. Port numbers lower than 1024 are restricted by the system.
EventName - The event Sub prefix name.

IsInitialized As Boolean

Returns `TRUE` if the object is initialized.

Listen

Starts listening in the background for incoming connections. When a connection is established, the `NewConnection` event is raised. If the connection is successful, a Socket object will be passed in the event. Calling `Listen` while the ServerSocket is listening will not do anything.

Socket

The Socket object is an endpoint for network communication. If you are connecting to a server, then you should initialize a Socket object and call **Connect** with the server address. The **Connected** event will be raised when the connection is ready or if the connection has failed.
Sockets are also used by the server. Once a new incoming connection is established, the **NewConnection** event will be raised and an initialized Socket object will be passed as a parameter.
Once a socket is connected, you should use its **InputStream** and **OutputStream** to communicate with the other machine.

Permissions:

android.permission.INTERNET

Event: Connected (Successful As Boolean)

Members:

- Close
- Connect (Host As String, Port As Int, TimeOut As Int)
- Connected As Boolean [read only]
- Initialize (EventName As String)
- InputStream As java.io.InputStream [read only]
- IsInitialized As Boolean
- OutputStream As java.io.OutputStream [read only]
- ResolveHost (Host As String) As String
- TimeOut As Int

Close

Closes the socket and the streams. It is safe to call this method multiple times.

Connect (Host As String, Port As Int, TimeOut As Int)

Tries to connect to the given address. The connection is done in the background. The Connected event will be raised when the connection is ready or if it has failed.
Host - The host name or IP.
Port - Port number.
TimeOut - Connection timeout. Value is specified in milliseconds. Pass 0 to disable the timeout.

Connected As Boolean [read only]

Returns **TRUE** if the socket is connected.

Initialize (EventName As String)

Initializes a new socket.

InputStream As java.io.InputStream [read only]

Returns the socket's InputStream which is used to read data.

IsInitialized As Boolean
Returns **TRUE** if the object was initialized.

OutputStream As java.io.OutputStream [read only]
Returns the socket's OutputStream which is used to write data.

ResolveHost (Host As String) As String
Resolves the host name and returns the IP address.
This method is deprecated and will not work properly on Android 4+ devices.

TimeOut As Int
Gets or sets the timeout of the socket's InputStream. Value is specified in milliseconds. By default there is no timeout.

UDPPacket
A packet of data that is being sent or received. To send a packet, call one of the Initialize methods and then send the packet by passing it to `UDPSocket.Send`. When a packet arrives, you can get the data in the packet from the available properties.

Members:
- Data() As Byte [read only]
- Host As String [read only]
- HostAddress As String [read only]
- Initialize (Data() As Byte, Host As String, Port As Int)
- Initialize2 (Data() As Byte, Offset As Int, Length As Int, Host As String, Port As Int)
- IsInitialized As Boolean
- Length As Int [read only]
- Offset As Int [read only]
- Port As Int [read only]
- toString As String

Data() As Byte [read only]
Gets the data array received.

Host As String [read only]
This method is deprecated and will not work properly on Android 4+ device.
Use HostAddress instead.

HostAddress As String [read only]
Gets the IP address of the sending machine.

Initialize (Data() As Byte, Host As String, Port As Int)
Initializes the packet and makes it ready for sending.
Data - The data that will be sent.
Host - The target host name or IP address.
Port - The target port.

Initialize2 (Data() As Byte, Offset As Int, Length As Int, Host As String, Port As Int)

Similar to Initialize. The data sent is based on the Offset and Length values.

IsInitialized As Boolean

Whether this object has been initialized by calling one of the `Initialize` methods.

Length As Int [read only]

Gets the length of available bytes in the data. This can be shorter than the array length.

Offset As Int [read only]

Gets the offset in the data array where the available data starts.

Port As Int [read only]

Gets the port of the sending machine.

toString As String

UDPSocket

UDPSocket supports sending and receiving UDPPackets. Sending packets is done by calling the `Send` method. When a packet arrives, the `PacketArrived` event is raised with the packet.

This example sends a string message to some other machine. When a packet arrives, it converts it to string and shows it:

```
Sub Process_Globals
  Dim UDPSocket1 As UDPSocket
End Sub
Sub Globals
End Sub
Sub Activity_Create(FirstTime As Boolean)
  If FirstTime Then
     UDPSocket1.Initialize("UDP", 0, 8000)
  End If
  Dim Packet As UDPPacket
  Dim data() As Byte
  data = "Hello from Android".GetBytes("UTF8")
  Packet.Initialize(data, "10.0.0.1", 5000)
  UDPSocket1.Send(Packet)
End Sub
Sub UDP_PacketArrived (Packet As UDPPacket)
  Dim msg As String
  msg = BytesToString(Packet.Data, Packet.Offset, Packet.Length,
"UTF8")
  Msgbox("Message received: " & msg, "")
End Sub
```

Permission: android.permission.INTERNET

Event: PacketArrived (Packet As UDPPacket)

Members:

- Close
- Initialize (EventName As String, Port As Int, ReceiveBufferSize As Int)
- IsInitialized As Boolean
- Port As Int [read only]
- Send (Packet As UDPPacket)
- toString As String

Close

Closes the socket.

Initialize (EventName As String, Port As Int, ReceiveBufferSize As Int)

Initializes the socket and starts listening for packets.
EventName - The name of the Sub that will handle the events.
Port - Local port to listen on. Passing 0 will cause Android to choose an available port automatically.
ReceiveBufferSize - The size of the receiving packet. Packets larger than this value will be truncated. Pass 0 if you do not want to receive any packets.

IsInitialized As Boolean

Returns **TRUE** if this object is initialized.

Port As Int [read only]

Gets the local port that this socket listens to.

Send (Packet As UDPPacket)

Sends a Packet. The packet will be sent in the background (asynchronously).

toString As String

NFC Library

This library, which is included in the IDE installation package, requires Android version 2.3.3 or above (API level 10 or above). It lets you read NFC tags formatted in NDEF form (NFC Data Exchange Format). You can find more about the internal process here:
http://developer.android.com/guide/topics/connectivity/nfc/nfc.html

---

List of types:

NdefRecord
NFC

NdefRecord

Members:

- GetAsTextType As String
- GetAsUriType As String
- GetPayload As Byte()
- IsInitialized As Boolean

GetAsTextType As String

Reads the payload and returns the stored text.

GetAsUriType As String

Reads the payload and returns the stored URI ("Uniform Resource Identifier" identifying the resource to get).

GetPayload As Byte()

Returns the whole payload.

IsInitialized As Boolean

Whether this object has been initialized.

NFC

Supports reading NDEF (NFC Data Exchange Format) tags.
See this tutorial (http://www.basic4ppc.com/forum/basic4android-getting-started-tutorials/14931-reading-ndef-data-nfc-tags.html) for more information.

Permissions:

android.permission.NFC

Members:

GetNdefRecords (Intent1 As Intent) As List

Retrieves the NdefRecords stored in the Intent object.

IsNdefIntent (Intent1 As Intent) As Boolean

Returns **TRUE** if the Intent contains data read from an NDef tag.

Phone Library

The Phone library contains all kinds of features related to the Android phone.
CallLog and **CallItem** give access to the phone calls log.
Contacts2 (page 459) (or the legacy **Contacts (page 458)**) give access to the stored contacts, retrieved as a **Contact (page 456)**.
ContentChooser (page 461) allows the user to choose content from other applications. For example, the user can choose an image from the Gallery application.
Email (page 461) helps with building an Intent that sends an email.
LogCat (page 462) tracks the internal phone logs.

PackageManager (page 463) allows you to retrieve information about the installed applications.
Phone (page 464) object includes information about the device and also other general features.
PhoneAccelerometer (page 469) and **PhoneOrientation (page 473)** objects are legacy objects, now replaced with **PhoneSensors (page 473)**.
PhoneEvents (page 469) allows you to handle all kinds of system events.
PhoneId (page 472) gives access to the the specific phone values.
PhoneIntents (page 472) and **PhoneCalls (page 469)** include several useful intents.
PhoneSensors (page 473) support many sensors such as accelerometer and orientation.
PhoneSms (page 476) supports sending Sms messages.
PhoneVibrate (page 477) vibrates the phone.
PhoneWakeState (page 478) allows you to force the screen and power to remain switched on.
RingtoneManager (page 478) allows you to control the ringtone.
SmsInterceptor (page 481) intercepts incoming Sms messages.
SmsMessages (page 482) together with **Sms (page 480)** support fetching messages from the phone database.
VoiceRecognition (page 483) converts speech to text.

CallItem

Represents a single call in the call logs. See CallLog for more information.

Members:

- CachedName As String
- CallType As Int
- Date As Long
- Duration As Long
- Id As Int
- Number As String
- TYPE_INCOMING As Int
- TYPE_MISSED As Int
- TYPE_OUTGOING As Int

CachedName As String

Returns the cached name assigned to this call number at the time of call.
Returns an empty string if no name was assigned.

CallType As Int

The call type. This value matches one of the TYPE constants.

Date As Long
The call date measured as ticks.

Duration As Long
The call duration in seconds.

Id As Int
The call internal id.

Number As String
The call phone number.

TYPE_INCOMING As Int
`CallType` for incoming calls.

TYPE_MISSED As Int
`CallType` for missed calls.

TYPE_OUTGOING As Int
`CallType` for calls made from this device.

CallLog

CallLog allows you to browse the call logs.
Retrieved calls are always ordered by descending date.
Usage example:

```
Dim Calls As List
Dim CallLog1 As CallLog
Calls = CallLog1.GetAll(10) 'Get the last 10 calls
For i = 0 To Calls.Size - 1
  Dim c As CallItem
  c = Calls.Get(i)
  Dim callType, name As String
  Select c.CallType
     Case c.TYPE_INCOMING
         callType="Incoming"
     Case c.TYPE_MISSED
         callType = "Missed"
     Case c.TYPE_OUTGOING
         callType = "Outgoing"
  End Select
  name = c.CachedName
  If name = "" Then name = "N/A"
  Log("Number=" & c.Number & ", Name=" & name _
     & ", Type=" & callType & ", Date=" & DateTime.Date(c.Date))
Next
```

Permissions:

android.permission.READ_CONTACTS

Members:

GetAll (Limit As Int) As List

- GetById (Id As Int) As CallItem
- GetSince (Date As Long, Limit As Int) As List

GetAll (Limit As Int) As List
Returns all calls, ordered by date (descending), as a List of **CallItems**.
Limit - Maximum number of **CallItems** to return. Pass 0 to return all items.

GetById (Id As Int) As CallItem
Returns the **CallItem** with the specified **Id**.
Returns **Null** if no matching **CallItem** found.

GetSince (Date As Long, Limit As Int) As List
Returns all **CallItems** with a date value on or after the specified **Date**.
Limit - Maximum number of items to return. Pass 0 to return all items.
Example:
```
Dim cl As CallLog
Dim logList As List
Dim startDate As Long
startDate = DateTime.DateParse("01/16/2013")
logList.Initialize2(cl.GetSince(startDate,0))
For Each call As CallItem In logList
 Log(DateTime.Date(call.Date))
Next
```

Contact
Represents a single contact. The Contacts or Contacts2 (page 459) objects should be used to get lists of Contact objects.
The available email types are identified by constants named EMAIL_x.
The available phone types are identified by constants named PHONE_x.

Members:
- DisplayName As String
- EMAIL_CUSTOM As Int
- EMAIL_HOME As Int
- EMAIL_MOBILE As Int
- EMAIL_OTHER As Int
- EMAIL_WORK As Int
- GetEmails As Map
- GetPhones As Map
- GetPhoto As BitmapWrapper
- Id As Int
- LastTimeContacted As Long
- Name As String
- Notes As String
- PHONE_CUSTOM As Int

- PHONE_FAX_HOME As Int
- PHONE_FAX_WORK As Int
- PHONE_HOME As Int
- PHONE_MOBILE As Int
- PHONE_OTHER As Int
- PHONE_PAGER As Int
- PHONE_WORK As Int
- PhoneNumber As String
- Starred As Boolean
- TimesContacted As Int

DisplayName As String
The displayed name. Equal to the Contact Name if the Name is not empty; otherwise equal to the contact's first email address.

EMAIL_CUSTOM As Int

EMAIL_HOME As Int

EMAIL_MOBILE As Int

EMAIL_OTHER As Int

EMAIL_WORK As Int

GetEmails As Map
Returns a Map with the email addresses of the Contact as keys and the email types as values. This will send a query to the device's contacts service, so it might be slow.

GetPhones As Map
Returns a Map with all the contact's phone numbers as keys and the phone types as values. This will send a query to the device's contacts service, so it might be slow.

GetPhoto As BitmapWrapper
Returns the contact photo or Null if there is no attached photo. This will send a query to the device's contacts service, so it might be slow.

Id As Int
Internal Id.

LastTimeContacted As Long
Last time that this contact was contacted. Value is given in ticks (page 285).

Name As String
Contact name.

Notes As String

PHONE_CUSTOM As Int

PHONE_FAX_HOME As Int

PHONE_FAX_WORK As Int

PHONE_HOME As Int

PHONE_MOBILE As Int

PHONE_OTHER As Int

PHONE_PAGER As Int

PHONE_WORK As Int

PhoneNumber As String
Primary phone number.

Starred As Boolean
Whether this contact is a "favorite" contact.

TimesContacted As Int
Number of times that this contact was contacted.

Contacts

This is a legacy object and has been replaced by Contacts2. For new projects, it might be better to consider using the ContactsUtils (http://bit.ly/180A35y) module with the ContentResolver Library (http://bit.ly/1djfesb) instead of Contacts or Contacts2.
The `Contacts` object allows you to access contacts stored on the device.

Permissions:

android.permission.READ_CONTACTS

Members:

FindByMail (Email As String, **Exact** As Boolean**)** As List
Returns a List of Contact objects with all contacts matching the given email.
Email - The email to search for.
Exact - If `True`, then only contacts with the exact **Email** address (case sensitive) will be returned, otherwise all contacts' email addresses that include the **Email** string (case insensitive) will be returned.

FindByName (Name As String, **Exact** As Boolean**)** As List
Returns a List of Contact objects with all contacts matching the given name.
Name - The name to search for.
Exact - If `True`, then only contacts with the exact **Name** value (case sensitive) will be returned, otherwise all contacts' names that include the **Name** string (case insensitive) will be returned.

GetAll As List
Returns a List of Contact objects with all the contacts. This list can be very large.

GetById (Id As Int) As Contact

Returns the Contact with the specified Id. Returns **Null** if no matching contact found.

Contacts2

The Contacts2 object allows you to access contacts stored on the device. **This type is based on a new API supported by Android 2.0 and above and supersedes the legacy Contacts type**. For new projects, it might be better to consider using the ContactsUtils (http://bit.ly/180A35y) module with the ContentResolver Library (http://bit.ly/1djfesb) instead of Contacts2.
The following example finds all contacts whose name contains the string "john", and print their fields to the Log. It will also fetch the contact photo and other details, if they exist:

```
Dim allContacts As Contacts2
Dim listOfContacts As List
listOfContacts = allContacts.FindByName("John", False, True,
True)
For i = 0 To listOfContacts.Size - 1
  Dim Contact1 As Contact
  Contact1 = listOfContacts.Get(i)
  Log(Contact1) 'will print the fields to the LogCat
  Dim photo As Bitmap
  photo = Contact1.GetPhoto
  If photo <> Null Then Activity.SetBackgroundImage(photo)
  Dim emails As Map
  emails = Contact1.GetEmails
  If emails.Size > 0 Then Log("Email addresses: " & emails)
  Dim phones As Map
  phones = Contact1.GetPhones
  If phones.Size > 0 Then Log("Phone numbers: " & phones)
Next
```

Permissions:

android.permission.READ_CONTACTS

Events:

Complete (ListOfContacts As List)

Members:

FindByMail (Email As String, Exact As Boolean, IncludePhoneNumber As Boolean, IncludeNotes As Boolean) As List

FindByName (Name As String, Exact As Boolean, IncludePhoneNumber As Boolean, IncludeNotes As Boolean) As List

GetAll (IncludePhoneNumber As Boolean, IncludeNotes As Boolean) As List

GetById (Id As Int, IncludePhoneNumber As Boolean, IncludeNotes As Boolean) As Contact

GetContactsAsync (EventName As String, Query As String, Arguments() As String, IncludePhoneNumber As Boolean, IncludeNotes As Boolean)

GetContactsByQuery (Query As String, Arguments() As String, IncludePhoneNumber As Boolean, IncludeNotes As Boolean) As List

FindByMail (Email As String, Exact As Boolean, IncludePhoneNumber As Boolean, IncludeNotes As Boolean) As List

Returns a List of Contact objects with all contacts matching the given **Email**.
Email - The email to search for.
Exact - If `True`, then only contacts with the exact **Email** address (case sensitive) will be returned, otherwise all contacts' email addresses that include the **Email** string (case insensitive) will be returned.
IncludePhoneNumber - Whether to fetch the default phone number.
IncludeNotes - Whether to fetch the notes field.

FindByName (Name As String, Exact As Boolean, IncludePhoneNumber As Boolean, IncludeNotes As Boolean) As List

Returns a List of Contact objects with all contacts matching the given name.
Name - The name to search for.
Exact - If `True`, then only contacts with the exact **Name** value (case sensitive) will be returned, otherwise all contacts' names that include the **Name** string (case insensitive) will be returned.
IncludePhoneNumber - Whether to fetch the default phone number.
IncludeNotes - Whether to fetch the notes field.

GetAll (IncludePhoneNumber As Boolean, IncludeNotes As Boolean) As List

Returns a List of Contact objects with all the contacts. This list can be very large.

GetById (Id As Int, IncludePhoneNumber As Boolean, IncludeNotes As Boolean) As Contact

Returns the Contact with the specified Id. Returns `Null` if no matching contact found.
IncludePhoneNumber - Whether to fetch the default phone number.
IncludeNotes - Whether to fetch the notes field.

GetContactsAsync (EventName As String, Query As String, Arguments() As String, IncludePhoneNumber As Boolean, IncludeNotes As Boolean)

This method is an asynchronous version of GetContactsByQuery. Once the list is ready, the `Complete` event will be raised. The **EventName** parameter sets the sub that will handle this event.

GetContactsByQuery (Query As String, Arguments() As String, IncludePhoneNumber As Boolean, IncludeNotes As Boolean) As List

Returns a list of contacts based on the specified query and arguments.
Query - The SQL query. Pass an empty string to return all contacts.

Arguments - An array of strings used for parameterized queries. Pass **`Null`** if not needed.
IncludePhoneNumber - Whether to fetch the phone number for each contact.
IncludeNotes - Whether to fetch the notes field for each contact.

ContentChooser

The ContentChooser object allows the user to select a specific type of content using other installed applications. For example, the user can use the internal Gallery application to select an image. If the user has installed a file manager, then the ContentChooser can be used to select general files. This object should usually be declared as a **`Sub Process_Globals`** object. After initializing the object, you can let the user select content by calling Show with the required MIME types.
The **`Result`** event will be raised with a **`Success`** flag and with the content **`Dir`** and **`FileName`**. Note that these values may point to resources other than regular files. Still, you can pass them to methods that expect **`Dir`** and **`FileName`**.
Only content types that can be opened with an **`InputStream`** are supported.

Event: Result (Success As Boolean, Dir As String, FileName As String)

Members:

- Initialize (EventName As String)
- IsInitialized As Boolean
- Show (Mime As String, Title As String)

Initialize (EventName As String)

Initializes the object and sets the Sub that will handle the Result event.
Example:

```
Dim CC As ContentChooser
CC.Initialize("CC")
```

IsInitialized As Boolean

Whether this object has been initialized by calling **`Initialize`**.

Show (Mime As String, Title As String)

Sends the request to the system. If there is more than one application that supports the given Mime, then a list with the applications will be displayed to the user. The Result event will be raised after the user chooses an item or cancels the dialog.
Mime - The content MIME type.
Title - The title of the chooser dialog (when there is more than one application).
Examples:

```
CC.Show("image/*", "Choose image")
CC.Show("audio/*", "Choose audio file")
```

Email

Using an Email object, you can create an intent that holds a complete email message. You can then launch the email application by calling StartActivity. Note that the email will not be sent automatically. The user will need to press on the “Send” button. Example:

```
Dim Message As Email
Message.To.Add("SomeEmail@example.com")
Message.Attachments.Add(File.Combine(File.DirRootExternal,
"SomeFile.txt"))
StartActivity(Message.GetIntent)
```

Members:

- Attachments As List
- BCC As List
- Body As String
- CC As List
- GetHtmlIntent As Intent
- GetIntent As Intent
- Subject As String
- To As List

Attachments As List

BCC As List

Body As String

CC As List

GetHtmlIntent As Intent

Returns the Intent that should be sent with StartActivity. The email message will be an HTML message.

GetIntent As Intent

Returns the Intent that should be sent with StartActivity.

Subject As String

To As List

LogCat

LogCat allows you to read the internal phone logs. Refer to the LogCat documentation (http://developer.android.com/intl/fr/guide/developing/tools/adb.html) for more information about the optional arguments. The LogCatData event is raised when there is new data available. You should use BytesToString to convert the raw bytes to string.
Note that the LogCatData event is raised in a different thread. This means that you can only log the messages.
You can also use the Threading library to delegate the data to the main thread.

Permissions:

android.permission.READ_LOGS

Event: LogCatData (Buffer() As Byte, Length As Int)

The LogCatData event is raised when there is new data available.

Members:

- LogCatStart (Args() As String, EventName As String)
- LogCatStop

LogCatStart (Args() As String, EventName As String)

Starts tracking the logs.
Args - Optional arguments passed to the internal LogCat command.
EventName - The Sub that will handle the LogCatData event.

LogCatStop

Stops tracking the logs.

PackageManager

The PackageManager allows you to find information about installed applications. Applications are referenced using their package name. You can get a list of all the packages by calling **`GetInstalledPackages`**.

Members:

- GetApplicationIcon (Package As String) As Drawable
- GetApplicationIntent (Package As String) As IntentWrapper
- GetApplicationLabel (Package As String) As String
- GetInstalledPackages As List
- GetVersionCode (Package As String) As Int
- GetVersionName (Package As String) As String
- QueryIntentActivities (Intent1 As Intent) As List

GetApplicationIcon (Package As String) As Drawable

Returns the application icon. Example:

```
Dim pm As PackageManager
Activity.Background = pm.GetApplicationIcon(
"com.google.android.youtube")
```

GetApplicationIntent (Package As String) As IntentWrapper

Returns an Intent object that can be used to start the given application. Example:

```
Dim In As Intent
Dim pm As PackageManager
In = pm.GetApplicationIntent("com.google.android.youtube")
If In.IsInitialized Then StartActivity(In)
```

GetApplicationLabel (Package As String) As String

Returns the application label.

GetInstalledPackages As List

Returns a list of the installed packages. Example:

```
Dim pm As PackageManager
Dim packages As List
packages = pm.GetInstalledPackages
For i = 0 To packages.Size - 1
  Log(packages.Get(i))
Next
```

GetVersionCode (Package As String) As Int

Returns the application version code.

GetVersionName (Package As String) As String

Returns the application version name.

QueryIntentActivities (Intent1 As Intent) As List

Returns a list of the installed activities that can handle the given intent. Each item in the list is the "component name" of an activity. You can use **`Intent.SetComponent`** to explicitly choose the activity. The first item is considered the best match. For example, the following code lists all the activities that can "view" a text file:

```
Dim pm As PackageManager
Dim Intent1 As Intent
Intent1.Initialize(Intent1.ACTION_VIEW, "file://")
Intent1.SetType("text/*")
For Each cn As String In pm.QueryIntentActivities(Intent1)
 Log(cn)
Next
```

Phone

Members:

- GetDataState As String
- GetMaxVolume (Channel As Int) As Int
- GetNetworkOperatorName As String
- GetNetworkType As String
- GetPhoneType As String
- GetResourceDrawable (ResourceId As Int) As Drawable
- GetRingerMode As Int
- GetSettings (Settings As String) As String
- GetSimOperator As String
- GetVolume (Channel As Int) As Int
- HideKeyboard (Activity As ActivityWrapper)
- IsAirplaneModeOn As Boolean
- IsNetworkRoaming As Boolean
- Manufacturer As String [read only]
- Model As String [read only]
- Product As String [read only]

- RINGER_NORMAL As Int
- RINGER_SILENT As Int
- RINGER_VIBRATE As Int
- SdkVersion As Int [read only]
- SendBroadcastIntent (Intent1 As Intent)
- SetMute (Channel As Int, Mute As Boolean)
- SetRingerMode (Mode As Int)
- SetScreenBrightness (Value As Float)
- SetScreenOrientation (Orientation As Int)
- SetVolume (page 468) (Channel As Int, VolumeIndex As Int, ShowUI As Boolean)
- Shell (page 468) (Command As String, Args() As String, StdOut As StringBuilder, StdErr As StringBuilder) As Int
- VOLUME_ALARM (page 468) As Int
- VOLUME_MUSIC (page 468) As Int
- VOLUME_NOTIFICATION (page 468) As Int
- VOLUME_RING (page 468) As Int
- VOLUME_SYSTEM (page 468) As Int
- VOLUME_VOICE_CALL (page 468) As Int

GetDataState As String

Returns the current cellular data connection state.
Possible values: DISCONNECTED, CONNECTING, CONNECTED, SUSPENDED.

GetMaxVolume (Channel As Int) As Int

Gets the maximum volume index (value) for the given channel.
Channel - One of the VOLUME constants given above.

GetNetworkOperatorName As String

Returns the name of the current registered operator. Returns an empty string if it is not available.

GetNetworkType As String

Returns the currently used cellular network type. Possible values:
1xRTT, CDMA, EDGE, EHRPD, EVDO_0, EVDO_A, EVDO_B, GPRS, HSDPA, HSPA, HSPAP, HSUPA, IDEN, LTE, UMTS, UNKNOWN.

GetPhoneType As String

Returns the phone radio type. Possible values: CDMA, GSM, NONE.

GetResourceDrawable (ResourceId As Int) As Drawable

Returns an internal drawable object. See this page (http://developer.android.com/intl/fr/reference/android/R.drawable.html) for a list of available resources.
Example:

```
Dim p As Phone
Dim bd As BitmapDrawable
bd = p.GetResourceDrawable(17301618)
Activity.AddMenuItem2("Menu1", "Menu1", bd.Bitmap)
```

GetRingerMode As Int

Returns the phone ringer mode. Value will be one of the RINGER constants.

GetSettings (Settings As String) As String

Returns the value of the phone settings based on the given key. The possible keys are listed here (http://developer.android.com/intl/fr/reference/android/provider/Settings.Secure.html) . The keys are lower cased. Example:

```
Dim p As Phone
Log(GetSettings("android_id"))
```

GetSimOperator As String

Returns the code of the SIM provider. Returns an empty string if it is not available.

GetVolume (Channel As Int) As Int

Returns the volume of the specified channel.
Channel - One of the VOLUME constants.

HideKeyboard (Activity As ActivityWrapper)

Hides the soft keyboard if it is displayed. Example:

```
Dim p As Phone
p.HideKeyboard(Activity)
```

IsAirplaneModeOn As Boolean

Returns **TRUE** if the phone "airplane mode" is on.

IsNetworkRoaming As Boolean

Returns **True** if the device is considered roaming on the current network.

Manufacturer As String [read only]

Model As String [read only]

Product As String [read only]

RINGER_NORMAL As Int

Normal phone ringer mode.

RINGER_SILENT As Int

Phone ringer will be silent and the device will NOT vibrate.

RINGER_VIBRATE As Int

Phone ringer will be silent and the device will vibrate.

SdkVersion As Int [read only]

Returns an integer describing the SDK version.

SendBroadcastIntent (Intent1 As Intent)

Sends an intent to all BroadcastReceivers that listen to this type of intent. Example of asking the media scanner to rescan a file:

```
Dim i As Intent
i.Initialize("android.intent.action.MEDIA_SCANNER_SCAN_FILE", _
  "file://" & File.Combine(File.DirRootExternal,
"pictures/1.jpg"))
Dim p As Phone
p.SendBroadcastIntent(i)
```

SetMute (Channel As Int, Mute As Boolean)

Mutes or unmutes the given channel.
Channel - One of the VOLUME constants.
Mute - Whether to mute or unmute the channel.

SetRingerMode (Mode As Int)

Sets the phone ringer mode.
Mode - One of the RINGER constants.
Example:

```
Dim p As Phone
p.SetRingerMode(p.RINGER_VIBRATE)
```

SetScreenBrightness (Value As Float)

Sets the brightness of the current activity. This method cannot be called from a service module.
Value - A float from 0 to 1. Set `-1` for automatic brightness.
Example:

```
Sub Process_Globals
  Dim phone1 As Phone
End Sub
Sub Globals
  Dim sb As SeekBar
End Sub
Sub Activity_Create(FirstTime As Boolean)
  sb.Initialize("sb")
  sb.Max = 100
  sb.Value = 50
  Activity.AddView(sb, 10dip, 10dip, 90%x, 30dip)
End Sub
Sub sb_ValueChanged (Value As Int, UserChanged As Boolean)
  phone1.SetScreenBrightness(Max(Value, 5) / 100)
End Sub
```

SetScreenOrientation (Orientation As Int)

Changes the current activity orientation. This method cannot be called from a service module.
Orientation - `-1` (minus 1) for unspecified, 0 for landscape and 1 for portrait.

SetVolume (Channel As Int, VolumeIndex As Int, ShowUI As Boolean)

Sets the volume of the specified channel.
Channel - One of the VOLUME constants.
VolumeIndex - The volume index. GetMaxVolume can be used to find the largest possible value.
ShowUI - Whether to show the volume UI windows.
Example:

```
Dim p As Phone
p.SetVolume(p.VOLUME_MUSIC, 3, True)
```

Shell (Command As String, Args() As String, StdOut As StringBuilder, StdErr As StringBuilder) As Int

Runs a native shell command. Many commands are inaccessible because of OS security restrictions. Returns the process exit value.
Command - Command to run.
Args - Additional arguments. Can be `Null` if not needed.
StdOut - A StringBuilder that will hold the standard output value. Can be `Null` if not needed.
StdErr - A StringBuilder that will hold the standard error value. Can be `Null` if not needed.
Example:

```
Dim p As Phone
Dim sb As StringBuilder
sb.Initialize
p.Shell("df", Null, sb, Null)
Msgbox(sb.ToString, "Free space:")
```

VOLUME_ALARM As Int

Alarms channel.

VOLUME_MUSIC As Int

Music channel.

VOLUME_NOTIFICATION As Int

Notifications channel.

VOLUME_RING As Int

Phone ring channel.

VOLUME_SYSTEM As Int

System sounds channel.

VOLUME_VOICE_CALL As Int

Voice calls channel.

PhoneAccelerometer

This is a legacy object and should not be used. The PhoneSensors (page 473) object provides greater functionality, supports all existing sensors and will be expanded to support future ones. That should be used instead.

PhoneCalls

This object creates an intent that launches the phone application. The reason that it is not part of the PhoneIntents library is that it requires an additional permission (page 83).

Permissions:

android.permission.CALL_PHONE

Member:

Call (PhoneNumber As String) As Intent

Creates an intent that will call a phone number.
Example:

```
Dim p As PhoneCalls
StartActivity(p.Call("1234567890"))
```

PhoneEvents

The Android OS sends all kinds of messages to notify applications of changes in the system. The PhoneEvents object allows you to catch such messages and handle those events in your program.
Usually, you will want to add this object to a **Service** module instead of an **Activity** module in order not to miss events that happen while your activity is paused. You should declare this object in **`Sub Process_Globals`** and initialize it in **`Sub Service_Create`**. For example, to monitor the level of the battery you could use:

```
Sub Process_Globals
 Dim phoneEvent As PhoneEvents
End Sub

Sub Activity_Create(FirstTime As Boolean)
 phoneEvent.Initialize("phoneEvent")
End Sub

Sub phoneEvent_BatteryChanged (Level As Int, Scale As Int, _
    Plugged As Boolean, Intent As Intent)
 Log(Intent.GetExtra("level"))
End Sub
```

Events:

Note that each event has an Intent (page 314), sent by Android, carrying extra information.

AirplaneModeChanged (State As Boolean, Intent As Intent)

Raised when the "airplane mode" state changes.
State - **`True`** when airplane mode is active.

Intent - this object is sent by Android.

BatteryChanged (Level As Int, Scale As Int, Plugged As Boolean, Intent As Intent)

Raised when the battery status changes.
Level - The current level.
Scale - The maximum level.
Plugged - Whether the device is plugged to an electricity source.
Intent - this object is sent by Android.

ConnectivityChanged (NetworkType As String, State As String, Intent As Intent)

There was a change in the state of the WIFI network or the MOBILE network (other network).
NetworkType - WIFI or MOBILE.
State - One of the following values: CONNECTING, CONNECTED, SUSPENDED, DISCONNECTING, DISCONNECTED, UNKNOWN.
Intent - this object is sent by Android.

DeviceStorageLow (Intent As Intent)

Raised when the device internal memory condition is low.
Intent - this object is sent by Android.

DeviceStorageOk (Intent As Intent)

Raised when the device internal low memory condition no longer exists.
Intent - this object is sent by Android.

PackageAdded (Package As String, Intent As Intent)

An application was installed.
Package - The application package name.
Intent - this object is sent by Android.

PackageRemoved (Package As String, Intent As Intent)

An application was uninstalled.
Package - The application package name.
Intent - this object is sent by Android.

PhoneStateChanged (State As String, IncomingNumber As String, Intent As Intent)

The phone state has changed.
State - One of the three values: IDLE, OFFHOOK, RINGING. OFFHOOK means that there is a call or that the phone is dialing.
IncomingCall - Available when the State value is RINGING.
Intent - this object is sent by Android.

ScreenOff (Intent As Intent)

The screen has turned off.
Intent - this object is sent by Android.

ScreenOn (Intent As Intent)
The screen has turned on.
Intent - this object is sent by Android.

SmsDelivered (PhoneNumber As String, Intent As Intent)
An Sms message sent by your application was delivered to the recipient.
PhoneNumber - The target phone number.
Intent - this object is sent by Android.

SmsSentStatus (Success As Boolean, ErrorMessage As String, PhoneNumber As String, Intent As Intent)
Raised after your application sends an Sms message.
Success - Whether the message was sent successfully.
ErrorMessage - One of the following values: GENERIC_FAILURE, NO_SERVICE, RADIO_OFF, NULL_PDU or OK.
PhoneNumber - The target phone number.
Intent - this object is sent by Android.

Shutdown (Intent As Intent)
The phone is shutting down (turned off, not just sleeping).
Intent - this object is sent by Android.

TextToSpeechFinish (Intent As Intent)
The Text-To-Speech engine has finished processing the messages in the queue.
Intent - this object is sent by Android.

UserPresent (Intent As Intent)
The user has unlocked the keyguard screen.
Intent - this object is sent by Android.

Members:
- Initialize (EventName As String)
- InitializeWithPhoneState (EventName As String, PhoneId As PhoneId)
- StopListening

Initialize (EventName As String)
Initializes the object and starts listening for events.
The PhoneStateEvent will not be raised. Use InitializeWithPhoneState instead if it is needed.

InitializeWithPhoneState (EventName As String, PhoneId As PhoneId)
Initializes the object and starts listening for events. The PhoneStateEvent will also be handled. Example:

```
Dim PhoneId1 As PhoneId
Dim PE As PhoneEvents
PE.InitializeWithPhoneState("PE", PhoneId1)
```

StopListening

Stops listening for events. You can later call **`Initialize`** to start listening for events again.

PhoneId

Permissions:

android.permission.READ_PHONE_STATE

Members:

GetDeviceId As String

Returns a unique device Id. Returns an empty string if the device Id is not available (usually on wifi only devices).

GetLine1Number As String

Returns the phone number string for line 1 as configured in the SIM card. Returns an empty string if it is not available.

GetSimSerialNumber As String

Returns the serial number of the SIM card. Returns an empty string if it is not available.

GetSubscriberId As String

Returns the unique subscriber Id. Returns an empty string if it is not available.

PhoneIntents

This object contains methods that create intents objects. An intent does nothing until you call StartActivity with the intent. Calling StartActivity sends the intent to Android.

Members:

OpenBrowser (URI As String) As Intent

Creates an intent that will open the specified URI.
URI – a “Uniform Resource Identifier” identifying the web address of the page to open.
Example:

```
StartActivity
(PhoneIntents.OpenBrowser("http://www.google.com"))
```

PlayAudio (Dir As String, File As String) As Intent

Creates an intent that will start playing the given audio file with the default player. This method cannot work with internal files.

PlayVideo (Dir As String, File As String) As Intent

Creates an intent that will start playing the given video file with the default player. This method cannot work with internal files.

PhoneOrientation

This is a legacy object and should not be used. The PhoneSensors object provides greater functionality, supports all existing sensors and will be expanded to support future ones. It should be used instead.

PhoneSensors

Most Android-powered devices have built-in sensors that measure motion, orientation, and various environmental conditions. See the Members list below for the possible sensor types. Bear in mind that most devices do not support all possible sensors. The **`StartListening`** method returns **`False`** if the requested sensor is not supported.

Sensors are capable of providing raw data with high precision and accuracy, and are useful if you want to monitor three-dimensional device movement or positioning, or you want to monitor changes in the ambient environment near a device.

The PhoneSensors object allows you to listen for changes in one of the device sensors.

Example to check accelerometer and show values:

```
Sub Process_Globals
 Dim accel As PhoneSensors
End Sub

Sub Globals
 Dim lbl As Label
End Sub

Sub Activity_Create(FirstTime As Boolean)
 If FirstTime Then
  ' Initialize accelerometer
  accel.Initialize(accel.TYPE_ACCELEROMETER)
 End If

 ' Prepare label to receive data
 lbl.Initialize("")
 lbl.TextColor = Colors.White
 Activity.AddView(lbl, 10dip, 10dip, 100%x - 10dip, 45dip)

End Sub

Sub Activity_Resume
 'Here we start listening for SensorChanged events.
 'By checking the return value we know if the sensor is
supported.

 If accel.StartListening("accel") = False Then
  lbl.Text = "Accelerometer is not supported."
  Log("Accelerometer is not supported.")
 End If
```

```
End Sub

Sub Activity_Pause (UserClosed As Boolean)
 'Stop listening for events.
 accel.StopListening
End Sub

Sub accel_SensorChanged (Values() As Float)
 Dim ps As PhoneSensors
 'Get the PhoneSensors object that raised this event.
 ps = Sender
 If Sender = accel Then
  lbl.Text = "Accelerometer data: " _
   & " X=" & NumberFormat(Values(0), 0, 3) _
   & ", Y=" & NumberFormat(Values(1), 0, 3) _
   & ", Z=" & NumberFormat(Values(2), 0, 3)
 Else
  Log ("xxx")
 End If
End Sub
```

See here (http://bit.ly/16oqRsm) for a more detailed example.

Event: SensorChanged (Values() As Float)

After initializing the object and calling **StartListening**, the **SensorChanged** event will be raised each time the sensor value changes. The value is passed as an array of Floats. Some sensors pass a single value and some pass three values. Example:

```
Sub Sensor_SensorChanged (Values() As Float)
 Dim ps As PhoneSensors
 Dim sd As SensorData
 Dim lbl As Label
 'Get the PhoneSensors object that raised this event.
 ps = Sender
 sd = SensorsMap.Get(ps) 'Get the associated SensorData object
 lbl = SensorsLabels.Get(ps) 'Get the associated Label
 If sd.ThreeValues Then
  lbl.Text = sd.Name & " X=" _
   & NumberFormat(Values(0), 0, 3) & ", Y=" &
NumberFormat(Values(1), 0, 3) _
   & ", Z=" & NumberFormat(Values(2), 0, 3)
 Else
  lbl.Text = sd.Name & " = " & NumberFormat(Values(0), 0, 3)
 End If
End Sub
```

Members:

- Initialize (SensorType As Int)
- Initialize2 (SensorType As Int, SensorDelay As Int)
- MaxValue As Float [read only]

- StartListening (EventName As String) As Boolean
- StopListening
- TYPE_ACCELEROMETER As Int
- TYPE_GYROSCOPE As Int
- TYPE_LIGHT As Int
- TYPE_MAGNETIC_FIELD As Int
- TYPE_ORIENTATION As Int
- TYPE_PRESSURE As Int
- TYPE_PROXIMITY As Int
- TYPE_TEMPERATURE As Int

Initialize (SensorType As Int)

Initializes the object and sets the sensor type (one of the **TYPE** constants).

Initialize2 (SensorType As Int, SensorDelay As Int)

Initializes the object and sets the sensor type and sensor events rate.
SensorType - One of the **TYPE** constants.
SensorDelay - A value from 0 (fastest rate) to 3 (slowest rate). This is only a hint to the system.

MaxValue As Float [read only]

Returns the maximum value for this sensor.
Returns **-1** if this sensor is not supported.

StartListening (EventName As String) As Boolean

Starts listening for sensor events. Returns **True** if the sensor is supported. Usually, you will want to start listening in **Sub Activity_Resume** and stop listening in **Sub Activity_Pause**.

StopListening

Stops listening for events.

TYPE_ACCELEROMETER As Int

A constant identifying the Accelerometer sensor.

```
Dim accel As PhoneSensors
accel.Initialize(accel.TYPE_ACCELEROMETER)
```

The SensorChanged event receives an array of three values when this type of sensor changes. See example above. The values give the acceleration measured in Meters / Second ^ 2 for each axis (X, Y and Z).

TYPE_GYROSCOPE As Int

A constant identifying the Gyroscope sensor. The SensorChanged event receives an array of three values when this type of sensor changes. See example above. The values give the angular velocity measured in Radians / Second around each of the three axis.

TYPE_LIGHT As Int

A constant identifying the Light sensor. The SensorChanged event receives a single value when this type of sensor changes. See example above. The values give the ambient light level measured in SI lux units.

TYPE_MAGNETIC_FIELD As Int

A constant identifying the Magnetic field sensor. The SensorChanged event receives an array of three values when this type of sensor changes. See example above. The values give the ambient magnetic field measured in micro-Tesla for the X, Y and Z axis.

TYPE_ORIENTATION As Int

A constant identifying the Orientation sensor. The SensorChanged event receives an array of three values when this type of sensor changes. See example above. The values give the orientation measured in degrees for azimuth, pitch and roll.

TYPE_PRESSURE As Int

A constant identifying the Pressure sensor. The SensorChanged event receives a single value when this type of sensor changes. See example above. The values give the atmospheric pressure in units of hectoPascals (hPa) or, equivalently, millibars (mbar).

TYPE_PROXIMITY As Int

A constant identifying the Proximity sensor. The SensorChanged event receives a single value when this type of sensor changes. See example above. The values give the proximity measured in centimeters. Most devices will return only two possible values representing "near" and "far".
"far" should match MaxRange and "near" should be a value smaller than MaxRange.

TYPE_TEMPERATURE As Int

A constant identifying the Temperature sensor. The SensorChanged event receives a single value when this type of sensor changes. See example above. The values give the ambient temperature in degrees Celsius.

PhoneSms

Permissions:

android.permission.SEND_SMS

Members:

Send (PhoneNumber As String, Text As String)

Sends an Sms message. Note that this method actually sends the message (unlike most other methods that create an intent object). You can use `PhoneEvents` to handle the `SmsSentStatus` and `SmsDelivered` events. This method is equivalent to calling `PhoneSms.Send2(PhoneNumber, Text, True, True)`

Send2 (PhoneNumber As String, Text As String, ReceiveSentNotification As Boolean, ReceiveDeliveredNotification As Boolean)

Sends an Sms message without notification. Note that this method actually sends the message (unlike most other methods that create an intent object). You can use **`PhoneEvents`** to handle the **`SmsSentStatus`** and **`SmsDelivered`** events.

ReceiveSentNotification - If True then the SmsSentStatus PhoneEvent will be raised when the message is sent.

ReceiveDeliveredNotification - If True then the PhoneEvent SmsDelivered will be raised when the message is delivered.

Example:

```
Sub Globals
 Dim Sms As PhoneSms
 Dim PE As PhoneEvents
 Dim btnTest As Button
 Dim strPhoneNumber As String = "01234567890"
End Sub

Sub Activity_Create(FirstTime As Boolean)
 PE.Initialize("PE")
 Sms.Send2(strPhoneNumber, "This sms was sent from
Basic4Android",  True, True)
End Sub

Sub PE_SmsDelivered (PhoneNumber As String, Intent As Intent)
 Log ("SMS delivered to " & PhoneNumber)
End Sub

Sub PE_SmsSentStatus (Success As Boolean, ErrorMessage As
String, PhoneNumber As String, Intent As Intent)
 If Success = True Then
  Log ("SMS Sent to " & PhoneNumber)
 Else
  Log ("Failed to send SMS to " & PhoneNumber & ". Error = " &
ErrorMessage)
 End If
End Sub
```

PhoneVibrate

Permissions:

android.permission.VIBRATE

Members:

Vibrate (TimeMs As Long)

Vibrates the phone for the specified duration.

PhoneWakeState

The PhoneWakeState object allows you to prevent the device from turning off the screen. Once you call **`KeepAlive`**, the phone screen will stay on till you call ReleaseKeepAlive. It is important to eventually release it. A **recommended usage** is to call KeepAlive in **`Activity_Resume`** and call **`ReleaseKeepAlive`** in **`Activity_Pause`**.
Note that the user can still turn off the screen by pressing on the power button. Calling **`PartialLock`** will prevent the CPU from going to sleep even if the user presses on the power button. It will not, however, affect the screen.

Permissions:

android.permission.WAKE_LOCK

Members:

KeepAlive (BrightScreen As Boolean)

Prevents the device from going to sleep. Call ReleaseKeepAlive to release the power lock.
BrightScreen - Whether to keep the screen bright or dimmed.

PartialLock

Acquires a partial lock. This will prevent the CPU from going to sleep, even if the user presses on the power button. **Make sure** to call ReleasePartialLock eventually to release this lock.

ReleaseKeepAlive

Releases the power lock and allows the device to go to sleep.

ReleasePartialLock

Releases a partial lock that was previously acquired by calling **`PartialLock`**.

RingtoneManager

The RingtoneManager object allows you to set or get the default ringtone. It also provides access to the default ringtone picker. The **`PickerResult`** event will be raised when the picker is closed with the URI ("Uniform Resource Identifier", ie the address) of the selected ringtone. **Note** that an empty string will be returned if the "Silence" option was selected. Example of playing the selected ringtone with MediaPlayer:

```
Sub Process_Globals
  Dim rm As RingtoneManager
  Dim mp As MediaPlayer
End Sub
Sub Globals
End Sub
Sub Activity_Create(FirstTime As Boolean)
  mp.Initialize
  rm.ShowRingtonePicker("rm", rm.TYPE_RINGTONE, True, "")
End Sub
Sub rm_PickerResult (Success As Boolean, URI As String)
  If Success Then
     If URI = "" Then
         ToastMessageShow("Silent was chosen", True)
     Else
         mp.Load(rm.GetContentDir, URI)
         mp.Play
     End If
  Else
     ToastMessageShow("Error loading ringtone.", True)
  End If
End Sub
```

Permissions:

android.permission.WRITE_SETTINGS

Event: PickerResult (Success As Boolean, URI As String)

URI – the “Uniform Resource Identifier” specifying the address of the selected ringtone.

Members:

AddToMediaStore (Dir As String, FileName As String, Title As String, IsAlarm As Boolean, IsNotification As Boolean, IsRingtone As Boolean, IsMusic As Boolean) As String

Adds a sound file to the internal media store and returns the URI (address) to the new entry.
Dir - The file folder. Should be a folder under the storage card (public folder).
FileName - The file name.
Title - The entry title.
IsAlarm - Whether this entry should be added to the alarms sound list.
IsNotification - Whether this entry should be added to the notifications sound list.
IsRingtone - Whether this entry should be added to the ringtones sound list.
IsMusic - Whether this entry should be added to the music list.
Example:

```
Dim r As RingtoneManager
Dim u As String
u = r.AddToMediaStore(File.DirRootExternal, "bounce.mp3",
"Bounce!", True, True, True, True)
r.SetDefault(r.TYPE_RINGTONE, u)
```

DeleteRingtone (URI As String)

Deletes the given entry.
URI – the "Uniform Resource Identifier" (the address) of the ringtone to delete.

GetContentDir As String

Returns a string that represents the virtual content folder. This can be used to play a Ringtone with MediaPlayer.

GetDefault (Type As Int) As String

Returns the URI (address) of the default ringtone of a specific type, or an empty string if no default is available. Example:

```
Dim mp As MediaPlayer
mp.Initialize
Dim r As RingtoneManager
mp.Load(r.GetContentDir, r.GetDefault(r.TYPE_NOTIFICATION))
mp.Play
```

SetDefault (Type As Int, URI As String)

Sets the default ringtone for the given type.
URI – the "Uniform Resource Identifier" (the address) of the new ringtone default. In order to get the URI, you should use **`AddToMediaStore`** (for new sounds) or **`ShowRingtonePicker`** (for existing sounds).

ShowRingtonePicker (EventName As String, Type As Int, IncludeSilence As Boolean, ChosenRingtone As String)

Shows the ringtone picker activity. The PickerResult will be raised after the user selects a ringtone.
EventName - Sets the sub that will handle the PickerResult event.
Type - Defines the type(s) of sounds that will be listed. Multiple types can be set using Bit.Or.
IncludeSilence - Whether to include the Silence option in the list.
ChosenRingtone - The URI (address) of the ringtone that will be selected when the dialog opens. Pass an empty string if not needed.

TYPE_ALARM As Int

TYPE_NOTIFICATION As Int

TYPE_RINGTONE As Int

Sms

Represents an SMS message. SMS messages are retrieved using an SmsMessages object.

Members:

- Address As String
- Body As String
- Date As Long
- Id As Int
- PersonId As Int
- Read As Boolean
- ThreadId As Int
- Type As Int

Address As String
The message address.

Body As String
Message body.

Date As Long
The date of this message.

Id As Int
Message internal Id.

PersonId As Int
The Id of the person who sent the message. It will be `-1` if this data is missing. You can find more information about this person by calling **`Contacts.GetById`**.

Read As Boolean
Whether this message has been read.

ThreadId As Int
Thread Id.

Type As Int
The message type. One of the SmsMessages constant values.

SmsInterceptor
Listens for incoming SMS messages. The MessageReceived event is raised when a new message arrives. Returning **`True`** from the MessageReceived event will cause the broadcasted message to be aborted.
This can be used to prevent the message from reaching the standard SMS application.
However, in order for your application to receive the message before other applications, you should use Initialize2 and set the priority value to a value larger than 0. It should be 999 according to the Android documentation.

Permissions:

android.permission.RECEIVE_SMS

Event: MessageReceived (From As String, Body As String) As Boolean

Members:

Initialize (EventName As String)

Initializes the object and starts listening for new messages.

Initialize2 (EventName As String, Priority As Int)

Initializes the object and starts listening for new messages. **Priority** defines the application priority compared to other applications that listen to incoming messages. According to the official Android documentation, in order to receive the message first, you should set **Priority** to 999. However, it is possible that a third party application has used a higher value. The highest possible value is the maximum value of an Int, 2147483647.

StopListening

Stops listening for events. You can later call Initialize to start listening again.

SmsMessages

Provides access to the stored SMS messages. **Note** that you can use PhoneSms to send SMS messages. Example of printing all messages from the last week:

```
Dim SmsMessages1 As SmsMessages
Dim List1 As List
List1 = SmsMessages1.GetAllSince(DateTime.Add(DateTime.Now, 0,
0, -7))
For i = 0 To List1.Size - 1
  Dim Sms1 As Sms
  Sms1 = List1.Get(i)
  Log(Sms1)
Next
```

Permissions:

android.permission.READ_SMS

Members:

- GetAll As List
- GetAllSince (Date As Long) As List
- GetBetweenDates (StartDate As Long, EndDate As Long) As List
- GetByPersonId (PersonId As Int) As List
- GetByThreadId (ThreadId As Int) As List
- GetByType (Type As Int) As List
- GetUnreadMessages As List

The following are the defined TYPE constants:

- TYPE_DRAFT As Int
- TYPE_FAILED As Int
- TYPE_INBOX As Int
- TYPE_OUTBOX As Int

- TYPE_QUEUED As Int
- TYPE_SENT As Int
- TYPE_UNKNOWN As Int

GetAll As List

Returns all stored messages.

GetAllSince (Date As Long) As List

Returns all messages with a date value on or after the given date.

GetBetweenDates (StartDate As Long, EndDate As Long) As List

Returns all messages between the given dates. Start value is inclusive and end value is exclusive.

GetByPersonId (PersonId As Int) As List

Returns a list with all messages received from the person with the given Id.

GetByThreadId (ThreadId As Int) As List

Returns a list with all messages with the given ThreadId.

GetByType (Type As Int) As List

Returns a list with all messages of the given type. The type should be one of the **TYPE** constants.

GetUnreadMessages As List

Returns all unread messages.

TYPE_DRAFT As Int

TYPE_FAILED As Int

TYPE_INBOX As Int

TYPE_OUTBOX As Int

TYPE_QUEUED As Int

TYPE_SENT As Int

TYPE_UNKNOWN As Int

VoiceRecognition

Most Android devices support voice recognition (speech to text). Usually, the service works by sending the audio stream to some external server which analyzes the stream and returns the possible results. Therefore, a data connection is required. You should declare a VoiceRecognition object as a `Sub Process_Globals` object and initialize it in `Activity_Create` when `FirstTime` is `True`. Later, when you call `Listen`, a dialog will be displayed, asking the user to speak.

Event: Result (Success As Boolean, Texts As List)

The `Result` event will be raised with a **Success** flag and a list with the possible results (usually one result). You will need a Sub to process the result:

```
Sub VR_Result (Success As Boolean, Texts As List)
 If Success = True Then
  ToastMessageShow(Texts.Get(0), True)
 End If
End Sub
```

Members:

- Initialize (EventName As String)
- IsSupported As Boolean
- Language As String [write only]
- Listen
- Prompt As String [write only]

Initialize (EventName As String)

Initializes the object and sets the Sub that will catch the Ready event. Example:

```
Dim VR As VoiceRecognition
VR.Initialize("VR")
```

IsSupported As Boolean

Returns **TRUE** if voice recognition is supported on this device.

Language As String [write only]

Sets the language used. By default, the device default language is used. Example:

```
VR.Language = "en"
```

Listen

Starts listening. The Ready event will be raised when the result arrives.

Prompt As String [write only]

Sets the prompt that is displayed in the "Speak now" dialog in addition to the "Speak now" message.

PreferenceActivity Library

The PreferenceActivity library (included in the IDE installation package) allows you to show the standard settings interface and provides an easy way to handle applications settings.

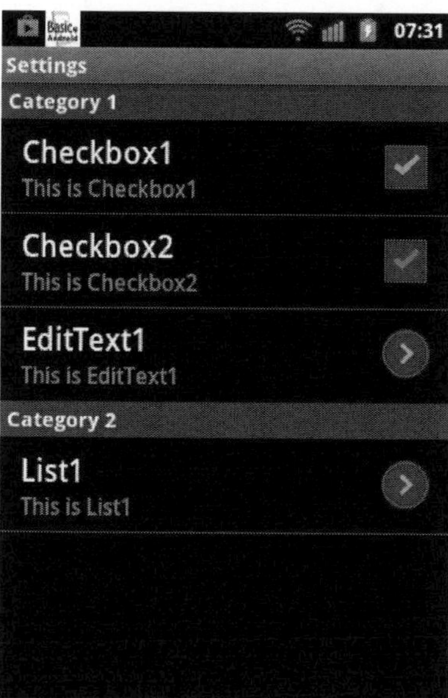

In order to use this library, you need to edit the manifest file (using the Manifest Editor (page 70)) and add the line:

```
AddApplicationText(<activity
android:name="anywheresoftware.b4a.objects.preferenceactivity"/>
)
```

See the tutorial (http://bit.ly/11jIyFd) (and the example project which it contains) for more information about how to use this library. **Note**: although the modification to the manifest is not visible in the example project (because the manifest is read-only), it is still required in any projects you create that use this library.

List of types:

PreferenceCategory
PreferenceManager
PreferenceScreen

PreferenceCategory

PreferenceCategory holds a group of other preferences.

Members:

- AddCheckBox (Key As String, Title As String, Summary As String, DefaultValue As Boolean)
- AddEditText (Key As String, Title As String, Summary As String, DefaultValue As String)
- AddList (Key As String, Title As String, Summary As String, DefaultValue As String, Values As List)
- AddPreferenceCategory (PreferenceCategory As PreferenceCategory)
- AddPreferenceScreen (PreferenceScreen As PreferenceScreen)
- CreateIntent As Intent

Initialize (Title As String)

AddCheckBox (Key As String, Title As String, Summary As String, DefaultValue As Boolean)

Adds a preference entry with a check box. The entry values can be either **`True`** or **`False`**.
Key - The preference key associated with the value.
Title - Entry title.
Summary - Entry summary (second row).
DefaultValue - The default value of this preference entry if the key does not already exist.

AddEditText (Key As String, Title As String, Summary As String, DefaultValue As String)

Adds a preference entry which allows the user to enter free text.
Key - The preference key associated with the value.
Title - Entry title.
Summary - Entry summary (second row).
DefaultValue - The default value of this preference entry if the key does not already exist.

AddList (Key As String, Title As String, Summary As String, DefaultValue As String, Values As List)

Adds a preference entry which allows the user to choose a single item out of a list.
Key - The preference key associated with the value.
Title - Entry title.
Summary - Entry summary (second row).
DefaultValue - The default value of this preference entry, if the key does not already exist. Should match one of the strings in **Values**.
Values - A list of strings with the possible values.

AddPreferenceCategory (PreferenceCategory As PreferenceCategory)

Adds a PreferenceCategory. A preference category is made of a title and a group of entries. **Note** that a PreferenceCategory cannot hold other PreferenceCategories.

AddPreferenceScreen (PreferenceScreen As PreferenceScreen)

Adds a secondary PreferenceScreen. When the user presses on this entry, the second screen will appear.

CreateIntent As Intent

Creates the Intent object that is required for showing the PreferencesActivity.
Example:

```
StartActivity(PreferenceScreen1.CreateIntent)
```

Initialize (Title As String)

Initializes the object and sets the category title.

PreferenceManager

Provides access to the saved settings. Using PreferenceManager, you can get the stored values and modify them.

Members:

- ClearAll
- GetAll As Map
- GetBoolean (Key As String) As Boolean
- GetString (Key As String) As String
- GetUpdatedKeys As List
- SetBoolean (Key As String, Value As Boolean)
- SetString (Key As String, Value As String)

ClearAll

Clears all stored entries.

GetAll As Map

Returns a Map with all the Keys and Values. Note that changes to this map will not affect the stored values.

GetBoolean (Key As String) As Boolean

Returns the Boolean value mapped to the given key. Returns `False` if the key is not found.

GetString (Key As String) As String

Returns the String value mapped to the given key. Returns an empty string if the key is not found.

GetUpdatedKeys As List

Returns a list with the keys that were updated since the last call to GetUpdatedKeys. Note that the updated keys may include keys with unchanged values. If, for example, the user changed the value of an item, and then restored it to the original value, this item would still be returned in the list of updated keys.

SetBoolean (Key As String, Value As Boolean)

Maps the given key to the given Boolean value.

SetString (Key As String, Value As String)

Maps the given key to the given String value.

PreferenceScreen

Members:

- AddCheckBox (Key As String, Title As String, Summary As String, DefaultValue As Boolean)
- AddEditText (Key As String, Title As String, Summary As String, DefaultValue As String)

AddList (Key As String, Title As String, Summary As String, DefaultValue As String, Values As List)
AddPreferenceCategory (PreferenceCategory As PreferenceCategory)
AddPreferenceScreen (PreferenceScreen As PreferenceScreen)
CreateIntent As Intent
Initialize (Title As String, Summary As String)

AddCheckBox (Key As String, Title As String, Summary As String, DefaultValue As Boolean)

Adds a preference entry with a check box. The entry values can be either **`True`** or **`False`**.
Key - The preference key associated with the value.
Title - Entry title.
Summary - Entry summary (second row).
DefaultValue - The default value of this preference entry if the key does not already exist.

AddEditText (Key As String, Title As String, Summary As String, DefaultValue As String)

Adds a preference entry which allows the user to enter free text.
Key - The preference key associated with the value.
Title - Entry title.
Summary - Entry summary (second row).
DefaultValue - The default value of this preference entry if the key does not already exist.

AddList (Key As String, Title As String, Summary As String, DefaultValue As String, Values As List)

Adds a preference entry which allows the user to choose a single item out of a list.
Key - The preference key associated with the value.
Title - Entry title.
Summary - Entry summary (second row).
DefaultValue - The default value of this preference entry if the key does not already exist. Should match one of the strings in **Values**.
Values - A list of strings with the possible values.

AddPreferenceCategory (PreferenceCategory As PreferenceCategory)

Adds a PreferenceCategory. A preference category is made of a title and a group of entries. Note that a PreferenceCategory cannot hold other PreferenceCategories.

AddPreferenceScreen (PreferenceScreen As PreferenceScreen)

Adds a secondary PreferenceScreen. When the user presses on this entry, the second screen will appear.

CreateIntent As Intent

Creates the Intent object that is required for showing the PreferencesActivity.
Example:

```
StartActivity(PreferenceScreen1.CreateIntent)
```

Initialize (Title As String, Summary As String)

Initializes the object and sets the title that will show. The summary will show for secondary PreferenceScreens.

RandomAccessFile Library

This library is included in the IDE installation package.

List of types:

AsyncStreams

The AsyncStreams object allows you to read from an InputStream and write to an OutputStream in the background without blocking the main thread.
See the AsyncStreams Tutorial (http://www.basic4ppc.com/forum/basic4android-getting-started-tutorials/7669-asyncstreams-tutorial.html).

Events:

NewData (Buffer() As Byte)

NewData event is raised only with full messages (not including the 4-bytes length value).

Error

Error event is raised when an error is encountered. You should check LastException to find the error.

Terminated

The Terminated event is raised when the other side has terminated the connection.

Members:

Close

Closes the associated streams.

Initialize (In As java.io.InputStream, Out As java.io.OutputStream, EventName As String)

Initializes the object. Unlike in prefix mode, the NewData event will be raised with new data as soon as it is available.
In - The InputStream that will be read. Pass `Null` if you only want to write with this object.
Out - The OutputStream that is used for writing the data. Pass `Null` if you only want to read with this object.
EventName - Determines the Subs that handle the NewData and Error events.

InitializePrefix (In As java.io.InputStream, BigEndian As Boolean, Out As java.io.OutputStream, EventName As String)
Initializes the object and sets it in "prefix" mode. In this mode, incoming data should adhere to the following protocol: every message should begin with the message length as an Int value (4 bytes). This length should not include the additional 4 bytes.
The NewData event will be raised only with full messages (not including the 4 bytes length value). The prefix Int value will be added to the output messages automatically. This makes it easier as you do not need to deal with broken messages.
In - The InputStream that will be read. Pass **`Null`** if you only want to write with this object.
BigEndian - Whether the length value is encoded in BigEndian or LittleEndian.
Out - The OutputStream that is used for writing the data. Pass **`Null`** if you only want to read with this object.
EventName - Determines the Subs that handle the NewData and Error events.

IsInitialized As Boolean
Returns **`TRUE`** if this object has been initialized.

OutputQueueSize As Int [read only]
Returns the number of messages waiting in the output queue.

Write (Buffer() As Byte) As Boolean
Adds the given byte-array to the output stream queue. If the object was initialized with **`InitializePrefix`**, then the array length will be added before the array.
Returns **`False`** if the queue is full and it is not possible to queue the data.

Write2 (Buffer() As Byte, Start As Int, Length As Int) As Boolean
Adds the given byte-array to the output stream queue. If the object was initialized with **`InitializePrefix`**, then the array length will be added before the array.
Returns **`False`** if the queue is full and it is not possible to queue the data.

CompressedStreams

The CompressedStreams object allows you to compress and decompress data using the **gzip** or the **zlib** compression methods. For more information about these, see http://en.wikipedia.org/wiki/Gzip and http://en.wikipedia.org/wiki/Zlib.
There are two options for working with CompressedStreams:

- Wrapping another stream by calling WrapInputStream or WrapOutputStream.
- Compressing or decompressing the data in memory.

The following example demonstrates the use of this object:

```
Sub Activity_Create(FirstTime As Boolean)
   Dim sb As StringBuilder
   sb.Initialize
   'Concatenation operations are much faster with StringBuilder
than with String.
   For i = 1 To 10000
      sb.Append("Playing with compressed streams.").Append(CRLF)
   Next
   Dim out As OutputStream
```

```
  Dim s As String
  Dim compress As CompressedStreams
  s = sb.ToString
  'Write the string without compressing it (we could have used
File.WriteString instead).
  out = File.OpenOutput(File.DirRootExternal, "test.txt", False)
  WriteStringToStream(out, s)

  'Write the string with gzip compression.
  out = File.OpenOutput(File.DirRootExternal, "test.gz", False)
  out = compress.WrapOutputStream(out, "gzip")
  WriteStringToStream(out, s)

  'Write the string with zlib compression
  out = File.OpenOutput(File.DirRootExternal, "test.zlib",
False)
  out = compress.WrapOutputStream(out, "zlib")
  WriteStringToStream(out, s)

  'Show the files sizes
  Msgbox("No compression: " & File.Size(File.DirRootExternal,
"test.txt") & CRLF _
     & "Gzip: " & File.Size(File.DirRootExternal, "test.gz") &
CRLF _
     & "zlib: " & File.Size(File.DirRootExternal, "test.zlib"),
"Files sizes")
  'Read data from a compressed file
  Dim in As InputStream
  in = File.OpenInput(File.DirRootExternal, "test.zlib")
  in = compress.WrapInputStream(in, "zlib")
  Dim reader As TextReader
  reader.Initialize(in)
  Dim line As String
  line = reader.ReadLine
  Msgbox(line, "First line")
  reader.Close

  'In memory compression / decompression
  Dim data() As Byte
  data = "Playing with in-memory compression.".GetBytes("UTF8")
  Dim compressed(), decompressed() As Byte
  compressed = compress.CompressBytes(data, "gzip")
  decompressed = compress.DecompressBytes(compressed, "gzip")
  'In this case the compressed data is longer than the
decompressed data.
  'The data is too short for the compression to be useful.
  Log("Compressed: " & compressed.Length)
  Log("Decompressed: " & decompressed.Length)
```

```
  Msgbox(BytesToString(decompressed,0, decompressed.Length,
"UTF8"), "")
End Sub
Sub WriteStringToStream(Out As OutputStream, s As String)
  Dim t As TextWriter
  t.Initialize(Out)
  t.Write(s)
  t.Close 'Closes the internal stream as well
End Sub
```

Members:

CompressBytes (Data() As Byte, CompressMethod As String) As Byte()

Returns a byte array with the compressed data.
Data - Data to compress.
CompressMethod - The name of the compression method (gzip or zlib).

DecompressBytes (CompressedData() As Byte, CompressMethod As String) As Byte()

Returns a byte array with the decompressed data.
CompressedData - The compressed data that should be decompressed.
CompressMethod - The name of the compression method (gzip or zlib).

WrapInputStream (In As java.io.InputStream, CompressMethod As String) As InputStreamWrapper

Wraps an input stream and returns an input stream that automatically decompresses the stream when it is read.
In - The original input stream.
CompressMethod - The name of the compression method (gzip or zlib).

WrapOutputStream (Out As java.io.OutputStream, CompressMethod As String) As OutputStreamWrapper

Wraps an output stream and returns an output stream that automatically compresses the data when it is written to the stream.
Out - The original output stream.
CompressMethod - The name of the compression method (gzip or zlib).

CountingInputStream

`CountingInputStream` and **`CountingOutputStream`** allow you to monitor the reading or writing progress. Counting streams wrap the actual stream and provide a **`Count`** property which allows you to get the number of bytes read or written.
Counting streams are useful when the reading or writing operations are done in the background. You can then use a timer to monitor the progress. This example logs the downloading progress:

```
Sub Process_Globals
  Dim hc As HttpClient
  Dim cout As CountingOutputStream
```

```
    Dim length As Int
    Dim timer1 As Timer
End Sub
Sub Globals
End Sub
Sub Activity_Create(FirstTime As Boolean)
    If FirstTime Then
        hc.Initialize("hc")
        timer1.Initialize("Timer1", 500)
    End If
    Dim req As HttpRequest
    req.InitializeGet("http://www.basic4ppc.com/android/files/b4a-
trial.zip")
    hc.Execute(req, 1)
End Sub
Sub hc_ResponseSuccess (Response As HttpResponse, TaskId As Int)
    cout.Initialize(File.OpenOutput(File.DirRootExternal, "1.zip",
False))
    Timer1.Enabled = True
    length = Response.ContentLength
    Response.GetAsynchronously("response", cOut, True, TaskId)
End Sub
Sub hc_ResponseError (Response As HttpResponse, Reason As
String, StatusCode As Int, TaskId As Int)
    Log("Error: " & Reason)
    If Response <> Null Then
        Log(Response.GetString("UTF8"))
        Response.Release
    End If
End Sub
Sub Response_StreamFinish (Success As Boolean, TaskId As Int)
    timer1.Enabled = False
    If Success Then
        Timer1_Tick 'Show the current counter status
        Log("Success!")
    Else
        Log("Error: " & LastException.Message)
    End If
End Sub
Sub Timer1_Tick
    Log(cout.Count & " out of " & length)
End Sub
```

Members:

BytesAvailable As Int

Close

Count As Long

Gets or sets the number of bytes read.

Initialize (InputStream As java.io.InputStream)
Initializes the counting stream by wrapping the given input stream.

IsInitialized As Boolean
Whether this object has been initialized by calling `Initialize`.

ReadBytes (arg0() As Byte, arg1 As Int, arg2 As Int) As Int

CountingOutputStream

See CountingInputStream for more information.

Members:

Close

Count As Long
Gets or sets the number of bytes written.

Flush

Initialize (OutputStream As java.io.OutputStream)
Initializes the counting stream by wrapping the given output stream.

IsInitialized As Boolean
Whether this object has been initialized by calling `Initialize`.

ToBytesArray As Byte()

WriteBytes (arg0() As Byte, arg1 As Int, arg2 As Int)

RandomAccessFile

This object allows you to non-sequentially access files and byte-arrays. You can also use it to encode numbers to bytes (and vice versa). **Note** that assets files (files added with the file manager) cannot be opened with this object as those files are actually packed inside the APK file. A short tutorial about the encryption methods is available here (http://bit.ly/159hDmT).

Members:

Close
CurrentPosition As Long
Flush
Initialize (Dir As String, File As String, ReadOnly As Boolean)
Initialize2 (Dir As String, File As String, ReadOnly As Boolean, LittleEndian As Boolean)
Initialize3 (Buffer() As Byte, LittleEndian As Boolean)
ReadBytes (Buffer() As Byte, StartOffset As Int, Length As Int, Position As Long) As Int
ReadDouble (Position As Long) As Double
ReadEncryptedObject (Password As String, Position As Long) As Object
ReadFloat (Position As Long) As Float

- ReadInt (Position As Long) As Int
- ReadLong (Position As Long) As Long
- ReadObject (Position As Long) As Object
- ReadShort (Position As Long) As Short
- ReadSignedByte (Position As Long) As Byte
- ReadUnsignedByte (Position As Long) As Int
- Size As Long [read only]
- WriteByte (Byte As Byte, Position As Long)
- WriteBytes (Buffer() As Byte, StartOffset As Int, Length As Int, Position As Long) As Int
- WriteDouble (Value As Double, Position As Long)
- WriteEncryptedObject (Object As Object, Password As String, Position As Long)
- WriteFloat (Value As Float, Position As Long)
- WriteInt (Value As Int, Position As Long)
- WriteLong (Value As Long, Position As Long)
- WriteObject (Object As Object, Compress As Boolean, Position As Long)
- WriteShort (Value As Short, Position As Long)

Close

Closes the stream.

CurrentPosition As Long

Holds the current file position. This value is updated automatically after each read or write operation.

Flush

Flushes any cached data.

Initialize (Dir As String, File As String, ReadOnly As Boolean)

Opens the specified file. **Note** that it is not possible to open a file saved in the assets folder with this object. If needed, you can copy the file to another location and then open it.

ReadOnly - Whether to open the file in read-only mode (otherwise, it will be readable and writable).

Example:

```
Dim raf As RandomAccessFile
raf.Initialize(File.DirInternal, "1.dat", false)
```

Initialize2 (Dir As String, File As String, ReadOnly As Boolean, LittleEndian As Boolean)

Same as Initialize with the option to set the byte order to Little Endian instead of the default Big Endian. This can be useful when sharing files with Windows computers.

Initialize3 (Buffer() As Byte, LittleEndian As Boolean)

Treats the given buffer as a random access file with a constant size. This allows you to read and write values to an array of bytes.

ReadBytes (Buffer() As Byte, StartOffset As Int, Length As Int, Position As Long) As Int

Reads bytes from the stream and into to the given array. Returns the number of bytes read (which is equal or smaller than Length).
Buffer - Array of bytes where the data will be written to.
StartOffset - The first byte read will be written to Buffer(StartOffset).
Length - Number of bytes to read.
Position - The position of the first byte to read.

ReadDouble (Position As Long) As Double

Reads a Double value stored at the specified position. Reads 8 bytes.

ReadEncryptedObject (Password As String, Position As Long) As Object

Reads an encrypted object from the stream.
Password - The password used when the object was written.
Position - Stream position.

ReadFloat (Position As Long) As Float

Reads a Float value stored at the specified position. Reads 4 bytes.

ReadInt (Position As Long) As Int

Reads an Int value stored at the specified position. Reads 4 bytes.

ReadLong (Position As Long) As Long

Reads a Long value stored at the specified position. Reads 8 bytes.

ReadObject (Position As Long) As Object

Reads an object from the stream. See `WriteObject` for supported types.

ReadShort (Position As Long) As Short

Reads a Short value stored at the specified position. Reads 2 bytes.

ReadSignedByte (Position As Long) As Byte

Reads a signed byte (-128 to 127) stored at the specified position.

ReadUnsignedByte (Position As Long) As Int

Reads an unsigned byte (0 to 255) stored at the specified position. The value returned is of type `Int` (because a `Byte` can only store values from -128 to 127).

Size As Long [read only]

Returns the file size.

WriteByte (Byte As Byte, Position As Long)

Writes a Byte value at the specified position. Writes 1 byte.

WriteBytes (Buffer() As Byte, StartOffset As Int, Length As Int, Position As Long) As Int

Writes the given buffer to the stream. The first byte written is Buffer(StartOffset) and the last is Buffer(StartOffset + Length - 1). Returns the numbers of bytes written.

WriteDouble (Value As Double, Position As Long)
Writes a Double value at the specified position. Writes 8 bytes.

WriteEncryptedObject (Object As Object, Password As String, Position As Long)
Similar to WriteObject. The object is encrypted with AES-256 and then written to the stream. **Note** that it is faster to write a single large object compared to many smaller objects.
Object - The object that will be written.
Password - The password that protects the object.
Position - The position in the file that this object will be written to.

WriteFloat (Value As Float, Position As Long)
Writes a Float value at the specified position. Writes 4 bytes.

WriteInt (Value As Int, Position As Long)
Writes an Int value at the specified position. Writes 4 bytes.

WriteLong (Value As Long, Position As Long)
Writes a Long value at the specified position. Writes 8 bytes.

WriteObject (Object As Object, Compress As Boolean, Position As Long)
Writes the given object to the stream. This method is capable of writing the following types of objects: Lists, Arrays, Maps, Strings, primitive types and user defined types. Combinations of these types are also supported. For example, a map with several lists of arrays can be written. The element type inside a collection must be a String or primitive type. Note that changing your package name may make older object files unusable (requiring you to write them again).
Object - The object that will be written.
Compress - Whether to compress the data before writing it. Should be `True` in most cases.
Position - The position in the file that this object will be written to.

WriteShort (Value As Short, Position As Long)
Writes a Short value (2 bytes) at the specified position.

Serial Library

This library is included in the IDE installation package.

List of types:

BluetoothAdmin
Serial

BluetoothAdmin

BluetoothAdmin allows you to administrate the Bluetooth adapter. Using this object, you can enable or disable the adapter, monitor its state and discover devices in range.

Permissions:

android.permission.BLUETOOTH
android.permission.BLUETOOTH_ADMIN

Events:

StateChanged (NewState As Int, OldState As Int)

The StateChanged event is raised whenever the adapter state changes. The new state and the previous state are passed. The values correspond to the STATE_xxxx constants.

DiscoveryStarted / DiscoveryFinished

The DiscoveryStarted and DiscoveryFinished events are raised when a discovery process starts or finishes.

DeviceFound (Name As String, MacAddress As String)

The DeviceFound event is raised when a device is discovered. The device name and MAC address are passed.

Members:

- CancelDiscovery As Boolean
- Disable As Boolean
- Enable As Boolean
- Initialize (EventName As String)
- IsEnabled As Boolean
- IsInitialized As Boolean
- StartDiscovery As Boolean

The following are STATE contants:

- STATE_OFF As Int
- STATE_ON As Int
- STATE_TURNING_OFF As Int
- STATE_TURNING_ON As Int

CancelDiscovery As Boolean

Cancels a discovery process.
Returns **`False`** if the operation has failed.

Disable As Boolean

Turns off the Bluetooth adpater. The adapter will not be immediately disabled. You should use the StateChanged event to monitor the adapter.
This method returns **`False`** if the adapter cannot be disabled or is already disabled.

Enable As Boolean

Turns on the Bluetooth adapter. The adapter will not be immediately ready. You should use the StateChanged event to find when it is enabled. This method returns **`False`** if the adapter cannot be enabled or is already enabled.

Initialize (EventName As String)
Initializes the object and sets the subs that will handle the events.

IsEnabled As Boolean
Returns **TRUE** if the Bluetooth adapter is enabled.

IsInitialized As Boolean
Returns **TRUE** if the object is initialized.

StartDiscovery As Boolean
Starts a discovery process. You should handle DiscoveryStarted, DiscoveryFinished and DeviceFound events to get more information about the process. Returns **False** if the operation has failed.

STATE_OFF As Int

STATE_ON As Int

STATE_TURNING_OFF As Int

STATE_TURNING_ON As Int

Serial

The Serial library allows you to connect with other Bluetooth devices using the Radio Frequency Communication protocol RFCOMM (http://bit.ly/1dgYl19), which emulates serial ports.
This library requires Android 2.0 (API level 5) or above.
The Serial object should be declared as a **Sub Process_Globals** object. After initializing the object you can connect to other devices by calling Connect with the target device MAC address. This can be done by first getting the paired devices map. This map contains the friendly name and address of each paired device.
To allow other devices to connect to your device, you should call **Listen**.
When a connection is established, the **Connected** event will be raised. There is no problem with both listening to connections and trying to connect to a different device (this allows you to use the same application on two devices without defining a server and client).
One Serial object can handle a single connection. If a new connection is established, it will replace the previous one. See this tutorial (http://bit.ly/19FCUCS) for more information.

Permissions:

android.permission.BLUETOOTH

Event: Connected (Success As Boolean)

The Connected event will be raised after the **Connect, Connect2, Listen** or **Listen2** command is issued, when the connection is ready (or fails).

Members:

Address As String [read only]

Connect (MacAddress As String)

- Connect2 (MacAddress As String, UUID As String)
- Connect3 (MacAddress As String, Port As Int)
- ConnectInsecure (Admin As BluetoothAdmin, MacAddress As String, Port As Int)
- Disconnect
- GetPairedDevices As Map
- Initialize (EventName As String)
- InputStream As java.io.InputStream [read only]
- IsEnabled As Boolean
- IsInitialized As Boolean
- Listen
- Listen2 (Name As String, UUID As String)
- ListenInsecure (Admin As BluetoothAdmin, Port As Int)
- Name As String [read only]
- OutputStream As java.io.OutputStream [read only]
- StopListening

Address As String [read only]

Returns the current device MAC address.

Connect (MacAddress As String)

Tries to connect to a device with the given address. The connection is done in the background. The Connected event will be raised when the connection is ready (or fails).

The UUID used for the connection is the default UUID: 00001101-0000-1000-8000-00805F9B34FB.

Connect2 (MacAddress As String, UUID As String)

Tries to connect to a device with the given address and UUID. The connection is done in the background. The Connected event will be raised when the connection is ready (or fails).

Connect3 (MacAddress As String, Port As Int)

This method is a workaround for hardware devices that do not connect with Connect or Connect2. See this issue (http://code.google.com/p/android/issues/detail?id=5427) for more information.

ConnectInsecure (Admin As BluetoothAdmin, MacAddress As String, Port As Int)

Tries to connect to a device over an unencrypted connection.

Admin - Object of type BluetoothAdmin.

MacAddress - The address of the remote device.

Port - RFCOMM (http://bit.ly/1dgYl19) channel.

Disconnect

Disconnects the connection (if such exists) and stops listening for new connections.

GetPairedDevices As Map

Returns a map with the paired devices' friendly names as keys and their addresses as values. The following code shows a list of available devices and allows the user to connect to one:

```
Dim PairedDevices As Map
PairedDevices = Serial1.GetPairedDevices
Dim l As List
l.Initialize
For i = 0 To PairedDevices.Size - 1
  l.Add(PairedDevices.GetKeyAt(i))
Next
Dim res As Int
res = InputList(l, "Choose device", -1) 'show list with paired
devices
If res <> DialogResponse.CANCEL Then
  Serial1.Connect(PairedDevices.Get(l.Get(res))) 'convert the
name to MAC address and connect
End If
```

Initialize (EventName As String)

Initialized the object. You may want to call IsEnabled before trying to work with the object.

InputStream As java.io.InputStream [read only]

Returns the InputStream that is used to read data from the other device. Should be called after a connection is established.

IsEnabled As Boolean

Returns **TRUE** if the Bluetooth is enabled.

IsInitialized As Boolean

Whether this object has been initialized by calling **Initialize**.

Listen

Starts listening for incoming connections using the default UUID. The Connected event will be raised when the connection is established. Nothing happens if the device is already listening for connections.

Listen2 (Name As String, UUID As String)

Starts listening for incoming connections. The Connected event will be raised when the connection is established. Nothing happens if the device is already listening for connections.

Name - An arbitrary string that will be used for internal registration.
UUID - The UUID defined for this record.

ListenInsecure (Admin As BluetoothAdmin, Port As Int)

Starts listening for incoming unencrypted connections.

Admin - An object of type BluetoothAdmin.
Port - The RFCOMM channel.

Name As String [read only]
Returns the current device friendly name.

OutputStream As java.io.OutputStream [read only]
Returns the OutputStream that is used to write data to the other device. Should be called after a connection is established.

StopListening
Stops listening for incoming connections. This will not disconnect any active connection.

Sip Library

The Sip library lets you make audio calls using Voice over IP (Voip) services. Sip features were added in Android 2.3 (API level 9). Note that not all devices above Android 2.3 support Sip features. In order to use this library, you will need to set android.jar in [Tools > Configure Paths] to platform-9 or above.
This library is included in the IDE installation package. A tutorial is available here (http://bit.ly/14tU0mz).

List of types:

Sip
SipAudioCall

Sip

Sip is the main object which manages the Sip services. Once you make a call or receive an incoming call, you will get a **`SipAudioCall`** object, which represents the call.

Permissions:

android.permission.USE_SIP
android.permission.INTERNET
android.permission.RECORD_AUDIO
android.permission.ACCESS_WIFI_STATE
android.permission.WAKE_LOCK
android.permission.MODIFY_AUDIO_SETTINGS

Events:

Registering

RegistrationDone (ExpiryTime As Long)

RegistrationFailed (ErrorCode As Int, ErrorMessage As String)

CallEstablished

CallEnded

Calling

CallError (ErrorCode As Int, ErrorMessage As String)

CallRinging (IncomingCall As SipAudioCall)

Members:

AutoRegistration As Boolean [write only]
Close
DisplayName As String [write only]
Initialize (EventName As String, User As String, Host As String, Password As String)
Initialize2 (EventName As String, URI As String, Password As String)
IsInitialized As Boolean [read only]
IsSipSupported As Boolean [read only]
IsVoipSupported As Boolean [read only]
MakeCall (TargetUri As String, TimeoutSeconds As Int) As SipAudioCall
OutboundProxy As String [write only]
Port As Int [write only]
ProfileName As String [write only]
Protocol As String [write only]
Register
SendKeepAlive As Boolean [write only]

AutoRegistration As Boolean [write only]

Sets whether the Sip manager will register automatically if needed.

Close

Closes the connection.

DisplayName As String [write only]

Sets the user display name.

Initialize (EventName As String, User As String, Host As String, Password As String)

Initializes the object.
EventName - Sets the subs that will handle the events.
User - User name.

Host - Host name or IP address.
Password - Account password.

Initialize2 (EventName As String, URI As String, Password As String)
Initializes the object.
EventName - Sets the subs that will handle the events.
URI – the "Uniform Resource Identifier" (address) of the profile resource, for example: "sip:zzz@iptel.org"
Password - Account password.

IsInitialized As Boolean [read only]
Returns **TRUE** if the object was initialized.

IsSipSupported As Boolean [read only]
Returns **TRUE** if Sip API is supported on the device.

IsVoipSupported As Boolean [read only]
Returns **TRUE** if Voip is supported on this device.

MakeCall (TargetUri As String, TimeoutSeconds As Int) As SipAudioCall
Makes an audio call. This method should only be called after registering.
TargetUri - The address of the target.
TimeoutSeconds - The timeout (measured in seconds).

OutboundProxy As String [write only]
Sets the outbound proxy address.

Port As Int [write only]
Sets the connection port.

ProfileName As String [write only]
Sets the user-defined profile name.

Protocol As String [write only]
Sets the protocol. Either "TCP" or "UDP".

Register
Sends a registration request to the server. The following events will be raised: either `Registering` and `RegistrationDone`, or `RegistrationFail`.

SendKeepAlive As Boolean [write only]
Sets whether keep-alive messages will be sent automatically.

SipAudioCall
Represents an audio call. This object is created by calling `Sip.MakeCall` or from the `CallRinging` event.

Members:

AnswerCall (TimeoutSeconds As Int)

Answers an incoming call.
TimeoutSeconds - Allowed time for the call to be established.

EndCall

Ends the current call.

IsInCall As Boolean [read only]

Returns **TRUE** if the call was established.

IsInitialized As Boolean

Whether this object has been initialized.

IsMuted As Boolean [read only]

Returns **TRUE** if the microphone is muted.

PeerUri As String [read only]

Gets the address of the peer.

SendDtmf (Code As Int)

Sends a Dtmf tone. Values can be 0-15, where 0-9 are the digits, 10 is '*', 11 is '# and 12-15 are 'A'-'D'.

SpeakerMode As Boolean [write only]

Sets the speaker mode.

StartAudio

Starts the audio for the call. Should be called in CallEstablished event.

ToggleMute

Toggles the microphone mute.

SQL Library

This library (included in the IDE installation package) allows you to create and manage SQLite databases. See the Databases Chapter (page 156) for more information.

List of types:

Cursor
SQL

Cursor

A cursor is the object returned from a database query. It consists of a set of records and a pointer to the current record.
It is similar to a **recordset** in Visual Basic.

Members:

Close

- ColumnCount As Int [read only]
- GetBlob (ColumnName As String) As Byte()
- GetBlob2 (Index As Int) As Byte()
- GetColumnName (Index As Int) As String
- GetDouble (ColumnName As String) As Double
- GetDouble2 (Index As Int) As Double
- GetInt (ColumnName As String) As Int
- GetInt2 (Index As Int) As Int
- GetLong (ColumnName As String) As Long
- GetLong2 (Index As Int) As Long
- GetString (ColumnName As String) As String
- GetString2 (Index As Int) As String
- IsInitialized As Boolean
- Position As Int
- RowCount As Int [read only]

Close

Closes the cursor and frees resources.

ColumnCount As Int [read only]

Gets the number of fields available in the result set.

GetBlob (ColumnName As String) As Byte()

Returns the blob stored in the given column. Example:

```
Dim Buffer() As Byte
Buffer = Cursor.GetBlob("col1")
```

GetBlob2 (Index As Int) As Byte()

Returns the blob stored in the column at the given ordinal. Example:

```
Dim Buffer() As Byte
Buffer = Cursor.GetBlob2(0)
```

GetColumnName (Index As Int) As String

Returns the name of the column at the specified index. The first column index is 0.

GetDouble (ColumnName As String) As Double

Returns the Double value stored in the given column. The value will be converted to Double if it is of different type. Example:

```
Log(Cursor.GetDouble("col2"))
```

GetDouble2 (Index As Int) As Double

Returns the Double value stored in the column at the given ordinal. The value will be converted to Double if it is of different type. Example:

```
Log(Cursor.GetDouble2(0))
```

GetInt (ColumnName As String) As Int

Returns the Int value stored in the given column. The value will be converted to Int if it is of different type. Example:

```
Log(Cursor.GetInt("col2"))
```

GetInt2 (Index As Int) As Int

Returns the Int value stored in the column at the given ordinal. The value will be converted to Int if it is of different type. Example:

```
Log(Cursor.GetInt2(0))
```

GetLong (ColumnName As String) As Long

Returns the Long value stored in the given column. The value will be converted to Long if it is of different type. Example:

```
Log(Cursor.GetLong("col2"))
```

GetLong2 (Index As Int) As Long

Returns the Long value stored in the column at the given ordinal. The value will be converted to Long if it is of different type. Example:

```
Log(Cursor.GetLong2(0))
```

GetString (ColumnName As String) As String

Returns the String value stored in the given column. The value will be converted to String if it is of different type. Example:

```
Log(Cursor.GetString("col2"))
```

GetString2 (Index As Int) As String

Returns the String value stored in the column at the given ordinal. The value will be converted to String if it is of different type. Example:

```
Log(Cursor.GetString2(0))
```

IsInitialized As Boolean

Whether this object has been initialized.

Position As Int

Gets or sets the current position (row). Note that the starting position of a cursor returned from a query is `-1`. The first valid position is 0. Example:

```
Dim SQL1 As SQL
Dim Cursor1 As Cursor
Cursor1 = SQL1.ExecQuery("SELECT col1, col2 FROM table1")
For i = 0 To Cursor1.RowCount - 1
  Cursor1.Position = i
  Log(Cursor1.GetString("col1"))
  Log(Cursor1.GetInt("col2"))
Next
Cursor1.Close
```

RowCount As Int [read only]

Gets the numbers of rows available in the result set.

SQL

The main object that accesses the SQLite database built-into Android. See the Databases Chapter (page 156) for more information.

Events:

QueryComplete (Success As Boolean, Crsr As Cursor)

NonQueryComplete (Success As Boolean)

Members:

- AddNonQueryToBatch (Statement As String, Args As List)
- BeginTransaction
- Close
- EndTransaction
- ExecNonQuery (Statement As String)
- ExecNonQuery2 (Statement As String, Args As List)
- ExecNonQueryBatch (EventName As String)
- ExecQuery (Query As String) As Cursor
- ExecQuery2 (Query As String, StringArgs() As String) As Cursor
- ExecQueryAsync (EventName As String, Query As String, StringArgs() As String)
- ExecQuerySingleResult (Query As String) As String
- ExecQuerySingleResult2 (Query As String, StringArgs() As String) As String
- Initialize (Dir As String, FileName As String, CreateIfNecessary As Boolean)
- IsInitialized (page 511) As Boolean
- TransactionSuccessful (page 511)

AddNonQueryToBatch (Statement As String, Args As List)

Adds a non-query statement to the batch of statements. The statements are (asynchronously) executed when you call ExecNonQueryBatch. **Args** can be **`Null`** if it is not needed. Example:

```
For i = 1 To 10000
     sql1.AddNonQueryToBatch("INSERT INTO table1 VALUES (?)",
Array As Object(Rnd(0, 100000)))
Next
sql1.ExecNonQueryBatch("SQL")
...
Sub SQL_NonQueryComplete (Success As Boolean)
   Log("NonQuery: " & Success)
   If Success = False Then Log(LastException)
End Sub
```

BeginTransaction

Begins a transaction (page 168). A transaction is a set of multiple "writing" statements for which either all or no changes will be saved to the database. Changes are held in a temporary form and, if there is an error, all changes are reversed so the database is restored to its original state. **It is very important** to handle transactions carefully and close them. The transaction is considered successful only if **`TransactionSuccessful`** is called. Otherwise, no changes will be saved.

Close
Closes the database. Does not do anything if the database was never opened or has already been closed.

EndTransaction
Ends the transaction.

ExecNonQuery (Statement As String)
Executes a single non query SQL statement. Example:
```
SQL1.ExecNonQuery("CREATE TABLE table1 (col1 TEXT , col2
INTEGER, col3 INTEGER)")
```
If you plan to do many "writing" queries one after another, then you should consider using **BeginTransaction** and **EndTransaction**, which will execute significantly faster.

ExecNonQuery2 (Statement As String, Args As List)
Executes a single non query SQL statement. The statement can include question marks which will be replaced by the items in the given list. Note that Basic4Android converts arrays to lists implicitly. The values in the list should be strings, numbers or byte-arrays. Example:
```
SQL1.ExecNonQuery2("INSERT INTO table1 VALUES (?, ?, 0)", Array
As Object("some text", 2))
```

ExecNonQueryBatch (EventName As String)
Asynchronously executes a batch of non-query statements (such as INSERT).
The NonQueryComplete event is raised after the statements are completed.
You should call AddNonQueryToBatch one or more times before calling this method to add statements to the batch. **Note** that this method internally begins and ends a transaction.

ExecQuery (Query As String) As Cursor
Executes the query and returns a cursor which is used to go over the results.
Example:
```
Dim SQL1 As SQL
Dim Cursor1 As Cursor
Cursor1 = SQL1.ExecQuery("SELECT col1, col2 FROM table1")
For i = 0 To Cursor1.RowCount - 1
  Cursor1.Position = i
  Log(Cursor1.GetString("col1"))
  Log(Cursor1.GetInt("col2"))
Next
```

ExecQuery2 (Query As String, StringArgs() As String) As Cursor
Executes the query and returns a cursor which is used to go over the results. The query can include question marks which will be replaced with the values in the array. Example:

```
Dim SQL1 As SQL
Dim Cursor1 As Cursor
Cursor1 = SQL1.ExecQuery2("SELECT col1 FROM table1 WHERE col3 =
?", Array As String(22))
```

SQLite will try to convert the string values based on the column types.

ExecQueryAsync (EventName As String, Query As String, StringArgs() As String)

Asynchronously executes the given query. The QueryComplete event will be raised when the results are ready. Example:

```
sql1.ExecQueryAsync("SQL", "SELECT * FROM table1", Null)
...
Sub SQL_QueryComplete (Success As Boolean, Crsr As Cursor)
  If Success Then
     For i = 0 To Crsr.RowCount - 1
         Crsr.Position = i
         Log(Crsr.GetInt2(0))
     Next
  Else
     Log(LastException)
  End If
End Sub
```

ExecQuerySingleResult (Query As String) As String

Executes the query and returns the value in the first column and the first row (in the result set). Returns **Null** if no results were found. Example:

```
Dim NumberOfMatches As Int
NumberOfMatches = SQL1.ExecQuerySingleResult("SELECT count(*)
FROM table1 WHERE col2 > 300")
```

ExecQuerySingleResult2 (Query As String, StringArgs() As String) As String

Executes the query and returns the value in the first column and the first row (in the result set). Returns **Null** if no results were found. Example:

```
Dim NumberOfMatches As Int
NumberOfMatches = SQL1.ExecQuerySingleResult2("SELECT count(*)
FROM table1 WHERE col2 > ?", Array As String(300))
```

Initialize (Dir As String, FileName As String, CreateIfNecessary As Boolean)

Opens the database file. A new database will be created if it does not exist and CreateIfNecessary is **True**. Example:

```
Sub Process_Globals
 Dim SQL1 As SQL
End Sub

Sub Activity_Create(FirstTime As Boolean)
 If FirstTime Then
 SQL1.Initialize(File.DirRootExternal, "1.db", True)
 End If
End Sub
```

IsInitialized As Boolean

Returns **TRUE** if the database is initialized and opened.

TransactionSuccessful

Marks the transaction as a successful transaction. No further statements should be executed till calling EndTransaction.

StringUtils Library

This library is included in the IDE installation package.

List of types:

StringUtils

StringUtils

Collection of string-related functions.

DecodeBase64 (Data As String) As Byte()

Decodes data from Base64 notation.

DecodeUrl (Url As String, CharSet As String) As String

Decodes an application/x-www-form-urlencoded string. See Text Encoding (page 304) for details of character sets.

EncodeBase64 (Data() As Byte) As String

Encodes the given byte-array into Base64 notation. Example:

```
Dim su As StringUtils
Dim encoded As String
encoded = su.EncodeBase64(data) 'data is a byte-array
```

EncodeUrl (Url As String, CharSet As String) As String

Encodes a string into application/x-www-form-urlencoded format.
Url - String to encode.
CharSet - The character encoding name. See Text Encoding (page 304) for details of character sets. Example:

```
Dim su As StringUtils
Dim url, encodedUrl As String
encodedUrl = su.EncodeUrl(url, "UTF8")
```

LoadCSV (Dir As String, FileName As String, SeparatorChar As Char) As List

Loads a CSV file and stores it in a list of string arrays.
Dir - CSV file folder.
FileName - CSV file name.
SeparatorChar - The character used in the original file to separate fields. For the tab character, use **Chr(9)**.
Example:

```
Dim lvTest As ListView
Dim lstCSV As List
Dim StrUtil As StringUtils
Dim strRow(), strOneLine As String
Dim iRowCount As Int

' prepare ListView to show data
lvTest.Initialize("")
Activity.AddView(lvTest, 0,0,100%x, 100%y)

 ' Read the csv file
lstCSV.Initialize
lstCSV = StrUtil.LoadCSV(File.DirAssets, "book2.csv", ",")

For iRowCount = 0 To lstCSV.Size - 1
 strRow = lstCSV.Get(iRowCount)
 strOneLine = ""
 For i = 0 To strRow.Length - 1
  strOneLine = strOneLine & strRow(i)
  If i < strRow.Length - 1 Then
   strOneLine = strOneLine & ", "
  End If
 Next
 lvTest.AddSingleLine(strOneLine)
Next
```

LoadCSV2 (Dir As String, FileName As String, SeparatorChar As Char, Headers As List) As List

Similar to LoadCSV, except that it loads the first row into the Headers list of strings.

MeasureMultilineTextHeight (TextView1 As TextView, Text As String) As Int

Returns the required height in order to show the given text in a label. This can be used to show dynamic text in a label. Note that the label must first be added to its parent and only then its height can be set. Example:

```
Dim Label1 As Label
Label1.Initialize("")
Label1.Text = "this is a long sentence, and we need to " _
  & "know the height required in order To show it completely."
Label1.TextSize = 20
Activity.AddView(Label1, 10dip, 10dip, 200dip, 30dip)
Dim su As StringUtils
Label1.Height = su.MeasureMultilineTextHeight(Label1,
Label1.Text)
```

SaveCSV (Dir As String, FileName As String, SeparatorChar As Char, Table As List)

Saves the table as a CSV file.
Dir - Output file folder.
FileName - Output file name.
SeparatorChar - Separator character. The character that will separate the fields in the output file.
Table - A List with arrays of strings as items. Each array represents a row. All arrays should be of the same length.
Example to create a CSV file:

```
Dim lstCSV As List
Dim StrUtil As StringUtils
Dim iRowCount As Int = 10
Dim iColCount As Int = 5

lstCSV.Initialize

' create a list of string arrays containing the data
For iRowCount = 0 To 9
 Dim strRow(iColCount) As String
 For iColCount = 0 To 4
  strRow(iColCount) = "Row " & iRowCount & ", Col " & iColCount
 Next
 lstCSV.Add(strRow)
Next

StrUtil.SaveCSV(File.DirDefaultExternal,"book2_output.csv", ",",
lstCSV)
```

SaveCSV2 (Dir As String, FileName As String, SeparatorChar As Char, Table As List, Headers As List)

Similar to SaveCSV, except the first row will come from the Headers list, which should be a list (or array) of strings.

TTS Library

This library (included in the IDE installation package) provides for text to speech (TTS). For an example program which performs both TTS and Voice Recognition, see this web page (http://bit.ly/14kXKG4).

TTS

Synthesizes text to speech and plays it. After initializing the object you should wait for the Ready event. See this example (http://bit.ly/11lo8KN).

Event: Ready (Success As Boolean)

Members:

Initialize (EventName As String)

Initializes the object. The Ready event will be raised when the text to speech engine is ready.
EventName - The Sub that will handle the Ready event.

IsInitialized As Boolean

Whether this object has been initialized by calling `Initialize`.

Pitch As Float [write only]

Sets the pitch value. Default is 1. Example:

```
TTS1.Pitch = 1.5
```

Release

Releases any resources related to this object. You will then need to initialize the object again before use. **Note** that it is safe to call this method with an uninitialized object.

SetLanguage (Language As String, Country As String) As Boolean

Sets the spoken language.
Language - Language code. Two lowercase letters.
Country - Country code. Two uppercase letters. Pass an empty string if not needed.
Returns `True` if a matching language is available. The country value will be ignored if the language code matches and the country code does not match.

Speak (Text As String, ClearQueue As Boolean)

Speaks the given text.
ClearQueue - If `True`, then all waiting texts are dismissed and the new text is spoken. Otherwise, the new text is added to the queue.

SpeechRate As Float [write only]

Sets the speech rate. Default is 1. Example:

```
TTS1.SpeechRate = 0.5
```

Stop

Stops speaking any currently-playing text (and dismisses texts in the queue).

USB Library

This library is included in the IDE installation package. Note that detailed explanation of this library is outside the scope of this book. A complete working example with a tutorial is available here (http://bit.ly/1deHpbH).

List of types:

MtpDevice
UsbAccessory
UsbDevice
UsbDeviceConnection
UsbEndpoint (page 518)
UsbInterface (page 519)
UsbManager (page 519)
UsbRequest (page 521)

MtpDevice

Members:

Close

Initialize (EventName As String, UsbDevice1 As UsbDevice)

IsInitialized As Boolean

Whether this object has been initialized by calling `Initialize`.

Open (Connection As UsbDeviceConnection)

test

UsbAccessory

Represents a Usb accessory.

Members:

Close
Description As String [read only]
InputStream As InputStreamWrapper [read only]
Manufacturer As String [read only]
Model As String [read only]
OutputStream As OutputStreamWrapper [read only]
Serial As String [read only]
URI As String [read only]
Version As String [read only]

Close

Closes the accessory. The accessory input and output streams should be individually closed first.

Description As String [read only]
Gets the description of the accessory.

InputStream As InputStreamWrapper [read only]
Gets the input stream for the accessory. When reading data from an accessory, ensure that the buffer that you use is big enough to store the USB packet data. The Android accessory protocol supports packet buffers up to 16384 bytes, so you can choose to always declare your buffer to be of this size for simplicity.

Manufacturer As String [read only]
Gets the manufacturer of the accessory.

Model As String [read only]
Gets the model name of the accessory.

OutputStream As OutputStreamWrapper [read only]
Gets the output stream for the accessory.

Serial As String [read only]
Gets the unique serial number for the accessory.

URI As String [read only]
Gets the URI (Internet address) for the website of the accessory.

Version As String [read only]
Gets the version of the accessory.

UsbDevice

Represents a Usb device.

Members:

- DeviceClass As Int [read only]
- DeviceId As Int [read only]
- DeviceName As String [read only]
- DeviceSubclass As Int [read only]
- GetInterface (Index As Int) As UsbInterface
- InterfaceCount As Int [read only]
- IsInitialized As Boolean
- ProductId As Int [read only]
- VendorId As Int [read only]

DeviceClass As Int [read only]
Gets the device class.

DeviceId As Int [read only]
Gets the device Id.

DeviceName As String [read only]
Gets the device name.

DeviceSubclass As Int [read only]
Gets the device subclass.

GetInterface (Index As Int) As UsbInterface
Gets the interface at the given index.

InterfaceCount As Int [read only]
Gets the number of interfaces.

IsInitialized As Boolean
Whether this object has been initialized.

ProductId As Int [read only]
Gets the product Id.

VendorId As Int [read only]
Gets the vendor Id.

UsbDeviceConnection
Represents a connection between the host and a client. UsbDeviceConnection is created by calling `UsbManager.OpenDevice`. Once connected, you should call `StartListening` to start listening for completed requests. Sending requests is done with `UsbRequest.Queue`. You should call `ContinueListening` to allow the listener to listen to the next completed request (after another IN request is sent).
Calling `StopListening` will close the connection. `ControlTransfer` method sends requests to endpoint zero which is the control endpoint. `ControlTransfer` is a blocking method (it waits for the transaction to finish, unlike `UsbRequest.Queue` which is asynchronous).

Event: NewData (Request As UsbRequest, InDirection As Boolean)
The NewData event is raised when a request completes. The request is passed as a parameter.

Members:

BulkTransfer (Endpoint As UsbEndpoint, Buffer() As Byte, Length As Int, Timeout As Int) As Int
Sends a synchronous request.
Endpoint - The endpoint for this transaction. The transfer direction is determined by this endpoint.
Buffer - Buffer for data to send or receive.
Length - The length of the data.
Timeout - Request timeout (in milliseconds).

CloseSynchronous
Like `StopListening`, `CloseSynchronous` closes the connection.
Note: this method should only be used when the asynchronous listener was not started.

ContinueListening
Notifies the listener to continue listening for completed requests.

ControlTransfer (RequestType As Int, Request As Int, Value As Int, Index As Int, Buffer() As Byte, Length As Int, Timeout As Int) As Int
Performs a control transaction on endpoint zero. Returns the number of bytes transferred.
RequestType - The request type. It should be either UsbManager.USB_DIR_IN or UsbManager.USB_DIR_OUT to set the request direction.
Request - Request Id.
Value - Value field.
Index - Index field.
Buffer - Buffer for data portion. Pass `Null` if not needed.
Length - The length of the data to send or receive.
Timeout - Timeout (in milliseconds).

GetRawDescriptors As Byte()
Returns the raw descriptors as an array of bytes.
This method is only available in Android 3.2 or above. It will return an empty array in Android 3.1 and earlier versions.

IsInitialized As Boolean
Returns `TRUE` if the object was initialized.

Serial As String [read only]
Returns the connected device serial number.

StartListening (EventName As String)
Starts listening for completed requests. When such are available, the `NewData` event will be raised.
EventName - The name of the sub that will handle the events.

StopListening
Stops listening to requests and closes the connection.

UsbEndpoint
Represents an endpoint in a specific interface.

Members:

Address As Int [read only]
Gets the endpoint address.

Attributes As Int [read only]
Gets the endpoint attributes.

Direction As Int [read only]
Gets the endpoint direction. Can be UsbManager.USB_DIR_IN or UsbManager.USB_DIR_OUT.

EndpointNumber As Int [read only]
Gets the endpoint number.

Interval As Int [read only]
Gets the interval field.

IsInitialized As Boolean
Whether this object has been initialized.

MaxPacketSize As Int [read only]
Gets the maximum packet size.

Type As Int [read only]
Gets the endpoint type.

UsbInterface

Represents a USB interface on a specific device.

Members:

EndpointCount As Int [read only]
Gets the number of endpoints available in this interface.

GetEndpoint (Index As Int) As UsbEndpoint
Gets the endpoint at the given index.

InterfaceClass As Int [read only]
Gets the interface class.

InterfaceProtocol As Int [read only]
Gets the interface protocol.

InterfaceSubclass As Int [read only]
Gets the interface subclass.

IsInitialized As Boolean
Whether this object has been initialized.

UsbManager

UsbManager gives access to the connected USB devices. It also holds the related constants. This library requires Android SDK 12 or above (Android 3.1 or above). You should configure Basic4Android to use android.jar from android-12 or above.

Members:

GetAccessories As UsbAccessory()
Returns an array of UsbAccessories with all the connected USB accessories.

GetDevices As UsbDevice()
Returns an array of UsbDevices with all the connected USB devices.

HasAccessoryPermission (Accessory As UsbAccessory) As Boolean
Returns `TRUE` if your application has permission (page 83) to access this accessory. Call `RequestAccessoryPermission` to receive such permission.

HasPermission (Device As UsbDevice) As Boolean

Returns `TRUE` if your application has permission (page 83) to access this device. Call `RequestPermission` to receive such permission.

Initialize

Initializes the object.

OpenAccessory (Accessory As UsbAccessory)

Connects to the given accessory

OpenDevice (Device As UsbDevice, Interface As UsbInterface, ForceClaim As Boolean) As UsbDeviceConnection

Connects to the given device and claims exclusive access to the given interface.
ForceClaim - Whether the system should disconnect kernel drivers if necessary.

RequestAccessoryPermission (Accessory As UsbAccessory)

Shows a dialog that asks the user to allow your application to access the USB accessory.

RequestPermission (Device As UsbDevice)

Shows a dialog that asks the user to allow your application to access the USB device.

USB_CLASS_APP_SPEC As Int

USB_CLASS_AUDIO As Int

USB_CLASS_CDC_DATA As Int

USB_CLASS_COMM As Int

USB_CLASS_CONTENT_SEC As Int

USB_CLASS_CSCID As Int

USB_CLASS_HID As Int

USB_CLASS_HUB As Int

USB_CLASS_MASS_STORAGE As Int

USB_CLASS_MISC As Int

USB_CLASS_PER_INTERFACE As Int

USB_CLASS_PHYSICA As Int

USB_CLASS_PRINTER As Int

USB_CLASS_STILL_IMAGE As Int

USB_CLASS_VENDOR_SPEC As Int

USB_CLASS_VIDEO As Int

USB_CLASS_WIRELESS_CONTROLLER As Int

USB_DIR_IN As Int

USB_DIR_OUT As Int

USB_ENDPOINT_DIR_MASK As Int

USB_ENDPOINT_NUMBER_MASK As Int

USB_ENDPOINT_XFER_BULK As Int

USB_ENDPOINT_XFER_CONTROL As Int

USB_ENDPOINT_XFER_INT As Int

USB_ENDPOINT_XFER_ISOC As Int

USB_ENDPOINT_XFERTYPE_MASK As Int

USB_INTERFACE_SUBCLASS_BOOT As Int

USB_SUBCLASS_VENDOR_SPEC As Int

USB_TYPE_CLASS As Int

USB_TYPE_MASK As Int

USB_TYPE_RESERVED As Int

USB_TYPE_STANDARD As Int

USB_TYPE_VENDOR As Int

UsbRequest

This object represents a USB request packet. The `Queue` method sends the request.

Members:

Buffer() As Byte [read only]

Returns the buffer associated with the request.

Initialize (Connection As UsbDeviceConnection, Endpoint As UsbEndpoint)

Initializes the request. The request will be binded to the given connection and endpoint. **Note** that for control transactions you should use: `UsbDeviceConnection.ControlTransfer`.

IsInitialized As Boolean

Whether this object has been initialized by calling `Initialize`.

Name As String

Gets or sets an arbitrary string that can be used to identify the request.

Queue (Buffer() As Byte, Length As Int)

Queues the request for sending. The `UsbDeviceConnection_NewData` event will be raised when the transaction completes.

UsbEndpoint As UsbEndpoint [read only]

XmlSax Library

This library (included in the IDE installation package) provides an XML Sax Parser.

XML

XML (Extensible Markup Language) is a way of encoding data into a document which can be read both by humans and computers. It is widely used to send structured data over the Internet. More information here (http://en.wikipedia.org/wiki/XML).

Sax

SAX (Simple API for XML) is a standard method of parsing (processing the elements of) an XML document. It is event-based (page 233). See this tutorial (http://bit.ly/143HXuY) for a working example.

List of types:

Attributes
SaxParser

Attributes

This object is passed in the **`StartElement`** event.

Members:

- GetName (Index As Int) As String
- GetValue (Index As Int) As String
- GetValue2 (URI As String, Name As String) As String
- IsInitialized As Boolean
- Size As Int [read only]

GetName (Index As Int) As String

Returns the name of the attribute at the specified index. **Note** that the order of elements can change.

GetValue (Index As Int) As String

Returns the value of the attribute at the specified index. **Note** that the order of elements can change.

GetValue2 (URI As String, Name As String) As String

Returns the value of the attribute in the namespace specified by the given **URI** (an empty string if no namespace is used) and **Name**. Returns an empty string if no such attribute was found.

IsInitialized As Boolean

Whether this object has been initialized.

Size As Int [read only]

Returns the number of attributes in this element.

SaxParser

A parser that sequentially reads a stream and raises events at the beginning and end of each element.

Events:

StartElement (URI As String, Name As String, Attributes As Attributes)

URI - Uniform Resource Identifier (address) of namespace, or an empty string if there is no namespace.
Name - The element name.
Attributes - An Attributes object holding the element's attributes.

EndElement (URI As String, Name As String, Text As StringBuilder)

URI - Uniform Resource Identifier (address) of namespace, or empty string if there is no namespace.
Name - The element name.
Text - The element text (if such exists).

Members:

Initialize

Initializes the object. Usually this object should be a `Sub Process_Globals` object.

Parents As List

A list that holds the names of the parent elements. During parsing you can use this list to recognize the current element.

Parse (InputStream As java.io.InputStream, EventName As String)

Parses the given InputStream.
EventName - The prefix of event subs.

Parse2 (TextReader As java.io.Reader, EventName As String)

Parses the given TextReader.
EventName - The prefix of event subs.

4.3 Additional Libraries and Modules

Introduction

Additional libraries are libraries which you either create yourself or download from the Basic4Android website or receive from somebody else. It is necessary to use a specific folder for Additional libraries. You need to specify this location within [Tools > Configure Paths]. In the following, we divide libraries into:

- Additional Official Libraries: libraries created by Anywhere Software (the makers of Basic4Android)
- Additional User Libraries (page 529): libraries which users have created and published on the Basic4Android website.

Note: some of the following are not actually libraries but code modules (classes or services) which you include directly in your project.

Additional libraries folder

You need to set up a special folder to save additional libraries, for example: C:\Basic4Android\AddLibraries. When you install a new version of B4A, all standard libraries are automatically updated, but the additional libraries are not included. The advantage of the special folder is that this folder is not affected when you install the new version of B4A. **Note** the additional libraries are not systematically updated with each new version of B4A. You might want to periodically check for updates.

Telling the IDE where to find additional libraries

When the IDE starts, it looks first for the available libraries in the Libraries folder of B4A and then in the folder for the additional libraries. You must specify your additional libraries folder in the IDE menu [Tools > Configure Paths]. The dialog allows you to specify the Additional Libraries folder.

List of Additional Libraries

The latest list of additional libraries is available here:
http://www.basic4ppc.com/android/wiki/index.php/Libraries

Additional Official Libraries

These libraries (only available if you have the Full version) were created by Anywhere Software, the makers of Basic4Android. We do not have the space to describe them all here. The links below will take you to the Basic4Android website where you can learn more about each library. Follow the first links to download the library.

Adiquity

(For more information see http://bit.ly/19UgZbZ)
this library adds support for AdiQuity (http://adiquity.com/) advertising.

AdMob

(For more information see http://bit.ly/11PfPuO)
this library lets you display Google ads in your applications.

AnotherDatePicker class

(For more information see http://bit.ly/GMbTE6)
a class module which provides a "web style" date picker.

AsyncStreamsText

(For more information see http://bit.ly/16FcRfw)
a class module which allows you to read a text stream over a network.

Analytics

(For more information see http://bit.ly/16FcTUT)
a library which adds the power of Google Analytics V2 to your application and track its usage.

Audio v1.31

(For more information see http://bit.ly/1gbwqlN)
a library which includes objects which let you record audio and video, play video, play beeps and choose short sounds from a pool, use the JetPlayer (http://developer.android.com/guide/topics/media/jetplayer.html) and stream audio over the Internet. Formal specification here (http://www.basic4ppc.com/android/help/audio.html).

Camera

(For more information see http://bit.ly/15ymkoe)
A library which allows access to the device's camera(s) and lets the user take and preview pictures. It is supported by Android 1.6+. If possible, it is recommended to work with the CameraEx class that wraps this object and adds many features. Formal specification here (http://www.basic4ppc.com/android/help/camera.html).

CameraEx

(For more information see http://bit.ly/16XWdKt)
This library extends the Camera library functionality. The CameraEx class requires Android 2.3+. It allows you to easily open the back or front camera, preview and save images, and includes methods to convert preview images to JPEG, to save the pictures taken, etc.

CustomListView

(For more information see http://bit.ly/Zoo9Rv)

A class module providing a flexible list based on ScrollView (page 379). It is suited for lists of up to 2000 items. Each item is made of a Panel that can hold any views. Each item can have a different height and the height can be set automatically based on the text.

DateUtils

(For more information see http://bit.ly/1gbwP7N)
A code module providing date and time related methods. Formal specification here (http://www.basic4ppc.com/android/help/dateutils.html).

DBUtils

(For more information see http://bit.ly/1eihJc5)
A code module providing database utilities which help you integrate SQLite databases in your program. We discuss this in the DBUtils (page 160) section of this book.

DropBox Sync

(For more information see http://bit.ly/11PhQap)
This library wraps the Dropbox Sync API (https://www.dropbox.com/developers/sync). Using this API, it is quite simple to store (and retrieve) data in a folder inside the user's Dropbox account.

Excel

(For more information see http://bit.ly/1cK2gDC)
This library wraps the open source jexcel (http://www.andykhan.com/jexcelapi/) project and allows you to read or write Excel workbooks. This library supports only XLS files; XSLX is not supported. Formal specification here (http://www.basic4ppc.com/android/help/excel.html).

GamePad

(For more information see http://bit.ly/GXt2ud)
This class module implements a multitouch gamepad made of two "joysticks".

Google Maps

(For more information see http://bit.ly/GXt3yj)
A library which allows you to add Google maps to your application. This library requires Android 3+ and will only work on devices with Google Play service. There is an on-line tutorial (http://bit.ly/10koqra) to support this library. Formal specification here (http://www.basic4ppc.com/android/help/googlemaps.html).

HttpServer

(For more information see http://bit.ly/16XWCg2)
A library which allows you to easily embed an HTTP server in your application. Formal specification here (http://www.basic4ppc.com/android/help/httpserver.html).

HttpUtils2

(For more information see
http://www.basic4ppc.com/forum/showthread.php?p=109068)
Two code modules (HttpUtils2Service and HttpJob) which allow you to use POST and GET to retrieve data from a web server, and then handle the data when it eventually arrives. Formal specification here (http://www.basic4ppc.com/android/help/httputils2.html).

InAppBilling

(For more information see http://bit.ly/19UidUJ)
This library is described elsewhere in this book (page 199).

JSch

(For more information see http://bit.ly/17ndfMr)
A library supporting SFTP (SSH File Transfer Protocol, also called Secured File Transfer Protocol). Formal specification here (http://www.basic4ppc.com/android/help/jsch.html).

JTidy

(For more information see http://bit.ly/16FdINo)
A library which allows you to convert an HTML page to XHTML. This can then be parsed with an XML parser, which can be more efficient than parsing the HTML using regular expressions (page 224). Formal specification here (http://www.basic4ppc.com/android/help/jtidy.html).

KeyValueStore

(For more information see http://bit.ly/1fu3UdE)
A class which uses an SQLite database to store and retrieve any kind of values you need to store persistently, such as user parameters, where each value is mapped to a key. A Keystore is very similar to a Map except that the data are stored in the file system. It can be used to store user preferences before Android calls **`Activity_Pause`**, then restore them on **`Activity_Resume`**. However, you might want to consider using StateManager for this purpose. See below.

Licensing

This library is described elsewhere in this book (page 200).

Net

(For more information see http://bit.ly/123LkwZ)
This library supports FTP, SMTP and POP3 protocols. Both regular connections and SSL connections are supported. Formal specification here (http://www.basic4ppc.com/android/help/net.html).

OAuth

(For more information see http://bit.ly/ZRSPuG)

A library which implements the OAuth protocol to allow you to sign HTTP requests (as required by some servers). Formal specification here (http://www.basic4ppc.com/android/help/oauth.html).

PayPal

(For more information see http://bit.ly/11PgPPN)
This library is a wrapper for the PayPal Mobile Payments Libraries (MPL) SDK. It allows users to pay for something using their PayPal account. Note that, as this book goes to press, PayPal is in the process of migrating to a new SDK named Mobile SDK (http://bit.ly/GXuDAq).

SearchView

(For more information see http://bit.ly/ZRU0Kz)
A class providing a more powerful alternative to AutoCompleteEditText (page 341). SearchView is quicker than AutoCompleteEditText and shows items that contain the input text anywhere, not just at the start of the item.

SMB

(For more information see http://bit.ly/165Yoqn)
This library provides access to a Microsoft Windows Network. There is a tutorial here (http://bit.ly/165YEWk) on how to use it. Formal specification here (http://www.basic4ppc.com/android/help/smb.html).

Speak Button

(For more information see http://bit.ly/11Pf1X2)
This class makes it easy to add a button which allows users to input data into an EditText field by speaking.

SQLCipher

(For more information see http://bit.ly/165Z6Uq)
This library allows you to encrypt an SQLite database.

StateManager

(For more information see http://bit.ly/10mRVZv)
A code module which takes care of handling the application UI state and settings including saving them to a file. It is available within the StateManagerExample which can be found here (http://bit.ly/10mRVZv), where documentation can also be found.

TableView

(For more information see http://bit.ly/165ZUIM)
This class makes it easy to add to your project and instantiate any number of tables in a layout. It is possible for tables to contain 500,000 cells. This is much better than implementing a table using a ScrollView (page 379).

Tap for Tap

Tap for Tap offers a way to promote your app and a way of generating ad revenue, or perhaps to do both. It is described elsewhere in this book (page 199).

USB Host

(For more information see http://bit.ly/11Pjzwu)
This library allows you to connect your device (Android 3.1 and above) to support USB host mode. With this feature you can connect to regular client usb devices. A tutorial is available here (http://bit.ly/11Pj3hZ). Formal specification here (http://www.basic4ppc.com/android/help/usb.html).

USBSerial

(For more information see http://bit.ly/11PiqoA)
This library supports various popular chips that support serial emulation over a USB connection and provides a common API to communicate with them all. Formal specification here (http://www.basic4ppc.com/android/help/usbserial.html).

XMLBuilder

(For more information see http://bit.ly/1663zXh)
This library allow you to create simple XML documents quickly and painlessly. Formal specification here (http://www.basic4ppc.com/android/help/xmlbuilder.html).

YouTube

(For more information see http://bit.ly/16648QF)
This library allows you to play YouTube videos inside your application. Formal specification here (http://www.basic4ppc.com/android/help/youtube.html).

Additional User Libraries

Introduction

There are many superb user-created libraries because the Basic4Android community is very fortunate to have some great library developers who love Basic4Android and want to share their work freely with others.
There are too many libraries for us to describe them all, and new ones are being added all the time. We provide links to lists of them and give details below of several of them to give a flavor of the types of libraries available.

List of libraries

Additional User Libraries

We give some examples of user-created libraries below. For a list of other user libraries with links to their documentation, see:
http://www.basic4ppc.com/android/documentation.html#libraries

Downloading User Libraries

For a list sorted by the user who created the library with links to the download page, see:
http://www.basic4ppc.com/android/wiki/index.php/Libraries

How to create a library

For details on how to create your own library, see here (page 406).

How to Share your Library

License

Unless otherwise stated, user-created libraries (jar files) which are uploaded to the Basic4Android website are licensed with the creative commons CC BY 3.0 license (http://creativecommons.org/licenses/by/3.0/). Only Basic4Android licensed users can use the JAR files and XML files to create apps, and distribute apps that have these libraries included, but the individual jar and XML files should not be distributed separately.

To load or update a library

- Download the library zip file somewhere.
- Unzip it.
- Copy the xxx.jar and xxx.xml files to either the
- - Basic4Android Library folder for a standard Basic4Android library or
- - Additional libraries folder for an additional library.
- Right-click the Lib Tab list to select Refresh.

Which ones does a project need?

To discover which additional libraries a project needs, you can open the Basic4Android (.b4a) file with a text editor. The libraries are listed in the file headers.
When you add libraries, you do not need to restart the IDE. You can just right-click on the list of libraries and select Refresh.

Dialogs Library

This library (written by Andrew Graham) contains several modal, that is blocking, dialogs by which the user can enter data. Presently, they are an InputDialog for text, a TimeDialog for times, a DateDialog for dates, both a ColorDialog and a ColorPickerDialog for colors, a NumberDialog for numbers, a FileDialog for folders and file names, and a CustomDialog.

Source

Download the library here (http://bit.ly/168SKTs).

Notes

Android does not provide modal dialogs, but Basic4Android has a special mechanism to permit them. The Android Activity lifetime system makes this support complicated because Activities can be created and destroyed at will by Android. To avoid stack runaway on the GUI thread when an Activity is destroyed, the stack must be unwound to the lowest level.

The Basic4Android modal mechanism does this by closing any modal dialog being shown and exiting the Sub that called the dialog, plus exiting any Sub that called that Sub, and so on, in order to return the main thread to the message loop. This means that the application does not necessarily receive a return value from the dialog and has its expected flow of execution interrupted. This will probably most often happen if the device is rotated while a modal dialog is displayed, so the Activity is destroyed and rebuilt with a new layout.

Because this may happen unexpectedly, applications (depending upon their logical structure) may need code in the **Pause** and **Resume** Subs to deal with the fact that modal dialog closure may not always be detected. For example, when a modal dialog is shown, you could set a Boolean as **True**. This variable would have to be declared within **Sub Process_Globals**. When the modal dialog returns you could clear the Boolean with some checking code in the **Resume** Sub.

The above discussion also applies to the Basic4Android modal dialogs **InputList**, **InputMultiList**, **Msgbox** and **Msgbox2**.

The value returned from the dialogs, called the "dialog return value" is:
-1 if the user clicks the left button (called "Positive" in the documentation below)
-3 if the user clicks the center button (called "Cancel" in the documentation below)
-2 if the user clicks the left button (called "Negative" in the documentation below)

List of types:

ColorDialog
ColorDialogHSV
ColorPickerDialog (page 534)
CustomDialog (page 535)
CustomDialog2 (page 536)
DateDialog (page 537)
FileDialog (page 538)
InputDialog (page 539)
NumberDialog (page 541)
TimeDialog (page 542)

ColorDialog

This modal dialog allows the user to define a color by its Red, Green and Blue components. This is an **`Activity`** object; it cannot be declared under **`Sub Process_Globals`**.

Members:

ARGB (Alpha As Int) As Int
Blue As Int
Green As Int
Red As Int
Response As Int [read only]
RGB As Int
Show (title As String, Positive As String, Cancel As String, Negative As String, icon As Bitmap) As Int
Version As Double [read only]

ARGB (Alpha As Int) As Int

Returns an integer value representing the color built from the three components and with the specified alpha value.
Alpha - A value from 0 to 255, where 0 is fully transparent and 255 is fully opaque.

Blue As Int

Sets the value of the blue component of the dialog when it is initially shown. Returns the value of the blue component of the dialog when it was closed.

Green As Int

Sets the value of the green component of the dialog when it is initially shown. Returns the value of the green component of the dialog when it was closed.

Red As Int

Sets the value of the red component of the dialog when it is initially shown. Returns the value of the red component of the dialog when it was closed.

Response As Int [read only]

Returns the response code that the dialog returned when it last closed.

RGB As Int

Sets the value of the red, green and blue components of the dialog when it is initially shown. Returns the color of the red, green and blue components of the dialog when it was closed. Alpha of the provided color is ignored; the alpha of the dialog is set to 255 (opaque).

Show (title As String, Positive As String, Cancel As String, Negative As String, icon As Bitmap) As Int

Shows a modal color dialog with the specified title.
Title - The dialog title.
Positive - The text to show for the "positive" button. Pass "" if you don't want to show the button.

Cancel - The text to show for the "cancel" button. Pass "" if you don't want to show the button.
Negative - The text to show for the "negative" button. Pass "" if you don't want to show the button.
Icon - A bitmap that will be drawn near the title. Pass **`Null`** if you don't want to show an icon.
Returns one of the DialogResponse values.

Version As Double [read only]

Returns the version of the library.

ColorDialogHSV

This modal dialog allows the user to define a color by its Hue, Saturation and Value components. This is an **`Activity`** object; it cannot be declared under **`Sub Process_Globals`**.

Members:

- ARGB (alpha As Int) As Int
- Hue As Float
- Response As Int [read only]
- RGB As Int
- Saturation As Float
- Show (title As String, Positive As String, Cancel As String, Negative As String, icon As Bitmap) As Int
- Value As Float
- Version As Double [read only]

ARGB (Alpha As Int) As Int

Returns an integer value representing the color built from the three components and with the specified alpha value.
Alpha - A value from 0 to 255, where 0 is fully transparent and 255 is fully opaque.

Hue As Float

Sets the value of the hue component of the dialog when it is initially shown. Returns the value of the hue component of the dialog when it was closed. The range of valid numbers for hue is 0.0 to 360.0.

Response As Int [read only]

Returns the response code that the dialog returned when it last closed.

RGB As Int

Sets the value of the red, green and blue components of the dialog when it is initially shown. Returns the color of the red, green and blue components of the dialog when it was closed. Alpha of the provided color is ignored and the alpha of the dialog is set to 255 (opaque).

Saturation As Float

Sets the value of the saturation component of the dialog when it is initially shown. Returns the value of the saturation component of the dialog when it was closed. The range of valid numbers for saturation is 0.0 to 1.0.

Show (title As String, Positive As String, Cancel As String, Negative As String, icon As Bitmap) As Int

Shows a modal color dialog with the specified title.
Title - The dialog title.
Positive - The text to show for the "positive" button. Pass "" if you don't want to show the button. **Cancel** - The text to show for the "cancel" button. Pass "" if you don't want to show the button.
Negative - The text to show for the "negative" button. Pass "" if you don't want to show the button.
Icon - A bitmap that will be drawn near the title. Pass `Null` if you don't want to show an icon.
Returns one of the DialogResponse values.

Value As Float

Sets the value component of the dialog when it is initially shown. Returns the value of the dialog when it was closed. The range of valid numbers for Value is from 0.0 to 1.0.

Version As Double [read only]

Returns the version of the library.

ColorPickerDialog

This modal dialog allows the user to select a color from a palette of colors. The color may be from a standard palette in the dialog or a custom programmed palette. This is an `Activity` object; it cannot be declared under `Sub Process_Globals`.

Members:

- ARGB (Alpha As Int) As Int
- GetPaletteAt (index As Int) As Int
- Palette() As Int
- ResetPalette
- Response As Int [read only]
- RGB As Int
- SetPaletteAt (index As Int, color As Int)
- Show (title As String, Positive As String, Cancel As String, Negative As String, icon As Bitmap) As Int
- Version As Double [read only]

ARGB (Alpha As Int) As Int

Returns an integer value representing the color built from the chosen color and with the specified alpha value.

Alpha - A value from 0 to 255 where 0 is fully transparent and 255 is fully opaque.

GetPaletteAt (index As Int) As Int

Gets the value of the color at the specified index in the current palette.

Palette() As Int

Copies the colors in the array provided to the palette of colors in the dialog. The provided array should contain 15 colors. Returns an integer array that is a copy of the present palette.

ResetPalette

Reset the palette of colors to the standard palette of the dialog.

Response As Int [read only]

Returns the response code that the dialog returned when it last closed.

RGB As Int

Sets the value of the chosen color of the dialog when it is initially shown. Returns the value of the chosen color of the dialog when it was closed.

SetPaletteAt (index As Int, color As Int)

Sets the value of the color at the specified index in the current palette. This allows replacing just one or two colors without defining an entire palette.

Show (title As String, Positive As String, Cancel As String, Negative As String, icon As Bitmap) As Int

Shows a modal color picker dialog with the specified title.
Title - The dialog title.
Positive - The text to show for the "positive" button. Pass "" if you don't want to show the button.
Cancel - The text to show for the "cancel" button. Pass "" if you don't want to show the button.
Negative - The text to show for the "negative" button. Pass "" if you don't want to show the button.
Icon - A bitmap that will be drawn near the title. Pass `Null` if you don't want to show an icon.
Returns one of the DialogResponse values.

Version As Double [read only]

Returns the version of the library.

CustomDialog

This modal dialog displays a custom set of controls laid out on a Basic4Android Panel. The Panel is displayed at an abolute position and size within the dialog. This is an **`Activity`** object; it cannot be declared under **`Sub Process_Globals`**.

Members:

AddView (view1 As View, left As Int, top As Int, width As Int, height As Int)

Adds the custom layout view, most probably a Panel, to the custom dialog. Although named AddView to match Basic4Android syntax, only one view can be added. Adding a view replaces any existing view previously added to the dialog.

Response As Int [read only]

Returns the response code that the dialog returned when it last closed.

Show (Title As String, Positive As String, Cancel As String, Negative As String, icon As Bitmap) As Int

Shows a modal custom dialog with the specified title.
Title - The dialog title.
Positive - The text to show for the "positive" button. Pass "" if you don't want to show the button.
Cancel - The text to show for the "cancel" button. Pass "" if you don't want to show the button.
Negative - The text to show for the "negative" button. Pass "" if you don't want to show the button.
Icon - A bitmap that will be drawn near the title. Pass `Null` if you don't want to show an icon. Returns one of the DialogResponse values.

Version As Double [read only]

Returns the version of the library.

CustomDialog2

This modal dialog displays a custom set of controls laid out on a Basic4Android Panel. The Panel will be automatically centred in the displayed dialog. This is an `Activity` object; it cannot be declared under `Sub Process_Globals`.

Members:

AddView (view1 As View, width As Int, height As Int)

Adds the custom layout view, most probably a Panel, to the custom dialog. Although named AddView to match Basic4Android syntax, only one view can be added. Adding a view replaces any existing view previously added to the dialog.

Response As Int [read only]

Returns the response code that the dialog returned when it last closed.

Show (Title As String, Positive As String, Cancel As String, Negative As String, icon As Bitmap) As Int

Shows a modal custom dialog with the specified title.
Title - The dialog title.
Positive - The text to show for the "positive" button. Pass "" if you don't want to show the button.

Cancel - The text to show for the "cancel" button. Pass "" if you don't want to show the button.
Negative - The text to show for the "negative" button. Pass "" if you don't want to show the button.
Icon - A bitmap that will be drawn near the title. Pass `Null` if you don't want to show an icon.
Returns one of the DialogResponse values.

Version As Double [read only]

Returns the version of the library.

DateDialog

This modal dialog allows the collection of user-entered data in the form of a date.
This is an `Activity` object; it cannot be declared under `Sub Process_Globals`.

Members:

DateTicks As Long
DayOfMonth As Int
Month As Int
Response As Int [read only]
SetDate (dayofmonth As Int, month As Int, year As Int)
Show (Message As String, Title As String, Positive As String, Cancel As String, Negative As String, icon As Bitmap) As Int
ShowCalendar As Boolean
Version As Double [read only]
Year As Int

DateTicks As Long

Sets the date value of the dialog when it is initially shown. Returns the date value in ticks of the dialog when it is closed.

DayOfMonth As Int

Sets the day of month value of the dialog when it is initially shown. Returns the day of month value of the dialog when it is closed.

Month As Int

Sets the month value of the dialog when it is initially shown. Returns the month value of the dialog when it is closed.

Response As Int [read only]

Returns the response code that the dialog returned when it last closed.

SetDate (dayofmonth As Int, month As Int, year As Int)

Sets the date values of the dialog when it is initially shown.

Show (Message As String, Title As String, Positive As String, Cancel As String, Negative As String, icon As Bitmap) As Int

Shows a modal date input dialog with the specified message and title.

Message - The dialog message.
Title - The dialog title.
Positive - The text to show for the "positive" button. Pass "" if you don't want to show the button.
Cancel - The text to show for the "cancel" button. Pass "" if you don't want to show the button.
Negative - The text to show for the "negative" button. Pass "" if you don't want to show the button.
Icon - A bitmap that will be drawn near the title. Pass `Null` if you don't want to show an icon.
Returns one of the DialogResponse values.

ShowCalendar As Boolean

Gets or sets a flag indicating whether to show the Calendar part of the DateDialog. This only works on devices supporting API 11 (Honeycomb 3.0.x) or later

Version As Double [read only]

Returns the version of the library.

Year As Int

Sets the year value of the dialog when it is initially shown. Returns the year value of the dialog when it is closed.

FileDialog

This modal dialog allows the user to choose a folder and choose or enter a filename. This is an `Activity` object; it cannot be declared under `Sub Process_Globals`.

Members:

- ChosenName As String
- FastScroll As Boolean
- FileFilter As String
- FilePath As String
- KeyboardPopUp As Boolean
- Response As Int [read only]
- ScrollingBackgroundColor As Int
- Show (Title As String, Positive As String, Cancel As String, Negative As String, icon As Bitmap) As Int
- ShowOnlyFolders As Boolean
- Version As Double [read only]

ChosenName As String

Sets the filename initially shown to the user. Returns the filename entered or chosen by the user.

FastScroll As Boolean

Gets or sets whether the fast scroll thumb (an indicator that can be dragged to quickly scroll through the list) is displayed by the dialog.

FileFilter As String
Gets or sets the filter values of the dialog. The filter can be a single value ".txt". The filter can also be a comma-separated list of values ".jpg,.png". Note that spaces in filter values are significant and are not ignored. If a filename contains the text of a filter value, the file will be displayed. A value of an empty string, the default, will show all files.

FilePath As String
Sets the file path of the dialog when it is initially shown. Returns the file path of the dialog when it is closed. Note that setting the file path also sets ChosenName to an empty string.

KeyboardPopUp As Boolean
Gets or sets whether the keyboard only pops up when the EditText is clicked.

Response As Int [read only]
Returns the response code that the dialog returned when it last closed.

ScrollingBackgroundColor As Int
Gets or sets the background color that will be used while scrolling the list. This is an optimization done to make the scrolling smoother. Set to Colors.Transparent if the background behind the list is not a solid color. The default is whatever is the default for the particular device.

Show (Title As String, Positive As String, Cancel As String, Negative As String, icon As Bitmap) As Int
Shows a modal file dialog with the specified title.
Title - The dialog title.
Positive - The text to show for the "positive" button. Pass "" if you don't want to show the button.
Cancel - The text to show for the "cancel" button. Pass "" if you don't want to show the button.
Negative - The text to show for the "negative" button. Pass "" if you don't want to show the button.
Icon - A bitmap that will be drawn near the title. Pass `Null` if you don't want to show an icon. Returns one of the DialogResponse values.

ShowOnlyFolders As Boolean
Gets or sets whether to show only folders and not files in the dialog.

Version As Double [read only]
Returns the version of the library.

InputDialog

This modal dialog allows the collection of user-entered data in the form of text. The default is free text, but the input can be restricted to numeric characters only or to signed numbers, including a decimal point. This is an `Activity` object; it cannot be declared under `Sub Process_Globals`.

Members:

Hint As String
HintColor As Int
Input As String
INPUT_TYPE_DECIMAL_NUMBERS As Int
INPUT_TYPE_NONE As Int
INPUT_TYPE_NUMBERS As Int
INPUT_TYPE_PHONE As Int
INPUT_TYPE_TEXT As Int
InputType As Int
PasswordMode As Boolean
Response As Int [read only]
Show (message As String, title As String, Positive As String, Cancel As String, Negative As String, icon As Bitmap) As Int
Version As Double [read only]

Hint As String

Gets or sets the text that will appear when the dialog is empty.

HintColor As Int

Gets or sets the hint text color.

Input As String

Sets the initial text when the dialog is shown and returns the text entered by the user.

INPUT_TYPE_DECIMAL_NUMBERS As Int

INPUT_TYPE_NONE As Int

This can be useful, for example, if you use a read-only **`InputDialog`** for which you do not want a keyboard to be displayed.

INPUT_TYPE_NUMBERS As Int

INPUT_TYPE_PHONE As Int

INPUT_TYPE_TEXT As Int

InputType As Int

Sets or returns the input type accepted by the input box. Possible values are:

- ThisDialogName.INPUT_TYPE_NUMBERS for integer numbers.
- ThisDialogName.INPUT_TYPE_DECIMAL_NUMBER for signed decimal numbers.
- ThisDialogName.INPUT_TYPE_TEXT for free text.
- ThisDialogName.INPUT_TYPE_PHONE for telephone numbers.

PasswordMode As Boolean

Sets or returns whether this dialog hides the actual characters entered by the user.

Response As Int [read only]
Returns the response code that the dialog returned when it last closed.

Show (message As String, title As String, Positive As String, Cancel As String, Negative As String, icon As Bitmap) As Int
Shows a modal text input dialog with the specified message and title.
Message - The dialog message. Title - The dialog title.
Positive - The text to show for the "positive" button. Pass "" if you don't want to show the button.
Cancel - The text to show for the "cancel" button. Pass "" if you don't want to show the button.
Negative - The text to show for the "negative" button. Pass "" if you don't want to show the button.
Icon - A bitmap that will be drawn near the title. Pass `Null` if you don't want to show an icon. Returns one of the DialogResponse values.

Version As Double [read only]
Returns the version of the library.

NumberDialog

This configurable modal dialog allows the user to enter a number. The dialog is configurable to show any number of digits between a minimum of one and a maximum of nine The display of a decimal point is optional and the character displayed as the decimal indicator is configurable. Note that the number accepted and returned by the dialog is an integer value and so may need scaling appropriately. This is an `Activity` object; it cannot be declared under `Sub Process_Globals`.

Members:

Decimal As Int
DecimalChar As Char
Digits As Int
Number As Int
Response As Int [read only]
Show (title As String, Positive As String, Cancel As String, Negative As String, icon As Bitmap) As Int
ShowSign As Boolean
Version As Double [read only]

Decimal As Int
Gets or sets the position of a displayed decimal point in the dialog. Zero (the default) displays no decimals, one indicates a single decimal, and so on.

DecimalChar As Char
Gets or sets the displayed decimal character in the dialog. The default is ".".

Digits As Int
Gets or sets the number of digits displayed in the dialog when it is open. One is the minimum, nine is the maximum. The default is five. If ShowSign is **`True`**, then the leftmost digit will display a "+" or "-" and only eight digits will be shown.

Number As Int
Sets the number initially displayed in the dialog when it is shown. If the number is negative and ShowSign is **`False`**, then the absolute value is displayed. Gets the number entered by the user after the dialog is closed. If ShowSign is **`True`**, the sign of the number corresponds to the sign entered by the user.

Response As Int [read only]
Returns the response code that the dialog returned when it last closed.

Show (title As String, Positive As String, Cancel As String, Negative As String, icon As Bitmap) As Int
Shows a modal number picker dialog with the specified title.
Title - The dialog title.
Positive - The text to show for the "positive" button. Pass "" if you don't want to show the button.
Cancel - The text to show for the "cancel" button. Pass "" if you don't want to show the button.
Negative - The text to show for the "negative" button. Pass "" if you don't want to show the button.
Icon - A bitmap that will be drawn near the title. Pass **`Null`** if you don't want to show an icon.
Returns one of the DialogResponse values.

ShowSign As Boolean
Gets or sets whether the displayed number includes a sign character. The default is **`False`**, so no minus sign is displayed if the number is negative.

Version As Double [read only]
Returns the version of the library.

TimeDialog
This modal dialog allows the collection of user entered data in the form of a time. The time may be entered in 12 or 24 hour format as determined by the programmer. This is an **`Activity`** object; it cannot be declared under **`Sub Process_Globals`**.

Members:
Hour As Int
Is24Hours As Boolean
Minute As Int
Response As Int [read only]
SetTime (hour As Int, minutes As Int, hours24 As Boolean)

Show (Message As String, Title As String, Positive As String, Cancel As String, Negative As String, icon As Bitmap) As Int
TimeTicks As Long
Version As Double [read only]

Hour As Int

Sets the hour value of the dialog when it is initially shown. Returns the hour value of the dialog when it is closed.

Is24Hours As Boolean

Sets or returns whether the dialog shows the time in 24 hour format.

Minute As Int

Sets the minute value of the dialog when it is initially shown. Returns the minute value of the dialog when it is closed.

Response As Int [read only]

Returns the response code that the dialog returned when it last closed.

SetTime (hour As Int, minutes As Int, hours24 As Boolean)

Sets the time values of the dialog when it is initially shown.

Show (Message As String, Title As String, Positive As String, Cancel As String, Negative As String, icon As Bitmap) As Int

Shows a modal time input dialog with the specified message and title.
Message - The dialog message.
Title - The dialog title.
Positive - The text to show for the "positive" button. Pass "" if you don't want to show the button.
Cancel - The text to show for the "cancel" button. Pass "" if you don't want to show the button.
Negative - The text to show for the "negative" button. Pass "" if you don't want to show the button.
Icon - A bitmap that will be drawn near the title. Pass `Null` if you don't want to show an icon.
Returns one of the DialogResponse values.

TimeTicks As Long

Sets the time value of the dialog when it is initially shown. Returns the time value in ticks of the dialog when it is closed.

Version As Double [read only]

Returns the version of the library.

Reflection Library

This library (written by Andrew Graham (http://www.basic4ppc.com/forum/members/agraham.html)) is perhaps one of the most useful user contributions. It contains the Reflector object which allows access to methods and fields of Android objects that are not exposed in the Basic4Android language. It does this by means of a facility called "Reflection" that uses meta-data for objects that are included in the application package and allows dynamic access to fields and methods at runtime.

Source

Download the library here (http://bit.ly/11f1e7K).

Notes

For more information about this library see here (http://www.basic4ppc.com/android/help/reflection.html),

List of types:

Reflector

Reflector

This is the object that does the reflection. In order to use this successfully, you will need an understanding of the use of Java classes and their fields and methods. Technical documentation (although often lacking useful explanatory details) is available on the Google Android website at http://developer.android.com.
Java is case sensitive and, as used for Android, does not support properties. Properties, as implemented in Basic4Android, are actually methods with lower-case prefixes 'set' and 'get'. 'set' methods take a single parameter and return void, 'get' methods take no parameters and return the requested values. Any other method signatures are exposed by Basic4Android as normal methods. For example, the Left property of a View is actually implemented in Java code as two methods, **`int getLeft()`** and **`void setLeft(int left)`**. The Basic4Android compiler makes them look like a single property to the programmer.

Events:

Click(ViewTag As Object); LongClick(ViewTag As Object) As Boolean; Focus(ViewTag As Object, Focus As Boolean); Key(ViewTag As Object, KeyCode As Int, KeyEvent As Object) As Boolean; Touch(ViewTag As Object, Action As Int, X As Float, Y As Float, MotionEvent As Object) As Boolean.

Example

```
Sub RegexReplace(Pattern As String, Text As String, Replacement
As String) As String
' example RegexReplace("abc(d)(e)", "abcde", "$2 $1")
 Dim m As Matcher
 m = Regex.Matcher(Pattern, Text)
 Dim r As Reflector
 r.Target = m
 Return r.RunMethod2("replaceAll", Replacement,
"java.lang.String")
End Sub
```

Members:

CreateObject (type As String) As Object

CreateObject2 (type As String, args() As Object, types() As String) As Object

GetActivity As Activity

GetActivityBA As BA

GetArray (indices() As Int) As Object

GetB4AClass (component As String) As Class

GetContext As Context

GetField (field As String) As Object

GetField2 (fieldinfo As Field) As Object

GetFieldInfo (field As String) As Field

GetMethod (method As String, types() As String) As Method

GetMostCurrent (component As String) As Object

GetProcessBA (component As String) As BA

GetProxy (page 548) (interfacenames() As String, b4asubname As String) As Proxy

GetPublicField (page 548) (field As String) As Object

GetStaticField (page 548) (classname As String, field As String) As Object

InvokeMethod (page 548) (instance As Object, method As Method, args() As Object) As Object

IsNull (page 548) As Boolean [read only]

RunMethod (page 548) (method As String) As Object

RunMethod2 (page 548) (method As String, arg1 As String, type1 As String) As Object

RunMethod3 (page 549) (method As String, arg1 As String, type1 As String, arg2 As String, type2 As String) As Object

RunMethod4 (page 549) (method As String, args() As Object, types() As String) As Object

RunPublicmethod (page 549) (Method As String, Args() As Object, types() As String) As Object

RunStaticMethod (page 549) (classname As String, method As String, args() As Object, types() As String) As Object
SetArray (page 549) (indices() As Int, value As String, type As String)
SetArray2 (page 549) (indices() As Int, value As Object)
SetField (page 550) (field As String, value As String, type As String)
SetField2 (page 550) (field As String, value As Object)
SetField3 (page 550) (fieldinfo As Field, value As String, type As String)
SetField4 (page 550) (fieldinfo As Field, value As Object)
SetOnClickListener (page 550) (sub As String)
SetOnCreateContextMenuListener (page 550) (sub As String)
SetOnFocusListener (page 550) (sub As String)
SetOnKeyListener (page 550) (sub As String)
SetOnLongClickListener (page 550) (sub As String)
SetOnTouchListener (page 551) (sub As String)
SetPublicField (page 551) (field As String, value As String, type As String)
SetPublicField2 (page 551) (field As String, value As Object)
SetStaticField (page 551) (classname As String, field As String, value As String, type As String)
SetStaticField2 (page 551) (classname As String, field As String, value As Object)
Target (page 551) As Object
TargetRank (page 551) As Int()
ToString (page 551) As String
TypeName (page 551) As String [read only]
Version (page 551) As Double [read only]

CreateObject (type As String) As Object

Creates and returns a new object of the specified type using the default constructor.

CreateObject2 (type As String, args() As Object, types() As String) As Object

Creates and returns a new object of the specified type using the constructor that matches the array of type names given and passes it the arguments provided. The array of type names is needed in order to find the correct constructor because primitives passed in the Args array are boxed and so CreateNew cannot tell whether to look for a target constructor that accepts a primitive parameter type or a boxed primitive object type.

GetActivity As Activity

Returns the current activity if any. To avoid memory leaks, this should not be used by a `Reflector` that is a `Sub Process_Globals` object. To use this requires a knowledge of the structure of a Basic4Android application.

GetActivityBA As BA

Returns the Activity BA of the current activity. To use this requires a knowledge of the structure of a Basic4Android application and an explanation is beyond the scope of this book. To avoid memory leaks this should not be used by a Reflector that is a `Sub Process_Globals` object.

GetArray (indices() As Int) As Object

Returns the Object at the position(s) in an array specified by the contents of **indices**.
indices - must be an integer array of the same rank as the Target array or an error will occur.

GetB4AClass (component As String) As Class

Returns the Java Class for the specified B4A Activity, Service or Code module. To use this requires a knowledge of the structure of a Basic4Android application.

GetContext As Context

Returns the Context of the Process to which the Reflection object belongs. This is the Application object returned from Activity.getApplicationContext().

GetField (field As String) As Object

Returns the value of the field of the current target. Protected and private fields may be accessed if allowed by any security manager which may be present. Target must be an instance of a Class, not a Class object.

GetField2 (fieldinfo As Field) As Object

Returns the value of the field of the current target. Target must be an instance of a Class, not a Class object.

GetFieldInfo (field As String) As Field

Finding a field from its string representation is expensive, so this method can be used to get the Field information object and save it for multiple accesses of the same field. Protected and private fields may be accessed if allowed by any security manager which may be present.

GetMethod (method As String, types() As String) As Method

Finding a method from its string representation is expensive, so this method can be used to get the Method information object and save it for multiple invocations of the same method.
The String array of type names is needed in order to find the correct variant of the method.

GetMostCurrent (component As String) As Object

Returns the current instance for the specified B4A Activity or Service module. This might return `Null` if the Activity or Service is not instantiated. Note that Code modules do not have a current instance. To use this requires a knowledge of the structure of a Basic4Android application.

GetProcessBA (component As String) As BA

Returns the processBA instance for the specified B4A Activity or Service module. To use this requires a knowledge of the structure of a Basic4Android application.

GetProxy (interfacenames() As String, b4asubname As String) As Proxy

In Java, you can generate an interface at runtime and have it run a pre-compiled method. Many events in Android are handled by an interface that typically has an "onXxxxx" method that is called with some parameters relevant to the event. The interface is typically set on an object using that object's "setOnXxxxxListener" method.
This GetProxy method dynamically creates a proxy instance that implements one or more specified interfaces and which contains the code to call a specified Basic4Android Sub when any of the interface methods are called.
Typically, this instance will implement one or more listeners and will then be assigned to an object instance using RunMethod4 and its setOnXxxxxListener method.
When a method of one of the specified interfaces is called, the proxy will call the specified Basic4Android Sub passing the method name as a string and any arguments in an object array.
Note that interfaces declared as internal to a class will need a "$" instead of a "." as their final separator and all interfaces need to be fully qualified. e.g android.view.View$OnTouchListener.
The Basic4Android Sub called must have the signature Sub WhateverName(method As String, anyargs() As Object) As Object.

GetPublicField (field As String) As Object

Returns the value of the public field of the current target. This is more efficient than GetField but can only access public fields. Target must be an instance of a Class, not a Class object.

GetStaticField (classname As String, field As String) As Object

Returns the value of the specified static field of the specified class. Protected and private fields may be accessed if allowed by any security manager which may be present. Static fields may also be accessed with GetField and an instance of the class.

InvokeMethod (instance As Object, method As Method, args() As Object) As Object

Invoke the provided Method on the provided object instance and return the result.

IsNull As Boolean [read only]

Returns `True` if the present value of Target is `Null`.

RunMethod (method As String) As Object

Runs the specified method on the current target. Protected and private methods may be accessed if allowed by any security manager which may be present.

RunMethod2 (method As String, arg1 As String, type1 As String) As Object

Runs the specified method on the current target passing it the argument provided. Protected and private methods may be accessed if allowed by any security manager which may be present.

RunMethod3 (method As String, arg1 As String, type1 As String, arg2 As String, type2 As String) As Object
Runs the specified method on the current object passing it the arguments provided. Protected and private methods may be accessed if allowed by any security manager which may be present.

RunMethod4 (method As String, args() As Object, types() As String) As Object
Runs the specified method on the current target passing it the arguments provided. Protected and private methods may be accessed if allowed by any security manager which may be present.
The String array of type names is needed in order to find the correct method because primitives passed in the Args array are boxed and so RunMethod cannot tell whether to look for a target method that accepts a primitive parameter type or a boxed primitive object type.

RunPublicmethod (Method As String, Args() As Object, types() As String) As Object
Runs the specified method on the current target passing it the arguments provided. This is more efficient that RunMethod4 but the method must be public.
The String array of type names is needed in order to find the correct method because primitives passed in the Args array are boxed and so RunMethod cannot tell whether to look for a target method that accepts a primitive parameter type or a boxed primitive object type.

RunStaticMethod (classname As String, method As String, args() As Object, types() As String) As Object
Runs the specified static method of the specified class passing it the arguments provided. Protected and private methods may be accessed if allowed by any security manager which may be present.
The String array of type names is needed in order to find the correct method because primitives passed in the Args array are boxed and so RunMethod cannot tell whether to look for a target method that accepts a primitive parameter type or a boxed primitive object type. For methods that take no parameters, `Null` may passed for args and types.

SetArray (indices() As Int, value As String, type As String)
Set the position(s) in an array specified by the contents of indices to the specified value. indices must be an integer array of the same rank as the Target array or an error will occur.

SetArray2 (indices() As Int, value As Object)
Set the position(s) in an array specified by the contents of indices to the specified value. indices must be an integer array of the same rank as the Target array or an error will occur.

SetField (field As String, value As String, type As String)
Sets the specified field of the current target to the value provided. Protected and private fields may be accessed if allowed by any security manager which may be present. Target must be an instance of a Class, not a Class object.

SetField2 (field As String, value As Object)
Sets the specified field of the current target to the value provided. Protected and private fields may be accessed if allowed by any security manager which may be present. Target must be an instance of a Class, not a Class object.

SetField3 (fieldinfo As Field, value As String, type As String)
Sets the specified field of the current target to the value provided. Target must be an instance of a Class, not a Class object.

SetField4 (fieldinfo As Field, value As Object)
Sets the specified field of the current target to the value provided. Target must be an instance of a Class, not a Class object.

SetOnClickListener (sub As String)
Target must be a View of some sort. In most cases, Basic4Android will have already exposed this as a Click event. Sets the OnClickListener of the view to a Sub that must have a signature of Sub Whatever(viewtag As Object).

SetOnCreateContextMenuListener (sub As String)
Target must be a View of some sort. This is included for completeness of all the Listeners that class View supports. Sets the OnCreateContextMenuListener of the view to a Sub that must have a signature of Sub Whatever(viewtag As Object, menu As Object, menuinfo As Object)

SetOnFocusListener (sub As String)
Target must be a View of some sort. Sets the onFocusChangeListener of the view to a Sub that must have a signature of Sub Whatever(viewtag As Object, focus As Boolean).
You should make sure not to call DoEvents, Msgbox or any modal Dialog inside this event as it will fail in Android 4.0.3 and above.
It may also fail if Debug is paused in the event in Android 4.0.3 and above.

SetOnKeyListener (sub As String)
Target must be a View of some sort. Sets the onKeyListener of the view to a Sub that must have a signature of Sub Whatever(viewtag As Object, keycode As Int, keyevent As Object) As Boolean.
This Sub must return `True` if it wants to consume the event or `False` otherwise.

SetOnLongClickListener (sub As String)
Target must be a View of some sort. In most cases Basic4Android will have already exposed this as a LongClick event. Sets the OnLongClickListener of the view to a Sub that must have a signature of Sub Whatever(viewtag As Object) As Boolean. This Sub must return `True` if it wants to consume the event or `False` otherwise.

SetOnTouchListener (sub As String)
Target must be a View of some sort. Sets the onTouchListener of the view to a Sub that must have a signature of Sub Whatever (viewtag As Object, action As Int, X As Float, Y As Float, motionevent As Object) As Boolean.
This Sub must return `True` if it wants to consume the event or `False` otherwise.
You should make sure not to call DoEvents, Msgbox or any modal Dialog inside this event as it will fail in Android 4.0.3 and above. If you want to do so, put the code in another sub and call this sub with CallSubDelayed.
It may also fail if Debug is paused in the event in Android 4.0.3 and above.

SetPublicField (field As String, value As String, type As String)
Sets the specified field of the current target to the value provided. This is more efficient than SetField but can only access public fields. Target must be an instance of a Class, not a Class object.

SetPublicField2 (field As String, value As Object)
Sets the specified field of the current target to the value provided. This is more efficient than SetField but can only access public fields. Target must be an instance of a Class, not a Class object.

SetStaticField (classname As String, field As String, value As String, type As String)
Sets the specified static field of the specified class to the value provided. Protected and private fields may be accessed if allowed by any security manager which may be present. Static fields may also be accessed with SetField and an instance of the class.

SetStaticField2 (classname As String, field As String, value As Object)
Sets the specified static field of the specified class to the value provided. Protected and private fields may be accessed if allowed by any security manager which may be present. Static fields may also be accessed with SetField and an instance of the class.

Target As Object
This field holds the object that is being reflected upon. The target object is assigned to this field where it can then be manipulated as required.

TargetRank As Int()
Returns an int array whose length is the number of dimensions of the array and whose contents are the length of the first element of each array dimension. A zero length integer array is returned if Target is not an array.

ToString As String
Returns the result of running the “toString()” method of the current object.

TypeName As String [read only]
Returns the name of the class of the current object.

Version As Double [read only]
Returns the version number of the library.

TabHostExtras Library

This library, created by WarWound (http://www.basic4ppc.com/forum/members/warwound.html), adds functionality to the TabHost (page 388) view.
For the library and a sample project, see here (http://bit.ly/16Bb09a).

getTabContentViewPadding (tabHost1 As TabHost) As RectWrapper

Gets the layout padding of tabHost1 TabContentView. Returns a Rect object containing pixel values.

getTabEnabled (tabHost1 As TabHost, index As Int) As Boolean

Get the Enabled state of TabIndicator #index in tabHost1.

getTabHeight (tabHost1 As TabHost) As Int

Get the height (in pixels) of the TabIndicators in tabHost1.

getTabHostPadding (tabHost1 As TabHost) As RectWrapper

Get the layout padding of tabHost1 container View. Returns a Rect object containing pixel values.

getTabTextSize (tabHost1 As TabHost) As Float

Get the text size (in pixels) of all TabIndicators.

getTabVisibility (tabHost1 As TabHost, index As Int) As Boolean

Get the visibility of TabIndicators #index in tabHost1.

setTabContentViewPadding (tabHost1 As TabHost, left As Int, top As Int, right As Int, bottom As Int)

Set the layout padding (in dip) of tabHost1 TabContentView.

setTabEnabled (tabHost1 As TabHost, enabled As Boolean)

Enable or disable all TabIndicators in tabHost1.

setTabEnabled2 (tabHost1 As TabHost, enabled As Boolean, index As Int)

Enable or disable TabIndicator #index in tabHost1.

setTabGradientDrawable (tabHost1 As TabHost, orientation As String, color1 As Int, color2 As Int, cornerRadius As Float)

Set a `GradientDrawable` as the background on all TabIndicators in tabHost1. All four corner radii of the `GradientDrawable` are set to the value of cornerRadius (in pixels).

setTabGradientDrawable2 (tabHost1 As TabHost, orientation As String, color1 As Int, color2 As Int, cornerRadius As Float())

Set a `GradientDrawable` as the background on all TabIndicators in tabHost1. Corner radii of the `GradientDrawable` are set individually (in pixels) based upon the number of elements in the array cornerRadius:
1 element defines all corner radii
2 elements define corner radii in order top left and right, bottom left and right
4 elements define corner radii in order top-left, top-right, bottom-right, bottom-left

setTabHeight (tabHost1 As TabHost, tabHeight As Int)

Set the height (in pixels) of all TabIndicators in tabHost1.

setTabHostPadding (tabHost1 As TabHost, left As Int, top As Int, right As Int, bottom As Int)

Set the layout padding (in dip) of tabHost1 container View.

setTabTextColor (tabHost1 As TabHost, Color As Int)

Set the color to be used for all tab indicators text.
This color will be used for all tab indicators regardless of their selected state.

setTabTextColorStateList (tabHost1 As TabHost, ColorStateListName As String)

Set a ColorStateList to be used for the text color of all tab indicators.
The ColorStateList must be defined in XML in your application Objects/res/drawable folder. Color for selected and not-selected tab state can be defined.

setTabTextSize (tabHost1 As TabHost, TextSize As Float)

Set the text size of all TabIndicators. TextSize is assumed to be in units of dip.

setTabTitle (tabHost1 As TabHost, Title As String, TabIndex As Int)

Set the Title text of TabIndicator #TabIndex in tabHost1.

---

setTabVisibility (tabHost1 As TabHost, visible As Boolean)

Set the visibility of all TabIndicators in tabHost1.

---

setTabVisibility2 (tabHost1 As TabHost, visible As Boolean, index As Int)

Set the visibility of TabIndicator #index in tabHost1.

Index

IsInitialized, 285
%x and %y, 82, 112
"Immediate Window" vs. "Logs" Tab, 269
1.1 Getting Started, 13
1.2 The Integrated Development Environment, 37
1.3 Upgrade to Full Version, 59
2.1 The Project, 68
2.10 Modules, 180
2.11 Publishing and Monetizing Your App, 193
2.12 Getting More Help, 203
2.2. Designing Your App, 74
2.3 Communicating with your User, 85
2.4 The Designer, 92
2.5 Designer Scripts Reference, 109
2.6 Compiling, Debugging & Testing, 119
2.7 Graphics and Drawing, 144
2.8 Databases, 156
2.9 Process and Activity Life Cycle, 173
3.1 Basic4Android's Language, 207
3.2 VB6 versus B4A, 262
3.3 Core Objects, 270
4.1 Libraries, 403
4.2 Standard Libraries included with Full Version, 408
4.3 Additional Libraries and Modules, 524
About Full Versions, 59
About the Author, 11
Abs, 242
Academic Licenses, 59
Accessibility Library, 409
Accessiblity, 409
Accessing other modules, 192
Accuracy, 435
AccuracyValid, 435
Acknowledgements, 10
ACos, 242
ACosD, 242
Acronyms, 8
Action, 315
Action Bar, 76
ACTION_APPWIDGET_UPDATE, 315
ACTION_CALL, 316
ACTION_DOWN, 274
ACTION_EDIT, 316
ACTION_MAIN, 316
ACTION_MOVE, 274
ACTION_PICK, 316
ACTION_SEND, 316
ACTION_UP, 274
ACTION_VIEW, 316
Activating Designer Scripts, 112
Activities vs Windows Forms, 182
Activity, 271
Activity Attributes, 174, 180
Activity Attributes Region, 46
Activity Events, 181, 272
Activity Global Variables, 222
Activity Globals, 175
Activity Members, 273
Activity Methods, 114
Activity Module, 174, 180
Activity.Finish vs ExitApplication, 178
Activity.RerunDesignerScript, 114
Activity_Pause and Activity_Resume, 173
Add, 286, 320, 386
Add a button, 30
Add a field, 172
Add code to button, 34
Add Elements, 319
Add Only Normalized Variants, 102
AddActivityText, 71
AddAll, 320, 386
AddAllAt, 321
AddApplicationText, 71
AddCatchAllState, 302
AddCategory, 316

AddCheckBox, 486, 488
AddEditText, 486, 488
AddHandleActionEvent, 442
AddHeightChangedEvent, 443
Adding a class module, 185
Adding a Standard Variant, 101
Adding Entry, 324
Adding Files to your Project, 303
Adding Other Variants, 101
Adding records, 170
Adding views by code, 81, 108
Additional Libraries, 65
Additional libraries folder, 403, 524
Additional Official Libraries, 403, 524
Additional User Libraries, 403, 529
AddList, 486, 488
AddManifestText, 71
AddMenuItem, 274
AddMenuItem2, 274
AddMenuItem3, 275
AddNonQueryToBatch, 508
AddPermission, 72
AddPreferenceCategory, 486, 488
AddPreferenceScreen, 486, 488
AddReceiverText, 71
AddReplacement, 72
Address, 481, 500, 518
AddServiceText, 71
AddSingleLine, 367
AddSingleLine2, 367
AddState, 302
AddState2, 302
AddTab, 390
AddTab2, 390
AddTabWithIcon, 390
AddTabWithIcon2, 391
AddToMediaStore, 479
AddTwoLines, 367
AddTwoLines2, 368
AddTwoLinesAndBitmap, 368
AddTwoLinesAndBitmap2, 368
AddView, 275, 372, 536
AddView menu, 93
Adiquity, 525
AdiQuity, 199
Administrator Library, 410
AdminManager, 411
AdMob, 198, 525
Advertising, 77
AHActionBar, 76
AirplaneModeChanged, 469
Alarms, 89
All Variants Script Area, 112
Allocating Values, 213
Allowed Characters, 69
Allowed Screen Orientation, 80
Alternative to an Activity, 189
Altitude, 435
AltitudeValid, 436
Always Private, 222
Amazon Appstore, 201
Analytics, 525
And, 279
Android Character Sets, 304
Android Themes, 77
Android Virtual Devices, 129
Android.jar, 65
Android's View of Services, 189
Animation, 412
Animation Library, 412
AnotherDatePicker class, 525
AnswerCall, 505
Anywhere Software, 203
APK File, 196
App Design Step by Step, 75
App or Widget ?, 83
Append, 338
Appending to a Map, 325
ApplicationLabel, 68
Approve the app on your device, 23
ApproximateScreenSize, 318
ARGB, 281, 532, 533, 534
Array, 242
Array Dimensions are Fixed, 218
Arrays, 216
Arrays of Objects, 218
Asc, 243
ASin, 243
ASinD, 243
AsyncStreams, 489
AsyncStreamsText, 525
ATan, 243

ATan2, 243
ATan2D, 243
ATanD, 243
Attachments, 462
Attributes, 518, 522
Audio Library, 415
Audio v1.31, 525
AudioRecordApp, 415
AutoCancel, 330
Autocomplete, 49
Autocomplete event subroutines, 50
Autocomplete Properties and Methods, 50
AutoCompleteEditText, 341
AutoFocus, 427
AutoRegistration, 503
AutoScale, 116
AutoScale Layouts for Different Sized Devices, 114
AutoScaleAll, 116
AutoScaleRate, 116
AVD Name, 130
Azimuth, 434
B4A Designer, 20
B4a Object Browser, 205
B4A-Bridge, 17, 127
B4AHelp, 205
Back, 399
Background, 109, 275, 343, 347, 350, 354, 357, 360, 362, 368, 372, 375, 377, 380, 382, 386, 391, 393, 396, 399, 425, 431
Background Property, 149
Backward Compatible, 74
BASIC, 207
Basic Design Principles, 75
Basic4Android, 207, 269
Basic4Android Enterprise Version, 59
Basic4Android Site License, 59
Basic4Android Standard Version, 59
BatteryChanged, 470
BCC, 462
Bearing, 436
BearingTo, 436
BearingValid, 436
Beep, 417
Beeper, 416
BeginTransaction, 508
Benefits of Classes, 183
Benefits of creating Libraries, 405
Bit, 278
Bitmap, 289, 291, 293, 360, 430
BitmapData, 430
BitmapDrawable, 291
BitmapsData, 431
Bitwise Operations, 278
Black, 281
Blue, 281, 532
Bluetooth connections, 19
BluetoothAdmin, 497
Body, 462, 481
Bookmarks, 47
Boolean, 209
Boolean Operations, 262
Bottom, 301
BOTTOM, 282
Branding and Marketing, 193
Breakpoint Limitations, 121
Breakpoints, 121
Bring To Front and Send To Back, 94
BringToFront, 343, 347, 350, 354, 358, 360, 362, 368, 372, 375, 377, 380, 382, 386, 391, 393, 396, 399, 425, 431
Buffer, 521
BulkTransfer, 517
Button, 346
By Email, 201
Byte, 209
BytesAvailable, 310, 493
BytesToString, 243
CachedName, 454
Call, 469
CallEnded, 503
CallError, 503
CallEstablished, 503
Calling, 503
Calling a sub, 264
Calling a Sub, 232
Calling a Sub from another module, 232
CallItem, 454

CallLog, 455
CallRinging, 503
CallSub, 244
CallSub2, 244
CallSub3, 244
CallSubDelayed, 244
CallSubDelayed2, 245
CallSubDelayed3, 245
CallType, 454
Camera, 427, 525
Camera Library, 426
CameraEx, 525
Cancel, 330
CANCEL, 282
CancelAutoFocus, 427
CancelDiscovery, 498
CancelScheduledService, 245
CanInstallToExternalStorage, 68
Canvas, 291, 429, 445
Canvas Object, 144
CaptureBitmap, 399
Case, 268
Casting, 220
Catch, 245
Caution Name cannot be changed, 70
CC, 462
cE, 245
Ceil, 245
CENTER, 282
CENTER_HORIZONTAL, 282
CENTER_VERTICAL, 282
CenterX, 301
CenterY, 301
Change an Element, 319
Change grid, 95
Changing Text Appearance, 365
Char, 210
CharAt, 335
CharsToString, 245
Charts Framework, 154
Chat Room, 203
Check if a Map contains an entry, 325
Check if the Java JDK is already installed, 59
CheckBox, 349
CheckChanged, 237
Checked, 350, 377, 394
CheckedChange, 376
ChosenName, 538
Chr, 245
Class Circle module, 186
Class module, 183
Class Square module, 186
Class_Globals, 222
Classes and Activity Object, 188
Classes Attributes, 406
Classes structures, 185
Classes vs Code Modules, 185
Classes vs Types, 185
Clear, 321, 326, 368, 386
Clear a List, 320
Clear all items from the map, 325
ClearAll, 487
ClearQueue, 418
Click, 236, 272, 346, 359, 362, 371, 389, 395
ClipPath, 293
Close, 310, 311, 312, 314, 448, 449, 452, 489, 493, 494, 495, 503, 506, 509, 515
CloseFile, 418
CloseMenu, 275
CloseSynchronous, 517
Code, 7
Code area, 45
Code header, 46
Code module, 188
Collapse the whole code, 46
Color, 275, 343, 347, 350, 354, 358, 360, 363, 368, 372, 375, 377, 380, 382, 386, 391, 394, 396, 399, 425, 431
Color Picker, 52
ColorDialog, 532
ColorDialogHSV, 533
ColorDrawable, 149, 299
ColorPickerDialog, 534
Colors, 264, 280
ColumnCount, 506
Combine, 307
Commenting and uncommenting code, 47

Comments, 207
Comments as Documentation, 51, 208
Common Windows XP Error, 64
Commonest View Events, 236
CompareTo, 335
Compilation Modes, 119
Compile and Run, 22
Compile Options, 41
Compiling, 119
Compiling the APK, 198
Complete, 420
CompressBytes, 492
CompressedStreams, 490
Conditional statements, 225
Configure Paths, 64
Configure your button, 32
ConfigureHomeWidget, 246
Connect, 449, 500
Connect the Designer to your device., 30
Connect the IDE to the device, 18
Connect to Device or Emulator, 95
Connect2, 500
Connect3, 500
Connected, 449
ConnectInsecure, 500
Connection Status, 97
ConnectivityChanged, 470
Constants, 208, 267, 270, 280
Contact, 456
Contacts, 458
Contacts2, 459
Contains, 335
ContainsKey, 326
ContentChooser, 461
ContentEncoding, 440
ContentLength, 440
ContentType, 440
Context Menu, 51
Context menus, 105
Continue, 229, 246
ContinueListening, 518
Controls vs. Views, 262
ControlTransfer, 518
Conventions Used in this Book, 7
Convert Array to List, 320
ConvertToMinutes, 436
ConvertToSeconds, 436
Copy, 307
Copy2, 307
CopyDBFromAssets, 161
Core Library, 403
Core Object Events, 233
Core Types, 210
CornerRadius, 299
Cos, 246
CosD, 246
Count, 493, 494
Count Records, 171
CountingInputStream, 492
CountingOutputStream, 494
cPI, 247
CPU ABI, 131
CreateIntent, 486, 488
CreateNew, 285
CreateObject, 546
CreateObject2, 546
CreateTable, 161
Creating a Device Definition, 134
Creating a Menu, 182
Creating a New Key, 197
Creating A Private Key, 197
Creating an AVD, 129
Creating Icons, 194
Creating Libraries, 404
Creating or Adding Modules, 180
Creating Tables, 161
Creating the Page, 181
Creating Tooltips for Subs, 233
Creating Your Own Types, 211
CRLF, 247
Current Variant Option, 111
CurrentOffsetX, 446
CurrentOffsetY, 446
CurrentPosition, 495
CurrentTab, 391
CurrentUserIdChanged, 418
Cursor, 168, 505
CustomBuildAction, 68
CustomDialog, 535
CustomDialog2, 536
CustomListView, 525

CustomView, 351
Cyan, 281
DarkGray, 281
Data, 450
Database, 156
Database Creation, 169
Database Administration, 159
Database Files, 158
Database fundamentals, 156
Date, 287, 455, 481
DateDialog, 537
DateFormat, 287
DateParse, 287
DateTicks, 537
DateTime, 285
DateTimeParse, 287
DateUtils, 526
Daydream, 428
Daydream Library, 428
DayOfMonth, 537
DBMS Tools, 159
DBUtils, 160, 526
DBUtils Field Types, 161
DBUtils Functions, 161
DBUtils Fundamentals, 160
Debug Legacy Mode, 119
Debug Rapid Mode, 119
Debugger Control, 121
Debugger Menus, 122
Debugging, 25, 120
Debugging Certificates, 196
Decimal, 541
DecimalChar, 541
Declare SQL Object, 159
Declaring a Sub, 232, 264
Declaring an Array, 216
Declaring Types, 219
Declaring Variables, 212
DecodeBase64, 511
DecodeUrl, 511
DecompressBytes, 492
Default, 221
DEFAULT, 285
DEFAULT_BOLD, 285
Defaults, 180
Delete, 307, 430
DeleteRecord, 162
DeleteRingtone, 480
Deleting data, 172
Density, 247
Description, 516
Designer, 40
Designer Main Tab, 97
Designer Scripting Basics, 111
Designer Scripts, 108
Designer Scripts and Activity Code, 109
Designer Scripts Tab, 103
Designer Status Line, 97
DestRect, 430
Detail Area, 53
Detecting Device Orientation, 80
Device, 131
DeviceClass, 516
DeviceDefaultDateFormat, 287
DeviceDefaultTimeFormat, 287
DeviceFound, 498
DeviceId, 516
DeviceName, 516
DeviceStorageLow, 470
DeviceStorageOk, 470
DeviceSubclass, 517
Diagrams Charts, 153
DialogResponse, 281
Dialogs Library, 88, 530
Differences between Basic4Android and Visual Basic, 226, 228, 229, 231
Different Layouts for Portrait and Landscape, 117
Digits, 542
Dim, 247, 262
Dim Statement, 212
Dimensions, 216
dip, 110
dips, 81
DipToCurrent, 82, 247
DirAssets, 307
DirDefaultExternal, 307
Direction, 518
DirInternal, 307
DirInternalCache, 307
DirRootExternal, 307

Disable, 411, 498
Disconnect, 500
Disconnect From Device, 96
Discovering the API of the current device, 74
DiscoveryStarted DiscoveryFinished, 498
DismissDropDown, 343
DisplayName, 457, 503
DistanceTo, 436
Distributing Apps elsewhere, 201
Divide by Zero, 266
Do not add too many variants, 101
Do Not Overwrite Manifest File Option, 73
Dock and Fill Strategy, 111
Does the device have a keyboard?, 82
DoEvents, 248, 264
Double, 209
Do-Until, 231
Do-While, 230
Do-While may not be executed, 230
Down, 346
Download and install Basic4Android, 63
Download Basic4Android Trial, 13
Downloading from a website, 202
Downloading User Libraries, 530
dpi dots per inch, 109
Drawables, 149
DrawBitmap, 145, 293
DrawBitmapFlipped, 294
DrawBitmapRotated, 145, 294
DrawCircle, 145, 295
DrawColor, 145, 295
DrawDrawable, 295
DrawDrawableRotate, 295
Drawing Bitmaps on Panels or ImageViews, 152
Drawing Methods, 149
Drawing Objects, 270, 289
DrawLine, 145, 295
DrawOval, 296
DrawOvalRotated, 296
DrawPath, 296
DrawPoint, 296
DrawRect, 145, 297
DrawRectRotated, 145, 297
DrawText, 145, 297
DrawTextRotated, 146, 297
DreamStarted, 428
DreamStopped, 428
DropBox Sync, 526
DropdownTextColor, 386
DropTable, 162
Duplicate Selected View, 94
Duration, 328, 413, 420, 425, 455
Edit menu, 39
Editing Code using the Rapid Debugger, 126
Editing Settings, 78
Editing Views in a program, 117
Editor commands, 71
Editor Highlighting, 57
EditText, 352
Elevation, 434
ElseIfEndIf, 263
Email, 461
EMAIL_CUSTOM, 457
EMAIL_HOME, 457
EMAIL_MOBILE, 457
EMAIL_OTHER, 457
EMAIL_WORK, 457
Emulation Options, 133
Enable, 411, 498
Enabled, 343, 347, 350, 354, 358, 360, 363, 368, 372, 375, 377, 380, 383, 386, 391, 394, 396, 399, 425, 431
Enabling Hardware Buttons, 138
EncodeBase64, 511
EncodeUrl, 511
Encrypting Databases, 158
EndCall, 505
EndElement, 523
End-of-Line Character, 305
EndpointCount, 519
EndpointNumber, 519
EndsWith, 335
EndTransaction, 509
EngineDestroyed, 447
EnterPressed, 342, 353
EqualsIgnoreCase, 335

Error, 489
Error Handling, 238
Error message “Are you missing a library reference?”, 404
Error Trapping, 269
Escaping end of string characters, 71
Event, 376, 385, 393, 416
Event AnimationEnd, 412
Event Complete, 327, 424
Event Connected, 449, 499
Event LogCatData, 462
Event MessageReceived, 482
Event NewConnection, 448
Event NewData, 517
Event PacketArrived, 452
Event PickerResult, 479
Event Ready, 514
Event RecordComplete, 423
Event Result, 461, 483
Event SensorChanged, 474
Event Tick, 339
Evolving Environment, 74
Example, 69, 81, 106, 117, 160, 183, 234, 244, 246, 339, 384, 442, 545
Example Code, 149
Example of a UI Cloud screen, 96
Example of If-Then, 225
Example of If-Then-Else, 225
Example Program, 146
Example Project, 151, 152
Examples, 249
Excel, 526
Exception, 303
Exceptions, 238
Exchanging files with the PC, 140
ExecNonQuery, 509
ExecNonQuery2, 509
ExecNonQueryBatch, 509
ExecQueries and ExecNonQueries, 168
ExecQuery, 509
ExecQuery2, 509
ExecQueryAsync, 172, 510
ExecQuerySingleResult, 510
ExecQuerySingleResult2, 510
Execute, 438
ExecuteCredentials, 438
ExecuteHtml, 162
ExecuteJSON, 163
ExecuteListView, 163
ExecuteMap, 164
ExecuteMemoryTable, 164
ExecuteSpinner, 164
Exists, 308
Exit, 229, 248, 263
Exit a Loop, 231
Exit Sub, 264
ExitApplication, 248
Explanation of Sub’s name, 34
Expressions and Operators, 223
ExternalReadable, 308
ExternalWritable, 308
ExtrasToString, 316
False, 248
FastScroll, 538
FastScrollEnabled, 368
Field, 156
Field Type, 157
File, 132, 248, 306
File locations, 303
File menu, 38, 92
File Object, 303
File Objects, 271
File.DirAssets, 304
File.DirDefaultExternal, 304
File.DirInternal
File.DirInternalCache, 304
File.DirRootExternal, 304
FileDialog, 538
FileFilter, 539
Filenames, 303
FilePath, 539
Files Tab, 54
FILL, 282
Filling an array using the Array keyword, 218
Filtering, 171
Find All References, 52
FindByMail, 458, 460
FindByName, 458, 460
Finish, 276, 429
FirstTime parameter, 176

Fixing Order in a Map, 325
Flags, 316
Flip, 430
FLIP_BOTH, 430
FLIP_HORIZONTALLY, 430
FLIP_NONE, 430
FLIP_VERTICALLY, 430
Float, 209
Floor, 248
Flush, 311, 314, 494, 495
FocusChanged, 342, 353
FocusDone, 427
For, 248
For – Next, 228
For Each, 249
For the Beginner, 5
For the Professional, 5
For...Next, 263
ForceDoneButton, 343, 354
For-Each, 229
Foreword by Erel Uziel, 4
Format, 264
Forum, 203
Forward, 399
Front Back Camera, 131
Fulfilling Wants and Needs, 74
FullScreen, 181, 429
FullScroll, 358, 380
FullWallpaperHeight, 446
FullWallpaperWidth, 446
Functions, 264
GamePad, 526
GameView, 430
GameView Library, 429
General, 270
Generate Members, 33, 93
Generating Your APK, 196
Get, 321, 326
Get the size of a List, 319
GetAccessories, 519
GetActivity, 546
GetActivityBA, 547
GetAll, 456, 458, 460, 483, 487
GetAllSince, 483
GetAllViewsRecursive, 276, 372
GetApplicationIcon, 463
GetApplicationIntent, 463
GetApplicationLabel, 463
GetArray, 547
GetAsTextType, 453
GetAsUriType, 453
GetAsynchronously, 440
GetB4AClass, 547
GetBetweenDates, 483
GetBlob, 506
GetBlob2, 506
GetBoolean, 487
GetById, 456, 459, 460
GetByPersonId, 483
GetBytes, 336
GetByThreadId, 483
GetByType, 483
GetColumnName, 506
GetContactsAsync, 460
GetContactsByQuery, 460
GetContext, 547
GetData, 316
GetDataState, 465
GetDayOfMonth, 287
GetDayOfWeek, 287
GetDayOfYear, 287
GetDBVersion, 165
GetDefault, 326, 480
GetDeviceId, 472
GetDeviceLayoutValues, 249
GetDevices, 519
GetDouble, 506
GetDouble2, 506
GetEmails, 457
GetEndpoint, 519
GetExtra, 316
GetField, 547
GetField2, 547
GetFieldInfo, 547
GetHeaders, 441
GetHour, 287
GetHtmlIntent, 462
GetInputStream, 441
GetInstalledPackages, 463
GetInt, 506
GetInt2, 507
GetIntent, 462

GetInterface, 517
GetItem, 368, 387
GetKeyAt, 326
GetLine1Number, 472
GetLong, 507
GetLong2, 507
GetMaxVolume, 465
GetMethod, 547
GetMinute, 288
GetMonth, 288
GetMostCurrent, 547
GetMyIP, 448
GetMyWifiIP, 448
GetName, 522
GetNdefRecords, 453
GetNetworkOperatorName, 465
GetNetworkType, 465
GetPairedDevices, 501
GetPaletteAt, 535
GetPayload, 453
GetPhones, 457
GetPhoneType, 465
GetPhoto, 457
GetPixel, 290
GetProcessBA, 547
GetProxy, 548
GetPublicField, 548
GetRawDescriptors, 518
GetResourceDrawable, 465
GetRingerMode, 466
GetSecond, 288
GetSettings, 466
GetSimOperator, 466
GetSimSerialNumber, 472
GetSince, 456
GetStartingIntent, 276
GetStaticField, 548
GetString, 441, 487, 507
GetString2, 507
GetSubscriberId, 472
getTabContentViewPadding, 552
getTabEnabled, 552
getTabHeight, 552
getTabHostPadding, 552
getTabTextSize, 552
getTabVisibility, 552
GetText, 308
GetTimeZoneOffsetAt, 288
Getting Help with Regular Expressions, 224
GetType, 249
GetUnreadMessages, 483
GetUpdatedKeys, 487
GetUserFontScale, 409
GetValue, 522
GetValue2, 522
GetValueAt, 326
GetVersionCode, 464
GetVersionName, 464
GetView, 276, 372
GetVolume, 466
GetYear, 288
Global Const, 263
Global Variables, 175
Global variables in Legacy Debugger, 123
Google Maps, 526
Google Play Developer Console, 201
Google Play Store Icon, 194
Google Play URL, 70
Goto Sub Declaration, 52
GPS, 433
GPS Library, 432
GPSEnabled, 434
GPSSatellite, 434
GpsStatus, 433
GradientDrawable, 149, 299
Gravity, 282, 291, 354, 360
Gravity, 343, 347, 350, 363, 377, 394
Gray, 281
Green, 281, 532
HandleAction, 442
HandleWidgetEvents, 333
Handling Long Lists, 88
Handling Modal Dialogs when your App Pauses, 89
HasAccessoryPermission, 519
HasExtra, 316
HasPermission, 520
HDPI, 195
Height, 276, 290, 318, 343, 347, 350, 354, 358, 360, 363, 368, 372, 375,

378, 380, 383, 387, 391, 394, 396, 399, 425, 432
HeightChanged, 442
Help area, 99
Help Menu, 44
Hex Literals, 210
HideKeyboard, 443, 466
Highlighting occurrences of words, 53
Hint, 343, 354, 540
HintColor, 344, 354, 540
HorizontalScrollView, 357
Host, 450
HostAddress, 450
Hour, 543
Hovering over Collapsed Code, 46
How AutoScale works, 115
How Basic4Android interacts with Emulated Devices, 128
How the Rapid Debugger Works, 125
How this Book is Organized, 6
How to Access Process_Globals Variables, 221
How to Compile a Library, 406
How to create a library, 530
How to Detect the Display Type, 80
How to Obtain this Book, 6
How to publish your library, 406
How to See the Effect of AutoScale, 115
How to See the Effect of AutoScale on Text Size, 116
How to Share your Library, 530
How to Start a Service, 189
How to upgrade, 129
How to use a List, 318
How to use a Map, 324
How to use Activity_Pause, 177
How to Use AutoScale, 116
HTTP Library, 437
HttpClient, 437
HttpRequest, 438
HttpResponse, 440
HttpServer, 526
HttpUtils2, 527
Hue, 533
Hungarian Notation, 216
Icon, 330
Icon Sizes, 195
Icons, 8, 49
Id, 455, 457, 481
IDE Options Sub-Menu, 43
If, 250
If – Then – Else – End If, 225
If you already have JDK 64 Bit, 60
Ignoring Warnings, 57
Image files, 99
ImageView, 359
IME, 442
IME Library, 441
Immutable Strings, 334
In the main module, 187
In-App Billing, 199
InAppBilling, 527
IncludeTitle, 181
Indentation, 48
Indeterminate, 375
Index, 555
IndexOf, 321, 336, 387
IndexOf2, 336
Initialization of Objects, 211
Initialize SQL Object, 160
Initialize2, 290, 298, 312, 314, 316, 321, 328, 380, 417, 428, 436, 444, 451, 475, 482, 495, 504
Initialize3, 290, 495
InitializeAcceptAll, 438
InitializeAlpha, 413
InitializeDelete, 439
InitializeFromBytesArray, 310
InitializeGet, 439
InitializeHead, 439
InitializeMutable, 290
InitializePost, 439
InitializePost2, 439
InitializePrefix, 490
InitializePut, 439
InitializePut2, 439
InitializeRotate, 414
InitializeRotateCenter, 414
InitializeSample, 290
InitializeScale, 414
InitializeScaleCenter, 414

InitializeToBytesArray, 311
InitializeTranslate, 414
InitializeWithPhoneState, 471
Initializing a Canvas, 144
Initializing a Recursive Type, 220
Input, 540
INPUT_TYPE_DECIMAL_NUMBERS, 344, 355, 540
INPUT_TYPE_NONE, 344, 355
INPUT_TYPE_NONE, 540
INPUT_TYPE_NUMBERS, 344, 355, 540
INPUT_TYPE_PHONE, 344, 355, 540
INPUT_TYPE_TEXT, 344, 355, 540
InputBox, 265
InputDialog, 539
InputList, 86, 250
InputMap, 87, 251
InputMultiList, 86, 251
InputStream, 310, 516
InputStream .io.InputStream, 449, 501
InputType, 344, 355, 540
Insert, 338
InsertAt, 321
InsertMaps, 165
Insistent, 331
Install and configure Basic4Android, 63
Install and Run the Trial, 13
Install the 32 bit Java JDK, 60
Install the Android SDK and a platform, 60
Install the B4A-Bridge app on your device, 18
Install the SDK, 60
Installation, 60
Installing .NET Framework, 13
Installing DBUtils, 160
Installing Icons, 195
Installing the Trial Version, 13
Instr, 268
Int, 209
Intent, 314
Interacting with your Virtual Device, 136
Interactive, 429
InterfaceClass, 519
InterfaceCount, 517
InterfaceProtocol, 519
InterfaceSubclass, 519
Internal Storage, 132
Interval, 340, 519
Introduction, 5, 128, 403, 408, 524, 529
Invalidate, 276, 344, 348, 350, 355, 358, 361, 363, 369, 372, 375, 378, 380, 383, 387, 391, 394, 397, 400, 425, 432
Invalidate2, 276, 344, 348, 350, 355, 358, 361, 363, 369, 373, 375, 378, 381, 383, 387, 392, 394, 397, 400, 425, 432
Invalidate3, 276, 344, 348, 351, 355, 358, 361, 363, 369, 373, 375, 378, 381, 383, 387, 392, 394, 397, 400, 425, 432
InvokeMethod, 548
Is, 252
Is24Hours, 543
IsAirplaneModeOn, 466
IsBackgroundTaskRunning, 252
IsDirectory, 308
IsEnabled, 499, 501
IsHardwareAccelerated, 432
IsInCall, 505
IsInitialized, 277, 290, 291, 299, 300, 301, 302, 303, 311, 312, 314, 317, 321, 327, 331, 338, 340, 345, 348, 351, 355, 358, 361, 363, 369, 373, 375, 378, 381, 383, 387, 392, 394, 397, 400, 414, 418, 421, 425, 432, 434, 435, 436, 438, 445, 451, 453, 461, 494, 501, 505,507, 514, 515, 517, 519, 521, 522
IsMuted, 505
IsNdefIntent, 453
IsNetworkRoaming, 466
IsNull, 548
IsNumber, 253
IsPaused, 253
IsPlaying, 328, 421, 425

IsPreview, 446
IsSipSupported, 504
IsSupported, 484
IsVisible, 446
IsVoipSupported, 504
ItemClick, 341, 366, 385
ItemLongClick, 366
Iterate a List, 319
Iteration, 324
Java JDK and Android SDK Installation, 59
Javac.exe, 64
JavaScriptEnabled, 400
JetPlayer, 417
JSch, 527
JSON Library, 443
JSONGenerator, 444
JSONParser, 444
JTidy, 527
KeepAlive, 478
Key Concepts, 109
Keyboard, 131
KeyboardPopUp, 539
KeyCodes, 282
KeyPress, 237
KeyPress and KeyUp, 181
KeyPress and KeyUp Events, 272
Keys, 327
Keys and Certificates, 196
Keystore Explorer, 198
KeyValueStore, 527
KeyValueStore Class, 158
Keywords, 242
Label, 362
Language, 484
LastException, 253
LastIndexOf, 336
LastIndexOf2, 336
LastModified, 308
LastTimeContacted, 457
Latitude, 436
Launcher Icon, 194
Layout as Overlay, 79
Layout Menu, 104
Layout variants, 100
LayoutValues, 80, 317
LDPI, 195
Left, 301, 345, 348, 351, 355, 358, 361, 363, 369, 373, 376, 378, 381, 383, 387, 392, 394, 397, 400, 426, 432
Left, 277
LEFT, 282
Left$ and Right$, 268
Legacy Debugger Information Area, 123
Legacy Debugging, 123
Len, 268
Length, 336, 338, 451
Lexical Rules, 207
Libraries Supporting Advertising, 198
Library and Tutorial, 199
Library Browsers, 204
Library compilation attributes, 69
Library specific attributes, 405
Libs Tab, 55
License, 64, 530
Licensing, 200, 527
Lifetimes of Process_Globals Variables, 221
Light, 331
LightGray, 281
Limitations of Classes, 188
Limitations of the Rapid Debugger, 124
LineTo, 300
Linked In, 204
List, 318
List of Additional Libraries, 524
List of Core Objects, 270
List of libraries, 529
List of Standard Libraries, 408
List of types, 409, 410, 412, 415, 426, 428, 429, 433, 437, 442, 443, 445, 447, 452, 485, 489, 497, 502, 505, 511, 515, 522, 531, 544
Listen, 448, 484, 501
Listen2, 501
ListenInsecure, 501
ListenToExternalTimeChanges, 288
ListFiles, 308
Lists, 218
ListView, 364

ListView as a Menu, 365
LiveWallpaper Library, 445
Load, 328, 421
Load the Layout, 35
LoadBitmap, 253
LoadBitmapSample, 253
LoadCSV, 512
LoadCSV2, 512
LoadFile, 418
LoadFromAssets, 285
LoadHtml, 400
LoadLayout, 277, 373
LoadUrl, 400
LoadVideo, 426
Local variables, 223
Local Variables, 174
Local variables in Legacy Debugger, 124
Location, 435
Location of Database, 161
LocationChanged, 433
LocationSettingsIntent, 434
LockScreen, 411
Log, 254
Logarithm, 254
LogCat, 462
LogCatStart, 463
LogCatStop, 463
Logging, 126
Logging Events, 27
Logical Operators, 224
Logs Tab, 55
Long, 209
LongClick, 236, 272, 346, 359, 362, 371, 389, 395
Longitude, 436
Loop structures, 228
Looping, 328, 421
Loops, If-Then, Select Case, 263
LWEngine, 445
LWManager, 446
Mac Keyboard Shortcuts, 137
Magenta, 281
Main Activity Excluded, 405
Main Properties, 98
MakeCall, 504
MakeDir, 308
Managing Permissions, 83
Managing Settings, 78
Manifest Editor, 70
Manifest Typing, 168
Manufacturer, 466, 516
Map, 323
Maps, 219
Mathematical expressions, 223
Matomy, 199
Max, 254, 383
Max and Min Values, 171
MaximumTimeToLock, 411
MaxPacketSize, 519
MaxTracks, 418
MaxValue, 475
MDPI, 195
Me, 254
Meaningful names, 208
MeasureMultilineTextHeight, 512
MeasureStringHeight, 298
MeasureStringWidth, 298
MediaControllerEnabled, 426
MediaPlayer, 327
MediaPlayerStream, 419
Member, 469
Memory Options, 132
Menu, 76
Menu and Toolbar, 38
Menu Overlay, 79
Merchant Account, 200
Message, 303
Methods, 114
Min, 254
Minute, 543
Missing Tabs, 129
Modal Dialogs, 85
Model, 466, 516
Module Attributes, 406
Modules, 40
Modules Tab, 54
Monetising Your App, 198
Monitor dpi, 135
MONOSPACE, 285
Month, 537
More about Debugging, 27

More about Designer, 36
More Advice, 78
More Complex Examples, 147
More Details, 144
More information, 73
More Information, 182
More Information Creating Libraries, 405
More Information on SQLite, 167
Most common Canvas functions, 144
Msgbox, 85, 254
MsgBox, 265
Msgbox2, 85, 254
MtpDevice, 515
Multiline, 250
Multiple activities, 79
Multiple Activity Modules, 182
Mutable Strings, 240, 334
Name, 457, 502, 521
Naming, 232
Naming of Variables, 215
Navigation Bar, 75
Navigation Drawer, 77
NdefRecord, 453
NEGATIVE, 282
Net, 527
Network Library, 447
NewData, 489
NextArray, 445
NextObject, 445
NextValue, 445
NFC, 453
NFC Library, 452
NinePatchDrawable, 152
NMEA, 433
No Home Screen Widget Libraries, 406
No Option Explicit, 213
No Scaling, 135
NO_GRAVITY, 282
Non-integer Iterators, 228
Non-Primitive Types, 210
NonQueryComplete, 508
Normalized Variants, 102
Not, 255, 263, 279
Note that type conversion does not always work, 210
Notepad and Notepad++, 305
Notes, 64, 458, 531, 544
Notes on Bluetooth Connection, 17
Notification, 329
Notification Icon Recommendations, 194
Notifications, 75, 90, 191
Notify, 331
Now, 288
Null, 255
Number, 331, 455, 542
Number formatting, 241, 334
NumberDialog, 541
NumberFormat, 255
NumberFormat2, 255
NumberOfViews, 277, 373
OAuth, 527
Objects, 211
Offset, 451
OffsetChanged, 447
OnGoingEvent, 331
On-line Documentation, 204
OnLine Link, 410
On-Line Tutorials, 204
Open, 515
Open Basic4Android, 64
OpenAccessory, 520
OpenBrowser, 472
OpenDevice, 520
OpenInput, 309
OpenMenu, 277
OpenOutput, 309
Or, 279
Ordering, 171
Other App Publishers, 202
Other Examples, 217
Other Keywords, 114
Other Properties, 114
OutboundProxy, 504
Output, 406
OutputQueueSize, 490
OutputStream, 311, 516
OutputStream .io.OutputStream, 450, 502

Overlays, 79
OverrideUrl, 398
Package name, 69
Package Name, 193
Package Options, 41
PackageAdded, 470
PackageManager, 463
PackageRemoved, 470
PageFinished, 398
Palette, 535
Panel, 358, 370, 381, 429
Parameterize the Command, 171
Parameters, 233
Parents, 523
Parse, 523
Parse2, 523
ParseInt, 279
Part 1 Basics, 12
Part 2 Creating Your App, 67
Part 3 Language and Core Objects, 206
Part 4 Libraries, 402
PartialLock, 478
Pass by Reference, 214
Pass by Value, 214
PASSWORD_QUALITY_ALPHABETIC, 412
PASSWORD_QUALITY_ALPHANUMERIC, 412
PASSWORD_QUALITY_NUMERIC, 412
PASSWORD_QUALITY_UNSPECIFIED, 412
PasswordMode, 345, 356, 540
PasswordSufficient, 412
Path, 300
Pause, 328, 418, 421, 422, 426
PayPal, 528
PC Keyboard Shortcuts, 137
PDF Guides, 204
PeerUri, 505
Percentage of Activity, 82
Permission
android.permission.INTERNET, 452
Permissions, 330, 398, 420, 427, 433, 437, 448, 449, 453, 455, 458, 459, 462, 469, 472, 476, 477, 478, 479, 481, 482, 498, 499, 502
PersonId, 481
PerXToCurrent, 82, 255
PerYToCurrent, 256
Phone, 464
Phone Library, 453
PHONE_CUSTOM, 458
PHONE_FAX_HOME, 458
PHONE_FAX_WORK, 458
PHONE_HOME, 458
PHONE_MOBILE, 458
PHONE_OTHER, 458
PHONE_PAGER, 458
PHONE_WORK, 458
PhoneAccelerometer, 469
PhoneCalls, 469
PhoneEvents, 469
PhoneId, 472
PhoneIntents, 472
PhoneNumber, 458
PhoneOrientation, 473
PhoneSensors, 473
PhoneSms, 476
PhoneStateChanged, 470
PhoneVibrate, 477
PhoneWakeState, 478
PictureTaken, 427
Pitch, 514
Pixel, 109
Play, 328, 418, 421, 422, 426
Play Store Compatibility Check, 74
PlayAudio, 472
Playing Safe, 74
PlayVideo, 472
Polymorphism, 186
Port, 451, 452, 504
Position, 329, 426, 507
POSITIVE, 282
Power, 256
PreferenceActivity Library, 484
PreferenceCategory, 485
PreferenceManager, 487
PreferenceScreen, 487

Preliminary SQL Steps, 160
Prepare Your App's Google Play Page, 200
Preparing the User's Device, 201
Preparing Your Library, 405
Prescribed Resolutions, 195
Preview, 427
Primary Key, 157
Primitive Types, 209
Prn, 435
Process, 173
Processing the SQL, 171
Product, 466
ProductId, 517
ProfileName, 504
Progress, 376
ProgressBar, 90, 374
ProgressDialog, 90
ProgressDialogHide, 256
ProgressDialogShow, 256
ProgressDialogShow2, 256
Project attributes, 405
Project Attributes, 68, 193
Project Attributes Region, 46
Project Icon, 69
Project menu, 40
Project Menu, 73
Prompt, 387, 484
Properties Editor, 97
Properties list, 97
Properties Within Scripts, 113
Protocol, 504
Public by Default, 221
Public vs Private Variables, 184
Purchase, 59
Put, 327
PutExtra, 317
QueryComplete, 508
QueryIntentActivities, 464
Queue, 521
QueuedSegmentsCountChanged, 418
QueueSegment, 418
QUOTE, 256
RadioButton, 376
RAM, 132
Random Numbers, 265
RandomAccessFile, 494
RandomAccessFile Library, 489
Randomize, 265
Rank, 211
Rapid Debugger Information Area, 125
Rapid Debugging, 124
Reacting to an Event, 233
Read, 312, 481
ReadAll, 313
ReadBytes, 311, 494, 496
ReadDouble, 496
ReadEncryptedObject, 496
ReadFloat, 496
Reading and Writing Excel Files, 305
ReadInt, 496
ReadLine, 313
ReadList, 309, 313
ReadLong, 496
ReadMap, 309
ReadMap2, 309
ReadObject, 496
ReadShort, 496
ReadSignedByte, 496
ReadString, 309
ReadUnsignedByte, 496
Ready, 313, 427
Record, 156, 416, 423
RecordComplete, 416
Rect, 300, 446
Recursive Types, 219
Red, 281, 532
ReDim, 262
Reference, 246
Reference SQL Library, 159
Reference to Non-Primitives, 210
Referencing Libraries, 404
Reflection Library, 543
Reflector, 544
Refresh, 446
RefreshAll, 446
Regex, 257
Regions, 45
Register, 504
Register as a Google Play Developer, 200

Registering, 503
Registering as a Google Play Developer, 200
RegistrationDone, 503
RegistrationFailed, 503
Regular Expressions, 224
Relational Data, 157
Relational Operators, 223
Release, 119, 329, 417, 419, 421, 422, 428, 441, 514
Release Mode, 119
ReleaseKeepAlive, 478
ReleasePartialLock, 478
Remote Compilation, 23
RemoteViews, 332
Remove, 327, 338
Remove an entry, 325
Remove Elements, 319
Remove Selected View, 95
RemoveAllViews, 277, 373
RemoveAt, 321, 369, 387
RemoveClip, 299
RemoveHeaders, 439
RemoveView, 345, 348, 351, 356, 358, 361, 363, 369, 373, 376, 378, 381, 383, 387, 392, 394, 397, 400, 426, 432
RemoveViewAt, 277, 373
Rename a table, 172
Renaming of Variables, 120
REPEAT_RESTART, 414
REPEAT_REVERSE, 414
RepeatCount, 414
Repeating Structures, 263
RepeatMode, 415
Replace, 268, 336
RequestAccessoryPermission, 520
RequestFocus, 345, 348, 351, 356, 359, 361, 363, 369, 373, 376, 378, 381, 383, 387, 392, 394, 397, 400, 426, 432
RequestFocus, 277
RequestNewPassword, 412
RequestPermission, 520
RerunDesignerScript, 277
ResetPalette, 535
ResetPassword, 412
Resolution, 109
ResolveHost, 450
Response, 532, 533, 535, 536, 537, 539, 541, 542, 543
ResponseError, 437
ResponseSuccess, 437
Restrictions, 244
Resume, 422
Retrieve Elements, 319
Retrieve Entry, 324
Retrieving data, 171
Return, 257
Returned value, 233
Returning from an Activity, 79
RGB, 281, 532, 533, 535
Right, 301
RIGHT, 282
RINGER_NORMAL, 466
RINGER_SILENT, 466
RINGER_VIBRATE, 466
RingtoneManager, 478
Rnd, 257, 265
RndSeed, 257, 265
Rotate, 430
Rotate your device, 25
Rotating Device, 221
Rotating the Emulator, 102
Round, 257, 266
Round2, 257
RowCount, 507
Run B4A-Bridge on your device, 18
Run Script, 96
Run Script Button, 111
Run your app, 35
RunMethod, 548
RunMethod2, 548
RunMethod3, 549
RunMethod4, 549
Running a Virtual Device and scaling for Real Size Emulation, 135
Running Subs in other modules, 222
Running the Designer, 29
Running your new app, 22
RunPublicmethod, 549
RunStaticMethod, 549

Runtime Errors, 238
Sample DBUtils Program, 166
Sample Projects Using Services, 192
Sample SQLite Program, 167
SANS_SERIF, 285
Saturation, 534
Save the program, 16
Save to and Load from a File, 325
Save to and Load from Files, 319
SaveCSV, 513
SaveCSV2, 513
Saving and Retrieving Data, 217
Saving and Retrieving Settings, 78
Saving Data, 177
Sax, 522
SaxParser, 523
Scale, 110, 318
Scale display to real size, 135
Scaling strategy, 117
Screen Size, 110, 112, 135
ScreenBright, 429
ScreenHeight, 446
ScreenOff, 470
ScreenOn, 471
Screens and Layouts, 78
ScreenWidth, 446
Script Language, 112
Scripting Areas, 111
ScrollingBackgroundColor, 369, 539
ScrollPosition, 359, 381
ScrollView, 379
SD Card, 132
SdkVersion, 466
SearchView, 528
SeekBar, 382
Select, 258
Select – Case, 226
SelectAll, 345, 356
SelectedIndex, 387
SelectedItem, 387
Selecting views, 106
Selecting Views, 94
SelectionStart, 345, 356
Self reference, 187
Selling Your App, 199
Send, 452, 476
Send To UI Cloud, 96
Send2, 477
SendBroadcastIntent, 467
SendDtmf, 505
Sender, 258
SendKeepAlive, 504
SendToBack, 277, 345, 348, 351, 356, 359, 361, 364, 369, 373, 376, 378, 381, 383, 388, 392, 395, 397, 400, 426, 432
Serial, 499, 516, 518
Serial Library, 497
SERIF, 285
ServerSocket, 448
Service, 333
Service Attributes, 47, 190
Service Code, 189
Service Module, 188
Services, 173
Set, 321
SetActivityAttribute, 72
SetActivityResult, 278
SetApplicationAttribute, 72
SetArray, 549
SetArray2, 549
SetBackgroundImage, 278, 345, 348, 351, 356, 359, 361, 364, 369, 373, 376, 378, 381, 383, 388, 392, 395, 397, 401, 426, 432
SetBoolean, 487
SetComponent, 317
SetContentDescription, 409
SetContentEncoding, 439
SetContentType, 439
SetCustomFilter, 443
SetDate, 537
SetDBVersion, 165
SetDefault, 480
SetField, 550
SetField2, 550
SetField3, 550
SetField4, 550
SetFocus, 266
SetHeader, 440
SetHttpParameter, 438
SetImage, 333

SetInfo, 331
SetInfo2, 331
SetItems, 345
SetItems2, 345
SetLanguage, 514
SetLayout, 278, 345, 348, 351, 356, 359, 361, 364, 369, 373, 376, 378, 381, 383, 388, 392, 395, 397, 401, 426, 432
SetManifestAttribute, 72
SetMute, 419, 467
SetNextFocusDown, 409
SetNextFocusLeft, 410
SetNextFocusRight, 410
SetNextFocusUp, 410
SetOnClickListener, 550
SetOnCreateContextMenuListener, 550
SetOnFocusListener, 550
SetOnKeyListener, 550
SetOnLongClickListener, 550
SetOnTouchListener, 551
SetPaletteAt, 535
SetPasswordQuality, 412
SetProgress, 333
SetProxy, 438
SetProxy2, 438
SetPublicField, 551
SetPublicField2, 551
SetRate, 422
SetReceiverAttribute, 72
SetRingerMode, 467
SetScreenBrightness, 467
SetScreenOrientation, 467
SetSelection, 369
SetServiceAttribute, 72
SetStaticField, 551
SetStaticField2, 551
SetString, 487
setTabContentViewPadding, 552
setTabEnabled, 552
setTabEnabled2, 552
setTabGradientDrawable, 553
setTabGradientDrawable2, 553
setTabHeight, 553
setTabHostPadding, 553
setTabTextColor, 553
setTabTextColorStateList, 553
setTabTextSize, 553
setTabTitle, 553
setTabVisibility, 554
setTabVisibility2, 554
SetText, 333
SetTextColor, 333
SetTextSize, 333
SetTime, 543
SetTimeZone, 288
Setting a breakpoint, 25
Setting Icons, 193
Setting Label Transparency, 267
Setting Your Project Parameters, 193
SetTrackMute, 419
SetType, 317
SetVisible, 333
SetVolume, 329, 421, 422, 468
Shared Event Handler, 234
Shell, 266, 468
ShiftLeft, 280
ShiftRight, 280
Short, 209
Show, 461, 532, 534, 535, 536, 537, 539, 541, 542, 543
Show Abstract Designer, 96
ShowCalendar, 538
ShowDropDown, 345
Showing Tables, 379
ShowKeyboard, 443
ShowOnlyFolders, 539
ShowRingtonePicker, 480
ShowSign, 542
Shutdown, 471
Signing, 196
Signing for Distribution, 197
Sin, 258
SinD, 258
Single line, 250
SingleLine, 345, 356
SingleLineLayout, 370
Sip, 502
Sip Library, 502
SipAudioCall, 504

Size, 132, 309, 321, 327, 370, 388, 496, 523
SizeChanged, 428, 447
Skin, 131
Skip, 313
Sliding Pages, 76
SMB, 528
Sms, 480
SmsDelivered, 471
SmsInterceptor, 481
SmsMessages, 482
SmsSentStatus, 471
Snapshot, 133
Snr, 435
Socket, 449
Sort, 321
Sort a List, 320
SortCaseInsensitive, 321
SortType, 322
SortTypeCaseInsensitive, 322
Sound, 332
SoundPool, 421
Source, 530, 544
Sources of Icons, 194
Speak, 514
Speak Button, 528
SpeakerMode, 505
Specifying Functional Arguments, 7
Specifying Menus, 7
SpeechRate, 514
Speed, 436
SpeedValid, 437
Spinner, 384
Splitting Long Lines, 208
SQL, 167, 507
SQL Library, 168, 505
SQL Object, 159, 160, 168
SQLCipher, 528
SQLite, 167
SQLite Commands, 169
SQLiteBrowser, 159
SQLiteExceptions, 168
SQLiteSpy, 159
Sqrt, 258
SrcRect, 430
Standard Libraries, 403
Standard Screen, 110
Standard Variant, 101
Starred, 458
Start, 415, 434
StartActivity, 177, 258
StartAudio, 505
StartDiscovery, 499
StartElement, 523
StartForeground, 334
StartListening, 475, 518
StartPreview, 428
StartService, 259
StartServiceAt, 259
StartsWith, 336
StartTicking, 447
State_Checked, 302
State_Disabled, 302
State_Enabled, 302
State_Focused, 302
STATE_OFF, 499
STATE_ON, 499
State_Pressed, 302
State_Selected, 302
STATE_TURNING_OFF, 499
STATE_TURNING_ON, 499
State_Unchecked, 302
StateChanged, 498
StateListDrawable, 151, 301
StateManager, 528
Statement Separator, 207
Status Bar, 75
StatusCode, 441
Step Value, 228
Stop, 329, 415, 421, 422, 426, 434, 514
StopForeground, 334
StopListening, 472, 475, 482, 502, 518
StopLoading, 401
Stopping B4A-Bridge, 21, 36
StopPreview, 428
StopService, 259
StopTicking, 447
Storage Card Folders, 304
StreamBuffer, 420
StreamError, 420
StreamReady, 420
String, 210, 334

String "Members", 267
String Functions Library, 334
String manipulation, 240
StringBuilder, 337
Strings obfuscation, 120
StringUtils, 511
StringUtils Library, 511
STYLE_BOLD, 285
STYLE_BOLD_ITALIC, 285
STYLE_ITALIC, 285
STYLE_NORMAL, 285
Sub, 259
Sub Activity_Create, 175
Sub Activity_Pause, 176
Sub Activity_Resume, 177
Sub DesignerCreateView, 352
Sub Globals, 175, 222
Sub Initialize, 352
Sub Process_Globals, 175, 221
SubExists, 260
Subject, 462
Subroutines, 222, 264
SubRoutines, 190
Subs, 232
Subscribing to Additional Library Updates, 404
SubString, 336
SubString2, 336
Support, 10
SupportedOrientations, 69
Syntax, 68
TAB, 260
Tabbed Views, 76
TabChanged, 389
TabCount, 392
TabHost, 388
TabHostExtras Library, 552
TabIndex, 267
Table, 156
Table creation, 169
Table of Contents, 3
TableView, 528
Tabs, 53
Tag, 278, 346, 348, 351, 356, 359, 361, 364, 370, 373, 376, 378, 381, 384, 388, 392, 395, 397, 401, 426, 432, 446
TakePicture, 428
Tan, 260
TanD, 260
Tap for Tap, 529
TapForTap, 199
Target, 131, 551
TargetRank, 551
Telling the IDE where to find additional libraries, 524
Telling the IDE where to find Additional Libraries, 404
Terminated, 489
test, 515
Testing your App, 127
Text, 346, 349, 351, 356, 379
Text, 364
Text encoding, 304
Text Properties, 113
Text Size, 110
TextChanged, 341, 353
TextColor, 346, 349, 351, 356, 379, 388, 395
TextColor, 364
TextOff, 395
TextOn, 395
TextReader, 312
TextSize, 346, 349, 351, 356, 379, 388, 395
TextSize, 364
TextToSpeechFinish, 471
TextWriter, 313
The Abstract Designer, 103
The Activity Concept, 173
The Activity Template, 174
The Android Screen, 75
The Designer, 79
The Emulator or Android Virtual Device Manager, 128
The KeyStore, 197
The Manifest, 70
The String functions, 240
The View and Layout Concepts, 28
The Warning Engine, 56
The warnings, 57

ThreadId, 481
Tick, 447
Ticks, 285
TicksPerDay, 288
TicksPerHour, 288
TicksPerMinute, 288
TicksPerSecond, 289
Time, 289, 437
TimeDialog, 542
TimeFormat, 289
Timeout, 440
TimeOut, 450
TimeParse, 289
Timer, 267, 338
TimesContacted, 458
TimeTicks, 543
TimeZoneOffset, 289
Tips, 72
Title, 278
Title Bar, 76
TitleColor, 278
To, 462
To load or update a library, 530
ToastMessageShow, 89, 260
ToBinaryString, 280
ToBytesArray, 311, 494
ToggleButton, 392
ToggleMute, 505
ToHexString, 280
ToLowerCase, 337
ToOctalString, 280
Toolbar, 44
Tools menu, 42
Tools Menu, 93, 105
Top, 301, 346, 349, 351, 356, 359, 361, 364, 370, 373, 376, 379, 381, 384, 388, 392, 395, 397, 401, 426, 432
Top, 278
TOP, 282
Top Most, 97
ToPrettyString, 444
toString, 318, 426, 451, 452
ToString, 338, 444, 551
Touch, 236, 272, 371, 447
Touch Event, 181
ToUpperCase, 337
Transactions, 168
TransactionSuccessful, 511
Transparent, 281
Trim, 268, 337
Troubleshoot Connection Problems, 143
True, 260
Try, 260
Try-Catch, 239
TTS, 514
TTS Library, 514
Tutorial, 366, 429
Twitter, 204
Two Versions, 13
TwoLinesAndBitmap, 370
TwoLinesLayout, 370
Type, 261, 481, 519
Type Checking, 213
Type Conversion, 210
Type variables, 219
TYPE_ACCELEROMETER, 475
TYPE_ALARM, 480
TYPE_DRAFT, 483
TYPE_FAILED, 483
TYPE_GYROSCOPE, 475
TYPE_INBOX, 483
TYPE_INCOMING, 455
TYPE_LIGHT, 476
TYPE_MAGNETIC_FIELD, 476
TYPE_MISSED, 455
TYPE_NOTIFICATION, 480
TYPE_ORIENTATION, 476
TYPE_OUTBOX, 483
TYPE_OUTGOING, 455
TYPE_PRESSURE, 476
TYPE_PROXIMITY, 476
TYPE_QUEUED, 483
TYPE_RINGTONE, 480
TYPE_SENT, 483
TYPE_TEMPERATURE, 476
TYPE_UNKNOWN, 483
Typeface, 284, 346, 349, 351, 356, 379, 395
Typeface, 364
TypeName, 551
Types, 209

Types of Libraries, 403
UDPPacket, 450
UDPSocket, 451
Uncaught Runtime Exceptions, 238
Unique name, 69
Unload, 422
UnsignedShiftRight, 280
Until, 261
Up, 346
UpdateRecord, 166
UpdateRecord2, 166
UpdateWidget, 333
Updating records, 170
Updating to a new version, 66
Upload your App to Google Play, 201
URI, 516
Url, 401
USB Debugging, 127
USB Host, 529
USB Library, 515
USB_CLASS_APP_SPEC, 520
USB_CLASS_AUDIO, 520
USB_CLASS_CDC_DATA, 520
USB_CLASS_COMM, 520
USB_CLASS_CONTENT_SEC, 520
USB_CLASS_CSCID, 520
USB_CLASS_HID, 520
USB_CLASS_HUB, 520
USB_CLASS_MASS_STORAGE, 520
USB_CLASS_MISC, 520
USB_CLASS_PER_INTERFACE, 520
USB_CLASS_PHYSICA, 520
USB_CLASS_PRINTER, 520
USB_CLASS_STILL_IMAGE, 520
USB_CLASS_VENDOR_SPEC, 520
USB_CLASS_VIDEO, 520
USB_CLASS_WIRELESS_CONTROLLER, 520
USB_DIR_IN, 520
USB_DIR_OUT, 521
USB_ENDPOINT_DIR_MASK, 521
USB_ENDPOINT_NUMBER_MASK, 521
USB_ENDPOINT_XFER_BULK, 521
USB_ENDPOINT_XFER_CONTROL, 521
USB_ENDPOINT_XFER_INT, 521
USB_ENDPOINT_XFER_ISOC, 521
USB_ENDPOINT_XFERTYPE_MASK, 521
USB_INTERFACE_SUBCLASS_BOOT, 521
USB_SUBCLASS_VENDOR_SPEC, 521
USB_TYPE_CLASS, 521
USB_TYPE_MASK, 521
USB_TYPE_RESERVED, 521
USB_TYPE_STANDARD, 521
USB_TYPE_VENDOR, 521
UsbAccessory, 515
UsbDevice, 516
UsbDeviceConnection, 517
UsbEndpoint, 518, 522
UsbInterface, 519
UsbManager, 519
UsbRequest, 521
USBSerial, 529
Use Host GPU, 133
Use of Unassigned Variables, 214
UsedInFix, 435
User Help, 193
User Support, 201
UserAndPasswordRequired, 398
UserClosed parameter, 177
UserEnabled, 433
UserPresent, 471
Using Integers as Boolean, 263
Using the Abstract Designer, 34
Using the Android Virtual Device Manager, 128
Using the Designer Tools, 33
Val, 266
Value, 384, 534
Values, 327
Variable Can Specify Dimensions, 217
Variables, 112, 208
Variables in other Activity Modules, 182
Variables in Subs, 223
Variables within an Activity, 174
Variant Specific Script Area, 112
VB6, 269

VendorId, 517
Version, 516, 533, 534, 535, 536, 537, 538, 539, 541, 542, 543, 551
Version of Basic4Android, 5
VersionCode, 69
Versioning, 160
VersionName, 69
Vibrate, 332, 477
Video Tutorials, 204
VideoRecordApp, 422
VideoView, 423
View, 395
View Drawables, 149
View Events, 235
View Selector, 97
View Variables Must be Here, 222
Views, 271, 340
Visibility and Lifetime of Variables and Subs, 220
Visibility Between Modules, 220
VisibilityChanged, 447
Visible, 346, 349, 351, 356, 359, 361, 364, 370, 373, 376, 379, 381, 384, 388, 392, 395, 397, 401, 426, 432
VM Heap, 132
VoiceRecognition, 483
VOLUME_ALARM, 417, 468
VOLUME_MUSIC, 417, 468
VOLUME_NOTIFICATION, 417, 468
VOLUME_RING, 417, 468
VOLUME_SYSTEM, 417, 468
VOLUME_VOICE_CALL, 417, 468
Warning Area, 55
Warning Bug in Emulator, 102
Warning Set Internal Properties before External, 113
Ways of Monetizing Your App, 198
We'd Like to Hear from You, 10
WebView, 398
What is a Class?, 183
What is a library?, 403
What You Need to Run Basic4Android, 5
When Does Android Kill a Process?, 189
When is Activity_Pause called?, 176
When the User Rotates a Device, 27
When to Use a Service, 191
When to use a Try-Catch, 239
Which ones does a project need?, 530
While, 261
White, 281
Who this Book is For, 5
Why this recommendation?, 102
Why use a Service, 188
Width, 278, 290, 318, 346, 349, 351, 356, 359, 361, 364, 370, 373, 376, 379, 381, 384, 388, 392, 395, 397, 401, 426, 432
Windows Character Sets, 305
Windows-1252, 305
Wireless connections, 19
Wrap, 346, 356
WrapAsIntentChooser, 317
WrapInputStream, 492
WrapOutputStream, 492
Write, 314, 490
Write2, 490
WriteByte, 496
WriteBytes, 312, 494, 496
WriteDouble, 497
WriteEncryptedObject, 497
WriteFloat, 497
WriteInt, 497
WriteLine, 314
WriteList, 310, 314
WriteLong, 497
WriteMap, 310
WriteObject, 497
WriteShort, 497
WriteString, 310
WriteToStream, 290
XHDPI, 195
XML, 522
XMLBuilder, 529
XmlSax Library, 522
Xor, 280
Year, 538
Yellow, 281
Your First App, 15
Your Second App Using the Designer, 28

Your Third App, 36
YouTube, 529
Zoom, 401
Zoom Menu, 105
ZoomEnabled, 401

Printed in Great Britain
by Amazon.co.uk, Ltd.,
Marston Gate.